AF479306

Van Gogh in America

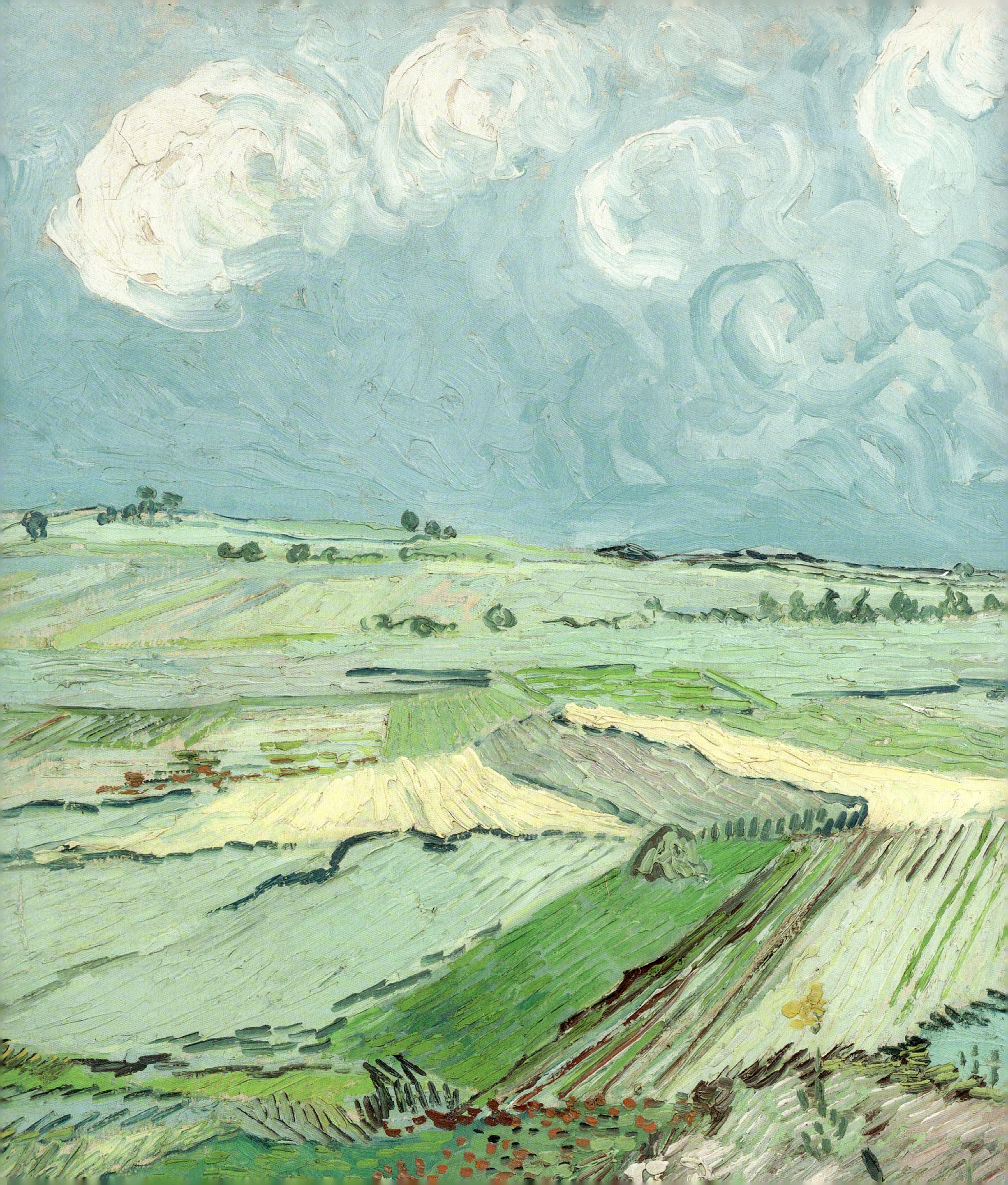

VAN GOGH in AMERICA

Edited by Jill Shaw

With essays by Rachel Esner, Joost van der Hoeven, Julia Krikke, Jill Shaw, Susan Alyson Stein, Chris Stolwijk, and Roelie Zwikker, and a chronology by Dorota Chudzicka

DETROIT INSTITUTE OF ARTS

DISTRIBUTED BY YALE UNIVERSITY PRESS
NEW HAVEN AND LONDON

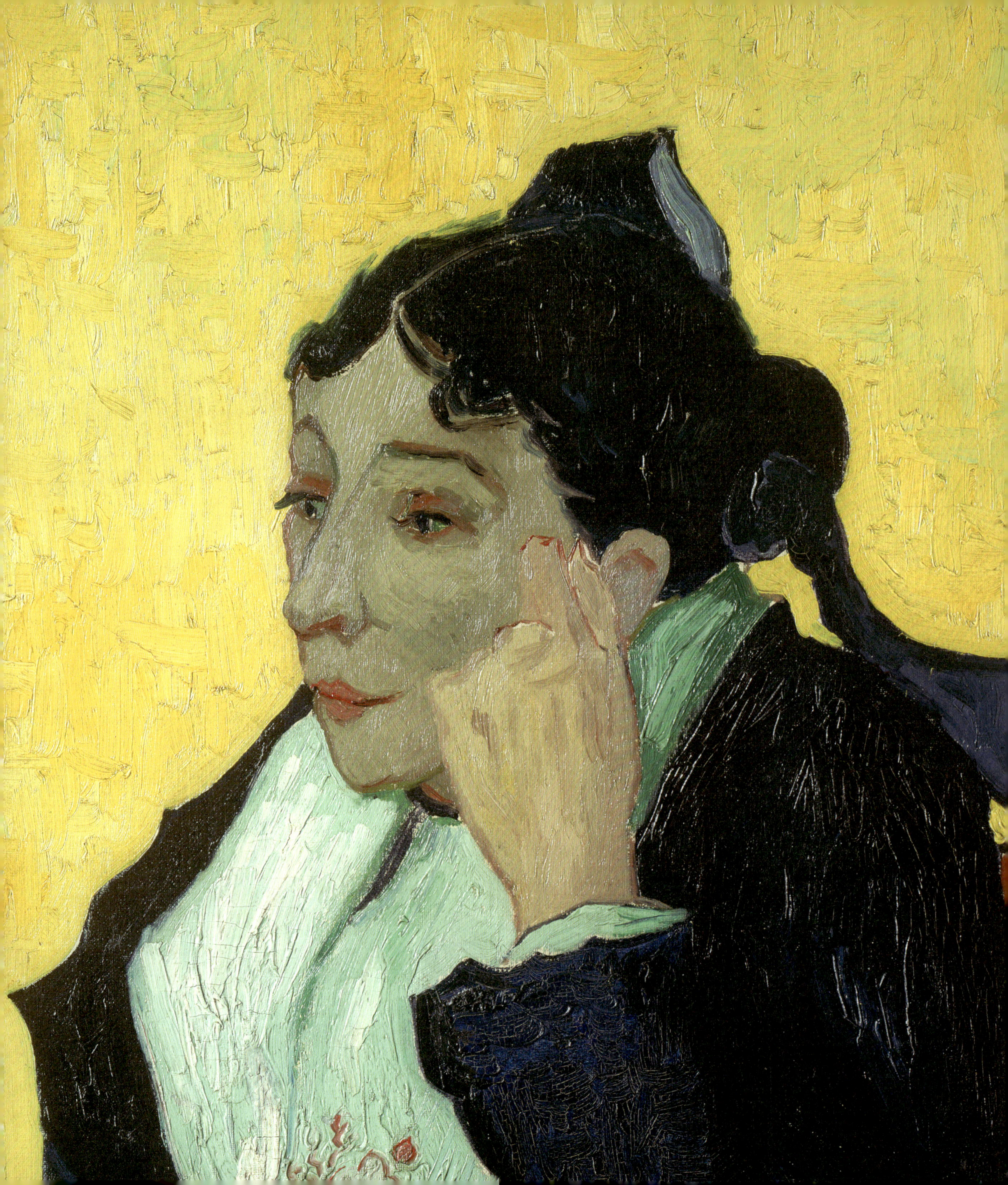

CONTENTS

Sponsors

Van Gogh in America is organized by the Detroit Institute of Arts and is part of the Bonnie Ann Larson Modern European Artists Series.

Lead support is generously provided by the Founders Junior Council, The J. Addison and Marion M. Bartush Family Foundation, Bank of America, Cadillac, and Nancy and Sean Cotton.

Major support is provided by the William H. and Patricia M. Smith Family, Kenwal Steel, Frances and Kenneth Eisenberg, Nicole and Stephen Eisenberg, Alex Erdeljan, James and Sally Scapa Foundation, Marjorie and Maxwell Jospey Foundation, Spencer & Myrna Partrich, Friends of Art & Flowers, Joanne Danto, Arnold Weingarden & Jennifer Danto Shore, Huntington, Ford Motor Company Fund, DTE Energy Foundation, Jennifer Adderley, and The Family of Christopher R.W.D. Stroh.

Additional support is provided by the Community Foundation for Southeast Michigan, Wells Fargo, Gilbert Family Foundation, Nancy S. Williams Trust and executor, Sharon Backstrom, and Aaron and Carolynn Frankel.

This exhibition is supported in part by the National Endowment for the Arts, as part of the Dutch Culture USA program by the Consulate General of the Netherlands in New York, and the European Paintings Council.

Funding is also provided by Mrs. William Clay Ford, Mr. and Mrs. John W. Ingle, Jr., Mr. and Mrs. John W. Ingle III, Mr. and Mrs. John M. Sullivan, Jr., Eleanor and Frederick Ford, and Kathleen and Robert Rosowski.

Major funding for the exhibition catalogue is generously provided by Jo Elyn and George M. Nyman.

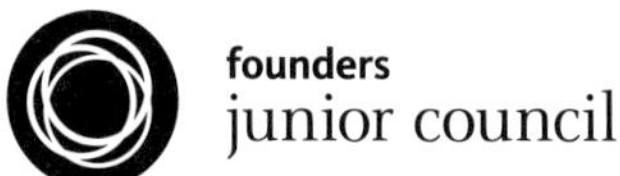

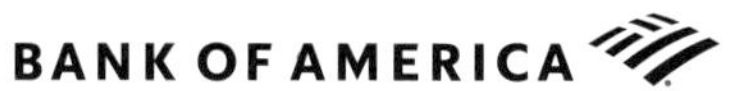

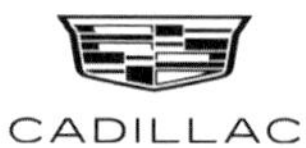

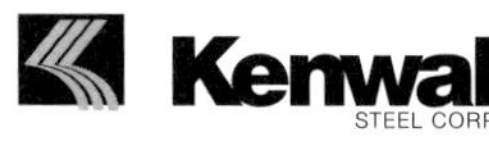

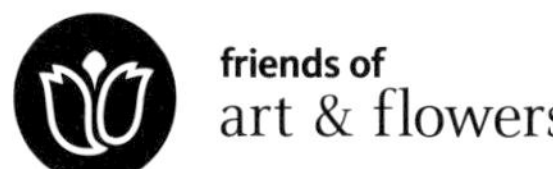

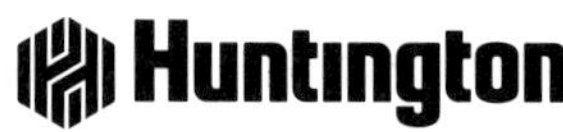

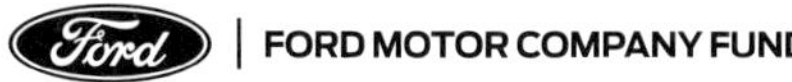

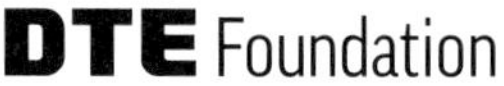

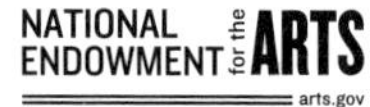

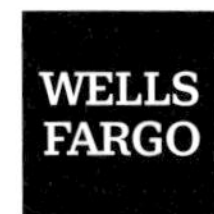

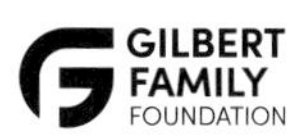

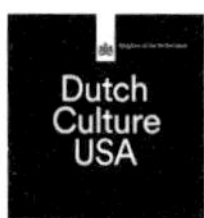

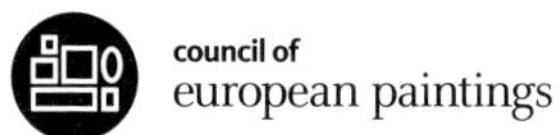

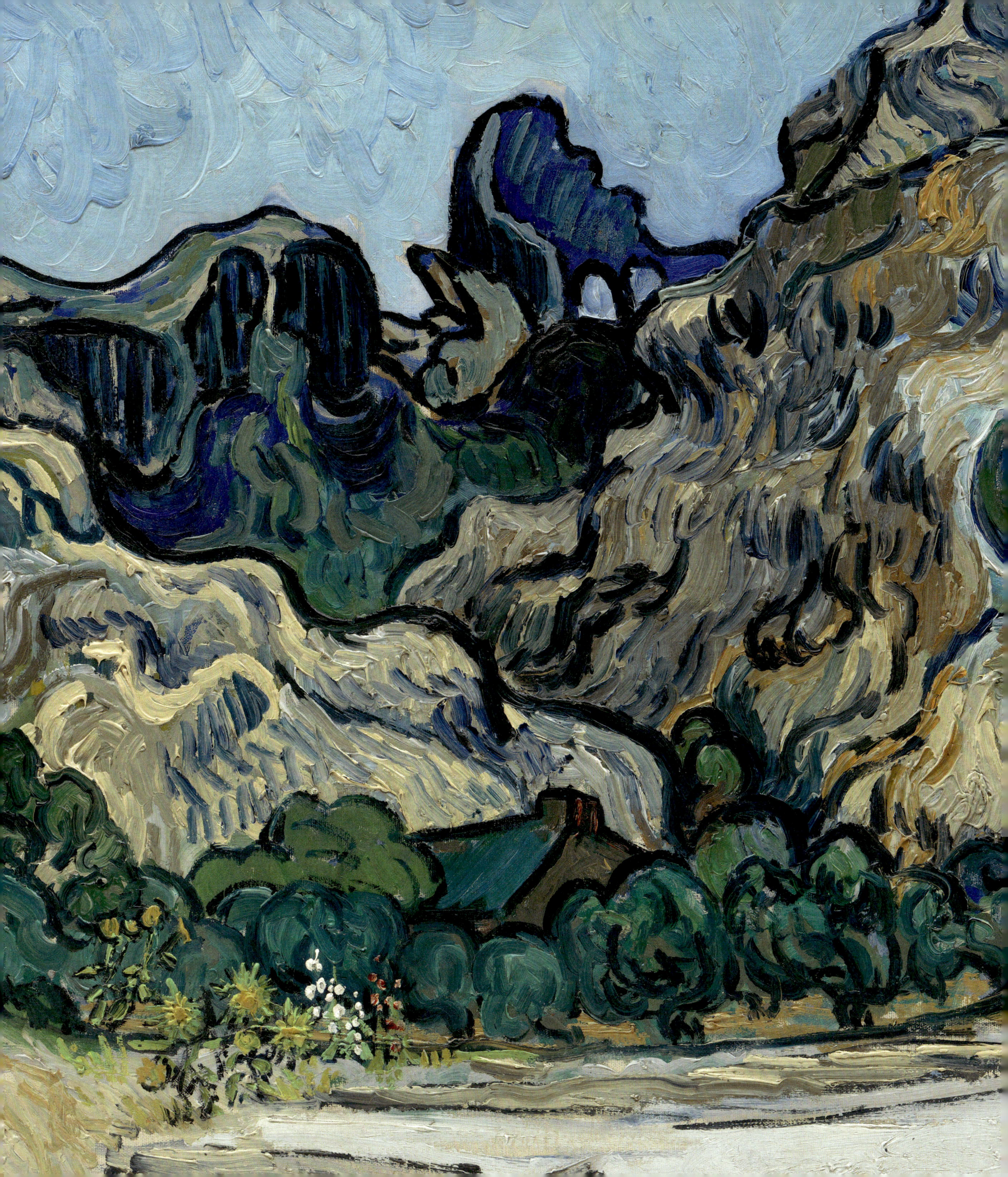

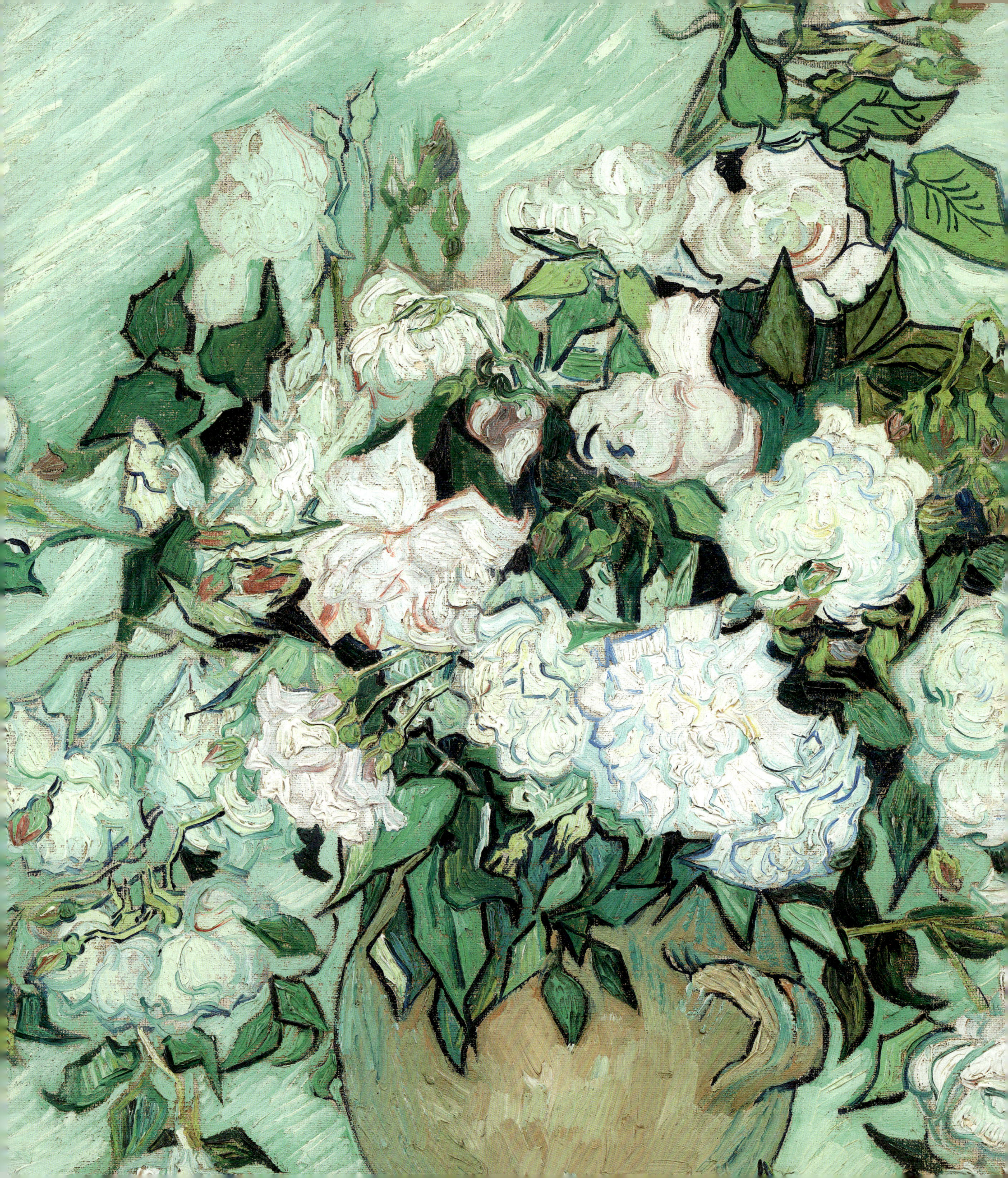

Foreword

On January 31, 1922, the Detroit Institute of Arts made history when Ralph H. Booth, president of the City of Detroit Arts Commission, attended the auction of dealer Dikran Kelekian's collection and successfully bid on Vincent van Gogh's *Self-Portrait*, 1887 (F526; plate 44). The purchase, described as "courageous" in contemporary press, would signify the first painting by the artist to be purchased by an American public museum. The DIA's trustees were motivated to build a collection that would give people access to established masterpieces as well as a broad spectrum of works of earlier, modern, and contemporary art.

One century later, it seems fitting that the DIA has organized the first exhibition dedicated to the early reception of his work in the United States. The artist's rise to fame in this country was not straightforward, and numerous actors played a role and shepherded the process: the Van Gogh family, artists, collectors, dealers, publishers, curators, scholars, filmmakers, and many others worked painstakingly through successes and failures to promote the artist and his work.

Presented only in Detroit, *Van Gogh in America* examines these efforts along with landmark moments, including the first public appearance of Van Gogh's art in America in the 1913 *International Exhibition of Modern Art* (commonly known as the Armory Show); his triumphant retrospective, organized by the Museum of Modern Art, New York, in the mid-1930s that traveled across the country; and the embrace of his art and a dramatic understanding of his life by Hollywood and the greater American public. After Vincente Minnelli's biopic *Lust for Life* (1956) arrived in the movie theaters of mid-century America, Van Gogh's mythic biography became fully integrated within the American collective imagination.

When our curator Jill Shaw proposed this exhibition and catalogue, it was immediately clear that this was not just *another* Van Gogh show and publication. The opportunity to study the artist in the context of American art collecting, which stemmed from the vision of our museum and its trustees in 1922, was compelling. To pursue this idea today, in the midst of our city's extraordinary resurgence, reinstates Detroit at the center of the art world, as it was in the 1920s, when art collecting and building a great museum "dedicated by the people of Detroit to the knowledge and enjoyment of art" was a civic priority. I am grateful to Jill Shaw for her passion, scholarship, and hard work in leading this project, as well as to Jennifer Paoletti, our director of exhibitions, who played a crucial role in the organization of the exhibition not only once, but twice. Originally scheduled to open in June 2020, *Van Gogh in America* was postponed to its current date due to the COVID-19 pandemic. I am also very proud of our entire team and their tremendous accomplishments.

An exhibition of this scope requires the collaboration of our many lenders and supporters. I would like to extend my profound thanks to the individual collectors and public institutions that have parted with their treasured works for this pioneering presentation. Furthermore, the exhibition, which is part of the DIA's Bonnie Ann Larson Modern European Artists Series, could not have been realized without the exceptional generosity of our sponsors: the Founders Junior Council, The J. Addison and Marion M. Bartush Family Foundation, Bank of America, Cadillac, Nancy and Sean Cotton, William H. and Patricia M. Smith Family, Kenwal Steel, Frances and Kenneth Eisenberg, Nicole and Stephen Eisenberg, Alex Erdeljan, James and Sally Scapa Foundation, Marjorie and Maxwell Jospey Foundation, Spencer & Myrna Partrich, Friends of Art & Flowers, Joanne Danto, Arnold Weingarden & Jennifer Danto Shore, Huntington, Ford Motor Company Fund, DTE Energy Foundation, Jennifer Adderley, The Family of Christopher R.W.D. Stroh, the Community Foundation for Southeast Michigan, Wells Fargo, Gilbert Family Foundation, Nancy S. Williams Trust and executor, Sharon Backstrom, Aaron and Carolynn Frankel, the National Endowment for the Arts, as part of the Dutch Culture USA program by the Consulate General of the Netherlands in New York, the European Paintings Council, Mrs. William Clay Ford, Mr. and Mrs. John W. Ingle, Jr., Mr. and Mrs. John W. Ingle III, Mr. and Mrs. John M. Sullivan, Jr., Eleanor and Frederick Ford, Kathleen and Robert Rosowski, and Jo Elyn and George M. Nyman.

Salvador Salort-Pons
DIRECTOR, PRESIDENT & CEO
DETROIT INSTITUTE OF ARTS

Acknowledgments

Van Gogh in America celebrates one of the many remarkable moments in the history of the Detroit Institute of Arts. Initiated in 2017, this major loan exhibition owes its success to Director, President & CEO of the Detroit Institute of Arts Salvador Salort-Pons, whose dedication to the project has been unwavering. When, in March 2020, the museum was forced to close its doors due to the COVID-19 pandemic, Salvador also made the difficult decision to cancel the opening of this exhibition, originally scheduled for June 2020. Yet, eliminating it from our exhibition schedule altogether never crossed his mind, and he encouraged our team to reschedule the exhibition and hone it based on the rich research compiled for the original catalogue that was pulled from the press just days before it was to print. To this end, *Van Gogh in America* has been refined and amplified and is presented in a celebratory year which marks the 100th anniversary of the museum's historic purchase of Vincent van Gogh's *Self-Portrait*, 1887 (F526; plate 44). Salvador's tremendous devotion to the DIA and his steadfast advocacy for this exhibition and scholarly catalogue have been essential to their realization.

Van Gogh's reception in America was orchestrated by an international team of players. Similarly, the story of that reception, told here for the first time, required the work of a significant number of scholars past and present, who have meticulously researched and documented the provenance and exhibition histories of Van Gogh's works. We are indebted to the efforts of these individuals, and while they are too numerous to list here, their endeavors are reflected in this scholarship.

Initial conversations with colleagues at the Van Gogh Museum, Amsterdam, were extraordinarily beneficial, and I am grateful for the early and ongoing support of that institution and the individuals who were so generous with their time, expertise, and resources, especially former director Axel Rüger and current director Emilie Gordenker, as well as Marije Vellekoop, Nienke Bakker, Louis van Tilborgh, Teio Meedendorp, Maite van Dijk, Monique Hageman, Hans Luijten, and their extraordinary colleagues in the Van Gogh Museum Library.

Equally important to the development and realization of the exhibition and catalogue were Susan Alyson Stein, Engelhard Curator of Nineteenth-Century European Painting, The Metropolitan Museum of Art, New York; and Chris Stolwijk, General Director RKD – Netherlands Institute for Art History / Professor of History of Dutch Art in an International Context, 1800–1940, Utrecht University. Their advice and guidance in all stages of the project were invaluable, and their catalogue essays will serve as foundational texts on this subject in the future, as will the important contributions by Dorota Chudzicka, Assistant Curator of Modern European Art, Detroit Institute of Arts; Rachel Esner, Associate Professor of Modern and Contemporary Art History, University of Amsterdam; Joost van der Hoeven, Researcher, Van Gogh Museum, Amsterdam; Julia Krikke, Research Assistant, Van Gogh Museum, Amsterdam; and Roelie Zwikker, Senior Researcher, Van Gogh Museum, Amsterdam.

The institutions around the world that loaned works to this important exhibition deserve particular recognition and thanks. These collections are listed on a separate page; however, the following past and present directors and curators deserve a special acknowledgment for their generous efforts: Janne Sirén, Cathleen Chaffee, and Holly E. Hughes, Albright-Knox Art Gallery, Buffalo; James Rondeau and Gloria Groom, The Art Institute of Chicago; Christopher Bedford and Katy Rothkopf, The Baltimore Museum of Art; Sam Keller and Raphaël Bouvier, Fondation Beyeler, Riehen/Basel; Eric Crosby, Sarah S. Minnaert, and Catherine Evans, Carnegie Museum of Art, Pittsburgh; Cameron Kitchin and Peter J. Bell, Cincinnati Art Museum; Olivier Meslay and Esther Bell, The Sterling and Francine Clark Art Institute, Williamstown; William Griswold, Heather Lemonedes, William Robinson, Emily J. Peters, and Britany Salsbury, The Cleveland Museum of Art; Deborah Swallow, Ernst Vegelin, and Karen Serres, The Courtauld Gallery, London; Agustín Arteaga and Nicole Myers, Dallas Museum of Art; Jeff Fleming, Alison Ferris, and Jared Ledesma, Des Moines Art Center; Richard Armstrong and Tracey Bashkoff, Solomon R. Guggenheim Museum, New York; Ann Philbin, Hammer Museum, Los Angeles; Martha Tedeschi, Joachim Homann, and Edouard Kopp, Harvard Art Museums, Cambridge; Norman E. Dascher Jr. and Jonathan Canning, The Hyde Collection, Glens Falls; Lisette Pelsers, Kröller-Müller Museum, Otterlo; Benno Tempel, Doede Hardeman, and

Frouke van Dijke, Kunstmuseum Den Haag, The Hague; Richard Aste and René Paul Barilleaux, McNay Art Museum, San Antonio; Max Hollein, Keith Christiansen, Stephan Wolohojian, Susan Alyson Stein, Nadine Orenstein, and Ashley Dunn, The Metropolitan Museum of Art, New York; Colin B. Bailey, John Marciari, and Isabelle Dervaux, The Morgan Library & Museum, New York; Christophe Leribault, Laurence des Cars, Sylvie Patry, Emmanuel Coquery, Claire Bernardi, and Isolde Pludermacher, Musée d'Orsay, Paris; Guillermo Solana, Museo Nacional Thyssen-Bornemisza, Madrid; Matthew Teitelbaum, Frederick Ilchman, and Katie Hanson, Museum of Fine Arts, Boston; Glenn Lowry and Ann Temkin, The Museum of Modern Art, New York; Gabriele Finaldi and Caroline Campbell, The National Gallery, London; Kaywin Feldman, Earl A. Powell III, Mary Morton, and Kimberly Jones, National Gallery of Art, Washington, DC; John Leighton, Christopher Baker, and Aidan Weston-Lewis, National Galleries of Scotland, Edinburgh; Klaus Biesenbach, Udo Kittelmann, Ralph Gleis, and Joachim Jäger, Nationalgalerie, Staatliche Museen zu Berlin; Julián Zugazagoitia and Aimee Marcereau DeGalan, The Nelson-Atkins Museum of Art, Kansas City; Stephen Snoddy, The New Art Gallery Walsall, United Kingdom; Gertrud Hvidberg-Hansen, Ny Carlsberg Glyptotek, Copenhagen; Timothy Rub and Jennifer Thompson, Philadelphia Museum of Art; Dorothy Kosinski and Susan Behrends Frank, The Phillips Collection, Washington, DC; John W. Smith and Maureen O'Brien, Museum of Art, Rhode Island School of Design, Providence; Michel Draguet, Royal Museums of Fine Arts of Belgium, Brussels; Min Jung Kim, Brent Benjamin, and Simon Kelly, Saint Louis Art Museum; Rein Wolfs, Jan Willem Sieburgh, and Beatrice von Bormann, Stedelijk Museum, Amsterdam; Maria Balshaw, Polly Staple, and Michael Raymond, Tate, London; Adam Levine, John Stanley, Brian Kennedy, and Lawrence Nichols, Toledo Museum of Art; Emilie Gordenker, Axel Rüger, Adriaan Dönszelmann, Nienke Bakker, and Marije Vellekoop, Van Gogh Museum, Amsterdam; the Van Gogh family and the Vincent van Gogh Foundation; Jeffrey N. Brown, Thomas Loughman, and Oliver Tostmann, Wadsworth Atheneum Museum of Art, Hartford; Marcus Dekiert and Barbara Schaefer, Wallraf-Richartz-Museum & Fondation Corboud, Cologne; Matthias Waschek, Jeffrey Forgeng, and Claire Whitner, Worcester Art Museum; Stephanie Wiles, Jock Reynolds, Laurence Kanter, Mark Mitchell, and Keely Orgeman, Yale University Art Gallery, New Haven.

I am also grateful to the private lenders to the exhibition: the Abelló Collection, the Nancy and Sean Cotton Collection, the Rudolf Staechelin Collection, and those who prefer to remain anonymous. The intermediaries who helped locate objects and facilitate loan requests were critical to this endeavor: Jonathan Boos; Till-Holger Borchert; Lauren and Gregory Fisher; Eugene A. Gargaro Jr.; Monique Hageman; Richard Manoogian; Takashi Omitsu; Monica Tachotte and Erica Schmatz, Almeida e Dale Galeria de Arte, São Paulo; Guy Agazarian and Pat Savage, Christie's, London; Max Carter, Cyanne Chutkow, Vanessa Fusco, Conor Jordan, David Kleiweg de Zwaan, Margaux Morel, and Allison Whiting, Christie's, New York; Christopher Eykyn and Susan Wallach, Eykyn Maclean, New York; Mary Arteche and Jim Carona, Heather James Fine Art, Palm Desert; Beatriz Moreno de Barreda; Conchita Romero; Natalie Alavi, Frances Asquith, Hannah Byers, Kayla Carlsen, Julian Dawes, Benjamin Doller, Edith Eustis, Elizabeth Goodridge, Brooke Lampley, Scott Niichel, Elizabeth Pisano, Lauren Powell, Katharine Richardson, Nina del Rio, Simon Shaw, Lucian Simmons, Molly Steiger, Liz Sterling, and August Uribe, Sotheby's, New York; Maria de Peverelli, Maria Edmée di Sambuy, and Johanna Schultheiss, Stonehage Fleming Financial Services, Ltd., London; and David Tunick, Inc., New York.

Other individuals providing assistance, advice, and research models include Martin Bailey, Geri Banik, Drew Erin Becker Lash, Mark Bowden, Lindsey Bright, Thomas Bruhn, Peter Buettner, Marisa Burgoin, Gabrielle Carlo, Danielle Carrabino, Theresa Kutasz Christensen, Jay A. Clarke, Tara C. Craig, Douglas Druick, James Finch, Meghan Gray, Tiffany Hamblin, Carol Jacobi, Erin Kinhart, Tara Laver, Nancy Norwood, Victoria Reed, Bart Ryckbosch, Keli Rylance, Kerry Schauber, Jenna Staut, Joel Stone, Gina Tecos, Clare Vasquez, Emily Vokt Ziemba, Debbie Webb, Gregory Wittkopp, Rachel Wixom, William Wixom, and Peter Zegers.

Closer to home, I am tremendously appreciative of the great support of the DIA's Board of Directors, led by Eugene A. Gargaro Jr., as well as the incredible commitment of our administration, especially Salvador Salort-Pons,

Robert Bowen, Elliott Broom, Judith Dolkart, Felicia Eisenberg Molnar, David Flynn, Christine Kloostra, Julie McFarland, Melissa Peña Gallis, Nina Sapp, and John Steele.

My debt of gratitude to Jennifer Paoletti, director of exhibitions, is enormous, and this project is a success because of her exceptional talent, professionalism, expertise, and dedication. Swarupa Anila, former director of interpretation, and Rachel Lewis, interpretative planner, have ensured that the visitor experience remained an ever-present priority. Dorota Chudzicka, assistant curator of modern European art, has been absolutely invaluable to all aspects of this exhibition's installation and catalogue. My colleagues in the curatorial division have been incredibly supportive, and I especially wish to acknowledge Judith Dolkart, deputy director, art, education, and programs, and curators Larry Baranski, Nancy Barr, Valerie Mercer, Kenneth Myers, Nii Quarcoopome, and Elliot Wilhelm. Additional thanks go to Iva Lisikewycz, Beverly Berry, James Miller, Alexandra Nickolaou, Stacie Durden, Samara Furlong, Carol George, and Celeste Goedert.

Many past and present DIA staff members have devoted extensive time and energy to this project. I am particularly indebted to the DIA's Research Library & Archives, especially director Maria Ketcham, archivist James Hanks, and interns Vasiliki Mitsiopoulos, Katherine Okonowski, and Louiza Taylor; in the Director's Office, Colleen Clinton and Rachael Goodwin; in Registration, Terry Segal, Kim Dziurman, Michelle Smith, and Amy Dunn; in Collections Management, Terry Birkett, James Johnson, and our dedicated group of museum technicians; in Exhibitions, Elena Berry, Everett Keyser, and Marc Langlois; in Conservation, Ellen Hanspach-Bernal, Christopher Foster, James Storm, and other members of the talented conservation team; in Development, Rose Gleeson, Jessica Trombley, Ed Maki-Schramm, Laticia Nelson-Clemons, Laura Orme, and their remarkable colleagues; in Protection Services, Eric Drewry and the many committed officers who serve under his leadership; in Marketing and Communications, Andi Schreiber, Megan Hawthorne, and their teams; in Learning and Audience Engagement, Jason Gillespie, Christine Mark, and their dedicated colleagues; in Environmental Services, Adam Pattison and his incredible staff; in Research and Evaluation, Kenneth Morris and Erin Wilcox; in Information Technology, Clinton Myers and Jamal Stallings; and in Photography, Eric Wheeler. Additional thanks go to Theodora Doulamis, who is responsible for the elegant exhibition design, and to exhibition materials editor Maia Rigas.

This beautiful and scholarly catalogue has been a labor of love for many individuals. I am especially thankful for the oversight of this catalogue's original editor Terry Ann R. Neff who ensured all of the complicated parts worked together seamlessly and provided critical feedback. Amanda Freymann expertly oversaw the challenging schedule and production elements. For the 2022 version of the catalogue, the above responsibilities were swiftly and ably brought to completion by Aaron Bogart. The thoughtful design is the product of designers Lorraine Wild, Tommy Huang, and Ching Wang of Green Dragon Office. We are also grateful for the translations provided by Lynne Richards and Diane Webb, as well as the contributions by proofreader Sheila Majumdar and indexer Jane Friedman. We are pleased to partner with Yale University Press on the distribution of the publication. We particularly thank Patricia Loiko, Indemnity Administrator, for her guidance during the indemnity application process.

The support of Bonnie Ann Larson, Rebecca A. Boylan, and Thomas W. Sidlik has been essential to this undertaking, and their tremendous advocacy of the DIA is inspiring. I am truly grateful for their support, excitement, counsel, and friendship.

Finally, I thank my family for their unwavering support throughout this challenging but endlessly rewarding project. Velma and Jack Shaw offered the kind of encouragement that only parents can provide, and I am deeply sorry that my father was unable to see it come to fruition; Claire Chase, who unwittingly traveled with me throughout Europe during all of my research trips, brought a joyous distraction to my research and writing; and Brad Chase was steadfast in his patience and understanding of the deep importance of this endeavor for me and for the DIA.

Jill Shaw
HEAD, THE JAMES PEARSON DUFFY DEPARTMENT OF MODERN AND CONTEMPORARY ART
REBECCA A. BOYLAN AND THOMAS W. SIDLIK CURATOR OF EUROPEAN ART, 1850–1970
DETROIT INSTITUTE OF ARTS

Lenders to the Exhibition

Abelló Collection
Albright-Knox Art Gallery, Buffalo
The Art Institute of Chicago
The Baltimore Museum of Art
Carnegie Museum of Art, Pittsburgh
Cincinnati Art Museum
The Cleveland Museum of Art
Nancy and Sean Cotton Collection
Dallas Museum of Art
Des Moines Art Center
Detroit Institute of Arts
Fondation Beyeler, Riehen/Basel
Hammer Museum, Los Angeles
Harvard Art Museums/Fogg Museum, Cambridge
The Hyde Collection, Glens Falls
Kröller-Müller Museum, Otterlo
Kunstmuseum Den Haag, The Hague
McNay Art Museum, San Antonio
The Metropolitan Museum of Art, New York
The Morgan Library & Museum, New York
Musée d'Orsay, Paris
Museo Nacional Thyssen-Bornemisza, Madrid
Museum of Art, Rhode Island School of Design, Providence
Museum of Fine Arts, Boston
The Museum of Modern Art, New York
National Galleries of Scotland, Edinburgh
The National Gallery, London
National Gallery of Art, Washington, DC
The Nelson-Atkins Museum of Art, Kansas City
The New Art Gallery Walsall
Ny Carlsberg Glyptotek, Copenhagen
Philadelphia Museum of Art
The Phillips Collection, Washington, DC
Royal Museums of Fine Arts of Belgium, Brussels
Saint Louis Art Museum
The Samuel Courtauld Trust, The Courtauld Gallery, London
Solomon R. Guggenheim Museum, New York
Staatliche Museen zu Berlin, Nationalgalerie
Rudolf Staechelin Collection
Stedelijk Museum, Amsterdam
The Sterling and Francine Clark Art Institute, Williamstown
Tate, London
Toledo Museum of Art
Van Gogh Museum, Amsterdam (Vincent van Gogh Foundation)
Wadsworth Atheneum Museum of Art, Hartford
Wallraf-Richartz-Museum & Fondation Corboud, Cologne
Worcester Art Museum
Yale University Art Gallery, New Haven

And private collectors who wish to remain anonymous

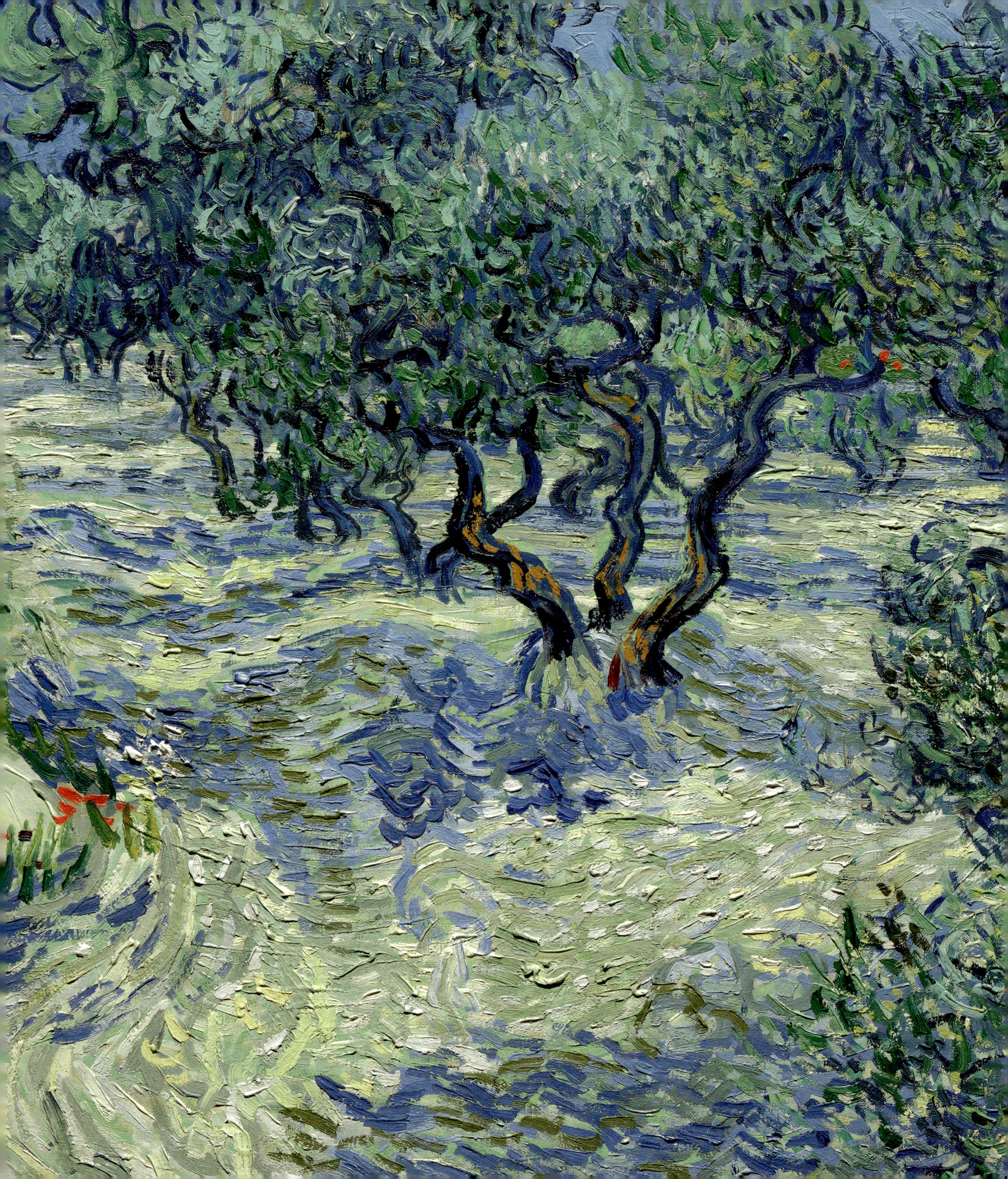

Note to the Reader

All works of art reproduced are by Vincent van Gogh (Dutch, 1853–1890) unless otherwise noted. Van Gogh's works are identified by their catalogue raisonné numbers: F for De la Faille 1970 and, in the checklist of the exhibition, JH for Hulsker 1996. Because Van Gogh often made several versions of the same subject, the F numbers are crucial elements of identification. Titles of works match institutional titles and are given in italics. In their absence, the titles from De la Faille 1970 are cited, also in italics; alternative titles, such as those in historical exhibition catalogues, press accounts, and archival materials, are in quotation marks. Titles in a language other than English are provided in translation.

All objects designated as plates are on view in the exhibition; they are listed in the checklist of the exhibition in chronological order, starting with the works by Van Gogh, followed by those of other artists.

All short-form reference titles throughout this catalogue appear in full citations in the selected bibliography. Van Gogh group and solo exhibitions referenced in this book are also listed in short forms, with the full citations in the exhibitions section of the selected bibliography. Archival collections consulted are referenced in full in the end-of-chapter notes. Van Gogh's letters are cited by the numbers used in Van Gogh Letters 2009, www.vangoghletters.org.

Originally planned to be published in 2020, this book is largely unchanged from then. A revised checklist and some research updates have been added.

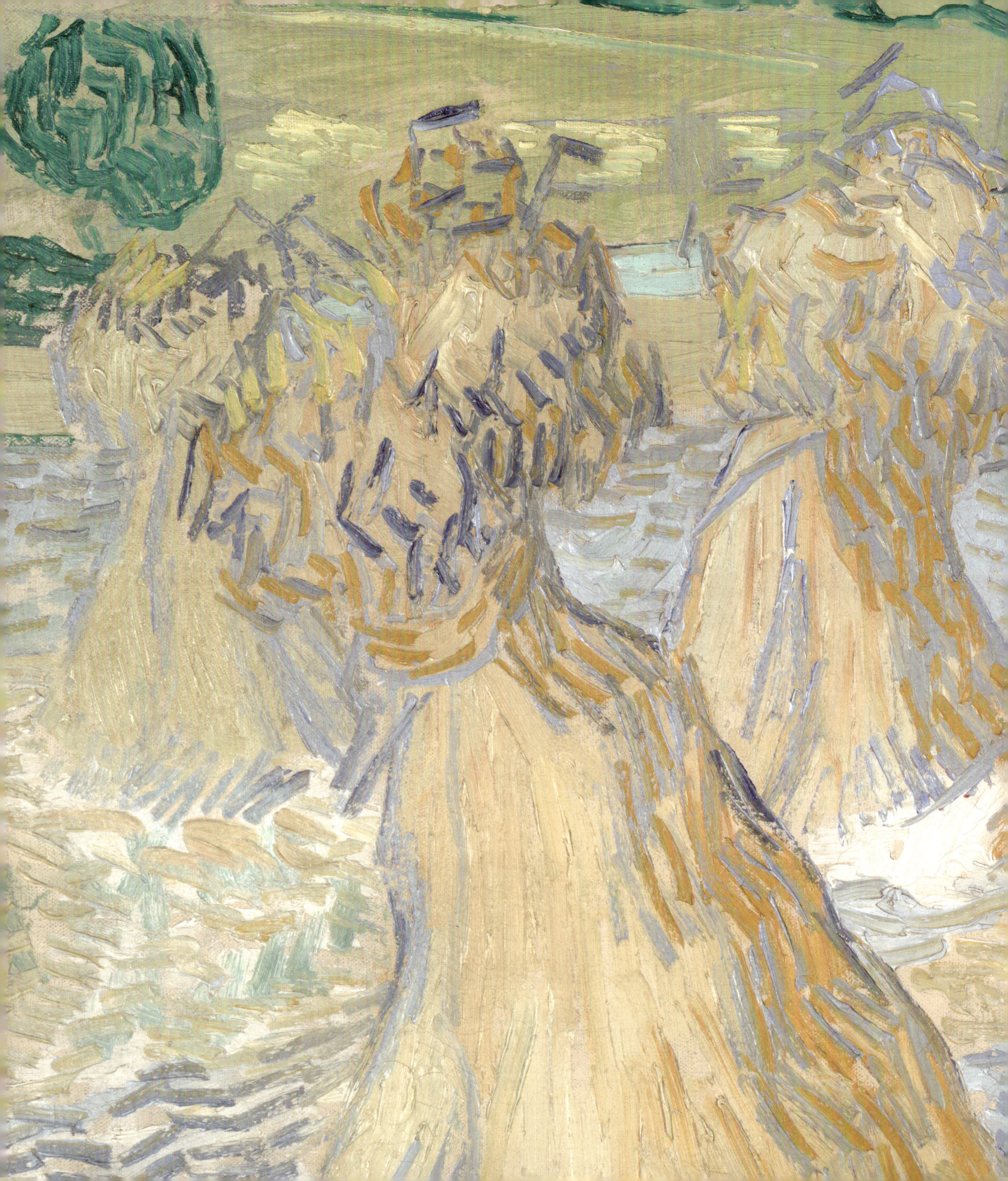

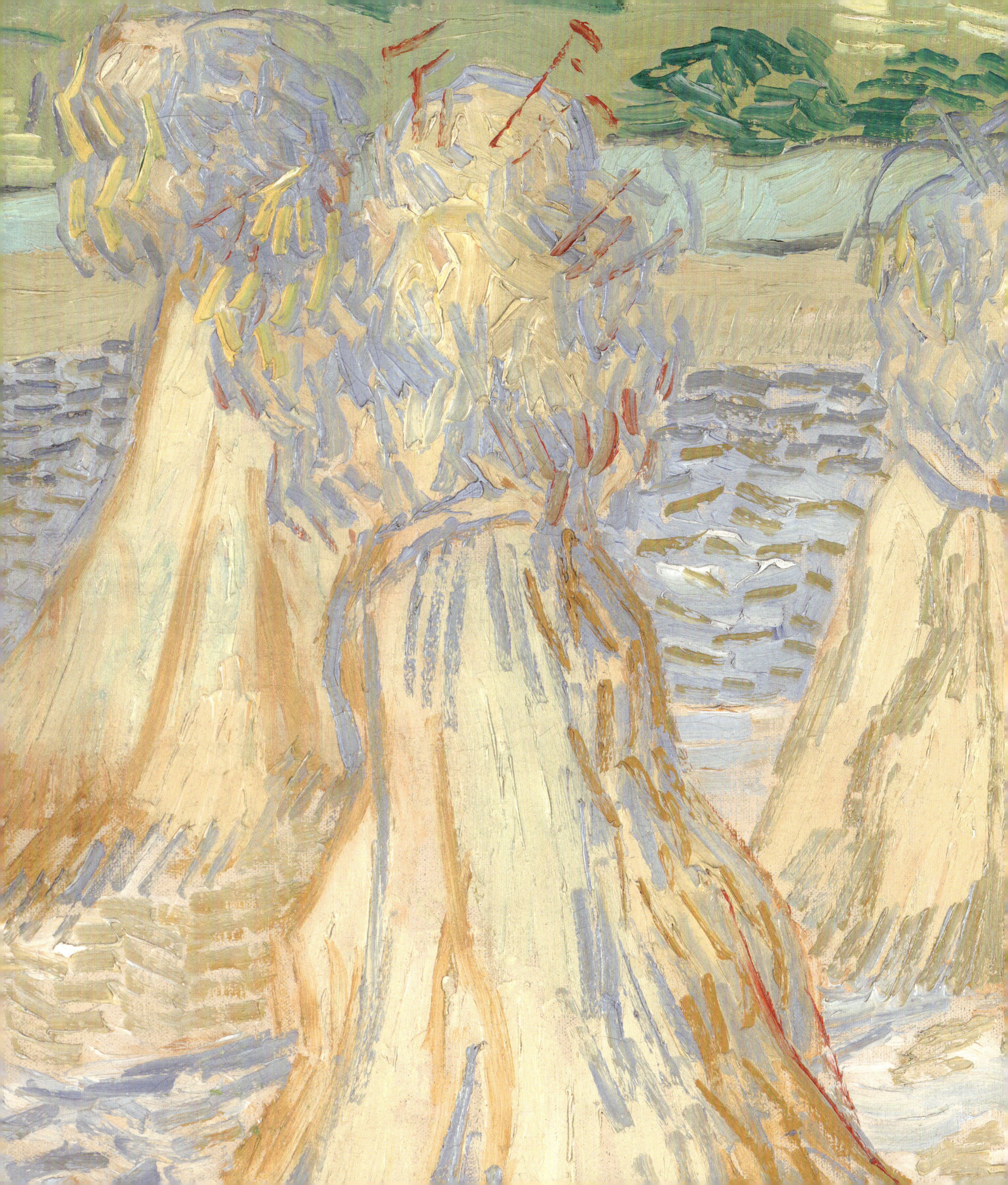

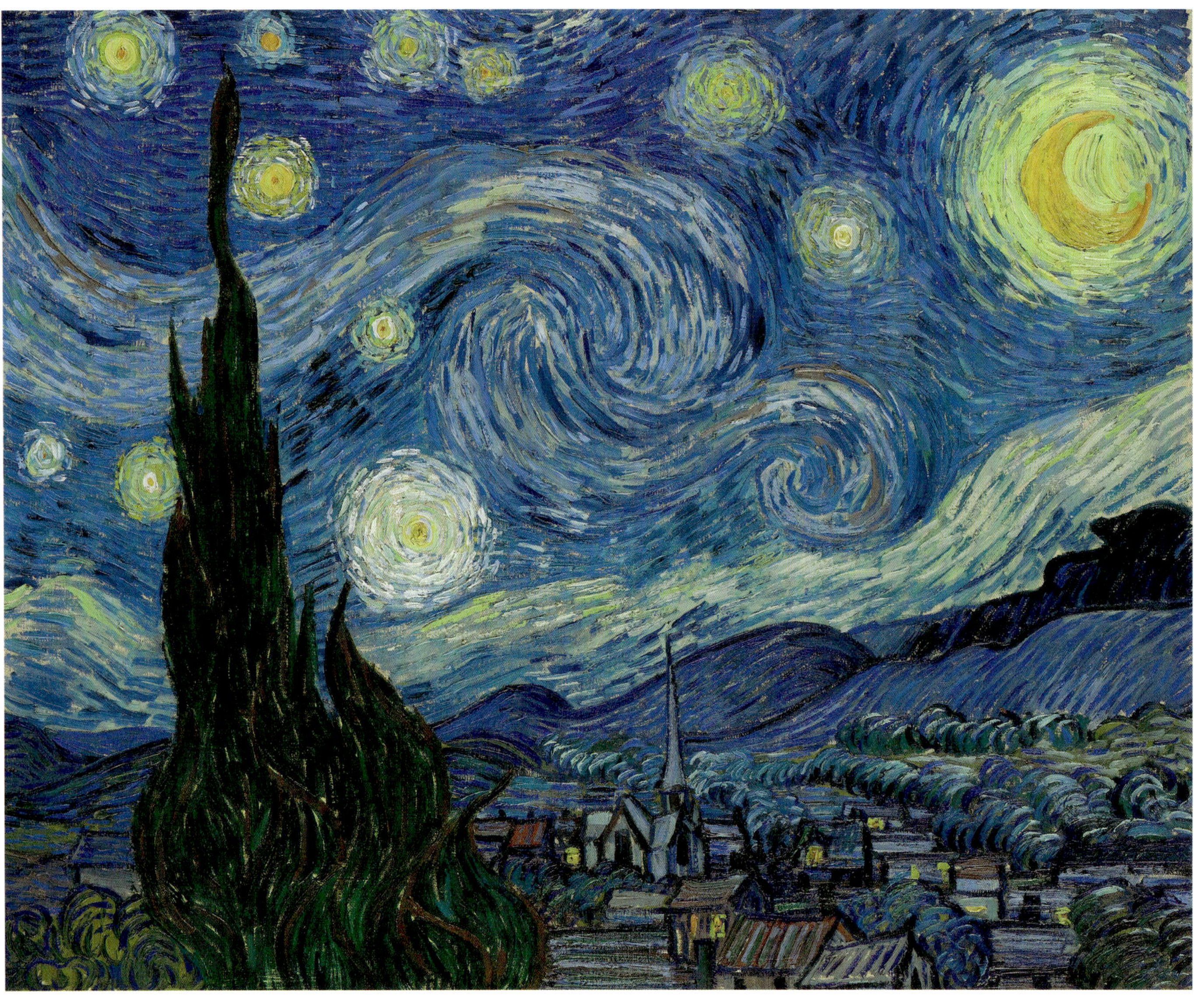

FIG. 1 *The Starry Night* (F612), 1889.
Oil on canvas, 29 × 36¼ in. (73.7 × 92.1 cm).
The Museum of Modern Art, New York.

JILL SHAW

America Wakes Up to Van Gogh

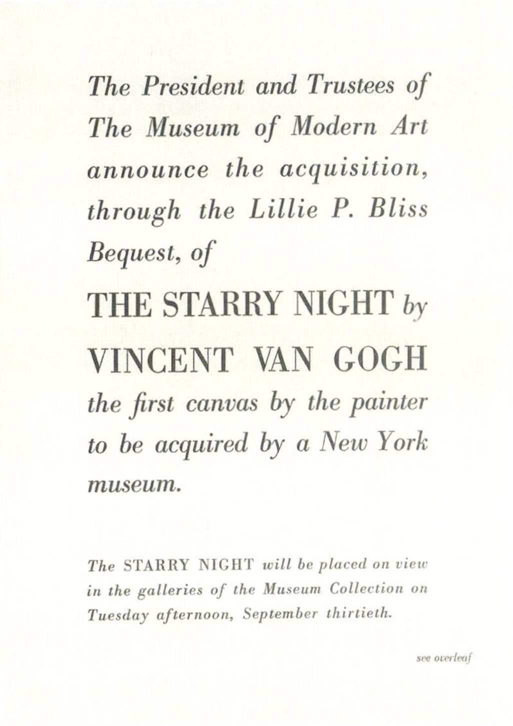

The President and Trustees of The Museum of Modern Art announce the acquisition, through the Lillie P. Bliss Bequest, of

THE STARRY NIGHT *by*

VINCENT VAN GOGH

the first canvas by the painter to be acquired by a New York museum.

The STARRY NIGHT *will be placed on view in the galleries of the Museum Collection on Tuesday afternoon, September thirtieth.*

see overleaf

FIG. 2 Announcement of the acquisition of *The Starry Night*, 1941.

Just over one hundred years ago, in 1920, the Montross Gallery in New York, with the support of Vincent van Gogh's family, mounted the first retrospective of the artist's work in America. On that occasion, art critic Henry McBride felt compelled to issue a damning remark about the reception of Van Gogh in the United States to date: "During the thirty years' nap in which our museum directors and collectors have been indulging, amateurs upon the other side of the water have not been asleep... To have bolted the doors so long against van Gogh, to have kept aloof from him during all the years in which he was, so to speak, upon trial, does not appear to throw a pretty light upon our museums."[1] McBride's words would ring true—at least for museum collections in New York—for more than twenty more years. It would not be until 1941 that the Museum of Modern Art would announce the landmark acquisition of *The Starry Night* (F612; fig. 1), touted as "the first canvas by the painter to be acquired by a New York museum" (fig. 2).[2]

It is hard today to imagine a time when America's premier modern art museum was not a site of pilgrimage for viewing what is arguably the most iconic Van Gogh painting in the world. Yet the story of how America came to embrace this artist to the point that the purchase of this masterpiece marks a significant event has until now remained largely untold.

Americans had the opportunity to learn about Van Gogh's life and work in advance of experiencing his achievements in a public forum on this side of the Atlantic. In the first decade of the twentieth century, the American press commented on major exhibitions of his work in Europe, and as early as 1908, anticipation of his arrival was building. As one critic observed: "What will happen to our nerves when Cézanne, Gauguin, Van Gogh appear?"[3] And just before Van Gogh finally did debut publicly in the United States in 1913 in the exhibition now commonly known as the Armory Show, the *New York Times* reported on the promise of a room of paintings by the artist "of whom we already have said much in these columns."[4] America's acceptance of Van Gogh, however, was neither easy nor straightforward.

In 1912, Albert C. Barnes, John Quinn, and Katherine S. Dreier were the first in the United States to recognize the power of Van Gogh's work and purchase examples of it for their personal collections. But they were exceptions; it would not be until the mid-to-late 1920s that private collectors in America, with the support of dealers committed to the cause, truly welcomed the artist into their homes.[5] And it was thanks to many of these collectors that Van Gogh's works ended up in American museums. More often than not, paintings crossed the Atlantic multiple times before occasionally finding an American buyer. Such was the fate of a number of the pictures on view at the Armory Show, including *Landscape with Figures* (F818; plate 1) and *Undergrowth with Two Figures* (F773; plate 2). Both works were lent by the Van Gogh family through their dealer Artz & De Bois; both took pride of place in the New York, Chicago, and Boston venues of the exhibition (see Stein, New York, fig. 3); and both were available for purchase but went back to Europe unsold. The two pictures returned to America for the artist's first United States gallery retrospective in 1920 at the Montross Gallery, but then again made the journey back to Europe to be exhibited in various cities in Switzerland, Germany, France, the Netherlands, and Great Britain. At last, in 1929, they were finally purchased by Americans.[6] *Landscape with Figures* went to Josef Stransky, the former conductor of the New York Philharmonic and an art collector and dealer; *Undergrowth with Two Figures* was sold to collector Gilbert E. Fuller, president of a travel agency headquartered in Boston. Neither picture would remain with its original owner: the former would be acquired in 1934 by notable Baltimore art collector Etta Cone; the latter would be purchased in the 1940s by Mary E. Johnston, a Procter & Gamble heir from Glendale, Ohio.[7] Thanks to their generosity, the works ended up in the collections of the Baltimore Museum of Art and the Cincinnati Art Museum, respectively. Their paths to a home in an American public museum had been long and hard.

Although the stories told in this catalogue take place well after Van Gogh's death, the artist was certainly aware of the international marketplace.[8] Before he dedicated himself to being an artist, Van Gogh worked with the art dealer Goupil & Co. at their branches in The Hague, London, and Paris; his brother Theo was also in the business.[9] And while the artist never visited America, he had a command of English and was exposed to American culture through multiple channels.[10] His rich letters reveal that he made the acquaintance of at least two American artists, Frank Myers Boggs and Dodge MacKnight.[11] He expressed his admiration for James McNeill Whistler and the illustrations featured in *Harper's Monthly*.[12] Moreover, as an avid reader, Van Gogh was known to peruse the poetry of Henry Wadsworth Longfellow and Walt Whitman.[13] Another powerful American book,

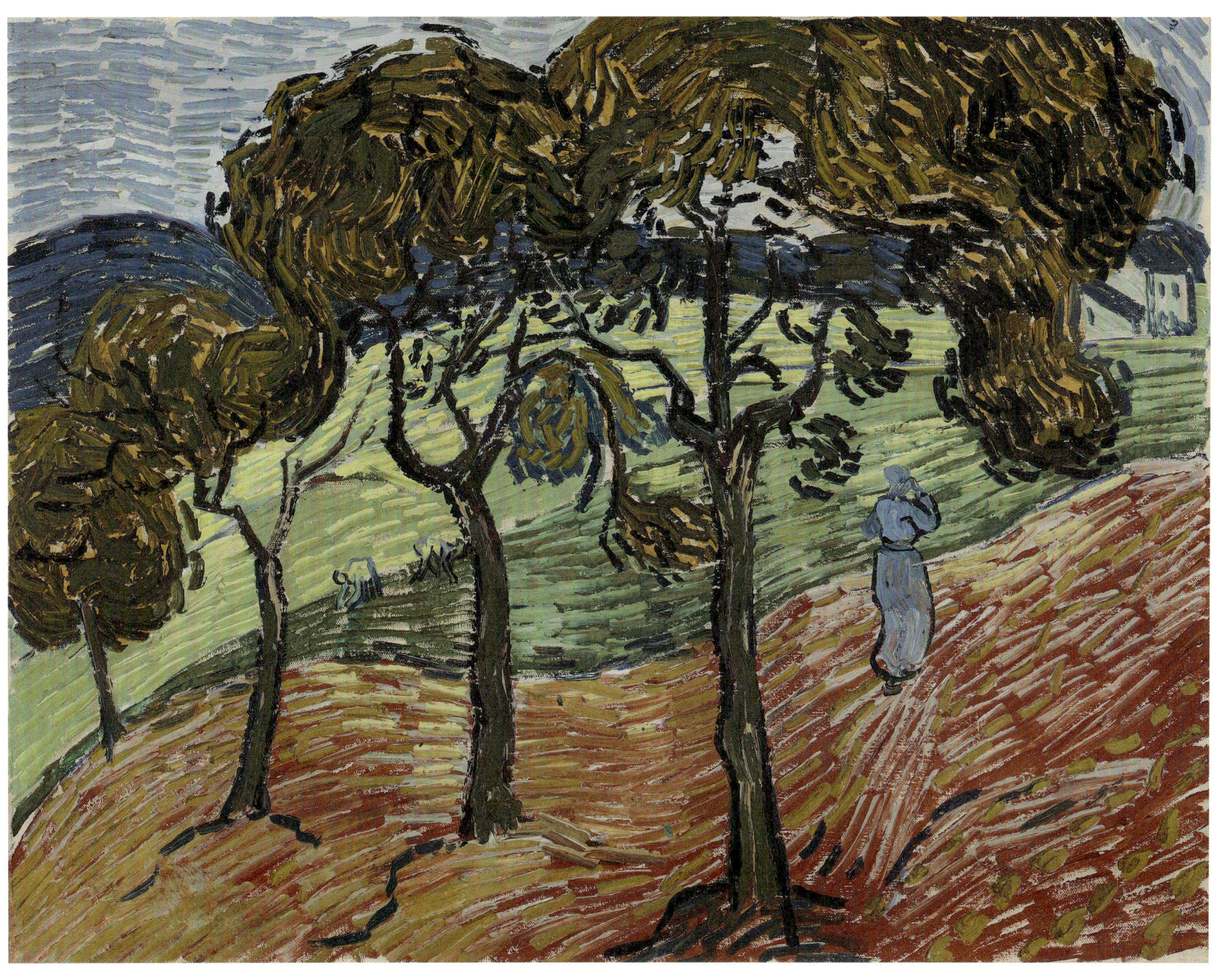

PLATE 1. *Landscape with Figures*, 1889 (CAT. 56)

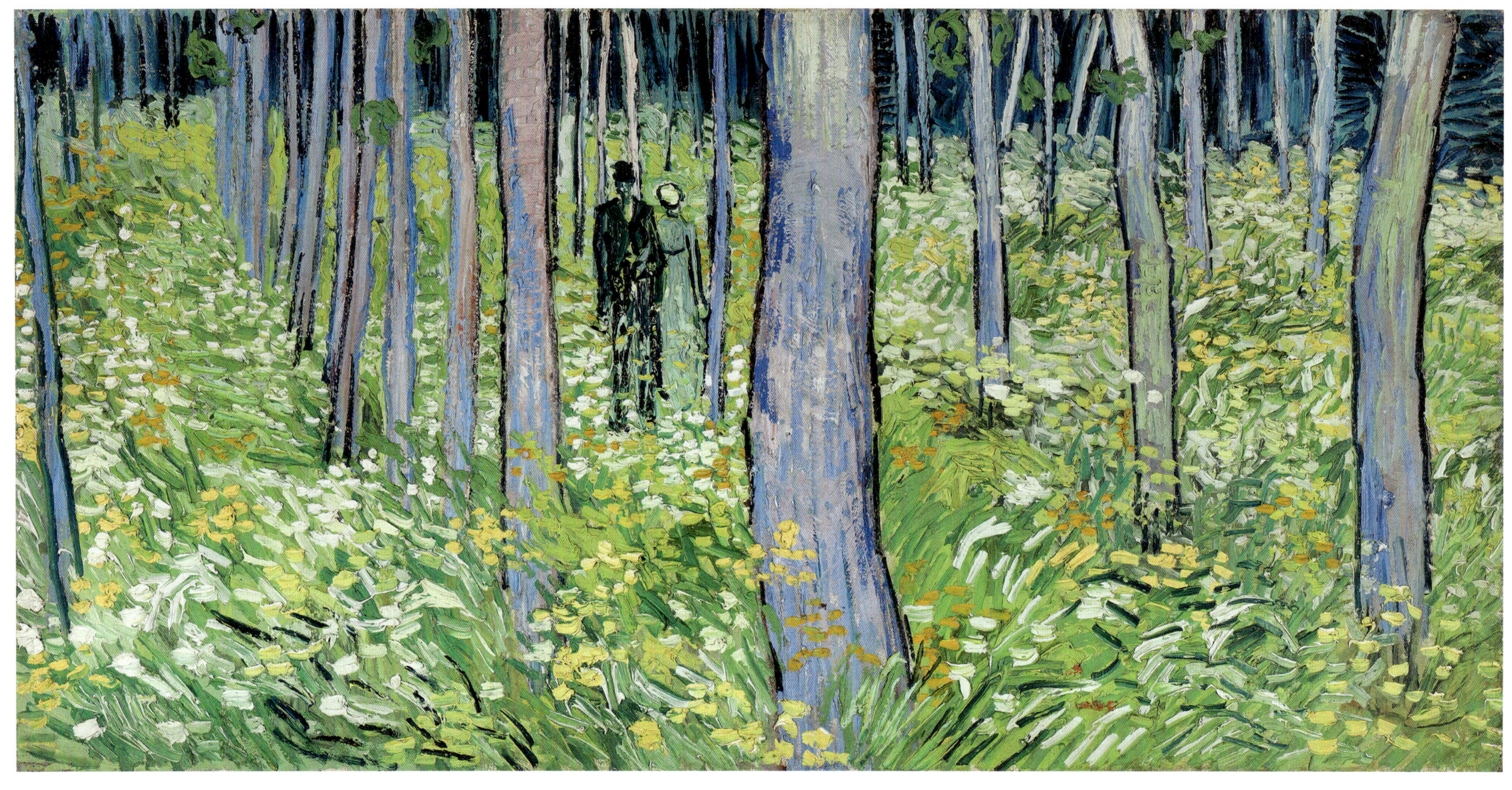

PLATE 2. *Undergrowth with Two Figures*, 1890 (CAT. 66)

Uncle Tom's Cabin (1852) by Harriet Beecher Stowe, had special meaning for the artist, so much so that he depicted a copy of the novel in his paintings of Arlésienne Madame Ginoux (F543; plate 41).[14]

This exhibition is the first to begin chronicling the considerable efforts made by early promoters of modernism here and in Europe to introduce Van Gogh's art to America. Insightful essays in this catalogue illuminate how Van Gogh's path to success in the United States was a circuitous one that included a combination of forward-thinking individuals, courage, and determination, and involved a series of false starts, sensational tales in print and film, the circulation of forgeries, and missed opportunities. America's delayed response, however, should in no way fuel the oft-repeated claim that the artist was unknown and sold only one picture in his lifetime—a myth recited and perpetuated, even in the most recent catalogue raisonné of the artist,[15] that numerous scholars have worked to discredit.[16] America's hesitation in coming around to the artist—as we see in this study—resulted from many factors, including a general reluctance to embrace modern art, and the high prices for Van Gogh's works thanks to demand for them in Europe even before his art was seen in the United States.

Yet in 1929, although the Detroit Institute of Arts and the Art Institute of Chicago were the only two public encyclopedic museums in the United States to own his paintings, it was noted that despite the fact that Americans "came late to Van Gogh, their power is so embracing that, their minds once made up, they get what they want."[17] By 1935, the year of his first retrospective exhibition in an American museum, individuals from coast to coast had welcomed Van Gogh into their private collections. Furthermore, the overwhelming enthusiasm for the artist began to solidify following the publication of American author Irving Stone's novel *Lust for Life* (1934). Loosely based on the life of the artist, the hugely popular book was adapted into film in 1956, famously featuring Kirk Douglas as Van Gogh. Undoubtedly Vincente Minnelli's film—as well as many others to follow—helped certain paintings, like the Detroit Institute of Arts' *Self-Portrait,* attain their iconic status (see fig. 3). These cultural productions have also

FIG. 3 *Lust for Life* press photo featuring Kirk Douglas as Vincent van Gogh in the guise of his *Self-Portrait* (F526; plate 44), now in the collection of the Detroit Institute of Arts.

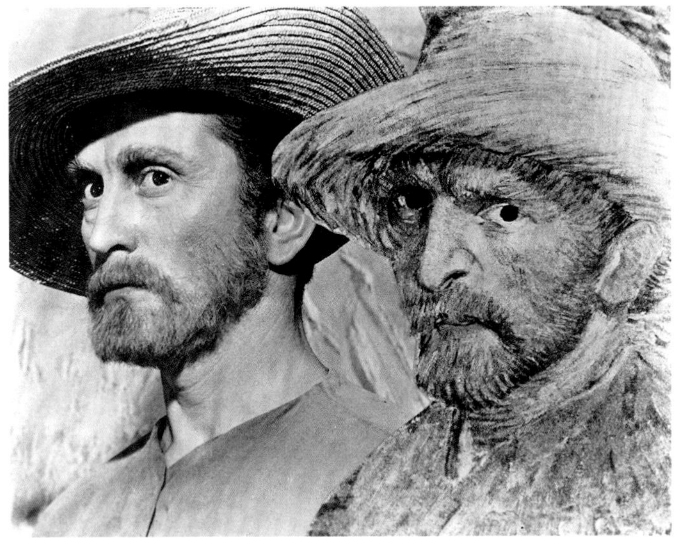

perpetuated ideas about the artist that scholars have been trying to correct for many years. This publication presents new research intended to reframe the popular narrative so deeply ingrained in the public imagination.

Van Gogh in America builds on the work of many predecessors who have isolated the "posthumous fate" of the artist and the market for his works as a subject of particular importance and interest.[18] It also should be considered a springboard for future studies on this subject. Indeed, new research has unearthed questions and avenues for exploration in regard to the many other collectors of Van Gogh's work that could not be treated at great length—or at all—in this publication. This catalogue focuses on the pioneering advocates for the artist's work up to around 1935—when Van Gogh received his first museum retrospective in the United States and was fully established within the art historical canon—and the landmark group or solo exhibitions of his work in America up to 1950. There is significant room to continue explorations about the propensity of women to promote and collect Van Gogh's work, including early American advocates such as Katherine S. Dreier (New York) and Alice Roullier (Chicago); later ones including Mary Batterman Booth (Detroit), Annie Swan Coburn (Chicago), Claribel and Etta Cone (Baltimore), Mary E. Johnston (Cincinnati), Adelaide Milton de Groot (New York), Effie Seachrest (Kansas City), and Dorothy Sturges (Providence); as well as Europeans like the artist's sister-in-law Jo van Gogh-Bonger (fig. 4) and Helene Kröller-Müller. Additional areas of inquiry include the several unsuccessful plans to bring Van Gogh's work to America before the Armory Show; the reception of the artist in non-English (especially German) American newspapers; the endless infatuation with his story in mass culture, most recently embodied by the number of Van Gogh "immersive experiences" dotting the world, but most especially in North America; and certainly—as has been explored in recent exhibitions focusing on the market for Van Gogh's works in other parts of the world, including Great Britain and Germany—the impact of his work on American artists, musicians, filmmakers, and writers.[19] Countless other avenues—including the market for his work in other North and South American countries—merit further attention as well. It is our hope that this publication inspires further work on the legacy of Van Gogh—an artist who slowly but surely captured the heart and imagination of America.

FIG. 4 Jo van Gogh-Bonger with her infant son Vincent Willem van Gogh, 1890. Van Gogh Museum, Amsterdam (Vincent van Gogh Foundation).

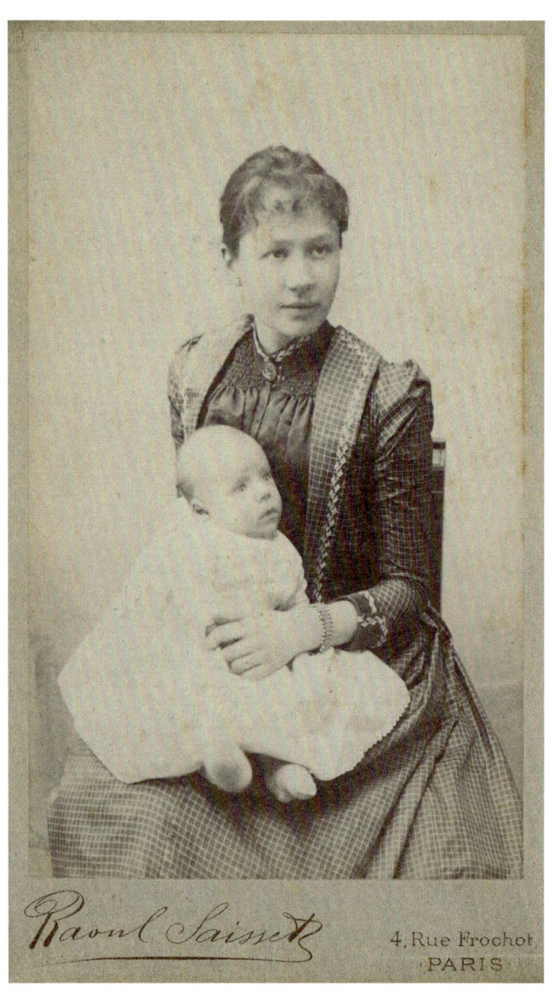

NOTES

1 McBride 1920b: 631. This article appeared in a section of *The Dial* called "Modern Forms," which was "devoted to exposition and consideration of the less traditional types of art."
2 *Bulletin of the Museum of Modern Art* 1941: 2.
3 *New York Sun* 1908: 8. Rewald 1989, 127n18 says the author is James G. Huneker, but the article is unsigned.
4 *New York Times* 1913: SM15.
5 For Dreier, experiencing Van Gogh's work in the 1912 Sonderbund exhibition in Cologne "was like stepping out of a stuffy room into glorious bracing air. What courage and conviction had produced this vitality—these pictures vibrant with life!" Dreier 1913, xiv.
6 W. Feilchenfeldt 2013, 257, 266.
7 For provenance on these two works, see Koldehoff and Stolwijk 2017, 176–77; and Prins 2016–17, 16.
8 Kelly 2012–13.
9 Bailey 2019, 15–18; and Amsterdam and Paris 1999–2000.
10 Pickvance 1970.
11 Boggs and MacKnight are mentioned in correspondence such as Van Gogh Letters 2009, nos. 570 and 598. See also Pickvance 1970 and Bailey 2007.
12 References appear in Van Gogh Letters 2009, nos. 267 and 273, among others.
13 Mention of Longfellow and Whitman can be found in correspondence such as Van Gogh Letters 2009, nos. 66 and 670.
14 For more on Van Gogh's reading of Harriet Beecher Stowe, see Pickvance 1970: 74; and Soth 1994.
15 Hulsker 1996, 370.
16 See, for example, W. Feilchenfeldt 1988, 8–9; Dorn 1990; W. Feilchenfeldt 1990, 39–40; Koldehoff 2003, 14; W. Feilchenfeldt 2013, 45; Van Tilborgh 2011, 18; and Kelly 2012–13. For Van Gogh myths, see Kōdera and Rosenberg 1993; Heinich 1996; and Koldehoff 2003.
17 Watson 1929: 147. This was published on the occasion of the first exhibition at the Museum of Modern Art, New York, that featured Van Gogh, along with Paul Cézanne, Paul Gauguin, and Georges Seurat. See New York 1929a, 30; and Shaw, Heartland, note 4.
18 Notable references include Rewald 1986; Dorn 1990; W. Feilchenfeldt 1990; Leeman 1990; Rabinow 2000; Stolwijk and Veenenbos 2002; Stein 2005; Warwickshire and Edinburgh 2006; Budapest 2006–2007; Koldehoff 2006–2007; Van Tilborgh 2011; Kelly 2012–13; W. Feilchenfeldt 2013; London 2019; and Frankfurt 2019–20. Numerous publications and exhibitions on dealers of modern art that handled Van Gogh's works have also contributed greatly to this dialogue. See W. Feilchenfeldt 1988; Jensen 1994; Amsterdam and Paris 1999–2000; New York, Chicago, and Paris 2006–2007; Patry 2015; and Koldehoff and Stolwijk 2017.
19 Most recently, London 2019 and Frankfurt 2019–20.

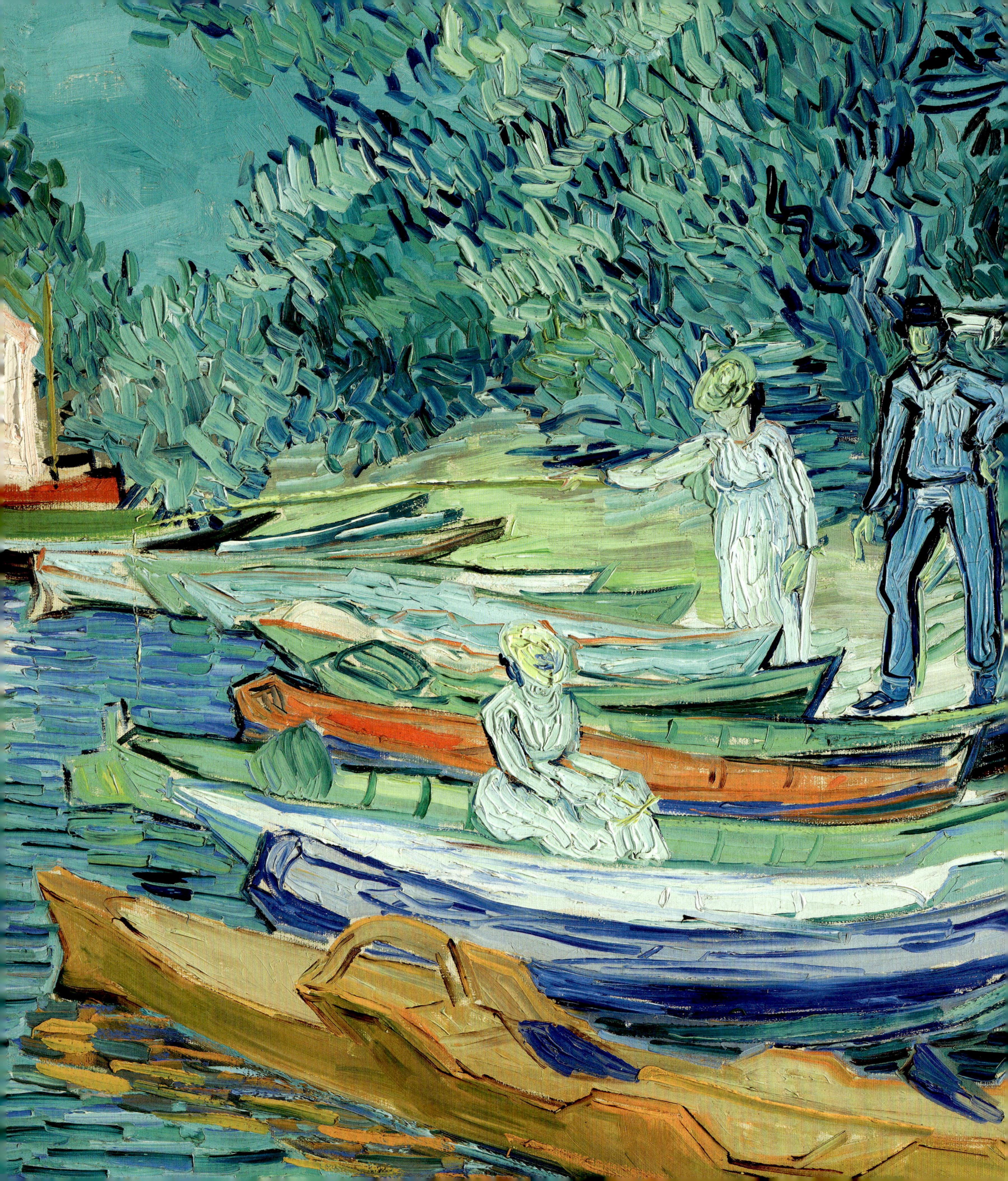

CHRIS STOLWIJK AND JULIA KRIKKE

Becoming the Most Popular Dutch Painter: Van Gogh in America, c. 1910–50

On January 17, 1950, the Dutch daily paper *De Volkskrant* reported with some national pride that Vincent van Gogh had become "the most popular painter in America."[1] Given some 302,000 visitors, *Van Gogh Paintings and Drawings: A Special Loan Exhibition* was the best attended exhibition in the history of New York's Metropolitan Museum of Art.[2] World War II had ended only a few years earlier. Van Gogh was presented as the artist who "transformed realism into a powerful, symbolic method," using "exaggerations of line and form" and, above all, color, to express a more universal significance reflecting his changing "emotional states." His art was a triumph "over misunderstanding, poverty, and pain," and his work brought "to a confused world…above all else: the power to reveal and to console."[3]

The exhibition was a national event. Eleanor Roosevelt mentioned that she had been to see it and that she had missed some works she had seen twenty years earlier at the Museum of Modern Art (MoMA).[4] She was referring to MoMA's inaugural show in 1929 organized by Alfred H. Barr Jr., in which Van Gogh appeared as a representative of the Modern French School along with Paul Cézanne, Paul Gauguin, and Georges Seurat, who supposedly laid the foundations of a more modern form of art in the last decades of the nineteenth century. In 1935–36 it was again MoMA under Barr's leadership that, with the successful exhibition simply titled *Vincent van Gogh*, firmly established Van Gogh's reputation in America.

Barr, MoMA's first director, took a formalist approach to the history of art, including modern art.[5] Van Gogh had introduced a new conception of line, form, and color. Although in the 1920s, many were still describing him as a French painter, Barr argued that Van Gogh was, rather, the archetype of expressionism:

"It is increasingly usual to call van Gogh a French painter...[however] the inner character of his work, trenchant, disproportioned, lacking in 'taste', but burning with a spiritual ardor, seems defiantly un-French...if any race may claim him, it should surely be Northern...Van Gogh is in fact the archetype of *expressionism*, of the cult of pure uncensored spontaneity."[6]

In his 1935–36 exhibition catalogue, Barr abandoned these sorts of classifications in favor of letting Van Gogh's life and work speak for themselves. He published excerpts from Van Gogh's correspondence, recent information about the places the artist stayed in the Netherlands, Belgium, and France, and details of his family history. As had been the case in the exhibition at New York's Montross Gallery in 1920, Van Gogh's Dutch period was acknowledged and explored: this time his *Potato Eaters* (F82; fig. 1) of 1885 was the most important work.

Whereas the American public was not really concerned at that moment about whether Van Gogh was a French modernist, a Northern expressionist, a Franco-Dutch artist, or a Dutch one, in the Netherlands the success of MoMA's 1935–36 exhibition was a confirmation that the nation's painting tradition had found a successor in Van Gogh—a successor, moreover, who could be regarded as one of the pioneers of an international modern art. "What does the average American know about Holland?...The Van Gogh exhibition in New York has made many people here realize that there is more to Holland than tulips, clogs, and small boys with their finger in the dike."[7]

FIG. 1 *The Potato Eaters* (F82), 1885. Oil on canvas, 32 × 44⅞ in. (82 × 114 cm). Van Gogh Museum, Amsterdam (Vincent van Gogh Foundation).

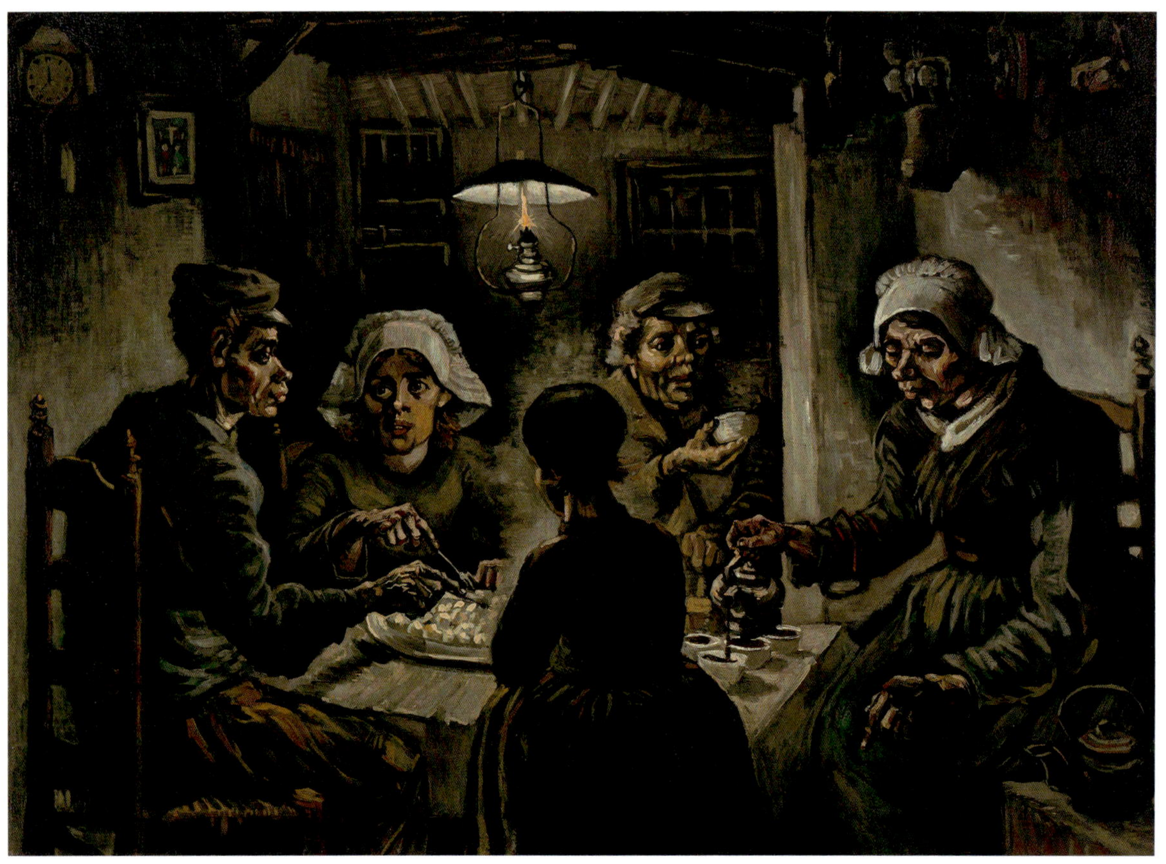

In today's world, an era marked by a crumbling sense of community and rising nationalist populism, it is important within the turbulent history of the early reception, distribution, and appreciation of Van Gogh to clarify *which* Van Gogh, under *which* circumstances, and at precisely *which* moment arrived on the American continent.

Setting the Scene

Around 1900 Van Gogh's reception and appreciation were anything but unequivocal; numerous institutional, ideological, national, and individual factors affected his reputation. The last quarter of the nineteenth century saw the emergence of an international professional art market filled with competing artists, dealers and galleries, exhibitions, collectors, and critics. This market established a foothold on American soil, where a group of newly wealthy buyers, usually with roots in Europe, were prepared to invest considerable sums in old and contemporary art. Although he came from a family of successful art dealers and was raised in the art trade, Van Gogh the artist had virtually no access to this international market. This, taken in conjunction with his unique work, his solitary existence, and his dramatic end, fueled the romantic image of a poor, tortured painter who was not accepted by his respectable family, the official art world, or society at large, and had to go his own way and die as a martyr for modern art.

Van Gogh's reception in America was also affected by a "battle of nations" in Europe around 1900 and the debate over what precisely was "modern art" in itself and vis-à-vis the possibilities of the international art market. This battle centered on the importance of a national art versus a universal art, on the relationship between a national tradition versus international modernity, and on the distinction between an art of realism rooted in the observation and experience of nature and in the present day versus a more symbolic approach.[8]

The many American artists who went to Europe during this period found themselves embroiled in this fight. Most went to Paris, the art capital of the world, and thus became instrumental in introducing contemporary, usually French, art to their countrymen.[9] They also went to the Low Countries, a cradle of painting regarded at that time as "sincere" and "healthily realistic" with its depiction of everyday subjects and sentiments.[10] As a consequence, from the last decades of the nineteenth century onward, a great many works in the Dutch tradition—by Old Masters and contemporary artists alike—found their way into American collections.

Around 1900 most Americans had virtually no access to knowledge about Van Gogh's life and work, particularly if he or she did not know Dutch, French, or German. Beginning in the early 1890s, articles about Van Gogh's letters had appeared in newspapers and art journals like *Mercure de France*, *Van Nu en Straks*, and *Kunst und Künstler*, but American readers had to wait until 1913 when the first significant body of selected letters by the artist were published in English translation.[11] Also in 1913, artist Katherine S. Dreier translated the memoirs of Van Gogh's sister Elisabeth du Quesne-Van Gogh from 1910, and Walter Pach collaborated with Van Gogh's sister-in-law Jo van Gogh-Bonger to publish a few letters in 1918–19.[12] The first two volumes of *The Letters of Vincent van Gogh to His Brother, 1872–1886* appeared in 1927.

Artistic Legacy in Europe

In addition to the dearth of resources in English was the fact that immediately after his death, Van Gogh's artistic legacy was dispersed among various sources within the Netherlands and France. A good deal of it was with his younger brother, Theo, an art dealer in Paris. From early 1884 on, Theo supported Vincent financially; in return he received his brother's output. In 1892 this substantial volume of work—around a thousand items—ended up in the Netherlands, where Theo's widow, Jo van Gogh-Bonger, settled with their infant son, Vincent Willem.[13] This "family collection" subsequently formed the basis of dozens of exhibitions, and Van Gogh's reputation began to spread in Europe and, after 1920, in America, too. Another Dutch source for Van Gogh's work was Oldenzeel, a gallery in Rotterdam, which in 1903 started selling unknown works from Van Gogh's Dutch period that he had left behind when he moved from the Netherlands to Antwerp.[14]

One more, not insignificant, part of the legacy had what might be called a French provenance. These were works that Van Gogh had entrusted to friendly dealers like Père Tanguy, had left in the "Studio of the South" in Provence, and had given to or exchanged with friends and other artists. In the 1890s Jo van Gogh-Bonger was still in direct contact with the French art market—in 1896, for instance, Ambroise Vollard staged a large gallery exhibition of Van Gogh works.

The dispersal of the legacy meant that interested parties at that time were obliged to go either to the "French" or to the "Dutch" sources. This geographical separation also led to an ideological one. From the early 1890s onward, France claimed Van Gogh as a French painter. Dutch art critics found it extremely difficult to place his work—which was virtually unknown in the country of his birth—within a national tradition, even though it had been shown in several smaller exhibitions in Paris, Brussels, and places in the Netherlands since 1889. In 1905 a critic reviewed the artist's retrospective at the Stedelijk Museum in Amsterdam: "His paintings come mainly from Nuenen in Brabant, from Paris, from Arles in the South of France, and from some other French places.... Most of them are entirely beyond what we here in Holland understand as painting. The intentions are

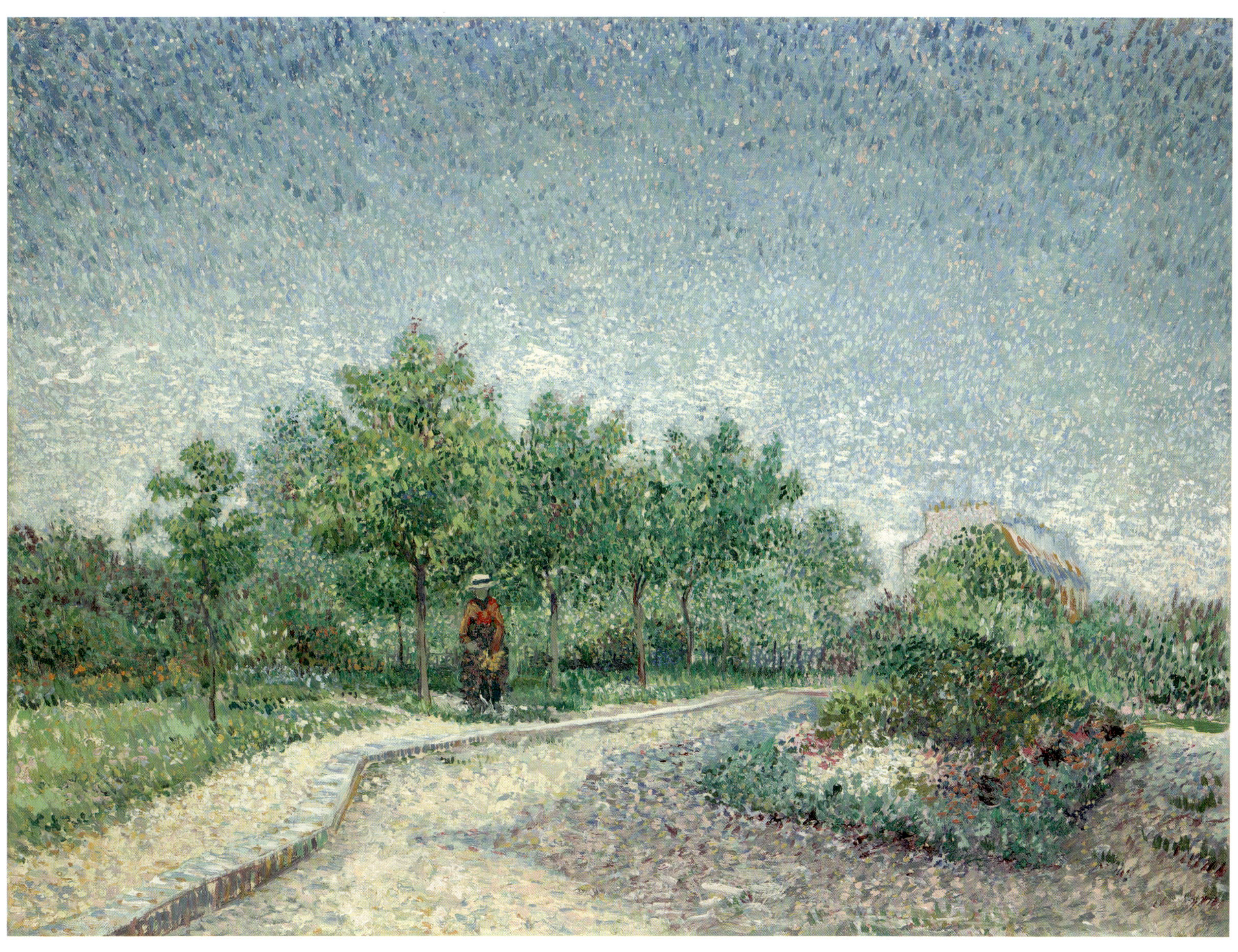

PLATE 3. *Square Saint-Pierre, Paris*, 1887 (CAT. 22)

different; the results are completely different" (see, for example, F276, F714, F793, F809; plates 3–6).[15] What was regarded as "modern" painting in Holland at that time differed fundamentally from the French view, although both, despite a huge diversity in conception and results, can be described as figurative, naturalistic art.[16]

In France, modern art—insofar as it was derived from art concepts based in realism, personal observation, and the present day—found its leading exponents in Eugène Delacroix, the Barbizon School, the Impressionists, and Post-Impressionists such as Cézanne, Gauguin, Seurat, and Van Gogh. Until the early twentieth century, Dutch contemporary painting was governed largely by a desire to showcase "Dutch glory" and engage with a national tradition rooted in the magnificent Golden Age.[17] Around 1900 this ambition was represented by the painters of the Hague School—Jozef Israëls, the Maris brothers, Anton Mauve, and Hendrik Mesdag, among others—then known internationally as the Modern Dutch School. A younger generation, including Jan Toorop, Kees van Dongen, Jan Sluijters, and Piet Mondrian, sought to connect with international modernity but initially found little response either in their own country or in France. Except for the work of the Barbizon painters, modern French art appealed to few in the Netherlands, despite some early initiatives and purchases by private individuals.[18]

Meanwhile, Van Gogh was gaining a reputation in Germany.[19] In 1901, in his Berlin gallery, Paul Cassirer staged the first solo exhibition of "works by the late Dutch painter Vincent van Gogh"; these paintings, "which had never before been exhibited in Germany," came from Jo van Gogh-Bonger's collection, as did *Bank of the Oise at Auvers* (F798; plate 7), later acquired by Cassirer in September 1905.[20] In 1905 Cassirer was given exclusive access to the family collection. Over the course of a quarter of a century, he placed dozens of works with (mostly) German collectors and museums (see, for example, F438; plate 8). The majority of them were scattered after Hitler came to power in 1933, and some found their way to America.

Cassirer organized numerous shows of earlier and contemporary art from Germany and beyond. His publishing house, Paul Cassirer Verlag, produced catalogues with in-depth art historical essays, illustrated magazines, and other art publications. In 1914, for instance, he issued a two-volume German edition of *Vincent van Gogh: Brieven aan zijn broeder* (Van Gogh Letters 1914), which had been published by Jo van Gogh-Bonger in the same year. This first extensive publication of the artist's correspondence included a biographical introduction that gave a nuanced picture of Van Gogh's life and work.[21]

Julius Meier-Graefe was among the writers on art who were in close contact with Cassirer and had a significant influence on Van Gogh's reputation in Germany. Meier-Graefe's 1910 German monograph on Van Gogh placed his Dutch period within a Dutch realist tradition of Van Ostade, Van der Neer, "and the other masters of subject matter."[22] In his French works, he was the "strongest, most healthy and most free" pupil of "Gauguin's Art School."[23] Some ten years later, promoting the

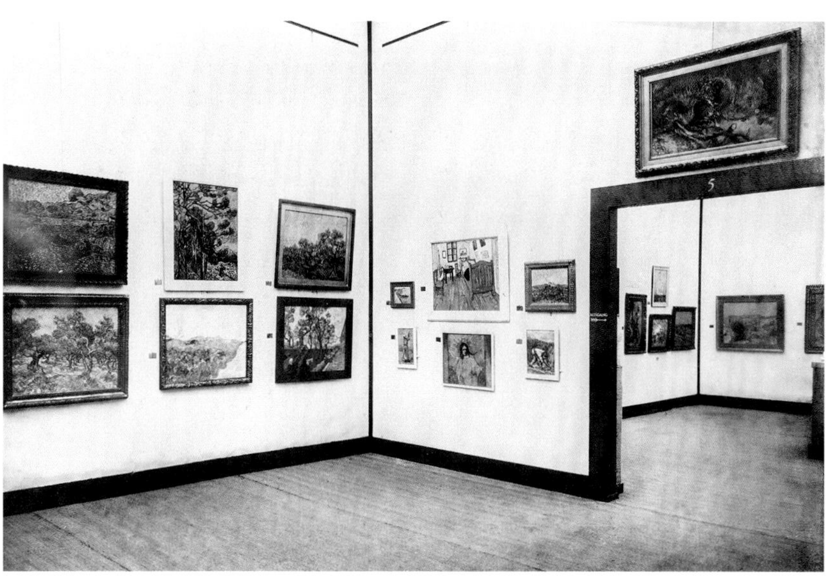

FIG. 2 Installation of works by Van Gogh in Rooms 5 and 6, Sonderbund exhibition, Cologne, 1912.

importance of German artists to modern art, Meier-Graefe presented Van Gogh as an exponent of the German Expressionism that was on the rise at that time—a view to which Barr also subscribed in 1929. To Meier-Graefe, Van Gogh was a "Germanic contribution to the development of modern European painting."[24]

Cassirer, on the other hand, like the dealers Heinrich and Justin Thannhauser, proved to have a more international outlook.[25] For him, Van Gogh was one of a select group of artists—including Cézanne, Gauguin, and Seurat—whose new art, based on their shared views of color, line, and form, was rooted in French Impressionism. It was this notion of art that gave a direction to a new generation of artists now known as German Expressionists. To those artists who belonged to Die Brücke and Der Blaue Reiter, Van Gogh was the prime example of a brilliant artist who came from the North, and despite isolation, poverty, social opposition, and physical and mental challenges, went his own way. In a unique new pictorial idiom "restricted to four or five basic colors," he had expressed his direct, emotional (subconscious) reaction to the often hostile world around him.[26] At the famous Sonderbund exhibition in Cologne in 1912, which served as the model for the organization of the Armory Show in New York in 1913, Van Gogh was described as the father of this "German" Expressionism (fig. 2). At the Sonderbund exhibition, more than 170 contemporary artists from ten European countries were represented, including the late Van Gogh (see, for example, F701; plate 9), Cézanne, and Gauguin. The intention was to show the current state of modern painting, which, according to the chairman of the exhibition, was moving away from naturalism and Impressionism toward simpler forms, new rhythm and color, and decoration and monumentality.[27]

Defining Van Gogh in America

Despite following on the heels of the Sonderbund exhibition, Van Gogh's debut in America at the Armory Show in 1913 presented him not as a "Dutch" artist, not as a "German Expressionist," but together with Cézanne and Gauguin as one of "the big three" of modern French painting. Save for two works from his Dutch period, all the works by Van Gogh in the show dated from his time in France.

According to Frederick James Gregg, the Armory Show's public relations director, the organizers wanted to introduce the American public to "the works of a number of foreign artists, who, though they are well known in Europe, are for the most part but names to New York and America." They did not, however, want "to throw our 'extreme' contemporaries at the heads of the public," but present them as worthy successors to a French tradition: "So Ingres was taken as the starting

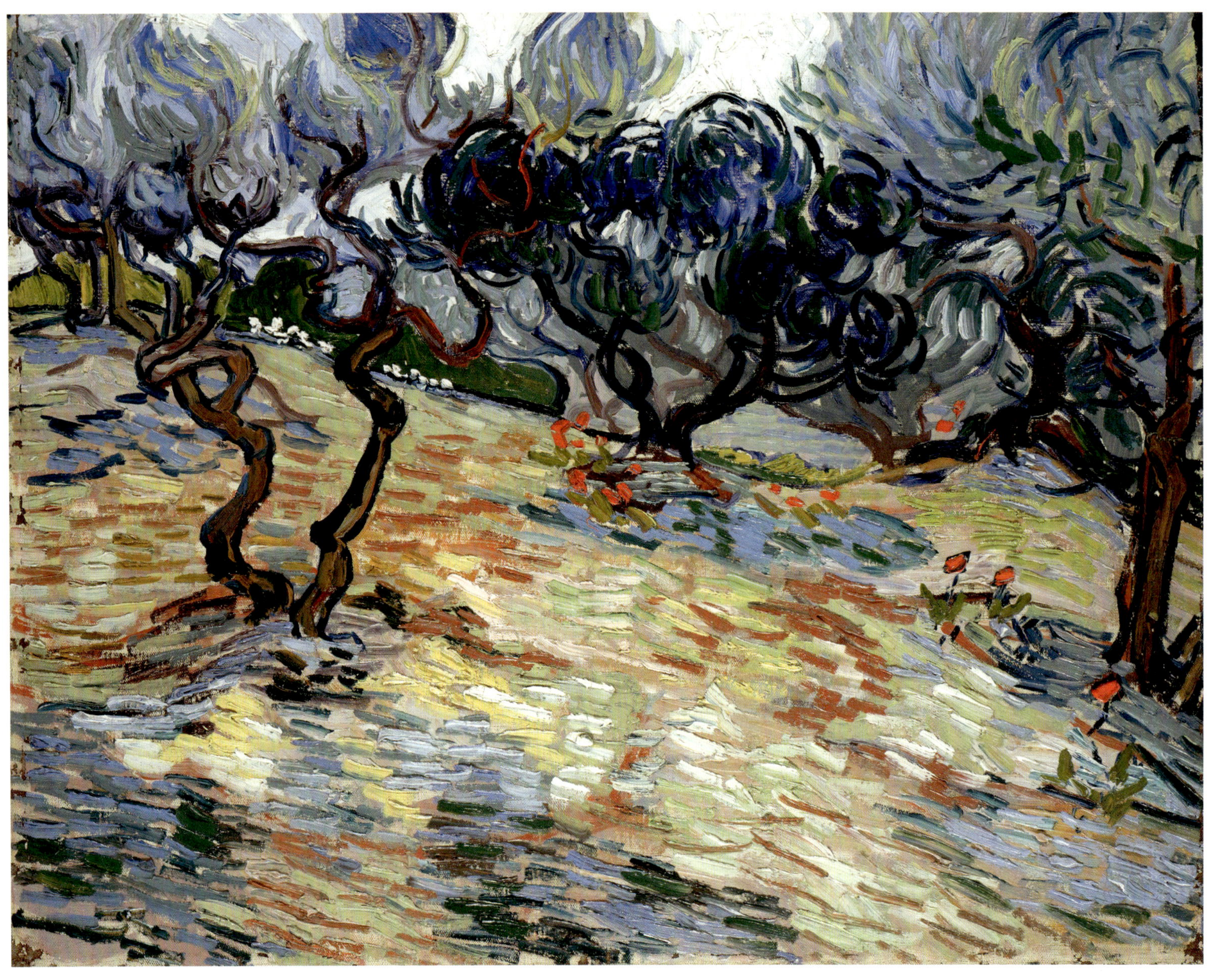

PLATE 4. *Olive Trees*, 1889 (CAT. 49)

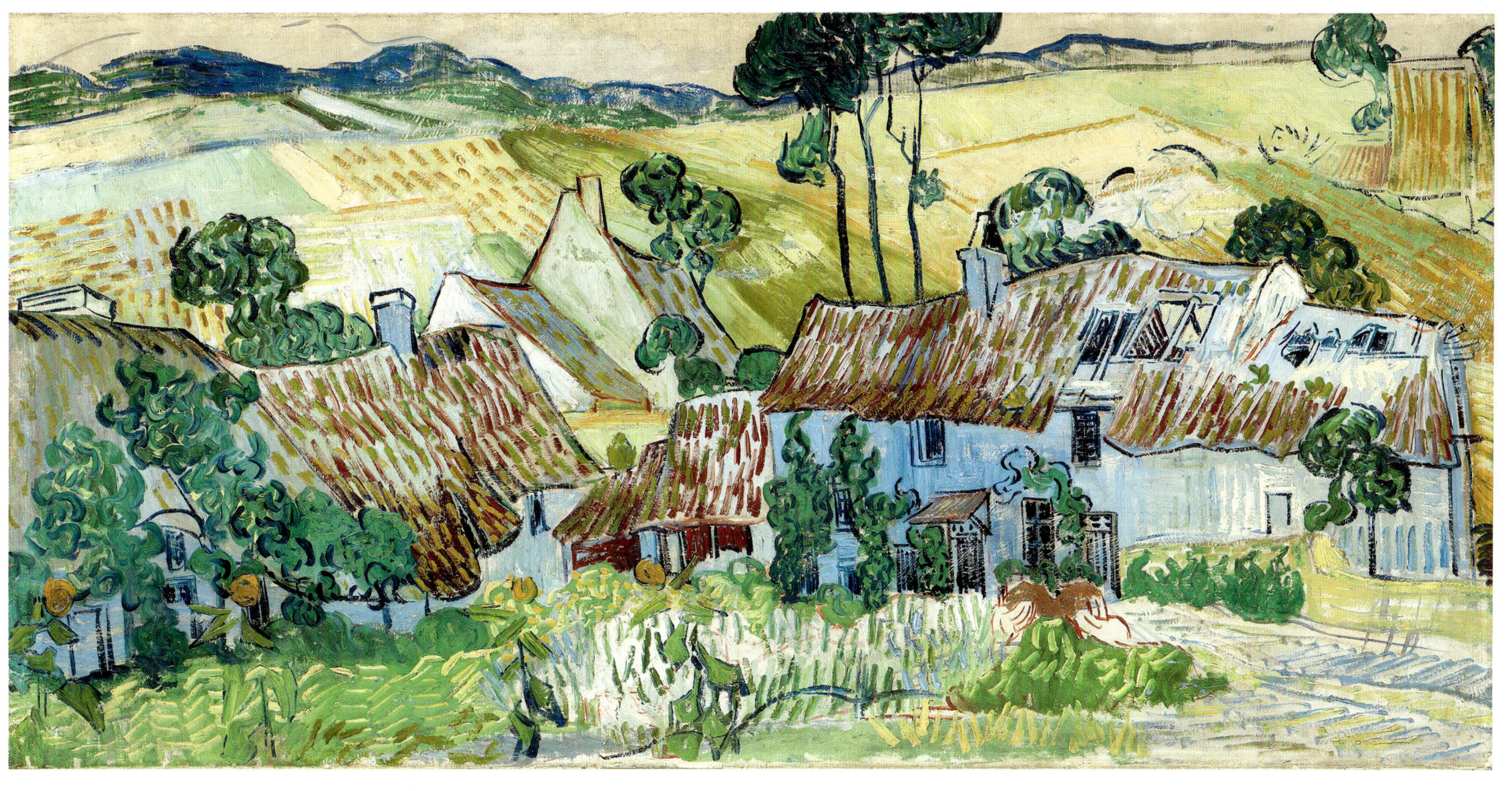

PLATE 5. *Farms near Auvers*, 1890 (CAT. 71)

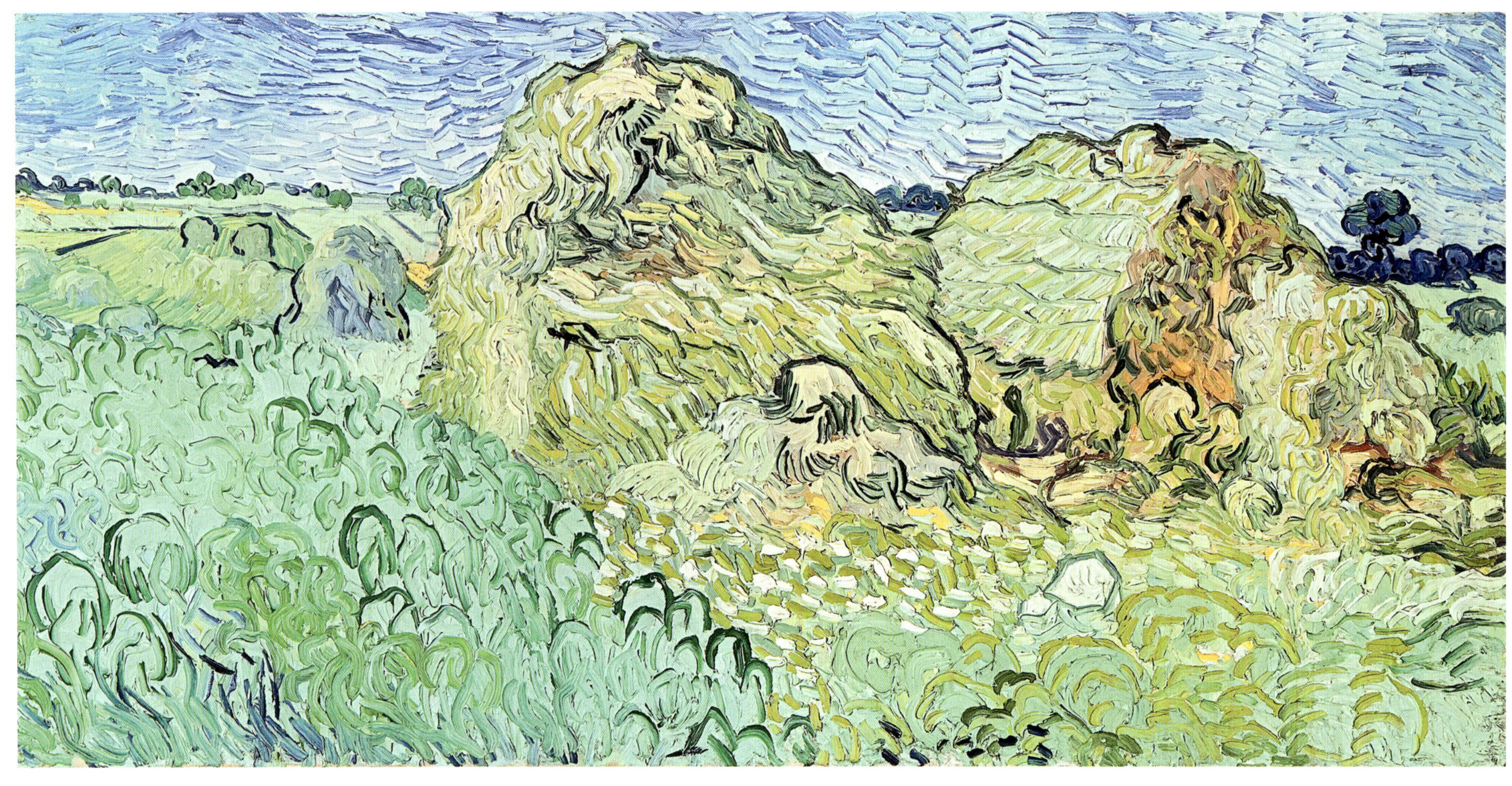

PLATE 6. *Wheat Stacks*, 1890 (CAT. 72)

point, the line continuing with Delacroix, Courbet, Corot, Daumier, Puvis de Chavannes, Degas, Renoir, Monet, Sisley, Pissarro, and so down to Cézanne, Gauguin, Van Gogh, Matisse, Picasso, and the 'Cubists.'"[28]

The artist Katherine S. Dreier, promoter of both Van Gogh and Mondrian, not only was a supporter of the Armory Show, she also spearheaded the English-language edition of *Personal Recollections of Vincent van Gogh* (1913) by his sister Elisabeth du Quesne-Van Gogh. In her lengthy introduction to the book, Dreier placed Van Gogh's struggles within the context of a general battle, starting in Paris, around the modern art "of various nations who are trying to express not only themselves but the spirit of to-day."[29] In his lonely quest, Van Gogh had found that universal "truth" by offering "a whole new vision of color construction," in other words, by "drawing in color—trying to give both light and form through color, as it has never been done before."[30] Although Dreier had lived and worked in the Netherlands when she was training as an artist, she placed Van Gogh's efforts in "the progress of color" in a Western, "classical" tradition of painting encompassing Giorgione, Botticelli, the (Flemish) Primitives, and "the men of the Renaissance," including Leonardo.[31] She said not a word about possible roots in a Dutch tradition.

In 1913, with scant knowledge about Van Gogh's life and work, the American public was served up an image of a virtually unknown, solitary French artist fighting for modern art. In one newspaper he was even presented as "the French schoolmaster, who began to paint at 40 and carried on the painting of sunlight from where Monet left off."[32]

In 1920 the Montross Gallery in New York staged the first retrospective exhibition in the United States centered on a wide selection of paintings, drawings, and lithographs for sale from the family collection that showed the "evolution" of the Dutch-born artist to the American public for the first time (see, for example, F111, F451, F771, F929a; plates 10–13). According to one critic, it also shed light on the influence of Mauve and the "Old Masters" of the Dutch tradition, "which Van Gogh studied for a long time."[33] Another critic wrote that the works of "the famous Dutch painter Vincent van Gogh, which are not yet very well known in America," elicited "admiration and appreciation."[34] For the time being, however, this did not translate into sales. After the exhibition, the gallery owner Newman E. Montross and Jo van Gogh-Bonger decided "to carry on displaying the works of the Dutch artist." Up through May 1921, apparently only three works were sold, all to the clergyman Theodore Pitcairn. One of them, the 1882 drawing *Sorrow* (F929a; plate 13), may have been the first work from Van Gogh's Dutch period to enter an American collection.[35]

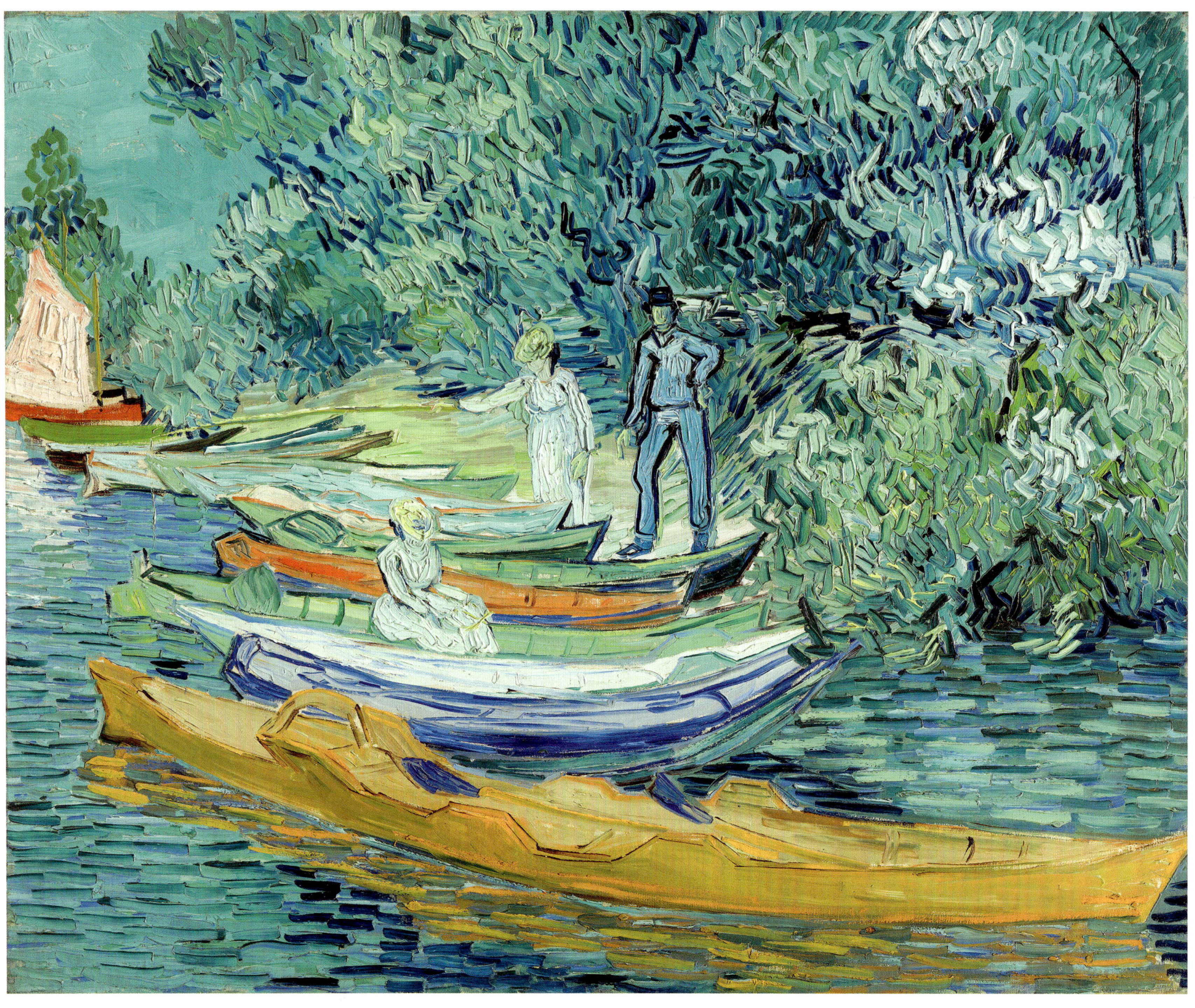

PLATE 7. *Bank of the Oise at Auvers*, 1890 (CAT. 62)

Walter Pach Plays a Part

It is thanks to the efforts of the artist, critic, consultant, and agent Walter Pach that Van Gogh's reputation grew in America after 1913. Pach had played a part in organizing the Armory Show, and through his good relationship with Jo van Gogh-Bonger was the de facto organizer of the Montross exhibition. He was thoroughly abreast of the developments taking place in the arts in Europe, which he visited almost every year beginning in 1903, when he was attending the famous painting lessons given by William Merritt Chase in Haarlem. There, Pach is said to have seen some Van Gogh drawings for the first time in 1906. In 1908, as a young artist, Pach had six works at the twenty-fourth *Salon des Indépendants* in Paris, where he also frequented the gatherings at Leo and Gertrude Stein's home.[36]

It was in this period that Pach published his first dedicated articles about painters of the "modern (French) tradition": Manet, Matisse, Monet, Cézanne, and Renoir. For half a century, Pach attempted in more synthesizing studies and articles to explain the importance and the significance of modern art (the Impressionists and Post-Impressionists, the Cubists, the Futurists, and others, and the art of his own day) specifically in relation to the development of contemporary American art—and place it in a broader, more universal tradition.

Van Gogh was one of the artists Pach was interested in early on. He wrote a number of lengthy articles about the Montross exhibition he had helped to organize. Pach saw his mission clearly: following the solo and group exhibitions he had been instrumental in organizing—Matisse (1915), Cézanne (1916, 1917), Gauguin (1920)—the Van Gogh exhibition, "aside from Seurat…rounded out fairly well the circle of great men who have been the initiators of the art of to-day."[37]

Pach presented Van Gogh as a wholly authentic artist, who "despite the influence of his predecessors and his contemporaries…was himself from the beginning to the end, so it is for himself that we want to study him to-day." He saw Van Gogh's greatest contribution to the development of modern art as the ultimate "control of the science of color which the Nineteenth Century had developed." If the artist was unique in his conception of color, where his mental state was concerned, Pach could not help thinking of Johan Barthold Jongkind, that other "great Dutchman of modern times, also an adoptive member of the French school, also a pioneer, a forerunner in modern art," who was "so deliberate, so precise" in his art, but lost his mind "the moment he quitted his easel."[38] In his "exploration of the enthralling mentality of Van Gogh," Pach also pointed to the fact that the artist constantly responded to the "great minds of the past." Rembrandt's "dark pictures," he asserted, always pursued him, "even as he works in that clearest sunlight of the South of France."[39] The Modern Dutch School, of which Rembrandt was regarded as the founder, was praised precisely for its "calm," "simplicity," and "sincerity."

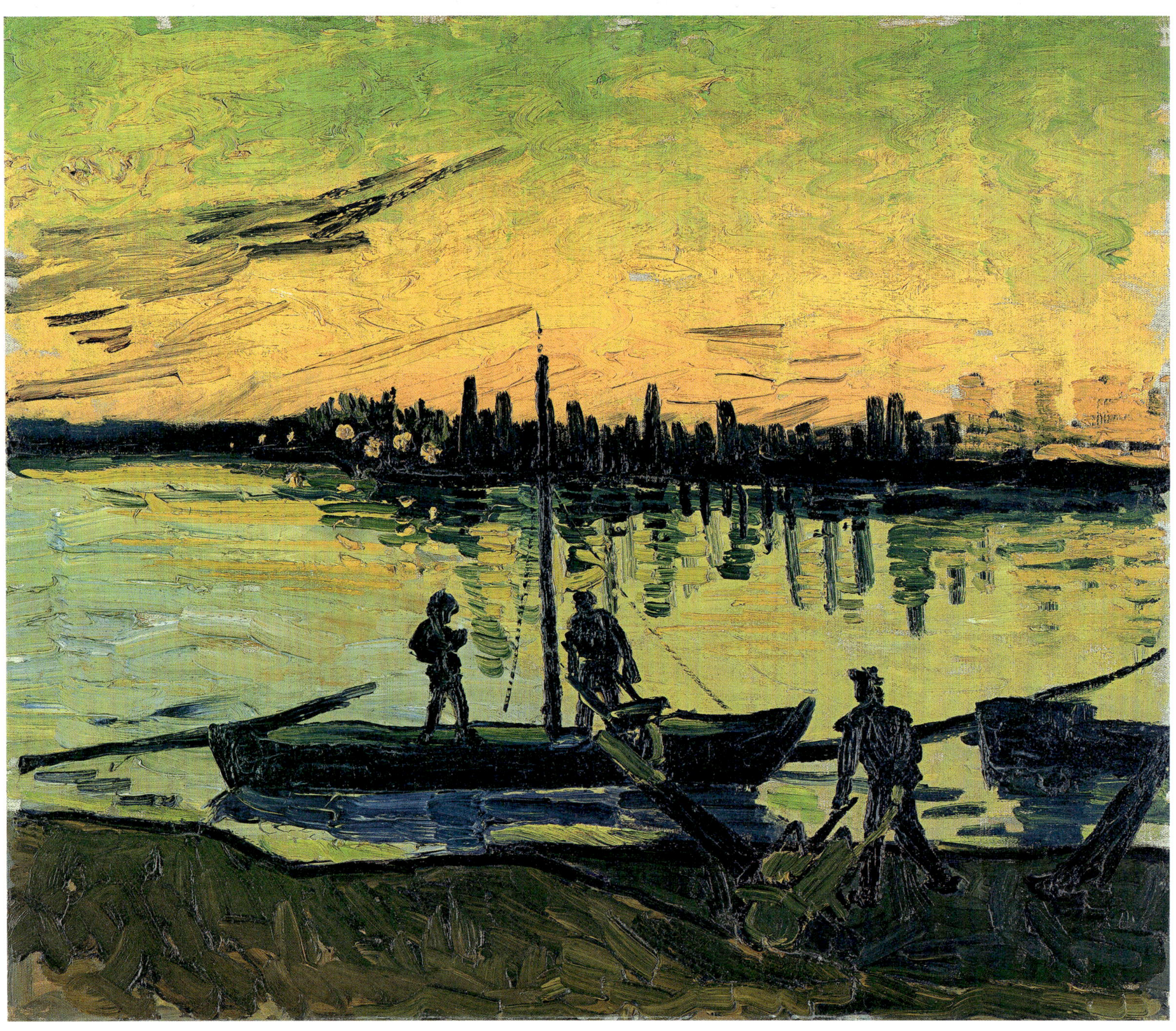

PLATE 8. *The Stevedores in Arles*, 1888 (CAT. 35)

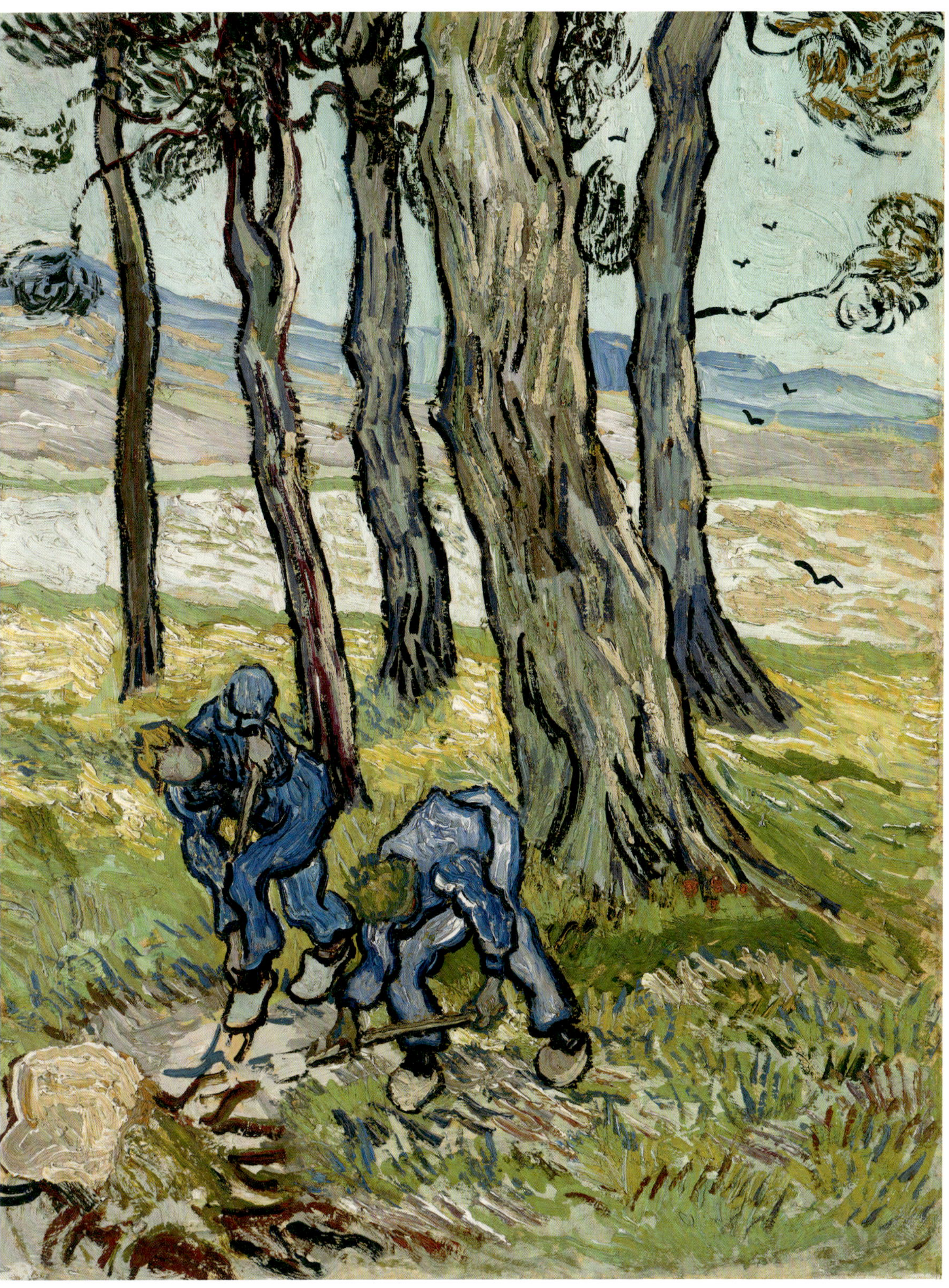

PLATE 9. *The Diggers*, 1889 (CAT. 55)

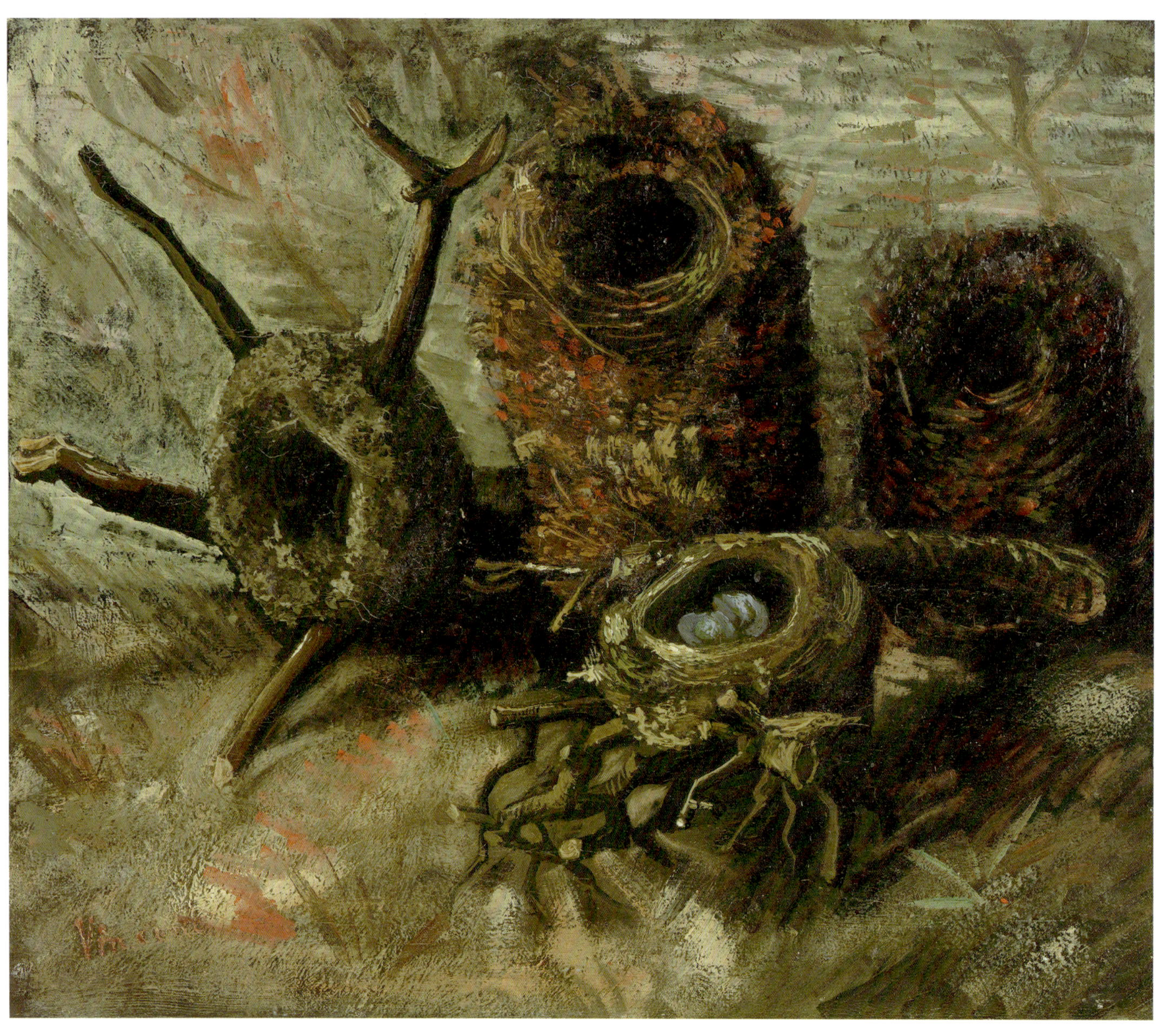

PLATE 10. *Birds' Nests*, 1885 (CAT. 13)

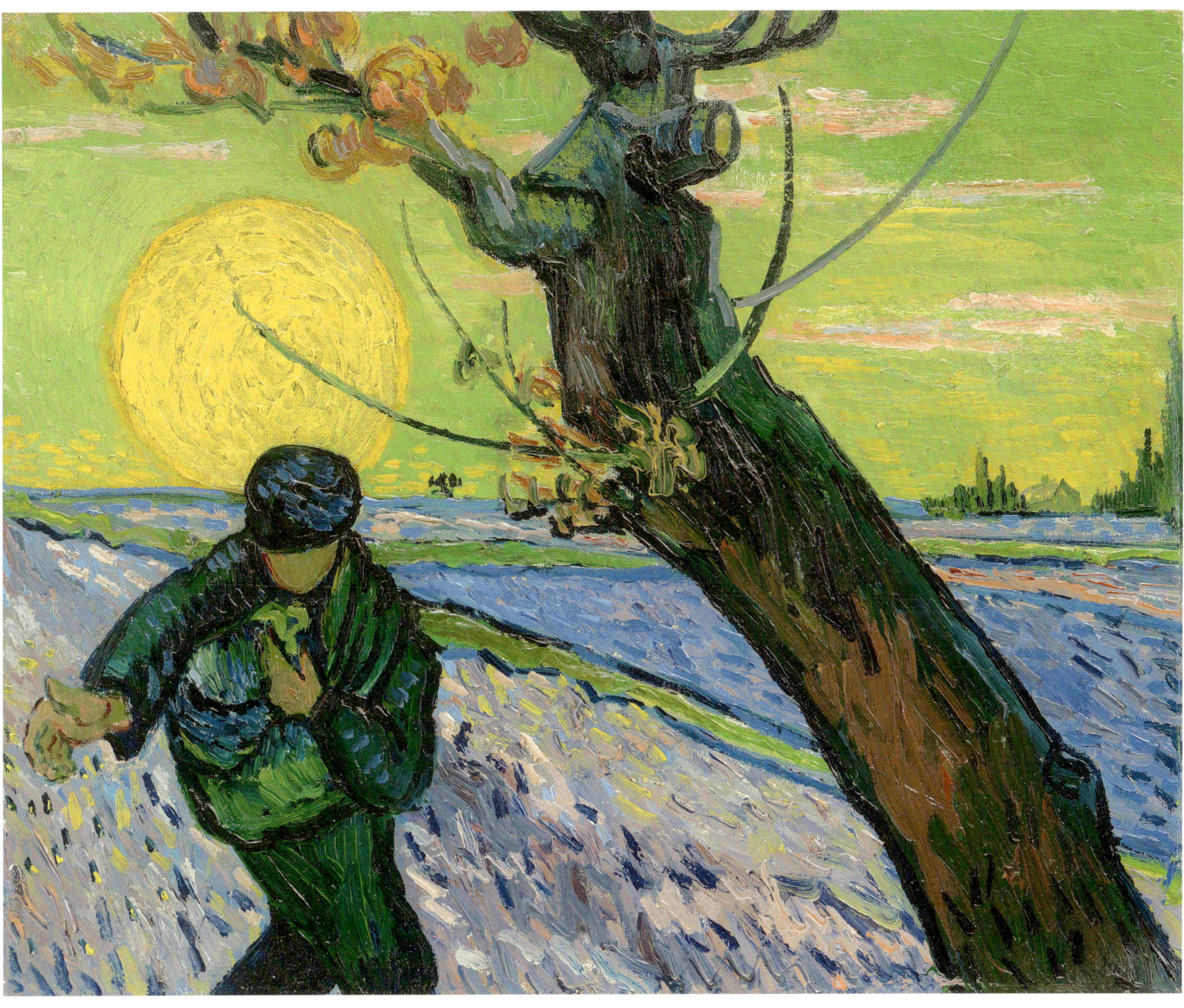

PLATE 11. *The Sower*, 1888 (CAT. 42)

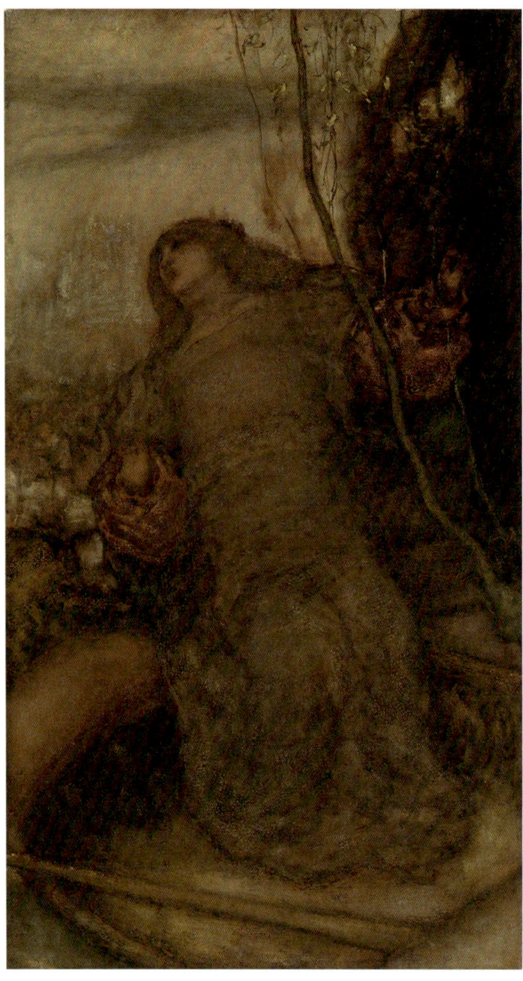

FIG. 3 Matthijs Maris (Dutch, 1839–1919). *The Lady of Shalott*, c. 1879–82. Oil on canvas, 22 × 10½ in. (55.9 × 26.7 cm). The Burrell Collection, Glasgow.

Pach subsequently nuanced his views of Van Gogh's mental state and placed his life and work in the context of the artist's own time.[40] However, psychologizing approaches remained in vogue, particularly in the popular media. In 1934, for instance, Irving Stone's novel *Lust for Life* seriously colored and distorted Van Gogh's image.

The Modern Dutch School in America, 1893–1915

The only other originally Dutch artist represented at the Armory Show was Matthijs ("Matthew") Maris, the middle of three successful artist brothers who were greatly admired by Van Gogh; Jacob and Willem became main representatives of the so-called Hague School, the leading subsection of the Modern Dutch School. The organizers of the Armory Show, however, evidently thought that representatives of the Modern Dutch School were no longer of any significance to what had meanwhile become known as modern art.

Like Van Gogh, Maris made work that was very difficult to place within a Dutch tradition. For the second half of his long life, taken under the wing of his art dealer, Daniel Cottier, he lived and worked in London. His dreamlike cityscapes and fairytale genre works found their way to international buyers, among them James G. Shepherd of Scranton, Pennsylvania, who was the only person to lend Maris's work to the Armory Show (fig. 3).[41] The Modern Dutch School was clearly losing the "battle of nations" and the fight for "modernity." Their struggle, which Van Gogh valued very highly, was now regarded as old-fashioned because its focus was too national, too impersonal, too bourgeois, too much based on a simple, naturalistic reproduction of a reality that no longer existed. Unlike his successful brothers, the unapproachable Matthijs Maris, like Van Gogh, had turned his back on this middle-class life and given universal significance to modern art by way of a more symbolic view.

Ironically, around 1900, the Modern Dutch School, represented chiefly by different generations of the Hague School, was internationally considered to be the most important contribution "Holland" had made to contemporary art, and its works were sought after by many American buyers. The American public and potential collectors knew almost nothing about Van Gogh, but they were well aware of the capability of the Modern Dutch School.

Some of this knowledge can be attributed to American world's fairs, the first of which was held in 1876 in Philadelphia. This Centennial Exhibition was followed by three more fairs, described by an American critic as cultural waves washing over the continent from coast to coast: Chicago in 1893, St. Louis in 1904, San Francisco in 1915.[42] These exhibitions offered an attractive opportunity to reach the wealthy American public, and Dutch artists sent works in great numbers. The Modern Dutch School was well received, and within the space of a few years the American market for paintings by the likes of Bernard Blommers, Israëls, Jacob and Willem Maris, Mauve (fig. 4), and Mesdag grew considerably.[43]

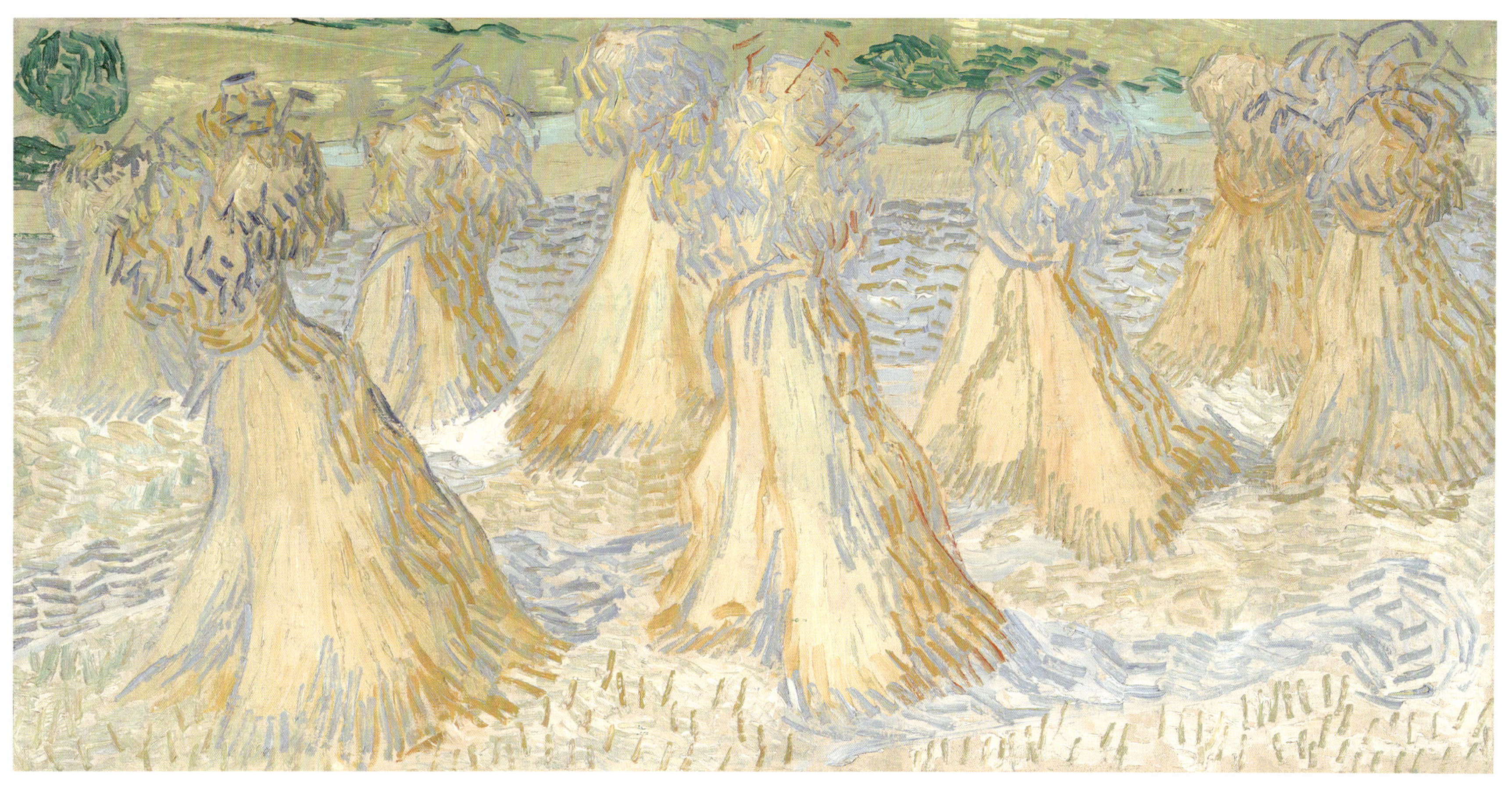

PLATE 12. *Sheaves of Wheat*, 1890 (CAT. 74)

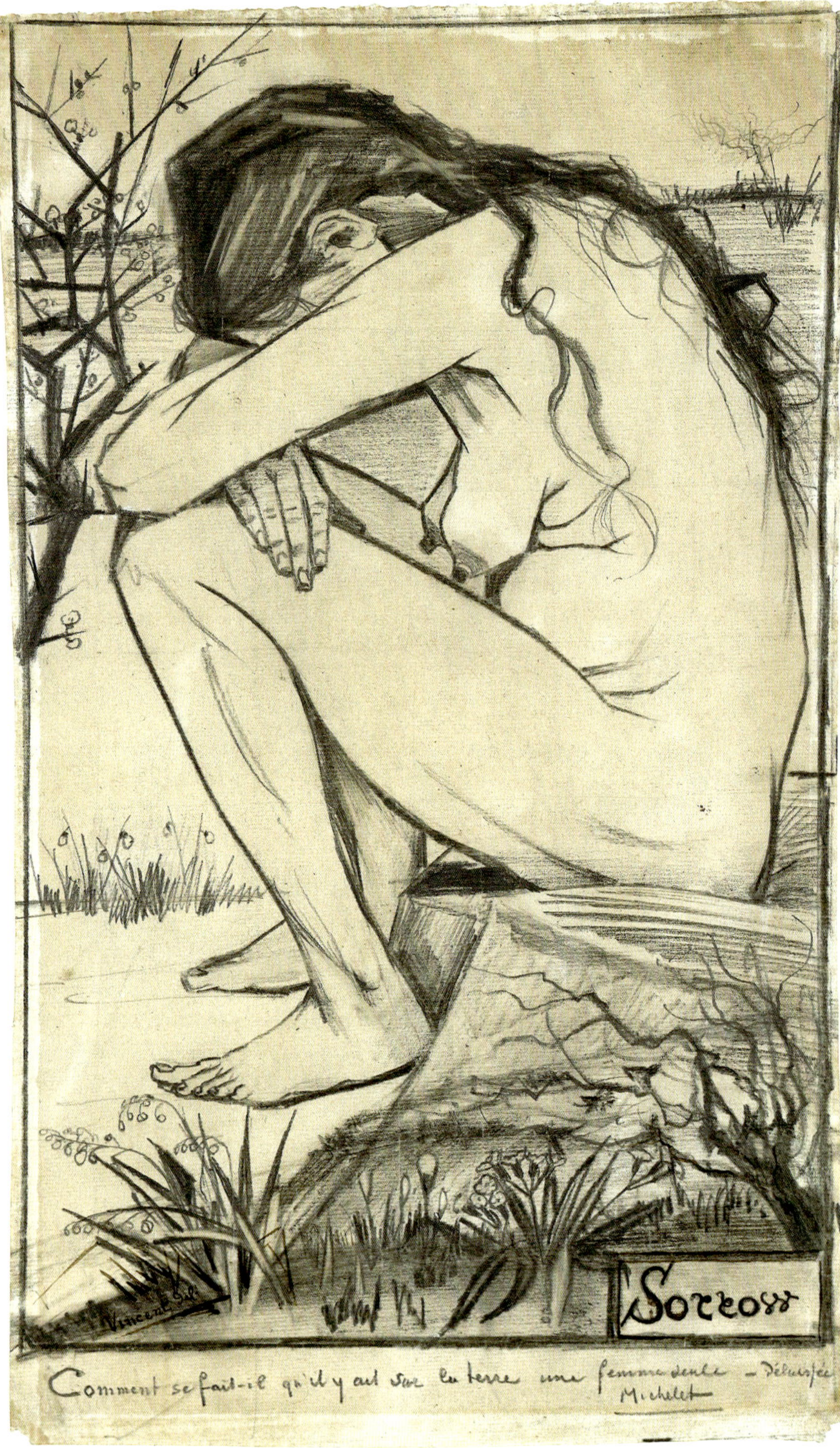

PLATE 13. *Sorrow*, 1882 (CAT. 2)

The organization of the Dutch sections of these exhibitions was largely in the hands of the artists themselves, who created a strong sense of harmony and affinity that the public appreciated. What linked the Dutch paintings was "a unity of purpose contrasting strongly with a distracting confusion in the other schools."[44] This assumed unanimity was generally attributed to the Dutch painters' collective endeavor to picture the landscape and everyday life in a realistic manner. A critic put it like this: "What it has to have to be really Dutch; it has to be an honest and faithful picture of the world. Otherwise it's not a Dutch painting. If a painting pretends to be something that it isn't in reality, it may be high art but it's not Dutch, that is: not honest art."[45]

This "honest" and "sincere" quality was invariably traced back to the Dutch art of the Golden Age. Time and again the Hague School was presented as the movement that, after an artistically unfruitful period, had returned to the principles of the illustrious masters of the Golden Age—and had done it in an entirely self-determining way without being dependent on foreign influences. In addition to being unpretentious and unaffected, the Modern Dutch School was also sober, friendly, and, above all, simple; democratic, too, for it was easily accessible to anyone who was prepared to look with their eyes open.[46]

Such traits were often directly associated with the character of the "Dutch" and their supposed "clear-sighted sense of reality."[47] In 1893 a reviewer for the *New York Herald Tribune* wrote that "sincerity and gravity" belonged to the nature and the works of Dutch born painters.[48] Yet again, we see the deeply rooted idea that the Modern Dutch School had an individual character that was inextricably bound up with a perceived national temperament and shared history.

Market Sales and Prices

The unprecedented success of the Chicago World's Fair of 1893 led to an exponential rise in the prices paid for art of the Modern Dutch School and Dutch (and Flemish) Old Masters on the American market.[49] Most of the artists concerned

FIG. 4 Anton Mauve (Dutch, 1838–1888). *Going to Pasture*, c. 1880–88. Oil on canvas, 22 × 29⅞ in. (55.9 × 75.9 cm). Detroit Institute of Arts.

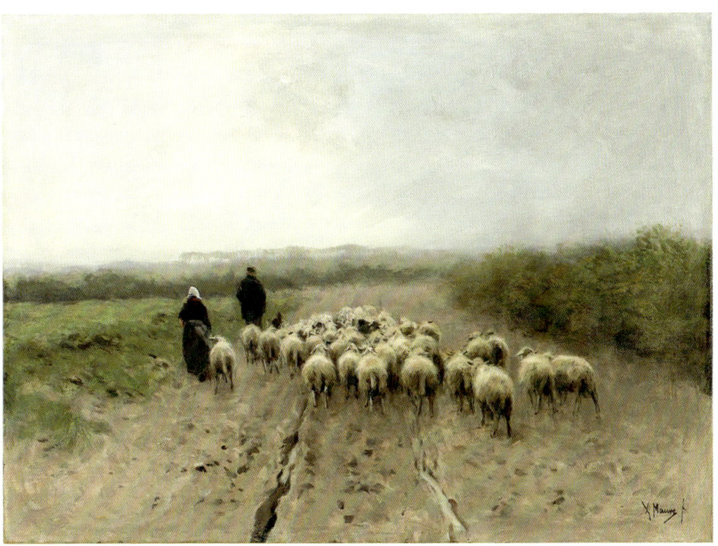

were by now famous painters of the Hague School and their immediate followers, such as Herman van der Weele and Evert Pieters. In St. Louis, painters of a younger generation, George Hendrik Breitner among them, made their appearance. Breitner, who had roamed The Hague sketching with Van Gogh in the early 1880s, won a gold medal with his Amsterdam cityscapes, one of which was *The Damrak, Amsterdam* (fig. 5). The work of these younger artists was well received in St. Louis and then in San Francisco, too, and took its place similarly in the same Dutch tradition.[50]

Some artists were missing, however—specifically the painters who had gone down a symbolist route, such as Toorop, Pieter Cornelis de Moor, and Matthijs Maris. They tried to capture not visible reality but its underlying universal principles. They took their inspiration from mysticism, dreams, and poetry. They were conspicuous by their absence from the Dutch exhibitions at American world's fairs. But they were represented at the *Panama-California International Exposition* in San Diego in 1916: a number of "moderns" from Holland were displayed alongside Dutch works that had been seen in San Francisco. Strikingly, these moderns were cited in the catalogue as the representatives of "the real Renaissance of modern art in Holland." According to the critic J. Nilsen Laurvik, it was not the recognized painters of the Modern Dutch School who "so eloquently reaffirmed the ancient gospel of their predecessors" that had started this renaissance, but Van Gogh.[51] Although Maris and Van Gogh were included in the United States section at the 1915 San Francisco *Panama-Pacific International Exposition*, it appears that none of Van Gogh's works were shown in San Diego. Nevertheless, he was extolled as the trailblazer for a new generation, which was "writing the new chapter in Dutch art begun by Vincent van Gogh."[52]

FIG. 5 George Hendrik Breitner (Dutch, 1857–1923). *The Damrak, Amsterdam*, 1903. Oil on canvas, 39⅜ × 59⅛ in. (100 × 150 cm). Rijksmuseum, Amsterdam.

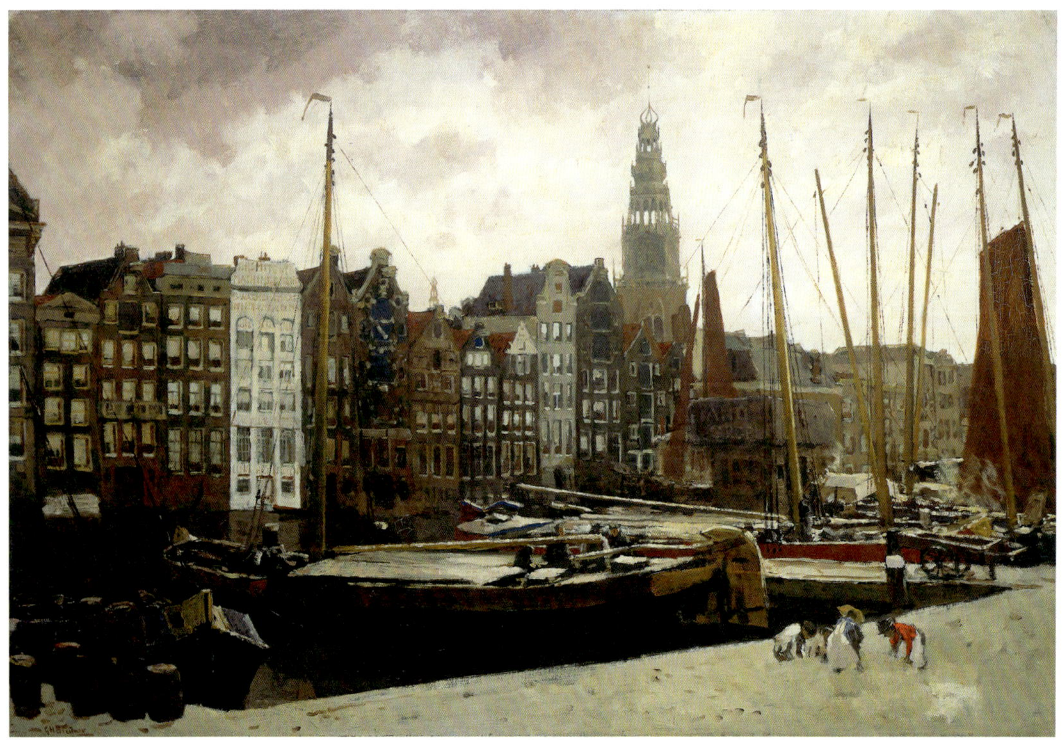

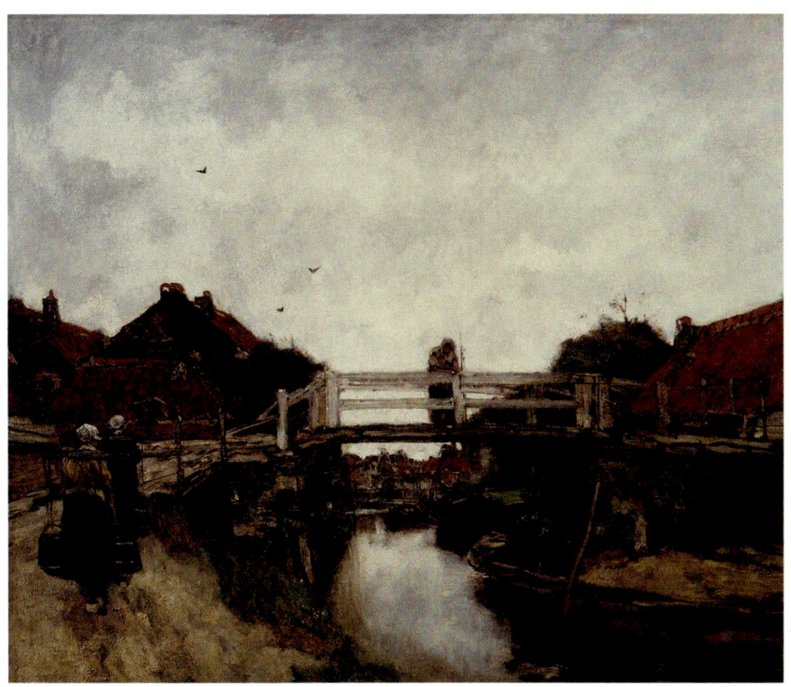

FIG. 6 Jacob Maris (Dutch, 1837–1899). *The Bridge*, 1885. Oil on canvas, 44⅜ × 54⅜ in. (112.7 × 138.1 cm). The Frick Collection, New York.

The confusion is stunning. At the Armory Show in New York in 1913, Van Gogh was one of the most important representatives of modern (French) art; the Modern Dutch School was nowhere to be seen. Three years later in San Diego, he was presented as the pioneer of Modern Dutch Art; in the exhibition, his works were nowhere to be seen.

The Modern Dutch School had enjoyed growing interest in the Netherlands, Germany, the United Kingdom, Central Europe, Canada, and the United States since the 1880s. During the Gilded Age, marked by changes in immigration, urbanization, economic expansion, and wealth, both the Dutch and Flemish Old Masters and the Modern Dutch School found their way into American collections. Their works took their place alongside art from other national schools. In 1906, for instance, Jacob Maris's *The Bridge* (fig. 6) found its way, through Knoedler, into the celebrated collection of Henry Clay Frick, as a pendant to his Salomon van Ruysdael's *River Scene*, which he had also acquired from Knoedler in 1905.

For decades, painters from the Golden Age and Modern Dutch School headed American collectors' wish lists. Sales figures reflected the interest. Between 1876 and 1910, prices rose for works on the American market. Whereas an "average" Modern Dutch School work cost around $180 in 1876–80, by 1906–10, a buyer had to be prepared to pay almost $520. In the case of the Old Masters, the rise was exponential: from an extremely meager $16 in 1876–80 to almost $9,500 in 1906–10.

At around $16,000, one of the most expensive Van Goghs in the 1913 Armory Show was *Mountains at Saint-Rémy* (F622; plate 14)—an asking price with little relationship to those for the Modern Dutch School.[53] The pricing of his works at this show was comparable to those for the other founders of the Modern French School, Cézanne and Gauguin, but only a fraction of the prices paid for Dutch and Flemish Old Master paintings. That same year, for example, Frick bought Anthony van Dyck's *James Stanley, Lord Strange, Later Seventh Earl of Derby, with His Wife, Charlotte, and Their Daughter* (c. 1636) for $350,000, while businessman Samuel Reading Bertron paid $77,500 for *Portrait of Saskia*, possibly by Rembrandt.

By around 1910 virtually all the leading figures of the Modern Dutch School had died. The ledgers of galleries Boussod & Valadon and Knoedler show that there was no new generation on hand to take up the baton. There is not even a trace of the Dutch modernists who are recognized today, such as Theo van Doesburg, Van Dongen, Bart van der Leck, Mondrian, and Sluijters, until after World War II.

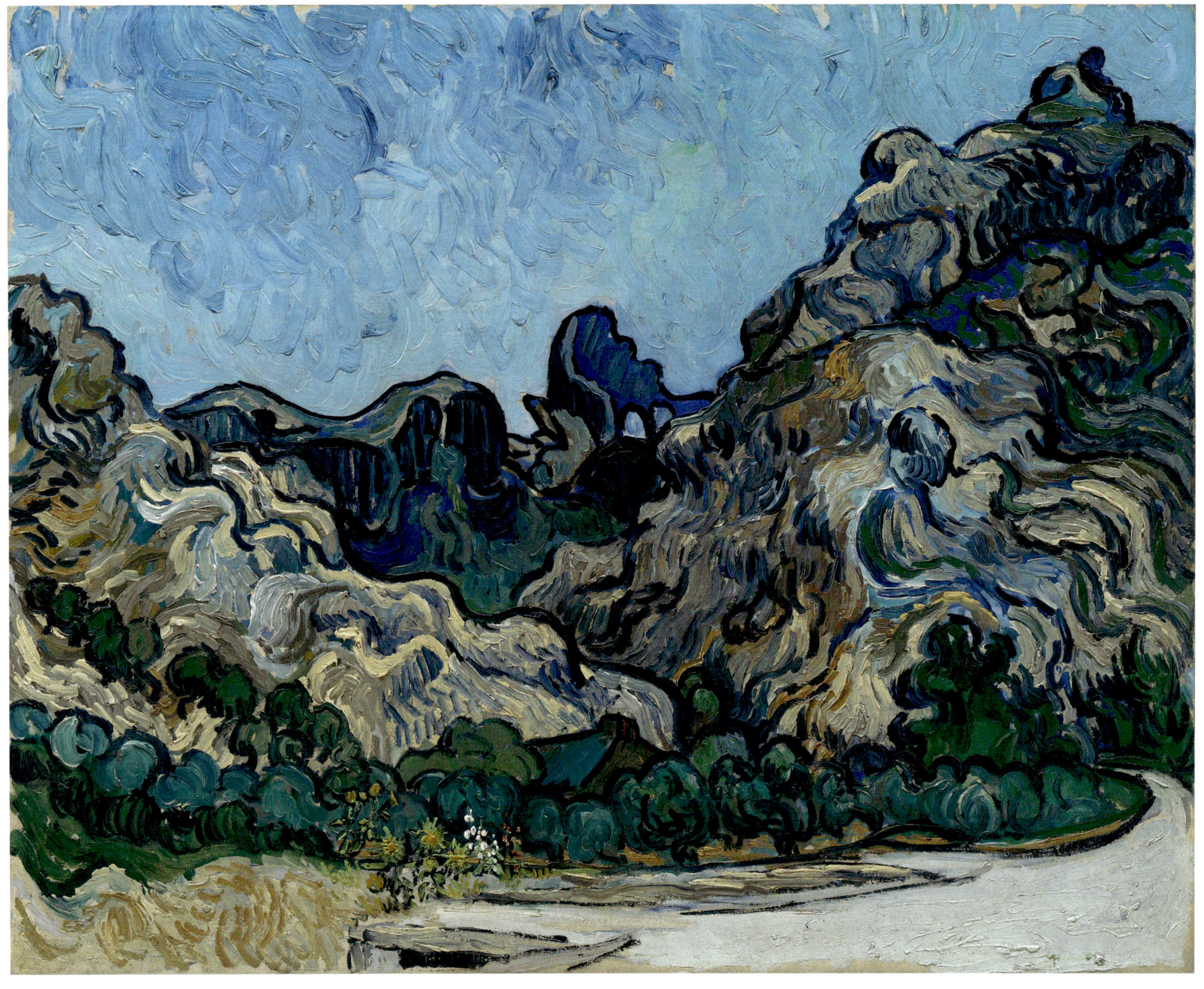

PLATE 14. *Mountains at Saint-Rémy*, 1889 (CAT. 52)

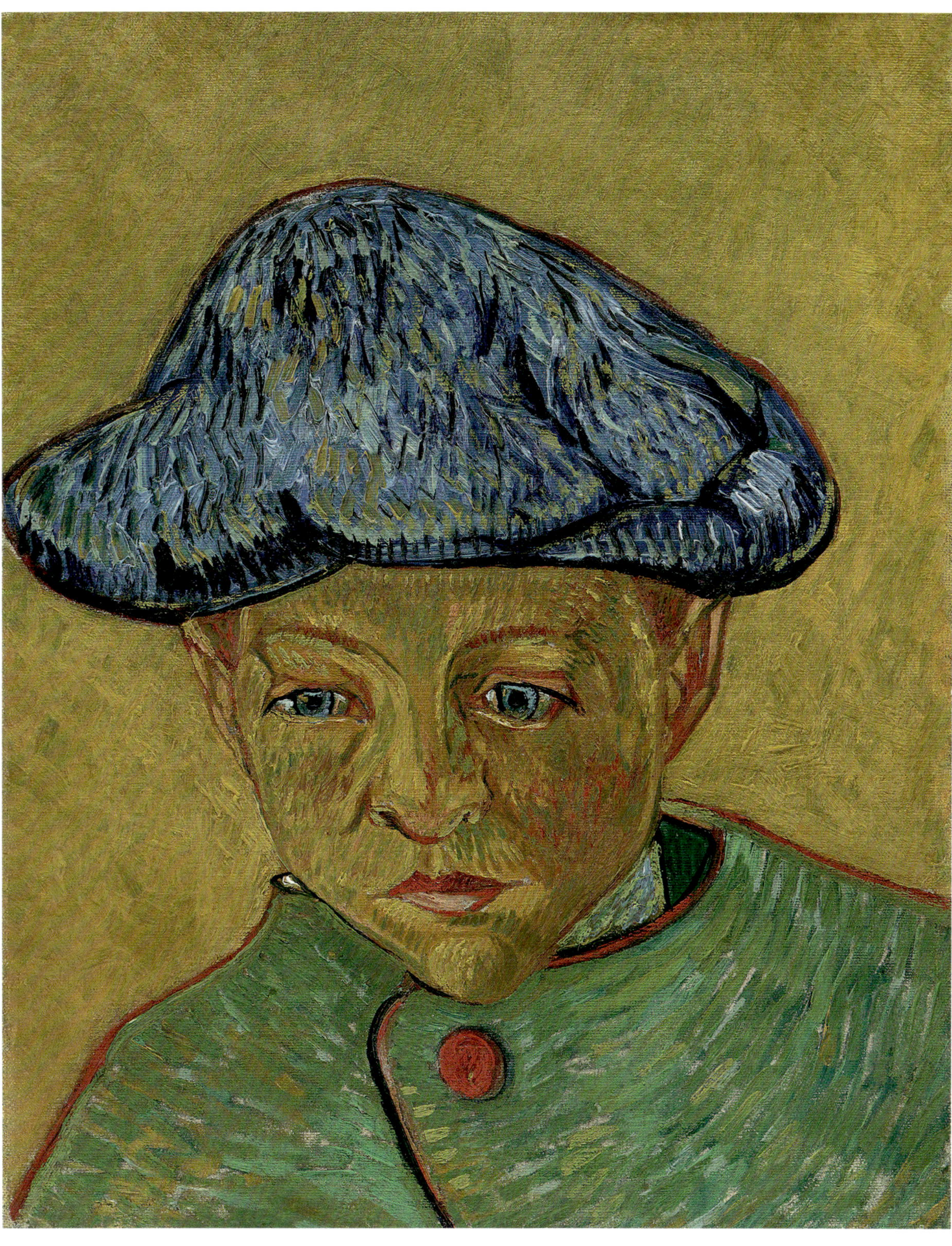

PLATE 15. *Portrait of Camille Roulin*, 1888 (CAT. 43)

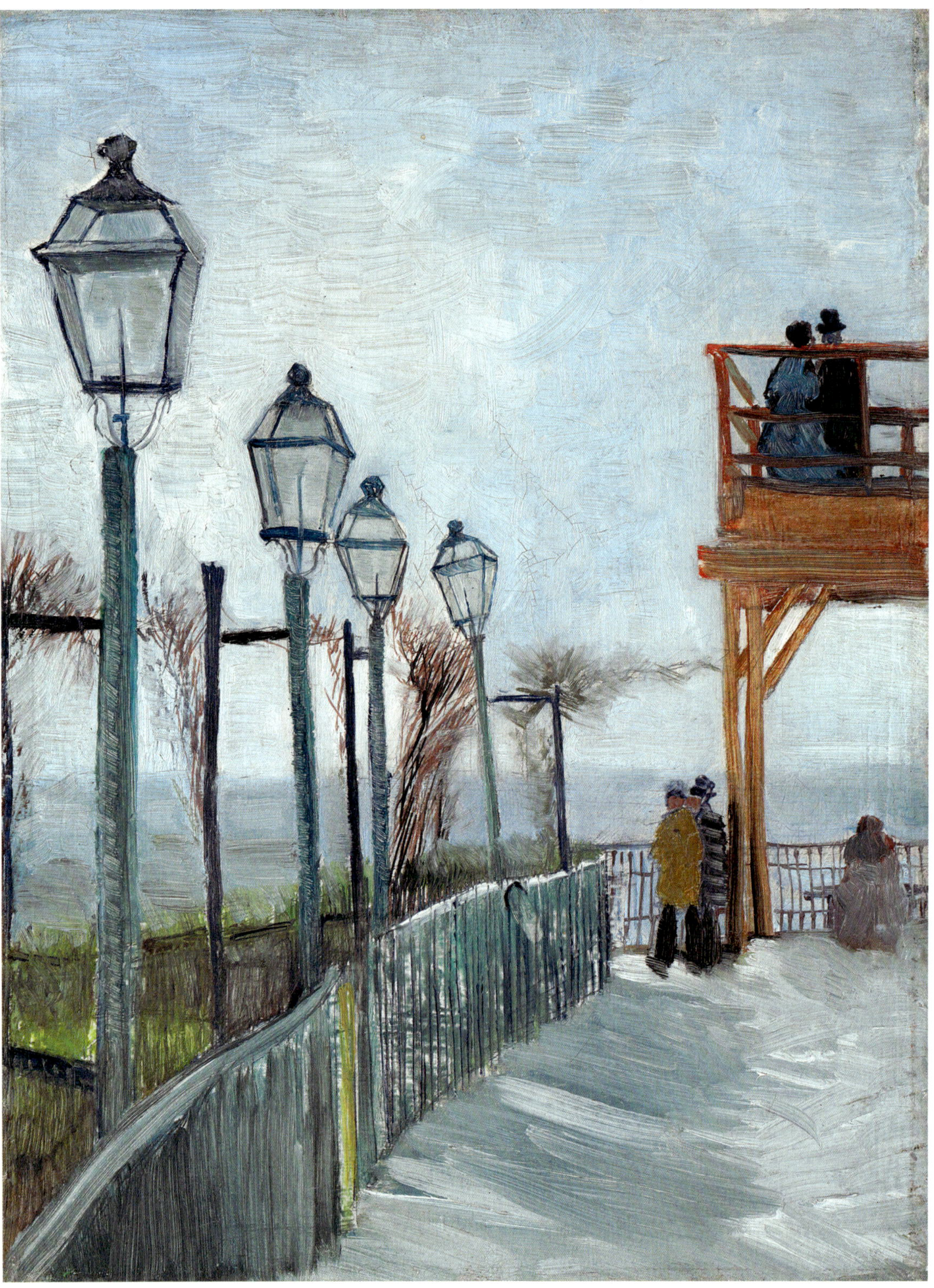

PLATE 16. *Terrace and Observation Deck at the Moulin de Blute-Fin, Montmartre*, 1887 (CAT. 21)

During World War I, Boussod & Valadon, a Parisian gallery that invested too late in what had already been termed "modern art," went under. Until the 1920s, Knoedler was still able to profit from the time lag following the passing of artists of the Modern Dutch School, whom Dreier wrote out of the history of modern art as uninspiring exponents of "contemporary art which is based on the past." In her view, modern art was based "on the same forces which have brought about the electricity and the radio." At that moment, she found those forces in Mondrian, whom she now placed in a Dutch tradition with Rembrandt and Van Gogh.[54]

A Sampling of Van Gogh Sales

While the Modern Dutch School market was in decline, Thannhauser's books, for example, reveal that around 1920 Van Gogh's works started to pick up in America. In 1919 Josef Stransky, collector, art dealer, and conductor of the New York Philharmonic, acquired *Portrait of Camille Roulin* (F537; plate 15) from Thannhauser. The painting had come from a French source and had previously belonged to Van Gogh's biographer Julius Meier-Graefe.[55] In 1924 Knoedler sold the early 1887 *Terrace and Observation Deck at the Moulin de Blute-Fin, Montmartre* (F272; plate 16) to the American artist and collector Frederic Clay Bartlett for £400 (around

FIG. 7 *Postman Joseph Roulin* (F432), 1888. Oil on canvas, 32 × 25¾ in. (81.3 × 65.4 cm). Museum of Fine Arts, Boston.

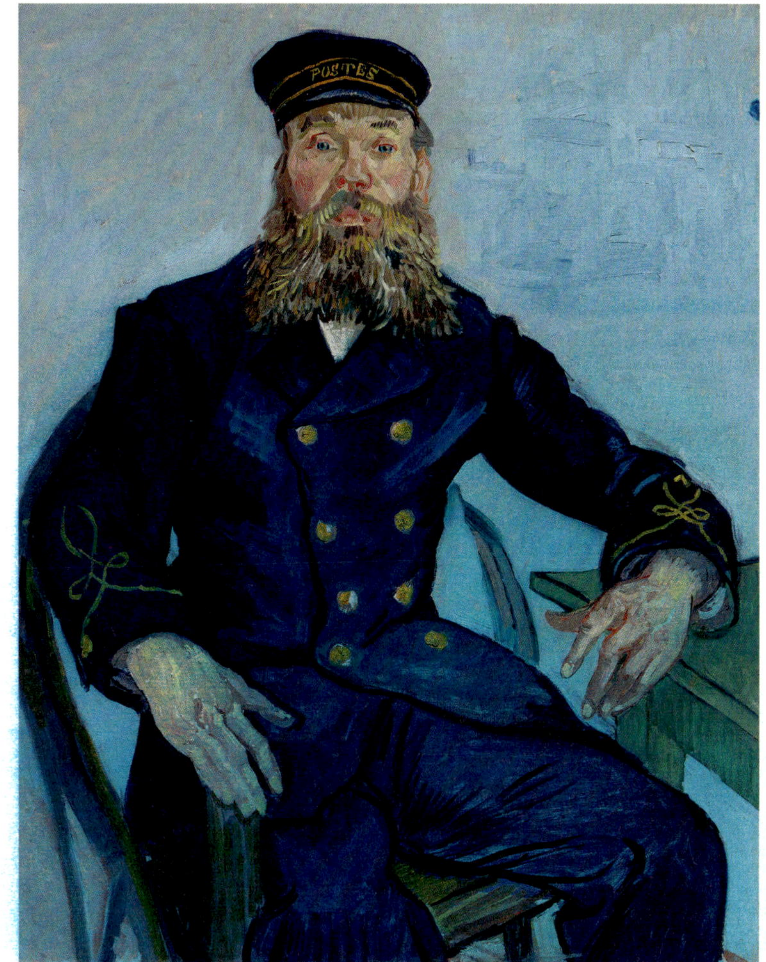

$1,450), a price similar to the sum Walter Spencer Morgan Burns paid in the same year for Edgar Degas's *Nude Woman in Bath*.[56] As a comparison, that year Knoedler sold a Pierre-Auguste Renoir still life to the New York dealers Scott and Fowles for £3,500.

In the space of just a few years, Van Gogh conquered the American market—almost exclusively with works from his French period, which, according to Pach, endorsed his contribution to the development of color. In 1928, for instance, Knoedler sold the famous *Postman Joseph Roulin* (F432; fig. 7) to Robert Treat Paine II for $48,000, and *Oleanders* (F593) to Anna Eugenia La Chapelle Clark for $47,500.[57] Cézanne was the only other "pioneer of modern art" at that time and later whose prices more or less kept pace with Van Gogh's. In 1929, for example, Stephen C. Clark bought Cézanne's *Still Life with Apples and Pears* (fig. 8) from Knoedler for $50,000.[58] By contrast, prices for works by the leading lights of the Modern Dutch School did not top the $3,500 mark (Anton Mauve), whereas some Dutch Old Masters fetched prices far in excess of $100,000, for example, Meindert Hobbema's *Hamlet in the Wood* of 1660–65, for which Horace O. Havemeyer paid $200,000 in 1928.[59] It was not until 1955 that Van Gogh broke through the $100,000 ceiling, when Knoedler sold his *Garden at Auvers* (F814) for $120,000 to the Morocco-based French industrialist Jacques Walter.

In just a few decades, Van Gogh's reputation in America was transformed from that of an unknown "French schoolmaster" into a trailblazer of modern art and one of the most popular artists born on Dutch soil—or elsewhere. The once very successful representatives of the Modern Dutch School he admired so much, who had "so eloquently reaffirmed the ancient gospel of their predecessors," were reduced from acknowledged teachers to mediocre students of an artist who, after an apprenticeship in the Netherlands, had eventually embarked on a "new chapter in Dutch art" in France.

FIG. 8 Paul Cézanne (French, 1839–1906). *Still Life with Apples and Pears*, c. 1891–92. Oil on canvas, 17⅝ x 23⅛ in. (44.8 x 58.7 cm). The Metropolitan Museum of Art, New York.

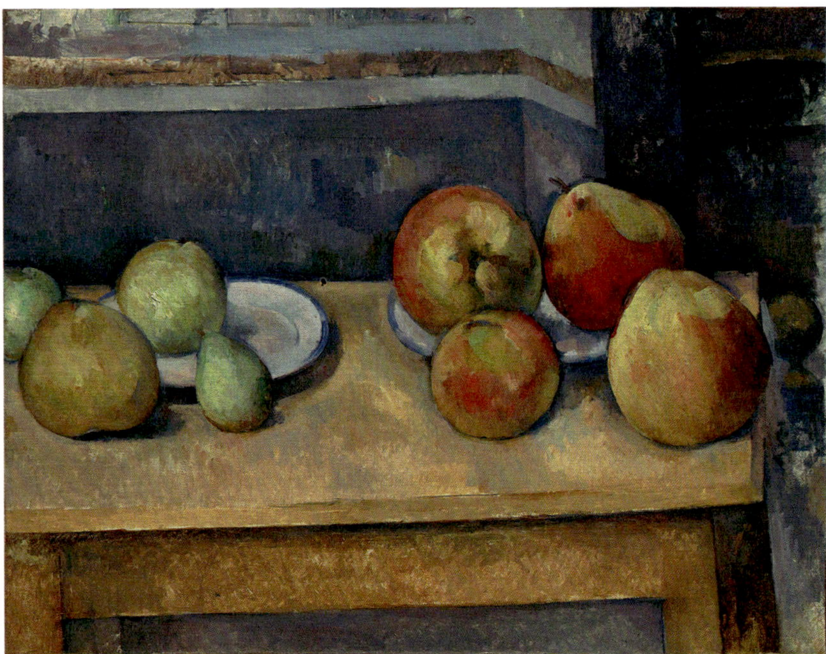

NOTES

Translated from the original Dutch by Lynne Richards.

1 *De Volkskrant* 1950, n.p.
2 There were also crowds at the Chicago venue for the New York and Chicago 1949–50 exhibition.
3 New York and Chicago 1949–50, 9–10.
4 See https://www2.gwu.edu/~erpapers/myday/displaydoc.cfm?_y=1949&_f=md001458, accessed March 2019.
5 For Barr, see especially Kantor 2002.
6 A. Barr 1929a, 17–18.
7 *Soerabaijasch Handelsblad* 1936. The reference to the boy who saved Holland comes from the colorful and popular bestselling novel *Hans Brinker; or, The Silver Skates: A Story of Life in Holland* (1865) by American author Mary Mapes Dodge, who never actually visited Holland.
8 This so-called "battle of nations" is largely discussed in Chris Stolwijk's inaugural lecture at Utrecht University; see Stolwijk 2018, https://issuu.com/humanitiesuu/docs/oratie-chris-stolwijk_2018_totaal, accessed March 2019.
9 Riopelle 2006, 208.
10 See Stott 1998.
11 See Van Gogh Letters 1913. This edition was a translation of Margarete Mauthner's *Briefe*, published by Bruno Cassirer in 1906. See http://vangoghletters.org/vg/publications_2.html#publications_2, accessed March 2019.
12 Extracts from letters were published in Carl Zigrosser's magazine *The Modern School* in 1918. They were selected by Jo van Gogh-Bonger, and she authorized the translation. With thanks to Hans Luijten, biographer of Jo van Gogh-Bonger.
13 For Jo van Gogh-Bonger, see Luijten 2019.
14 For the provenance of these works, see Stolwijk and Veenenbos 2002; W. Feilchenfeldt 2013; and Op de Coul 2002, 104–19.
15 In 1903 Marius wrote that in the 1890s Van Gogh had fallen like "a meteor…on the parched fields" of Dutch art. As far as his French work was concerned, he was "a descendant of Rubens," and in his Dutch period he was an "old Dutch master." Marius 1903, 493–511. For the 1905 review, see *Het Volk* 1905: n.p.
16 Thomson 2012, 310.
17 Krul 2006. See https://doi.org/10.18352/bmgn-lchr.652, accessed March 2019.
18 For the reception of modern art in the Netherlands in the twentieth century, see especially Van Adrichem 2001.
19 Manheim 1989.
20 *Vossische Zeutung* 1901, Beilage (supplement).
21 For Cassirer and Van Gogh, see W. Feilchenfeldt 1988. The works published by Cassirer Verlag are listed in R. Feilchenfeldt and Brandis 2002. The publication history of Van Gogh's correspondence is treated at length in Van Gogh Letters 2009. See http://vangoghletters.org/vg/publications_1.html, accessed March 2019.
22 Meier-Graefe 1910, 14.
23 Ibid., 5–6.
24 Meier-Graefe 1921, vol. 1, 9.
25 For Thannhauser, see Koldehoff and Stolwijk 2017.
26 Stolwijk 2006–2007, 29.
27 Cologne 2012, 9. For this exhibition, see also Amsterdam and New York 2006–2007; Stolwijk 2006–2007, 29–36; and Oslo and Amsterdam 2015–16.
28 Gregg 1913, 17.
29 Dreier 1913, xiii.
30 Ibid., xvi.
31 Ibid., xvii. Dreier exhibited her own work in New York, October 14–27, 1913. See Macbeth Gallery 1913.
32 *Christian Science Monitor* 1913. See https://www.aaa.si.edu/collections/items/detail/walt-kuhn-scrapbook-press-clippings-documenting-armory-show-vol-2-14643, accessed March 2019.
33 *Algemeen Handelsblad* 1920: 10.
34 *De Volksvriend* 1921: 41. *De Volksvriend* was, according to its colophon, "published weekly on Thursdays, in Orange City, Iowa."
35 Stolwijk and Veenenbos 2002, 152, note 19/10.
36 McCarthy 2011, 170–72.
37 Pach 1920a: xiii.
38 Ibid., xiv.
39 Pach 1920b: 303.
40 Pach 1936b.
41 Around 1900 Shepherd put together a collection: "with the exception of two French pictures the collection [was] evenly divided between the work of American and Modern Dutch Painters…Maris, Mauve, Israëls, and Weissenbruch." See *Collector and Art Critic* 1906: 78.
42 Brinton 1915b: xcvi.
43 Tibbe 2016: 339, 350; Dekkers 1996: 61–70.
44 *Modern Art* 1893: n.p.
45 Flack (pseud.) 1904: 1.
46 These notions appeared in articles in newspapers, art journals, and collectors' magazines and were echoed in catalogues and exhibition guides. See, for example, G. Davis et al. 1893, 377; Ives 1904, xvii; Laurvik 1915.
47 Laurvik 1915, 102.
48 [Cortissoz] 1893: 2.
49 Dekkers 1996: 67–73; and Washington 1982, 26. The sales figures presented in this essay are based on "Dutch and Flemish" sales by Goupil (Boussod & Valadon), 1860–1917, and by Knoedler, c. 1860–1960. These sales, 13,718 in total, are mentioned in the ledgers of the abovementioned galleries in the Getty Research Institute in Los Angeles. See for Goupil's stock books, http://archives.getty.edu:30008/getty_images/digitalresources/goupil/goupil.htm, and for Knoedler's archives https://www.getty.edu/research/special_collections/notable/knoedler.html.
50 See, for example, Caffin 1904: cccxxxi; Brinton 1915a: xlviii.
51 Laurvik 1916, 2.
52 Ibid., 3.
53 Koldehoff and Stolwijk 2017, 172–73, no. 38.
54 Katherine S. Dreier, "Before the Members of the School Art League at the Brooklyn Museum," Lecture, November 20, 1926, Brooklyn Museum, New York. See https://brbl-dl.library.yale.edu/vufind/Record/3684292, accessed March 2019.
55 Koldehoff and Stolwijk 2017, 144–45, no.. 23.
56 See Lowrey 2007, 47.
57 For *Oleanders*, see https://www.metmuseum.org/art/collection/search/436530, accessed March 2019.
58 Sterling et al. 1966, vol. 2, 109, inv. no. 61.101.03, and see https://www.metmuseum.org/art/collection/search/435883, accessed March 2019.
59 See https://www.brooklynmuseum.org/opencollection/objects/72403, accessed March 2019.

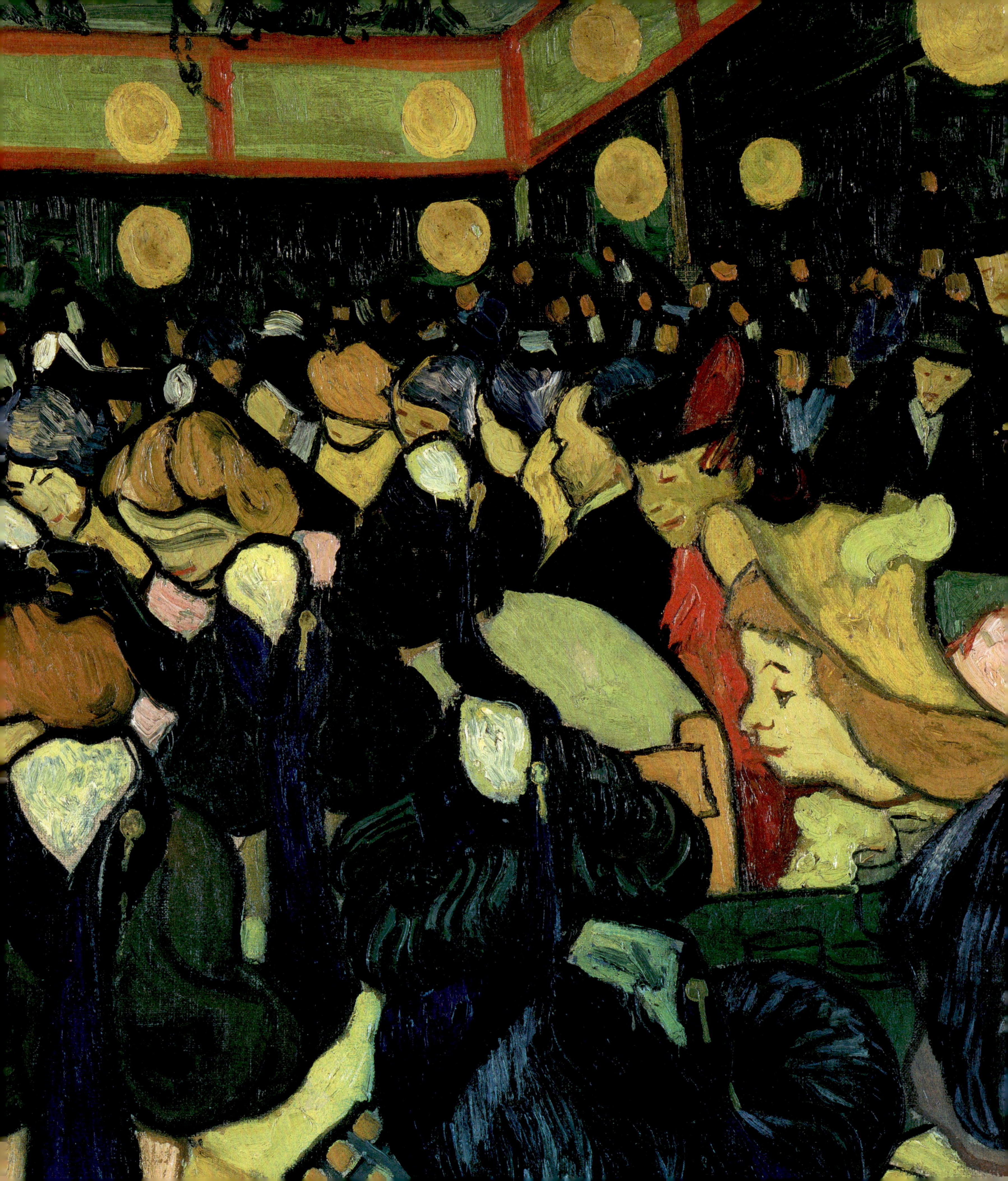

SUSAN ALYSON STEIN

Van Gogh in New York: Picturing the First Years, 1912–29

It may be long before "the good public" finds in his hard won achievements anything other than "caricature" but it is well worth while to make him known in a country unaccustomed to such intensity as his.
—*The New York Times*, September 15, 1912[1]

By the time America enjoyed its first glimpse of works by Vincent van Gogh in 1913, his pictures had been featured in some two hundred venues abroad. They had attracted a strong following among artists, collectors, and dealers in France, the Netherlands, Russia, and especially in Germany where interest and prices were booming. Van Gogh's bold use of color and line had claimed the adulation of the Fauves and the Expressionists; weathered the mockery and shock of British audiences; and cemented his fame, alongside Paul Cézanne and Paul Gauguin, as one of the trailblazers of modern art. Closer to home, news that Van Gogh's works were coming to this country proved topical enough for a *New York Times* reporter to announce the "worth while" prospect with ample fanfare in a full-page, illustrated spread.

Van Gogh's reputation abroad assured him top billing and a prominent central gallery when he debuted in the United States at the eye-opening *International Exhibition of Modern Art.* Nicknamed for Manhattan's cavernous Sixty-Ninth Regiment Armory, which hosted the 1,300-work New York venue in February 1913, the Armory Show traveled in smaller versions to Chicago and Boston. This ambitious undertaking was spearheaded by American artists

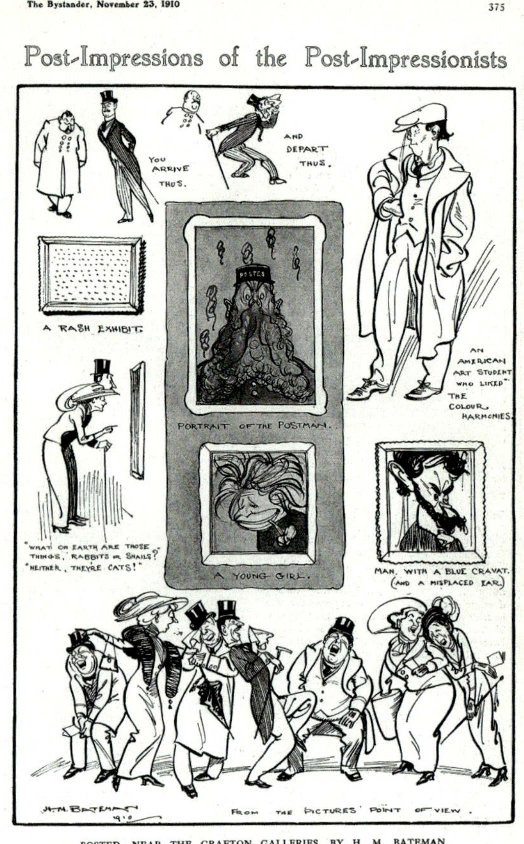

FIG. 1 "Posted, near the Grafton Galleries," by H. M. Bateman. Cartoon in the *Bystander* (November 23, 1910): 375.

Arthur B. Davies, Walt Kuhn, and Walter Pach in the wake of groundbreaking exhibitions that had already jumpstarted the collecting of Van Gogh's work. Taking heed from the blockbuster *Manet and the Post-Impressionists* exhibition organized by former Metropolitan Museum of Art curator and British art critic Roger Fry for the Grafton Galleries in London (1910–11), and the stunning international modern art survey held at the Sonderbund in Cologne (1912), these artists placed great stock in having "Van Gogh make a good showing" stateside.[2] Kuhn piloted the effort to secure loans in late September 1912. He followed on the heels of three American collectors and another team of artists who had already rallied to introduce Van Gogh's works on this side of the Atlantic.

In 1912–13 five paintings by Van Gogh left France and the Netherlands to take their place in American collections newly launched along the eastern seaboard by the pharmaceutical tycoon Albert C. Barnes, attorney John Quinn, and painter Katherine S. Dreier—a *Who's Who* of notable patrons of modern art. Three of the paintings would make their way to Philadelphia and later to Barnes's suburban estate in Merion, where they veritably disappeared from view, never lent and reproduced only in black and white for much of the century. The two other paintings, both portraits, were destined to become—like their owners—well-known figures on the New York art scene, playing a key role in introducing Van Gogh to the public, indeed, from the start, in the 1913 Armory Show.

Barnes bought his first Van Gogh, *The Postman (Joseph-Étienne Roulin)* (F435), sight unseen, in the spring of 1912. It was part of a cache of thirty-three modern pictures that American artists William Glackens (acting as advisor) and Alfred Maurer (as resident scout) had rounded up in a whirlwind shopping mission in Paris, funded to the tune of $20,000. The Parisian dealer Eugène Druet had recently loaned the portrait to the Grafton Galleries' exhibition in London where the "Postman" became the poster boy for a show that caused spirited waves of controversy (figs. 1 and 2). Barnes made successive trips to Paris in 1912, acquiring two more Van Goghs sourced by Maurer: *The Smoker* from Druet (F534), and *The Factory* (F318) from the Galerie Bernheim-Jeune. Barnes had the means and the appetite to buy four more Van Goghs between 1922 and 1933, becoming the earliest of the artist's American collectors and owning the largest number of his works—although they were a relatively marginal part of a collection brimming with enthusiasm for Pierre-Auguste Renoir, Cézanne, and Henri Matisse.[3]

New York collector John Quinn was keenly interested in Fry's London exhibition, which put the term "Post-Impressionism" into circulation and set the presses rolling. The high-profile coverage of the *succès de scandale* by the New York dailies ushered in a newfound appreciation for Van Gogh. He became a "must see" artist for the general public and a "must have" artist for Quinn. During the run of the London show, Quinn resolved to acquire examples by each of the pioneering

Post-Impressionists. He kept to his pledge, buying Van Gogh's *Self-Portrait* (F268; plate 17) along with paintings by Gauguin and Cézanne from the Parisian dealer Ambroise Vollard in September 1912.[4] They would be cornerstone acquisitions for a legendary collection of more than two thousand works that would reflect Quinn's dedicated commitment to advancing the cause of modernism through a continual show of hands-on support. Quinn would serve as legal counsel and a driving force behind the Armory Show from the inception of the idea, which both he and gallerist and photographer Alfred Stieglitz floated in the winter of 1911,[5] through its realization in the wake of the great modern art exhibition held in 1912 at the Sonderbund in Cologne—which marked a triumph for Van Gogh and would bring another New York collector into the fold: Katherine S. Dreier.

Dreier visited the Sonderbund toward the end of an extended stay abroad. Even Cézanne and Gauguin basked in the reflected glory of the dazzling display of some 125 works by Van Gogh, which spilled over to five rooms of this international survey. Dreier was so struck by the power of Van Gogh's genius—which she described as "stepping out of a stuffy room into glorious, bracing air"—that

FIG. 2 *The Postman (Joseph-Étienne Roulin)* (F435), 1889. Oil on canvas, 25⅞ × 21¾ in. (65.7 × 55.2 cm). The Barnes Foundation, Philadelphia.

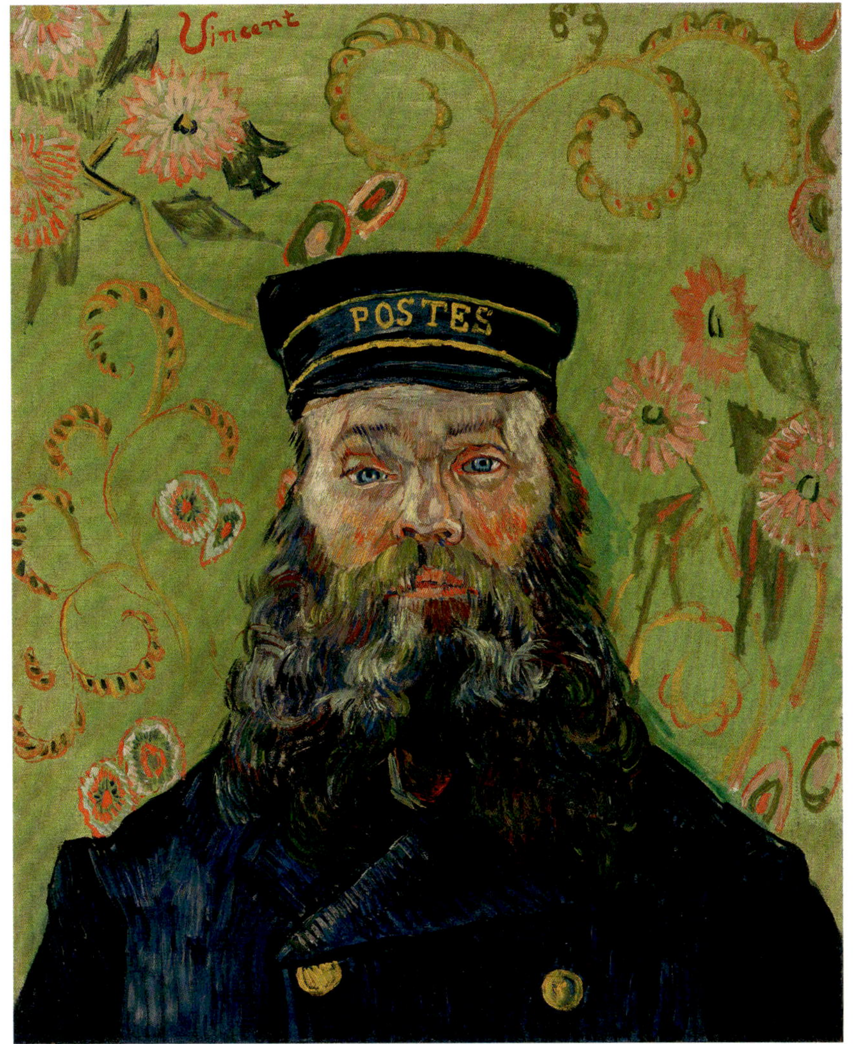

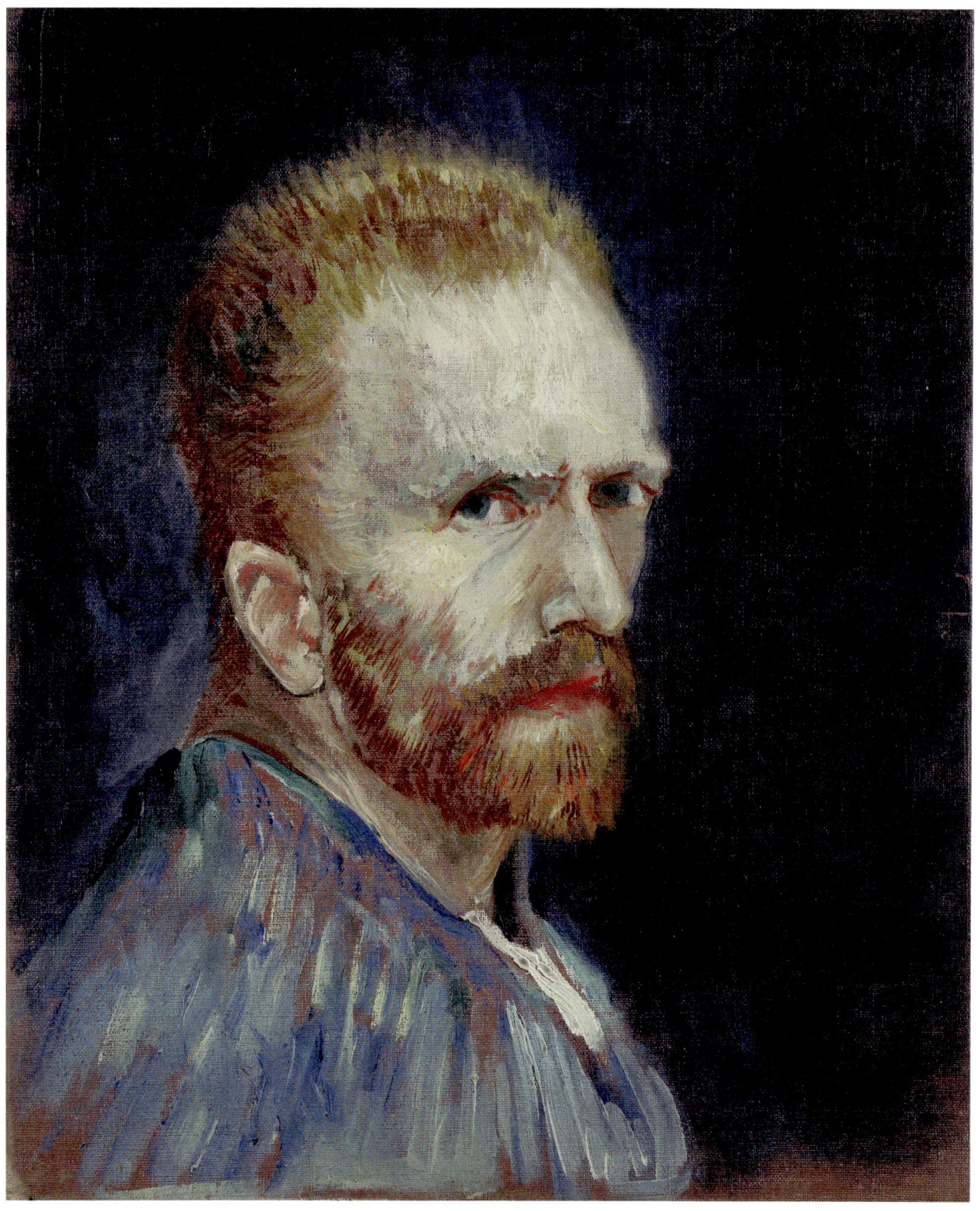

PLATE 17. *Self-Portrait*, 1887 (CAT. 24)

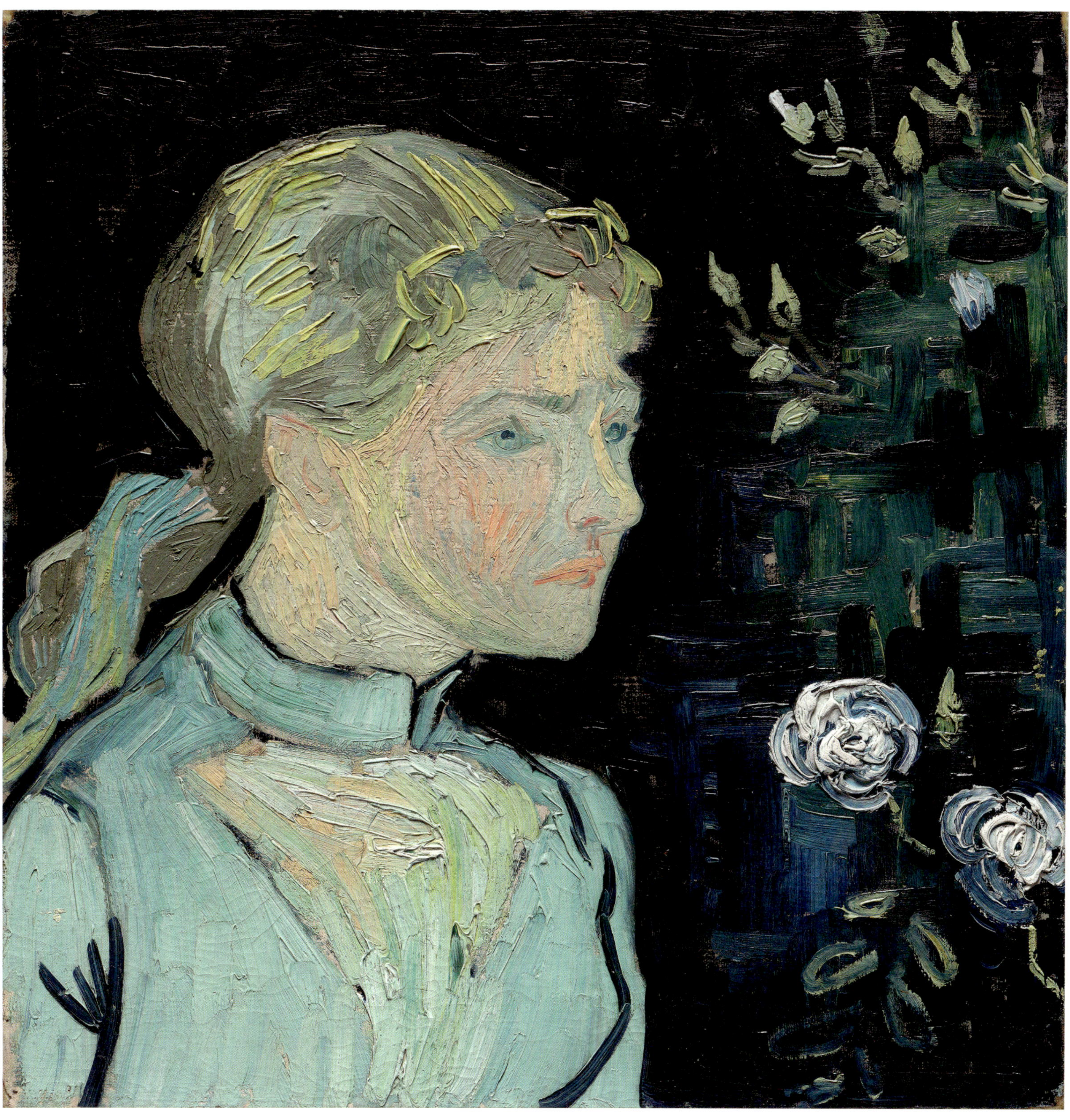

PLATE 18. *Adeline Ravoux*, 1890 (CAT. 65)

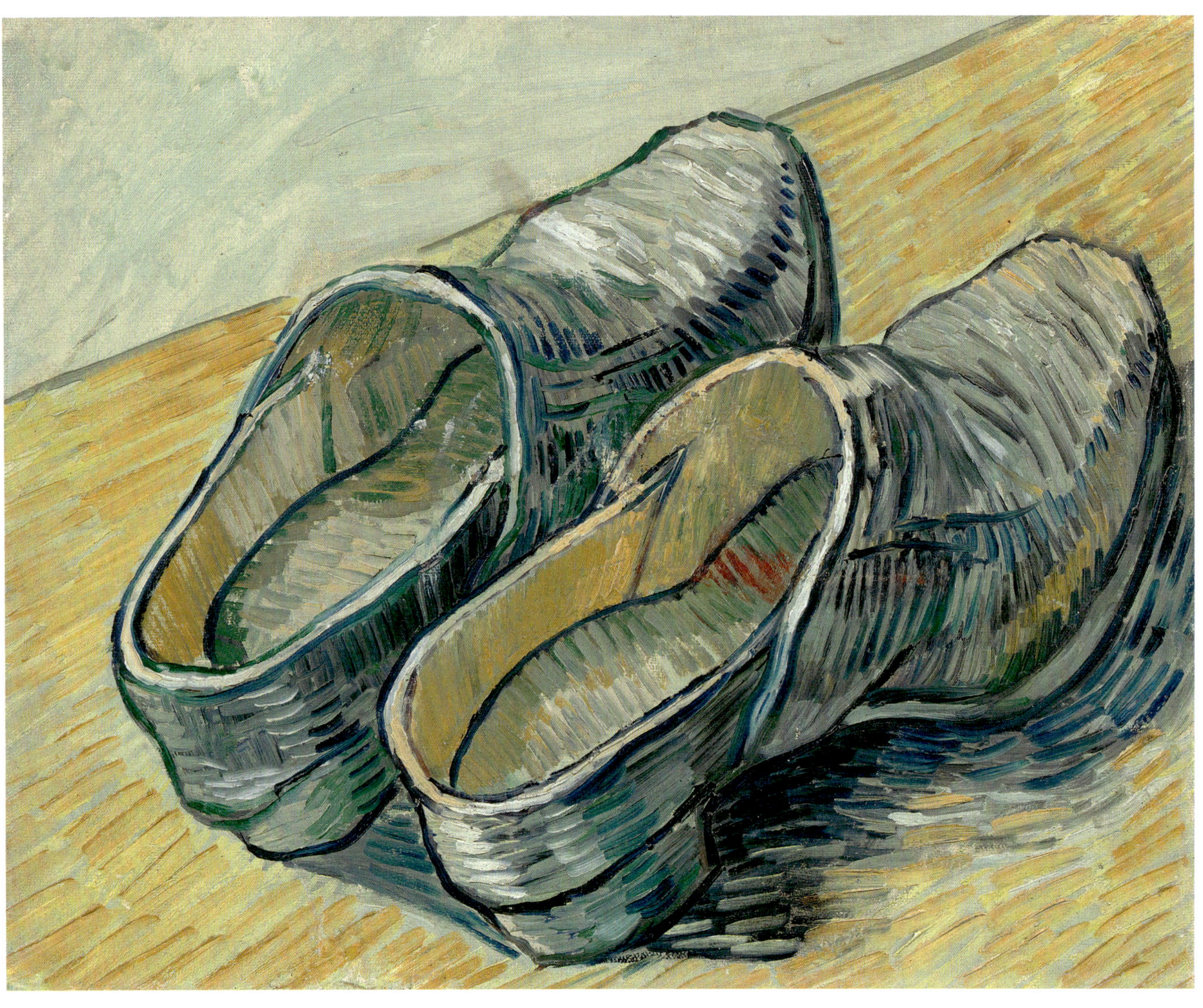

PLATE 19. *A Pair of Leather Clogs*, 1889 (CAT. 54)

she felt compelled to go straight to the source.[6] Traveling to the Netherlands, she bought *Adeline Ravoux* (F786; plate 18), one of the loans from the Van Gogh family collection, through their Dutch representative, the dealer Artz & De Bois; she also initiated plans to publish an English translation of the reminiscences of the artist's younger sister. Dreier returned to New York with portrait and manuscript in hand, armed to play a role in presenting the American public with "an intimate and sincere introduction to the life and work of the man...who was deeply impressing and influencing artists and critics in many countries."[7] A participant and active promoter of the Armory Show, Dreier, like Quinn, would emerge as an illustrious patron of modern art as she directed her passion toward fostering the recognition of living innovators, from Wassily Kandinsky to Marcel Duchamp.

In the Armory Show, Van Gogh held his own with eighteen works to his name from five lenders primed to support the initiative of introducing his art to a provincial audience. Quinn and Dreier contributed their new acquisitions. Artz & De Bois sent ten paintings from the family collection (including F607; plate 19) overseen by the artist's sister-in-law, Jo van Gogh-Bonger, who had devoted herself to shepherding it to renown through exhibitions and sales. The Parisian dealer Druet, who had just sold two portraits to Barnes, lent a less expensive option for first-time buyers, *The Zouave* watercolor (F1482; plate 20), and two standout paintings: *The Dance Hall at Arles* (F547; plate 21), which seems to have "made the most impression on the public,"[8] and the "much studied and wondered over" *Mountains at Saint-Rémy* (F622; plate 14), said to arrest "visitors...by its novel lines and treatment."[9] Another three loans came from the dealer Stephan Bourgeois, who had moved from Paris to New York to establish a market for the "giants" of modern art. He opened a gallery bearing his name in 1914, so that artists like Van Gogh could receive "the attention which is due them" in the United States.[10]

Van Gogh was represented by a respectable, if somewhat quirky, selection of pictures divided among still life, figure painting (two made under the spell of Gauguin), and landscapes, including two views of Montmartre and two of olive groves. Reflecting something of the scramble involved in assembling the loans, the group was an imperfect basis for sizing up his achievement—as reviewers variously recognized. Van Gogh's staunchest admirers, set to give him a hero's welcome, lamented the shortfall of masterworks, like *La Berceuse* (see, for example, F508; plate 22), that would show what he was truly "capable of,"[11] while his

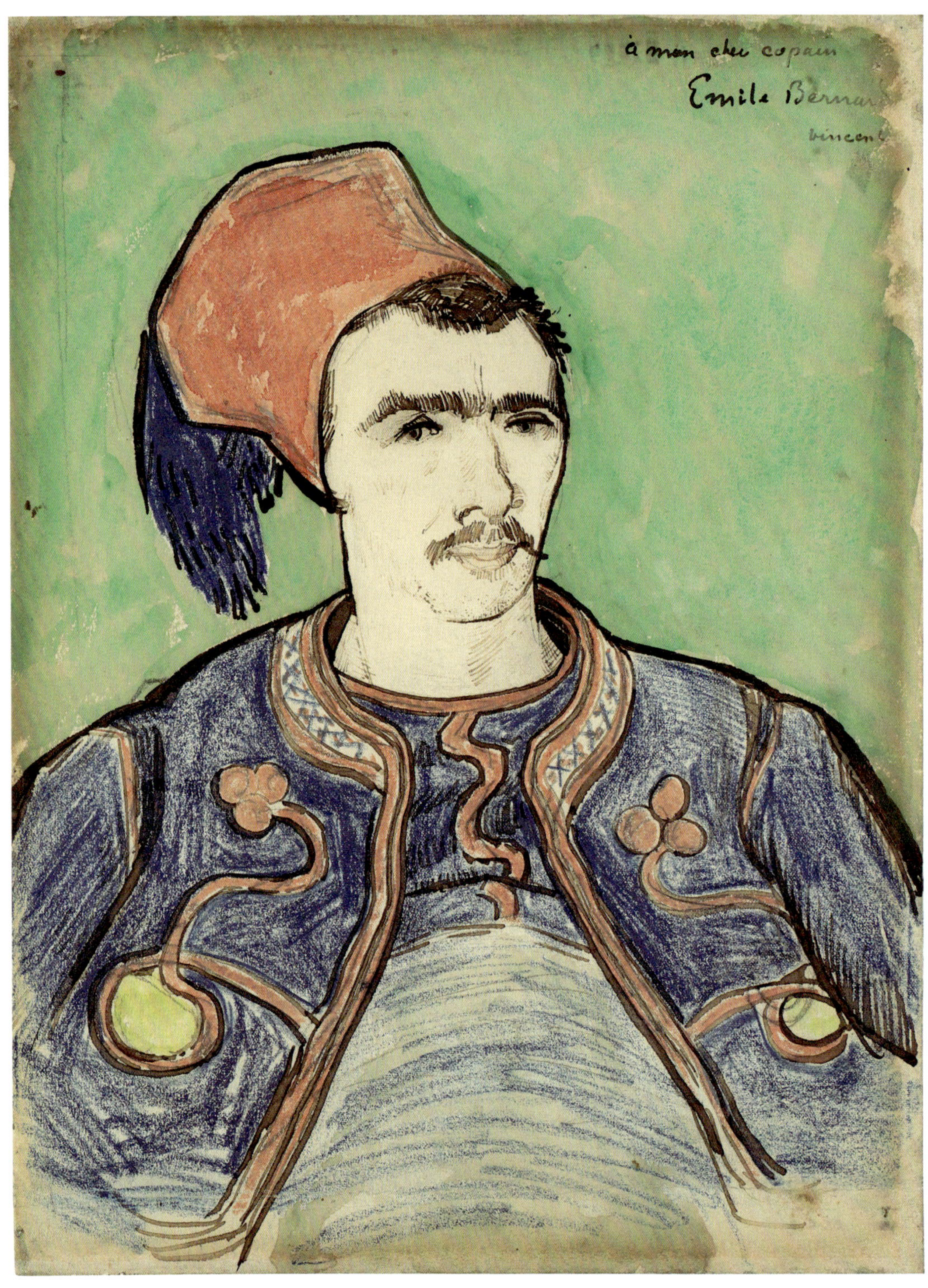

PLATE 20. *The Zouave*, 1888 (CAT. 33)

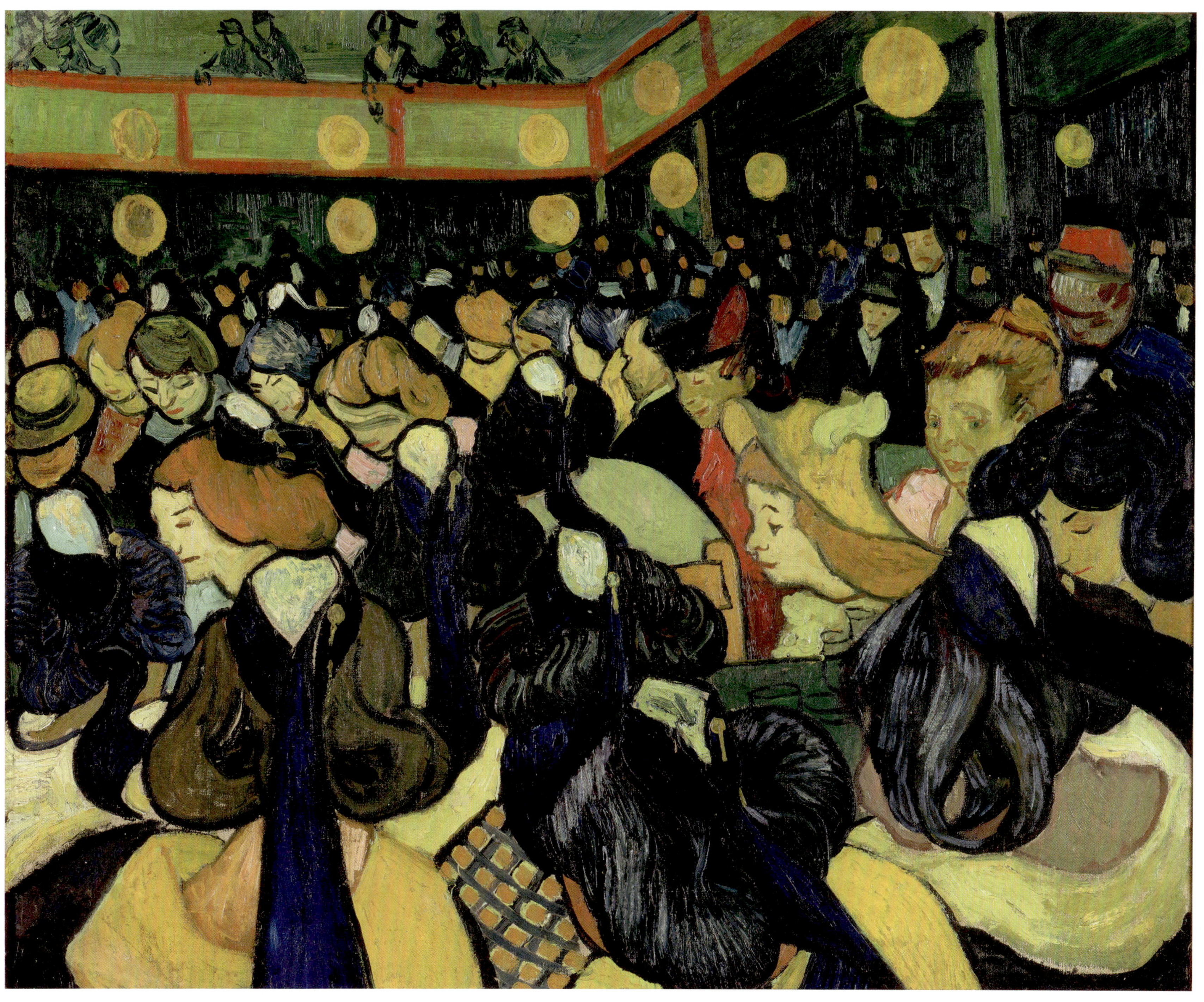

PLATE 21. *The Dance Hall at Arles*, 1888 (CAT. 44)

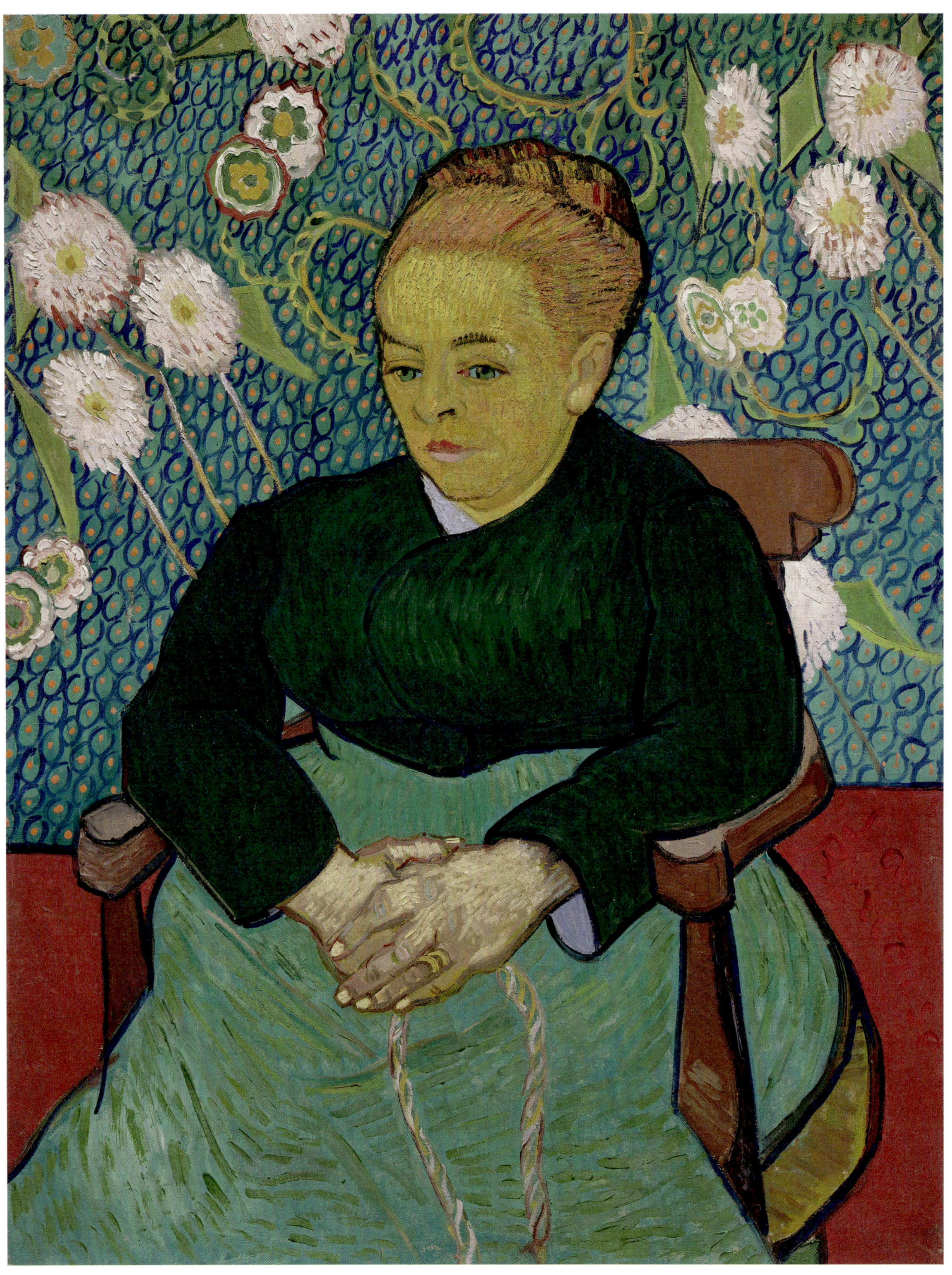

PLATE 22. *Lullaby: Madame Augustine Roulin Rocking a Cradle (La Berceuse)*, 1889 (CAT. 46)

toughest critics, eager to judge whether he lived up to the hype, resolved that he was no more than a "moderately competent Impressionist, who was heavy-handed, had little if any sense of beauty and spoiled a lot of canvas with crude, quite unimportant pictures."[12]

All but two of the eighteen works listed in the catalogue have been securely identified;[13] thirteen are documented in an installation view of the Chicago venue (fig. 3). Curiously, the largest painting, and with an asking price of $26,000 by far most expensive, "Montmartre," has yet to be identified. Yet, arguably, only one picture fits the bill: Van Gogh's *Kitchen Gardens on Montmartre* (F350; fig. 4). Originally shown at the Salon des Indépendants in 1888, it was a staple on loan lists from the Van Gogh family collection for more than a dozen venues, where it was routinely distinguished by its "groote" size and hefty price tag.[14] At the Armory Show, the painting caught the eye of a reviewer, who offered a brief but apt account of the scene: "There is one landscape in particular, a broad expanse of country, with a road and red-roofed buildings, which has an astonishingly living quality. It seems actually to throb with life."[15] This leaves one riddle: the "Lilies," one of the three last-minute entries lent by Stephan Bourgeois. It may represent the bouquet Van Gogh described in a letter of August 1886 (presumed lost, or painted over),[16] or it was simply a poor substitute for the real thing, not unlike various still lifes that peppered the marketplace during World War I, among them a study of lilacs, which may well have been mistitled when it was added to the catalogue in haste.[17]

FIG. 3 Installation view of works by Van Gogh at the Chicago venue of the 1913 Armory Show. Top row, left to right: F607 (plate 19), F256, F271, F708, F786 (plate 18), F818 (plate 1), F1482 (plate 20); bottom row: F547 (plate 21), F711, F622 (plate 14), F268 (plate 17), F773 (plate 2), F279 (plate 24).

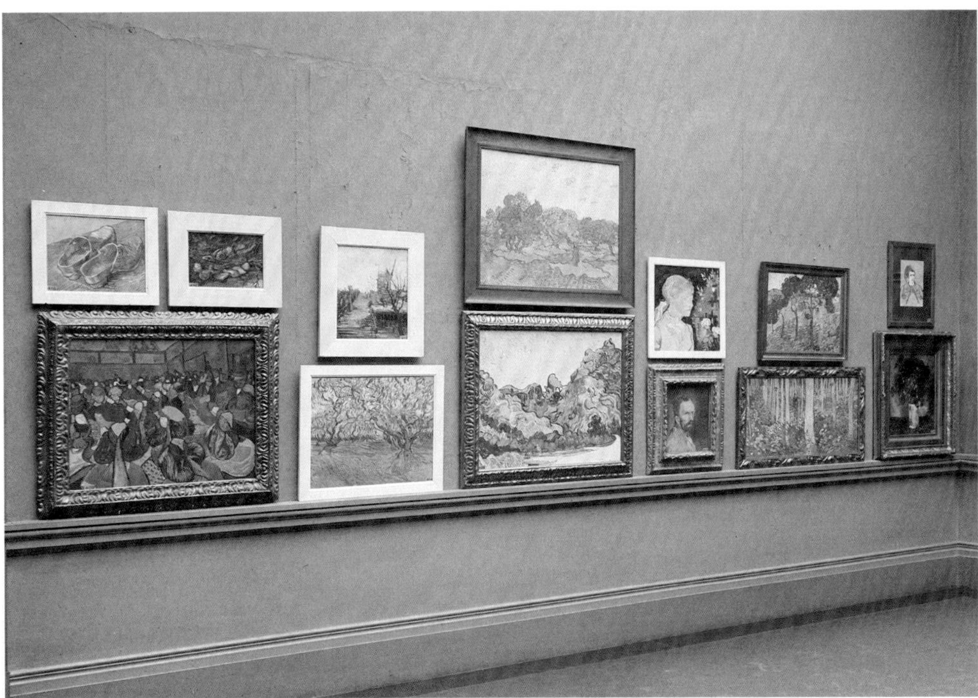

It is likely that at least three other loans never made it into the catalogue at all. Apparently, Walt Kuhn's efforts to coax the cooperation of German dealers and collectors—so richly represented in the Sonderbund exhibition—was not entirely in vain. One painting seems to have eventually come through, from Bernhard Koehler of Berlin: *Two Peasant Women Digging* (F695). It was prominently illustrated in two reviews of the show, including one by the seasoned critic Frank Jewett Mather Jr., who later quipped how tough it was to keep up with a show that "shifts bewilderingly day by day through changes of hanging and admission of new pictures."[18] As for other latecomers, the Dutch period (represented by two still lifes [F49, plate 23; and F99]) appears to have been fleshed out with a "woman of the low country" not unlike the large "Hollandaise" exhibited at the Modern Gallery in 1915 and the period Van Gogh worked in Auvers (represented by F786, plate 18; and F773, plate 2) by "Young Girl with a Cornflower—which she holds by its stem in her teeth" (F787).[19]

The Armory Show set a precedent for how Van Gogh would "become known and appreciated in a country unaccustomed to such intensity as his."[20] The vast majority of works that served to cultivate an early appreciation for Van Gogh came from the two countries the so-called "Franco-Dutchman" called home. The middling French interest in the artist's works made Parisian dealers more receptive to entertaining the first signs of enthusiasm across the Atlantic, and over the next decade pictures regularly made their way from France to test the waters of a new market, including some that put American naiveté to the test. By the same token,

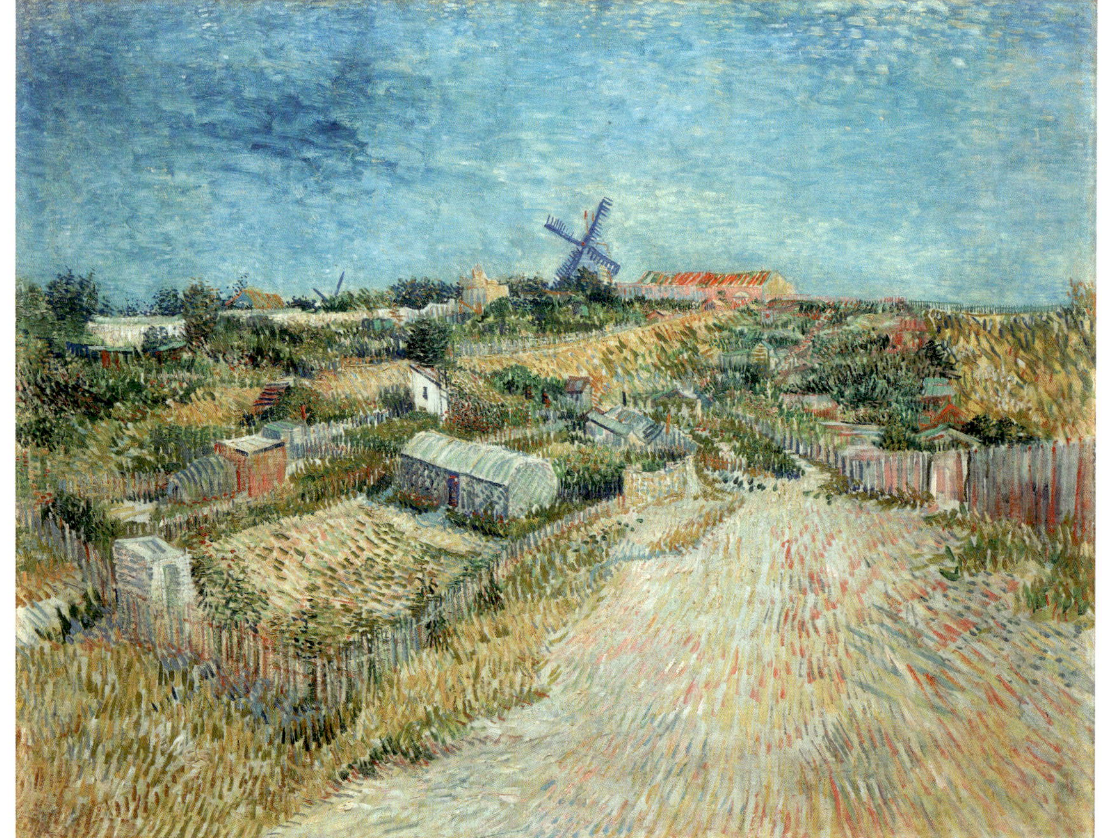

FIG. 4 *Kitchen Gardens on Montmartre* (F350), 1887. Oil on canvas, $37^{13}/_{16} \times 47^{1}/_{4}$ in. (96 × 120 cm). Stedelijk Museum, Amsterdam.

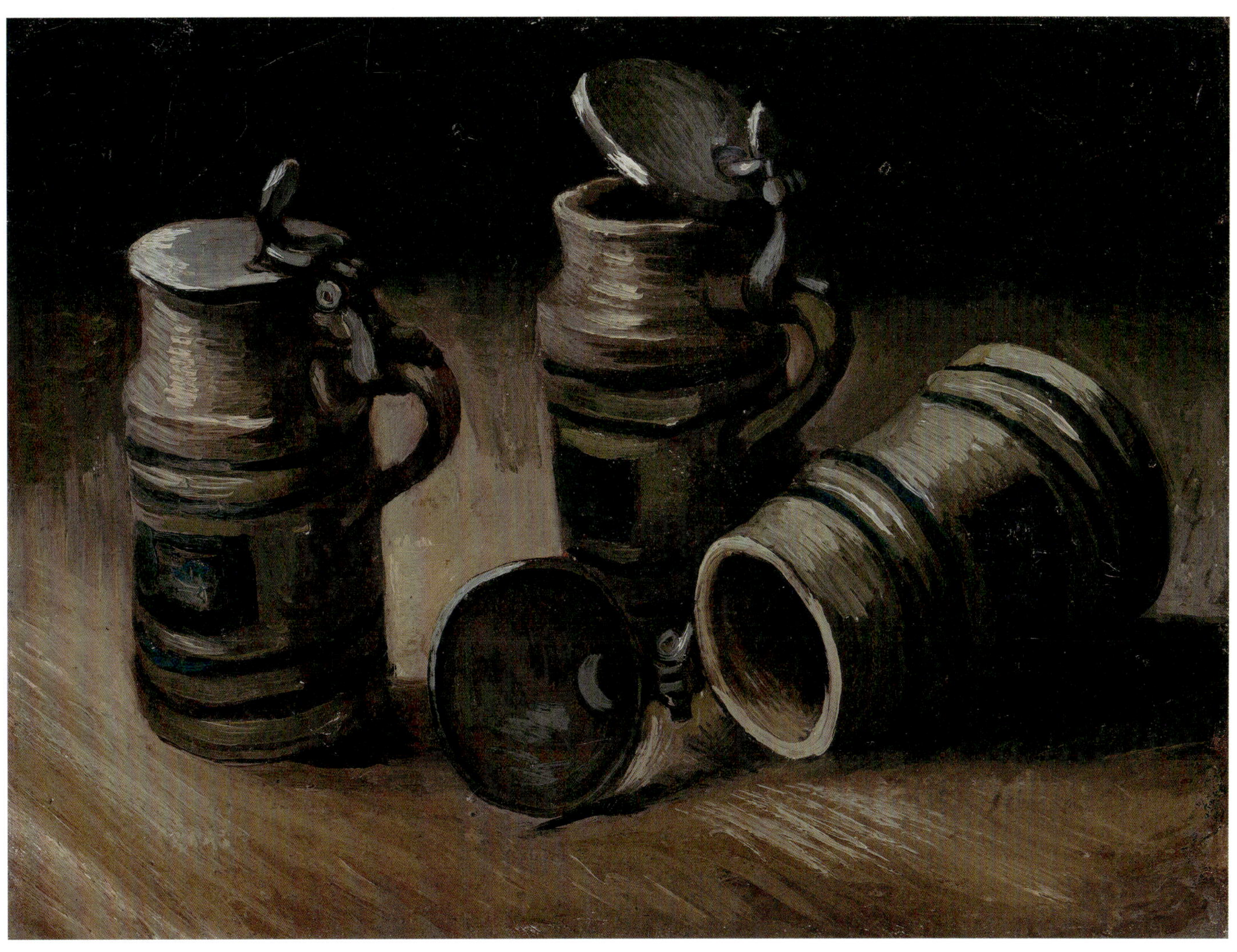

PLATE 23. *Beer Tankards*, 1885 (CAT. 12)

the booming market in Germany—which raised pricing to Old Master ranks and the number of Van Gogh paintings in collections to 120 (versus our five) by World War I[21]—doubtless forecast the lack of cooperation the Armory Show initiative received not only from the organizers of the Sonderbund exhibition but also from Van Gogh's most important dealer, Paul Cassirer in Berlin.[22] Indeed, had it not been for the strong show of support from the Dutch side, Davies, Kuhn, and Pach would have been hard-pressed to make up the difference between their aim of having "Van Gogh make a good showing" and the result. The same would hold true for New York dealers who mounted this country's first monographic shows in 1915 and 1920, and for museum curators in the 1920s who ensured that "slowly" but surely Van Gogh "arrived at the high places of American esteem."[23]

Works from the Van Gogh family collection played a decisive role in filling in the blanks on walls that would otherwise have been bare—or barely representative of his art—in exhibitions held in New York between 1913 and 1923. Some of these pictures were hand-delivered: Jo van Gogh-Bonger and her son, Vincent Willem van Gogh, spent the World War I years in New York. Other works were placed on extended loan, allowing for the kind of exposure Pach imagined it would take—through "repeated viewings of so epitomized an art as Van Gogh's to arrive at a judgement of its value."[24] With prices that were as foreign to American sensibility as the pictures themselves, Van Gogh was a hard sell. "Like the French, who have established the key-note of our taste in painting...neither our laymen nor our artists take quickly to tumultuous painting."[25] Nor did Van Gogh immediately catch on with local collectors. "Almost more than any other modern painter he is felt to be an alien...[his] appeal is so simple and direct. It is just this simplicity that makes him appear strange. The simplicity of a child and the white hot fervour of an evangelist are indeed strange in New York."[26]

In the decade after the Armory Show, more than one hundred works by Van Gogh arrived in New York from France and the Netherlands. All but a handful returned unsold. The influx of pictures was spurred on by the exigencies of war: with the Parisian market practically closed, and the loss of their best clients, start-up Manhattan galleries functioned as outlets for selling modern art. Enthusiastically sourced by hook or by crook, the French offerings were bolstered by Dutch imports that came with a solid provenance. While Americans were partial to figure paintings—as may be traced from the first acquisitions to the frontispiece images for landmark exhibition catalogues—still lifes held a certain appeal, particularly as a kind of gateway acquisition. For example, before New York businessman and collector Stephen C. Clark ventured to buy the great *Night Café* (F463; see Chudzicka, fig. 19) in 1933, he treaded more lightly, with a still life (later returned).[27] Ironically, the seemingly safer bet sometimes proved a risky proposition. When it came to discriminating between the good, the bad, and the ugly ("ugliness" being a common refrain), critics, dealers, and would-be buyers were all on unfamiliar ground. Inevitably it was a bit of a gamble for all involved, and fakes were part of the bargain.

Contrary to expectations and current documentation, Van Gogh enjoyed a discernible presence on the New York art scene during the war years. This was largely owing to two enterprising dealers who introduced more than two dozen works by (or said to be by) the artist into the marketplace: Stephan Bourgeois, formerly of the Rue de Rivoli in Paris, and Marius de Zayas, former advisor to Alfred Stieglitz and his "291" gallery in New York.

The first Van Goghs for sale on Fifth Avenue were exhibited in "luxurious surroundings"—or as "innocently as possible on lovely damask walls"[28]—at the Bourgeois Galleries' opening show of "old and modern masters," in 1914. Included among the "four examples of the virile art of Vincent van Gogh"[29] were *Vase with Poppies* (F279; plate 24), which had been lent to the Armory Show (with the less elegant title "Red Flowers"); a second floral piece; a "delightful sketch of the 'Moulin de la Galette'" (F228; plate 63); and "a charming Provençal landscape"[30] with "carmine outlines to the flowering fruit trees"(F513)[31] that was "alone worth the trip to the gallery."[32] One such trip to the premises resulted in a sale. "Field Flowers in a Vase" caught the eye of Philadelphia lawyer and collector John G. Johnson, whose illustrious bequest to his hometown museum in 1917 would include this bouquet, which, however, bears a spurious signature and was destined to wilt in storage.[33] The three other works failed to entice buyers, and were auctioned off in Europe the same year.[34] Before they left, *Le Moulin de la Galette* was sent to San Francisco, where it made a cameo appearance on the West Coast at the 1915 *Panama-Pacific International Exposition*.[35]

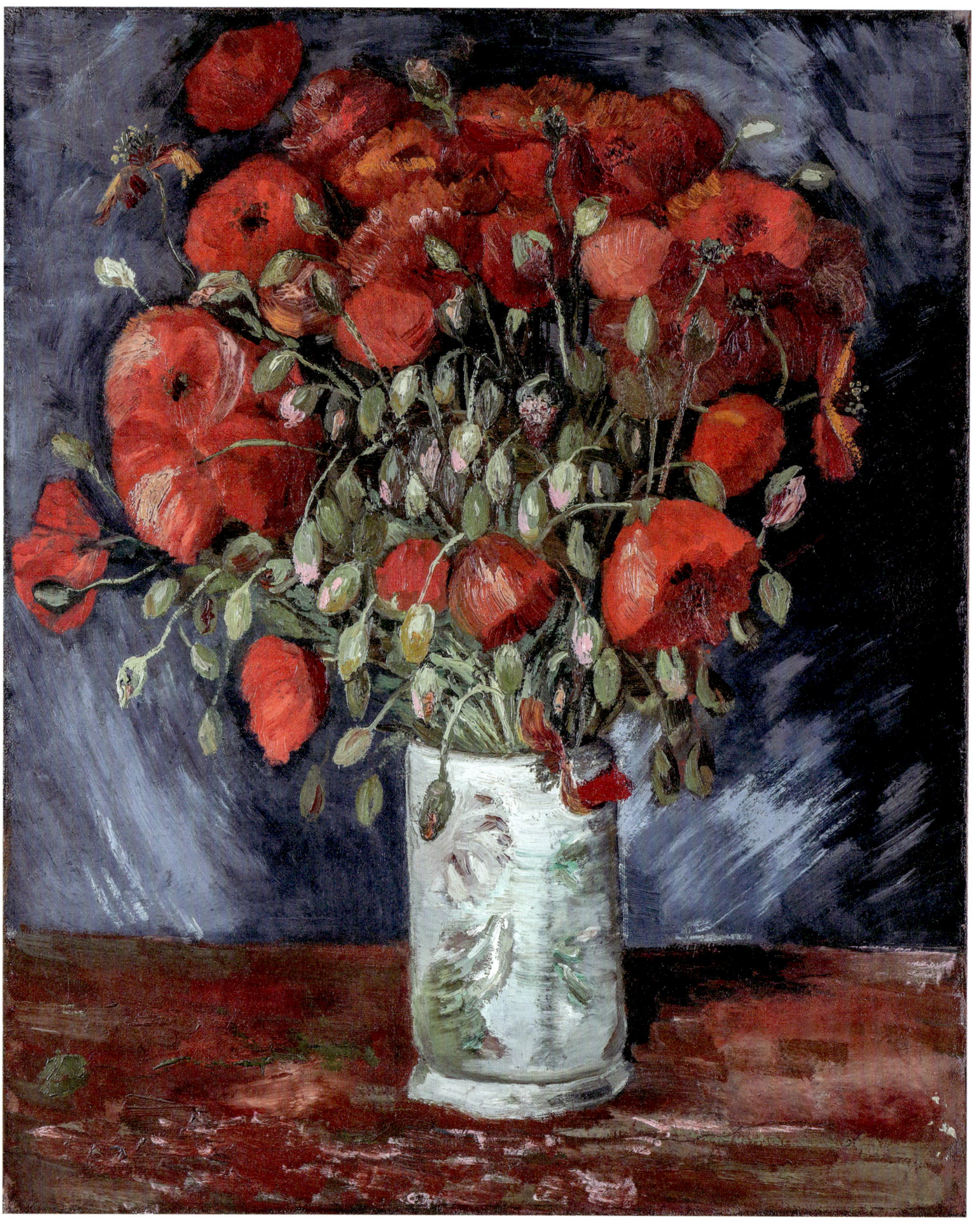

PLATE 24. *Vase with Poppies*, 1886 (CAT. 16)

Bourgeois introduced new works by Van Gogh in his *Exhibition of Modern Art* held in April 1916: two paintings, "Still Life" and "Iris," and five drawings that ranged from early subjects such as "The Weaver" and "Garden at Nuenen" to the later "Butterfly."[36] Reviewers hastened to mention them only in passing, so the titles—if telling—provide only a clue regarding this fresh infusion of works. Presumably they were relatively modest in scale and portable enough to be brought across the Atlantic by the artist's family members who spent the war years in New York. The artist's nephew, Vincent Willem van Gogh, and his wife Josina, arrived in mid-October 1915, just in time to double the contents of the artist's first solo show in America. (His mother, Jo van Gogh-Bonger, joined them in late August 1916.[37])

The Van Gogh exhibition held at the Modern Gallery in late 1915 capped off Marius de Zayas's first year in business running the commercial offshoot of Stieglitz's "291." Applauding his resourcefulness in bringing "from Paris eight examples of Van Gogh's painting,"[38] the press was quick to report in late November 1915: "Van Gogh reigns supreme in a little show, now on at the Modern Gallery."[39] Writers could not have been more enthusiastic or more earnest in their efforts to grapple with a selection that presented "the most striking contrasts imaginable."[40] No wonder. As far as one can gather, it seems to have been divided between works by, and not by, Van Gogh. On the plus side, De Zayas had landed one of the five versions of the "famous picture" *La Berceuse* (F505)[41] and two Arles landscapes: a "snow scene" showing "a wide expanse of level country...beyond which, at the skyline a city rises with dark buildings" (F391);[42] and "a roughly effective look over some poppy fields in France, with an excessively tormented sky" (F575).[43] On the other hand (not Van Gogh's), there was a mountainous landscape "Les Baux" (F725)[44] and the real show-stealer: a "masterly group of flowers on a garden path" (fig. 5).[45] Critics were ineluctably drawn to the "lyric joy" of this

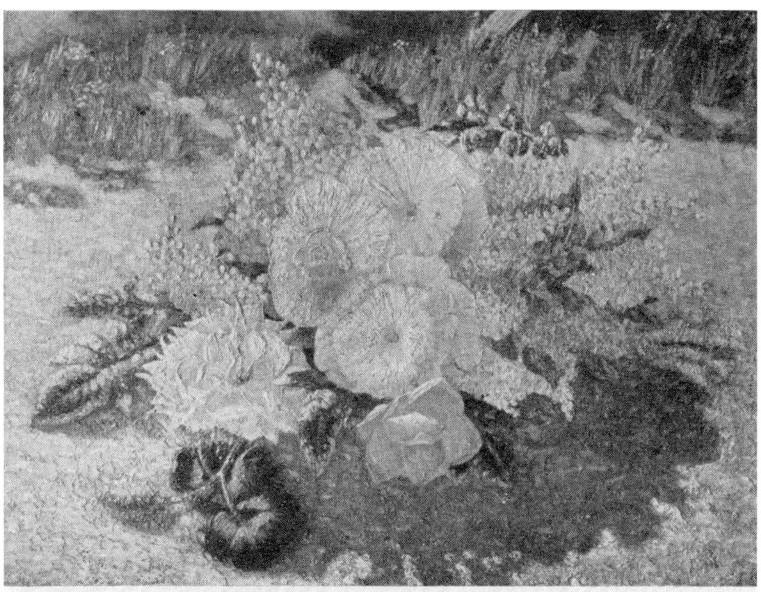

FIG. 5 Illustration in *Arts and Decoration*, January 1916. Artist unknown, shown as "Fleurs Lilas" by Van Gogh at the Modern Gallery, New York 1915 and 1916.

"harmoniously grouped" arrangement of lilacs with its "delightfully handled"[46] color schemes that was reproduced (with a "291" caption) in the January 1916 issue of *Arts and Decoration* just before its reshowing in a group exhibition at the Modern Gallery the following month.[47] Overall, the still lifes and flowers were ranked as the "sanest and calmest" and most satisfying of the artist's works.[48] Insofar as a picture of herrings was given a slight edge over the "almost equally beautiful" sunflowers,[49] we may be fairly certain that the "Vase de Soleils" was not one of the iconic Arles bouquets. But only further research into this cache of paintings may serve to puzzle out if they—and the large, early figure picture called "La Hollandaise"—are or are not by Van Gogh. For now, we can wonder if this is the same group of "8 Van Goghs"—"several fine, one 'La Berceuse' a beauty—others—landscapes"—that the artist Marsden Hartley signaled in a letter to Stieglitz of April 13, 1912, written upon Hartley's arrival in Paris.[50]

Gallery records indicate that the Modern Gallery's 1915 Van Gogh exhibition included eight paintings and ran from November 22 to December 12,[51] but the newspapers tell a different story. The final tally was seventeen. The initial selection also included "a small sketch of a woman seated, a comparatively unimportant work."[52] Around the scheduled close date, journalists reported that the show was "supplemented by a number of sketches and drawings from the family of the artist,"[53] or, more precisely, "eight additions...procured from the nephew of the famous artist."[54] The writer for the *Brooklyn Daily Eagle* elaborated: "The drawings are mellow and interesting. The color studies include scenes of work, a man in

FIG. 6 *The Sower* (F1441), 1888. Pencil, pen, and reed pen and ink on paper, 9⅝ × 12⅝ in. (24.4 × 32 cm). Van Gogh Museum, Amsterdam (Vincent van Gogh Foundation).

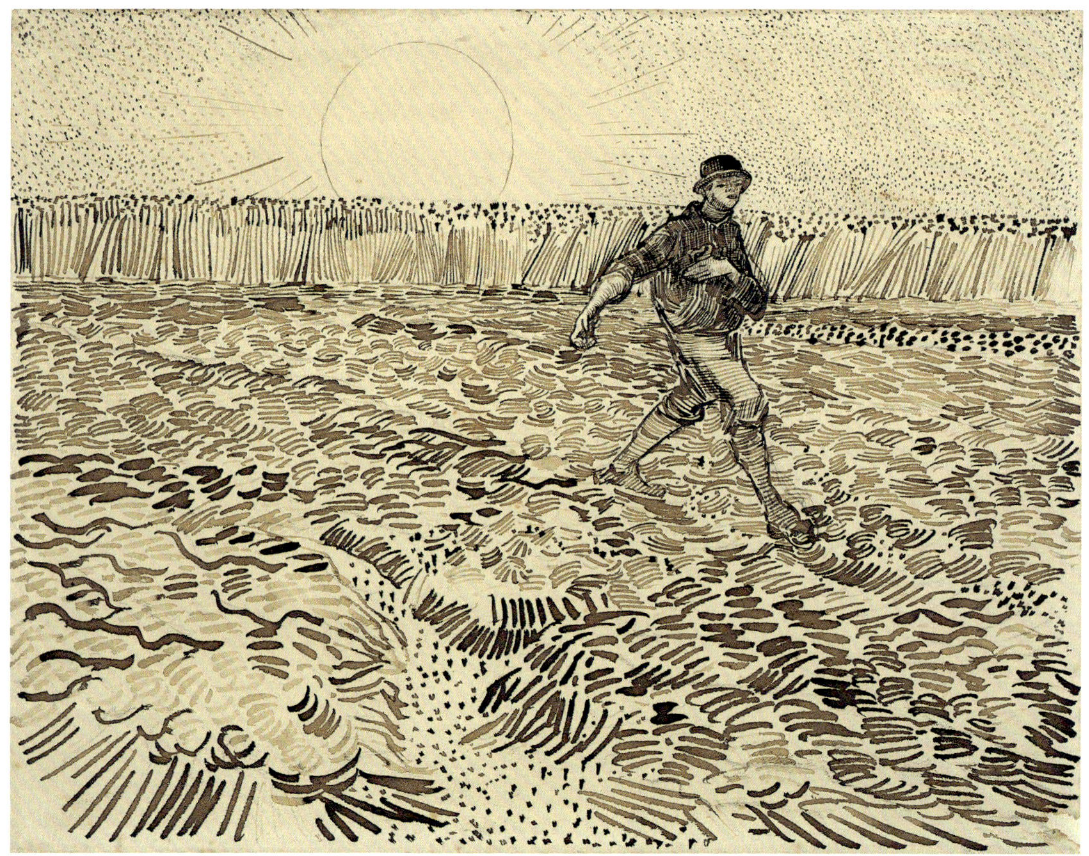

blue stooping, a peasant woman at work out of doors, a color study of grass and poppies in a landscape scene [F748; see Van der Hoeven and Zwikker, fig. 1] and other scenes depicted in the artist's individual style."[55] Fortunately, the writer for the *New York Times* was intrigued enough by Van Gogh's "clearly thought out method" to describe these other scenes in such sharp detail as to allow for the identification of half the group. He noted a drawing of a sower in which "the sky is covered with dots...closely sprinkled over the paper," which become "less close" as they near the sun (F1441; fig. 6). He marveled at how "the schematic waving lines" in a small late landscape are "used in foliage, grasses, clouds, and wherever movement is suggested" (F1624?). And he went on to remark that the "lovely study in color of a butterfly on a large flower of the orchid variety [F610] is supplemented by the black and white sketch made as a preliminary study for the butterfly [F1523]" in the spirit of William Blake's "passion for 'minute appropriate execution.'"[56]

While Van Gogh had been kept afloat along the Hudson during the war years, his reputation would advance on more solid—even hallowed (museum)—ground in the 1920s. The tides turned at the start of the decade owing to the large shipment of works—sixty-seven in all—that the artist's family placed on loan to the Montross Gallery, which hosted the "most comprehensive exhibition of the art of Vincent van Gogh ever held in America"[57] beginning in late October 1920. Hailed as "the outstanding event of the art season so far,"[58] and even as "an event unsurpassed in its way since the international show of modern art at the Armory, in 1913,"[59] the exhibition was seen as rendering a "great service"[60] by laying bare "the whole experimental and creative career of the plodding mercurial Hollander."[61]

The novelty of discovering Van Gogh's early works "in grave Dutch tones that seem a far remove from the later brilliantly light and colorful studies of Arles" made them "the chief surprise."[62] The Paris period paintings, represented by such familiar motifs as the Moulin de la Galette (F346), proved the most "pleasing," especially for pundits like Royal Cortissoz, who took a dim view of the artist's later achievement and looked to sniff out the charm that "still peeps through" in floral still lifes and landscapes that retain "something of the light touch" and "springlike gamut of color."[63] No word was more bandied about than "ugliness," but few failed to mention the virility of his drawing, the intensity of his expression, or his evident sincerity. Van Gogh's portraits—with their vitality of "rough truth" and "vividness of characterization"—registered even with his most reluctant fans.[64] The savviest critics quoted from Van Gogh's letters to highlight his admiration for Jean-François Millet, as reflected in *Two Peasants Digging* (F648; plate 25) and *Snow-Covered Field with a Harrow (after Millet)* (F632; see Shaw, Heartland, fig. 1), or

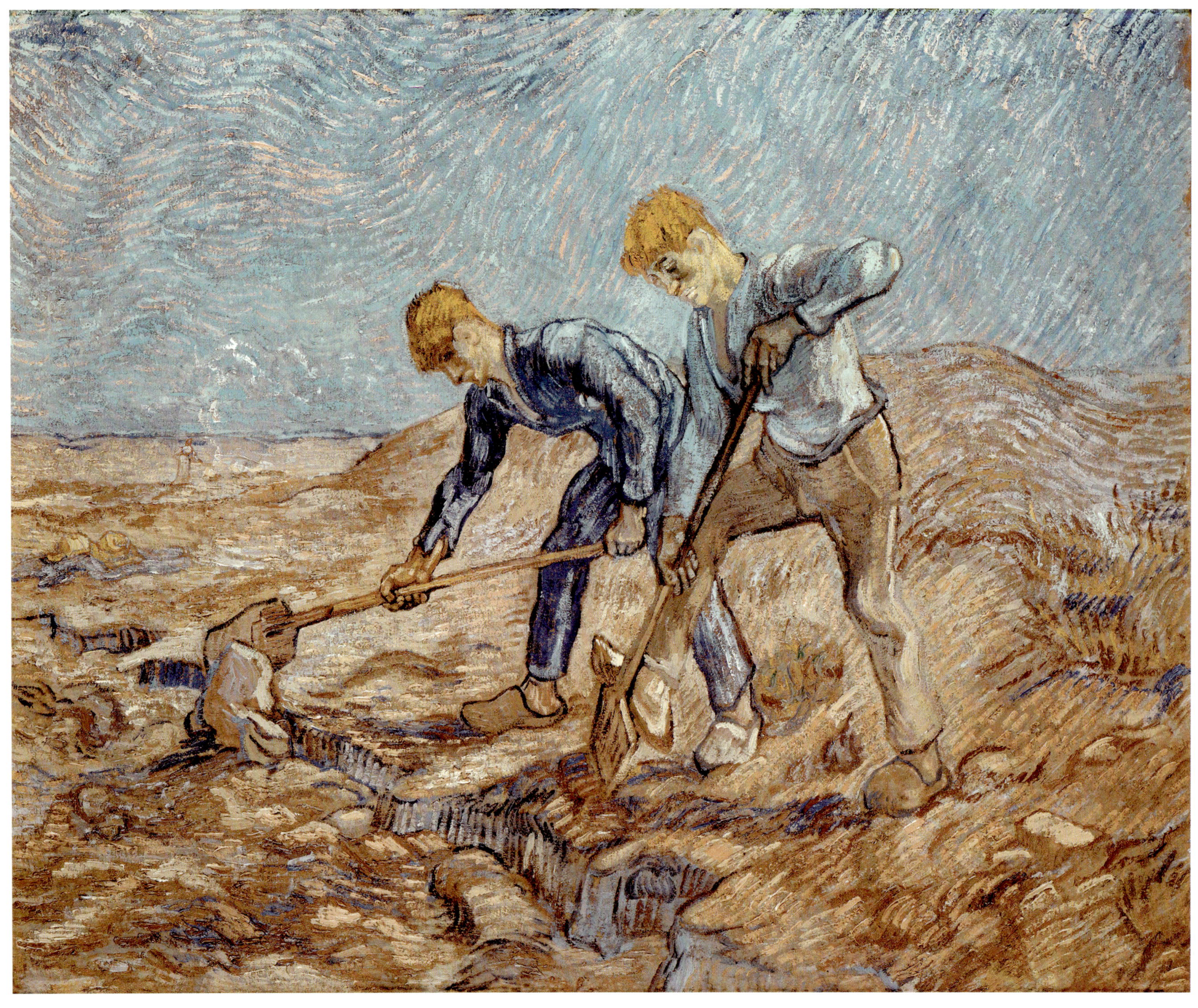

PLATE 25. *Two Peasants Digging*, 1889 (CAT. 57)

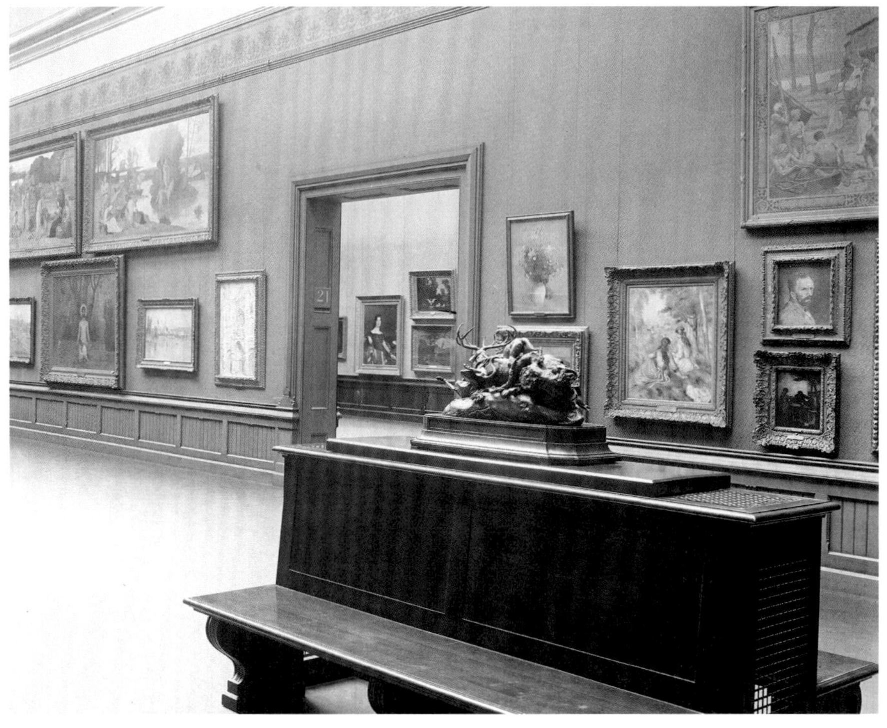

FIG. 7 Installation view of the *Fiftieth Anniversary Exhibition*, The Metropolitan Museum of Art, New York, 1920, featuring *Self-Portrait* (F268; plate 17), lent by John Quinn.

his expressive use of color in Provence when the "nuances and refinements of his Paris technique" give way to a broad style and direct approach "of irresistible power."[65] With an air of familiarity, writers reminded their audience of other works that had been shown along Fifth Avenue. One took note of the relationship between the "characteristic" self-portrait on view (F356) to the one lent—by John Quinn (F268; plate 17)—earlier that year to the Metropolitan Museum's *Fiftieth Anniversary Exhibition*, where it became the first work by the artist to grace the walls of the venerable institution (fig. 7).[66] Another remarked on the style of the "flat, decorative portraits" of *The Zouave* (F423) and of "Postman" *Joseph Roulin* (F436) "done in the robust manner of the famous Berceuse" that was shown "some years ago" at De Zayas's Modern Gallery.[67] But mostly, they urged their readers to put aside "much of the preposterous nonsense in detraction and adulation" to view the works "unclouded by either haze."[68]

The thirty-two paintings and thirty-five works on paper from the Van Gogh family collection that comprised the contents of this milestone exhibition would make a decisive impact—beyond what may be gleaned from the critical response to the two-month-long showing. The fact is, the group of loans remained in town for *three years*. During this period, Newman E. Montross extended the initial run of the retrospective, restaged it twice (in early 1921 and in the spring of 1923), and routinely included Van Gogh in group shows in his gallery.[69] Moreover, the contents furnished loans to high-profile venues in New York and Chicago, including the Metropolitan Museum's 1921 foray into exhibiting modern art, which was enriched by seven loans (four paintings and three drawings).[70]

Nor were these the only works from the Van Gogh family collection in town; others, including the *Pietà (after Delacroix)* (F630; see Van der Hoeven and Zwikker, fig. 2) and the glorious *Irises* (F678), were lent to the *Modern Art of Holland* exhibition held in 1921 at the Anderson Galleries in New York, and five more were featured at the same gallery, in the spring of 1923, as part of a traveling exhibition of Dutch and Flemish art.[71] The former show, which ran from April 23 through May 7, 1921, fell into a lineup of exhibitions that kept Van Gogh in the public eye as his works took their place "in the company of canonized immortals" on the walls of public institutions.[72] The Brooklyn Museum led the way in "opening its doors to the Post-Impressionists of France" in March 1921 with its *Modern French Masters* exhibition, which included Van Gogh's *Self-Portrait* (F526; plate 44) and *Women Picking Olives* (F655; see Shaw, Heartland, fig. 3), on loan from the collection of

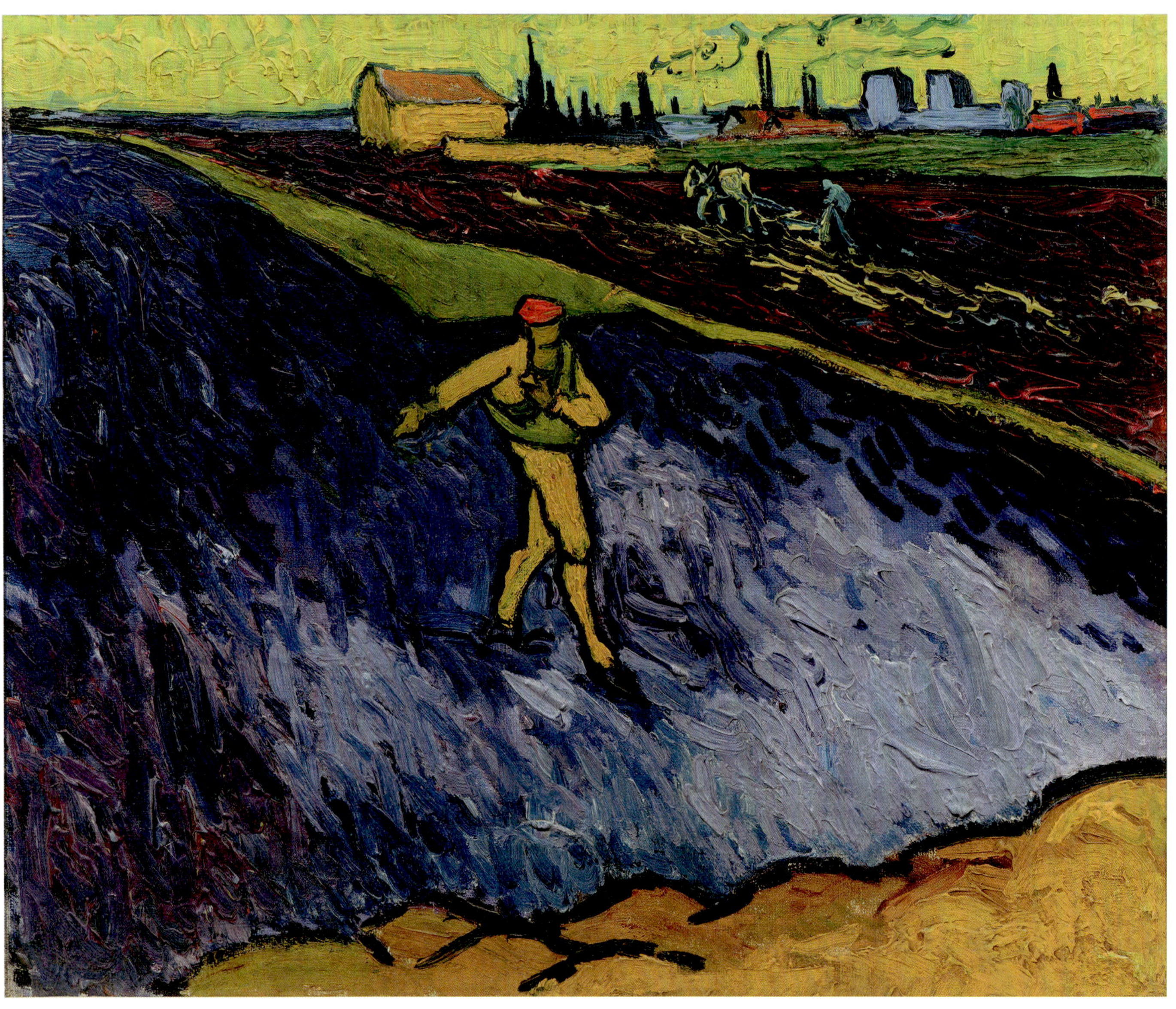

PLATE 26. *The Sower*, 1888 (CAT. 41)

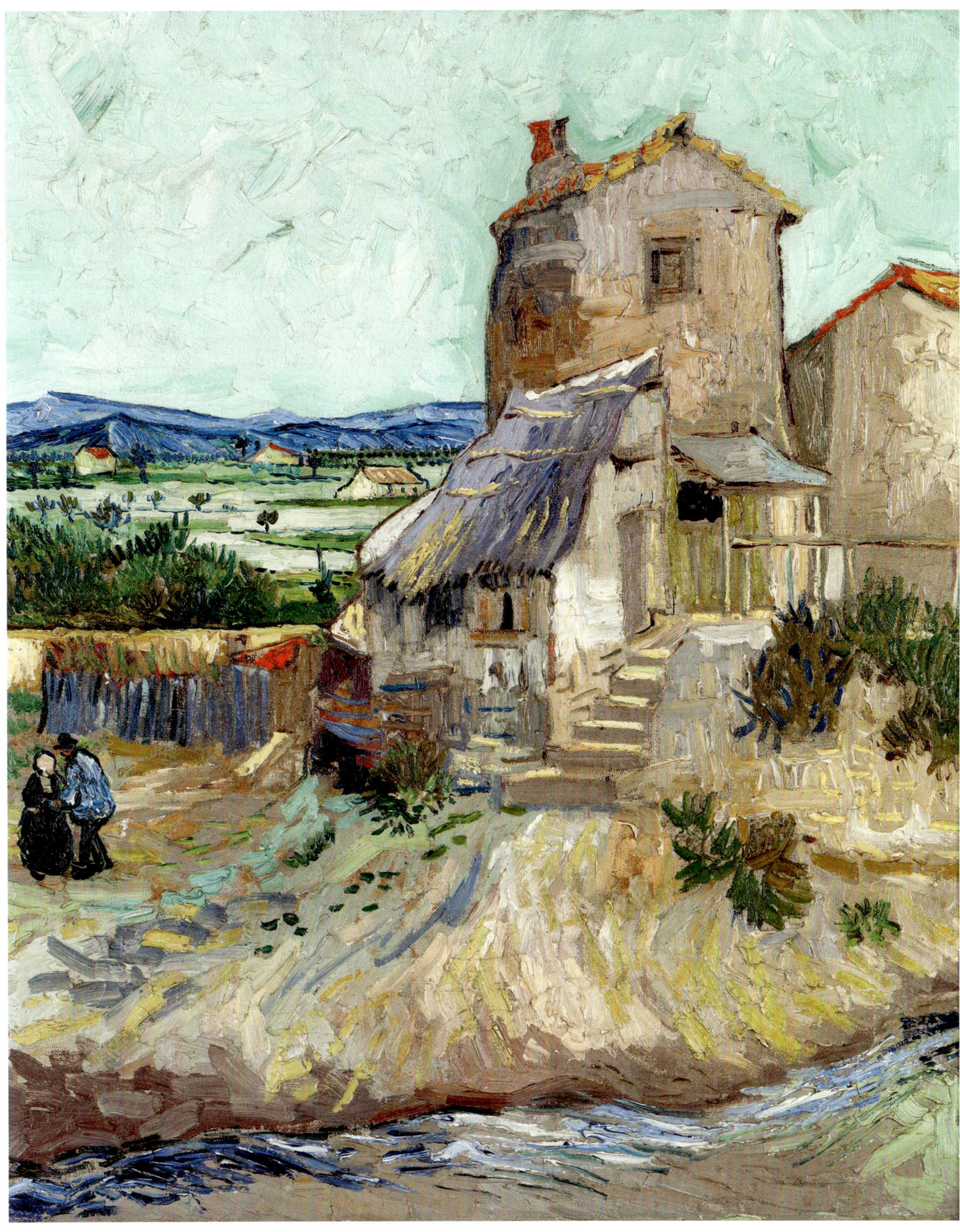

PLATE 27. *House on the Crau (The Old Mill)*, 1888 (CAT. 36)

veteran New York dealer Dikran Kelekian. Once "officialdom in New York was finally awake," as Stieglitz put it, Brooklyn's "big neighbor in Manhattan" kept the momentum going that summer through the fall.[73]

The Metropolitan Museum's *Loan Exhibition of Impressionist and Post-Impressionist Paintings* was held at the urging of John Quinn and other like-minded collectors eight years after the Armory Show gave New York its first large-scale introduction to modern art and eight years before the Museum of Modern Art's inaugural exhibition launched plans for giving it a permanent home. A keen barometer and galvanizer of the cause, the 1921 exhibition was seen as doubly important: "first, from the fact that it affords the best basis for an estimate of Post-Impressionism that this country has yet had; second, from the recognition of Modernism by a great institution like the Metropolitan Museum."[74]

Of the seven Van Gogh loans on display (fig. 8), four had enjoyed their fair share of press coverage during the run of the Montross show: *Still Life—Lemons and Carafe* (F340), *Van Gogh's Chair* (F498; plate 47), *Snow-Covered Field with a Harrow (after Millet)* (F632; see Shaw, Heartland, fig. 1), and especially, the *Portrait of Joseph Roulin* (F436), which had sparked interest from a potential buyer. Two other pictures, lent anonymously, were short-term acquisitions of Marius de Zayas: *Portrait of Camille Roulin* (F537; plate 15) and *Farmhouse in Auvers* (F623), perhaps the "very good landscape" on view at his gallery earlier that year.[75] (Cash-strapped De Zayas sold both works at auction in 1923, closed up shop in New York, and moved abroad.) John Quinn contributed his *Self-Portrait* (F268; plate 17). Arguably the best-known Van Gogh in the city, it had been a mainstay of the New York art scene for the past seven years, from the 1913 Armory Show to its more recent showing at the Metropolitan Museum's *Fiftieth Anniversary Exhibition*.

FIG. 8 Installation view of the *Loan Exhibition of Impressionist and Post-Impressionist Paintings*, The Metropolitan Museum of Art, New York, 1921, featuring works by Van Gogh. Right to left, top row: F340, F498 (plate 47), F623; bottom row: F537 (plate 15), F632, F268 (plate 17); and F436 on spur wall to right.

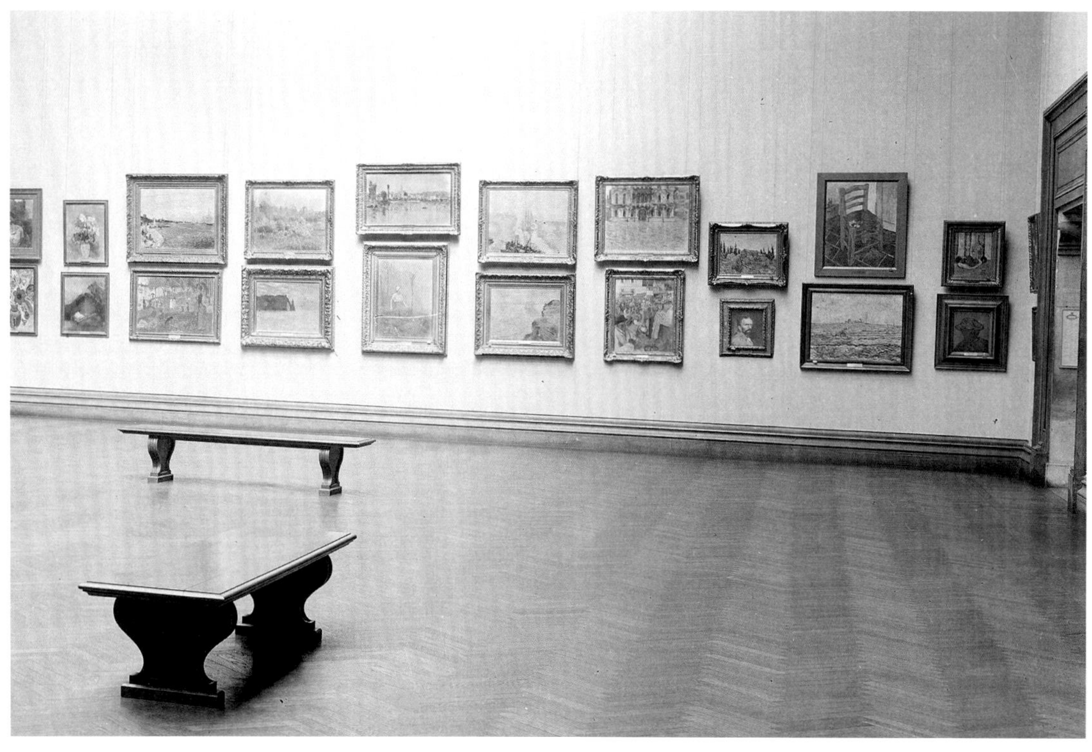

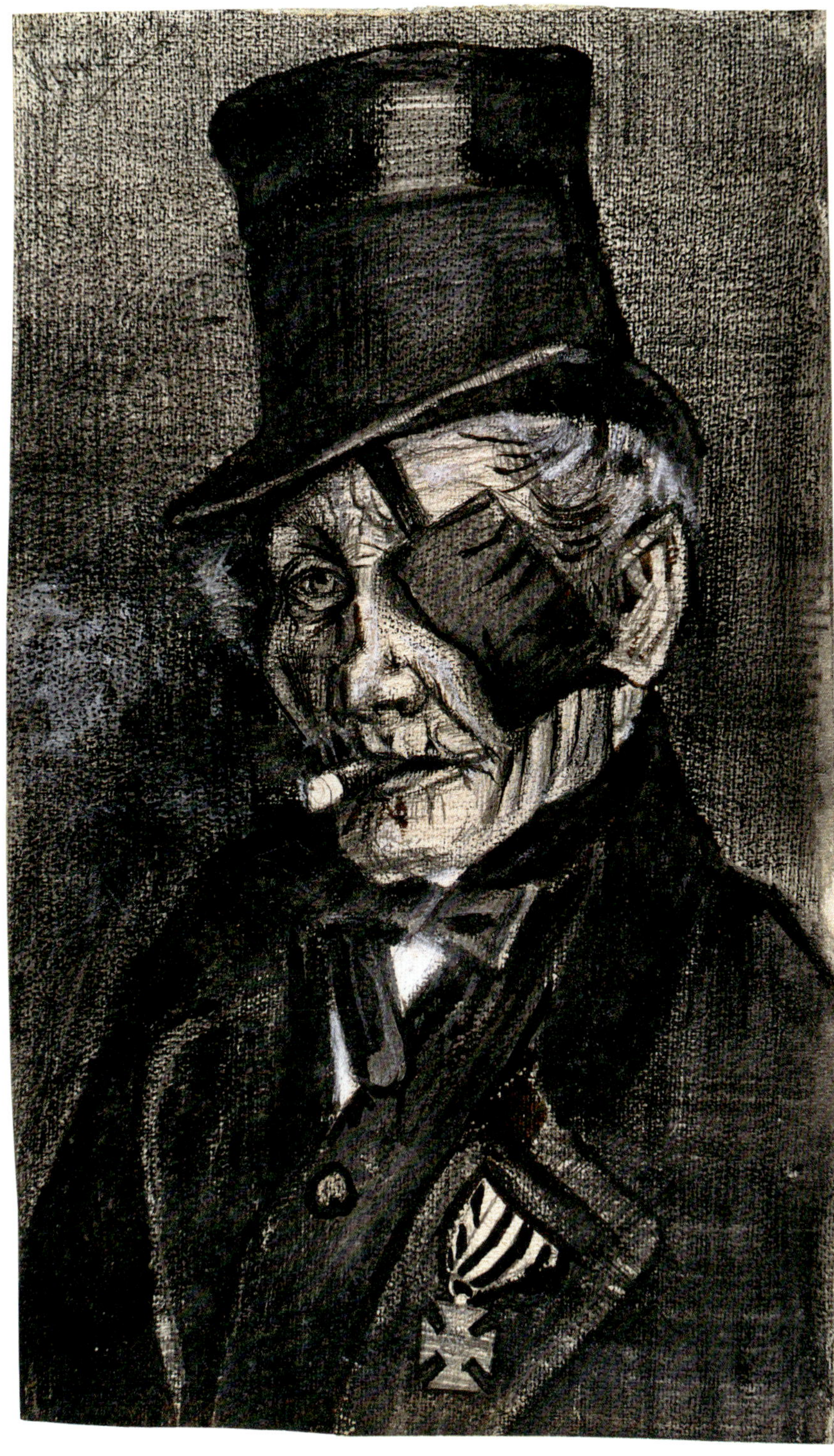

PLATE 28. *The Wounded Veteran*, c. 1882–83 (CAT. 6)

Another work was destined to be a familiar fixture: "A still life painting by Van Gogh added to the exhibition from the collection of Frederick [*sic*] Clay Bartlett."[76] Formerly owned by the French critic and dealer Théodore Duret, this still life (fig. 9) seems to have floated between the Montross and Carroll galleries in 1914–15 before it found a buyer, through Walter Pach, who unwittingly promoted and brokered its sale.[77] Who was to know that Duret, once the great champion of Manet and the Impressionists, had become a great purveyor of fakes? The picture enjoyed its heyday in the 1920s. It was a "favorite" of critic Forbes Watson, who found any number of occasions to highlight its charms. Within a decade bracketed by its showing at the Metropolitan Museum and its return to New York for MoMA's inaugural exhibition in 1929, the still life had entered the Art Institute of Chicago as part of the cornerstone Birch Bartlett bequest—along with "the famous Grande Jatte" by Georges Seurat and such signature Van Goghs as *The Bedroom* (F484; plate 45) and *Madame Roulin Rocking the Cradle (La Berceuse)* (F506). What's more, it held its own: it was seen as having the same intensity of vision and directness of *La Berceuse* and, indeed, fared better than the "third wispy but charming canvas, 'On Montmartre' [F272; plate 16], from the hand of the sensitive 'Vincent.'"[78]

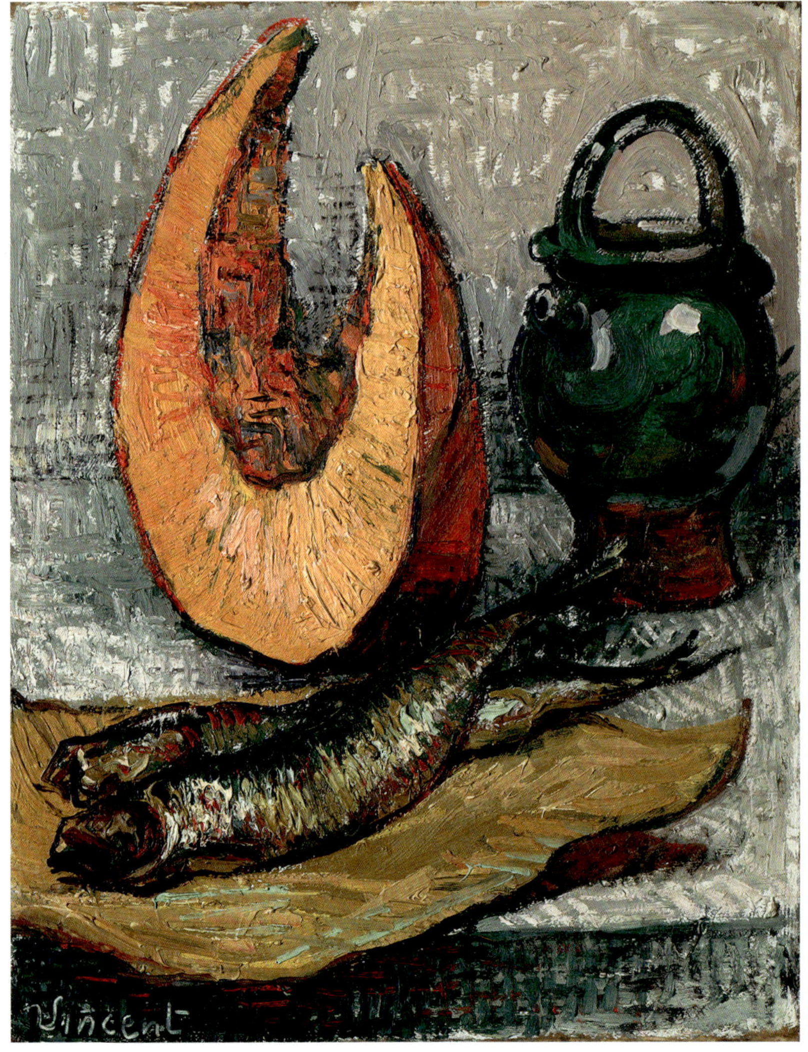

FIG. 9 Artist unknown, *Still Life: Melon, Fish, Jar*, n.d. Oil on panel, 21¾ × 18¼ in. (55.2 × 46.3 cm). The Art Institute of Chicago.

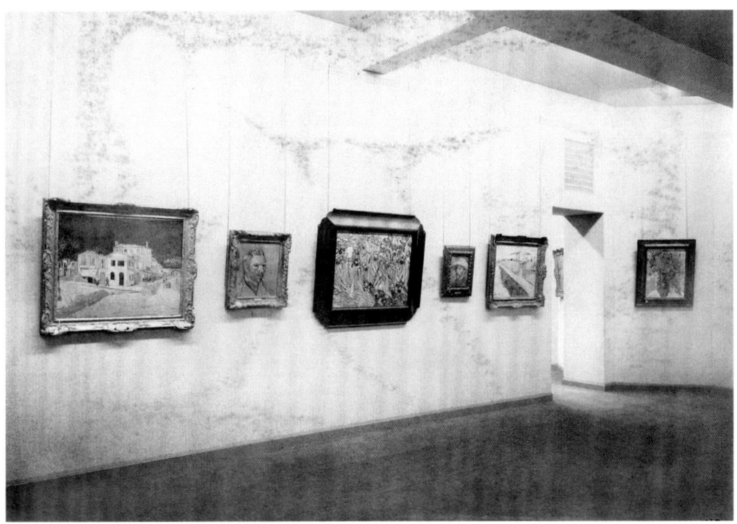

FIG. 10 Installation view featuring Van Gogh works in the *First Loan Exhibition: Cézanne, Gauguin, Seurat, van Gogh*, The Museum of Modern Art, New York, 1929. Left to right: F464, F501, F608, F526 (plate 44), F400, F280.

Notwithstanding these missteps along the way, by the mid-September close date of the Metropolitan Museum's 1921 exhibition, Van Gogh had gained a real foothold in the cultural landscape of New York. Indeed, since the previous fall, his works had been featured in an almost seamless run of displays along Fifth Avenue and, in the spring of 1923, even in overlapping venues before they left town. Beyond a lasting impression, they left little trace behind.

Over the course of three years, despite the dealer's valiant efforts, Jo van Gogh-Bonger's abiding good will and price reductions, and their mutual optimism that prospects would improve, only three works were sold and to a single buyer: the Reverend Theodore Pitcairn, whose acquisitions in 1921 placed him in the company of fellow Philadelphian Barnes as the only other American owner of multiple Van Goghs, and quite nearby, in the outlying Philadelphia suburb Bryn Athyn.

Pitcairn's inherited fortune allowed him to indulge his love of antiquities and the arts of Asia on a grand scale and to buy the occasional picture that struck his fancy, including Monet's *Garden at Sainte-Adresse* (one of the glories of the Metropolitan Museum of Art) and in 1927 Van Gogh's *Portrait of the Artist's Mother* (F477). Had it not been for a snafu at the Kelekian auction, he might have also owned a fifth Van Gogh—the *Self-Portrait* (F526; plate 44) in Detroit.[79] Pitcairn's 1921 purchase of the drawing *Sorrow* (F929a; plate 13), the oil painting *The Sower* (F575a; plate 26), and a portrait of Adeline Ravoux (F769)—the so-called "Blue Girl," which was the catalogue's frontispiece and a frontrunner in the critical praise column—marked the first sale of works from the Van Gogh family collection since the outbreak of war in 1914,[80] and the second to an American collector. The initial sale was to Katherine S. Dreier, whose portrait of Ravoux (F786; plate 18) made its reappearance on the New York art scene in the months leading up to the Montross retrospective when it was shown in the spring 1920 inaugural exhibition of the Société Anonyme, the "experimental museum" she cofounded with Marcel Duchamp and Man Ray.

In 1921, as a writer for the *International Studio* observed, "Van Gogh's day in America is not yet."[81] Within the next few years, his works took hold and increasingly gained traction with collectors. By the end of the decade, our newfound "wealth in Van Goghs"[82] was given memorable form in MoMA's *First Loan Exhibition: Cézanne, Gauguin, Seurat, van Gogh* of 1929 (fig. 10). All but a handful of the twenty-seven works by Van Gogh came from American lenders, including a dozen from New Yorkers and five from Bostonians, whose names were called out—like

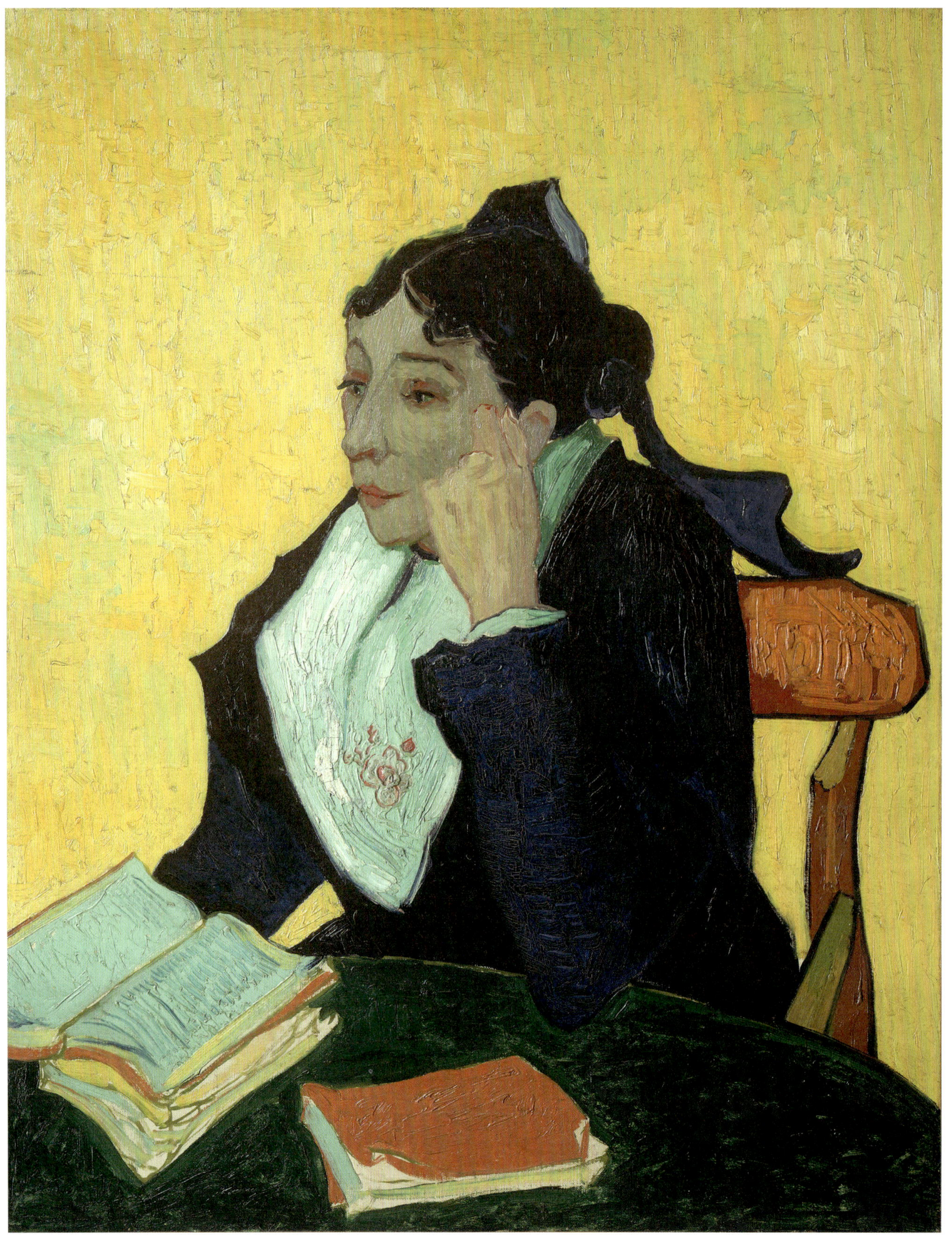

PLATE 29. *L'Arlésienne: Madame Joseph-Michel Ginoux (Marie Julien, 1848–1911)*, 1888–89 (CAT. 45)

an honor roll—in paragraph-long lists that governed the press releases and coverage of the show. Of great topical interest, if not a point of pride, was the fact that Van Gogh was now represented in a number of private collections along the eastern seaboard and in museums located in the Midwest. As Forbes Watson put it: "Undoubtedly an outstanding development in recent American collecting has been our acquisition of first-rate Van Goghs."[83]

Most of the loans were new to the "interested spectators" who piled into the Heckscher building at 730 Fifth Avenue[84]—a few blocks and a decade away from MoMA's permanent site—but there were some familiar faces among the crowds, such as the portrait *Adeline Ravoux* (F786; plate 18) and *The Zouave* (F1482; plate 20) of Armory Show fame, and also the Detroit *Self-Portrait* (F526; plate 44), which made local news as a loan and sale from the Kelekian collection in 1921–22. New Englanders had an edge over the MoMA crowd. In the spring of 1929, seven of the loans secured by MoMA were shown in the *Exhibition of French Painting* held at Harvard's Fogg Art Museum in Cambridge, which was reprised in large part for a summer show at the Museum of Fine Arts, Boston. This mini-preview included *House on the Crau (The Old Mill)* (F550; plate 27), lent by A. Conger Goodyear of Buffalo; *Street in Auvers* (F805), lent by John T. Spaulding of Boston; *The Wounded Veteran* (F1003; plate 28), lent by Meta and Paul J. Sachs of Cambridge; "portrait of an azure letter-carrier" (F432; see Stolwijk and Krikke, fig. 7), which was "found thrilling by many lady visitors at the Museum,"[85] lent by Mr. and Mrs. Robert Treat Paine II, of Boston; and last but not least, *L'Arlésienne: Madame Joseph-Michel Ginoux (Marie Julien, 1848–1911)* (F488; plate 29), lent by New Yorker Adolph Lewisohn, which was destined to become one of the best-known and loved Van Goghs in town.[86]

In the decade between Lewisohn's purchase of *L'Arlésienne* in 1926 (through his art advisor Stephan Bourgeois) and its star turn as the cover image of MoMA's 1935–36 *Vincent van Gogh* blockbuster (fig. 11), the painting would be featured in no less than eight exhibitions on the New York art scene. In 1929 Edward Alden Jewell, writing for the *New York Times,* went so far as to say: "No Van Gogh group could be called really worthy that did not contain the grand *L'Arlésienne* (Mme. Ginoux)...She is present, with her unconquerable vitality and the splendor of her yellow background and the books she may or may not read."[87] Even as recalcitrant a fan as Royal Cortissoz of the *Herald Tribune* considered it one of the artist's "curious best."[88]

Fast-forward to the present, and *L'Arlésienne* is one of five works lent to MoMA in 1929 that enjoys pride of place in the permanent collection of the Metropolitan Museum of Art.[89] Other loans have since entered museums in Boston, Cambridge, Chicago, Cleveland, and Washington, DC. By and large, once the pictures earned their keep with first-generation collectors, they were here to stay. Each of the pioneering purchases made by Barnes, Dreier, and Quinn in 1912 and two-thirds of the loans to MoMA in 1929 have become part of the cultural heritage of museumgoers in America. As fate would have it, New York—the first port of call for Van Gogh's works on this side of the Atlantic—would become a destination site for the appreciation of the "hard won achievements" of an artist who eventually, if unpredictably, won over the "good public." It would take a while, as a writer for the *New York Times* forecast back in 1912—or roughly a quarter of a century.[90] By the time of MoMA's retrospective in New York in 1935–36, Van Gogh had become, in the eyes of those monitoring the record-breaking crowds, "more popular" than "any other artist of the past or present."[91] The rest is all history.

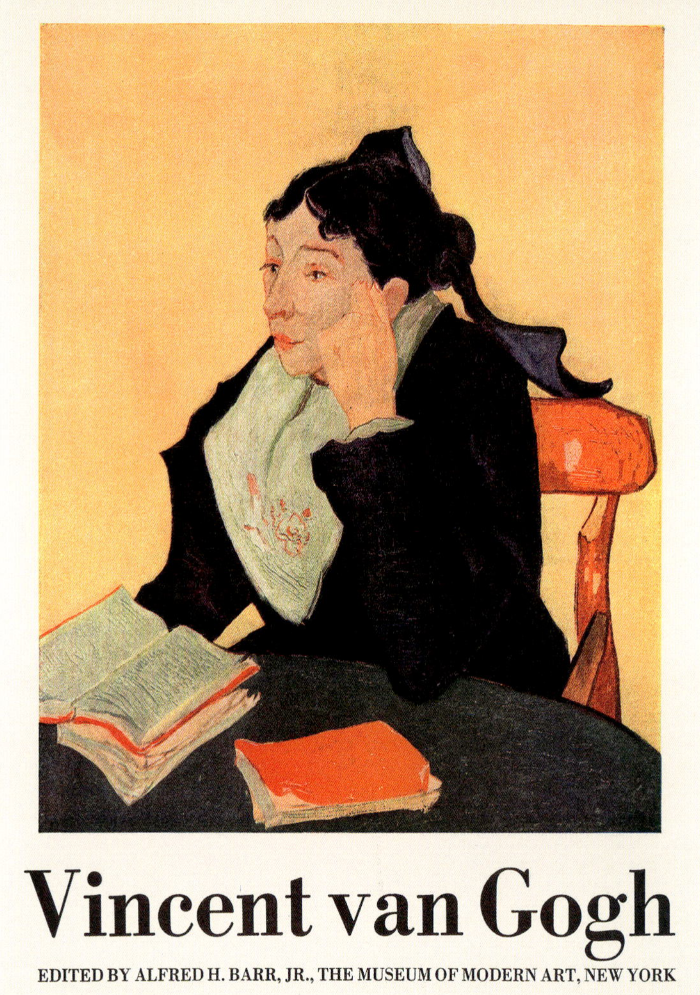

FIG. 11 Cover of the *Vincent van Gogh* retrospective exhibition catalogue, The Museum of Modern Art, New York, 1935.

NOTES

1 *New York Times* 1912. The article advised readers of the *Times* that "a collection of pictures by Van Gogh" was slated to be shown "as early in the season as is found possible to assemble them" at the galleries of the American branch of the Berlin Photographic Company. The reporter seems to have rushed to press with the newsworthy item, giving the story full-page coverage, replete with art historical details and illustrations (F82, see Stolwijk and Krikke, fig. 1; F493; F525; F1325), presumably acting on an inside scoop from the young dealer Martin Birnbaum. Fresh from a visit to the Sonderbund exhibition in Cologne, Birnbaum doubtless assumed that it would be possible to introduce to the galleries he managed at 505 Madison Avenue, some measure of the stunning array of Van Goghs on view. Armory Show organizer Walt Kuhn had the same idea and in fact, a month later, learned that Birnbaum "had been over here ahead of me trying to get Van G's. From what I hear he has not been successful." Walt Kuhn, letter to Vera Kuhn, October 8, 1912, https://www.aaa.si.edu/collections/items/detail/walt-kuhn-letter-to-vera-kuhn-14498. The exhibition Birnbaum planned never came to fruition; it was literally a no-show. Kuhn also left Germany empty-handed.

2 Walt Kuhn, letter to J. H. de Bois, November 29, 1912, https://edan.si.edu/slideshow/slideshowViewer.htm?damspath=/CollectionsOnline/kuhnwalt/Box_0001/Folder_017.

3 For the March buying trip and Barnes's relationship with Maurer, see Wattenmaker 2010, especially 18–22, 127–30. I am immensely grateful to my colleague Cindy Kang, curator at the Barnes Foundation, for generously providing me with information concerning the acquisition history of the seven paintings by Van Gogh in the collection and for clarifying that Barnes owned three before World War I (not two, as is given elsewhere in the literature, most recently in W. Feilchenfeldt 2013, 27). Barnes saw *The Smoker* (F534) with Maurer at Druet's in June, asked Maurer to negotiate a purchase price, and bought it in September. *The Factory* (F318) was acquired on November 15, 1912, from Bernheim-Jeune, as documented by a letter and copy of the check. In July 1922, Barnes bought F674 from Paul Gachet *fils*, followed by the purchases of F330 on July 19, 1924; F478 by 1926; and F600 on March 1, 1933.

4 Zilczer 1978, 18, 23. The sale of the "three Paintings" to Quinn is recorded in the Vollard gallery Date Book (*Agenda de la galerie*), Archives des Musées Nationaux, Paris, Fonds Vollard, MS 421 (5, 8), fol. 163, under an entry dated September 17, 1912, which reads: "Vendu à M Quinn trois Tableaux/Mad Cezanne Cezanne 25,000 frs/Gauguin Tahiti 16,000/Van Gogh portrait 8,000." An entry from the previous day notes that Vollard had sold Quinn a book of Van Gogh letters ("Vendu à Mr John Q[uinn] 1 livre de Van Gogh lettres"). Vollard did not ship the paintings to Quinn until January 29, 1913, as documented by Rabinow and Warman 2006–2007, 286, 302, no. 244. Quinn, who later referred to Vollard as the "great procrastinator," had sent a telegram to the dealer on January 25, asking him to send the three works; see Dumas 2006–2007 (albeit, erroneously referring to them as loan requests for the Armory Show as opposed to purchases), 21, 27n130. Quinn is quoted in Groom 2006–2007, 99n69.

5 See Nathanson 1985: 6–8.

6 Dreier 1913, xiv.

7 Ibid.

8 Hale 1913: 455.

9 Pattison 1913: 295.

10 Stephan Bourgeois, letter to Walter Pach, June 19, 1913, quoted in Brown 1963, 190.

11 MacColl 1913: 24.

12 [Cortissoz] 1913b: 6.

13 However, the correlation between titles and loans remains a bit of a muddle when it comes to the three landscapes with trees. The most convincing assignments were published by Heijbroek and Wouthuysen 1993, 192–94, 197–200, who have identified "L'Olivier"/"The Olive Tree" (no. 428) as F711; "Le Grand Olivier"/"The Big Olive Tree" (no. 430) as F708; and "Paysage d'Arles"/"Landscape, Arles" (no. 434) as F818. W. Feilchenfeldt 2013, 231, 236, 257, provides identifications that contradict the relevant documentation he furnishes from loan lists (which, in fact, support the assignments above). The recent exhibition catalogue New York 2013–14 relies on Feilchenfeldt's identifications.

14 See Heijbroek and Wouthuysen 1993, 194; W. Feilchenfeldt 1988, 350.

15 *Evening Post* 1913: 9. The presence of the picture at the Sonderbund in Cologne is still debated; see Cologne 2012, 553, as possibly exhibited hors catalogue. While the painting has not yet been identified as being shown in London at the Grafton Galleries in 1910–11, this may be confirmed by the spot-on descriptions of reviewers cited in Robins 2010: 789, for example: "C. J. Holmes described 'a dusty road among allotment gardens' while the *Graphic* pointed out the 'wide road going up to the mill.'" In addition, Robins notes that a picture called "groote Montmartre" was included on the first list of loans and "Montmartre 1200" (the highest-valued work) was included on the second list. Apparently it was shown either hors catalogue or mistitled "View of Arles" (no. 64) in the catalogue.

16 See Van Gogh Letters 2009, no. 568, http://vangoghletters.org/vg/letters/let568/letter.html.

17 See note 47.

18 As Laurette E. McCarthy persuasively traced through these illustrations and citations in McCarthy 2013. It was not strictly speaking, however, a "new discovery." Brown 1988, 237, no. 434, identified the painting, albeit in a confused entry that provides the De la Faille number (F708) for the Metropolitan Museum's *Olive Trees*.

19 A reviewer of the New York Modern Gallery 1915 exhibition wrote: "A large work, 'Hollandaise,' shows a woman of the low country of Northern Europe; its style, though more decorative as to back ground, is similar to his work seen at the Lexington avenue, Manhattan, Armory exhibition some years ago." See *Brooklyn Daily Eagle* 1915a: 18. The unidentified painting is listed as no. VII, "Hollandaise," in the catalogue checklist published in De Zayas 1996, 135. Here, it was shown with a version of *La Berceuse* (F505)—or precisely the example of "human portraiture" that a critic felt would give a true indication of what Van Gogh was "capable of." See note 11. This early call-out of the motif and the dealer's canny response give pause for reflection, especially as three of the five versions of the painting are in American museums today (see, for example, F508; plate 22). The painting is described and illustrated in a review of the Armory Show in *Current Opinion* 1913; see also Borgmeyer 1913: 471. I am grateful to Jill Shaw for bringing these articles to my attention.

20 See note 1.

21 W. Feilchenfeldt 2013, 29.

22 On this subject, see Walt Kuhn, letter to Vera Kuhn, October 8, 1912, https://www.aaa.si.edu/collections/items/detail/walt-kuhn-letter-to-vera-kuhn-14498.

23 Watson 1929: 147.

24 Pach 1920a: xiii.

25 Watson 1929: 148.

26 *International Studio* 1921b: III.

27 Lees 2006–2007, 328, no. 144, *The Night Café* (F463), purchased in 1933; and no. 145, *Zinnias* (F592), purchased in 1928 and returned in 1929.

28 *The Sun* 1914: 2.

29 *American Art News* 1914: 1. The exhibition New York 1914 was accompanied by a catalogue, *Exposition de tableaux anciens et modernes*. The four pictures are illustrated and described in short entries.

30 Ibid.

31 *The Sun* 1914: 2.

32 *Arts and Decoration* 1914: 240. Stephan Bourgeois, letter to Walter Pach, June 10, 1913, mentions having recently purchased this work: "Je viens encore d'acheter dernièrement un magnifique paysage de Van Gogh, un potager dans toute sa fraicheur matinale" and hopes that he has the chance to show it to Pach. Walt Kuhn, Armory Show papers, Archives of American Art, Smithsonian Institution, Washington, DC (hereafter AAA, SI); letter translated in Brown 1988, 221–22. Ten Berge et al. 2003, 215, records Bourgeois labels on the reverse of the painting.

33 This still life is part of the John G. Johnson Collection, Philadelphia Museum of Art, inv. no. 2322. Per correspondence with curator Joseph Rishel, it has long been classified as "Imitator of Van Gogh." An old label on the stretcher has the name "Bourgeois," with an address, "4 Lincoln St."

34 *M. X. artiste-peintre*, sale cat., Amsterdam, Frederick Muller, June 19, 1917, lots 36–38. Apparently they were sold from the collection of Leonardus Nardus, who is listed in the Bourgeois catalogue as the former owner.
35 San Francisco 1915, no. 4031.
36 New York 1916b. The Van Goghs are listed as nos. 44, 45, and 77–81.
37 According to information kindly provided by Roelie Zwikker, Vincent Willem van Gogh and Josina van Gogh-Wibaut stayed in New York from October 17, 1915, until early spring 1918, and again, upon their return from trips to the West Coast and Japan, from September 1919 until January 31, 1920. Jo van Gogh-Bonger was in New York from August 27, 1916, until April 23, 1919.
38 *Brooklyn Daily Eagle* 1915a: 18.
39 *American Art News* 1915: 6.
40 *Evening Post* 1915: 9.
41 The version now in the Metropolitan Museum (F505) was illustrated in the press: *The Sun* 1915: 7. On the basis of its provenance at the time, presumably the picture was sent (on consignment) by the Galerie Bernheim-Jeune.
42 *Brooklyn Daily Eagle* 1915a: 18.
43 *American Art News* 1915: 6.
44 Regarding its deattribution, see Ten Berge et al. 2003, 362–66.
45 *American Art News* 1915: 6.
46 *Evening Post* 1915: 9.
47 See *Arts and Decoration* 1916: 136; and see fig. 5. The painting, "Fleurs Lilas," was shown again in New York 1916a as no. 4.
48 *New York Times Magazine* 1915a: 17.
49 *Evening Post* 1915: 9.
50 In the same breath, Hartley notes "four Cezannes at Vollard's." For Hartley's letter to Stieglitz, see https://www.philamuseum.org/exhibitions/2009/312.html?page=2. The Van Gogh landscapes (F391 and F575) were sold from the collection of the Hungarian Marcell von Nemes in 1918, along with two other works (F286 and F815). See Molnos and Geskó 2006–2007, 152–53, 155n50–54.
51 See De Zayas 1996, 135, which publishes the catalogue checklist for the eight works shown.
52 *Evening Post* 1915: 9.
53 *New York Times Magazine* 1915b: 22.
54 *Brooklyn Daily Eagle* 1915b: 9.
55 Ibid. Hans Luijten, who is preparing a biography on Jo van Gogh-Bonger, was kindly able to confirm that Vincent Willem van Gogh and Josina van Gogh-Wibaut brought "some Van Goghs to New York and lent at least one small painting [F748] to this exhibition," noting that the loan is recorded in a letter Van Gogh-Bonger sent to the couple in February 1916 (b8697). According to email correspondence with Hans Luijten, November 8, 2018, and Roelie Zwikker, November 20, 2018, it is not possible, on the basis of existing documentation, to confirm my suspicion that works from the family collection were also lent to the New York 1916b exhibition, which included a watercolor or drawing of a butterfly (no. 81). Two of the drawings brought by the Van Goghs to New York were left with the Montross Gallery and required new frames before they were shown in the 1920 retrospective (New York 1920b). See Stein, Appendix, note 3.
56 *New York Times Magazine* 1915b: 22.
57 Field 1920a: 39.
58 *Art and Archaeology* 1920: 198.
59 *Christian Science Monitor* 1920: 12.
60 [Field] 1920b: 26.
61 *Christian Science Monitor* 1920: 12.
62 McBride 1920a, section 3, p. 8.
63 Cortissoz 1920: 7.
64 Ibid.
65 *Christian Science Monitor* 1920: 12.
66 Ibid. Apparently both self-portraits were on view at Montross (at least at the time of the opening). Henry McBride remarks: "The self-portrait lent by the American owner Mr. John Quinn, to top out the exhibition, is one of the superb things." See McBride 1920a.
67 McBride 1920b: 631.
68 Lloyd 1920: 33.
69 See Stein, Appendix for an account of these exhibitions.
70 See ibid., note 13.
71 New York 1921c included nine works by Van Gogh, nos. 28–36. It is likely that in addition to the illustrated works (F630 and F678), the four other paintings and three drawings listed in the catalogue also came from the Van Gogh family collection. While this cannot be confirmed on the basis of documentation at the Van Gogh Museum (per email correspondence with Hans Luijten, November 8, 2019, and Roelie Zwikker, November 20, 2019), the titles are suggestive. Perhaps the pen drawing "Landscape in the Provence" (no. 29) represents the work Jo van Gogh-Bonger gave to Walter Pach (F1518) as a token of friendship, formed during her stay in New York (in the suburb of Far Rockaway, where they met in the summer of 1917), and in appreciation for his onsite assistance with the Montross retrospective and the traveling exhibition organized by the dealer Jacques Goudstikker (see St. Louis and other cities 1922–23).
72 *New York Evening Telegram* 1920, quoted in Rewald 1989, 317.
73 Stieglitz 1921: 107.
74 *American Art News* 1921c: 5.
75 *Brooklyn Daily Eagle* 1921: 34; see McBride 1921, section 2, p. 5. The De Zayas Gallery (1919–21) succeeded the Modern Gallery.
76 According to the *New York Tribune* 1921: 11.
77 *Still Life: Melon, Fish, Jar*, The Art Institute of Chicago (1926.201) bears a handwritten note on the reverse that reads: "'Still Life' by Vincent van Gogh/Brought from Paris in 1920 by Walter Pach from Théodore Duret to whom it was originally given by Van Gogh. Presented to me by my wife Helen Birch Bartlett on Jan 22 1921/Frederic Clay Bartlett." The picture was recognized as a fake in De la Faille 1930, 10, no. 78 (ex coll. Duret). Several sources refer to its showing at the Montross Gallery in 1914, including *Les Arts* 1928: 147; and Watson 1929: 147. It seems quite plausible that it was also the "still life" shown in New York 1915a as no. 8, Van Gogh, *Still Life*. (There is an annotated copy of the catalogue, with pricing, in the Walter Pach papers, AAA, SI.) Just after the run of this show, Duret wrote Pach on May 22, 1915, to inquire if the Van Gogh painting he had loaned to an exhibition had been sold; on December 29, Duret asks again if Pach had been able to sell it. See https://sova.si.edu//details/AAA.pachwalt2.
78 See Watson 1926: 310 (describes it as one of his "favorites"); *Bulletin of the Art Institute of Chicago* 1925: 82; see also Watson 1929: 147.
79 Raymond Pitcairn, letter to (his brother) Theo Pitcairn, February 15, 1922, notes: "I put a bid in for the VanGogh's [*sic*] self portrait which I intended to give to you if I got it. The sad story of how I missed it will appear in the enclosed letter from Mr. Kirby of the American Art Association gallery. I shall try to obtain an extra copy of the illustrated catalogue." Unfortunately, the enclosed letter referring to the Kelekian sale held two weeks earlier (January 30–31, 1922), which included the *Self-Portrait* (F526; plate 44) that went to the Detroit Institute of Arts, is lost. The letter referenced above and other unpublished documents concerning the Pitcairn collection were generously shared with me by Gregory A. Jackson, archivist for the Glencairn Museum, Bryn Athyn, Pennsylvania.
80 Stolwijk and Veenenbos 2002, 29–30.
81 *International Studio* 1921b: III.
82 Watson 1929: 147.
83 Ibid.
84 Mechlin 1929: 4, remarks that it was so crowded on a Saturday afternoon that it was difficult to see the paintings.
85 *American Magazine of Art* 1929: 591.
86 Cambridge 1929: Van Gogh nos. 89–96, 124, and 125. The works mentioned were shown as nos. 91–93, 95, and 125. Regarding the midsummer Boston show, see *American Magazine of Art* 1929: 591.
87 Jewell 1929c: X14.
88 Cortissoz 1929: 10.
89 The others are *Cypresses* (F613; see Chudzicka, fig. 4), *The First Steps, after Millet* (F668), *The Zouave* (F1482; plate 20), and *Hospital Corridor at the Asylum* (F1529), which were shown as nos. 85, 88, 96, and 97, respectively. *L'Arlésienne* (F488; plate 29) was no. 73.
90 See note 1.
91 *Art Digest* 1936: 9.

Appendix: Montross Correspondence, 1920–23

Two dozen letters between Newman E. Montross, Jo van Gogh-Bonger, and Vincent Willem van Gogh, preserved in the Van Gogh Museum in Amsterdam, offer an intimate glimpse of the backstory behind the group of sixty-seven works lent to the Montross Gallery for the artist's first major exhibition in the United States.[1]

The pictures had been "ready to go" in early February 1920, but a longshoremen's strike delayed their arrival until August 8.[2] Even before the show opened in October—"the earliest date for any particular interest in Art"—Montross registered concern about pricing and inquired about the possibility of reductions, for example, a "concession in price" for museums.[3] It would be a frequent topic. "Our collectors are unanimous in feeling the prices are too high. They do not realize the value of the work," Montross advised at the initial sign of a potential buyer in November.[4] But even with a "first sale" discount from $10,000 to $8,000[5] on the *Portrait of Joseph Roulin* (F436) that was of interest, it remained unsold. The high valuation also made the insurance expense "prohibitive" for prospective borrowers, notably, "the leading Art museum of Chicago," which otherwise would have liked "to have the collection for exhibition."[6] "It will be a great sorrow to me if none of them are kept for this country," Montross confided, repeating the same sentiments six weeks later: "I love the pictures more than ever as I have further acquaintance with them and earnestly wish that many of them might remain in the country."[7]

While the Montross exhibition was a "great success in public interest,"[8] enjoyed the longest run of any show held at the gallery, and the dealer continued to court would-be customers—devoting a gallery to featuring a selection in January 1921—"the results have been very disappointing," the "few who were advanced enough to want them" balked at the prices and made unacceptable low-ball offers. Montross was keen to try for another year to "do all I can to make them better known."[9] Jo van Gogh-Bonger conceded, "Once they are in America, we shall be glad to have them become better known and of course that must take some time."[10] They agreed to reduce the prices by 20 percent in the hope of "perhaps more chance of sale,"[11] and by late May, the dealer was "glad to report some business" as a result: namely, the sale of three works to the Reverend Theodore Pitcairn of Pennsylvania (who failed to pay the balance of $14,800 until October).[12]

There was added reason for optimism in the spring of 1921. Montross had arranged for the loans of four paintings and three drawings to the Metropolitan Museum of Art.[13] "Judging from the catalogue," which curator Bryson Burroughs had prepared to accompany the *Impressionist and Post-Impressionist Paintings* show, Jo van Gogh-Bonger sensed it was a "wonderful exhibition. Van Gogh has become so much better known in America this last year." She was hopeful that this might bode well for future sales.[14] Montross chimed in: the show had "created a great deal of interest and we are likely to have some benefits from it this coming season."[15] Still, faced with the "great drawback" of the insurance cost, he had not been able to organize "exhibitions for other cities as yet," as he lamented in October.[16] This changed by year's end: he succeeded in sending a half-dozen paintings, including the *Portrait of Joseph Roulin* (F436) and *Snow-Covered Field with a Harrow (after Millet)* (F632; see Shaw, Heartland, fig. 1) to a "very impressive" group show held at the Arts Club of Chicago, assembled by the critic Forbes Watson, which ran from November 21 to December 12, 1921.[17] In the interim, Montross had taken matters into his own hands: "I am devoting one of my principal Galleries to the display of pictures and hope to steadily increase the knowledge and interest in the work."[18]

At the start of 1922, Montross confessed he had "nothing of importance to report in regard to [the] pictures" but he was planning to show "a number of vanGogh [*sic*]" in an upcoming "special exhibition" (New York 1922).[19] Held in April, it featured "an exquisite little picture" of Montmartre (F346) and an "ugly" flower sketch, according to one critic.[20] While business conditions were unfavorable to selling, Montross felt "the interest in modern things is gradually increasing and will surely bring results." He imagined that the January sale of "the very important Kelekian collection"—which included two Van Goghs, *Women Picking Olives* (F655; see Shaw, Heartland, fig. 3) and the *Self-Portrait* (F526; plate 44) bought by the Detroit Institute of Arts—might "greatly stimulate buying."[21] Sensing prospects on the horizon, Jo van Gogh-Bonger agreed to "leave the pictures in [his] care for another year," through May 1923, and was willing to make a "small reduction of prices" to "effectuate a sale."[22]

Over the course of the year, no sales were consummated, but the pictures left with Montross became more widely known. By the time May came around, Montross admitted: "I cannot report any business done this Winter, although I have made another special showing of them for three weeks which brought them to the knowledge of a good many people who had not seen them before."[23] It would be their last hurrah. On view from March 27 to April 14, 1923, the exhibition, as critics noted, was essentially a reprisal of the original 1920 retrospective, albeit somewhat smaller in scale (minus, for example, the three works sold to Pitcairn).[24]

Montross knew of no "prospects for purchasers" but felt "it is always possible that some may appear" and was even hopeful that the English-language edition of Julius Meier-Graefe's influential book, *Vincent van Gogh: A Biographical Study*, "may have some good result."[25] Montross was willing to renew the loan, but as "it is three years since van Gogh's pictures are in NewYork [*sic*]," Jo van Gogh-Bonger asked for their return, unless he thought it worth keeping four (or six, penciled in) of his choice for another year or so.[26] In the end, only the "Mill on Montmartre" (F346?) stayed behind, but it was apparently returned, as requested, when it failed to sell by the following February.[27] "After a few years we might try again to show Vincent's works to the American public," she wrote to Montross on May 28, 1923.[28] A week later the loans were "all packed and ready to go," and set sail on the S.S. *Veendam* on June 9.[29]

NOTES

1 Monique Hageman of the Van Gogh Museum, Amsterdam, kindly brought this correspondence to my attention. Letters are located in the Van Gogh Museum Documentation, Amsterdam (hereafter VGMD).

2 Vincent Willem van Gogh, letter to Newman E. Montross, May 29, 1920 (b6249); and Newman E. Montross, telegram to Vincent Willem van Gogh, August 8, 1920 (b6253), reporting "pictures safely received," VGMD.

3 Newman E. Montross, letter to Vincent Willem van Gogh, September 10, 1920 (b6255), VGMD. Apparently the shipment included thirty-three of the thirty-five works on paper. In the same letter, Montross notes that the "two drawings that were here I have had to have simply framed." A likely candidate for one of these works is *The Sower* (F1441; see Stein, New York, fig. 6), formerly shown at the Modern Gallery in 1915 (New York 1915b), which appears in the Montross catalogue as no. 34 of the "Water Colors [*sic*], Drawings, and Lithographs" on view in Gallery One. The last drawing listed (no. 35) is *Landscape with Cottages and a Mill* (F1345).

4 Newman E. Montross, letter to Jo van Gogh-Bonger, December 7, 1920 (b6259), VGMD.

5 Vincent Willem van Gogh, telegram to Newman E. Montross, November 2, 1920 (b6258), VGMD.

6 Montross to Van Gogh-Bonger, December 7, 1920 (b6259).

7 Newman E. Montross, letter to Jo van Gogh-Bonger, January 25, 1921 (b6261), VGMD.

8 Montross to Van Gogh-Bonger, December 7, 1920 (b6259).

9 Montross to Van Gogh-Bonger, January 25, 1921 (b6261).

10 Jo van Gogh-Bonger, letter to Newman E. Montross, February 17, 1921 (b6262), VGMD.

11 Jo van Gogh-Bonger, letter to Newman E. Montross, March 23, 1921 (b6263), VGMD.

12 Newman E. Montross, letter to Jo van Gogh-Bonger, May 27, 1921 (b4085); and October 7, 1921 (b4087), VGMD, noting that he "has finally received the money in payment for the sale...amounting to $14,800."

13 Montross to Van Gogh-Bonger, May 27, 1921 (b4085). The Metropolitan Museum mounted a complementary show of works on paper, *French Prints and Drawings of the Last Hundred Years*, at the time of the New York 1921d exhibition; it ran from May 17 to September 15, 1921. The three drawings are recorded in a "List of Exhibitions" ledger in the museum's Department of Drawings and Prints. They may be identified as: *Winter Garden* (F1128); *Rocks and Trees, Montmajour* (F1447); and *Cottages, Saintes-Maries-de-la Mer* (F1437) as noted in Stein 2005, 37. However, the third work Montross named was the *Hospital Corridor at the Asylum* (F1529). Apparently this substitute was made after the list was prepared. Writing on May 27, 1921, ten days after the show had already opened, Montross noted: "I have loaned them the Winter-Garden, Le Rocher, and Hospital at Arles."

14 Jo van Gogh-Bonger, letter to Newman E. Montross, June 20, 1921 (b4084), VGMD.

15 Newman E. Montross, letter to Jo van Gogh-Bonger, September 19, 1921 (b4086), VGMD.

16 Montross to Van Gogh-Bonger, October 7, 1921 (b4087).

17 Newman E. Montross, letter to Jo van Gogh-Bonger, January 28, 1922 (b6266), VGMD, reporting: "The only showing that I was able to arrange for them was in Chicago where five of them were in a very impressive group of works by modern artists but no sales were made." This letter was written six weeks after the close date of the exhibition (Chicago 1921), which, in fact, included a half-dozen Van Gogh loans. See Shaw, Heartland, p. 136.

18 Montross to Van Gogh-Bonger, October 7, 1921 (b4087).

19 Montross to Van Gogh-Bonger, January 28, 1922 (b6266).

20 *Brooklyn Daily Eagle* 1922: 40.

21 Montross to Van Gogh-Bonger, January 28, 1922 (b6266).

22 Jo van Gogh-Bonger, letter to Newman E. Montross, February 22, 1922 (b6267), VGMD.

23 Newman E. Montross, letter to Jo van Gogh-Bonger, May 11, 1923 (b6269), VGMD.

24 In sizing up the exhibition, reviewers variously described it as a smaller version of the 1920 retrospective (New York 1920b) and attributed the "many" or "few" missing works to presumed sales in the interim. For a relatively detailed account of the pictures shown, see *Art News* 1923b: 2; see also *New York Times* 1923b: X7; and *Brooklyn Daily Eagle* 1923: 24. The 1923 Montross show overlapped in date with a traveling exhibition of Dutch and Flemish art that toured the Midwest before making its final stop at the Anderson Galleries in New York (see St. Louis and other cities 1922–23). It was organized by Jacques Goudstikker, "one of the most important art-dealers in Holland," as Jo van Gogh-Bonger would refer to him, when she asked Montross to support the project with loans (October 25, 1922, b6268). Ultimately, however, the Goudstikker selection, which included five Van Goghs, did not draw upon the Montross Gallery's holdings. See Shaw, Heartland, p. 148.

25 Montross to Van Gogh-Bonger, May 11, 1923 (b6269). See Meier-Graefe 1922.

26 Jo van Gogh-Bonger, letter to Newman E. Montross, May 11, 1923 (b6270), VGMD. Their letters of the same date must have crossed in the mail. See note 25.

27 Vincent Willem van Gogh, letter to Newman E. Montross, August 30, 1923 (b6275), VGMD.

28 Jo van Gogh-Bonger, letter to Newman E. Montross, May 28, 1923 (b6271), VGMD.

29 Newman E. Montross, letter to Jo van Gogh-Bonger, June 6, 1923 (b6272), VGMD.

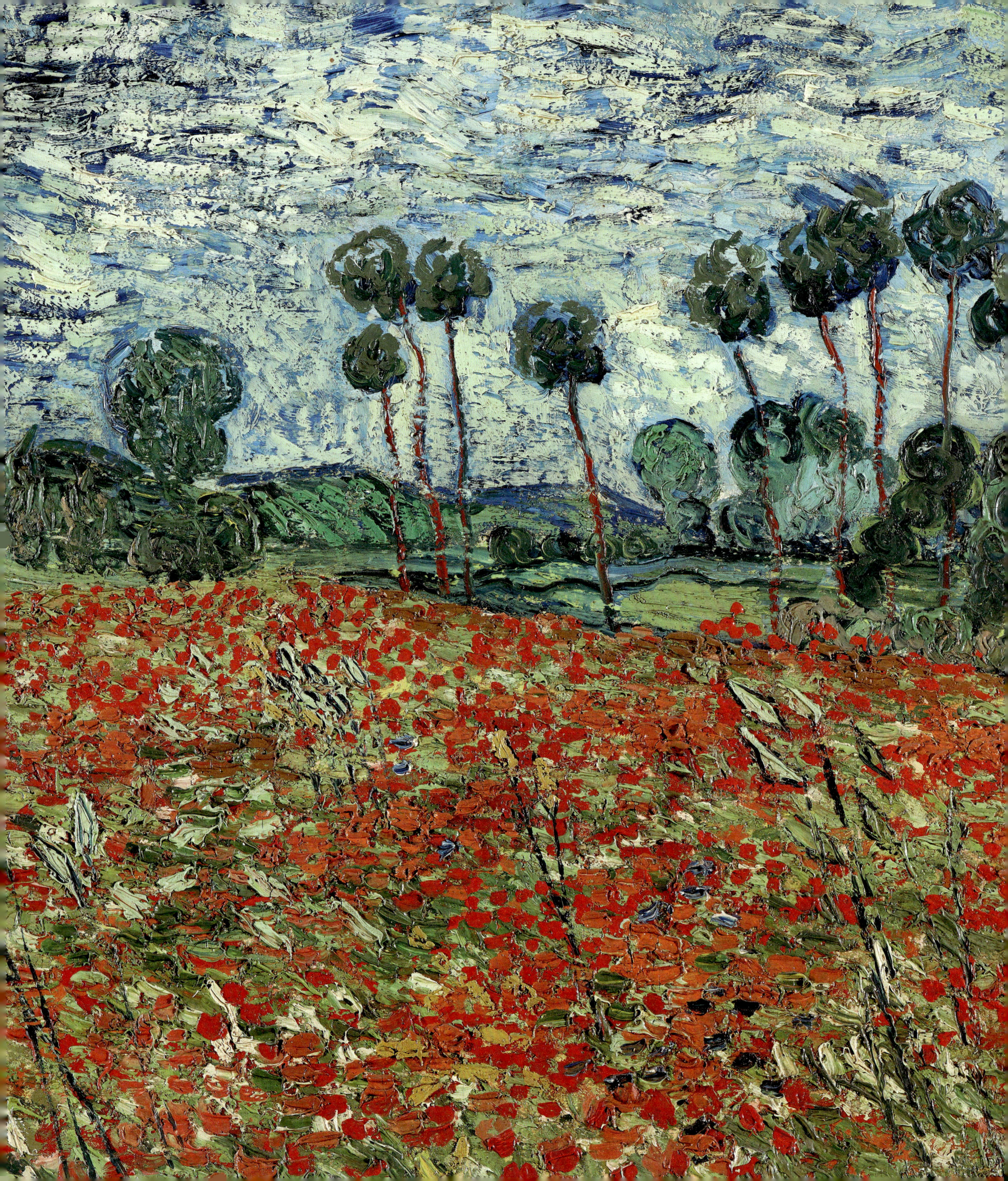

JOOST VAN DER HOEVEN AND ROELIE ZWIKKER

The Dutch Connection: The Role of Vincent Willem van Gogh and Helene Kröller-Müller in the Presentation of Van Gogh in America

On October 21, 1949, an impressive Van Gogh exhibition opened at the Metropolitan Museum of Art in New York. The lion's share of the paintings and drawings had come from the two important Van Gogh collections in the Netherlands: that of the engineer Vincent Willem van Gogh, son of the art dealer Theo van Gogh and nephew of the artist, and the holdings of the Kröller-Müller Museum in Otterlo.[1] The artworks traveled from the Netherlands on *De Westerdam* in the care of Bram Hammacher, director of the Kröller-Müller Museum, and Vincent Willem van Gogh. After arriving in New York on October 3, the sealed crates were transferred to two trucks. Under the supervision of four armed museum guards and a police escort with sirens blaring, the trucks drove from Hoboken to the Metropolitan Museum on the Upper East Side.[2]

Van Gogh's fame reached unprecedented heights in the United States in the first half of the twentieth century. In the light of history, the traveling retrospective exhibition mounted by New York's Museum of Modern Art in 1935–36 marked the turning point at which the artist was embraced by the general public. By 1949 success was assured. Dutch efforts to build up Van Gogh's reputation in America, a story in which the two collections mentioned above played a key role, were fundamental to this promotional enterprise.

The collection of Vincent Willem van Gogh, the artist's namesake, comprised the estates of the artist and his brother, Theo van Gogh, who died shortly after Vincent. Theo's widow, Jo van Gogh-Bonger, and her young son, Vincent Willem, inherited all the paintings, drawings, prints, and letters. Van Gogh-Bonger carried

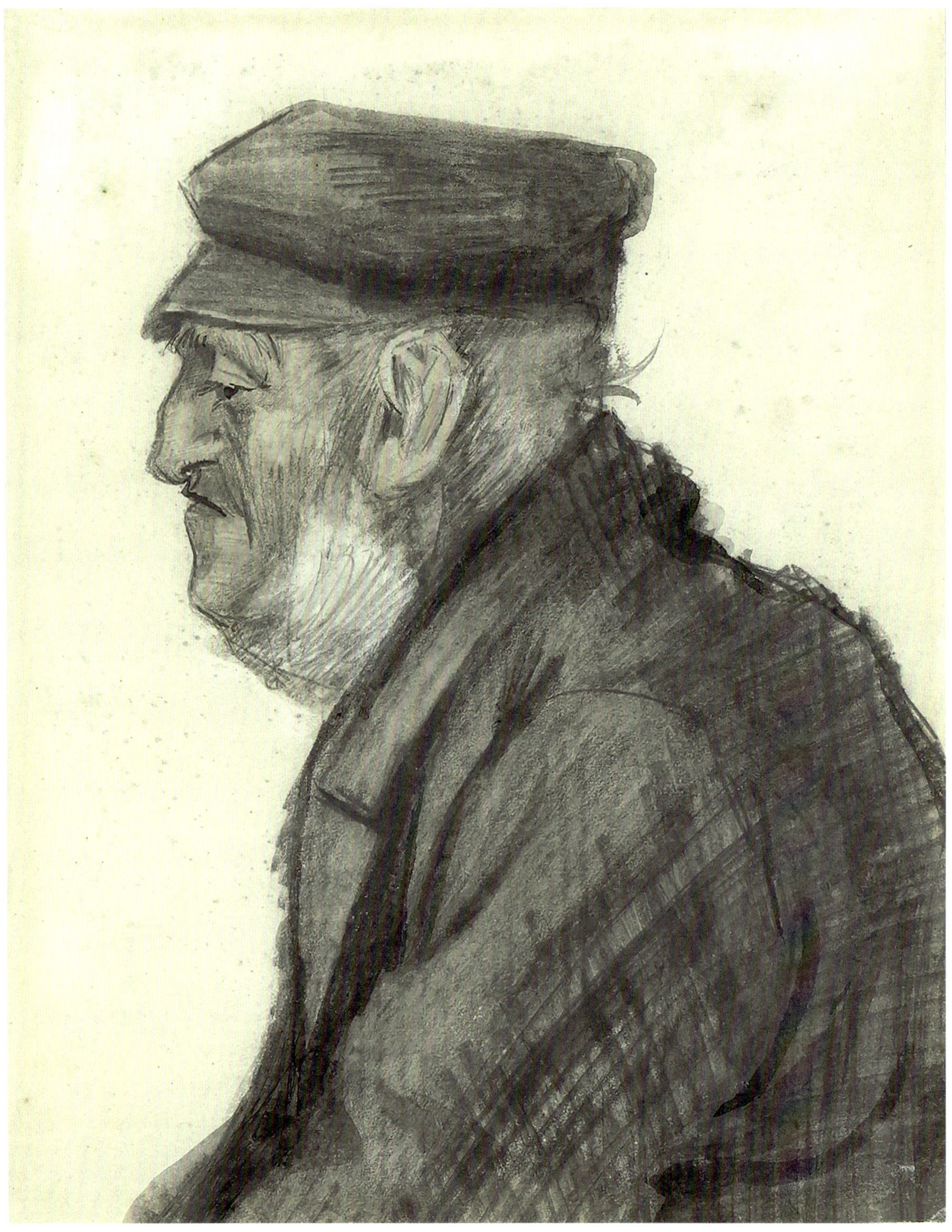

PLATE 30. *Orphan Man*, 1882–83 (CAT. 5)

on her late husband's mission and set herself the goal of making Van Gogh's art widely known and appreciated. She sold some of the work, organized exhibitions, and published *Vincent van Gogh: Brieven aan zijn broeder* (*Letters to His Brother*) in 1914. Young Vincent Willem grew up surrounded by his uncle's artworks. From his teenage years he was involved in activities relating to the collection; later on, he was consulted on important decisions. He pursued a career in engineering, and together with a former fellow student, started the first management consultancy in the Netherlands—a pioneering enterprise in a field that had come to Europe from America. After the death of his mother in 1925, responsibility for the estate rested entirely on his shoulders. He was a frequent lender to exhibitions, but largely stopped selling artworks.[3] Although always involved with the collection, he did not explicitly present himself as its keeper until after World War II. In 1960 he set up the Vincent van Gogh Foundation. Two years later he sold the estate—which included, among other things, 203 paintings and 497 drawings by Van Gogh—to the Van Gogh Foundation. The Dutch government financed the purchase and the city of Amsterdam made available a tract of land on the large grassy square known as Museumplein, where the Van Gogh Museum opened its doors in June 1973.[4]

The Kröller-Müller collection, formed between 1908 and 1928 by German-born Helene Kröller-Müller, ultimately comprised 88 paintings and more than 180 works on paper. It is the second-largest Van Gogh collection in the world, and together with the Van Gogh family estate, accounts for nearly one-third of the artist's total oeuvre. There was, however, no contact between Kröller-Müller and the Van Gogh family. Both their backgrounds and their relation to Van Gogh's artworks differed greatly. Jo van Gogh-Bonger and her son were socialists, and as heirs to the Van Gogh estate, they had a personal affinity with the artworks. Kröller-Müller, on the other hand, could afford to surround herself with Van Goghs by making purchases, all of which were mediated by art dealers or other go-betweens. According to the art critic Gustave Coquiot, Kröller-Müller once tried—without success, despite offering an unlimited sum—to purchase the entire collection from Van Gogh-Bonger.[5]

Helene Kröller-Müller could collect art on a large scale. Her Dutch husband, Anton Kröller, as director of her family's shipping company, Müller & Co., amassed a large fortune in the early decades of the twentieth century. She used the money to pursue her ambitious goal of forming a collection that would provide an overview of the development of modern art.[6] She acquired not only Van Goghs, but also a wide range of primarily French and Dutch works. In realizing her objective, Kröller-Müller was assisted by her personal advisor, H. P. Bremmer—also a collector of Van Gogh's art (see, for example, F1018; plate 30)—from 1905.[7]

In Bremmer's view, no individual in modern art was more important than Van Gogh, and Kröller-Müller followed her teacher's example in considering him "the absolute."[8] Together with Bremmer, and often accompanied by her husband as well, Kröller-Müller visited many art auctions in the Netherlands and abroad. She caused a stir, both by purchasing so many Van Goghs and by paying such large sums for them.[9] It was her wish ultimately to house the collection in a museum whose focal point would be Van Gogh. That wish was fulfilled in 1938 with the construction of a small museum in the Veluwe region near the village of Otterlo in the province of Gelderland. Kröller-Müller became the first director, a position she held until her death the following year. In 1948, after several directors had followed one another in rapid succession, Bram Hammacher took up the reins.

The First Exhibitions in the United States

America's overwhelming reception of Van Gogh's works in 1949 was in stark contrast to the circumstances in 1915, the year of the very first solo exhibition of the artist's work in the United States. In October of that year, twenty-five-year-old Vincent Willem van Gogh and his wife Josina van Gogh-Wibaut moved to New York. They left Europe because of the war and Vincent Willem planned to work as an engineer in New York. At the beginning of November, they moved into a room on Madison Avenue and 121st Street, opposite Mount Morris Park.[10] They decorated it with several Van Gogh works, including the small painting *Butterflies and Poppies* (F748; fig. 1).[11] The decision to take several drawings and paintings with them to America was no doubt connected with the mission that Jo van Gogh-Bonger had embarked on when her son was still a toddler: to ensure that Van Gogh's work became widely known and appreciated. This was already the case in Europe, but art lovers on the other side of the Atlantic still had to be won over.

The life and work of Van Gogh had already been introduced to the American public. A selection of Van Gogh's letters had appeared in an English translation in the United States in 1913.[12] In addition, Elisabeth du Quesne-Van Gogh, a sister of the artist, had published her personal recollections of her brother in 1910; the English version of her book was published in 1913. In contrast to the original Dutch edition, which contained only one illustration, this English version featured twenty-four reproductions (including F163, plate 31; F508, plate 22; and F82, see Stolwijk and Krikke, fig. 1; for a lithograph of the last subject, see F1661, plate 32) and its cover was graced with one version of *Sunflowers* (F457).[13] The artist and collector Katherine S. Dreier wrote the introduction and translated the text. Arthur B. Davies—like Dreier, a passionate promoter of modern art in America—wrote the foreword. Both had also been involved in the legendary *International Exhibition of Modern Art*, known as the Armory Show, held in New York, Chicago, and Boston in 1913, in which Van Gogh's work was well represented.[14]

Having his sister's recollections published in English that same year was certainly good timing. Even though the book promises to provide an extensive firsthand account of Du Quesne-Van Gogh's recollections of her brother, it mainly reads as a biography in which only Van Gogh's teenage years could have been based on actual memories. In his later life, the two were hardly in touch.[15] Nevertheless, the book sparked an interest in Van Gogh's life story, as the childhood recollections are studded with lyrical references to the artist's supposed budding genius, which Du Quesne-Van Gogh makes us believe already surfaced frequently during his youth.

FIG. 1 *Butterflies and Poppies* (F748), 1889. Oil on canvas, 13¾ × 10$\frac{1}{16}$ in. (35 × 25.5 cm). Van Gogh Museum, Amsterdam (Vincent van Gogh Foundation).

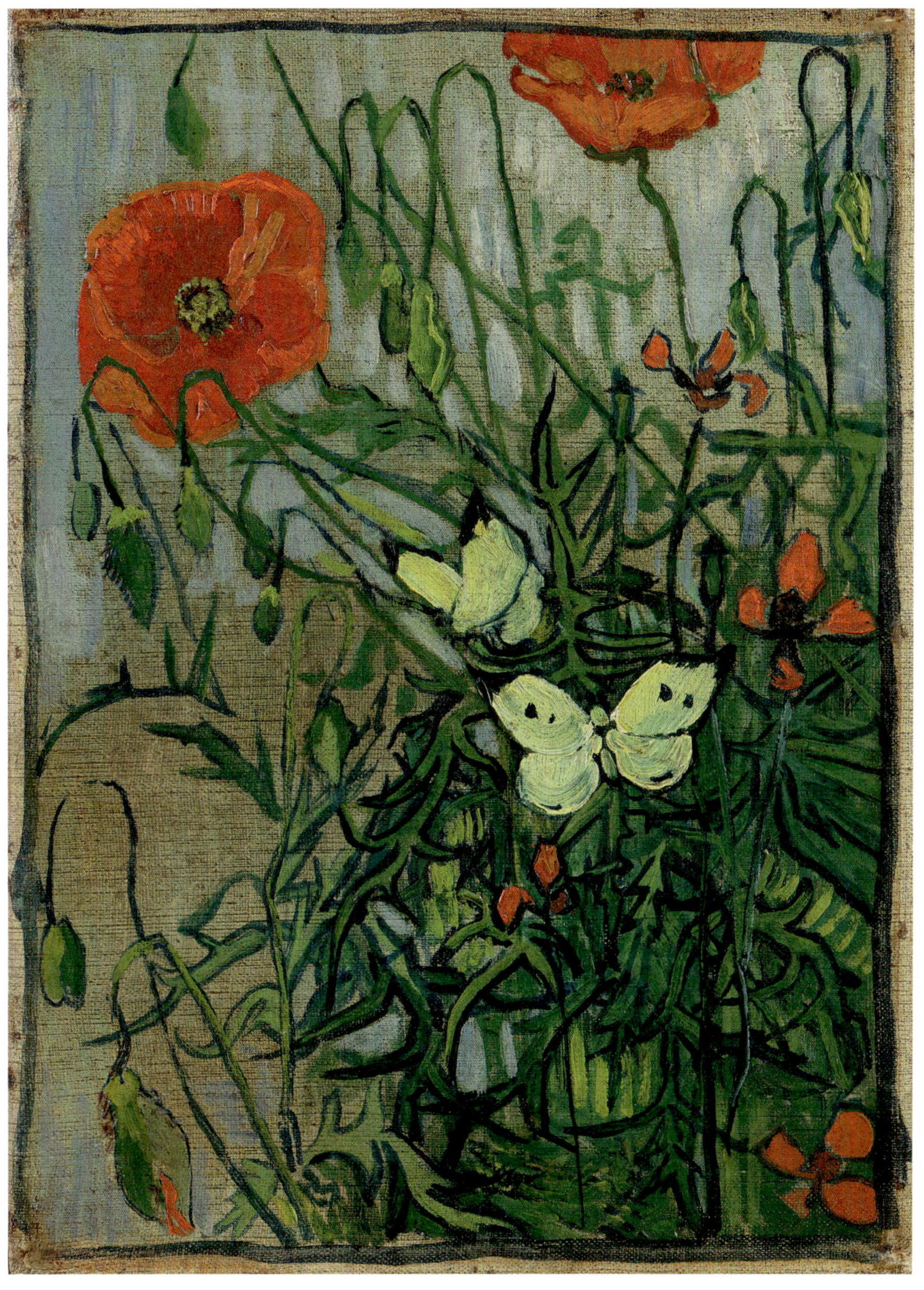

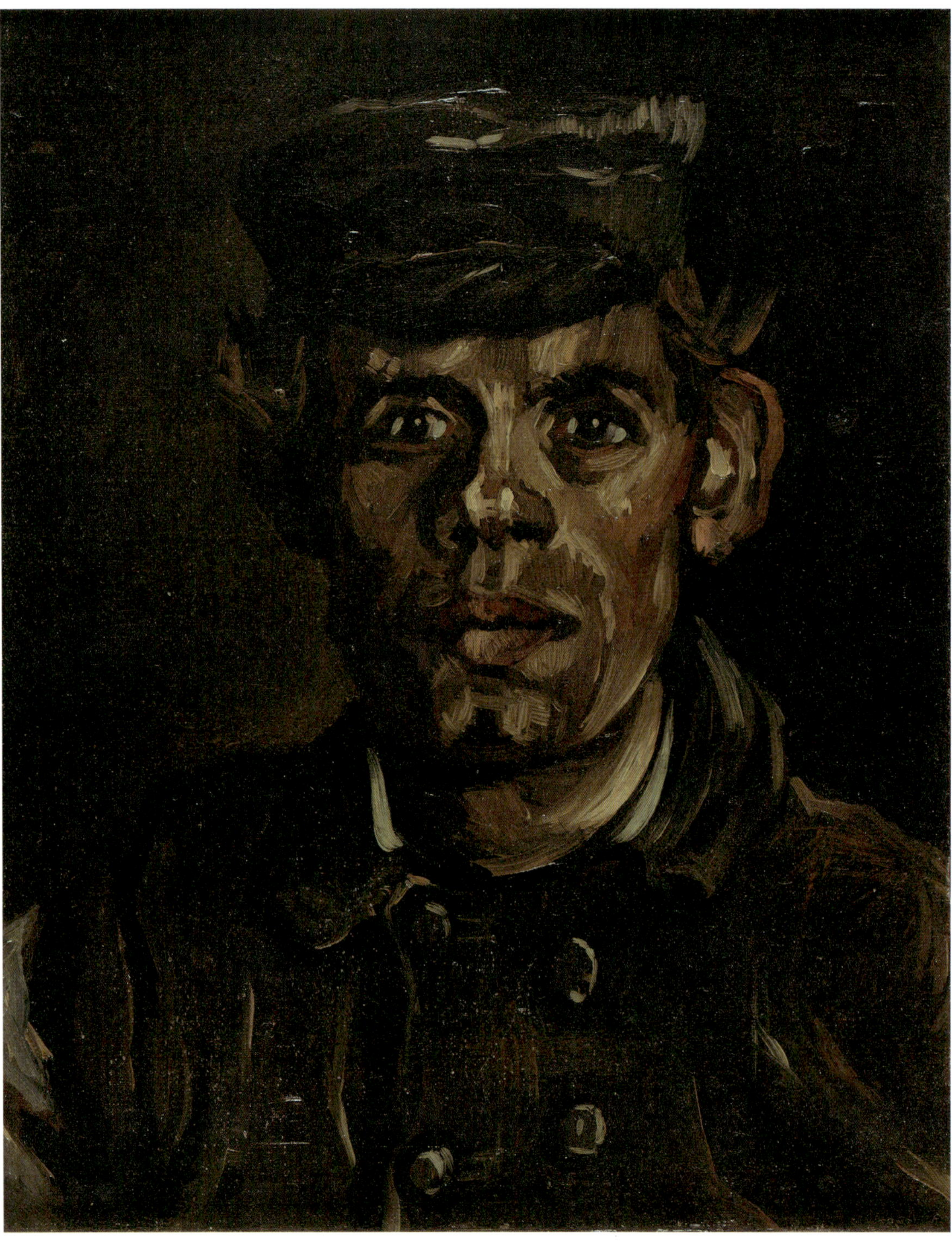

PLATE 31. *Head of a Peasant*, 1885 (CAT. 9)

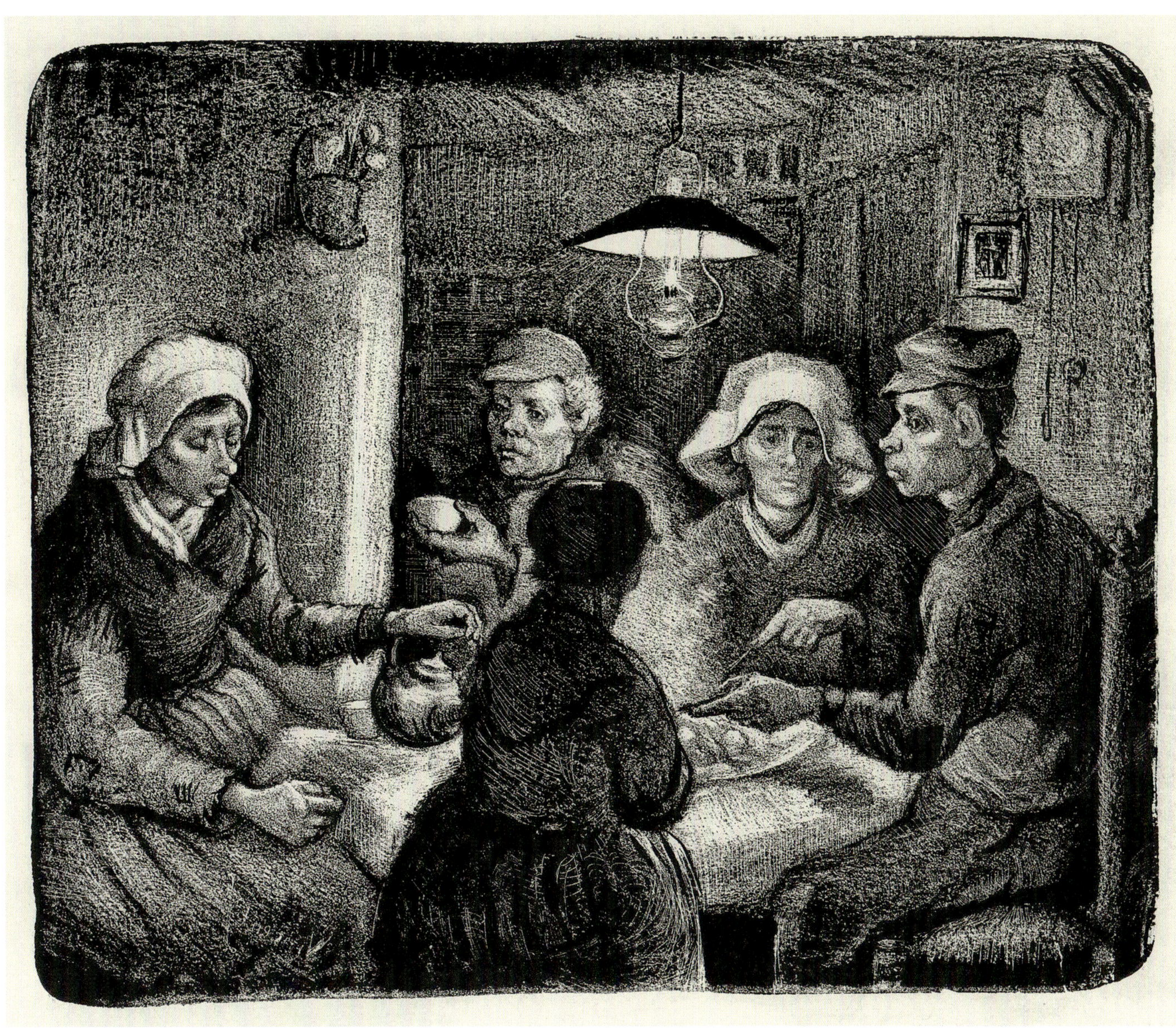

PLATE 32. *The Potato Eaters*, 1885 (CAT. 10)

Even though American tastes remained conservative, the Armory Show did generate a growing interest in avant-garde art. The "291" gallery, an initiative of Alfred Stieglitz, preceded even the Armory Show with exhibitions on Matisse, Toulouse-Lautrec, and Picasso in 1909, 1910, and 1911, respectively. But after the Armory Show, more modern art galleries emerged on the scene. In 1914, for example, the Bourgeois Galleries and the Washington Square Gallery opened their doors in New York, followed in early October 1915 by the Modern Gallery on the corner of Fifth Avenue and 42nd Street. All three galleries aimed to promote and sell modern art.[16]

One morning around a month after he arrived in New York in 1915, Vincent Willem van Gogh was walking down 42nd Street when he discovered, to his great surprise, an exhibition of works by his uncle in a "little art dealership" on the second floor of a modest building. He went upstairs, spoke to the art dealer, and timidly asked whether he was interested in augmenting his collection with "the four small Van Goghs" he had with him.[17] This "little art dealership" was the Modern Gallery, and the Van Gogh exhibition was an initiative of the Mexican artist and critic Marius de Zayas, who was responsible for the day-to-day operation of the gallery.[18] De Zayas had originally planned to exhibit Gauguin as well, but had failed to secure the desired works. Through art dealers in Paris, however, he had managed to get eight paintings by Van Gogh on loan for three weeks. This chance addition of the works supplied by Vincent Willem van Gogh helped to amplify the small gallery's presentation.[19]

The added works included several drawings and the painting *Butterflies and Poppies* (F748; fig. 1). "How very fortuitous, that exhibition of Uncle Vincent's taking place just now," Jo van Gogh-Bonger reacted enthusiastically, "and good that you added that small picture to it." She encouraged her son to explore the art market. "If you can sell a drawing for the museum, I would *certainly* do it, there are so many of them!" It is not known which museum she was referring to, but she was clear about the price: her son should not ask "too little": "I should think 1,000 dollars at the least."[20]

Considering Jo van Gogh-Bonger's ambition to enhance Van Gogh's reputation, placing his work in a museum collection would have been a good strategic move, but the time was not yet ripe. Vincent Willem van Gogh felt that in 1915 the New York art world had given itself over "heart and soul" to Gauguin. Cézanne was "much less in demand" and "one scarcely looked at" Van Gogh. It is hardly surprising, then, that there was little enthusiasm for the exhibition at the Modern Gallery: "No one took any notice of it."[21]

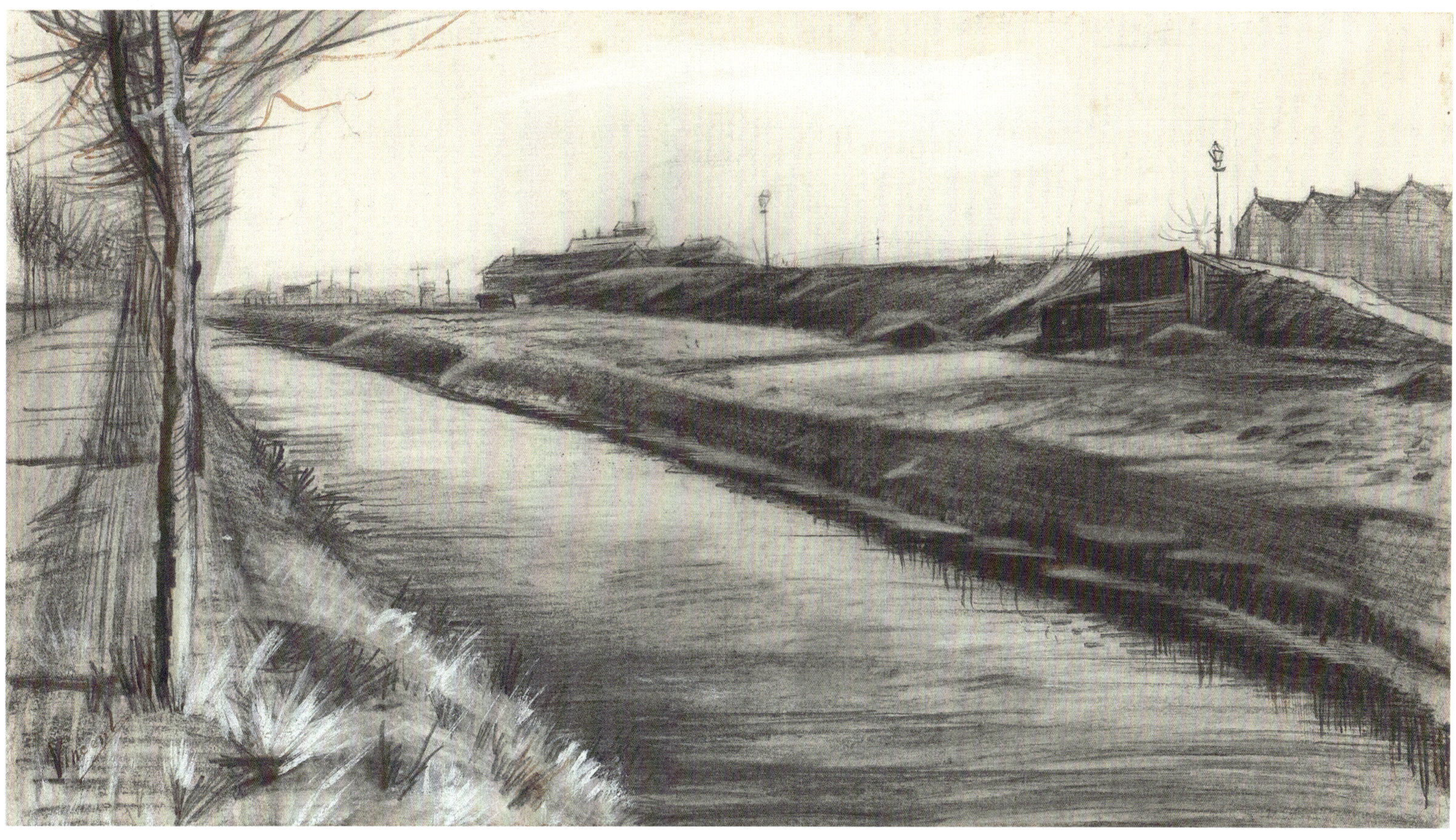

PLATE 33. *Ditch along Schenkweg*, 1882 (CAT. 1)

Even so, a request soon came for a loan to another exhibition in New York. In the spring of 1916, the Van Goghs received a visit from the American art critic and painter Walter Pach, who had been instrumental in organizing the Armory Show, and the art dealer Stephan Bourgeois of the Bourgeois Galleries. They had come to select drawings for an exhibition being put together by a group of European and American painters and sculptors.[22] As explained in the accompanying catalogue: "The pictures by Cézanne, Van Gogh and Seurat are hung with those of the living exhibitors to mark the tradition the latter regard as the greatest of the immediate past." The exhibition, which ran April 3–29 at the Bourgeois Galleries, included five drawings and two paintings by Van Gogh.[23]

Bourgeois learned from Vincent Willem van Gogh that there were many more paintings by Van Gogh in Amsterdam, and he was very keen to have works shipped over for exhibitions he planned to organize in the United States. The artist's nephew and his wife felt, however, that it would be better to wait until after the war, given the dangers it posed to shipping.[24] Meanwhile, they had received a parcel of facsimiles from Jo van Gogh-Bonger, who shared their opinion. Shipping good copies was a safer way to market Van Gogh's work and for people who could not afford real art, it was a good way to enjoy his work. Van Gogh-Bonger hoped that the Washington Square Gallery would "place a large order" for them.[25]

In August 1916, Van Gogh-Bonger followed her son and daughter-in-law to New York, and during her two years and eight months there, she made a start on the English translation of Van Gogh's letters.[26] Vincent Willem van Gogh, who from May 1918 had spent several months in San Francisco, and subsequently lived and worked in Japan through August 1919, left New York with his wife and returned to Amsterdam in January 1920.

Dutch Eyes on America

Shortly after Vincent Willem van Gogh's return to the Netherlands, his mother received a telegram from the art dealer Newman E. Montross, one of the family's contacts in the New York art world, with a proposal for organizing an exhibition.[27] They had already left two drawings with him, but now another thirty-three works on paper and thirty-two paintings were shipped to America.[28]

The exhibition, which ran from the fall into the winter of 1920, did not go unnoticed in the Netherlands. The correspondent for the *Nieuwe Rotterdamsche Courant* wrote: "The exhibition held at the Montross Galleries includes the work that Van Gogh's relatives kept in the Netherlands and saved from the violence of the whirlwind that seized the oeuvre at some point and scattered it to every corner of the world, except the corner of official America." The collection was "large enough to convince America," and a "look at the press" gave reason for optimism: "The literary supplements of the large papers are devoting columns of print to the exhibition, several of them illustrating the text with reproductions."[29] The Dutch newspaper *Het Vaderland* stated that the magazine *Current Opinion* called the Van Gogh show at the Montross Gallery "the first important exhibition" of his work in America.[30] And despite the show's lack of sales, Montross acted as an intermediary for additional exhibitions held in this period.

The Dutch press also gave enthusiastic reports in the early 1920s about other initiatives that intentionally presented Van Gogh in the context of Dutch artists. For the Dutch government and the Dutch business sector, initiating exhibitions abroad was a means of enhancing the prestige of the Netherlands. Around 1920 the Netherlands Committee for Arts, Science and Friendly Relations—a department of the Chamber of Commerce—conceived the plan to mount an exhibition of Dutch art in New York. This led to the founding of the Holland-America Society for Arts, Science and Friendly Relations, which assumed responsibility for organizing an exhibition at the Anderson Galleries.

FIG. 2 *Pietà (after Delacroix)* (F630), 1889. Oil on canvas, 28¾ × 23$^{13}/_{16}$ in. (73 × 60.5 cm). Van Gogh Museum, Amsterdam (Vincent van Gogh Foundation).

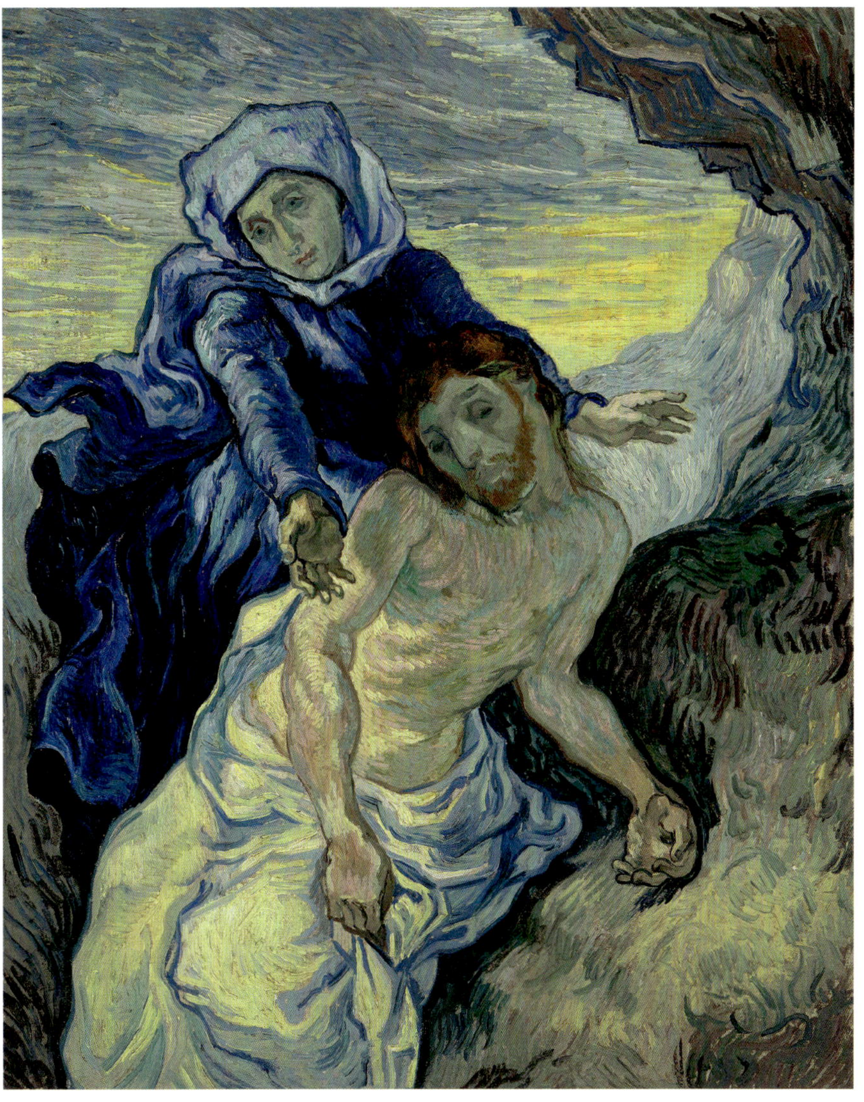

Henrik Cramer, the New York correspondent for the *Nieuwe Rotterdamse Courant*, traveled in early January 1921 to the Netherlands charged with putting together a collection of modern Dutch paintings.[31] Jo van Gogh-Bonger and Vincent Willem van Gogh were happy to contribute to such an undertaking, and lent, among other works, *Irises* (F678) and *Pietà (after Delacroix)* (F630; fig. 2).[32] "Holland takes great pains to send the masterpieces of its art abroad," Van Gogh-Bonger wrote to her friend Paul Gachet.[33] The Royal Dutch Lloyd shipping company conveyed, free of charge, the 135 selected artworks, including those from the Van Gogh family, to America on the steamship *Gaasterland* at the end of February.[34]

The newspaper *Algemeen Handelsblad* devoted a great deal of attention to the exhibition at the Anderson Galleries, which was seen as "a first attempt" to give America a comprehensive overview of Dutch painting from the period after the "widely known" Hague School. Until this time, following the show at the Montross Gallery in 1920, Van Gogh had been "the most important" Dutch artist to have a solo exhibition in the United States. "But," the New York correspondent observed, "America does, or did, not actually see Van Gogh as a Dutchman." His name was so tied to those of Cézanne and Gauguin that one had begun to forget that he was not French. Now that Van Gogh's work was displayed next to that of such artists as George Hendrik Breitner, Isaac Israëls, Jan Sluijters, and Kees van Dongen, New York could not help but accord him the place he deserved, that is to say, "at the forefront of our Dutch masters of the modern age."[35]

Both the organization and the installation of the exhibition were in Dutch hands. The "hanging committee" consisted of three journalists; Gijs Bosch-Reitz, curator of the Department of Asian Art at the Metropolitan Museum of Art; and Adriaan J. Barnouw of Columbia University in New York, who wrote the introductory essay for the catalogue and also gave several lectures on Van Gogh.[36] The *Algemeen Handelsblad* describes how the gentlemen accomplished their "difficult task": in their shirtsleeves they stood "in front of the stacks of paintings from which Van Dongen's white, Van Gogh's yellow, and Sluijters's red, green, and blue burst out with a fierceness that seemed to consume the gold dust of [Gerrit Willem] Dijsselhof's fish, the soft azure of [Jan] Voerman's skies, and the sketchy palette of Isaac Israëls. There was lugging and arranging and rearranging. The canvases were placed along the wall. But in the end they found the combination. And the three rooms of the Anderson Galleries became a crescendo of color." Upon entering the first room, viewers looked straight at the "jubilation of color" in Van Gogh's *Irises*, "in the face of whose hundredfold-greater vitality the real tulips in a vase, which had been placed somewhere to decorate the room, were reduced

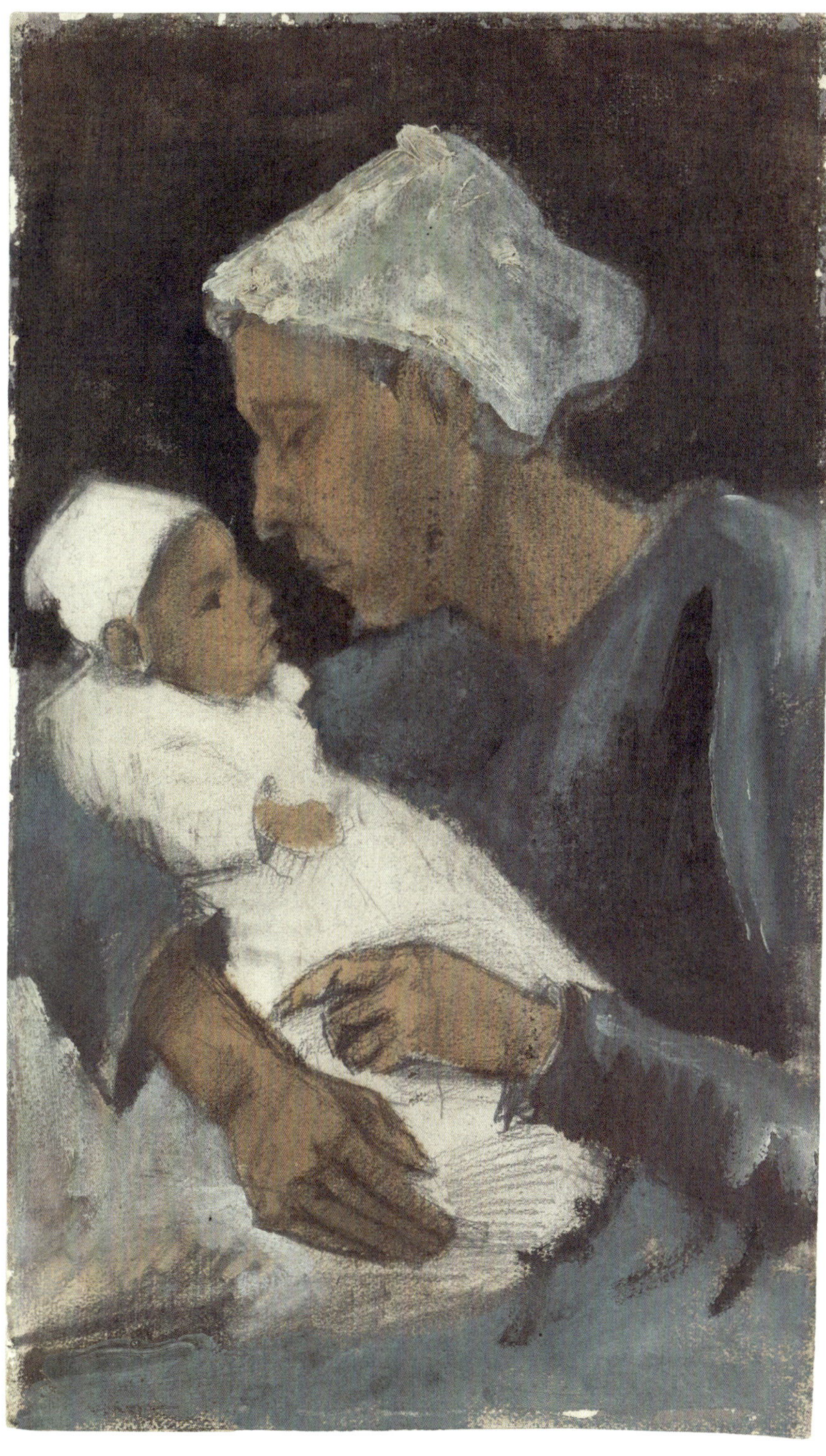

PLATE 34. *Mother with Child*, 1882 (CAT. 3)

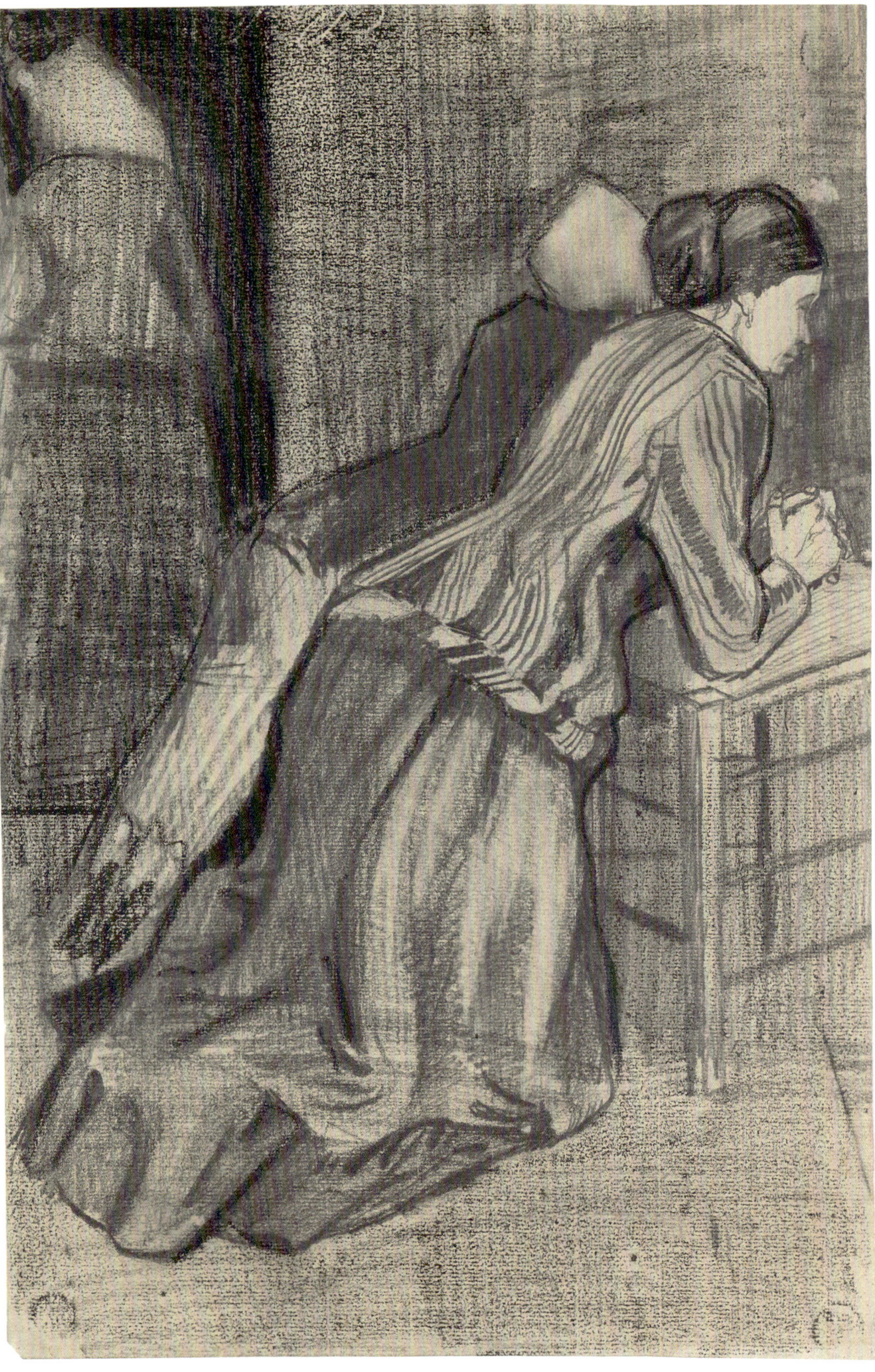

PLATE 35. *Two Women Praying*, 1882 (CAT. 4)

to absolute powerlessness." On opening day the public appeared to be "moved," "charmed," "shocked," and constantly "interested." "And that is more than can be said of many exhibitions of paintings."[37]

Two years later the Dutch press reported another "typically Dutch undertaking," namely the exhibition of the famous Goudstikker collection. This show was held under the auspices of the Netherlands-America Affiliation, the Netherlands Chamber of Commerce in New York, and the Netherland-America Foundation (NAF). After traveling to St. Louis, Cleveland, and Detroit, the collection was displayed in New York from March 10 to April 7, 1923, again at the Anderson Galleries. The exhibition included approximately two hundred paintings and provided an overview of six hundred years of Flemish and Dutch painting. Among the works on display were "five very strong Van Goghs, including a self-portrait from his last period."[38] These works were not part of the Goudstikker collection, but had been lent to Goudstikker by Jo van Gogh-Bonger.[39]

In addition to the joy occasioned by the positive reviews in all the leading American newspapers, there was pride in the large number of visitors in New York. "Collectors and museum directors from Boston, Philadelphia, Baltimore and Washington were willing to spend a day traveling in order to view the collection," according to *De Telegraaf*. The reporter also expressed his surprise at the large crowds of people, and conveyed his impression that in general Americans were mainly occupied with matters such as building houses, constructing roads, fattening up pigs, and reading accounts of baseball games: "only a small part" of the population took an interest in art. Three explanations were given by the same reporter as to why so many interested people flocked to the exhibition. For one thing, Jacques Goudstikker, by his own account, had received important institutional support from the Netherlands Chamber of Commerce. Moreover, there had been a great deal of publicity in the New York papers. But above all, the reporter concluded that the success was a result of the composition of the collection: "The many first-rate paintings increased the value of the exhibition and piqued the curiosity of the difficult, spoiled, used-to-everything American, New York public."[40]

The *Algemeen Handelsblad* also drew attention to a possible downside of the show's great popularity, namely, that it might lead to the sale of important Dutch paintings, which would then be lost to the Netherlands: "In this respect we send up a quick prayer with a very uneconomic wish for the art market."[41]

After this, all was quiet for a while with regard to loan requests from the United States. In 1927, two years after the death of Jo van Gogh-Bonger, Montross again attempted to have paintings from the family collection sent to America. But in the meantime Vincent Willem van Gogh had promised to lend a large number of works to the Rijksmuseum in Amsterdam, and he told Montross that he did not wish to sell any paintings for this reason.[42]

The Museum of Modern Art, New York (MoMA)

When the Paris art dealership of Bernheim-Jeune & Cie. informed Vincent Willem van Gogh in 1929 that a museum of modern art was to be founded in New York, his immediate reaction was positive: "I'm fully inclined to lend pictures."[43] Alfred H. Barr Jr. became the director of this new museum, where he would play an important role in making avant-garde art accessible to a broad public.[44] The museum's inaugural exhibition on Cézanne, Gauguin, Seurat, and Van Gogh that autumn included Vincent Willem van Gogh's loan of four paintings: *Pietà (after Delacroix)* (F630; fig. 2), *The Yellow House (The Street)* (F464; fig. 3), *The Langlois Bridge* (F400), and *Wheatfield under Thunderclouds* (F778).[45] Although Barr himself

FIG. 3 *The Yellow House (The Street)* (F464), 1888. Oil on canvas, 28⅜ × 36 in. (72 × 91.5 cm). Van Gogh Museum, Amsterdam (Vincent van Gogh Foundation).

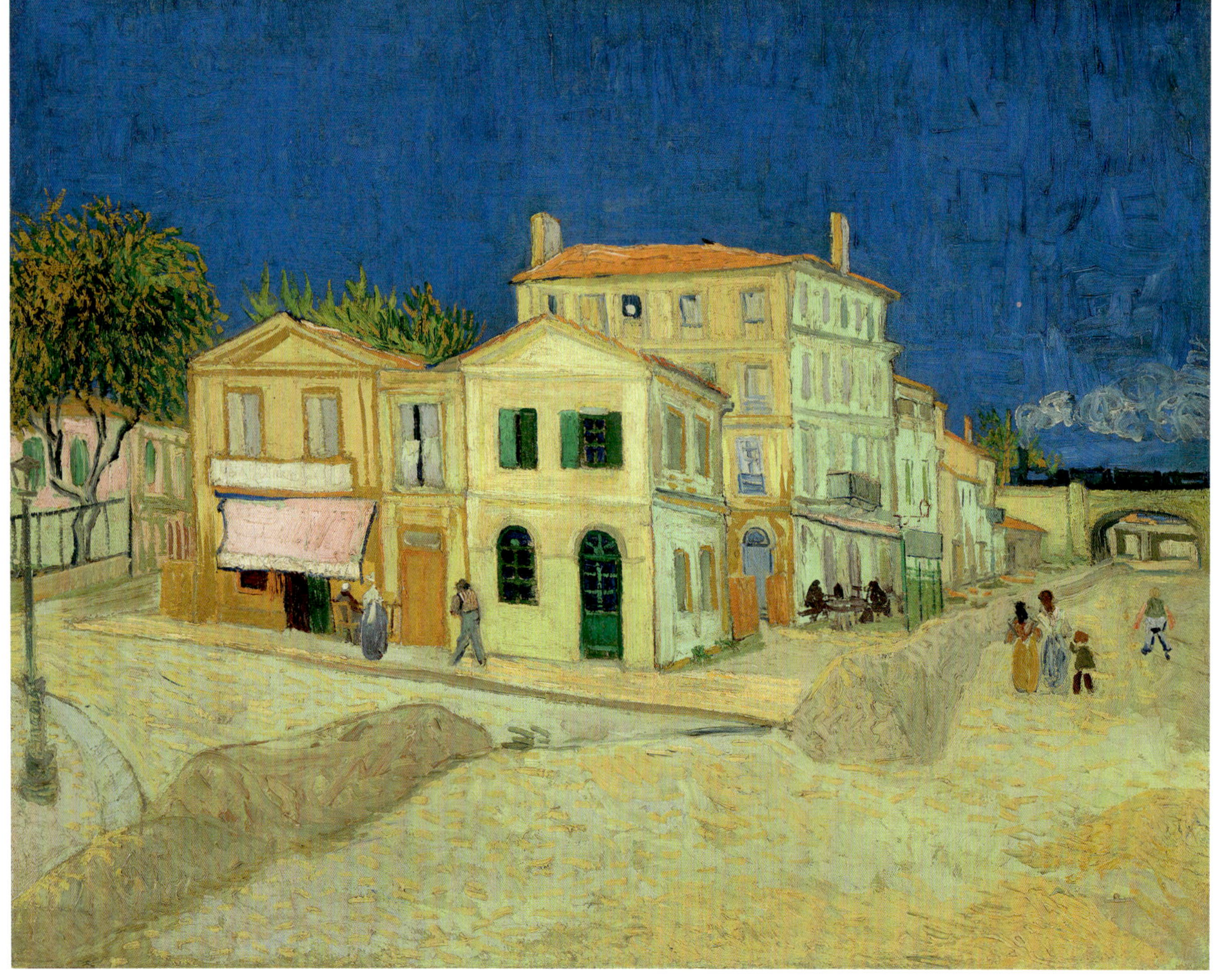

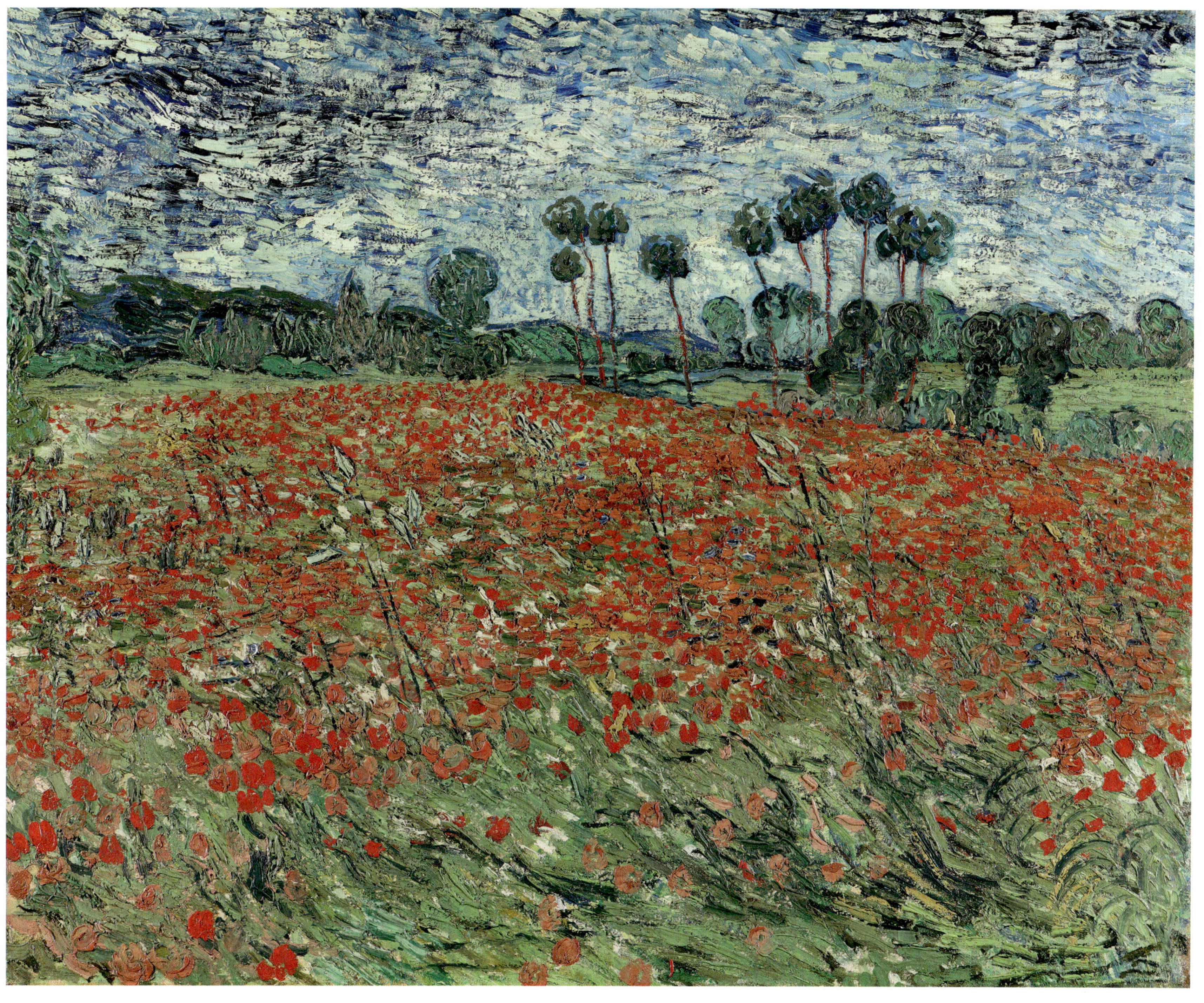

PLATE 36. *Poppy Field*, 1890 (CAT. 63)

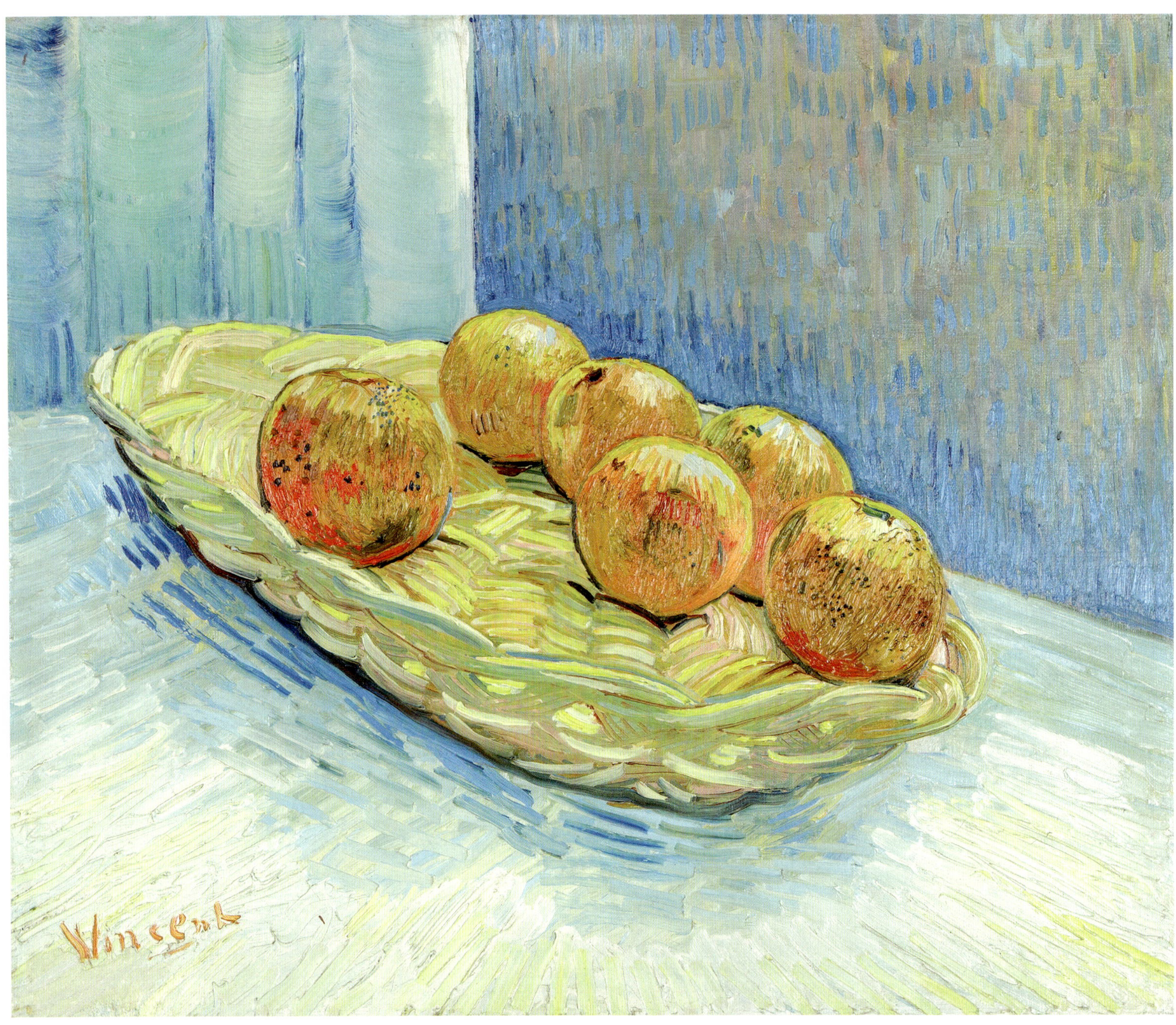

PLATE 37. *Basket with Oranges*, 1888 (CAT. 27)

preferred to open the museum with a show of paintings by nineteen contemporary American artists, it was the founding trustees, among them Abby Aldrich Rockefeller and Lillie P. Bliss, who were adamant on opening with the artists they all saw as the pioneers of modern art.[46] Within this milieu sympathetic to modern art, Van Gogh's acceptance in the canon was beyond discussion.[47]

Not long after this first exhibition, Barr, together with MoMA's president, Anson Conger Goodyear, decided to devote more attention to Van Gogh in 1935 by means of a solo exhibition. They knew that sizable loans from the two large Van Gogh collections in the Netherlands would be indispensable to such a project. If Vincent Willem van Gogh and Helene Kröller-Müller could not be persuaded to become involved, the venture would probably not succeed.[48]

Van Gogh's reputation in America had grown enormously, owing in part to the best-selling novel *Lust for Life* (1934), Irving Stone's fictionalized and romanticized story of Van Gogh's life. Barr sought to ride this wave of popularity.[49] But the pioneering work done by Montross and others in the 1920s should not be underestimated. It contributed a great deal to the appreciation of Van Gogh's work in America. Barr had been on good terms with Vincent Willem van Gogh since MoMA's opening exhibition in 1929, and he knew that a large loan from Helene Kröller-Müller was also a possibility. After all, she had already sent her collection on a "grand tour" of Switzerland, Germany, and Belgium in 1927, 1928, and 1929.[50]

At the time of this tour, filled with high expectations, on November 1, 1927, Barr visited the Kröller-Müller collection, which was then exhibited in several rooms at the headquarters of Müller & Co. in The Hague. He was hugely disappointed to learn that all the works by Van Gogh were out on loan.[51] Yet he was greatly impressed by the rest of the collection, "which astonished [him] by its courage and its variety."[52] Unfortunately, Kröller-Müller was not present, so he could not compliment her personally on the quality of her collection.[53]

A few years later, in New York, Barr met Sam van Deventer, Kröller-Müller's confidant and right-hand man, and himself the owner of several Van Goghs.[54] It is possible that they spoke about the Van Gogh exhibition MoMA hoped to mount. Barr had undoubtedly heard that Kröller-Müller's personal collection had been subsumed into the Kröller-Müller Foundation in 1928.[55] Although Van Deventer was secretary of the foundation, it was incumbent on Barr to approach Kröller-Müller herself with all due respect if he was to have any chance of success.[56] He also discovered that it would be better for him to meet with her separately from Vincent Willem van Gogh. This became clear during a large retrospective exhibition of Van Gogh's work at the Stedelijk Museum in Amsterdam in 1930. Both collectors were lenders,[57] but the Kröller-Müller loans had to be shown in separate rooms, and Helene Kröller-Müller even had a separate catalogue printed for her part of the exhibition.[58]

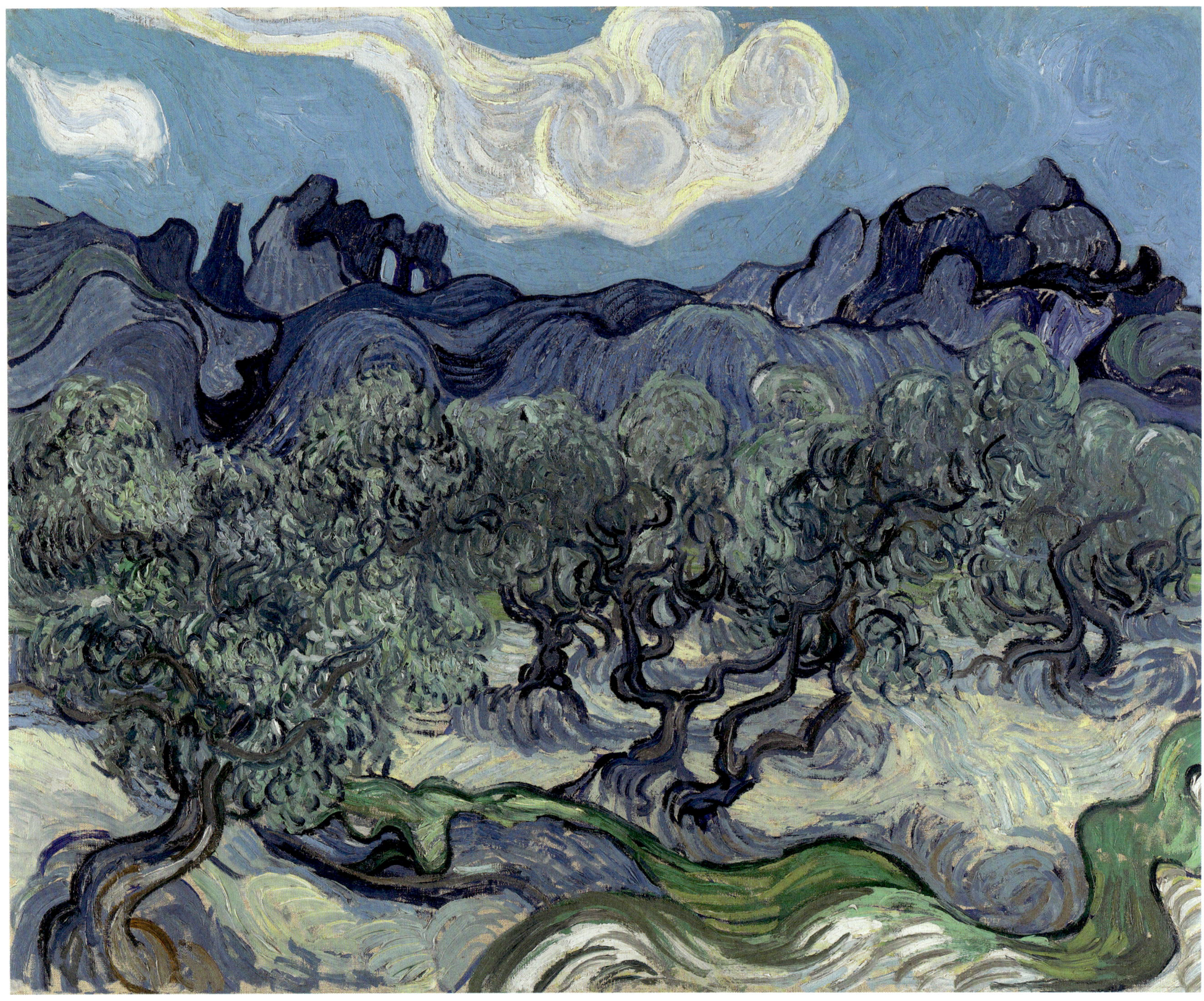

PLATE 38. *The Olive Trees*, 1889 (CAT. 51)

In June 1935, when Barr approached both parties with loan requests, he handled the situation very adroitly. In his initial letter to the Kröller-Müller Foundation, he had told them that in his view they owned "the foremost collection of Van Gogh's art" and that the Van Gogh family's holdings were "less important."[59] But after Barr had visited both owners and seen their collections, he wrote to Vincent Willem van Gogh: "I feel more strongly than ever that there are many paintings in your collection which are quite unparalleled in hers."[60]

His flattery and personal visits to the owners paid off. Barr succeeded in creating good relations not only with the family but also with the dour Kröller-Müller. The latter even provided Barr with a temporary office, where he could study the collection for days on end, in order to make a well-considered selection of loans.[61] This was an unprecedented state of affairs for her. She generally exercised a great deal of influence on the selection and presentation of her loans. Her trust in Barr is characteristic of their close working relationship at the outset and also during the later stages of the project.[62]

The time and effort Barr invested in these relations ultimately resulted in sizable loans. From the Kröller-Müller Foundation, he received thirty-three paintings and thirty-five drawings (among them, F921, F1061, F1058, F636; plates 33–36), including the loaned works belonging to Van Deventer (for example, F395, plate 37; and F712, plate 38); from Vincent Willem van Gogh, thirteen paintings and eight drawings (including F413; plate 39). Together, these two loans accounted for more than two-thirds of the entire exhibition, with the rest coming from private collectors in the United States (among them, F1548, F543, F1664, F1516, plates 40–43; and F681, plate 59) and three from American museums.[63] Vincent Willem van Gogh's

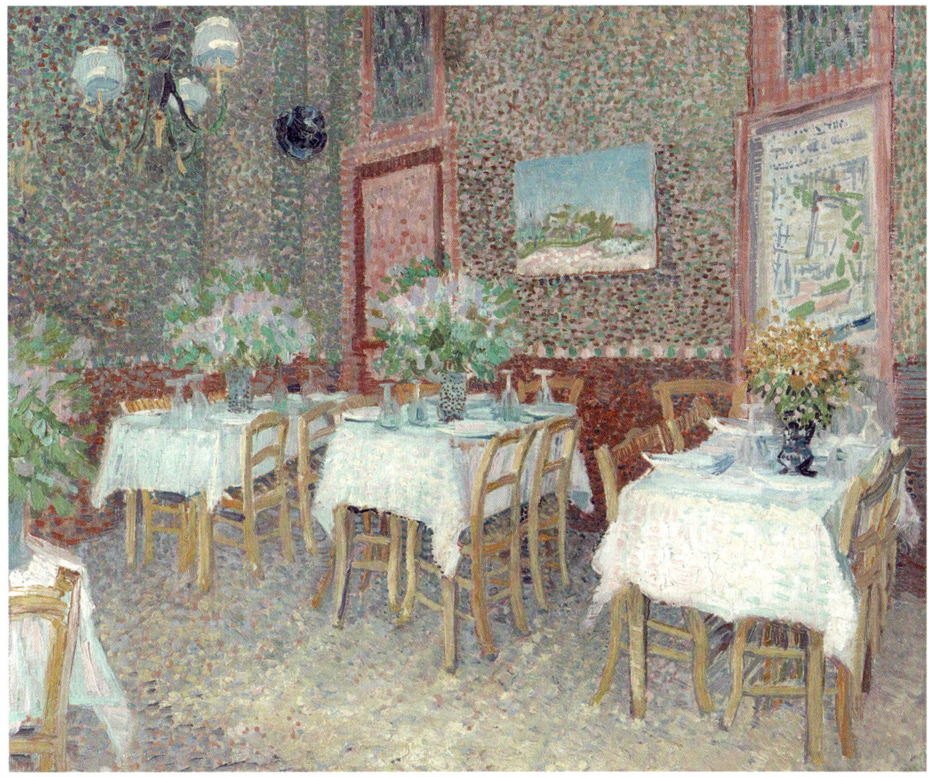

FIG. 4 *Interior of a Restaurant* (F342), 1887. Oil on canvas, 17 15/16 × 22 1/16 in. (45.5 × 56 cm). Kröller-Müller Museum, Otterlo.

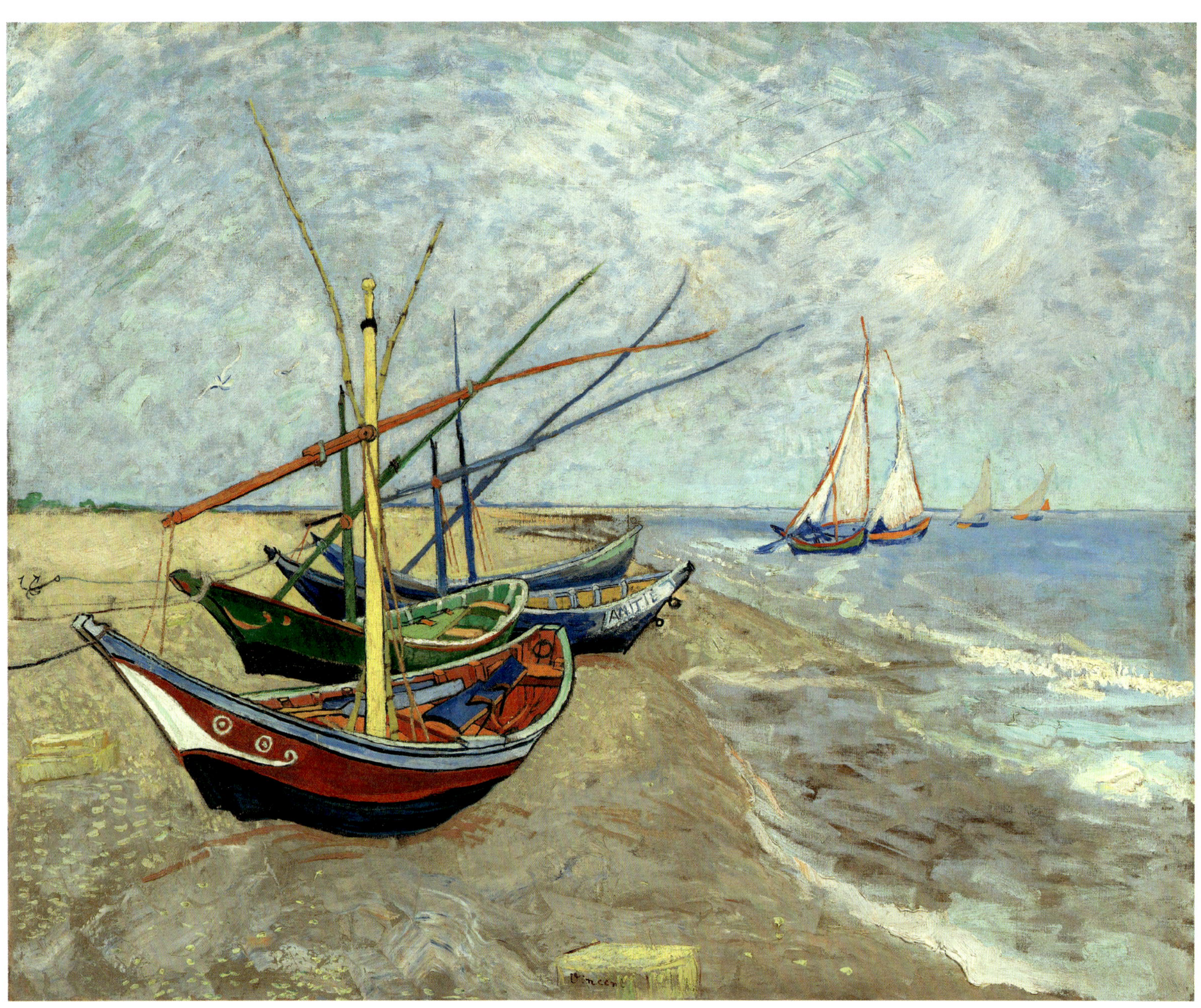

PLATE 39. *Fishing Boats on the Beach at Les Saintes-Maries-de-la-Mer*, 1888 (CAT. 31)

loans included many first-rate works, such as *The Potato Eaters* (F82; see Stolwijk and Krikke, fig. 1), *The Bedroom* (F482), and *Wheatfield with Crows* (F779), but the Kröller-Müller paintings were no less impressive, including *Interior of a Restaurant* (F342; fig. 4), *Terrace of a Café at Night (Place du Forum)* (F467; fig. 5), and *La Berceuse (Portrait of Madame Roulin)* (F504).

Kröller-Müller's generosity was largely due to her plans to build a museum and to the financial straits in which she and her husband had increasingly found themselves since the mid-1920s. The large losses suffered by Müller & Co. meant that they were compelled to turn to the Dutch government for financial support to build their museum. Kröller-Müller thought that an international tour of their paintings would influence public opinion and help persuade the Dutch officials to contribute to the building costs. This had also been the motive behind the European tour in the 1920s.[64] Moreover, the loan included a payment of $7,500 to the Kröller-Müller Foundation as compensation for the absence of the works by Van Gogh at their headquarters. This money would be put toward the construction of the museum.[65]

FIG. 5 *Terrace of a Café at Night (Place du Forum)* (F467), 1888. Oil on canvas, 31¾ × 25¹¹⁄₁₆ in. (80.7 × 65.3 cm). Kröller-Müller Museum, Otterlo.

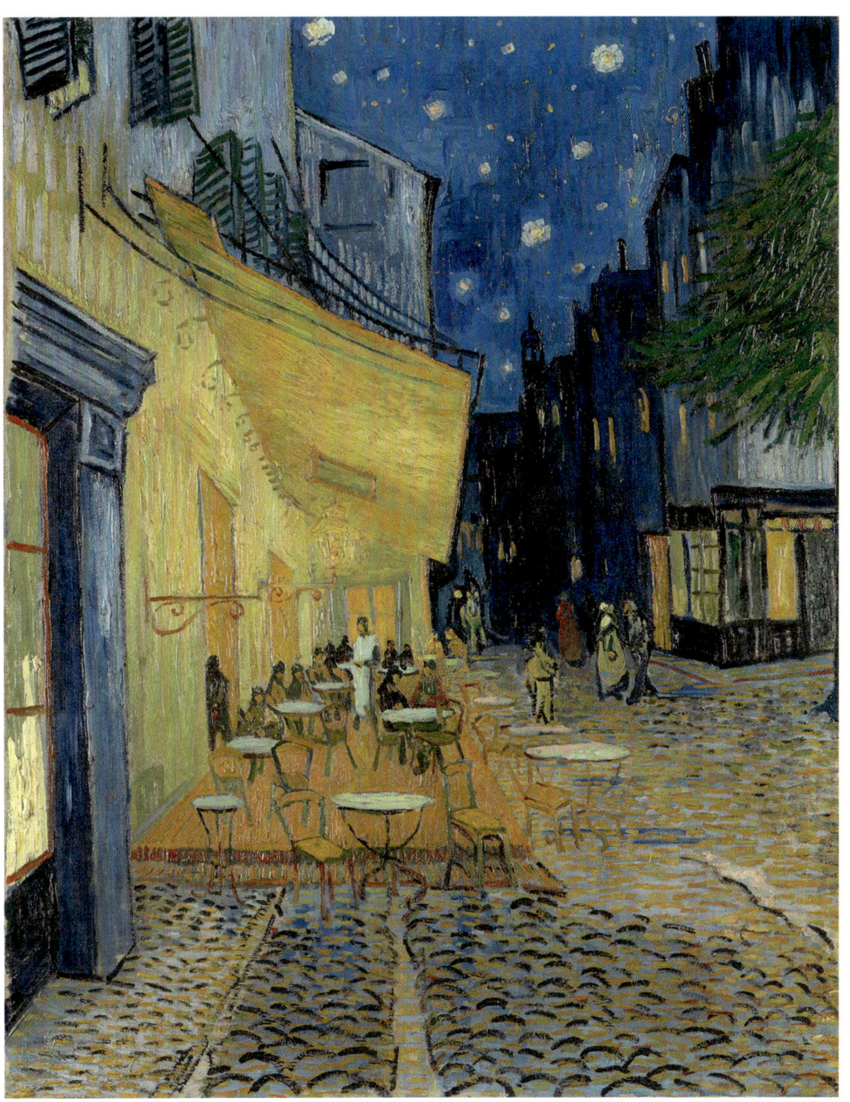

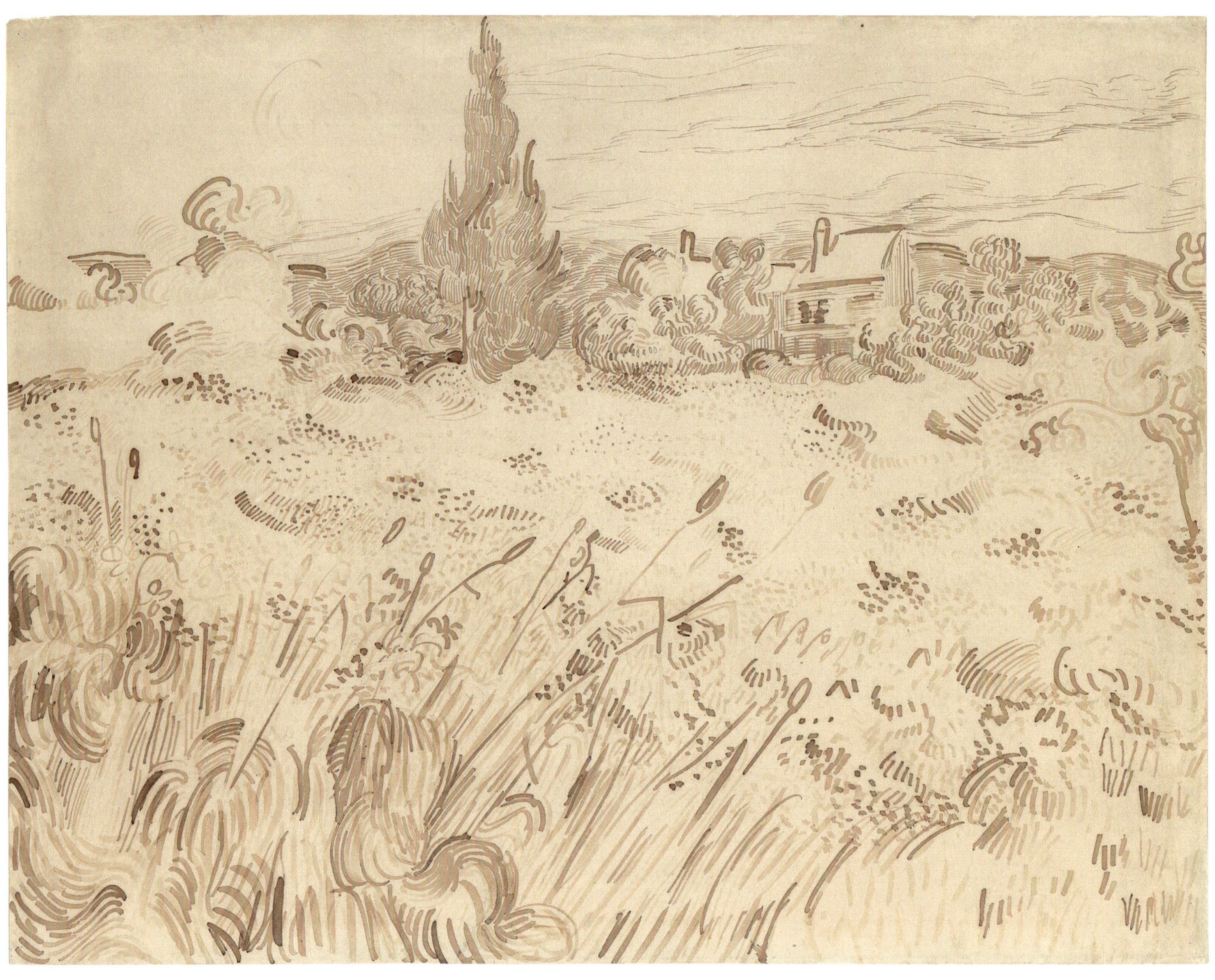

PLATE 40. *Wheatfield, Saint-Rémy de Provence*, 1889 (CAT. 48)

Vincent Willem van Gogh's decision to lend works to this exhibition was less opportunistic. His consent was in line with his mother's objectives: to enhance the reputation and reception of Van Gogh. He did not ask for any financial compensation.

The works from both collections were shipped from Rotterdam to New York on October 5, 1935.[66] After their arrival, MoMA heightened the excitement by circulating a press release that emphasized the extraordinary nature of the exhibition and the uniqueness of the loans from the Netherlands. To fire the imagination, they reported that the insured value of the works exceeded one million dollars.[67]

Immediately after the opening on November 4, it was clear that the exhibition would be a great success. There were more than 3,200 visitors on the very first day—a record for MoMA.[68] People stood in line outside waiting to get in, then moved in a tight procession past the paintings (fig. 6).[69] This level of enthusiasm had never before been seen in an American museum. It was a blockbuster *avant la lettre*. Saks Fifth Avenue even went so far as to decorate its shop windows in "Van Gogh colors."[70]

The press also devoted a great deal of attention to the exhibition. Newspapers in New York and farther afield discussed it extensively, generally offering nothing but praise. The value of the works on loan from the Netherlands was often mentioned. A topic of universal interest was the tragedy of Van Gogh's life, and almost every article lamented the fact that he had sold only a single painting in his lifetime.[71] A frequent question concerned why Van Gogh's popularity was experiencing such an astronomical rise given that fifteen years earlier there had been very little interest in him.[72] Many journalists concluded that *Lust for Life* must have been the deciding factor, and that curiosity and sensation were the main impetus behind the torrent of visitors.[73] Barr had been right when he judged that the time was ripe for America's first large retrospective exhibition of

FIG. 6 Installation view of the *Vincent van Gogh* exhibition at the Museum of Modern Art, New York, 1935. Left to right: F455, F650, F620, F661, F488 (plate 29), and F712 (plate 38).

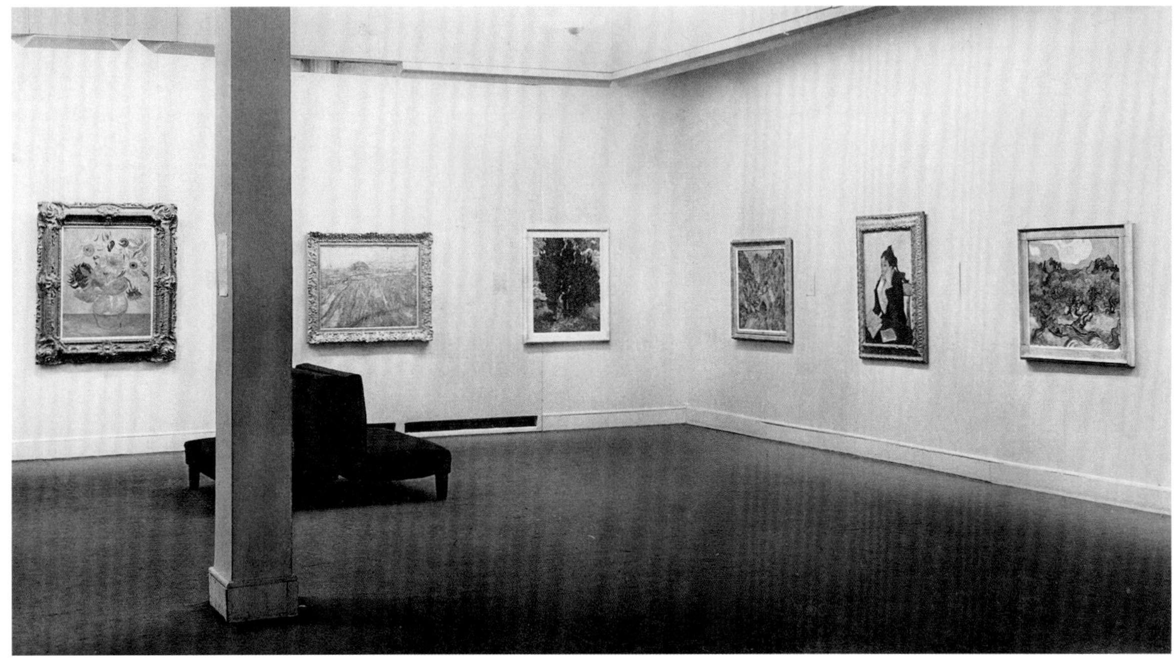

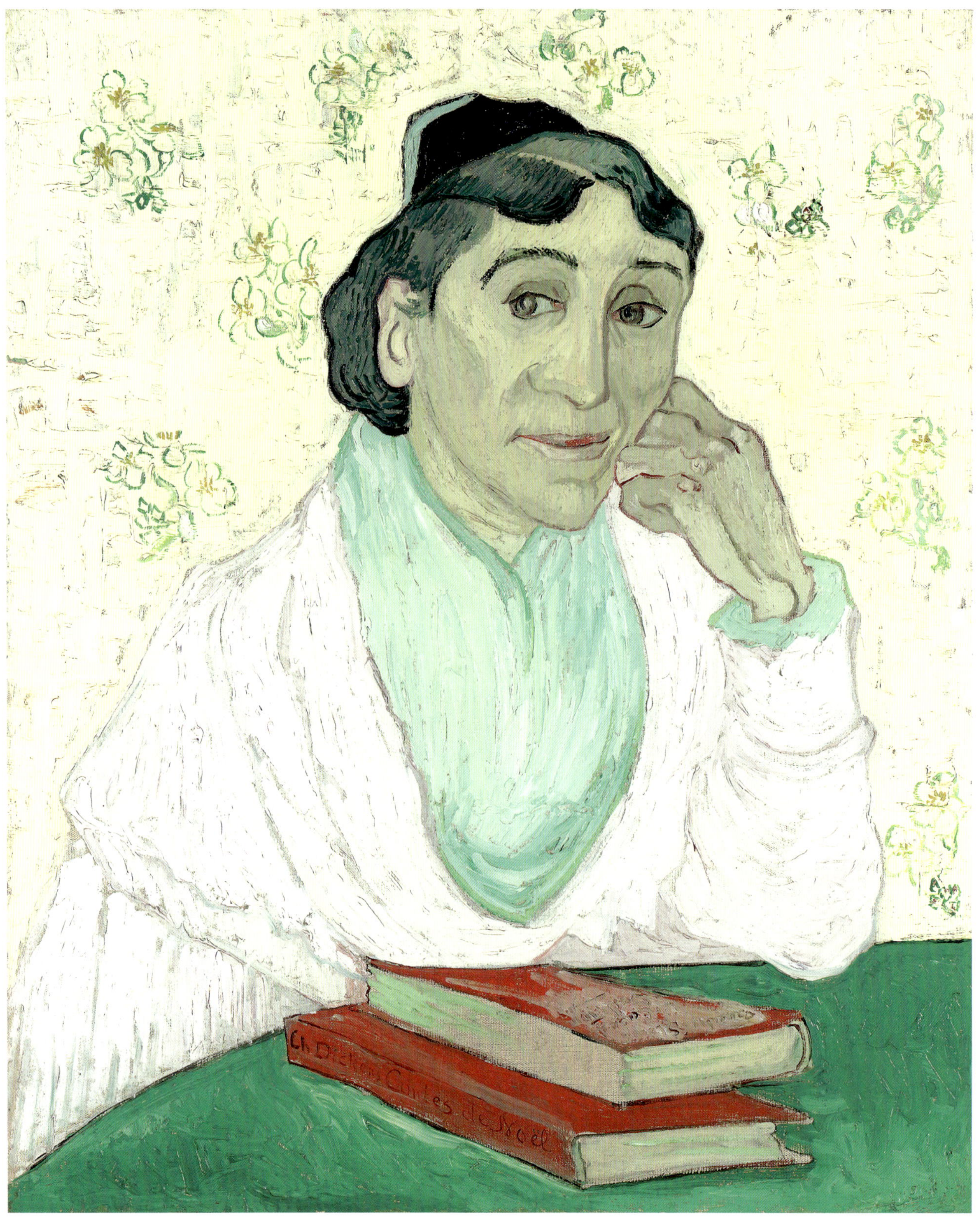

PLATE 41. *L'Arlésienne, Madame Ginoux*, 1890 (CAT. 58)

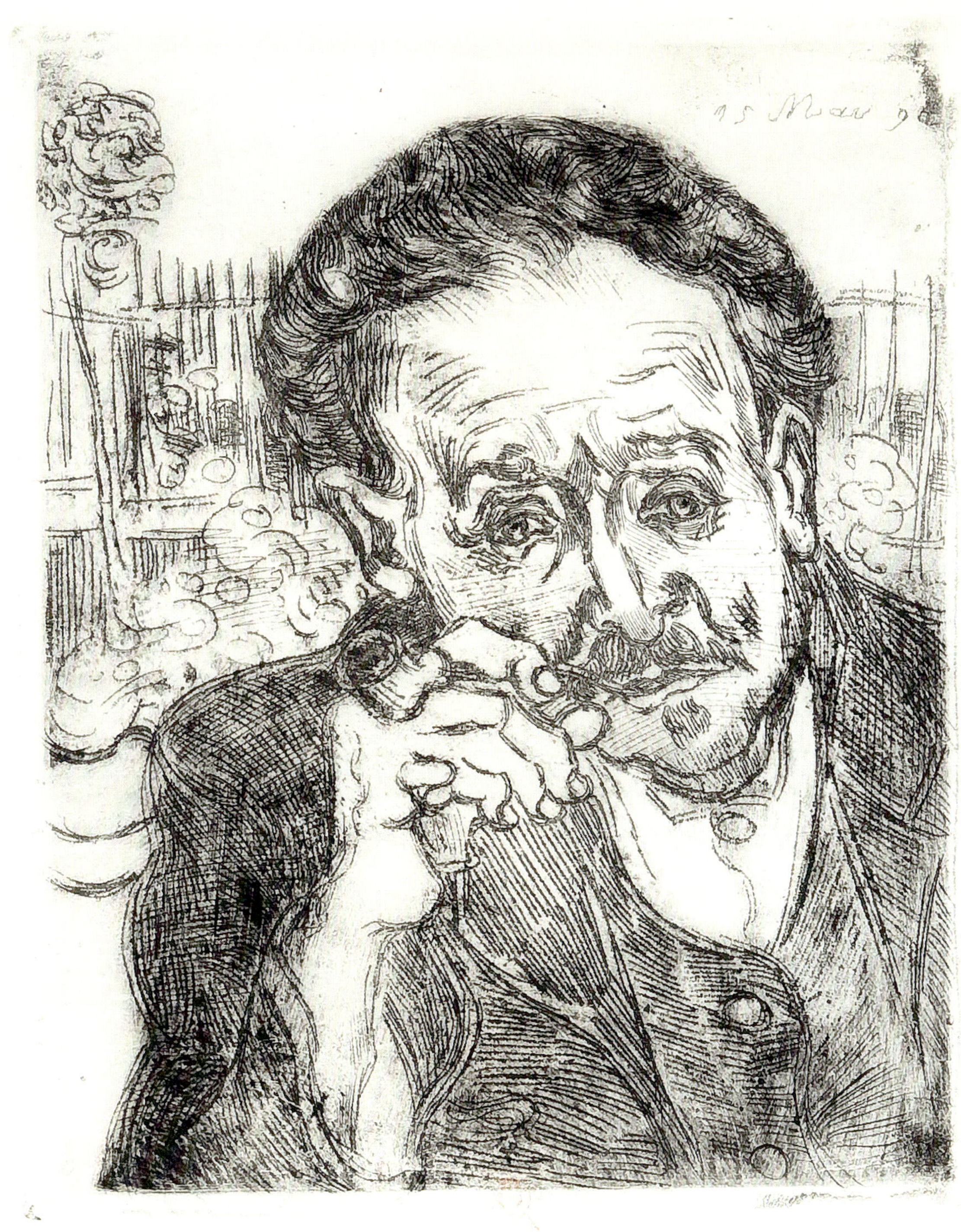

PLATE 42. *Portrait of Dr. Gachet (Man with a Pipe)*, 1890 (CAT. 64)

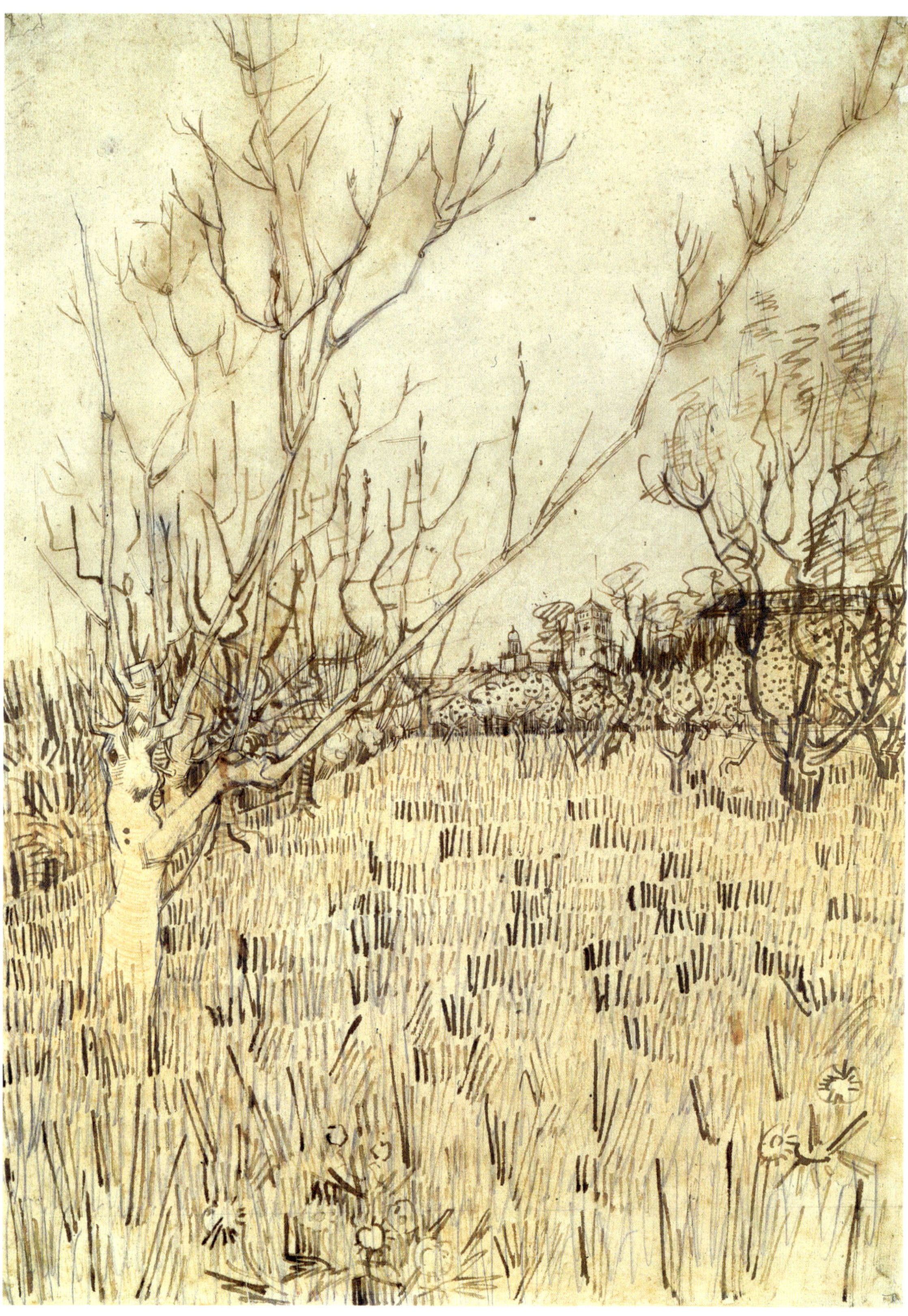

PLATE 43. *Orchard with Arles in the Background*, 1888 (CAT. 28)

Van Gogh. No fewer than 123,339 visitors flocked to the museum during the two months of the show.[74] During the last days, it was even necessary to close the doors temporarily, owing to the crush of people in the galleries.[75]

Barr had the newspaper articles and the attendance numbers sent to his Dutch lenders. The Kröller-Müller Foundation, in particular, was pleased. Barr received an enthusiastic letter, telling him that they would be using the information "for the purpose of informing the Government so as to impress upon them what that part of the collection means."[76] The loan had the desired effect for the foundation: the support of international opinion to demonstrate the inestimable value of their holdings. On April 15, 1937, the Kröller-Müller Foundation and the Dutch government signed an agreement whereby the latter committed itself to building a museum for the collection.[77] It cannot be said for certain, but it is quite possible that the success of the exhibition at MoMA and other American venues was an important factor in winning government support.

Vincent Willem van Gogh, by contrast, did not like sensationalism, and it disturbed him when articles gave incorrect information.[78] He was not happy either about the public announcement of the insured value of the loans. Indeed, he confessed in his diary that he almost regretted his collaboration as a lender to the exhibition.[79] He was, however, full of praise for the catalogue, in which Barr let the artist speak for himself by quoting passages from the letters previously translated into English by Jo van Gogh-Bonger. He also placed great value on the fact that the catalogue had been dedicated to his father, Theo van Gogh.[80] He wrote to Barr: "I congratulate you with the fine book you have published; it will have a lasting value for those who have it in their possession."[81]

After its New York venue, the exhibition traveled with great success to Philadelphia, Boston, Cleveland, and San Francisco, where it closed May 24, 1936. MoMA bore responsibility for the entire tour.[82] In Boston, there were 100,376 visitors to the show, and in San Francisco 227,540.[83] The spectacular level of interest prompted another forty-eight American museums to contact Barr in hopes of taking the show.[84] Barr wanted to accommodate five of these museums, and he sought a six-month extension. Vincent Willem van Gogh had other obligations, and his works were returned to the Netherlands, but the Kröller-Müller Foundation saw this as an opportunity to generate additional support and revenues.[85] For the sum of $5,000, they agreed to let their works travel on to Kansas City, Minneapolis, Chicago, Detroit, and Toronto, together with several of the works on loan from American collections: *Portrait of Père Tanguy* (F364; see Esner, fig. 1), *Adeline Ravoux* (F786; plate 18), *Orchard with Arles in the Background* (F1516; plate 43), *Cypresses* (F1525), *Haystacks near a Farmhouse* (F1427), and *Portrait of Dr. Gachet (Man with a Pipe)* (F1664; for example plate 42).[86] There was great frustration in the cities that missed out. In Los Angeles, where a special "Van Gogh Exhibition Committee" had been set up, they were "bitterly disappointed" at not securing the exhibition.[87]

The extension of the show was in fact a great burden on Barr's shoulders, as he had to act as liaison between the new venues and the Kröller-Müller Foundation. The latter held him accountable for all the proceedings.[88] Simultaneously, Barr was informed by Van Deventer that Bob Kröller, Kröller-Müller's son who had lent his *Poppy Field* (F636; plate 36) to the exhibition, wanted to sell the work in America.[89] Initially they wanted Barr to find them a buyer, but when he refused to act as salesman, Van Deventer asked him to withdraw the work from the exhibition so that it could be shipped to an art dealer in New York.[90] This put Barr in an equally awkward position, as the museums had paid the Kröller-Müller Foundation for the display of the entire group of Van Gogh works that was touring the United States. Barr proposed that the Kröller-Müller Foundation provide a replacement (*Sorrowing Old Man ["At Eternity's Gate"]*, F702) which would account for the absence of *Poppy Field*.[91] The foundation agreed, and in September 1936, when the exhibition was in Chicago, *Poppy Field* was taken from the wall and sent to New York to be sold, and *Sorrowing Old Man ("At Eternity's Gate")* was hung in its place.[92]

None of the parties involved thought it would be challenging to find a buyer for the work, since Van Gogh's popularity had grown considerably in the United States.[93] Americans had taken Van Gogh into their hearts. By the time the Kröller-Müller paintings arrived back in the Netherlands at the end of the tour, in February 1937, they had been viewed by nearly one million Americans.[94]

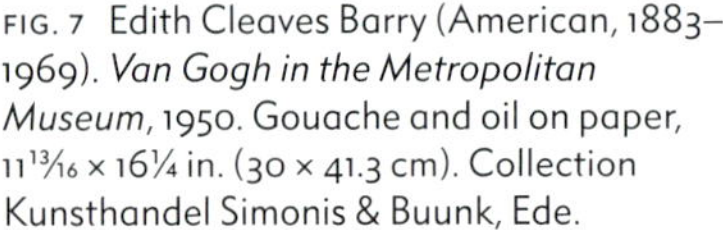

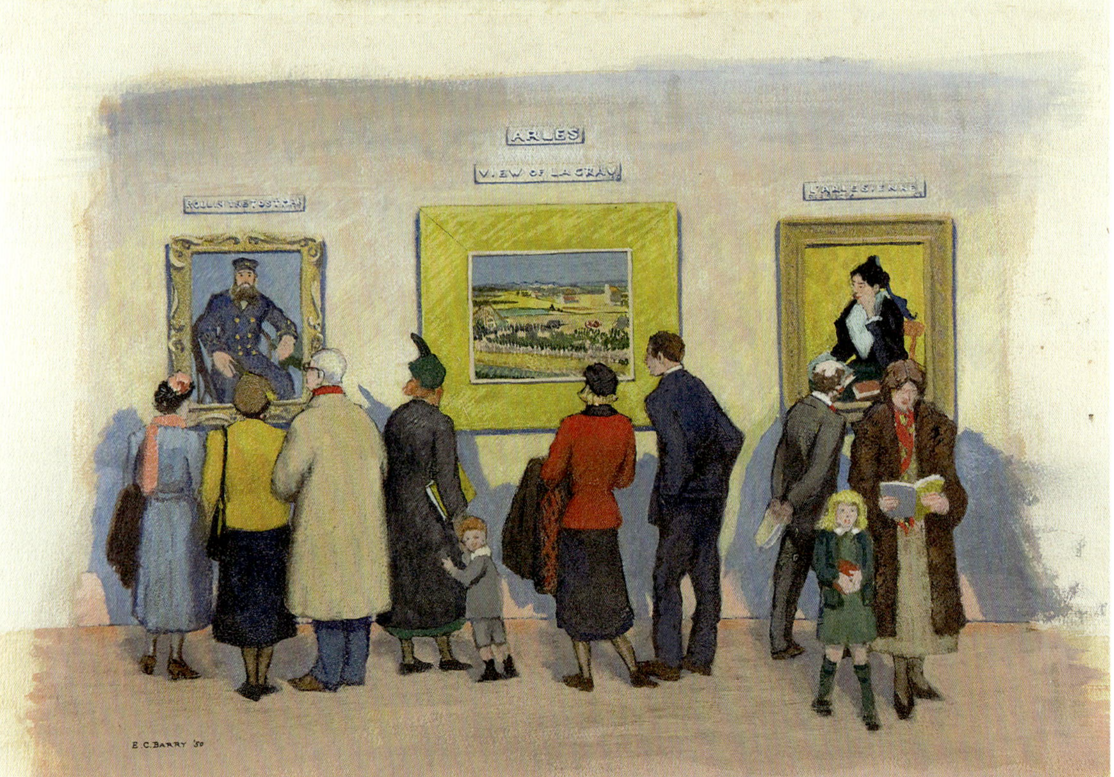

FIG. 7 Edith Cleaves Barry (American, 1883–1969). *Van Gogh in the Metropolitan Museum*, 1950. Gouache and oil on paper, 11 13/16 × 16¼ in. (30 × 41.3 cm). Collection Kunsthandel Simonis & Buunk, Ede.

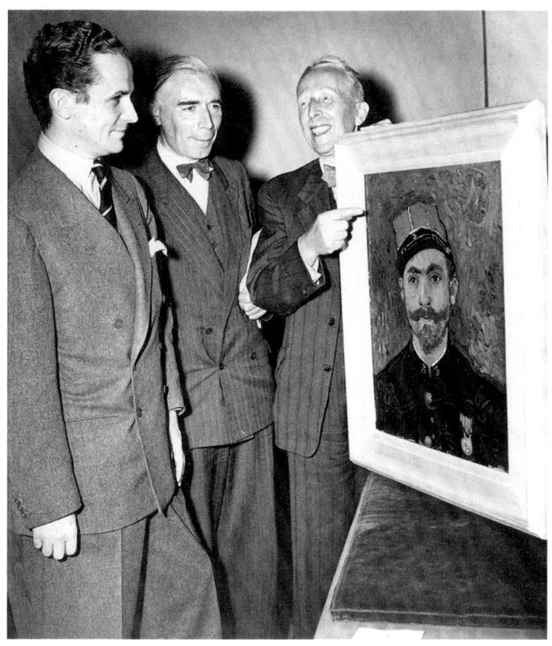

FIG. 8 Metropolitan Museum of Art curator Theodore Rousseau Jr., Kröller-Müller director A. M. (Bram) Hammacher, and Vincent Willem van Gogh unpacking works for the New York venue of *Van Gogh Paintings and Drawings: A Special Loan Exhibition*, 1949.

A Tour during the War Years

In 1939 Vincent Willem van Gogh made fourteen paintings available for an international exhibition in San Francisco, where they were on display for eight months. The selection included *The Yellow House (The Street)* (F464; fig. 3), *Self-Portrait with a Grey Felt Hat* (F344), *Wheatfield under Thunderclouds* (F778), *Cypresses and Two Women* (F621), and *Farmhouse* (F806).[95] After the *Golden Gate International Exposition*, these five works were put on display in the same city, at the M. H. de Young Memorial Museum.[96]

When World War II broke out in Europe, and Germany invaded the Netherlands on May 10, 1940, the fourteen works remained in the United States. They were brought from San Francisco to New York, where they were exhibited June 6–28, 1940, in the gallery at Holland House, which had opened its doors the previous year in the recently built Rockefeller Center. The Dutch Chamber of Commerce and the Dutch Consulate were housed there, as were the offices of the Netherland-America Foundation (NAF), which had previously sponsored the Goudstikker exhibition in the Anderson Galleries in 1923.[97]

After a tour of no fewer than twenty-seven venues in the United States and Canada, the exhibition of the fourteen Van Gogh paintings was scheduled to end in the summer of 1945 at MoMA.[98] A press release placed the presentation in the context of the prior exhibitions at the museum: at MoMA's opening in 1929, "the Dutch artist was presented in this country for the first time by an adequate number of paintings."[99] They neglected to mention the exhibitions that had taken place in the early 1920s, particularly the show mounted by Montross, who had exhibited sixty-seven pieces from the family's collection as early as 1920.

The tour of the paintings during the war years indicates some continuity in Dutch involvement in the promotion of Van Gogh in America, but it could not compare with the level of ambition and success of the traveling exhibition of 1935–36. That thread was picked up again in 1949 with the large retrospective exhibition at the Metropolitan Museum of Art in New York and the Art Institute of Chicago (fig. 7).[100] Unlike in 1935, both Van Gogh collections from the Netherlands were now cooperating as lenders.[101] The new director of the Rijksmuseum Kröller-Müller got along well with Vincent Willem van Gogh, and together they presented themselves as ambassadors of the artist (fig. 8). From this time onward, the keepers of the two collections would collaborate more frequently to bring Van Gogh to the art-loving public.[102]

NOTES

Translated from the original Dutch by Diane Webb.

1 New York and Chicago 1949–50.
2 Vincent Willem van Gogh was accompanied by his second wife, Nel van der Goot. His first wife, Josina van Gogh-Wibaut, died in 1933. *De Telegraaf* 1949: 1; *De Volkskrant* 1949: 3. The exhibition ran until January 15, 1950, then traveled to the Art Institute of Chicago, which co-organized the exhibition. De Ruiter 2000, 251–53.
3 Vincent Willem van Gogh did part with several more works, giving some away as gifts and using others as a means of exchange during the war. He also sold a few works. The Van Gogh Museum contains documentation concerning these transactions: see Van Gogh Museum Documentation, Amsterdam (hereafter VGMD).
4 J. van Gogh, "Chronologisch overzicht van het leven van Ir. Dr. V. W. van Gogh 31 januari 1890–28 januari 1978," September 1995, n.p., VGMD; J. van Gogh 1987, 1–8.
5 Ten Berge et al. 2003. See, for example, the provenance of inv. no. KM 110.056 on p. 207, which applies to the provenances of all paintings described in this catalogue of the Van Gogh paintings in the collection of the Kröller-Müller Museum. The provenance likewise applies to all Van Gogh works on paper in the Kröller-Müller Museum that are listed in Meedendorp 2007. Gustave Coquiot, Notebook (b3348), VGMD, p. 20: "Elle a refusé de vendre à Mme Kröller-Müller toute l'oeuvre de Vincent, bien que Mme Kröller fit une somme illimitée!" See also Zwikker 2020.
6 In her own words: "Formed for the benefit and enjoyment of the community, this collection serves to give an overview of the development of both the individual modern artist and the art of our day in general" ("Tot nut en genot der gemeenschap bijeengebracht, dient deze verzameling, om een aanschouwelijk beeld te geven der ontwikkeling zoowel van den individueelen modernen kunstenaar als de kunst onzer dagen in het algemeen"). See the document drawn up by Helene Kröller-Müller in "De Kunstverzameling," 1932, 2 (HA415388), Kröller-Müller Museum, Historical Archive, Otterlo (hereafter KMM).
7 Balk 2006, 155.
8 Helene Kröller-Müller, letter to Sam van Deventer, November 12, 1910, quoted in Rovers 2010, 109.
9 Rovers 2010, 190–93.
10 They lived at the home of Anna and Sergius Ingerman, both physicians and fervent socialists, located at 1843 Madison Avenue. Vincent Willem van Gogh, "Dagboek (Diary)," July 22 and 23, 1972, Van Gogh Museum.
11 Jo van Gogh-Bonger, letter to Vincent Willem van Gogh and Josina van Gogh-Wibaut, November 14–18, 1915 (b3717), VGMD; Jo van Gogh-Bonger, letter to Vincent Willem van Gogh and Josina van Gogh-Wibaut, December 29, 1915 (b8294), VGMD.
12 Van Gogh Letters 1913. The book was based on the fourth edition (1911) of *Briefe*, first published by Bruno Cassirer in 1906.
13 Du Quesne-Van Gogh 1910 and 1913.
14 Heijbroek and Wouthuysen 1993, 45.
15 Hulsker 1985, 18.
16 Zilczer 1978, 31.
17 For the events of 1915, see *De Telegraaf* 1949; *De Volkskrant* 1949.
18 Scott and Rutkoff 1999, 62.
19 The exhibition ran for at least three weeks, with Vincent Willem van Gogh's works on view for part of that time. Rewald 1989, 287, 309. The Paris dealers remain unknown. For additional information on New York 1915b, see Stein, New York, pp. 73–75.
20 Van Gogh-Bonger to Vincent Willem van Gogh and Van Gogh-Wibaut, December 29, 1915 (b8294); Vincent Willem van Gogh, letter to Mark Edo Tralbaut, November 1, 1955 (b7787), VGMD.
21 *De Telegraaf* 1949; Vincent Willem van Gogh to Tralbaut, November 1, 1955 (b7787).
22 Josina van Gogh-Wibaut, letter to Jo van Gogh-Bonger, March 20, 1916 (b3112), VGMD.
23 New York 1916b, 3, 11, 13. It is possible that all of the Van Gogh works were from the family's collection.
24 Van Gogh-Wibaut to Van Gogh-Bonger, March 20, 1916 (b3112).
25 These were W. van Meurs's facsimiles, first published in 1904, which were highly valued in the Netherlands. Marius 1907: 6; Jo van Gogh-Bonger, letter to Vincent Willem van Gogh and Josina van Gogh-Wibaut, April 17, 1916 (b3715), VGMD; Van Gogh-Wibaut to Van Gogh-Bonger, March 20, 1916 (b3112).
26 Jo van Gogh-Bonger died in 1925. The three-volume publication would appear in 1927–29. See Van Gogh Letters 1927–29.
27 Newman E. Montross, telegram to Jo van Gogh-Bonger, January 22, 1920 (b3150), VGMD.
28 New York 1920b lists thirty-five works on paper and thirty-two paintings: nos. 34 "Sower" and 35 "Landscape with Farm" must already have been with Montross, because Jo van Gogh-Bonger wrote these titles by hand on her own typed list of the works on paper (b6246), VGMD. Moreover, Montross wrote to Vincent Willem van Gogh, September 10, 1920 (b6255), VGMD, that he was having the two drawings already in his keeping framed. He augmented the exhibition with Van Gogh's *Self-Portrait* (F268; plate 17) from the holdings of the famous collector John Quinn. See McBride 1920a: 8; Zilczer 1978, 100–101, no. 30.
29 *Nieuwe Rotterdamsche Courant* 1920: B9.
30 *Het Vaderland* 1921: 6.
31 The exhibition opened on April 23 and lasted two weeks. See *Algemeen Handelsblad* 1921: 9; *Nieuwe Tilburgsche Courant* 1921: 2; Edelman 2012, 7–8.
32 New York 1921c, nos. 34, 35.
33 Jo van Gogh-Bonger compared the exhibition in New York to the exhibition of Dutch art that took place that same spring at the Jeu de Paume in Paris. This had been organized by the Dutch Ministry of Education, Arts and Sciences (OKW) with the intention of enhancing the prestige of the Netherlands. Jo van Gogh-Bonger and Vincent Willem van Gogh were lenders to that exhibition as well. Jo van Gogh-Bonger, letter to Paul Gachet Jr., May 2, 1921 (b1517), VGMD: "La Hollande ce donne beaucoup de peine pour envoyer les chefs d'oeuvre de son art à l'étranger." See also Minister of OKW, letter to Vincent Willem van Gogh, January 15, 1921 (b5778), VGMD; Vincent Willem van Gogh, letter to Minister of OKW, January 19, 1921 (b5779), VGMD. A letter to a friend testifies to Van Gogh-Bonger's recognition of the efforts made by the Chamber of Commerce. See Jo van Gogh-Bonger, letter to Annie van Gelder, October 6, 1921 (b3719), VGMD.
34 *Nieuwe Tilburgsche Courant* 1921.
35 *Algemeen Handelsblad* 1921.
36 *De Telegraaf* 1921: 9; *Algemeen Handelsblad* 1921. Adriaan J. Barnouw, letter to Jo van Gogh-Bonger, January 12, 1922 (b6265), VGMD. During this period, Van Gogh-Bonger tried in vain to find an American publisher for Van Gogh's letters; she had been in contact about this with Barnouw, among others.
37 *Algemeen Handelsblad* 1921.
38 *Algemeen Handelsblad* 1923: 9.
39 These five Van Goghs (four paintings and a watercolor) were shipped with the other artworks from the Goudstikker collection and had been obtained through the mediation of Cornelis Baard, director of the Stedelijk Museum. See "List of paintings for Mr. Goudstikker," October 25, 1922 (b5500 and b5501), VGMD, of which the latter includes prices. Van Gogh-Bonger lent the works to ensure that Van Gogh would be represented in the show. In addition, she put Goudstikker in touch with Montross, who still had works from the family collection in his gallery and might also be able to lend pieces to Goudstikker. Jo van Gogh-Bonger, letter to J. Goudstikker, October 25, 1922 (b5502), VGMD; J. Goudstikker to Jo van Gogh-Bonger, October 25, 1922 (b5503), VGMD; and St. Louis and other cities 1922–23, nos. 149–53 (New York catalogue).
40 When he gave this impression of Americans, the reporter was quoting from a text written by the Dutch historian Hendrik Willem van Loon, who lived in America. *De Telegraaf* 1923: 7.
41 *Algemeen Handelsblad* 1923.
42 Newman E. Montross, letter to Vincent Willem van Gogh, July 5, 1927 (b6279), VGMD; Vincent Willem van Gogh, letter to Newman E. Montross, n.d. (draft of letter) (b6280), VGMD.
43 J. Bernheim-Jeune, letter to Vincent Willem van Gogh, August 30, 1929 (b6281), VGMD; Vincent Willem van Gogh, letter to J. Bernheim Jr., September 4, 1929 (b6282), VGMD: "Je suis tout disposé à prêter des tableaux."
44 Kantor 2002, 216.
45 Loan receipt, November 15, 1929 (b6283), VGMD; New York 1929a, nos. 78, 80, 81, 89.
46 Goodyear 1943, 15–16.
47 New York 1929a, 11.
48 Alfred H. Barr Jr., letter to Sam van Deventer, before June 15, 1935 (HA412900), KMM.
49 Alfred H. Barr Jr., letter to Helene Kröller-Müller, June 15, 1935 (HA412902), KMM: "There has now grown in America a great popular interest in Van Gogh and an immense desire to see his paintings."
50 Ibid.: "I am encouraged to make this request by the memory of the 'grand tour' of European cities made by your Van Gogh collection in 1927–1928." Barr apparently wasn't aware the collection was on view at the Hamburger Kunstverein from March 14 to May 21, 1929.
51 Alfred H. Barr Jr., letter to Helene Kröller-Müller, November 1, 1927 (HA411370), KMM.
52 Ibid.
53 It emerges from the correspondence in KMM that Barr had not met Kröller-Müller before 1935.
54 Barr to Van Deventer, before June 15, 1935 (HA412900): "I think it is now three or four years ago we last talked about Van Gogh in New York."
55 Rovers 2010, 382.

56 This is apparent from the fact that Barr was very circumspect in approaching Helene Kröller-Müller. He first wrote to Van Deventer, asking him to sound her out about the possibility of a loan, before approaching her himself. See Barr to Van Deventer, before June 15, 1935 (HA412900).

57 Amsterdam 1930.

58 Rovers 2010, 393–95; in regard to this exhibition, Kröller-Müller was in contact with the Stedelijk Museum only, and not with her fellow lender.

59 Barr to Kröller-Müller, June 15, 1935 (HA412902); Barr to Van Deventer, before June 15, 1935 (HA412900).

60 Alfred H. Barr Jr., letter to Vincent Willem van Gogh, June 25, 1935 (b5287), VGMD.

61 M. Barr 1987, 41.

62 When Sam van Deventer and Alfred H. Barr Jr. were exchanging pleasantries shortly before the opening of the exhibition, Van Deventer confessed to Barr that "she [Helene Kröller-Müller] only consented to the sending over because she had confidence in your dealing with this matter." Sam van Deventer, letter to Alfred H. Barr Jr., November 1, 1935 (HA412933), KMM.

63 See the "Master checklist," a list of exhibited works that was annotated and supplemented by Alfred H. Barr Jr., The Museum of Modern Art, New York, Archives (hereafter MoMA Archives). The three American museums that lent a Van Gogh were: the Metropolitan Museum of Art (F1625), the Art Institute of Chicago (F1524), and the Fogg Art Museum (F1003, even though this work was bequeathed and came into the museum's full possession in 1965). Barr also maintained ties with the Stedelijk Museum, which had had a large part of Vincent Willem van Gogh's collection on long-term loan since 1930.

64 See the minutes of the January 1933 meeting of the Kröller-Müller Foundation, 4–8 (HA414732), KMM.

65 Sam van Deventer, letter to Alfred H. Barr Jr., July 11, 1935 (HA412905), KMM.

66 Sam van Deventer, telegram to Alfred H. Barr Jr., October 2, 1935 (HA417336), KMM.

67 MoMA press release, October 14, 1935, MoMA Archives.

68 Anson Conger Goodyear, telegram to Helene Kröller-Müller, November 6, 1935 (HA412935), KMM.

69 *Brooklyn Daily Eagle* 1936: 7: "So crowded was the museum that none was allowed to linger in front of a painting. In a double line the art-minded public was conducted around like a moving belt."

70 *De Maasbode* 1936: "One of the largest fashion stores, Saks on Fifth Avenue, filled twelve windows with fabrics in characteristic 'Van Gogh colors!'"

71 McMahon 1935: 16: "The contrast between his life and his fame after death is elementary and sensational. Great popular interest today, and poverty, suffering, obscurity during his lifetime. Almost no earnings during his active years, and great wealth now represented by his work." The subtitle of a long piece in the *New York Times Magazine*, written by none other than Irving Stone, read: "Van Gogh Sold Only One of His Paintings and Ended His Unhappy Career By Suicide, Yet Posterity Has Discovered That He Was a Genius." Stone 1935: 12.

72 Bonte 1936: 12: "Why are Van Gogh paintings popular? One is tempted to say that his popularity depends on those very qualities which shocked and puzzled people not only during his lifetime, but for 30 or 40 years after his death....Only a few years ago, for instance, the leading art critic of the leading morning paper of one of our large cities wrote: 'Van Gogh was a crazy galoot...whose paintings...at their worst represent the crude elemental expressions which nit-wits affix to sidewalks, barn doors and elsewhere.'"

73 Dooley 1935: "Few artists since Leonardo da Vinci have 'caught on' so enthusiastically with that section of an appreciative public which would have a dramatic martyr for its hero. How much of Van Gogh's following in this country has been brought on by Irving Stone's best-selling novel 'Lust for Life'...is easily surmised."

74 MoMA press release, n.d. (after January 5, 1936), MoMA Archives.

75 *New York Times* 1936a: 15: "On each of the final days the galleries had to be closed several times while the crowd inside thinned out."

76 Sam van Deventer, letter to Alfred H. Barr Jr., December 13, 1935 (HA412941), KMM.

77 Rovers 2010, 433–34.

78 Vincent Willem van Gogh, letter to Mr. Rowland, October 28, 1935 (b6298), VGMD.

79 Vincent Willem van Gogh, "Dagboek (Diary)," October 27, 1935, Van Gogh Museum.

80 Alfred H. Barr Jr., letter to Vincent Willem van Gogh, October 24, 1935 (b6297), VGMD.

81 Vincent Willem van Gogh, letter to Alfred H. Barr Jr., December 5, 1935 (b6303), VGMD.

82 See the agreement between the Kröller-Müller Foundation and MoMA, that was drawn up in The Hague, August 3, 1935 (HA412891), KMM.

83 MoMA press release, n.d. (after August 17, 1936), MoMA Archives. One reason San Francisco had so many visitors was because, in contrast to New York, admission was free.

84 Alfred H. Barr Jr., letter to William A. Bryan, director of the Los Angeles Museum of History, Science and Art, February 17, 1937 (HA416233), KMM: "In spite of the extension many museums had to be disappointed – forty-three to be exact." Adding the five institutions that succeeded in getting the exhibition brings the number to forty-eight.

85 Alfred H. Barr Jr., letter to Vincent Willem van Gogh, January 7, 1936 (b6306), VGMD.

86 Van Deventer, letter to Barr, December 13, 1935 (HA412941). Russell Plimpton (then director of the Minneapolis Institute of Arts), letter to Edward Buckman, July 6, 1936, VGMD.

87 Merle Armitage, chairman of the Los Angeles Van Gogh Committee, telegram to Sam van Deventer, quoted in Sam van Deventer, letter to Alfred H. Barr Jr., February 8, 1937 (HA412991), KMM.

88 Van Deventer, letter to Barr, December 13, 1935 (HA412941).

89 Sam van Deventer, letter to Alfred H. Barr Jr., April 16, 1936 (HA412964), KMM.

90 Alfred H. Barr Jr., letter to Sam van Deventer, April 16, 1936 (HA412965), KMM: "If Robert Kröller wants to sell the picture soon, I would advise him to put it in the hands of a reputable American dealer...."

91 Alfred H. Barr Jr., letter to Sam van Deventer, July 11, 1936 (HA412973), KMM: "As to withdrawing the picture from the tour in the autumn I find myself slightly embarrassed since we are under an engagement with the other museums to send each of them a complete group of paintings from the Kröller-Müller Foundation as they were exhibited in New York. Since the museums are paying a large fee most of which is passed on to the Kröller-Müller Foundation I am not quite sure what we should do. Would it be possible—I suggest this quite tentatively, to send to America a painting to substitute for the Poppies. I suggest, for example, the painting of the old man seated with chin on his hands, painted I think at S. Rémy after one of the Dutch drawings."

92 Alfred H. Barr Jr., letter to Sam van Deventer, October 3, 1936 (HA412982), KMM.

93 Sam van Deventer, letter to Alfred H. Barr Jr., October 8, 1936 (HA413092), KMM.

94 Before the works were shown for several more weeks in New York in 1937, a total of 878,719 Americans had seen the exhibition. See Jewell 1937: 17.

95 The other works were *Evening (after Millet)* (F647), *Seascape near Les Saintes-Maries-de-la-Mer* (F415), *Wheatfield with Partridge* (F310), *Daubigny's Garden* (F765), *Sprig of Flowering Almond in a Glass* (F392), *The Reaper (after Millet)* (F687), *Landscape with Rabbits* (F739), *Vase with Chinese Asters and Gladioli* (F234), and *Basket of Potatoes* (F116). The selection had been made by the Dutch government. Before they were sent to San Francisco, these paintings had been part of an exhibition in Batavia (now Jakarta) in the Dutch East Indies (present-day Indonesia). See "Schilderijen van Vincent van Gogh voor de tentoonstelling te Batavia," March 15, 1938 (b6335), VGMD; *De Indische Courant* 1938: 13.

96 San Francisco 1939, nos. 169–82; San Francisco 1939–40, nos. Y-122, L-123, L-125, L-126, Y-127.

97 Adriaan J. Barnouw, organizer of the exhibition at Holland House, had written the introduction to the catalogues of the exhibitions in the Anderson Galleries in 1921 and 1923. *De Telegraaf* 1921; Barnouw, letter to Van Gogh-Bonger, January 12, 1922 (b6265); Edelman 2012, 6–9, 16–17, 26–28; New York 1940; *Algemeen Handelsblad* 1940: 2.

98 "Showings of collection of fourteen Van Gogh paintings in the United States Under the Jurisdiction of the Netherlands Information Bureau in New York" (b6321), VGMD.

99 "Fourteen Van Gogh Paintings to be shown at Museum of Modern Art for Three Weeks" (b6320), VGMD.

100 *Het Parool* 1949: 5; *De Tijd* 1949: 3; Trouw 1949: 5.

101 This time Vincent Willem van Gogh's share of the loan was much larger than Kröller-Müller's. He gave forty-six paintings and fifty drawings on loan to the exhibition, whereas the Rijksmuseum Kröller-Müller made available "only" twenty-one paintings and seventeen drawings. New York and Chicago 1949–50, 20–89.

102 In this way they organized, on the basis of both collections, an exhibition to commemorate the centenary of Van Gogh's birth on March 30, 1853; St. Louis, Philadelphia, and Toledo 1953–54. De Ruiter 2000, 253. "Gegevens over de werkzaamheden van Ir. Dr. V. W. van Gogh in verband met het organiseren van tentoonstellingen in Amerika, verzameld uit de jaarverslagen van de Vincent van Gogh Stichting," memorandum, VGMD.

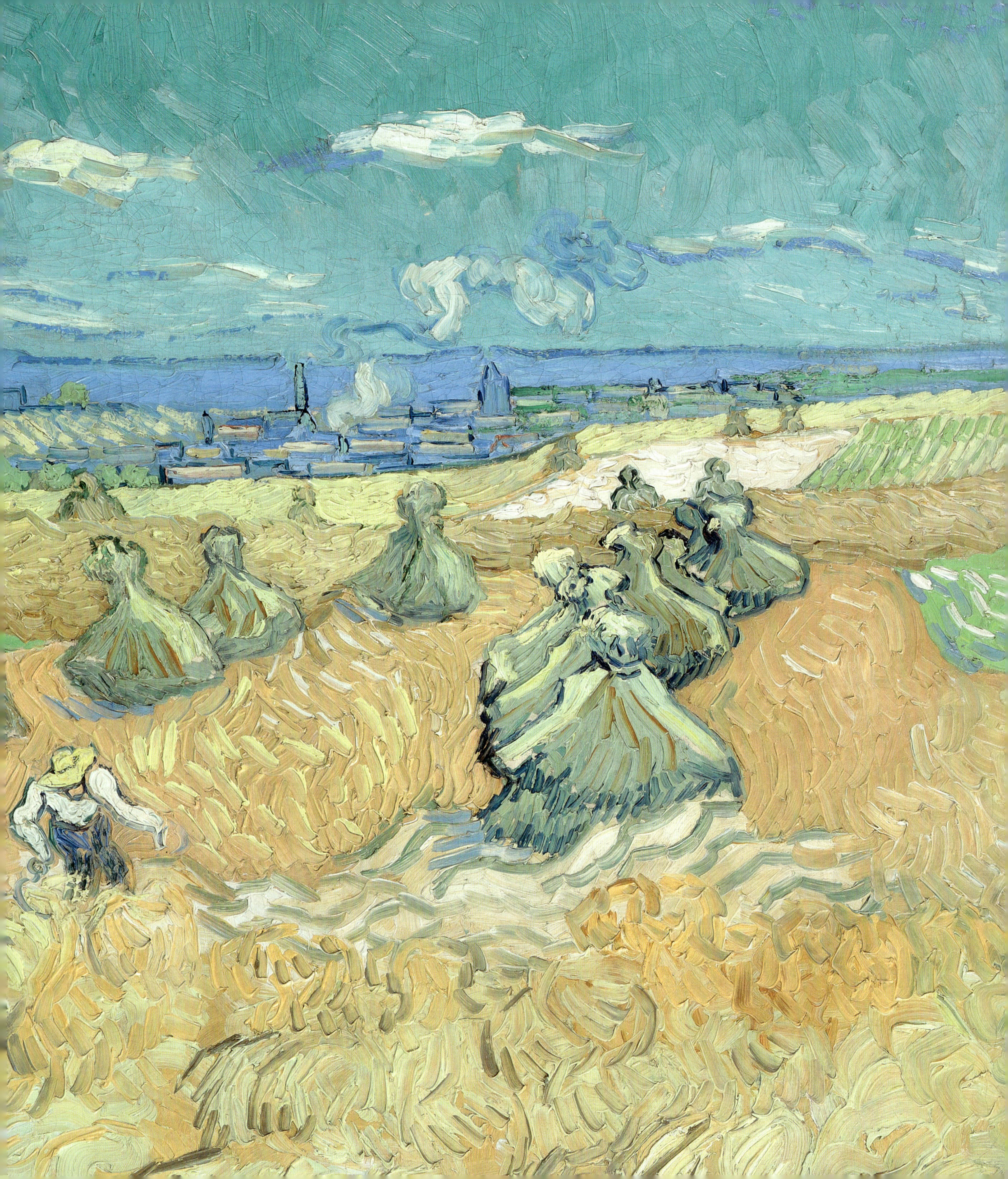

JILL SHAW

The Heartland Steps Up: Van Gogh in the Midwest, 1913–36

In a 1929 article in *Vogue*, Alfred H. Barr Jr., the founding director of the Museum of Modern Art (MoMA) in New York, laid out the case for a new museum in the city that would focus on promoting and exhibiting modern and contemporary art. He appealed directly to his readers:

> And now our most important question—our museums—what have they done? Have they kept pace with the progressive spirit of our collectors and critics, and the general public?
>
> The answer to this question embodies strange contradictions. In Detroit, Dr. Valentiner has brought together a very stimulating collection of modern paintings, American, German, and French. The Chicago Art Institute houses the magnificent Birch-Bartlett room of masterpieces by Cézanne, Seurat, Picasso, and Matisse...San Francisco, Cleveland, Minneapolis, and Worcester have excellent modern pictures of the non-academic kind. But in New York, that vast, that exceedingly modern metropolis, we discover a curious anomaly. The Metropolitan, the foremost museum in America, owns no Van Gogh, no Gauguin, no Seurat, no Toulouse-Lautrec, men long dead....[1]

Despite its hyperbolic promotional agenda, Barr's statement is enlightening for reasons *not* having to do with New York. Notably and likely surprisingly, many of the American institutions mentioned as leading promoters of modern art were Midwestern ones: Detroit, Chicago, Cleveland, and Minneapolis. Other press surrounding the opening of MoMA likewise cited the importance of "America's Middle West, where, oddly enough, modern art has enjoyed the most success."[2]

Such was the case specifically with advocacy of Vincent van Gogh. Only two American public institutions lent works by Van Gogh to MoMA's inaugural 1929 exhibition: the Detroit Institute of Arts (F526; plate 44) and the Art Institute of Chicago (F484; plate 45).[3] Moreover, they were the only encyclopedic museums in America at that point that *could* lend to the exhibition, for they were the only ones that had accessioned paintings by the artist into their permanent collections.[4] Other notable forward-thinking Midwestern collectors, institutions, and cities—including Cleveland, Kansas City, Minneapolis, St. Louis, and Toledo—exhibited or acquired the artist's work before or in 1935, the year MoMA staged the first monographic exhibition of Van Gogh's art in a United States museum. Thus, for all intents and purposes, an examination of the early reception of Van Gogh in America must consider the efforts of the Midwest, for it promoted Van Gogh in ways that at times surpassed those on the East Coast or anywhere else in the country.

Chicago—Second City, First Museum

While MoMA is recognized as the first museum in the United States to host a Van Gogh retrospective, it was a Midwestern one that was the first to display his work. Following its inaugural installation at New York's Sixty-Ninth Regiment Armory, the 1913 *International Exhibition of Modern Art* (better known as the Armory Show)—where the American public first saw Van Gogh—traveled in a reduced version to Chicago and Boston. Perhaps most significant about the exhibition in the second city was the venue itself: the hallowed Art Institute of Chicago. While the circumstances of the Chicago showing—the only version to take place in a museum setting—and the overwhelmingly mixed response to the works on view are well documented, Van Gogh's role in the exhibition merits special consideration.[5]

The person most responsible for bringing the exhibition to Chicago was art patron Arthur T. Aldis, who met the Armory Show's main drivers, Arthur B. Davies, Walt Kuhn, and Walter Pach, in Paris while they were scouting out works. Aldis essentially committed the Art Institute to take the exhibition, but he had to convince its director, William M. R. French, and trustees. Other public voices also called for the show to come to Chicago. Reviewing the New York installment of the exhibition, Harriet Monroe, progressive Chicago art critic and founder and editor of the avant-garde publication *Poetry: A Magazine of Verse*, reported: "At last an important group of our artists rebels against the provincialism, and the academic prejudices which govern most exhibitions in this country.... The intelligent public of the west may reasonably ask why this exhibition, or a part of it, should not come to Chicago."[6]

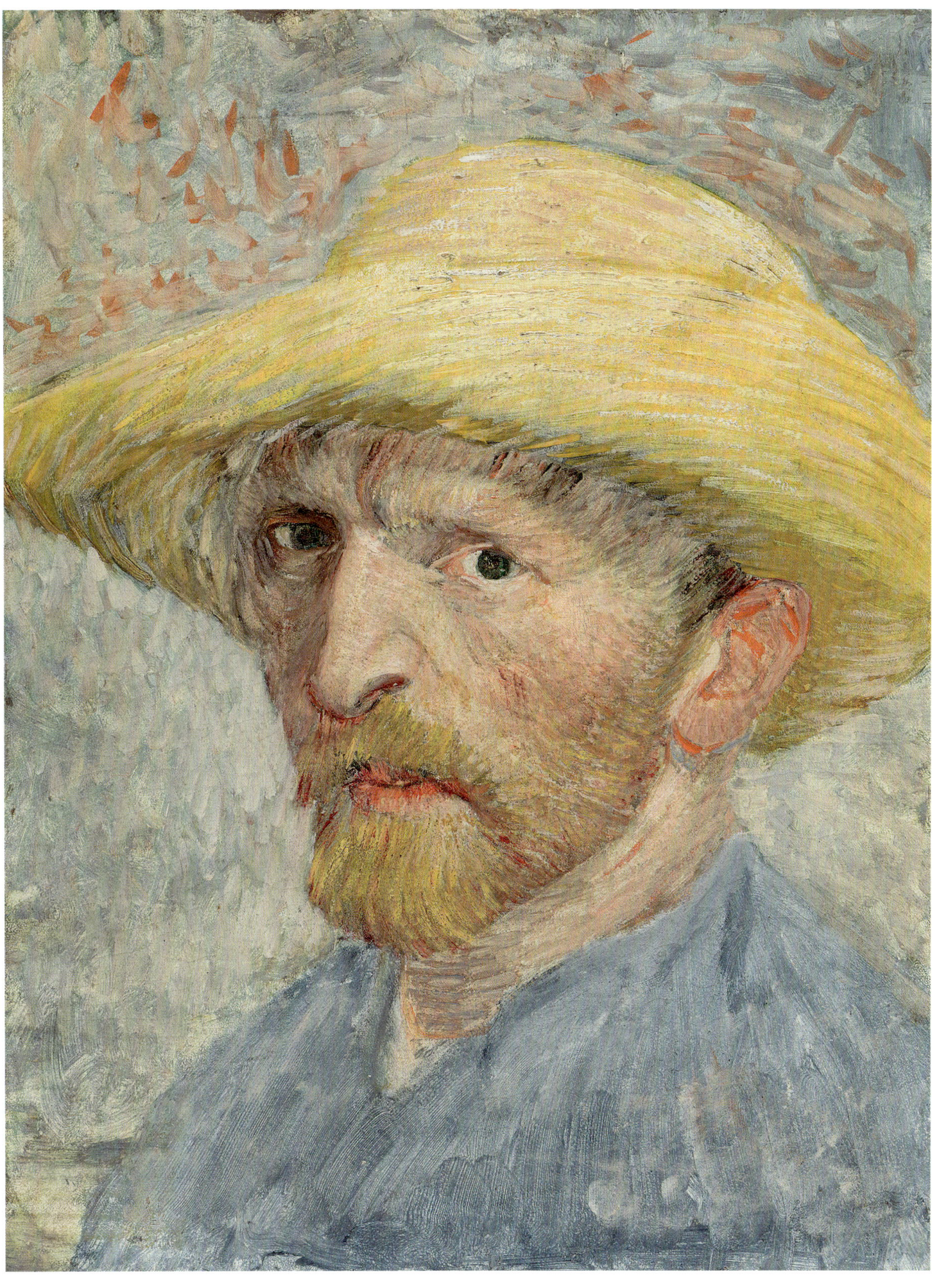

PLATE 44. *Self-Portrait*, 1887 (CAT. 25)

Aldis piqued French's interest, but the Chicago director signaled his reservations in a letter to the president of the board, Charles Hutchinson, written on a train home following his visit to the Armory Show in New York: "With regard to the desirability of bringing the exhibition to Chicago, my opinion has changed... I still think it would be reasonable and right for us to exhibit a single gallery.... But when it comes to bringing a large part of the exhibition here... I hesitate. We cannot make a joke of our guests."[7]

Despite the reluctance to take the whole exhibition, Chicago's desire to feature certain artists—including Van Gogh—was clear. Concerned that Boston's participation not affect Chicago's, Aldis advocated for the artist from the start. "Please be sure to give us a 'square deal' in this," he wrote to Kuhn. "We were first to ask to come in. Let us have our full half of Cézanne, Gaguin [*sic*], Van Gogh, Matisse, and Picasso, et al., which our students and our public here would not otherwise have a chance to see... Mr. Davies told me that the heart and genius of American Art were situated in the Middle West. Therefore, let's make 'em throb!"[8] And even though Director French did not seem to think fondly of the European modernists—and specifically judged Van Gogh to be one of the "eccentrics... actually unbalanced and insane, who really believe what they profess and practice"—he echoed Aldis, reiterating the desire to have "the more novel part of the exhibition... Matisse, Gauguin, Redon, Duchamp, Cézanne, Picasso, Van Gogh, Rousseau... and the rest of the well known and extraordinary foreigners."[9]

In the end all eighteen Van Gogh works included in the catalogue of the New York exhibition came to Chicago (see Stein, New York, fig. 3). Press—both positive and negative—abounded, especially since Chicago had the "advantage" of being able to anticipate the exhibition based on the reporting of the New York show. Although Van Gogh's appearance was overshadowed by the harsh criticism of Henri Matisse, the Cubists, and those among "the great circus of insurgent souls,"[10] progressive critics celebrated that America was finally being introduced to his work, along with that of Paul Cézanne and Paul Gauguin, "the three acknowledged masters whom the post-impressionists claim as the founders of their school."[11] A number of Van Goghs, especially the landscapes, prompted comment. "Hills at Arles" (F622; plate 14) was "much studied and wondered over" and visitors were said to be "arrested by its novel lines and treatment."[12] For other reviewers, "Van Gogh painted the hills at Arles as they were, are and shall be evermore," and revealed "Van Gogh's genius."[13] Figure paintings were also featured in the press: "Ball at Arles" (F547; plate 21), illustrated in the *Chicago Daily Tribune*, seemed to have "made the most impression on the public."[14] That same "patterned" painting, in addition to "the green 'Woman Reading' [F497; plate 46] and the 'Young Woman' portrait [F786; plate 18]" (a photo of which also appeared in the press), seemed, for another critic, to be "more experimental."[15]

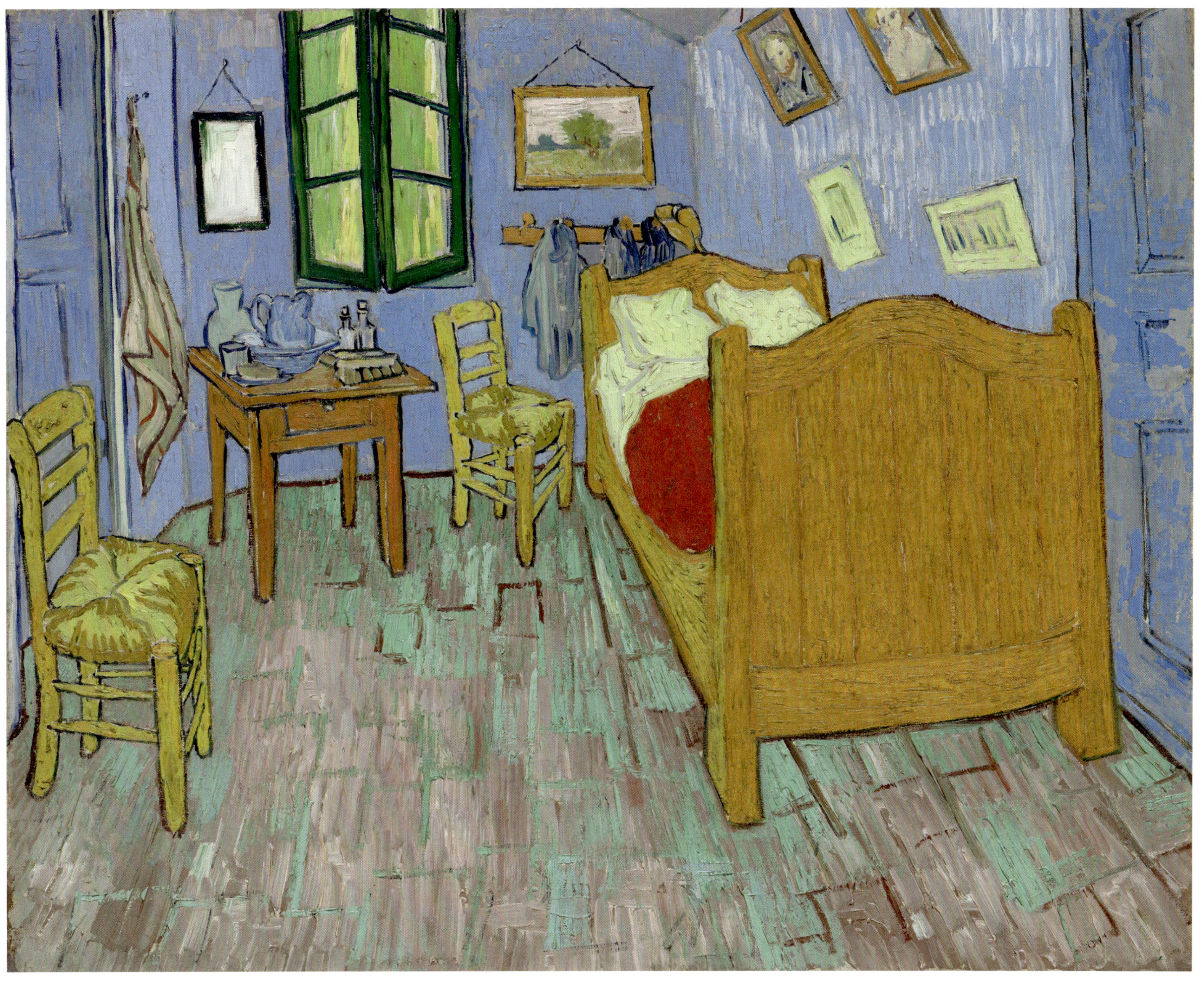

PLATE 45. *The Bedroom*, 1889 (CAT. 53)

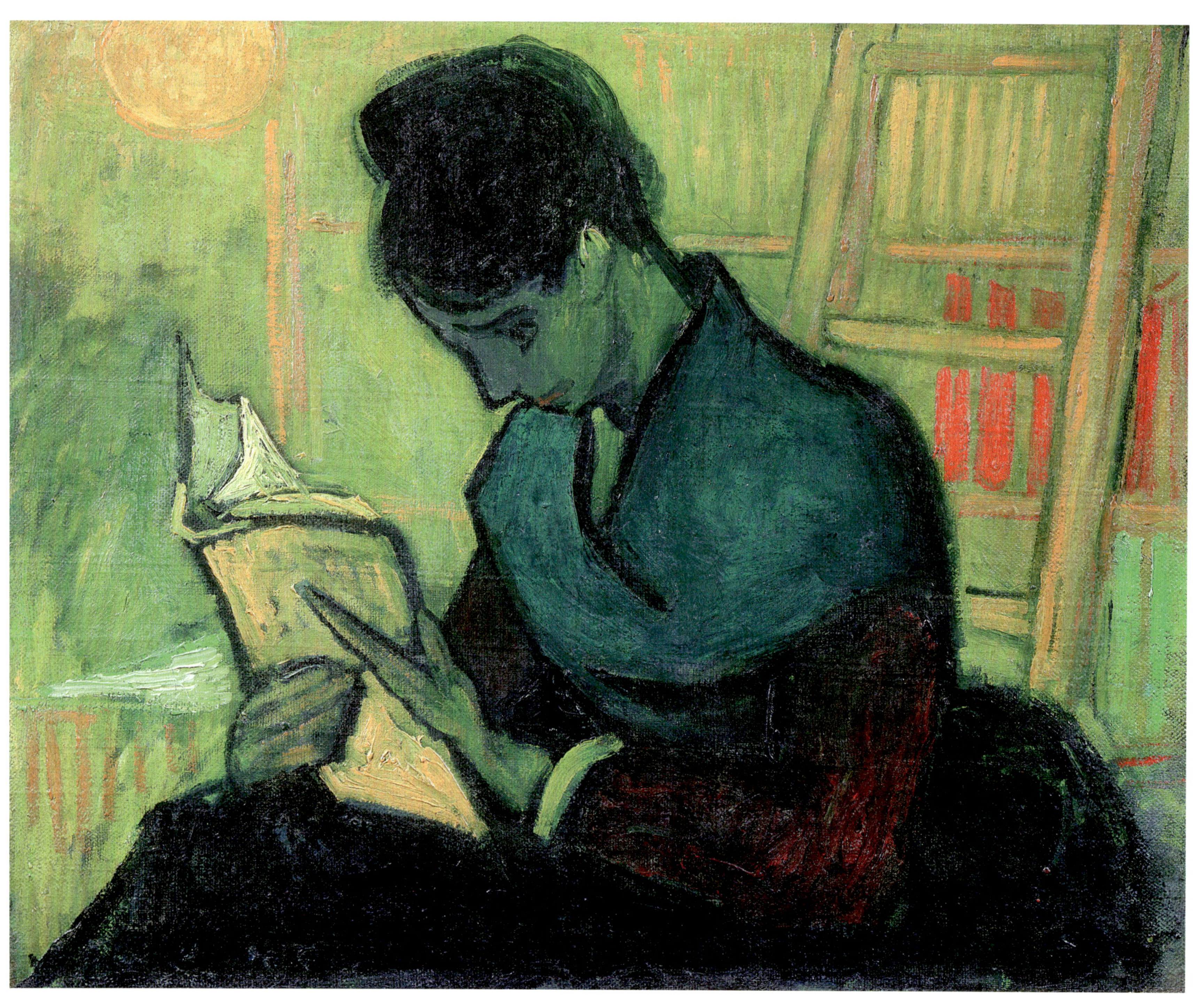

PLATE 46. *The Novel Reader*, 1888 (CAT. 39)

However, the artist's biography—especially his mental health—caught the attention of reviewers, perhaps even more than his art. For conservative critics and artists, it offered a way to further dismiss the avant-garde art in the exhibition by those who came after him. In a talk at the Art Institute, artist Charles Francis Browne declaimed that Van Gogh, Cézanne, and Gauguin "were much saner than their followers...[but] have been described as 'unbalanced, enthusiastic, unskilled, and possessing the zeal of martyrs.'"[16] About Van Gogh specifically, another critic reported that "his succession of works reveal a mind going it knows not whither."[17]

But there were also writers who, while not necessarily fond of Van Gogh's work, felt the need to provide a corrective to this narrative. Out of Chicago came one of the first substantial American reviews of Anthony M. Ludovici's English translation of a selection of the artist's letters. Following the Art Institute's presentation of the Armory Show, the review, published by Edward Hale in Chicago's progressive literary magazine *The Dial*, addressed the issue head-on: "The air is so full at present of utterances concerning Futurists, Cubists, Neo-Impressionists, and Post-Impressionists, that it seems wrong to add anything to the dust," he wrote. "Still we believe that...[a] reading of these letters will certainly do something to clear away the extravagances which now cloud the public mind."[18] Through Van Gogh's letters, as Hale explained to his readers, he found a man "now at the centre of the cyclonic duststorm," yet who "lived rather a simple, direct, straightforward kind of life, unconfused by the ideas of other people or by movements."[19] Although he opined that the artist "does not seem to have been able to paint anything very well," Hale attempted to give Van Gogh—the man—back his voice, and advocated for a look at his art through his own words and experiences rather than trying to view it in "the light of what has come to pass."[20]

Another Chicagoan, Arthur Jerome Eddy, would similarly call upon Van Gogh's letters as an antidote to those "critics and opponents of his work [that] have seized upon his madness as proof of lack of sanity in what he painted."[21] A lawyer, modern art collector, and fervent supporter of the Armory Show, Eddy tried his hand at shaping the discourse in his *Cubists and Post-Impressionism*, one of the earliest books on modern art to appear in the United States. He illustrated four paintings by Van Gogh and placed him within the group of artists, including Cézanne, Gauguin, Rousseau, and Matisse, that he argued were the leaders of Fauvism.[22] But despite his literary advocacy of Van Gogh and his importance for the art that would follow him, Eddy surprisingly never collected the artist's work. Eddy purchased a total of twenty-five works from the Armory Show's New York and Chicago venues, second only to famed New York collector John Quinn, but none were by Van Gogh. Although his collection changed, shifted, and grew into the hundreds, extant partial lists indicate that no Van Gogh (or Cézanne or Gauguin, for that matter) was ever part of it. It was perhaps because Eddy, at this point, was keen on supporting living artists, and he was especially interested in Wassily Kandinsky and the German Expressionists.[23] But it is also possible he never purchased Van Gogh because Quinn—considered to be a rival—already owned the artist's *Self-Portrait* (F268; plate 17) that was included in the Armory Show. Eddy surely wanted to develop a collection as distinct as possible from Quinn's, for he never wanted to do anything anyone else was doing.[24]

It would be a number of years until Chicago would see Van Gogh again, this time at the Arts Club of Chicago, an organization founded in 1916 in the wake of the Armory Show to bring to the city art that "had come up for exhibition and active discussion elsewhere" and was identified as "the Art of the 20th Century *in the making*."[25] It was largely due to the efforts of Rue Winterbotham Carpenter (Arts Club president, 1918–31) and Alice Roullier (chairman of its Exhibition Committee through the early 1940s) that avant-garde exhibitions were brought to Chicago in the days when modern art was still highly controversial.[26] And despite some failed early attempts—some in real time, some in retrospect—the Arts Club was key for the early exhibition of Van Gogh's work in the Midwest.

While it is possible Van Gogh was exhibited at the Arts Club earlier, its first known showing of a work attributed to the artist was in a group show of modern paintings and sculpture in December 1919.[27] The paintings purportedly came from New York's Bourgeois Galleries, and the lone work attributed to Van Gogh received scant press. However, one critic's reference to the "solid, coarse, realistic" still life and snide query, "whose soul is stirred by herrings and melon?" suggest that the painting was *Still Life: Melon, Fish, Jar* (see Stein, New York, fig. 9).[28] This work, now deemed inauthentic, had been on view previously in New York and would enter the collection of Chicagoans Helen Birch and Frederic Clay Bartlett in early 1921.[29]

There was further interest on the part of the Arts Club to exhibit works by Van Gogh in 1921, when Roullier considered taking an exhibition prepared by Katherine S. Dreier and the Société Anonyme, the New York art organization that worked to promote modern art in America. Roullier had received a list of modern paintings available for exhibition by way of American sculptor John Storrs, but she clarified her interest in the show very directly in a letter to the Société Anonyme: "We would not...be interested," she wrote, "unless we could have the big names represented—Matisse, Van Gogh, Picabia, Derain, Picasso, and Kandinsky."[30] Roullier doubled down on this request after hearing from Dreier that some of the works on her wish list might not be possible; although one Van Gogh was available—certainly this was Dreier's *Adeline Ravoux* (F786; plate 18)—the Matisse, André Derain, and Pablo Picasso loans were in question.[31] While the Arts Club was eager to host the exhibition, Roullier said it was "most necessary...to emphasize the big names." She continued: "We are a long ways from the east in all that pertains to modern art matters; the Arts Club is practically the only gallery open to things of this character."[32] But because of scheduling and a failure to come to terms on the checklist, Roullier graciously declined the exhibition.[33]

Roullier did secure a show, curated by New York critic Forbes Watson, for later that same year that suited the needs of the Arts Club. "Big names" were included in the fifty-nine works by American and "French" painters on view—

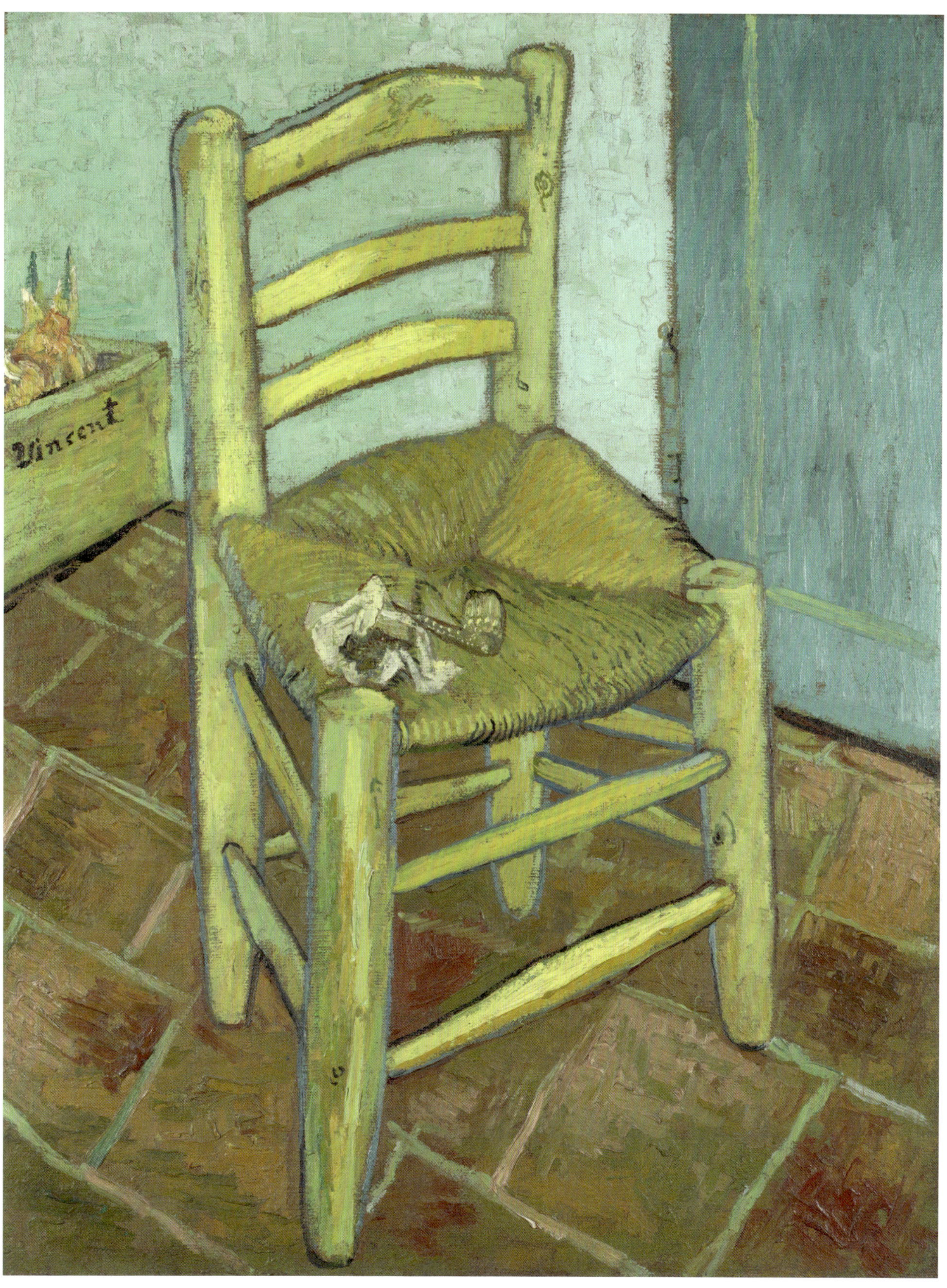

PLATE 47. *Van Gogh's Chair*, 1888 (CAT. 40)

including six Van Goghs—illustrating "the various steps in the development of modern painting."[34] Watson did not intend the exhibition to be sensational, explaining in the catalogue that "the time to 'shock the bourgeois' has passed, and the discerning know that the keynote of art will be found, not in schools or dates or propaganda, but in the vitality of the work itself."[35]

Nonetheless, the exhibition proved "provocative of discussion" and "an awakener that opens wide our eyes, makes us take a full, deep breath and be glad we are alive."[36] The Van Goghs were especially noted. In advance of the opening, Chicago society columnist Mme. X (pseudonym for Caroline Kirkland) reported that Van Gogh, the "rarest of modern painters to find in an exhibit today," would be included.[37] "All told," Hi Simons wrote, "Chicago has not seen in all the last ten years so numerous nor so various works by him as are here together."[38]

The six Van Goghs came from the Van Gogh family collection and had been part of the artist's first American retrospective at the Montross Gallery the previous year (see Stein, Appendix, p. 89).[39] Three paintings received especially glowing reviews, even from Chicago's more conservative critics: "The Plow" (F632; fig. 1), for example, was "a powerful piece of realism, painted strongly and with feeling" and played as a "foil" to the "quaint" Picasso landscape (fig. 2) in the adjacent room; "The Chair" (F498; plate 47) showed "Van Gogh's power in romancing the unromanceable."[40] "The Postman" (F436)—"fulsome with beauty"—was additionally noted for its "gusto."[41] The exhibition was also a success with artists, like Raymond Jonson, who sent his congratulations: "It makes one feel that after all there is a little leak, in the prison wall of this city, where fresh air, sunshine and life can get in."[42] But despite the accolades, none of the Van Goghs in the exhibition sold.[43]

FIG. 1 *Snow-Covered Field with a Harrow (after Millet)* (F632), 1890. Oil on canvas, 28⅜ × 36¼ in. (72.1 × 92 cm). Van Gogh Museum, Amsterdam (Vincent van Gogh Foundation).

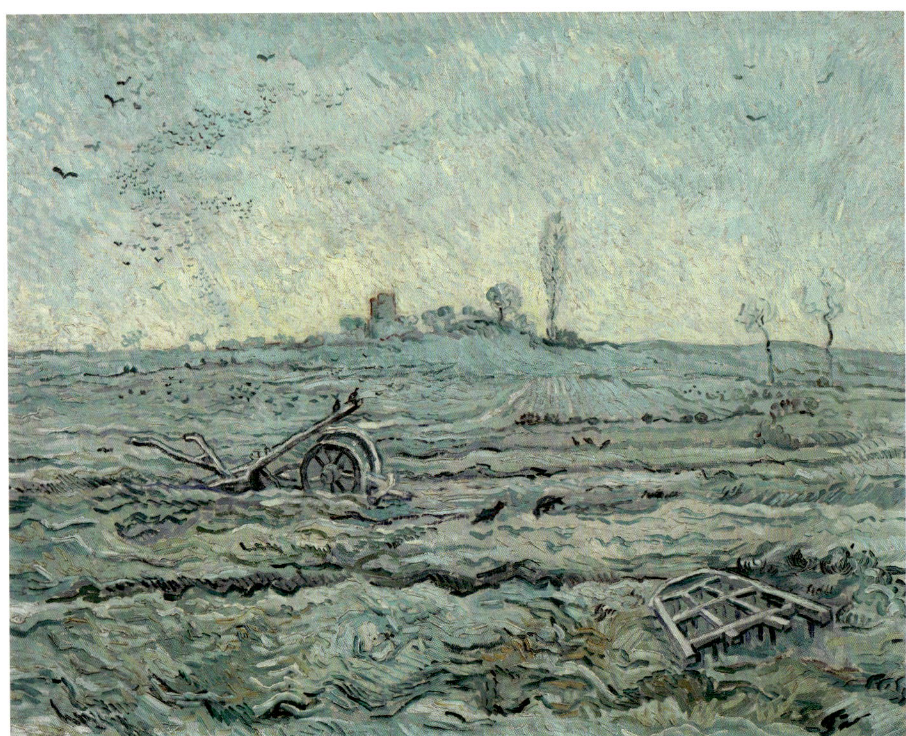

Detroit's Courage

In the fall of 1921, Midwestern cities were following the controversy surrounding the Metropolitan Museum of Art's *Loan Exhibition of Impressionist and Post-Impressionist Paintings*. "The exhibit is termed degenerate," wrote conservative Chicago critic Eleanor Jewett, "and the painters of the canvases are relegated to the class of the insane" by certain physicians whose claims, she reported, "are sustained by the New York public in a pamphlet denouncing Gauguin, Van Gogh, Toulouse-Lautrec, and other cubists, tubists, and futurists."[44] In Detroit, the pamphlet was discussed in further detail, and the press noted that at least three of the painters whose works were in the "mooted exhibition" were represented on the walls of the Detroit Institute of Arts: Pierre-Auguste Renoir, Camille Pissarro, and Claude Monet.[45] Perhaps it was this commentary that stoked the museum's interest in acquiring more of these controversial artists included in the Metropolitan Museum's exhibition. Just a few months later, at the January 30–31, 1922 auction of the Dikran Kelekian collection of modern art, the Detroit museum would purchase works by Davies, Derain, Raoul Dufy (plate 48), Matisse (plate 49), and Van Gogh (F526; plate 44).

Kelekian's modern art collection was widely known and had been very visible in the lead-up to the auction. Van Gogh's *Self-Portrait* (F526; plate 44) and *Women Picking Olives* (F655; fig. 3) were featured in an exhibition at the Brooklyn Museum in 1921; works by other artists were shown that year at the Metropolitan Museum and the Arts Club of Chicago.[46] The collection was also on free public view at the American Art Galleries beginning January 24 until January 30, the first day of the sale.[47] Publicity abounded, and individual works were discussed. *Self-Portrait*, for example, was touted by the *American Art News* as "one of the finest things in the collection and a superb example of [Van Gogh's] art."[48]

FIG. 2 Pablo Picasso (Spanish, 1881–1973), *Landscape with Dead and Live Trees*, 1919. Oil on canvas, 19 7/16 × 25 3/4 in. (49.4 × 65.4 cm). Bridgestone Museum of Art, Tokyo.

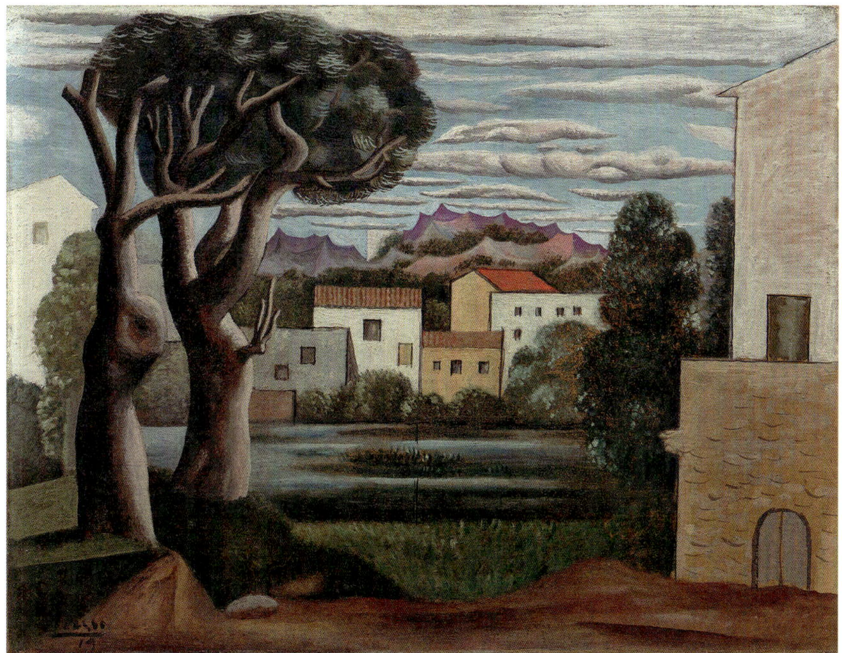

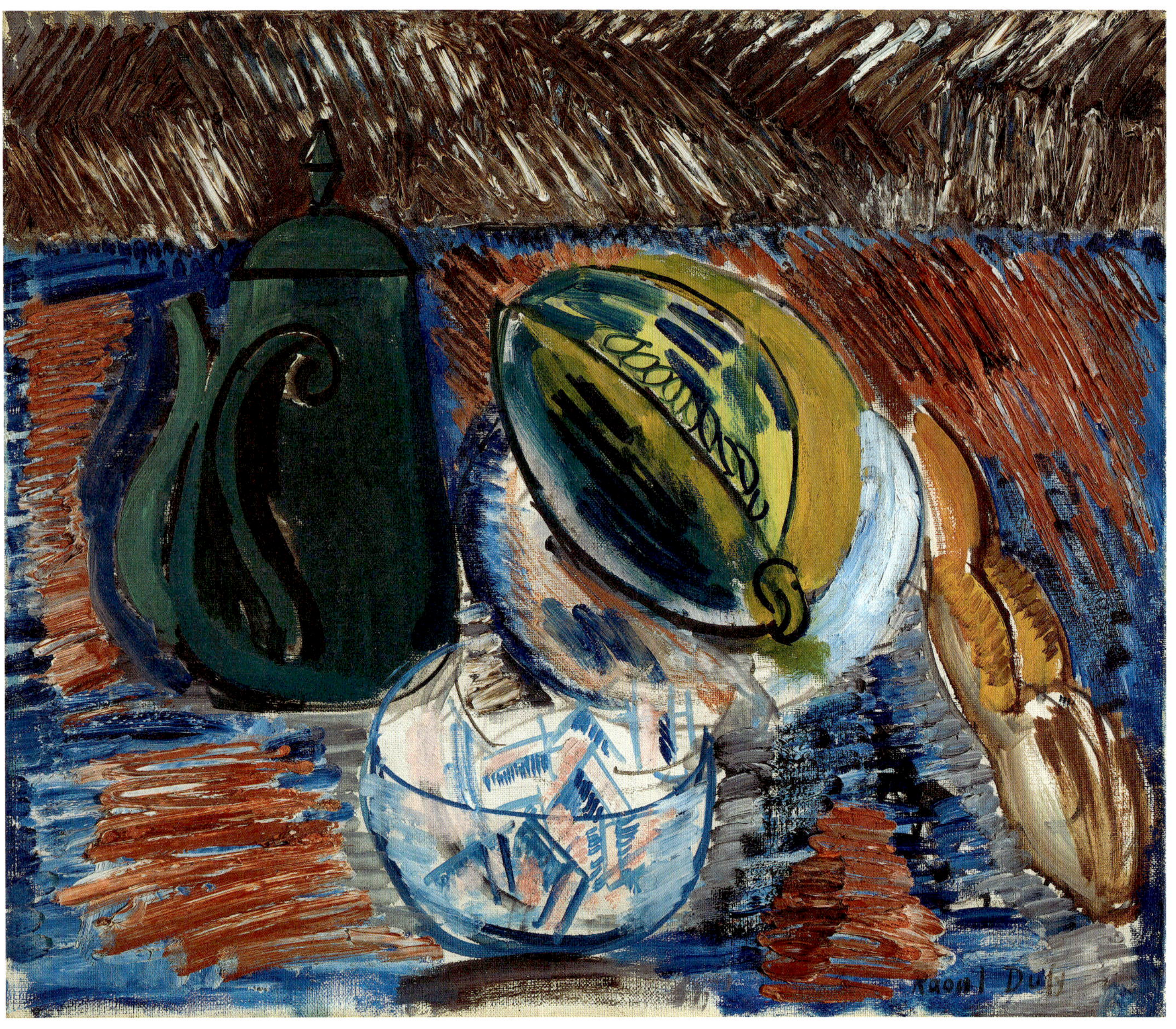

PLATE 48. Raoul Dufy (French, 1877–1953), *Still Life*, c. 1914 (CAT. 78)

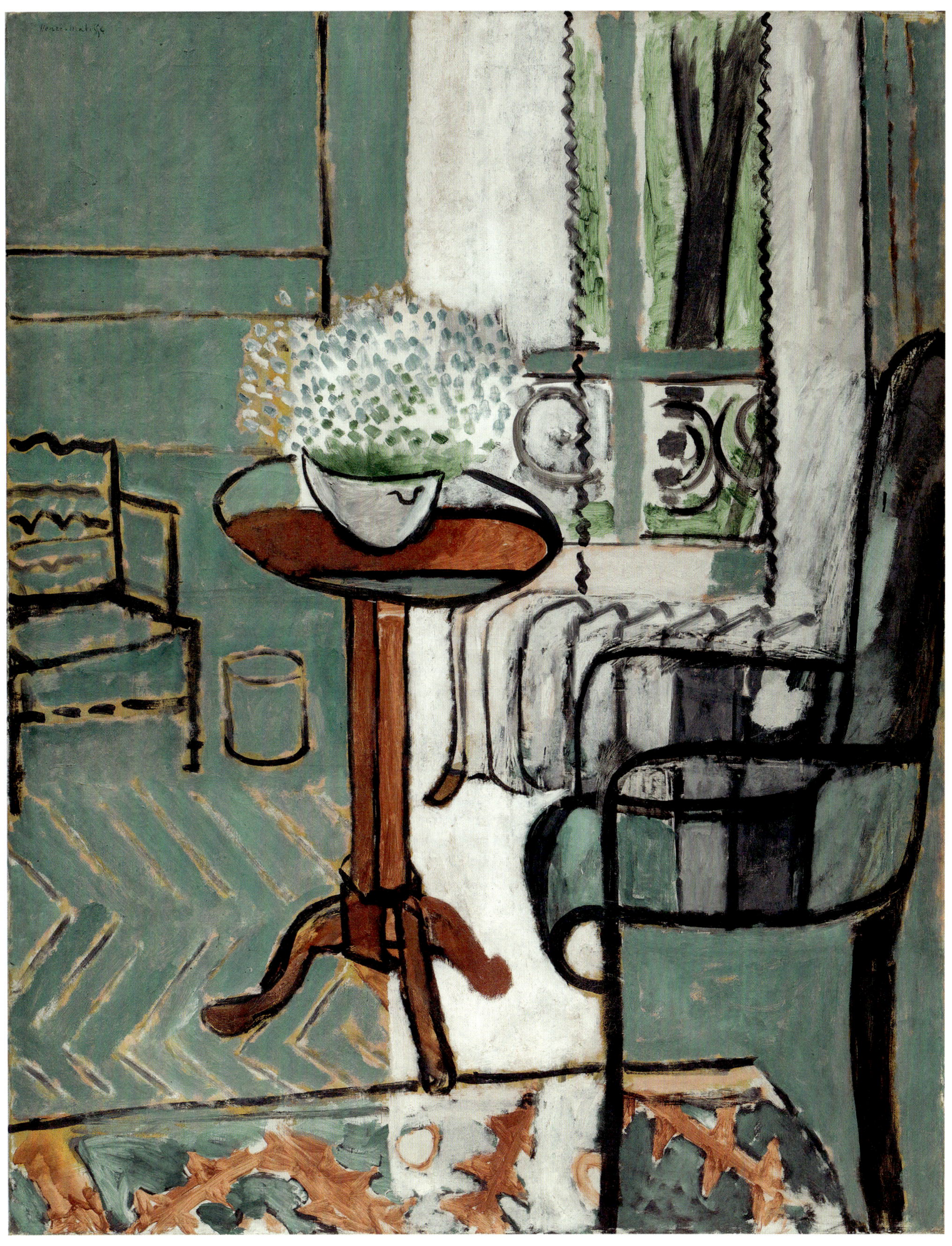

PLATE 49. Henri Matisse (French, 1869–1954), *The Window*, 1916 (CAT. 79)

Along with the hype, however, was concern that Americans would not attend and bid. The editor of *The Arts* worried that France and Germany would be more competitive than the Americans and that the "masterpieces" would return to Europe.[49] But Americans did show up and with "more enthusiasm…than [had] been seen for a long time at a sale of paintings in New York," and "everybody in New York art circles attended."[50] Among the buyers were three American public museums, the Metropolitan Museum of Art, the Brooklyn Museum, and the Detroit Institute of Arts, which was, according to one critic, "the most courageous, for it dared" to buy Van Gogh's "notable" *Self-Portrait* (F526; plate 44), the first painting by the artist to be purchased for an American public museum collection.[51]

Although newspapers reported that Ralph H. Booth, president of the Arts Commission of the City of Detroit, purchased the works on behalf of the museum, Wilhelm (William) Valentiner, art adviser to the Detroit Institute of Arts (and its director beginning in 1924), is often mistakenly credited for the accomplishment.[52] Valentiner had begun in 1921 to advise the museum in its quest to build the collection for an anticipated new building. And he was a Van Gogh enthusiast, having taken an interest in the artist well before he moved from Germany to America in 1908 to become curator of decorative arts at the Metropolitan Museum of Art. According to his reminiscences, he acquired a Van Gogh drawing in Holland that he brought with him to America (it was lost during World War I), and he also

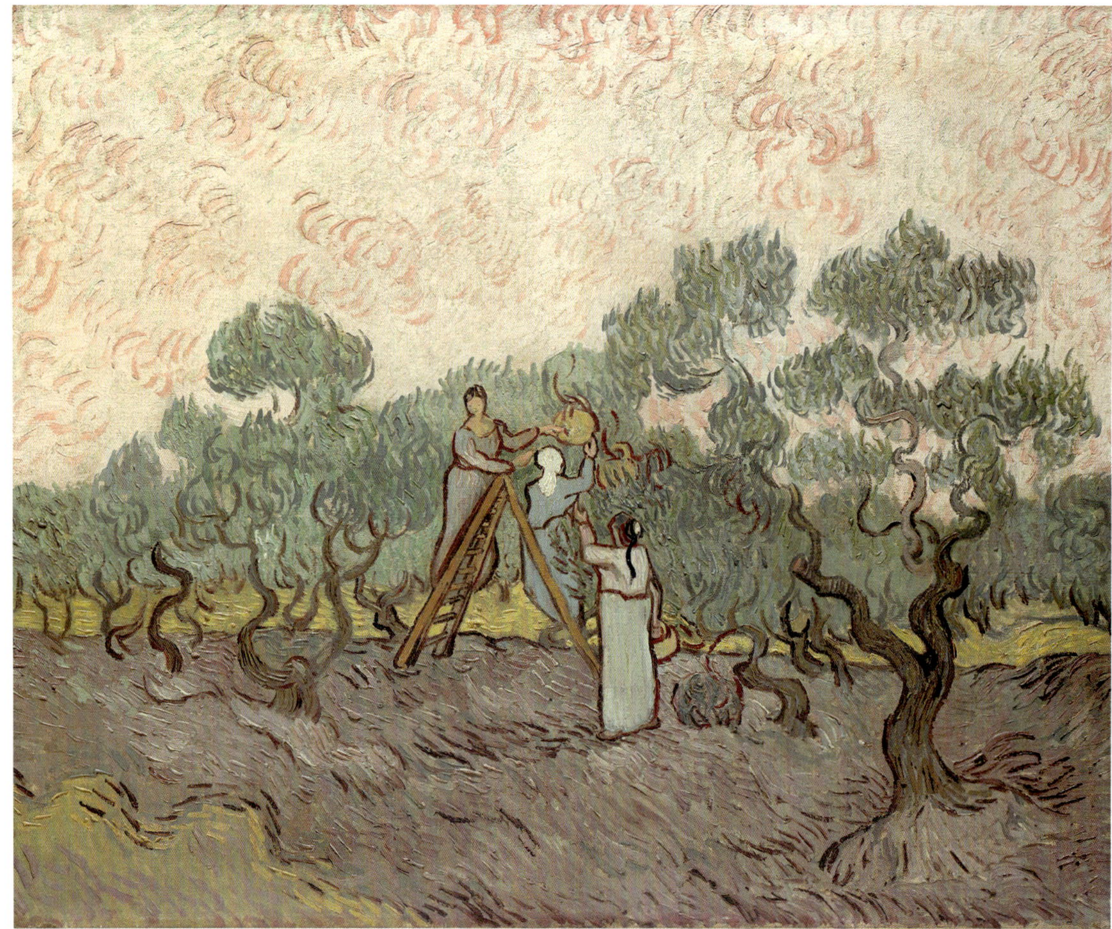

FIG. 3 *Women Picking Olives* (F655), 1889. Oil on canvas, 28⅝ × 36 in. (72.7 × 91.4 cm). The Metropolitan Museum of Art, New York.

recounted his unsuccessful efforts to promote Van Gogh's early Dutch drawings with collectors and museum directors in Munich and Frankfurt.[53] Valentiner's interest in Van Gogh continued in America. Letters exchanged as early as February 1912 between Jo van Gogh-Bonger, custodian of the Van Gogh family collection, and their Dutch dealer Artz & De Bois suggest an ongoing conversation about organizing an exhibition of the artist's work in America for 1913.[54] No such exhibition seems to have come to pass—perhaps because of the staging of the Armory Show that year.

But a note from Valentiner to Booth two months after the Kelekian auction confirms Booth *did* act independently of Valentiner. "I congratulate the Museum," Valentiner remarked. "It seems very courageous to buy works by these remarkable masters—especially Van Gogh seems to me one of the great ones. I hope it will be appreciated by the people in Detroit if not now, I do not doubt, some time in the future."[55] Other congratulations rolled in. Forbes Watson was "delighted" to learn that Booth had bought the Van Gogh for the museum, for his "knowledge and courage are not only going to help Detroit but [will] awaken many other museums which have gone to sleep and stimulate the whole situation."[56] Worcester Art Museum Director Raymond Wyer echoed Watson's sentiments about the Van Gogh: "I congratulate you for your courage...such acquisitions will bring distinction to Detroit" (see Chudzicka, fig. 8).[57]

Archival records, however, suggest that the Detroit museum—perhaps with guidance from Valentiner—was on the hunt for a Van Gogh much earlier. Representatives from the museum hoped to visit the 1920 Van Gogh retrospective exhibition at the Montross Gallery before it opened to the public, although it is not known whether the visit took place and nothing was acquired.[58] Discussion was also underway with other galleries about possible Van Gogh acquisitions. Documentation in the Thannhauser Gallery archives suggests that possibly before August 25, 1921, the museum was specifically looking for a Van Gogh landscape.[59] As well, in that same year, Berlin gallery Van Diemen & Co. offered the museum Van Gogh's *Landscape with Wheelbarrow* (F1100; plate 50). It was only *after* the Kelekian sale that Detroit responded to the offer, stating: "At this time we are so heavily in debt on account of recent purchases that we are unable to consider any new accessions, but I am very glad to have brought to our attention such important things."[60] Nonetheless, Booth continued his search for additional Van Gogh works—whether for the museum or for his personal collection. Notable Van Goghs offered by Thannhauser, for example, but that were passed over included *Sunflowers* (F375); *Portrait of Joseph Roulin* (F436); *L'Arlésienne, Madame Ginoux* (F543; plate 41); and *Bank of the Oise at Auvers* (F798; plate 7).[61] The museum was fortunate to receive another version of *Portrait of Postman Roulin* (F433; plate 51) from Mr. and Mrs. Walter Buhl Ford II in 1996, and *Bank of the Oise at Auvers* (F798; plate 7) ultimately made its way into the collection through Robert H. Tannahill, who purchased the work in 1935 from the Knoedler Gallery and bequeathed it to the museum in 1970.

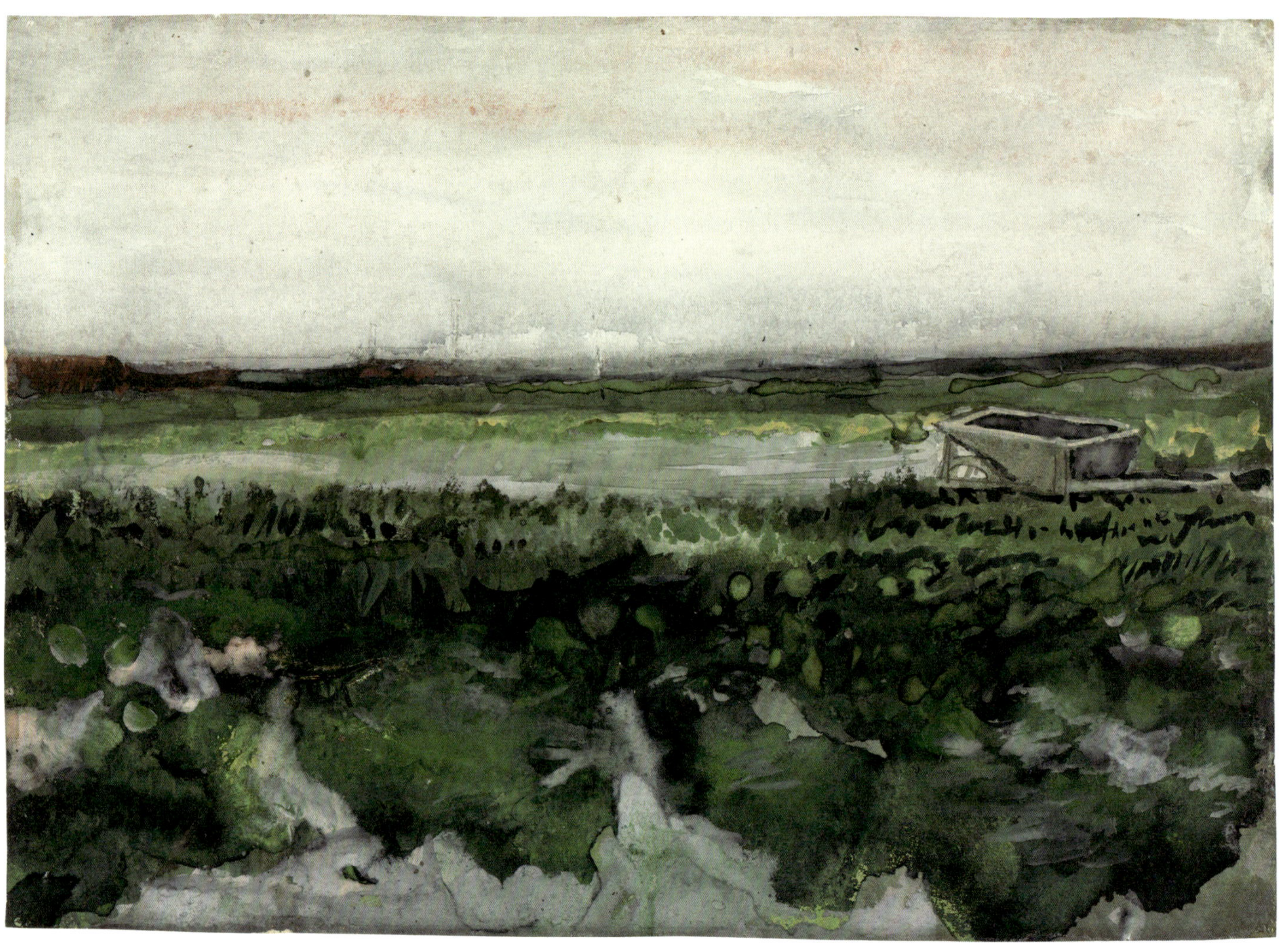

PLATE 50. *Landscape with Wheelbarrow*, 1883 (CAT. 7)

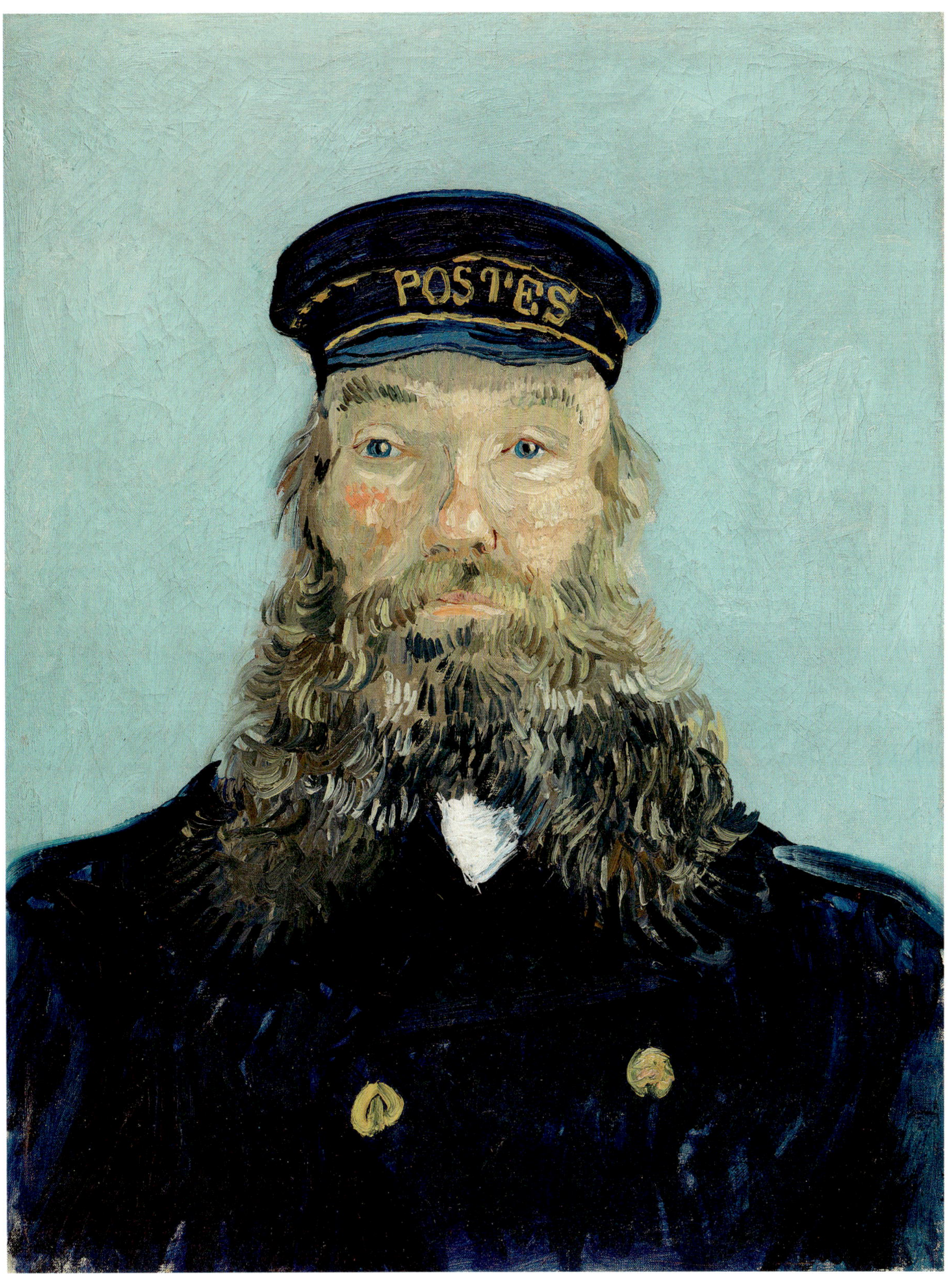

PLATE 51. *Portrait of Postman Roulin*, 1888 (CAT. 34)

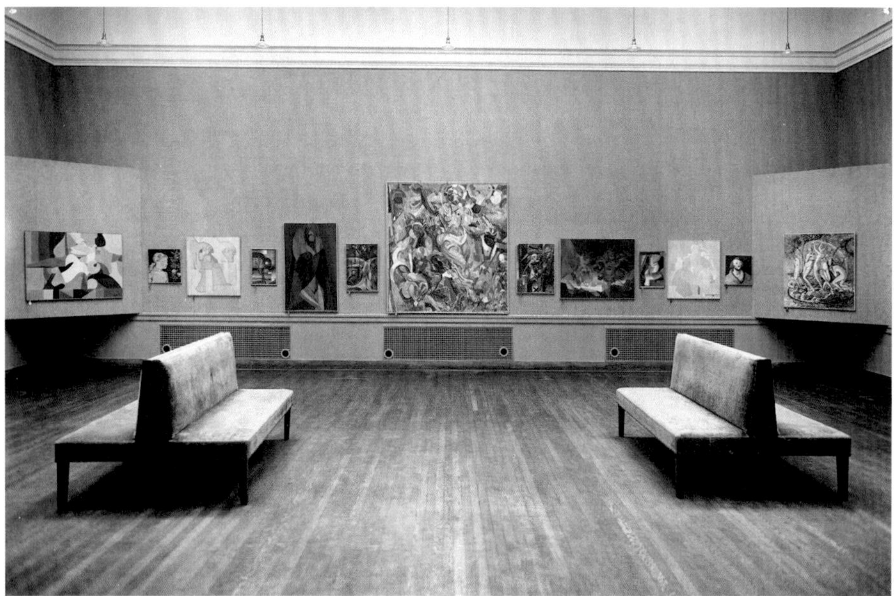

FIG. 4 Installation view of the Société Anonyme exhibition, Worcester Art Museum, Worcester, Massachusetts, November–December 1921, featuring *Adeline Ravoux* (F786; plate 18) second from the left.

Van Gogh's *Self-Portrait* was first installed in the museum among the Old Master paintings. The press remarked that even though it was a small canvas, it "holds its own."[62] Most local commentary, however, was enveloped in the chatter surrounding an exhibition of modern art to be held at the museum in March 1922—the same one organized by Dreier and the Société Anonyme that had been offered unsuccessfully to the Arts Club of Chicago and numerous other museums.[63] Detroit showed interest in the exhibition as early as June 1921, but did not confirm its participation until the end of December.[64] The museum's delay was certainly because administrators wanted to hear feedback from the Worcester Art Museum about their experience hosting the exhibition, which included works by (mostly) living avant-garde European and American artists (fig. 4). In response to Detroit's inquiry about the exhibition, Worcester director Raymond Wyer advised: "[It] is quite good of its kind... I was able to have it because the only people to be considered were the Trustees, we being independent of the city. If you show it in Detroit I shall consider you very courageous.... There is no compromising in the exhibition and that is an important point."[65] Shortly after receiving this message, Detroit sent word to the Société Anonyme that they wanted to secure the same exhibition shown at the Worcester "in its entirety."[66]

But because Detroiters had not had the opportunity to experience any of the newer artistic movements after Impressionism, the Detroit Institute of Arts expanded its presentation to include some local artists as well as recent acquisitions, including the new Van Gogh.[67] The museum also sought to borrow additional Van Goghs as well as works by artists including Cézanne, Matisse, Henri de Toulouse-Lautrec, Picasso, Maurice de Vlaminck, and Derain, in order to connect the dots between Impressionism and the more recent works from the Société Anonyme. To this end, the museum reached out to private collectors, dealers, and museums including the Minneapolis Institute of Arts, where Russell Plimpton, the new director and a great supporter of modern art, had shown two Van Gogh paintings—"Head of a Boy" (F537; plate 15) and "The Farmhouse at Auvers" (F623), borrowed from New York dealer Marius de Zayas—in their *Modern French Paintings* exhibition the previous fall.[68]

In the end Detroit secured just three works listed as Van Gogh in the exhibition: the recently purchased *Self-Portrait*; the Bartletts' still life painting (now considered inauthentic; see Stein, New York, fig. 9); and Dreier's "Adolescence" (F786; plate 18), described in the press as "a well-known head of a young girl...pale against a dark background."[69] The Van Goghs were exhibited in the first (and smaller)

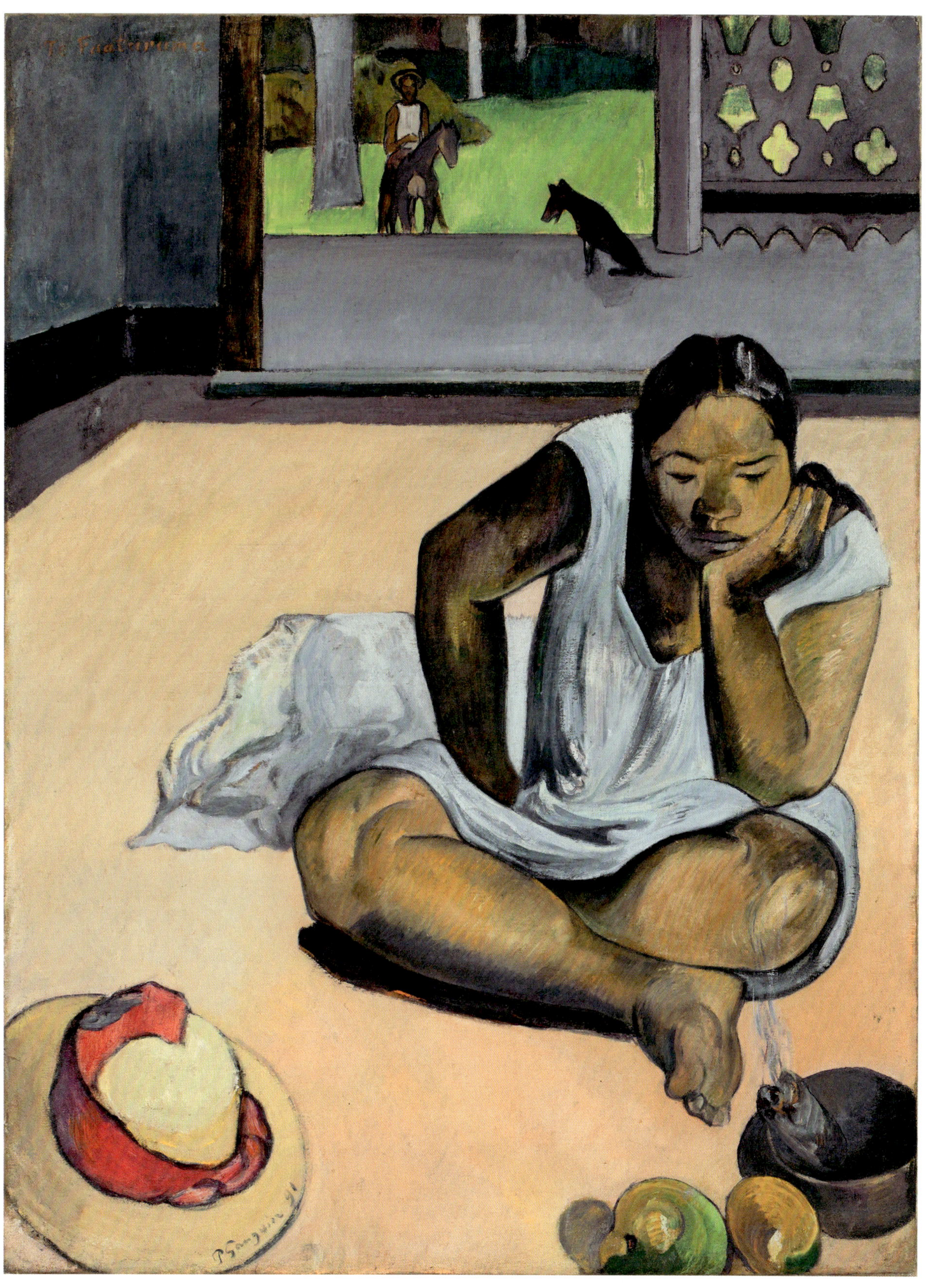

PLATE 52. Paul Gauguin (French, 1848–1903), *The Brooding Woman (Te Faaturuma)*, 1891 (CAT. 75)

of two galleries along with two Gauguins (including one from the Worcester Art Museum; plate 52), two works listed as Cézanne, three Matisses (Detroit's recent acquisition was included; plate 49), and "others who are either really fine artists or who represent the saner and more skilled section of the extremists."[70]

It was the artists in the second room of the exhibition—"the wild men"—juxtaposed with African sculpture "as if to show one of the influences of the extremists," that received the harshest criticism.[71] American artist Joseph Stella took the brunt of the negative commentary; his monumental *Battle of Lights, Coney Island, Mardi Gras* (plate 53) was singled out for its incomprehensibility.[72] Other works also drew bewildered responses: Man Ray's contribution (fig. 5), for one critic, looked like "a discarded mattress, ripped down the middle," while Dadaist Georges Ribemont-Dessaignes's painting (plate 54) resembled "a wireless apparatus in difficulty, together with a couple of tooth brushes, a ratchet and a pair of pliers thrown in to make the significance more significant."[73]

Despite these comments, the reaction to the exhibition on the ground was surprisingly subdued. One reporter commented: "We loitered among the Post-Impressionists on the opening day of the bizarre exhibit at the Art Institute listening for disgusted comments and looking for startled expressions. We heard and saw neither. Mostly the throng—the gallery was crowded—went about from picture to picture with puzzled, disappointed faces. They took it all so seriously and seemed to be trying so hard to understand."[74] Another observed: "Detroiters are visiting the Institute of Arts these days who never heard of the place before or, if they had, never imagined they would voluntarily plunge into such an abyss of boredom. The reason for this local renaissance is that the word has gone forth that there are goings-on in the galleries—that walls are shrieking, that the post-impressionists, dadists [*sic*], futurists, cubists, simultanists, and otherists have plastered...their propaganda and that if you go inside you will be able to see just how crazy an artist can be." The reporter continued: "The audiences have so

FIG. 5 Man Ray (Emmanuel Radnitzky, American, 1890–1976), *The Rope Dancer Accompanies Herself with Her Shadows*, 1916. Oil on canvas, 52 × 73⅜ in. (132.1 × 186.4 cm). The Museum of Modern Art, New York.

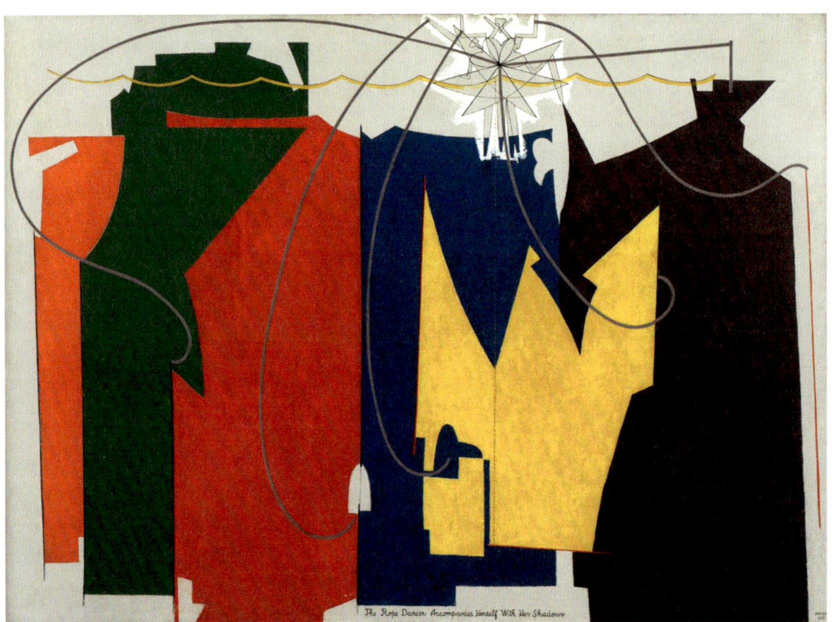

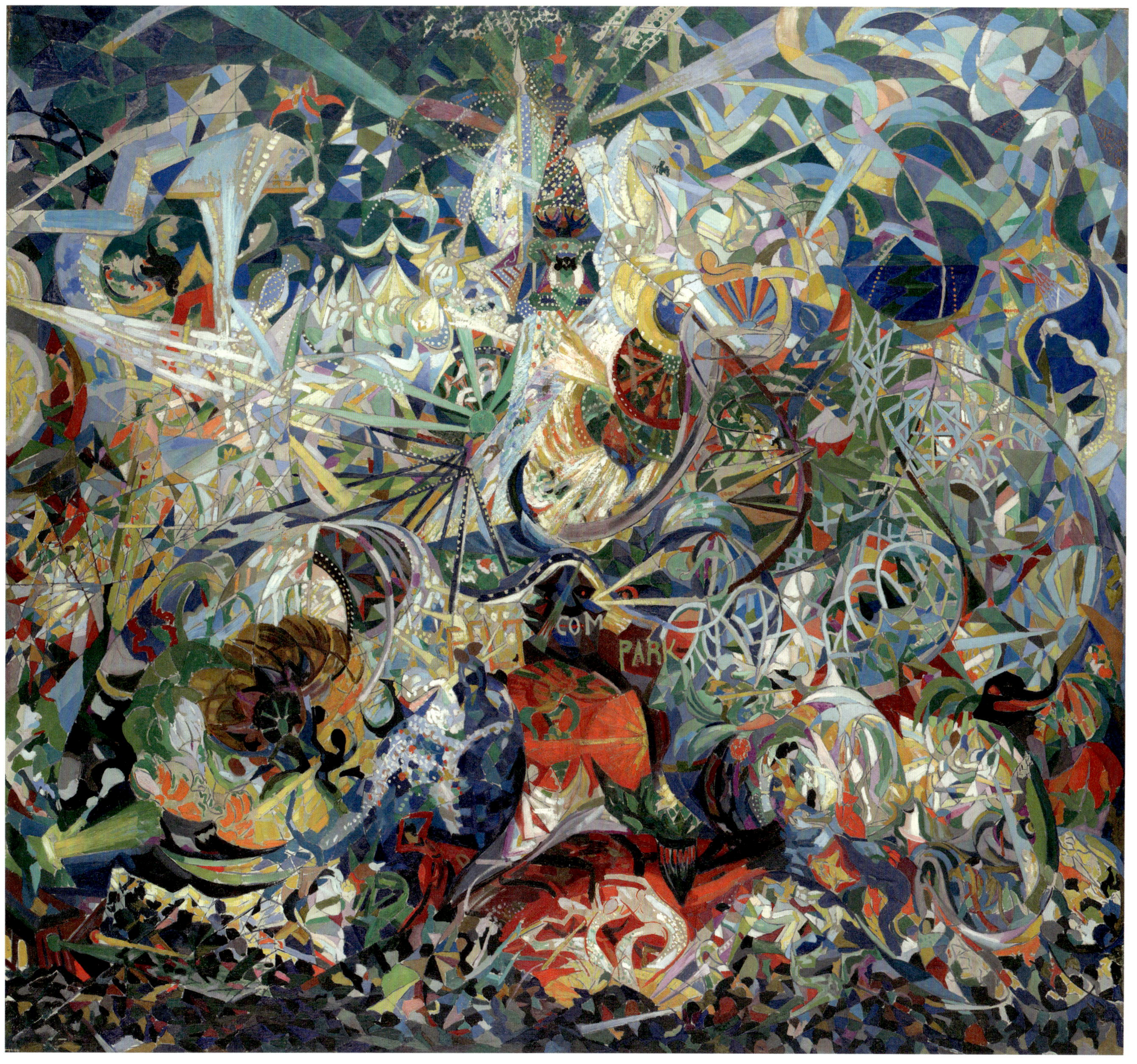

PLATE 53. Joseph Stella (American, 1877–1946), *Battle of Lights, Coney Island, Mardi Gras*, 1913–14 (CAT. 77)

far consisted of 99 per cent utter amazement, 1 per cent of humorless people who think the taxpayers' money is being wasted and one man who announced that he understood what it was all about. But he was led out quietly without doing any harm."[75]

It was perhaps this response that encouraged the museum to exhibit more modern pictures—including five additional Van Goghs—the following year. The paintings were part of the touring exhibition of the Goudstikker collection of Dutch and Flemish pictures from the fifteenth to the twentieth century, which came to America under the auspices of the Netherlands-America Affiliation and traveled to St. Louis, Cleveland, Detroit, and New York.[76] The Van Goghs, however, were not part of the collection, but were lent by the Van Gogh family because Jo van Gogh-Bonger strongly felt that "modern Dutch art cannot be represented without Van Gogh."[77] Although she asked art dealer Newman E. Montross to contribute loans from the stock she had entrusted to him in New York (see Stein, Appendix, p. 91n24), archival documentation and details in the catalogue for the Detroit venue as well as local press indicated that the paintings on view in the touring exhibition were likely new works shipped from the Netherlands (including F631, fig. 6; F320; F358; and possibly F819, plate 58).[78]

Moreover, each venue crafted their own checklist based on preference and available space. Evidence suggests that only Detroit and New York included the five Van Goghs, or, for that matter, any modern art at all. That St. Louis and Cleveland did not choose to include modern pictures is perhaps why Goudstikker, when pitching the show to Detroit, especially touted them. Certainly because of its recent acquisition and exhibition history, he knew the museum was "very much interested in modern art too."[79]

Expanding Midwestern (Private and Public) Collections

In 1926 paintings by Van Gogh would enter the permanent collection of a second public, encyclopedic, and notably Midwestern museum: the Art Institute of Chicago. This time the acquisition came as a gift—from Frederic Clay Bartlett in honor of his late wife, Helen Birch (1883–1925). The original proposal included three works listed under Van Gogh's name: *Still Life: Melon, Fish, Jar* (acquired by the Bartletts in 1921; Stein, New York, fig. 9); *Madame Roulin Rocking the Cradle (La Berceuse)* (F506; acquired 1923); and *Terrace and Observation Deck at the Moulin de Blute-Fin, Montmartre* (F272; acquired 1924; plate 16).[80] A fourth work, the iconic *The Bedroom* (F484; acquired 1926; plate 45), was added shortly thereafter.[81] The Helen Birch Bartlett Memorial Collection contains what are now considered to be major Post-Impressionist and modern masterpieces, although reportedly the gift was accepted by only a narrow vote.[82]

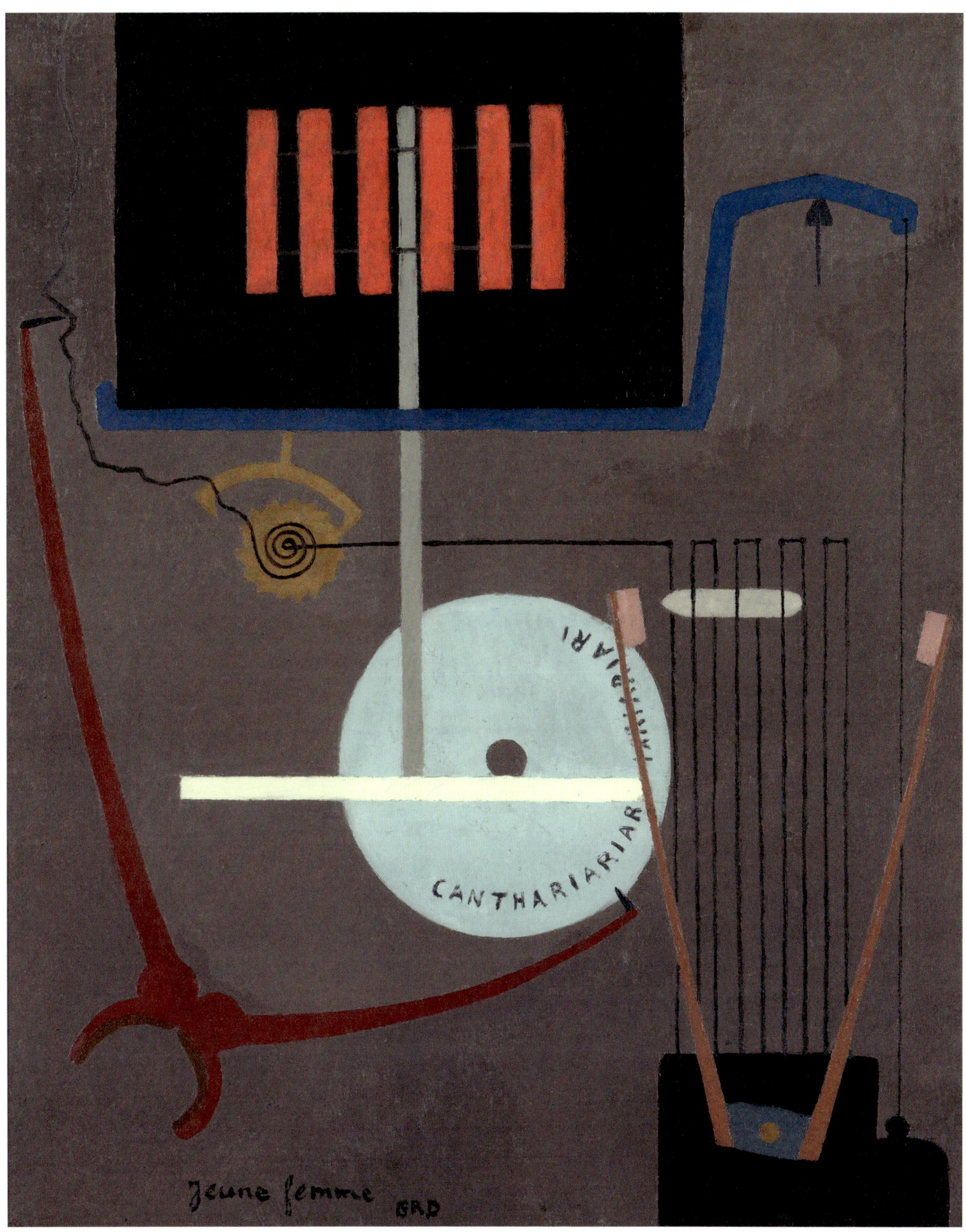

PLATE 54. Georges Ribemont-Dessaignes (French, 1884–1974), *Young Woman*, 1919 (CAT. 80)

The collection had been on view multiple times in various stages before it was installed at the museum in May 1926 following approval of the gift. Its initial showing in the fall of 1923 included *Madame Roulin Rocking the Cradle (La Berceuse)* (F506; for a similar work, see plate 22); about this work, one contemporary critic expressed "dread."[83] And while the Art Institute's newsletter encouraged its readers to visit the loan show, it also recalled the "tremendously shocked" and "thoroughly outraged" visitors to the 1913 Armory Show and remarked that "since then the public has softened very little toward post-impressionism."[84] Perhaps for this reason, the author carefully created a distance between Bartlett and the works he collected, noting: he has "acquired some of the canvases, not because he is a convert to the revolutionary theories of the post-impressionists, but because he wished to make a thorough study of their methods first hand."[85] Bartlett himself was an academically trained artist and, coincidentally, had an exhibition at the Montross Gallery in January 1921, immediately after

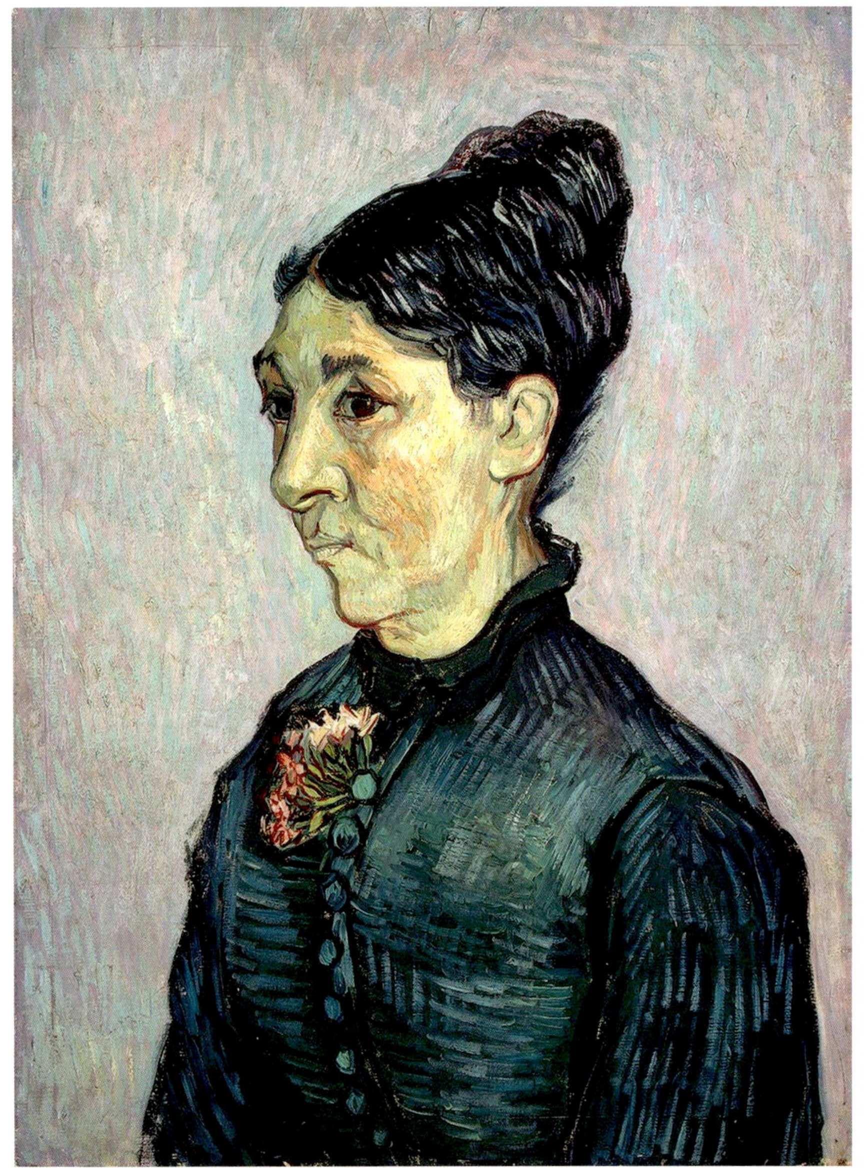

FIG. 6 *Portrait of Jeanne Trabuc* (F631), 1889. Oil on canvas, 25¼ × 19¼ in. (64 × 49 cm). Hermitage Museum, St. Petersburg.

Van Gogh's retrospective there. And while his own work did not incorporate the bold character of Post-Impressionist art which he once, self-admittedly, thought was "absurd," he came to understand and appreciate it.[86]

By 1924, when their collection was exhibited a second time at the Art Institute, the Bartletts were thinking about making it a permanent gift, "if it be found acceptable to the taste of the day."[87] It was becoming more well known, and other institutions began to request the collection for loan.[88] In 1925 it traveled to the Minneapolis Institute of Arts and the Boston Art Club, as well as once again to the Art Institute. The subsequent gift in 1926 was publicized widely, and Bartlett received many congratulatory letters, including one from Paul J. Sachs, who had trained numerous museum professionals in his Museum Course at Harvard. "I know of no room anywhere which gives one a better idea of the modern movement than the room that you have created," he conveyed. "I think that all of us are very much in your debt."[89]

FIG. 7 *The Park of Saint Paul's Hospital* (F640), 1889. Oil on canvas, 25½ × 19¼ in. (64.5 × 49 cm). Private Collection.

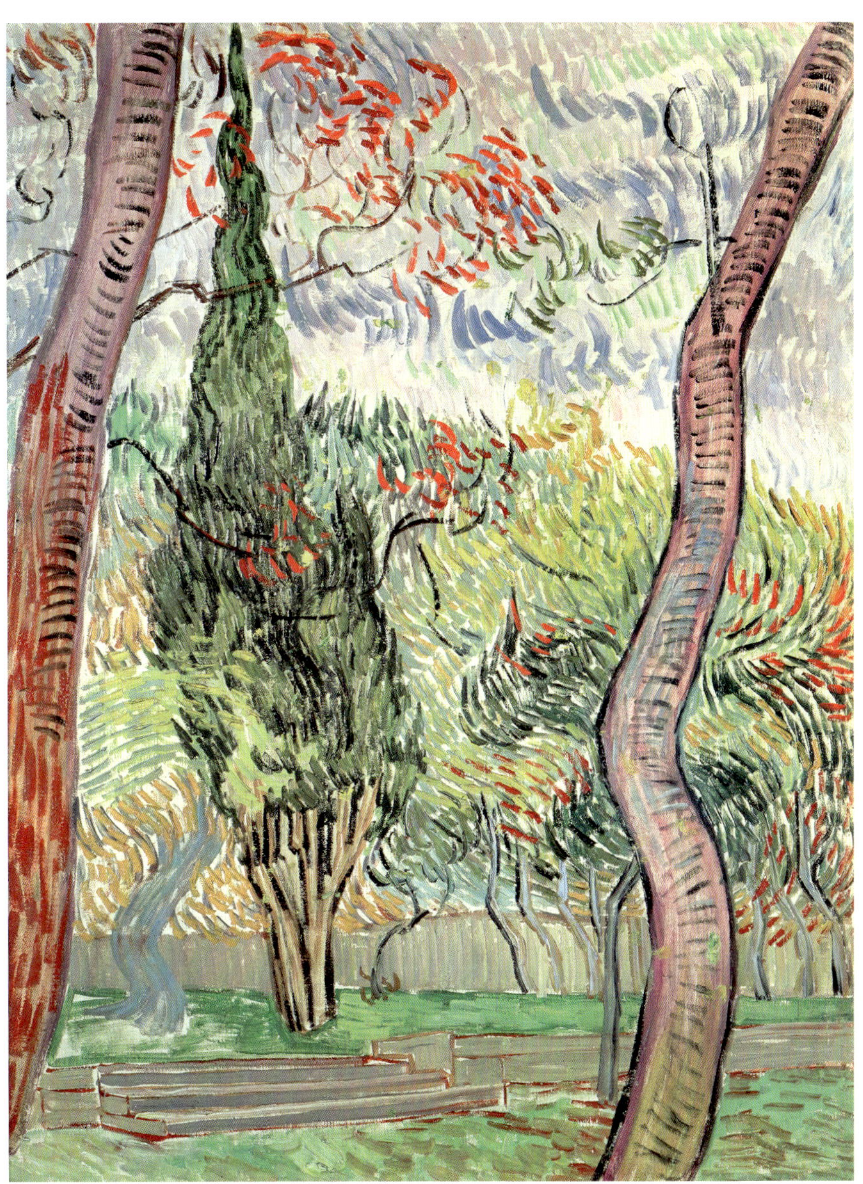

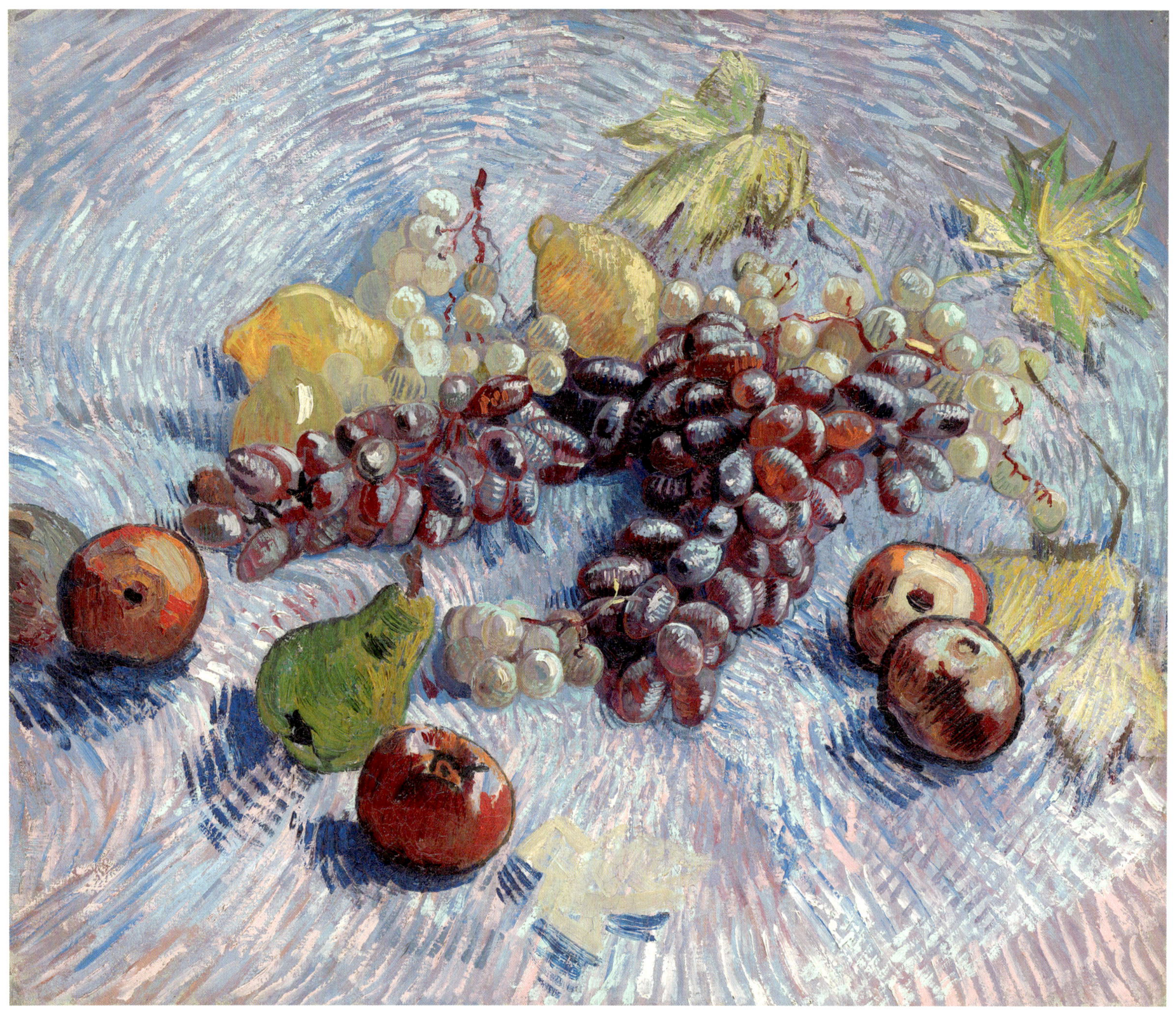

PLATE 55. *Grapes, Lemons, Pears, and Apples*, 1887 (CAT. 26)

Such an accomplishment certainly encouraged other Midwestern collectors in the second half of the 1920s. Robert Allerton, an Art Institute trustee and a generous donor of art, gifted the Van Gogh drawing *Cypresses* (F1524) to the museum in 1927.[90] And by the end of the decade, the names of other Midwestern Van Gogh collectors were becoming known to the world. Cleveland collector of modern art Ralph M. Coe would lend *The Park of Saint Paul's Hospital* (F640; fig. 7)—a painting included in the Arts Club of Chicago's 1921 exhibition but that he did not purchase until 1927—to an exhibition at the Cleveland Museum of Art in 1929.[91] Chicagoans Walter S. and Kate L. Brewster contributed their Van Gogh *Grapes, Lemons, Pears, and Apples* (F382; plate 55)—a work once owned by Edgar Degas that they purchased from the Chester H. Johnson Gallery in Chicago in September 1928—to multiple exhibitions in 1929: the Arts Club of Chicago's *Loan Exhibition of Modern Paintings Privately Owned by Chicagoans*; the Fogg Art Museum's "finest exhibition of modern French painting since the Armory Show"; and MoMA's *First Loan Exhibition: Cézanne, Gauguin, Seurat, van Gogh*, where Alfred H. Barr Jr. was so "overpowered" by it that he would laud the Midwest as the only region of the country that could demonstrate the inclusion of Van Gogh paintings in private collections as well as public, encyclopedic museums.[92]

It was also in 1929 that the Brewsters acquired a second Van Gogh, a drawing called "Landscape" (F1642) that came from another great Chicago collector of modern art, Annie Swan Coburn, whose remarkable collection was exhibited at the Art Institute of Chicago in 1932.[93] The two works in that exhibition attributed to Van Gogh, "Soleil du Midi" (F468, see fig. 8; and Chudzicka, fig. 17) and "Self-Portrait with a Pipe" (F527a; now determined to be inauthentic), were likely purchased in the second half of the 1920s and were divided up following her death: the Art Institute received the former and the Fogg Art Museum the latter, probably because the Art Institute director Robert Harshe never believed that "Self-Portrait with a Pipe" was by Van Gogh's hand.[94]

Midwest Matters

It was in the decade of the Great Depression, however, that Van Gogh's popularity would soar to new heights in the United States. Again, the Midwest played a central role, in both collecting *and* exhibiting the artist's work. Considering the increased visibility of Van Gogh's art in America in the mid-to-late 1920s—in gallery and museum group shows as well as in private collections, some of which were partially open to the public (including those of Duncan Phillips and Albert Barnes)—it is perhaps surprising that it was not until the 1930s that the second, third, fourth, and fifth Van Gogh paintings would finally be purchased by public, encyclopedic museums in America. Notably, all were in the Midwest.

Kansas City led the pack in 1932 when advocates of modern art in the city went to great lengths to encourage the purchase of *Olive Trees* (F715; plate 56) for the new public art museum that was being built thanks to the combined estates of *Kansas City Star* co-founder William Rockhill Nelson (1841–1915) and his heirs, as well as that of Mary McAfee Atkins (1836–1911), schoolteacher and widow of a successful entrepreneur in the mill and real-estate industries. Faced with the daunting challenge of purchasing an encyclopedic collection for the new museum—for which funds were left in Nelson's bequest—the institution enlisted Harold Woodbury Parsons as art adviser. He encountered difficulties with respect to collecting modern art for the museum as the Nelson funds were restricted to be used for works by artists deceased for at least thirty years. Luckily for Kansas City, Parsons and local art dealer and schoolteacher Effie Seachrest set their sights on acquiring a work by Van Gogh, who died young and, unlike many of his peers, met the thirty-year requirement set by the Nelson Trust.[95]

FIG. 8 Interior of Annie Swan Coburn's apartment at the Blackstone Hotel, Chicago, c. 1925. Van Gogh's *Poet's Garden* (F468) is on the floor, second from the left.

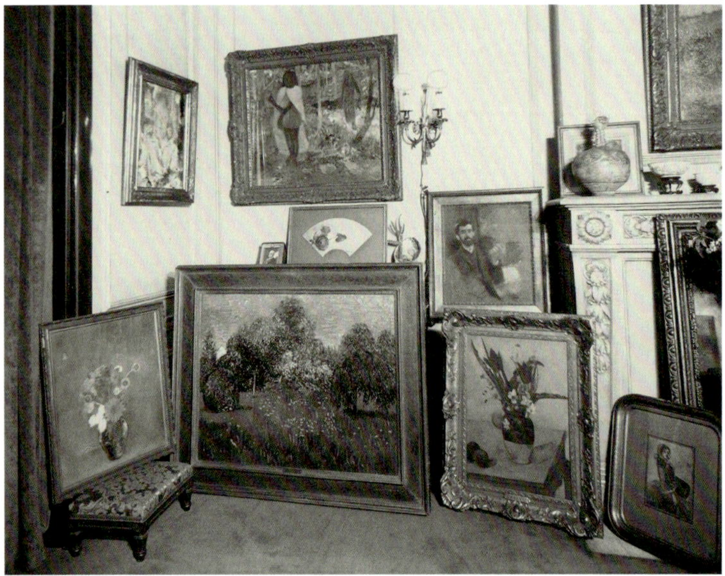

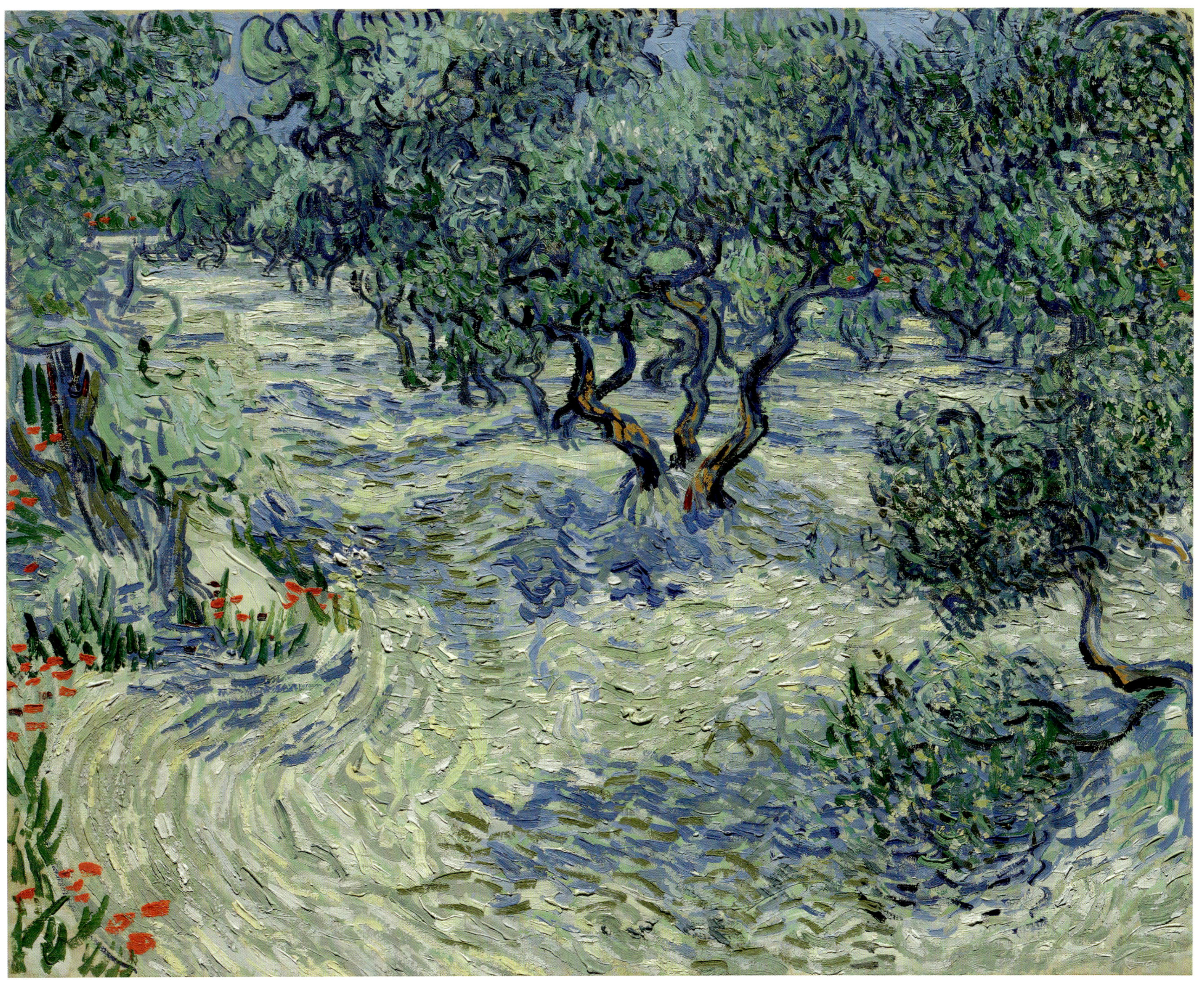

PLATE 56. *Olive Trees*, 1889 (CAT. 50)

Despite knowing that the work might not appeal to Nelson trustees, in 1931 Parsons asked if he could send a "masterpiece" by Van Gogh to Kansas City on approval and for temporary exhibition. *Olive Trees* (F715; plate 56), a painting that he and Seachrest saw at Durand-Ruel in New York, was on view at the Kansas City Art Institute by April 4.[96] But the purchase decision was very protracted. The trust hesitated, thinking that art prices might fall should the market continue its downward trend, but Parsons argued passionately for the painting, emphasizing the rarity of works available: "The Van Gogh is a well established masterpiece and he is perhaps the most difficult of all the modern men to acquire since his life was short and his works are greatly sought after."[97] He amplified his argument by mentioning that Duncan Phillips was selling several Daumiers in order to purchase another Van Gogh.

Seachrest also chimed in, writing to the Nelson Trust about a petition started by a member of her class. "I don't want to fight," she wrote. "I want to help to get great pictures for Kansas City…I feel that this painting would stimulate art here and bring dissenting forces together."[98] That Van Gogh was a figure Seachrest could imagine bridging the gap between conservative *and* avant-garde art lovers is indicative of the major change in attitude toward Van Gogh since his first Midwestern appearance in Chicago in 1913.

This effort proved successful: after no fewer than eight months of deliberation, "at least two hundred admirers" who signed petitions, and pressure from Durand-Ruel to make a decision or return the painting, an offer was made for Van Gogh's *Olive Trees*.[99] It was lower than Durand-Ruel's bottom price, and the fact that it ultimately was accepted at a loss to the dealer is an indication that the art market—even for Van Gogh—was suffering.[100] Public support accompanied by shrewd negotiation landed the Nelson-Atkins the distinction of being the second encyclopedic museum in the United States to have purchased a painting by Van Gogh.

Despite the harsh economic times, the Midwest was determined—with its upcoming World's Fair in Chicago—to celebrate American accomplishments, including its success in collecting art. The strides made to acquire Post-Impressionist art was certainly evident at the Museum of Modern Art's inaugural exhibition in 1929. And it was this incredible pride in American collectors that was ultimately brought to the fore in the Art Institute of Chicago's *Exhibition of Paintings and Sculpture* that accompanied the city's *Century of Progress* exhibition in 1933. The museum's director, Robert Harshe, visited Europe in summer 1929 to begin planning, but soon thereafter—in large part because the economic crash of that year impacted the budget and scope of the exhibition—he limited the checklist to

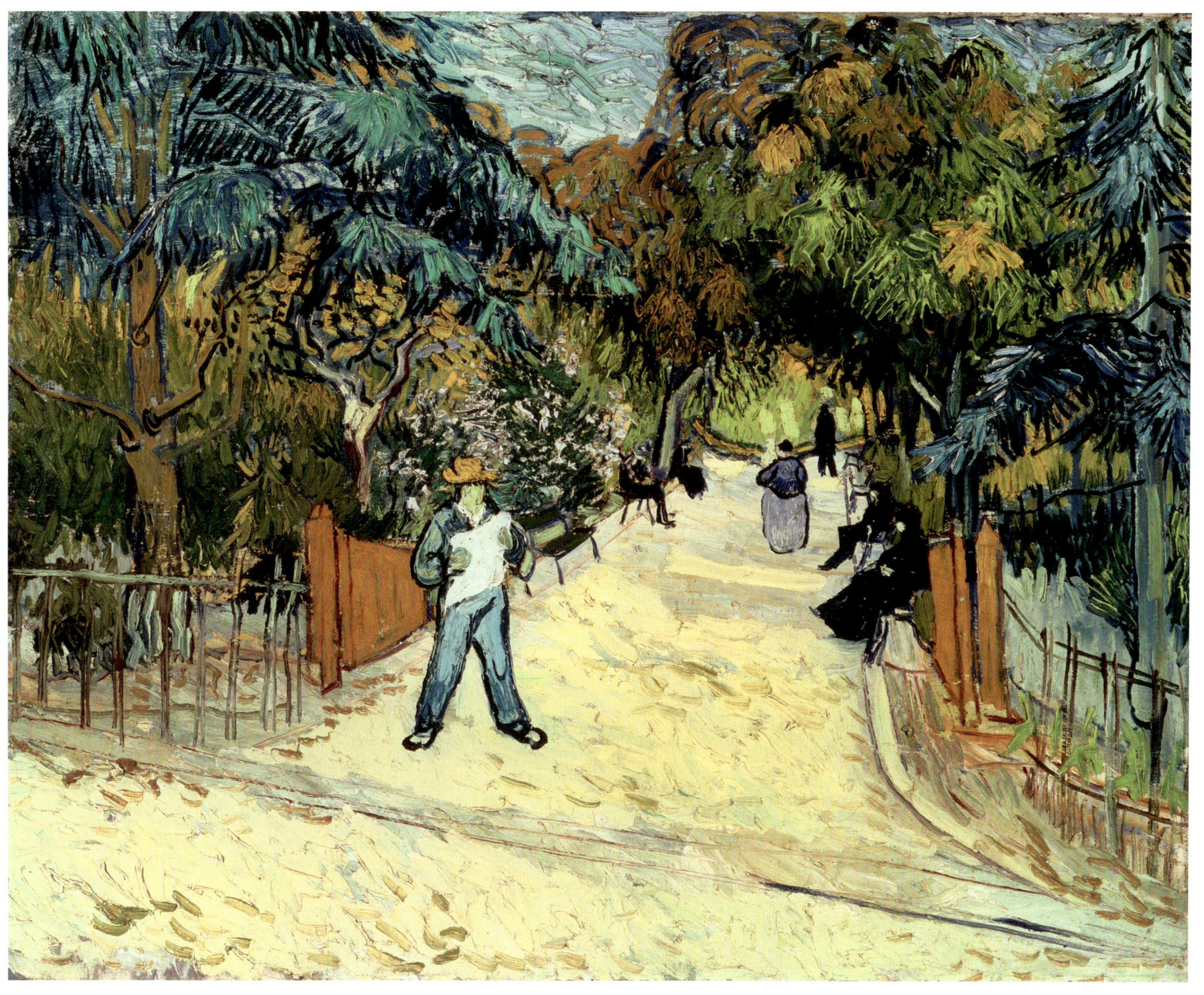

PLATE 57. *Entrance to the Public Gardens in Arles*, 1888 (CAT. 38)

feature primarily "the very finest things from American museums and collectors."[101] And he succeeded. The exhibition of more than twelve hundred works of art—all but one from American collections—included European art from the thirteenth century to European and American art of the present day, and aimed to showcase "not only art of the last century, but a hundred years' progress in American collecting."[102] One of the most distinctive characteristics of this "century of progress" was that for the first time, the Art Institute arranged all of the works chronologically and treated modern art as part of the long trajectory of history.[103] This organizational structure would eventually lead the museum to reinstall its galleries in chronological order rather than by donor.[104]

The massive exhibition featured twenty-seven rooms dedicated to modern art. Gallery 47 hosted Toulouse-Lautrec and Van Gogh, but Van Gogh dominated the space with thirteen works (versus Toulouse-Lautrec's four), and it was said to be the most popular "modern" room in the exhibition.[105] Five works listed as Van Gogh were from the Art Institute of Chicago's collection, and in response to the rallying cry to celebrate American collecting, some important collectors of Van Gogh's work participated: Julius Oppenheimer, New York (F668 and F737); Anson Conger Goodyear, New York (F550; plate 27); Chester Dale, New York (F431); Duncan Phillips (The Phillips Memorial Gallery), Washington, DC (F566; plate 57); Robert Treat Paine II, Boston (F432, of which the AIC director stated: "it will be, in my opinion, the most important work by that master shown [see Stolwijk and Krikke, fig. 7]"); and one anonymous lender (F658).[106] Although unidentified in the catalogue, Dorothy Sturges of Providence, Rhode Island, lent "Pavers: Street in St. Remy" (F658; see Chudzicka, fig. 16), a work that would be purchased by Duncan Phillips in 1949.[107]

The exhibition was not just a display of bounty, but a marketplace—for collectors as well as dealers. Sturges offered to lend an additional work by Dufy to the exhibition because she thought it would be a good way to sell it; she had hopes of replacing it with another Van Gogh.[108] Galleries also lent. Works available for purchase were noted in the catalogue, and the Art Institute maintained a sales force during the exhibition and charged a 15 percent commission.[109] But there were no Van Goghs sold—at least not from the exhibition. "Banks of the River: La Grenouillere [*sic*]" (F798; plate 7), offered by the Knoedler Gallery, went back to New York, only to return to the Midwest two years later when it was purchased by Detroit collector Robert H. Tannahill.[110] "Women of the Fields" (F819; plate 58), lent by Chicago's Chester H. Johnson Galleries (and previously in the collection of fellow lender Duncan Phillips), also did not find a buyer. Indeed, the current economy was an issue, for late in the run of the exhibition Marie Harriman, whose gallery contributed "White Roses" (F681; plate 59) to the exhibition, told

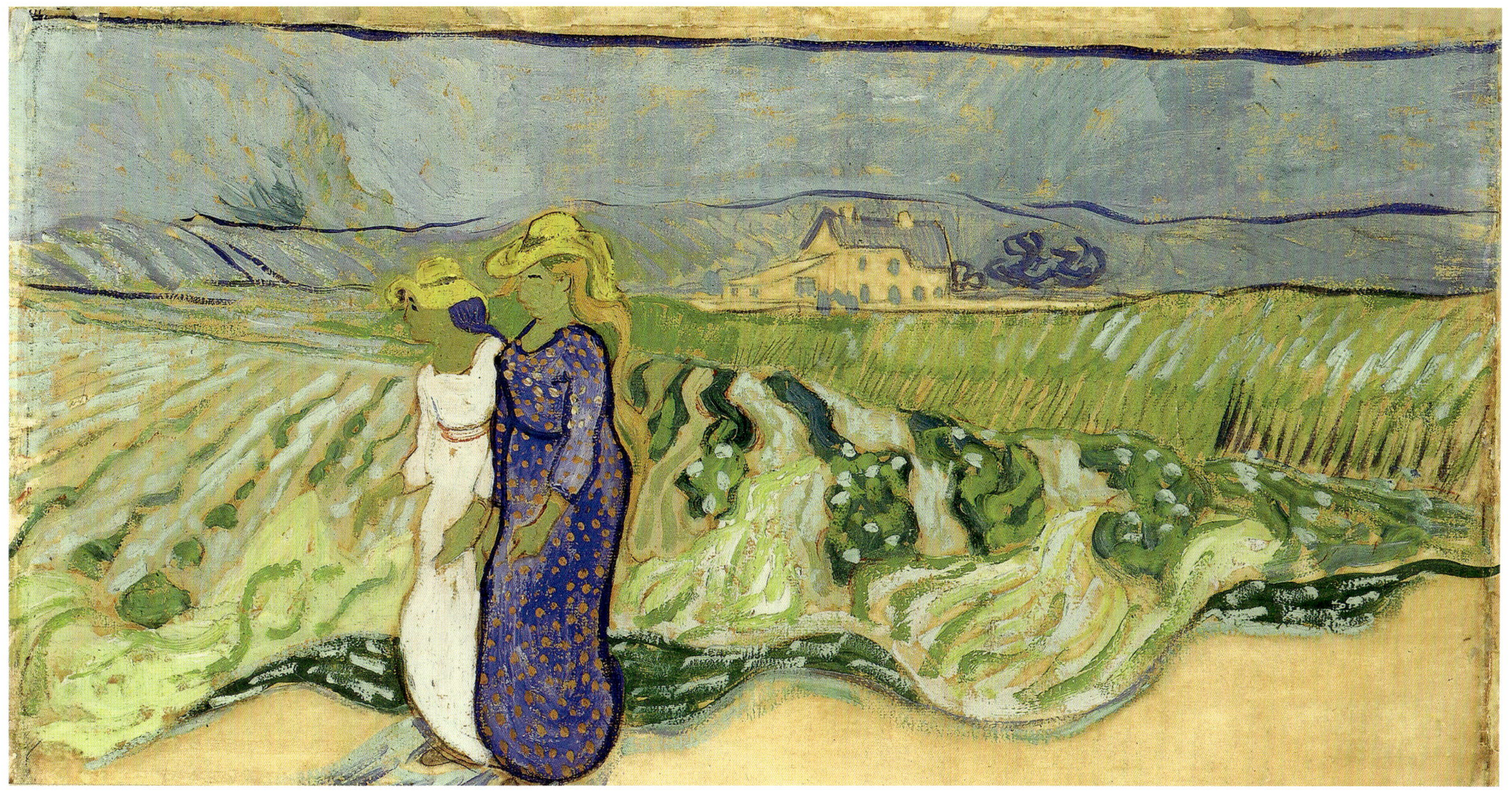

PLATE 58. *Women Crossing the Fields*, 1890 (CAT. 68)

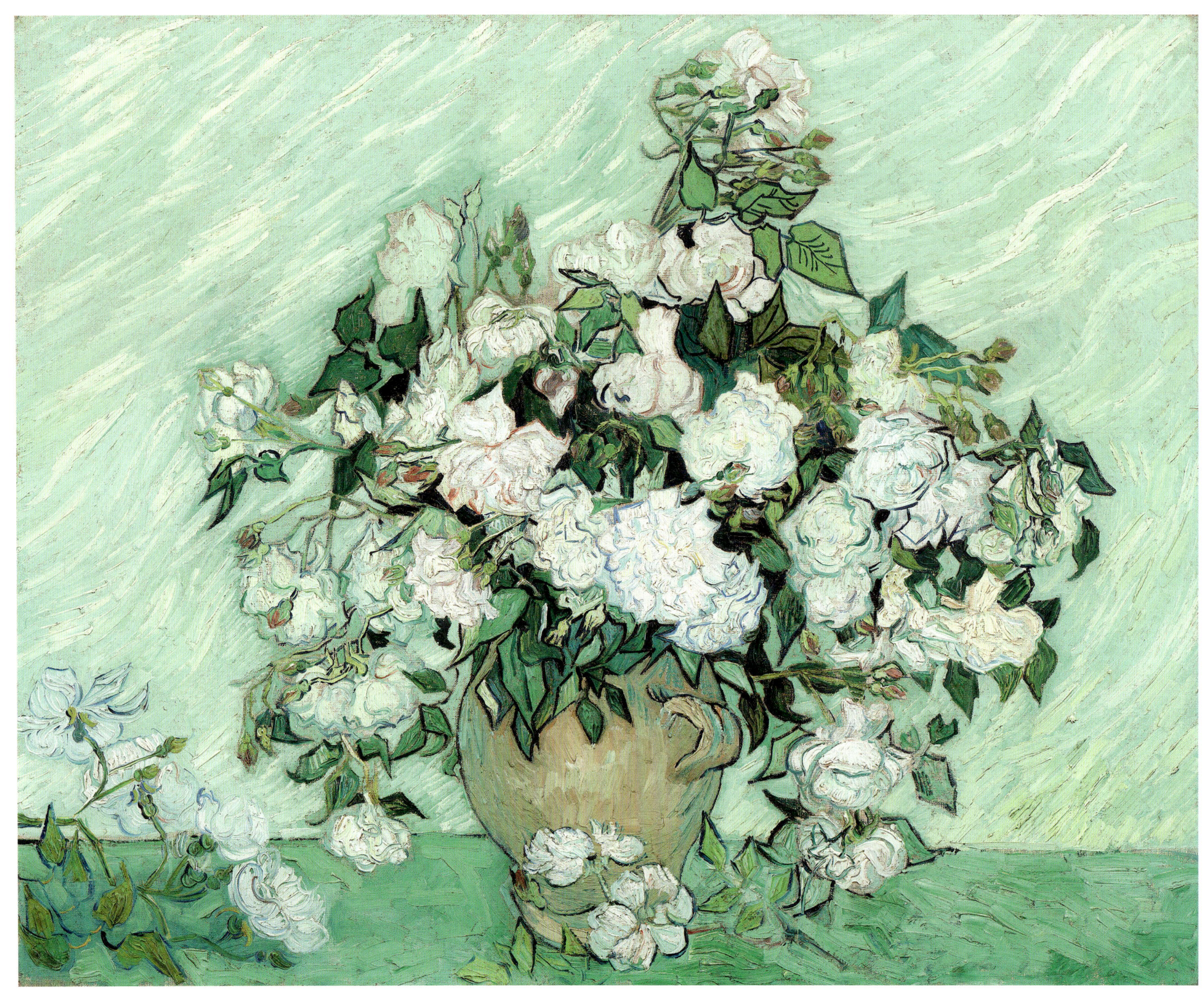

PLATE 59. *Roses*, 1890 (CAT. 59)

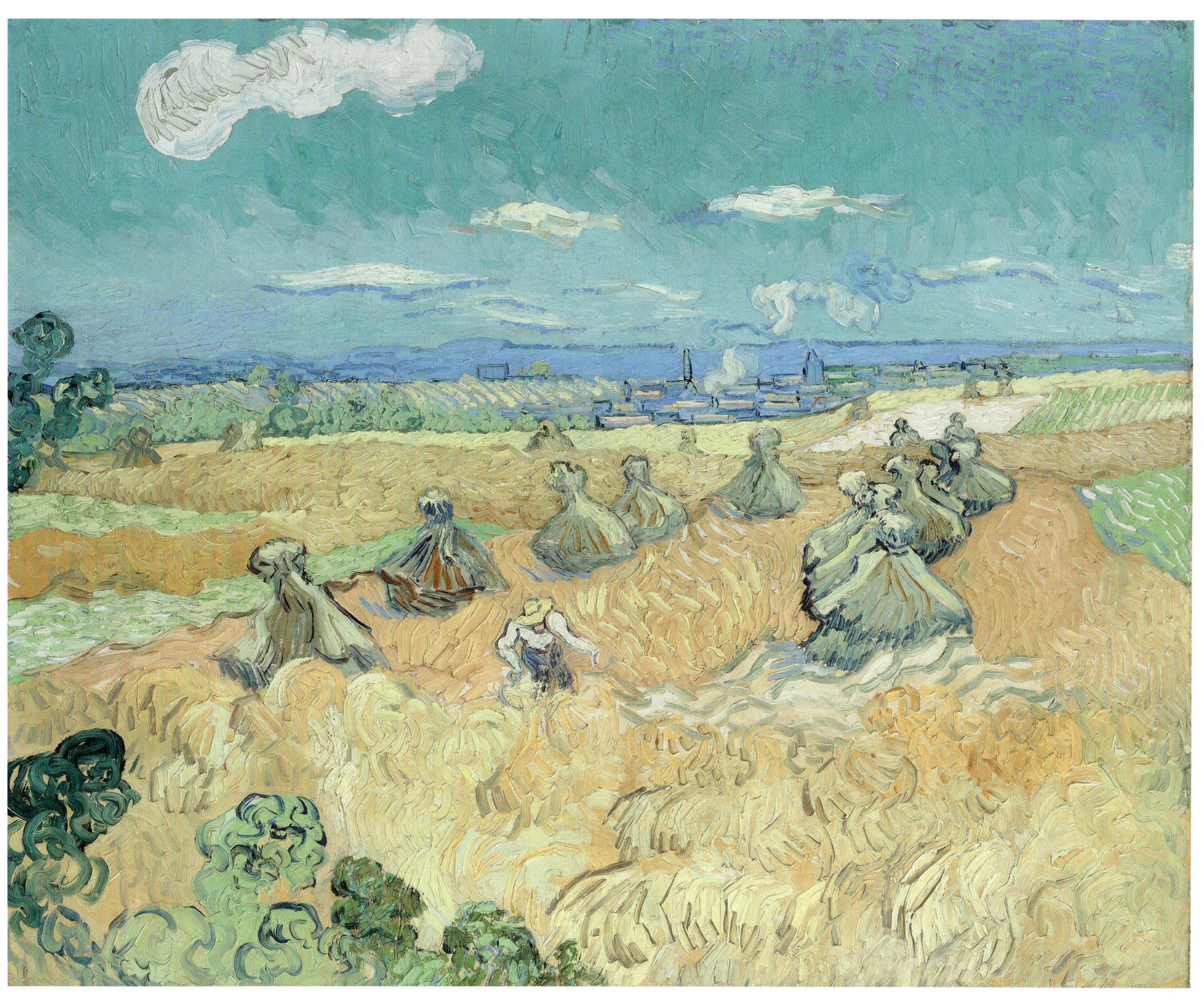

PLATE 60. *Wheat Fields with Reaper, Auvers*, 1890 (CAT. 60)

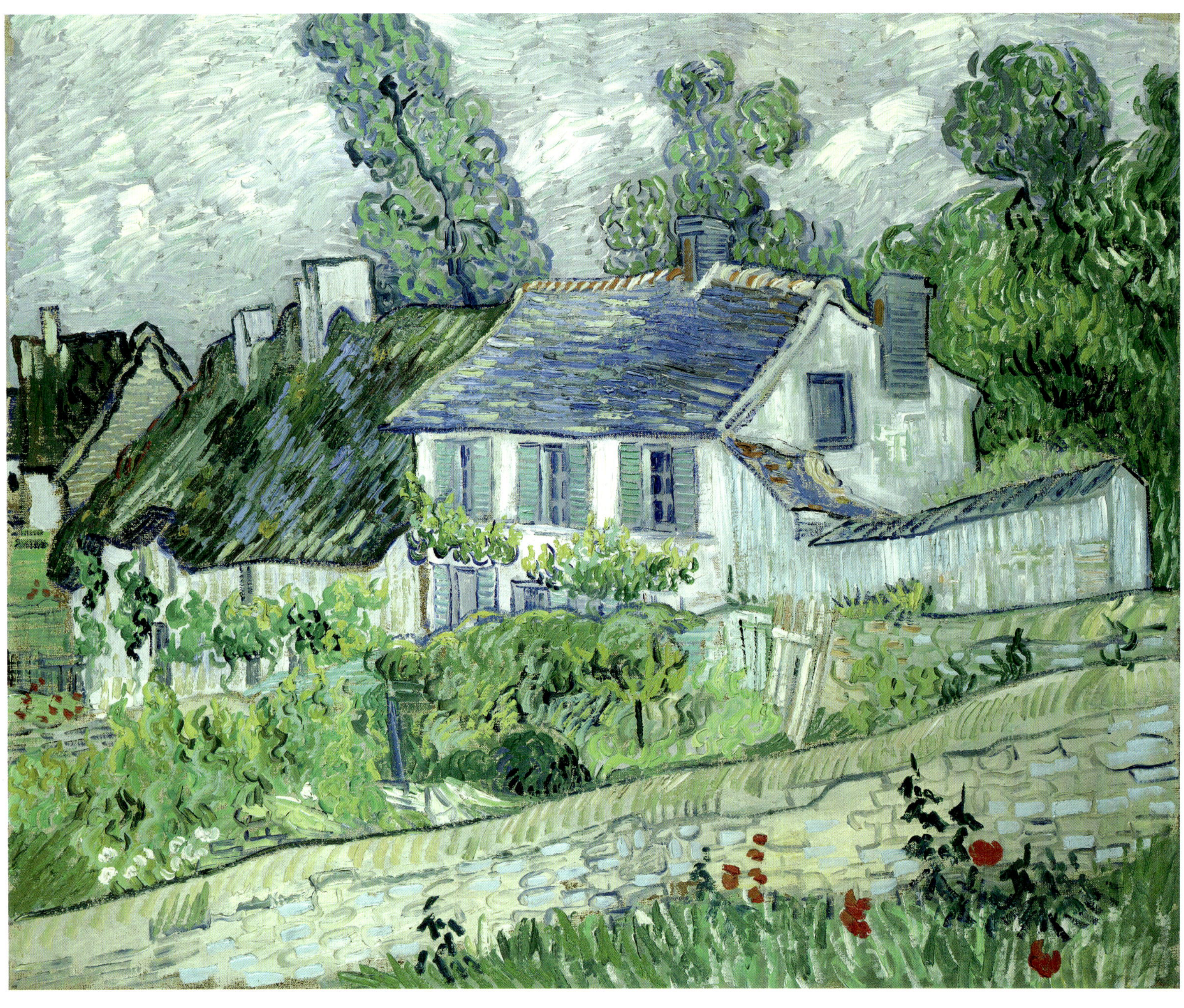

PLATE 61. *Houses at Auvers*, 1890 (CAT. 61)

Harshe that "I no longer care to sell them on account of the depreciation of the dollar in relation to the franc."[111]

Although it was not a financial success for dealers—at least in terms of Van Gogh—the *Century of Progress* exhibition was a critical success, attracting international attention, congratulatory letters, and reportedly, over its six-month run, a staggering 1,500,000 visitors to the Art Institute. The World's Fair as a whole was so successful that it reopened in 1934 and inspired a second exhibition at the museum, dedicated this time to American painting from the eighteenth century to the present as well as some works—including seven Van Goghs which shared a gallery with Ferdinand Hodler, Henri Rousseau, Georges Seurat, and Toulouse-Lautrec—that "either originally belonged to the great European collections and museums or have at one time hung on their walls."[112] In addition to three Birch Bartlett Van Gogh paintings was Annie Swan Coburn's recent bequest to the Chicago museum, "Sunny Midi" (F468; see Chudzicka, fig. 17). "Le Café de Nuit" (F463; see Chudzicka, fig. 19), lent anonymously by Stephen Clark, who had bought it just the previous year; the Detroit Institute of Arts' *Self-Portrait* (F526; plate 44); and Wildenstein's "Wheat Fields near Arles" (F559; plate 60) rounded out the list.

Following the close of the exhibition, "Wheat Fields near Arles" was sent to the Toledo Museum of Art, along with "The Bedroom at Arles" from Chicago (F484; plate 45), and "House at Auvers" (F759; plate 61) from Durand-Ruel for their November 1934 exhibition *French Impressionists and Post-Impressionists*.[113] In a coup for the Midwest, that same month the City Art Museum of St. Louis (later renamed the Saint Louis Art Museum) purchased *Stairway at Auvers* (F795; plate 62) from dealer Paul Rosenberg. Toledo was on their coattails and accessioned the two dealer loans in their exhibition shortly thereafter (F559, plate 60; and F759, plate 61), effectively making the first five purchases of Van Gogh paintings by encyclopedic museums in the United States to be all by Midwestern institutions.[114]

It seems fitting, then, that when MoMA organized the first American museum retrospective of Van Gogh's work in 1935–36 and circulated it across the country, the Midwest would be among the venues to host. And indeed that was the case: the Cleveland Museum of Art was one of five institutions to receive the full exhibition. And of the over fifty institutions that reportedly requested the reduced version of the show, four of the five museums selected were Midwestern: Kansas City, Minneapolis, Chicago, and Detroit.[115] Van Gogh had truly "made it" in the eyes of America, and it was in no small part because of the efforts of its heartland. For indeed, all of the aforementioned events and acquisitions took place before Van Gogh's *The Starry Night* (F612; see Shaw, America Wakes Up, fig. 1)—arguably the artist's most iconic painting—even set foot in America.[116] Remarkably, it would not be until 1941 that that painting would become the first one by the artist to enter the Museum of Modern Art's collection—nearly twenty years after the Detroit Institute of Arts' historic purchase of *Self-Portrait*.

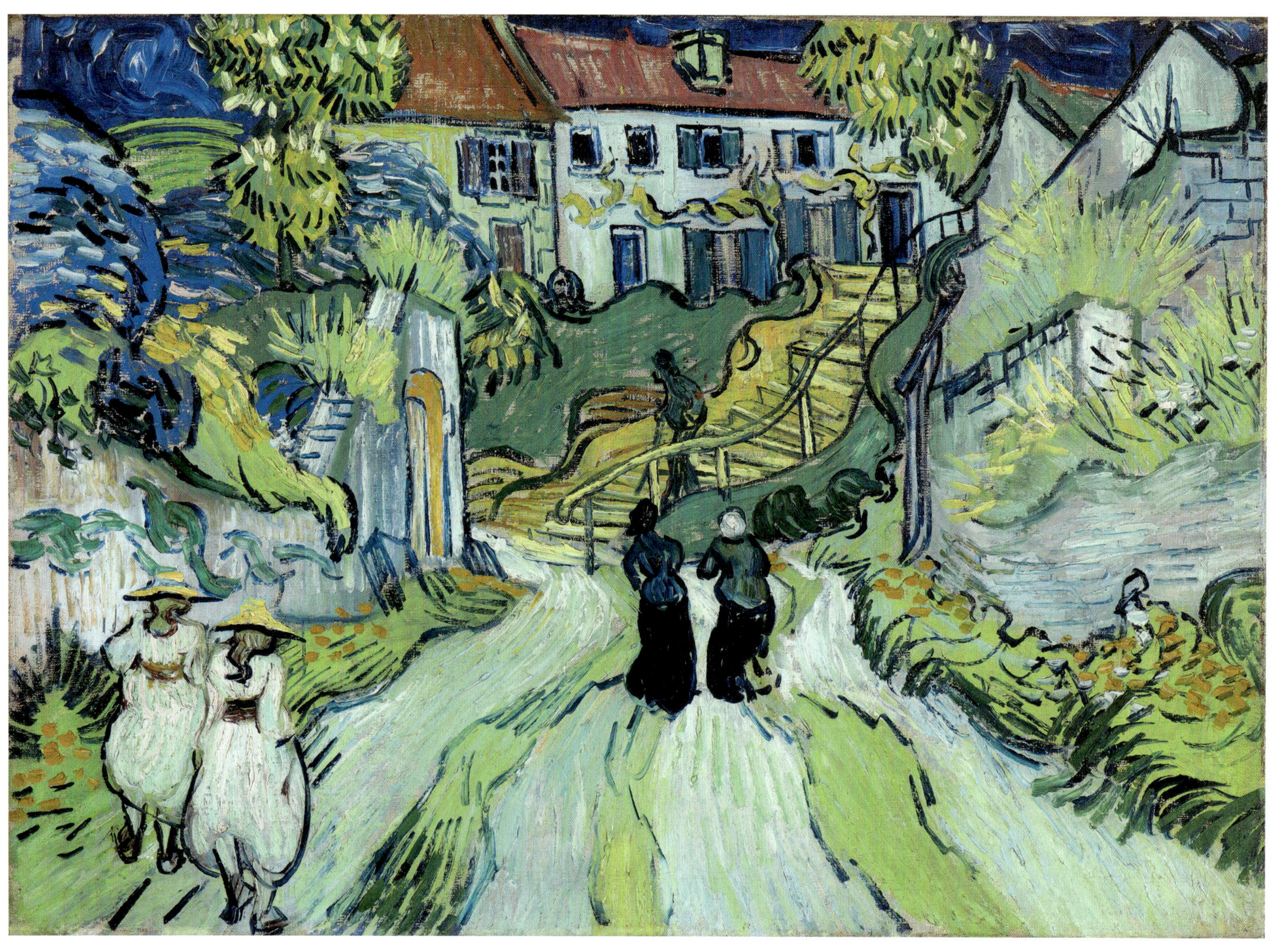

PLATE 62. *Stairway at Auvers*, 1890 (CAT. 67)

NOTES

I would like to thank Dorota Chudzicka for her assistance in the research for this essay. Thanks are also due to the staff of the Van Gogh Museum for their support and access to research materials, as well as Susan Alyson Stein for her guidance and scholarly insight. Douglas Druick and Peter Zegers instilled in me a deep understanding of the meticulous research required for a study of Van Gogh, and for that, I am grateful.

1 A. Barr 1929b: 108.
2 Jewell 1929b: SM7. Chicagoans were also proud of this, as society page columnist Caroline Kirkland (Mme. X) noted: "We of Chicago…[are] pioneers of many years standing where New York is just beginning to step out." See [Kirkland] 1929: H2. Midwestern support of Impressionist-era art in the late nineteenth and early twentieth centuries is well documented. See Sweet 1966; Erens 1979; Johnston 1992; Zafran 2007; Shaw and Chudzicka 2008; Groom and Shaw 2014; Thompson 2015; Hendren 2019; and others.
3 New York 1929a lists under Van Gogh's name, nos. 72 (F526; Detroit), 79 (F484; Chicago), and 91 (Chicago). The last work was called "Still Life: Melon, Fish, Jar" and has been downgraded to an imitator of Van Gogh.
4 At this time, Van Gogh's work was also in the collections of Albert C. Barnes (Barnes Foundation, Merion, Pennsylvania) and Duncan Phillips (Phillips Memorial Gallery, Washington, DC). While open to the public to a certain extent, those collections were considered private institutions by Barr, as they were formed by private collectors. See New York 1929a, 30.
5 See Brown 1963; Brettell and Prince 1990; Martinez 1993; Barter 2013; Hendrickson 2013; Olson 2017; and Marshall 2018. D'Alessandro 2013 is also helpful for understanding the early landscape for modern art in the city.
6 Martinez 1993: 36; Monroe 1913a: B4.
7 Martinez 1993: 57. The full transcript of William French, letter to Charles Hutchinson, February 22, 1913, ibid.: 56–57.
8 Ibid.: 38, citing Arthur Aldis, letter to Walt Kuhn, February 17, 1913.
9 Ibid.: 57. For French's response, see ibid.: 40, citing William French, letter to Arthur B. Davies, March 6, 1913.
10 Landon 1913: 2.
11 Monroe 1913b: B5. Others commented that Van Gogh, Cézanne, and Gauguin, once confounding to the public, now look like "old masters" compared to the new movements. See, for example, *Chicago Daily Tribune* 1913a: 12.
12 Pattison 1913: 295.
13 Dell 1913; Monroe 1913d: B5.
14 *Chicago Daily Tribune* 1913b: 7; Hale 1913: 455.
15 Monroe 1913d: B5.
16 *Chicago Daily Tribune* 1913c: 15.
17 McCauley 1913.
18 Hale 1913: 455. *The Dial* was started by Francis F. Browne in Chicago in 1880; it would move to New York in 1918. See Brooker and Thacker 2012, 35.
19 Hale 1913: 455, 456.
20 Ibid.: 457, 458.
21 Eddy 1914, 40.
22 Ibid., 40, 56, 120, 121 illustrates "Portrait of Self" (F529); "Café" (F463; see Chudzicka, fig. 19); "Woman with Frying Pan" (F176); "Chair with Pipe" (F498; plate 47).
23 See especially Kruty 1987: 43–46; Paul Kruty, email to the author, June 17, 2019; and Germer 1990: 181–86.
24 On their supposed rivalry, see Brown 1963, 99; Zilczer 1982: 59–60; Kruty 1987: 40, 45; and Rewald 1989, 225.
25 [Alice Roullier], "The Arts Club of Chicago: A Report of the Exhibition Committee Submitted by the Chairman," March 16, 1922. Arts Club Records, The Newberry Library, Chicago (hereafter Arts Club Records), Series 1, Box 1, Folder 14.
26 Olson 2017, 123. For the Winterbotham family's contribution to modern art in Chicago, see Delliquadri 1994. By 1933 Joseph Winterbotham Jr. acquired *The Drinkers* (F667); see Koldehoff and Stolwijk 2017, 236. He purchased *Self-Portrait* (F345) by June 1935; see his letter to Robert Harshe, June 10, 1935, in the Winterbotham-Harshe correspondence file, The Art Institute of Chicago Archives (hereafter AIC Archives). My thanks go to Bart Ryckbosch and Debbie Webb at the Art Institute for their generous help with Chicago's archival materials.
27 Chicago 1919 was reported in Jewett 1919: C11; and Stuart 1920: 5. It is possible Van Gogh was included in the Arts Club's *Exhibition of French Post-Impressionists* (April 9–23, 1919), but little archival information about the exhibition has surfaced.
28 "Report of the Exhibition Committee, Season 1919–1920," Arts Club Records, Series 1, Box 1, Folder 8; Eleanor Jewett, "Art," no date, clipping, ibid., Series 12, Box 1, Folder 2.
29 See Stein, New York, note 77. The Bartletts lent the painting to New York 1921d; see *New York Times* 1921a: 8. By October 6, 1921, the work was on view at the Art Institute of Chicago. See the Art Institute's registration card for the work, copy in Curatorial Object File 1926.201, The Art Institute of Chicago (hereafter AIC).
30 Arts Club of Chicago (Alice Roullier), letter to Société Anonyme Inc., February 5, 1921, in Katherine S. Dreier Papers / Société Anonyme Archive, Beinecke Library, Yale University, New Haven, YCAL MSS 101 (hereafter Dreier Papers / Société Anonyme Archive), Box 3, Folder 75.
31 See Katherine S. Dreier, letter to Alice Roullier, February 9, 1921, ibid.
32 Alice Roullier, letter to Katherine S. Dreier, February 22, 1921, ibid.
33 Alice Roullier, letter to Katherine S. Dreier, March 14, 1921, ibid.
34 Chicago 1921, nos. 51–56. See "Formal Opening of Arts Club Gallery Monday Afternoon," clipping, Arts Club Records, Series 12, Box 1, Folder 4.
35 Watson 1921, n.p.
36 Katharine Eggleston Roberts, "At the Galleries," November 23, 1921, clipping, Arts Club Records, Series 12, Box 1, Folder 4.
37 [Kirkland] 1921: G4.
38 Simons 1921: 97.
39 Four of the six works in the Arts Club exhibition had just been shown in New York 1921d: F340; F436; F498, plate 47; and F632, fig. 1. The two other works were: "Moulin de la Galette" (F346) and "The Park in Autumn" (probably F640; fig. 7). The identification of F346 is based on Cortissoz 1920: 7, which illustrated the work by the same title in the Montross exhibition. "The Park in Autumn" was identified as F640 in W. Feilchenfeldt 2013.
40 Jewett 1921b: G12. The Picasso "Landscape" (Chicago 1921, no. 29) was lent by Dikran Kelekian and was illustrated in *Arts* 1921b: 134.
41 Simons 1921: 97.
42 Raymond Jonson, letter to Arts Club of Chicago, March 24, 1922, Arts Club Records, Series 1, Box 1, Folder 13.
43 See Newman E. Montross, letter to Jo van Gogh-Bonger, January 28, 1922 (b6266), Van Gogh Museum Documentation, Amsterdam (hereafter VGMD).
44 Jewett 1921a: F8.
45 F. Davis 1921: 8.
46 Seymour de Ricci, "The Kélékian Collection: A Foreword," in *Illustrated Catalogue of the Notable Collection…Formed by…Dikran Khan Kélékian…*, sale cat., New York, American Art Association, January 30–31, 1922, n.p.
47 *New York Herald* 1922a: 3.
48 *American Art News* 1922a: 7. The *Self-Portrait* was also described as "remarkable" in an earlier exhibition of the Kelekian collection in Paris; see *American Art News* 1920b: 4.
49 *Arts* 1921b: 132.
50 *New York Times* 1922a: 27; and *Arts* 1922: 246.
51 *Arts* 1922: 246; and *New York Herald* 1922b: 8. For auction results, see also *New York Times* 1922a: 27. By the time of Detroit's purchase, at least two other works thought to be by the artist—but now considered inauthentic—had entered American museum collections as *gifts*. The first was John G. Johnson's 1917 donation of a painting to the Philadelphia Museum of Art (*Still Life with a Vase of Flowers*, inv. no. 2322). I thank Philadelphia Museum of Art curator Jennifer Thompson for bringing this to my attention; see Thompson, email to the author, April 18, 2018. The second was a drawing given to the Art Institute of Chicago by the Friends of American Art that was on view at the museum by December 1921; see *American Art News* 1921e: 9. About the purchase, see Art Institute of Chicago newsletter, December 30, 1921, AIC Archives; *Bulletin of the Art Institute of Chicago* 1922: 11 (ill.), 12; Receipt no. R. 2355, dated February 5, 1926, AIC Archives; and note 105. I thank Emily Vokt Ziemba at the Art Institute for her kind assistance with this research.
52 *New York Times* 1922a; *New York Herald* 1922b. According to the Detroit Arts Commission Meeting Minutes from February 7, 1922, in the Detroit Institute of Arts Research Library & Archives (hereafter DIA Archives), Booth purchased it "on his own initiative." Booth's role has also been acknowledged in Peck 1991, 71.
53 M. Sterne 1980, 66–67.

54 See J. H. de Bois, letter to Jo Cohen Gosschalk-Bonger [Jo van Gogh-Bonger], February 8, 1912 (b5482); and J. H. de Bois, letter to Jo Cohen Gosschalk-Bonger [Jo van Gogh-Bonger], December 11, 1912 (b5488), VGMD. My thanks go to Joost van der Hoeven for helping with the translation of these letters.

55 W. R. Valentiner, letter to Ralph Booth, March 23, 1922, DIA Archives, Clyde H. Burroughs Records (hereafter Burroughs Records), Series 1, Box 23, Folder 11.

56 Forbes Watson, letter to Clyde H. Burroughs, February 3, 1922, ibid., Folder 12.

57 Raymond Wyer, telegram to Clyde H. Burroughs, February 5, 1922, Detroit Institute of Arts, Registration Records, Object File 22.14.

58 Clyde H. Burroughs, letter to Newman E. Montross, October 25, 1920, in DIA Archives, Burroughs Records, Series 1, Box 18, Folder 4.

59 Thannhauser recorded a visit by Booth on August 25, 1921, but above the notes for that visit is an annotation (presumably from an earlier conversation) that Detroit was looking for a "Van Gogh landscape," among other works. Galerien Thannhauser records, ZADIK Archive, Cologne, A077_XIX_0033_002a.

60 See Van Diemen & Co., letter to Ralph Booth, December 8, 1921, DIA Archives, Burroughs Records, Series 1, Box 23, Folder 10; Van Diemen & Co., letter to Ralph Booth, December 13, 1921, ibid., Folder 9; and Clyde H. Burroughs, letter to Van Diemen & Co., February 23, 1922, ibid., Folder 10.

61 Koldehoff and Stolwijk 2017, 156, 180, 204, 228. Ralph H. Booth did not have good fortune when it came to acquiring Van Goghs for his personal collection. Two works he purchased from Galeries Matthiesen, Berlin—"Two Shoes" (probably purchased around 1925–26) and "Landscape in the Provence" (F729; purchased by October 1927)—turned out to be inauthentic. See Galerien Thannhauser records, ZADIK Archive, Cologne, A077_XIX_0033_0017; Koldehoff 2006–2007: 81n4; and W. Feilchenfeldt 2005, 102. Booth's wife, Mary Batterman Booth, proved more successful in her efforts. Following her husband's death, she owned *Poppy Field at Arles* (F1494), *Zinnias* (F592), and *Olive Trees* (F710). See French Art Galleries, invoice to Mary Booth, November 11, 1939, in Virginia Kingswood Booth Vogel Papers, Cranbrook Archives, Cranbrook Center for Collections and Research, Bloomfield Hills, Michigan, Series 3, Box 9, Folder 16; French Art Galleries, invoice to Mary Booth, February 3, 1941; and French Arts Associates, invoice to Mary Booth, November 17, 1944, both ibid., Series 3, Box 8, Folder 14.

62 *Detroit Free Press* 1922: D4.

63 The Société Anonyme hoped for other Midwestern museums to host the exhibition as well, especially Cleveland, Cincinnati, and Chicago. See Katherine S. Dreier, letter to Mary Knoblauch, June 14, 1921, in Dreier Papers / Société Anonyme Archive, Box 20, Folder 585. According to Edith Cowles, letter to Clyde H. Burroughs, February 24, [1922], DIA Archives, Burroughs Records, Series 6, Box 12, Folder 11, there was also a possibility that the exhibition would go to Kansas City after Detroit, however the works were shipped back to the original owners following the DIA's exhibition. See Mary Knoblauch, telegram to Clyde H. Burroughs, April 5, 1922; and Clyde H. Burroughs, letter to Detroit Insurance Company, April 7, 1922, both ibid.

64 See Reginald Poland, letter to Sheldon Cheney, June 2, 1921; and Katherine S. Dreier, letter to Reginald Poland, June 7, 1921, both ibid., Series 1, Box 19, Folder 5. See also note 66.

65 Raymond Wyer, letter to Clyde H. Burroughs, December 14, 1921, ibid., Series 6, Box 12, Folder 10.

66 Clyde H. Burroughs, letter to Mary Knoblauch, December 30, 1921, ibid.

67 See Detroit 1922; and [Burroughs] 1922: 61.

68 For correspondence with private collectors John Quinn, Frederic Clay Bartlett, and Martin Ryerson, see DIA Archives, Burroughs Records, Series 1, Box 22, Folder 25 and Series 6, Box 12, Folder 10. For letters with dealers Bourgeois Galleries and Wildenstein & Co., see ibid., Folder 10. Detroit also contacted the Cleveland Museum of Art, the Art Institute of Chicago, and the Minneapolis Institute of Arts; see ibid. The Van Goghs in Minneapolis 1921 (nos. 17, 18) were listed as anonymous loans, but certainly came from New York dealer Marius de Zayas. Plimpton, who had just come to Minneapolis from the Metropolitan Museum of Art, was likely able to secure them because of his connection to his former institution; the Metropolitan Museum had just shown the paintings in New York 1921d. For Plimpton's career, see Brettell 1983: 238–40.

69 Detroit 1922, nos. 77, 78, 78a; Speyer 1922: 12.

70 Worcester's Gauguin is listed in Detroit 1922 as no. 34, "Woman Seated"; see Speyer 1922: 12.

71 "Detroit," *American Art News*, March 18, [1922], clipping, DIA Scrapbook 1919–1923.

72 See Florence L. Smith, "Cubistitis Hits Old, Young At 'Art' Show," March 16, [1922], clipping, ibid.

73 The comment about the Man Ray is from ibid.; the Ribemont-Dessaignes description is from Dud Carson, "Dud Finds Cubicles Puzzle Him More than Tax Blank," March [10?], [1922], clipping, ibid.

74 Clipping, March 12, [1922], ibid.

75 Ralph Holmes, "Artists and Other 'Ists' Show Weird Work At The Art Institute," March 11, [1922], clipping, ibid.

76 *New York Times* 1923a. The DIA also wrote to the Art Institute of Chicago and the Metropolitan Museum of Art recommending the exhibition for their consideration, though those efforts seem not to have come to fruition. See Reginald Poland, letter to Edward Robinson, February 23, 1923; and Reginald Poland, letter to Robert B. Harshe, January 27, 1923, DIA Archives, Burroughs Records, Series 6, Box 13, Folder 9.

77 Jo van Gogh-Bonger, letter to Newman E. Montross, October 25, 1922 (b6268), VGMD.

78 See list b5500 in Anderson Gallery, New York, 1923 exhibition file, VGMD; St. Louis and other cities 1922–23 (Detroit catalogue), nos. 24–28; and St. Louis and other cities 1922–23 (New York catalogue), nos. 149–53. The modern paintings were not illustrated in the catalogues, but three (possibly four) of the Van Goghs can be identified from press accompanying the exhibition in Detroit: "Self Portrait" and "Portrait of a Lady" were illustrated in Ralph Holmes, "Modern Dutch Pictures to be Shown," *Detroit Free Press*, January 28, 1923, clipping, DIA Scrapbook 1923–1925; they can be identified as F631 (fig. 6) and F320, respectively. A third picture, "Still Life with Books," is probably F358, given the dimensions listed in the catalogue (21 × 29 in.) and the description in the press of a painting "simply of piles of paper-covered books in yellow, orange, green and violet"; see [Poland] 1923a: 12. A fourth painting "with its walking women, the green tree and rolling fields," was also described. Listed in the Detroit catalogue as 12¾ × 24 in., this work may be F819 (plate 58), although the description is not an exact match.

79 Jacques Goudstikker, letter to Clyde H. Burroughs, December 16, 1922, DIA Archives, Burroughs Records, Series 6, Box 13, Folder 9. The St. Louis museum director specified that they did not exhibit modern paintings; see Samuel L. Sherer, letter to Clyde H. Burroughs, November 25, 1922, ibid. Archival documentation indicates that all five Van Goghs that shipped with the exhibition from St. Louis to Cleveland remained in storage during the latter city's presentation. See "Special Exhibition of Dutch Pictures, Collection Goudstikker" document in Registrar's Records, The Cleveland Museum of Art. I am grateful to Peter Buettner and Mary Suzor of the Cleveland Museum of Art for providing critical documentation.

80 See note 29. *La Berceuse* arrived at the Art Institute from France in August 1923 via De la Rancheraye shipping company; see document dated August 20, 1923, Birch Bartlett file, AIC Archives. *Montmartre* arrived in August 1924 through M. Knoedler & Co., New York; see document dated August 25, 1924, Birch Bartlett file, AIC Archives.

81 Bartlett made his first payment on the painting in May 1926 and the final installment in December of the same year. See The Art Institute of Chicago's Memorandum, May 21, 1927, in Curatorial Object File 1926.417, AIC.

82 See Erens 1979, 112; and Donnell 1986: 93. Much has been written about the Bartletts and the gift of their collection to the Art Institute of Chicago. See Sweet 1966: 196–97; Erens 1979, 100–14; Brettell 1986; and Donnell 1986.

83 Jewett 1923: F4.

84 Art Institute of Chicago newsletter, October 6, 1923, AIC Archives.

85 Art Institute of Chicago newsletter, October 13, 1923, ibid.

86 *Paintings of China by Frederick* [*sic*] *Clay Bartlett*, ran January 12–29, 1921; see *International Studio* 1921a: 4. For more on Bartlett as an artist, see Donnell 1986. Bartlett also recounts his work as an artist in his posthumously published memoir; see Bartlett 1965. In an unpublished part of his manuscript, he described his about-face with modern art while living in New York. See Frederic Clay Bartlett, "Pencil Book #2," 18, AIC Archives.

87 [Kirkland] 1924: G1.

88 For Minneapolis's request, see Frederic Clay Bartlett, letter to Robert [Harshe], October 27, 1924, Birch Bartlett file, AIC Archives.

89 Paul J. Sachs, letter to Frederick [*sic*] [Clay] Bartlett, February 17, 1928, Frederic Clay Bartlett file, AIC Archives.

90 Allerton purchased the work from Thannhauser in February 1927; the bill was sent to the Art Institute to be paid out of the Allerton fund. See Receipt no. R. 3323, dated May 4, 1927, in Curatorial Object File 1927.543, AIC; and Koldehoff and Stolwijk 2017, 174.

91 A drawing, "Boats" (F1462), was also lent to the exhibition by Edith Wetmore; see *Bulletin of the Cleveland Museum of Art* 1929: 168. For Coe's purchase of F640, see Koldehoff and Stolwijk 2017, 178. The Cleveland Museum of Art included Van Gogh in an earlier exhibition as well: *Fifty Years of French Art* in 1926 contained "an early flower piece, lent by Scott and Fowles" and "*Les Oliviers,* of Wildenstein and Company." See Milliken 1926: 337.

92 Brewster made a down payment on the painting on September 18, 1928, and paid the remainder on December 21. See Chester H. Johnson, invoice to Walter S. Brewster, December 19, 1928 [annotated December 21, 1928], in Mr. and Mrs. Walter Brewster General Correspondence file, AIC Archives. See Chicago 1929, no. 18; Cambridge 1929, no. 94; New York 1929a, no. 94; and Alfred H. Barr Jr., letter to Walter S. Brewster, October 7, 1929, in Mr. and Mrs. Walter Brewster General Correspondence file, AIC Archives.

93 It is likely that Coburn purchased the drawing from C. W. Kraushaar Art Galleries, New York, in 1928. A Kraushaar label once on the verso and bearing the title "Landscape" is preserved in Curatorial Object File 1949.382, AIC. And when Brewster thanked Coburn for selling them this work, he indicated that Coburn would have had it in her possession in the fall of 1928. See [Walter Brewster], letter to Mrs. Lewis L. Coburn, May 1, 1929, in Mr. and Mrs. Walter Brewster General Correspondence file, AIC Archives. The work is possibly New York 1928, no. 72. For more information about Coburn, see "Mrs. Lewis Larned (Annie Swan) Coburn," in Groom and Shaw 2014, https://publications.artic.edu/monet/reader/paintingsanddrawings/section/136368/136368_anchor.

94 F468 was in Coburn's collection by May 28, 1928, when it came to the Art Institute as a loan; see Receipt no. R.3778, May 28, 1928, copy in Curatorial Object File 1933.433, AIC; it was probably acquired from Howard Young after 1925 according to the AIC's registration card for the work; copy, ibid. "Self-Portrait with Pipe," was acquired by September 5, 1927, when it was endorsed by De la Faille; it was published by him as a forgery in De la Faille 1930, no. 527bis, pl. XV. Julius Meier-Graefe also endorsed the work and considered it "one of the most beautiful Self Portraits." Copies of these authentications are located in the Vincent van Gogh file, AIC Archives.

95 For a succinct early history of the Nelson-Atkins, see "Ready for Art: The 1933 Opening of the Nelson-Atkins Museum of Art," https://g.co/arts/gZYzxFmgW8Fco8oU7, accessed November 2019. My thanks go especially to Aimée Marcereau DeGalan, Meghan Gray, and Tara Laver for providing access to Nelson-Atkins archival materials. Comprehensive provenance for *Olive Trees* can be found at: https://art.nelson-atkins.org/objects/8083/olive-trees?ctx=e2438ad6-ad8e-424a-a918-b2e413990327&idx=0 and is included in Marcereau DeGalan 2021.

96 *Kansas City Star* 1931: E.

97 J. C. Nichols, letter to Harold W. Parsons, March 13, 1931; and Harold W. Parsons, letter to J. C. Nichols, May 2, 1931, copies in Curatorial Object File 32.2, The Nelson-Atkins Art Museum, Kansas City (hereafter Nelson-Atkins).

98 Effie Seachrest, letter to J. C. Nichols, May 17, 1931, in The Nelson-Atkins Museum of Art Archives (hereafter NAMA Archives), William Rockhill Nelson Trust Office Records (RG 80/05), Series II: Objects Offered, 1926–33, Box 7, Folder 12.

99 See Minutes of the Meeting of Trustees, January 12, 1932, copy in Curatorial Object File 32.2, Nelson-Atkins.

100 Durand-Ruel's initial price on June 4, 1931, was $60,000, however they offered it to the museum for $47,500 because "Nelson was one of our old clients." On June 8, the trust responded that they were not interested in the painting at $47,500 because "we believe that even supreme works of art will suffer the same depression in prices as other things." By January 25, 1932, Durand-Ruel had accepted the offer of $25,000 despite the fact that their Paris office initially had set their lowest price at $38,000 and they were taking a loss. See Edwin C. Holston (Durand-Ruel, New York), letter to J. C. Nichols, June 4, 1931; J. C. Nichols, letter to Edwin C. Holston, June 8, 1931; and Durand-Ruel, letter to J. C. Nichols, January 25, 1932, all in NAMA Archives, RG 80/05, Series II, Box 7, Folder 12. Indeed, the painting's initial price was already a good deal. In April 1931, the Valentine Gallery had offered *Portrait of Patience Escalier* (F444) to the Nelson-Atkins for $100,000, which was promptly declined. See Valentine Dudensing, letter to Harold W. Parsons, April 1, 1931; and Harold W. Parsons, letter to Valentine Dudensing, April 6, 1931, copies in Curatorial Object File 32.2, Nelson-Atkins.

101 See AIC Director [Robert Harshe], letter to Joseph Winterbotham, September 30, 1929, in Winterbotham-Harshe correspondence file, AIC Archives; AIC Director [Robert Harshe], letter to Joseph Winterbotham, September 30, 1932, ibid.; and Smith 1993: 63.

102 Chicago 1933, xiii.

103 Prince 1990b, 111–12; Brettell and Prince 1990, 222–23.

104 Much to the chagrin of some donors, including Frederic Clay Bartlett, who was very particular in the way he wanted to see the Birch Bartlett Memorial Collection hung. See Brettell and Prince 1990, 223; Smith 1993: 63, 106n17.

105 See Chicago 1933, nos. 375–87, 880–81. Two drawings listed as Van Gogh—"Cypresses" (F1524) and "Pastoral (Harvesting)" from the Art Institute's collection—were likely exhibited separately in a corridor; see Chicago 1933, xiv. The work called "Pastoral (Harvesting)" was a gift to the Art Institute in 1921 and has since been downgraded to an imitator of Van Gogh; see note 51. For the popularity of the Van Gogh room in Chicago 1933, see unidentified clipping, William Rockhill Nelson Gallery of Art and Atkins Museum, Kansas City, 1936 exhibition file, VGMD.

106 AIC Director [Robert Harshe], letter to Robert Treat Paine II, December 27, 1932, in Robert Harshe Papers, Century of Progress, 1933 Correspondence P–Q File, AIC Archives.

107 AIC Director [Robert Harshe], letters to Dorothy Sturges, December 4, 1932, and December 27, 1932, ibid., 1933 Correspondence Sti–Sz File. These letters suggest that the other version of this painting (F657) was also slated to be in the exhibition, but that would not come to pass. The painting had to be returned to France because of "legal complications."

108 See Dorothy Sturges, letter to Robert Harshe, December 5, [1932], ibid.

109 AIC Director [Robert Harshe], letter to M. Knoedler, December 30, 1932, ibid., 1933, Correspondence K File.

110 Knoedler acknowledged the return of the painting after the exhibition. See Charles R. Henschel, letter to Robert Harshe, November 20, 1933, ibid. Tannahill would bequeath the painting to the Detroit Institute of Arts in 1970.

111 Marie Harriman, letter to Robert Harshe, October 20, 1933, ibid., 1933, Correspondence H–I File. The catalogue does not list any of the works that Harriman lent as being for sale.

112 For 1933 attendance and the 1934 exhibition theme, see Robert Harshe, letter to Clyde H. Burroughs, January 31, 1934, ibid., 1934, Correspondence D–Dr File. See also Chicago 1934, ix, and nos. 310–16.

113 Toledo 1934, nos. 24–26.

114 See https://www.slam.org/collection/objects/33826/, accessed August 2019; *Art News* 1935a: 8; and *Art News* 1935b: 8.

115 *New York Times* 1936b: X7.

116 See https://www.moma.org/documents/moma_press-release_325262.pdf, accessed July 2019.

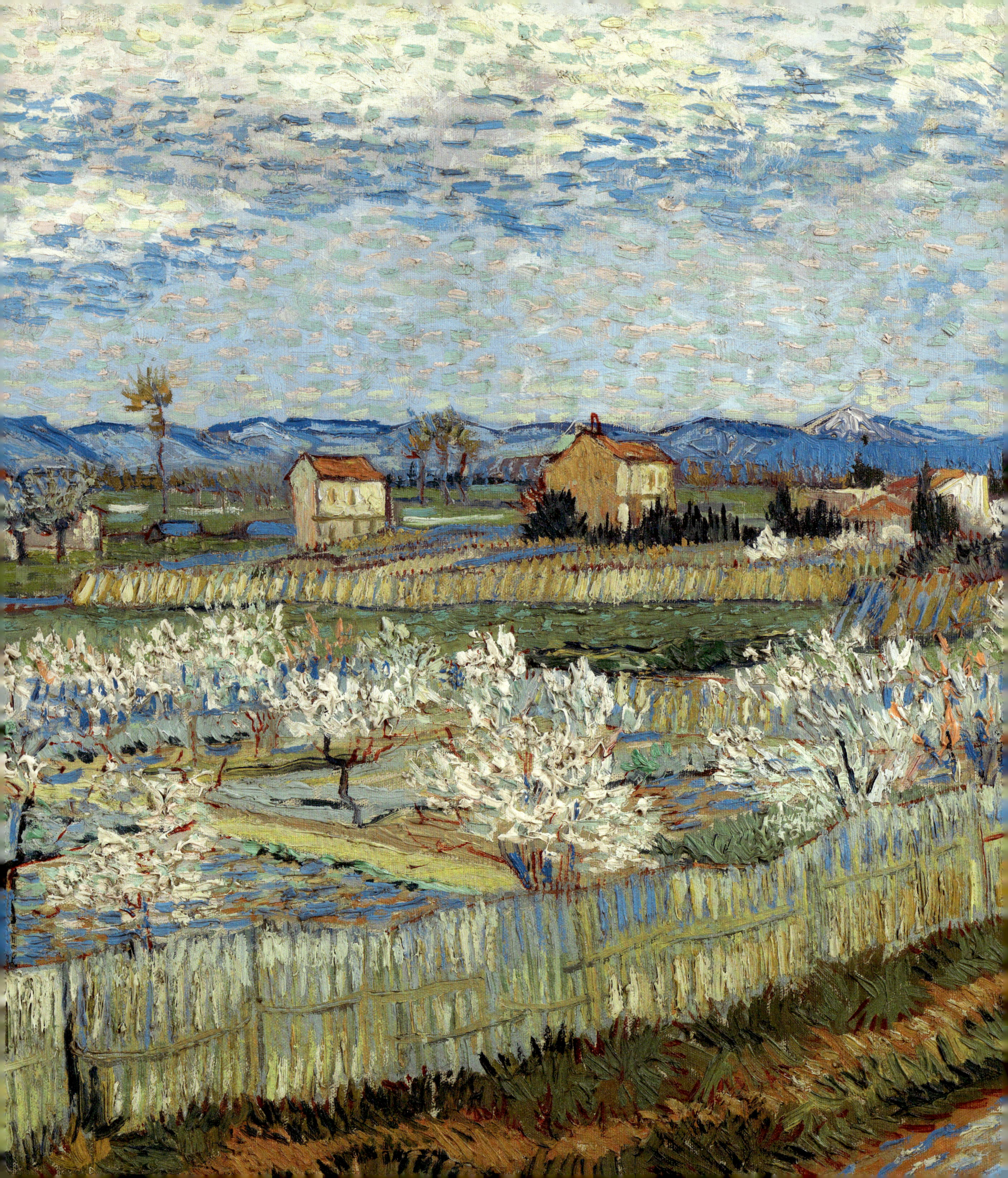

RACHEL ESNER

Van Gogh in (and around) Hollywood, 1920–70

Two men are seated at a table with what looks at first glance to be a sketchbook by the world's most famous modern artist: Vincent van Gogh. The man on the left, his shirt casually unbuttoned, places the gloved hand of his companion on one of the drawings, pressing it down firmly on the paper. The second man, red-headed, his eyes closed, has his other hand on his heart. A concentrated but serene smile plays across his lined face. This image, published in *Monaco-Matin* in March 2019,[1] shows the artist and film director Julian Schnabel and the actor Willem Dafoe during a presentation of what some scholars have claimed to be a group of previously unknown Van Gogh drawings,[2] "discovered" some years before by Franck Baille, president of the Hôtel des Ventes de Monte-Carlo, in a ledger said to have belonged to Van Gogh's Arles landlady, Madame Ginoux.

The "sketchbook," which was categorically rejected by the Van Gogh Museum in Amsterdam in 2016,[3] plays a central role in Schnabel and Dafoe's film, *At Eternity's Gate* (2018), which purports to trace the last years of Van Gogh's life in Arles and Auvers. The photograph thus takes on a peculiar significance. In essence, it depicts Dafoe "channeling" Van Gogh through his art, the actor somehow "becoming" the artist. This transmogrification is subsequently evidenced in Dafoe's convincing—and incidentally rather moving—performance in the film. Despite an age gap of more than thirty years, the actor strongly resembles the painter, while the film's sense of authenticity is further underlined by the camerawork, which depicts the world largely through the eyes of its protagonist. As film historians have pointed out, the indexicality of the filmic medium, a strong physical resemblance between the Hollywood star and the person he (or occasionally, she) portrays, and the embodied authenticity of the performance all combine in biopics to create what appear to be irrefutable facts, which in turn shape the public's understanding of historical figures.[4] And so it is in *At Eternity's Gate*. The film deploys every means possible to appear as true and thereby to retroactively authenticate not only this specific (and controversial) account of Van Gogh's last years, in particular the question of whether he was accidentally murdered or took his own life,[5] but also the sketchbook itself. Having lived intensely in Van Gogh's world for almost two hours, how could the viewer fail to be convinced that what she had just witnessed was in fact what had actually happened? And indeed, at the end of the film, as a prelude to the credits, we are treated to a conclusive statement: "Madame Ginoux never knew Van Gogh had returned the account ledger to her having filled it with 65 drawings. The ledger was found 126 years later, in 2016." This intertwining of fact and fiction, as well as the use of Van Gogh and the many myths surrounding his life for a variety of purposes having little to do with art, is typical of the reception the artist enjoyed on the West Coast in the twentieth century, especially during the years 1920–70, the Golden Age of Hollywood cinema, and a time when both San Francisco and Los Angeles sought to establish themselves on a cultural footing equal with that of New York and other art centers on the eastern seaboard.

The Exhibitions

Despite his popularity as the subject of films, television, and documentaries, and of his work among Hollywood collectors, Van Gogh began his conquest of the West Coast not in Los Angeles, but in San Francisco. During the 1915 *Panama-Pacific International Exposition*, his *Moulin de la Galette* (F228; plate 63) was on display.[6] Here we find the artist situated in the United States section along with other (mainly French) modernists, rather than in the Dutch section proper. In his catalogue introduction to the 1916 San Diego version of the San Francisco show (which, however, did not include any work by Van Gogh), art critic J. Nilsen Laurvik writes:

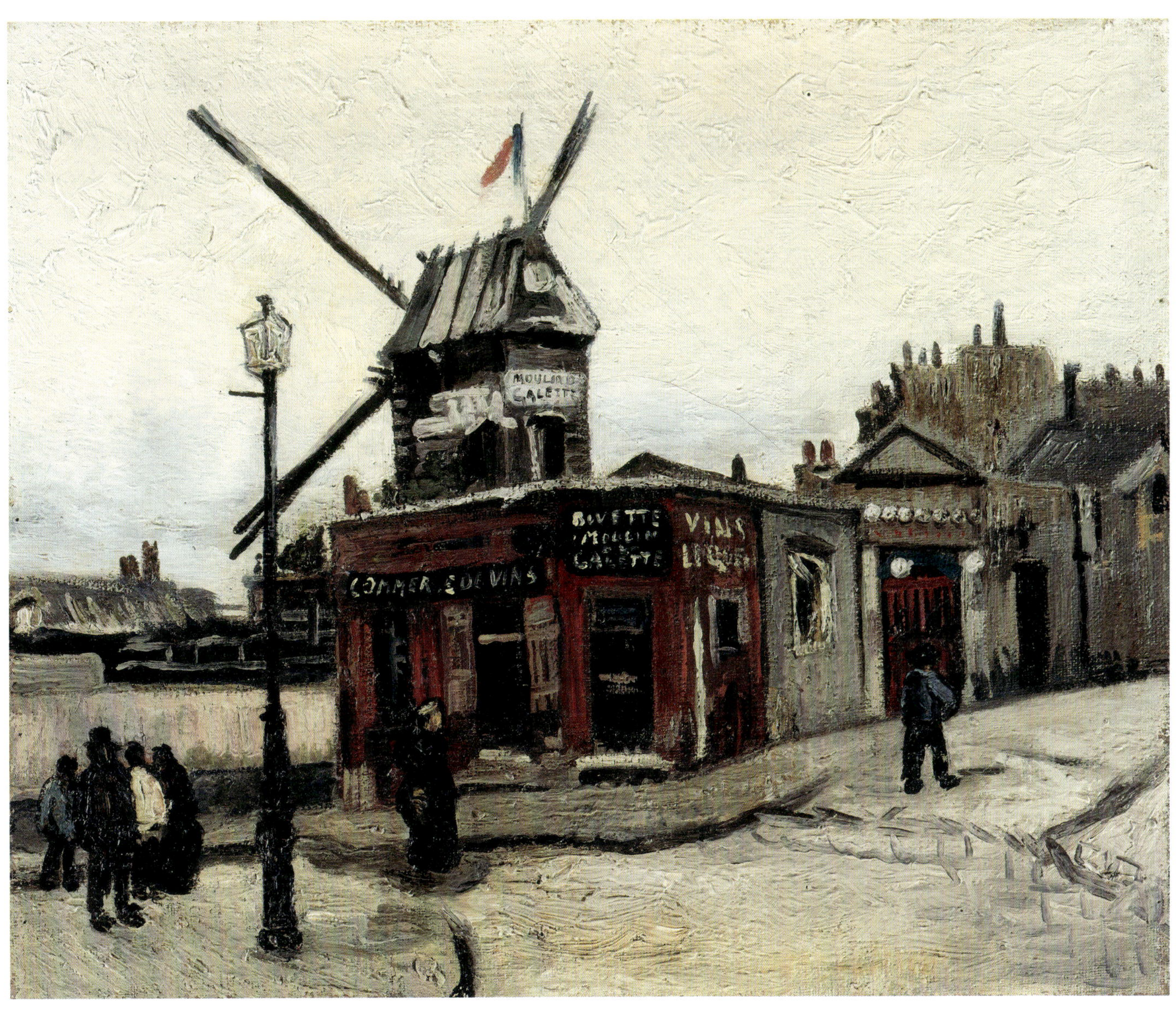

PLATE 63. *Le Moulin de la Galette*, 1886 (CAT. 19)

> However, the real Renaissance of modern art in Holland begins not with these men [the Hague School] who so eloquently reaffirmed the ancient gospel of their predecessors; its birth dates, phoenix-like, from the death of Vincent van Gogh.... This extraordinary luminary who disappeared so sadly in the West was soon to rise again in the East and eclipse the lunar lights who had made the dark night of modern Dutch art bright with their presence. The saffron-streaked dawn of the day approaches, and with it those exponents of a more luminous, colorful palette that threatens to completely change the face of art in Holland as it has elsewhere in the world.[7]

Although his work was included in another California exhibition in 1924–25,[8] Van Gogh's first Hollywood appearance would have to wait until 1933, when the Los Angeles Museum exhibited *Portrait of Père Tanguy (Julien Tanguy, 1825–1894)* (F364; fig. 1)—a work that would soon come into the collection of the actor

FIG. 1 *Portrait of Père Tanguy (Julien Tanguy, 1825–1894)* (F364), 1887–88. Oil on canvas, 25⁹⁄₁₆ × 20¹⁄₁₆ in. (65 × 51 cm). Stavros Niarchos Collection.

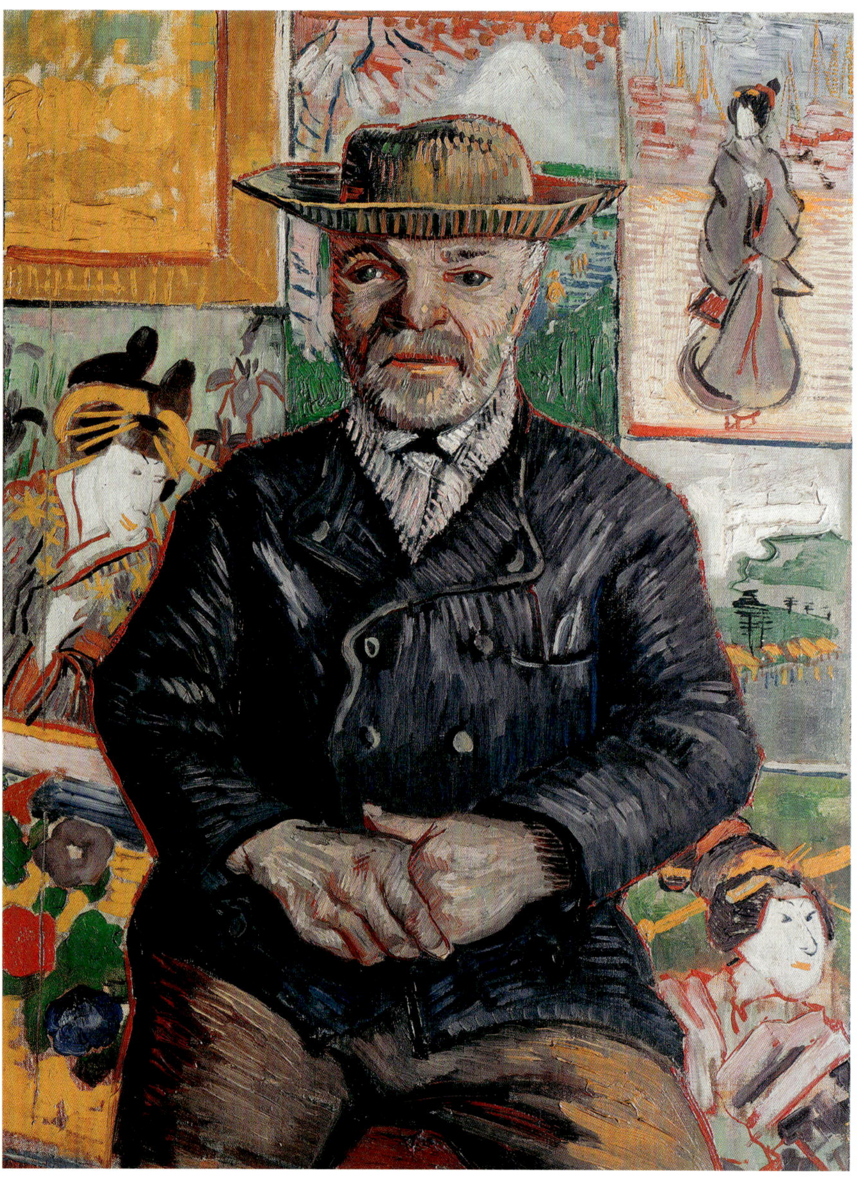

Edward G. Robinson—and *Wheat Fields with Reaper, Auvers* (F559; plate 60) in a show entitled *Five Centuries of European Painting*. Here again the artist is placed among his French rather than Dutch contemporaries, but is also labeled as an exponent of what is described as "typically Northern, Germanic" art; for the author Ernst L. Tross, Van Gogh represented "the ideal of Northern, of Gothic art."[9]

Although his pictures appeared sporadically in exhibitions during the following years,[10] on the West Coast as elsewhere, Van Gogh's real breakthrough came in 1935–36, with the arrival in California of the grand retrospective prepared by Alfred H. Barr Jr. and the Museum of Modern Art in New York.[11] Once again, however, it was San Francisco that had the privilege of hosting the show, much to the chagrin of a group of "distinguished representative members of Museum Art Association film producers directors executives collectors etc.," who cabled the organizers several times in a desperate attempt to bring the exhibition to Los Angeles, even offering to double the required loan fee.[12] In addition to the works borrowed from the collections of Vincent Willem van Gogh and Helene Kröller-Müller, the San Francisco venue included four more works, two of which came from the California collectors Mr. and Mrs. W. W. Crocker: *Cypress and Olive Trees, St. Rémy* (F743) and *Ploughing* (F625). Also present was *Portrait of Père Tanguy* (F364), again lent by Wildenstein.[13]

As had been the case elsewhere, the show was a resounding success, receiving some 227,540 visitors in four weeks and forcing the Palace of the Legion of Honor to extend its hours.[14] On April 26, just before the opening, the *San Francisco Chronicle* reprinted the article by Irving Stone that had accompanied the exhibition at its other venues, based on his bestseller *Lust for Life* (1934). Titled "Van Gogh Exhibition Is Symbol in Pigment of a Spiritual Epic," the article describes the discrepancy between the value of Van Gogh's work in Stone's own time and when it was made, explaining this phenomenon through the dramatic details of the artist's biography. For Stone, Van Gogh's life and work were inseparably intertwined: the artist may have been "a pioneer" and "a precursor" whose works were "painted in hot blood," but they were above all symbols of the painter's spiritual journey as a man.[15] This approach to Van Gogh was not without its dangers, as noted several weeks later by the *Chronicle*'s critic Alfred Frankenstein, who sought to differentiate between understanding a life and understanding an artwork: "I would suggest that the story of van Gogh's life is only part of the whole

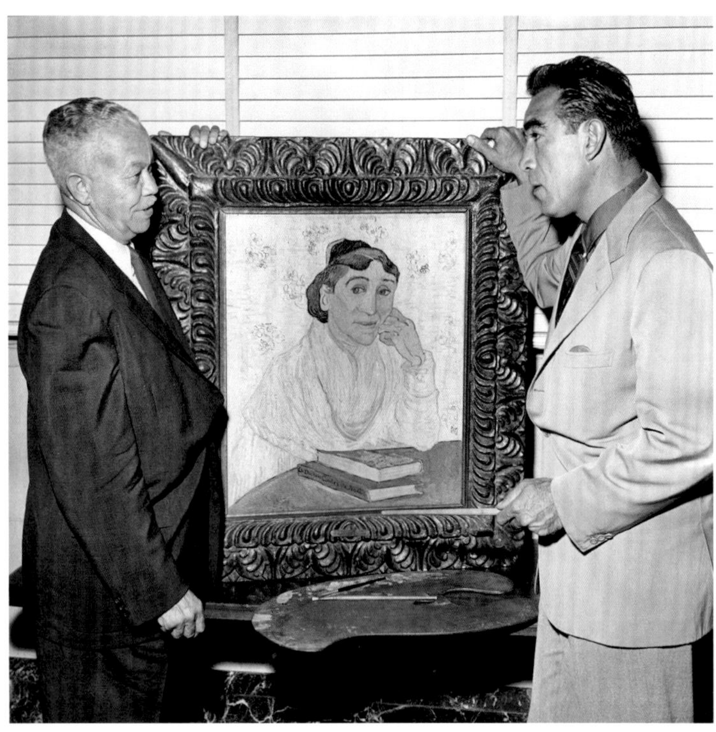

FIG. 2 Actor Anthony Quinn and president of the Municipal Art Commission of Los Angeles Paul R. Williams viewing *L'Arlésienne, Madame Ginoux* (F543; plate 41) before it was installed in *Vincent van Gogh: A Loan Exhibition of Paintings and Drawings* at the Municipal Art Gallery, Los Angeles, 1957.

story, and that the clue to what a genius does in paint is more likely to be found in the paint than in what he does with his right ear."[16] Far more significant for Frankenstein was that, thanks to the huge number of visitors, many of them bused in from as far away as Seattle and Portland, "the show [had] probably done more to break down popular prejudices against modern art than an army of lecturers terrible with polysyllables and colored slides, and in this respect its ultimate, general effects will be felt for a long time."[17] This was undoubtedly true, but the indissoluble link Stone had created between the artist's biography and his oeuvre, and the myths this gave rise to, were to prove far more powerful in determining how Van Gogh was understood by the American public.

Van Gogh's pictures, including several from California collections, could be seen in both San Francisco and Los Angeles in the following years,[18] but the next major shows would not take place until 1957 (fig. 2) and 1958–59.[19] Significant for the reception of these two events—the latter a kind of repeat performance of the 1935–36 touring exhibition featuring the collection of Vincent Willem van Gogh[20]—was undoubtedly the release in 1956 of Vincente Minnelli's *Lust for Life*. The film's formative power on the audience's understanding of Van Gogh should not be underestimated. It had a rich visual language and included reproductions of scores of the artist's paintings and drawings from all phases of his career (for example, F141, F348a, F474, F514, F777, F781; plates 64–69). Moreover, the intense performance of the movie's lead, Kirk Douglas, added a new, colorful, living and breathing dimension to Irving Stone's already influential book: the man on screen was the real Van Gogh. From this point forward, Douglas's portrayal, troubled and extreme in all respects, became the abiding image of the artist. Van Gogh's more reflective and intellectual side, his concern for solving artistic rather than emotional problems with his painting—both of which are fully manifest in the letters—would henceforth be entirely ignored by the public and scholars alike.

This is already evident in art historian John Rewald's introduction to the catalogue of the 1957 show. Here Rewald abandons any pretense of academic distance, trading in his normally sober writing style for something significantly more flamboyant. The introduction opens with the artist's suicide and a description of his suffering. Van Gogh is "the very symbol of the artist who risks his life and sanity for a calling to which he devotes himself with consummate fervor but

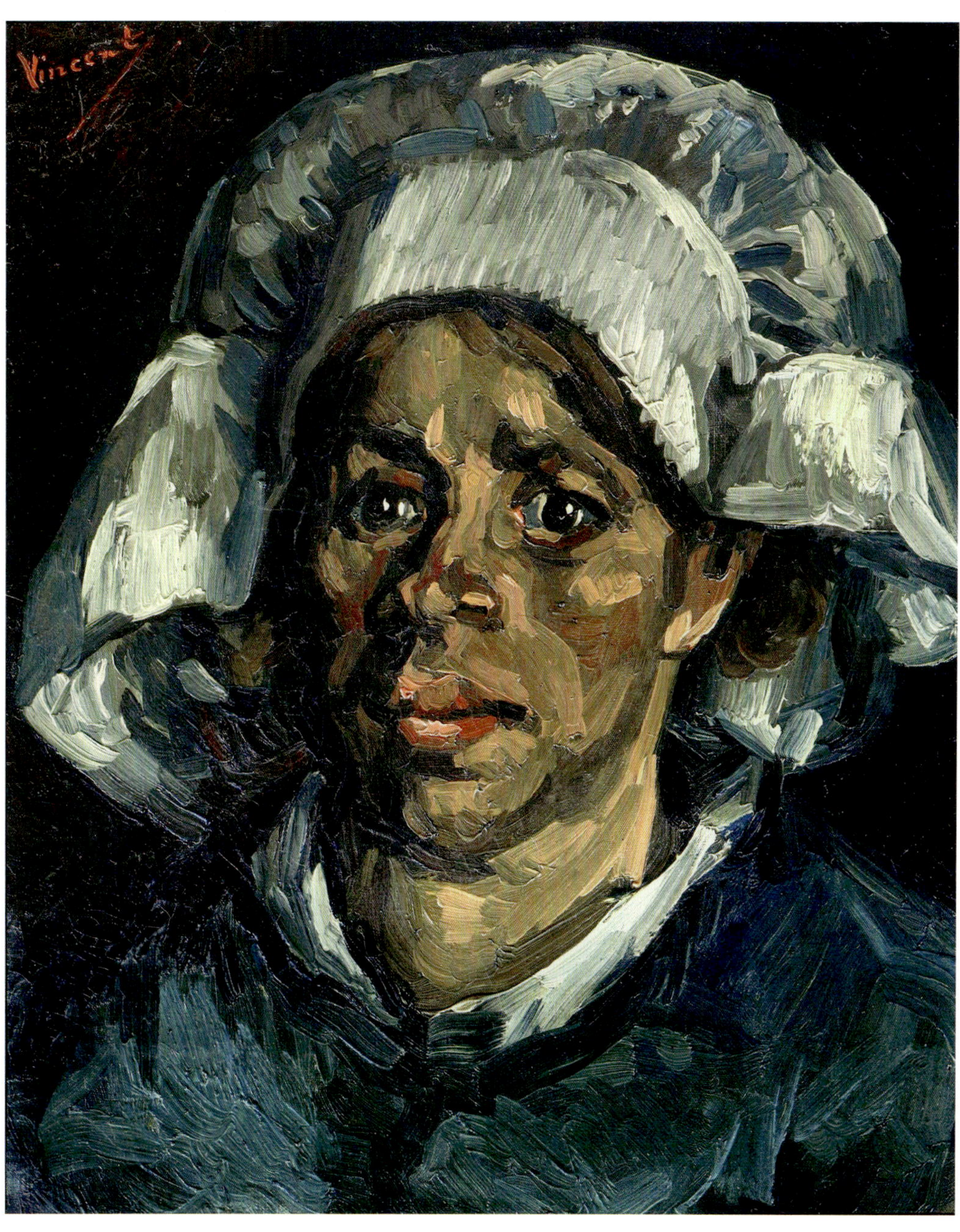

PLATE 64. *Head of Gordina de Groot*, 1885 (CAT. 11)

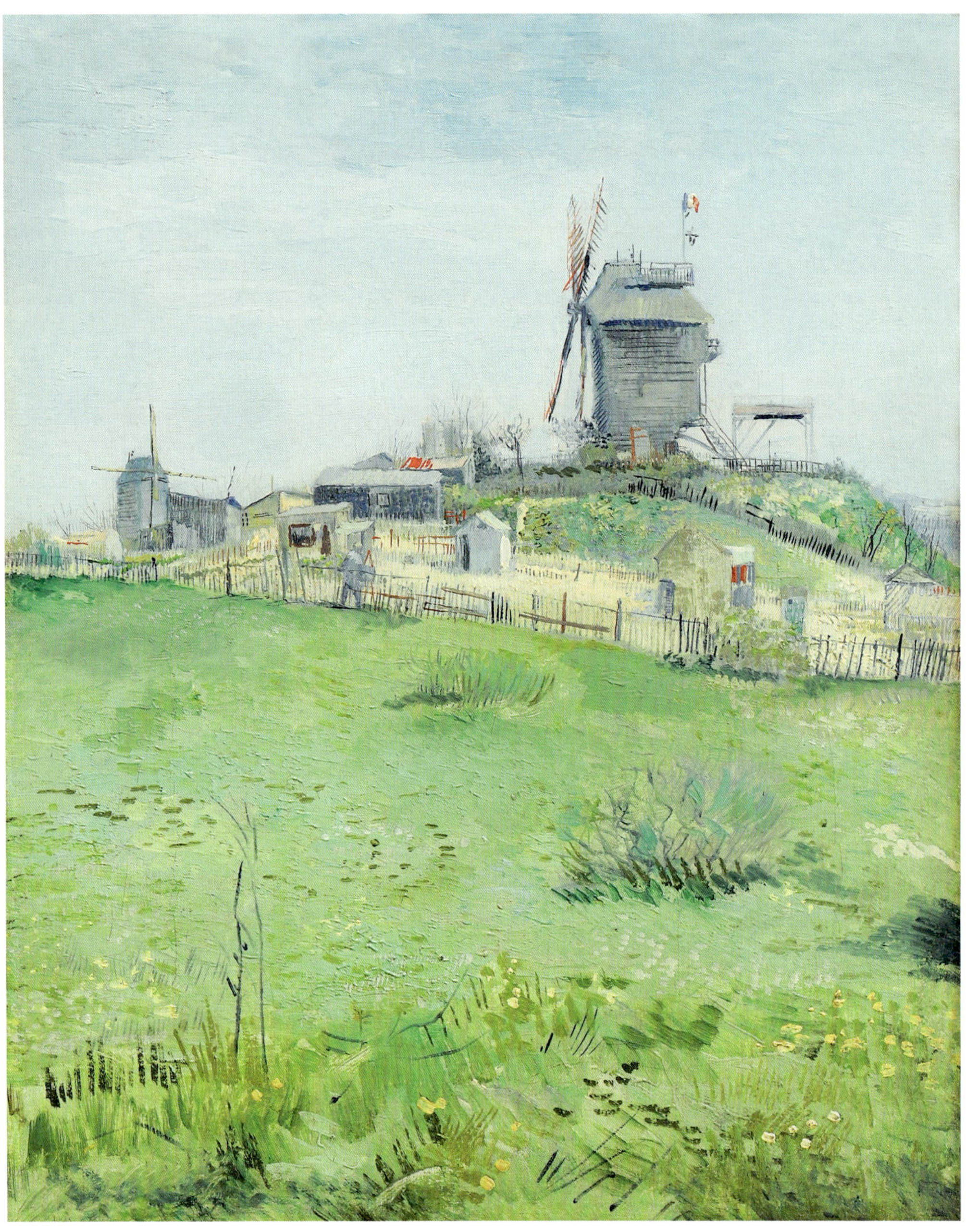

PLATE 65. *Le Moulin de la Galette*, 1886–87 (CAT. 15)

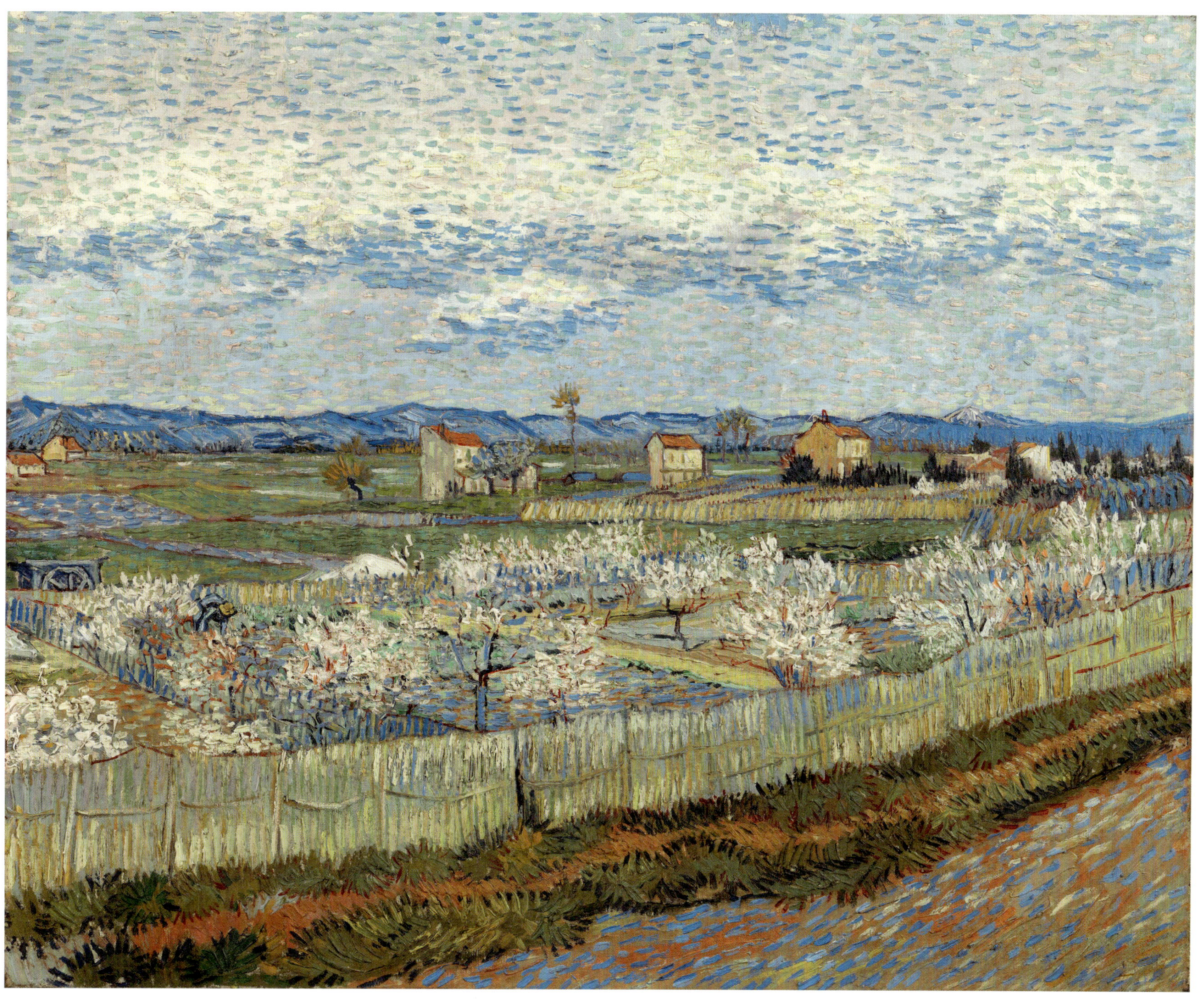

PLATE 66. *Peach Trees in Blossom*, 1889 (CAT. 47)

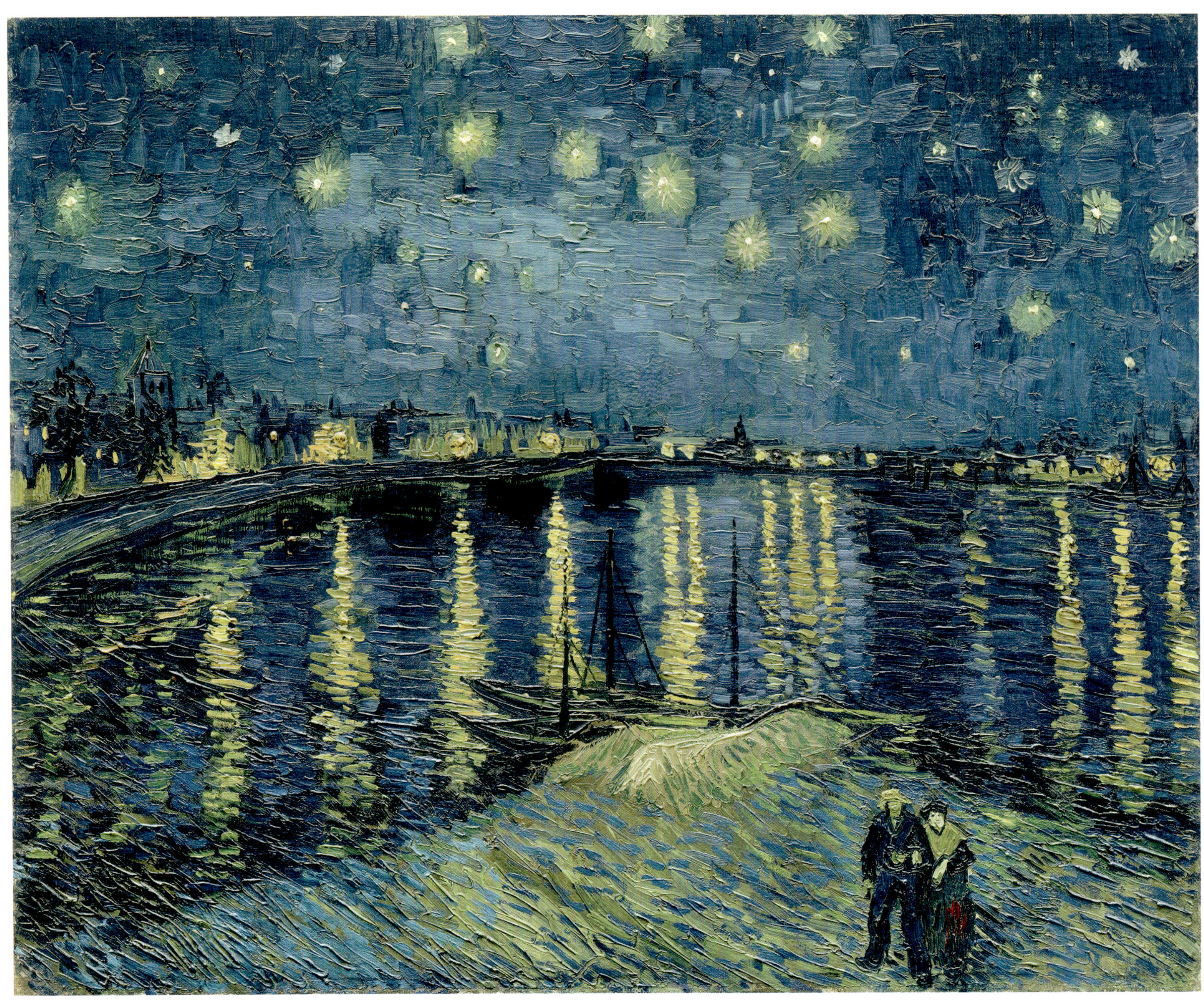

PLATE 67. *Starry Night*, 1888 (CAT. 37)

whose rewards are posthumous only." Rewald speaks of Van Gogh's "singular destiny," describing his life as "a Horatio Alger story of an artist"—taking his fate into his own hands and transforming himself into a painter only "by willpower." "Van Gogh became an artist because he *wanted* to be one," Rewald writes, and as such could "serve as a beacon for future generations."[21] This association of the artist with the myth of "the self-made man" is also one of the major tropes in Minnelli's film, making Van Gogh a role model for postwar American audiences.

The 1958–59 exhibition was important for other reasons. Striking in the reception in both San Francisco and Los Angeles is the attention paid to the social ramifications of the show and the different meanings the two cities attached to them. In the run-up to the San Francisco venue, for example, the newspapers were full of photographs of local socialites preparing for the show's arrival; note was taken of restaurants serving Dutch meals and shops decorating their windows in Van Gogh's honor.[22] The city was extremely proud of its role as host, understanding it not only in cultural but also economic terms; with a final attendance of 440,767, local businesses had apparently flourished, and some employers even felt that the show was so important they gave their staff time off to visit it.[23] Much was made of the exhibition's enormous and broad appeal (fig. 3). As the museum's newsletter, the *De Young Muse*, noted: "Newspapers and magazines have devoted reams of copy to [the exhibition] and radio and television stations have given hours of time. Several movie theaters riding on the crest of the ... exhibition's popularity have brought back Van Gogh's biographical film 'Lust for Life'...." Teenage girls had been spotted "buzzing excitedly" from one picture to another—one of them exclaiming "breathlessly, 'How immortal can you get!'" For the museum, it was the social makeup of the crowds that was of paramount interest and importance. According to "Art Makes Return to Man on Street," a tellingly titled article in the *Petaluma Argus Courier*: "Anybody who still thinks that

FIG. 3 Crowds gathered in front of the M. H. de Young Memorial Museum in San Francisco to view the *Vincent van Gogh: Paintings and Drawings* exhibition, *San Francisco Examiner*, October 13, 1958.

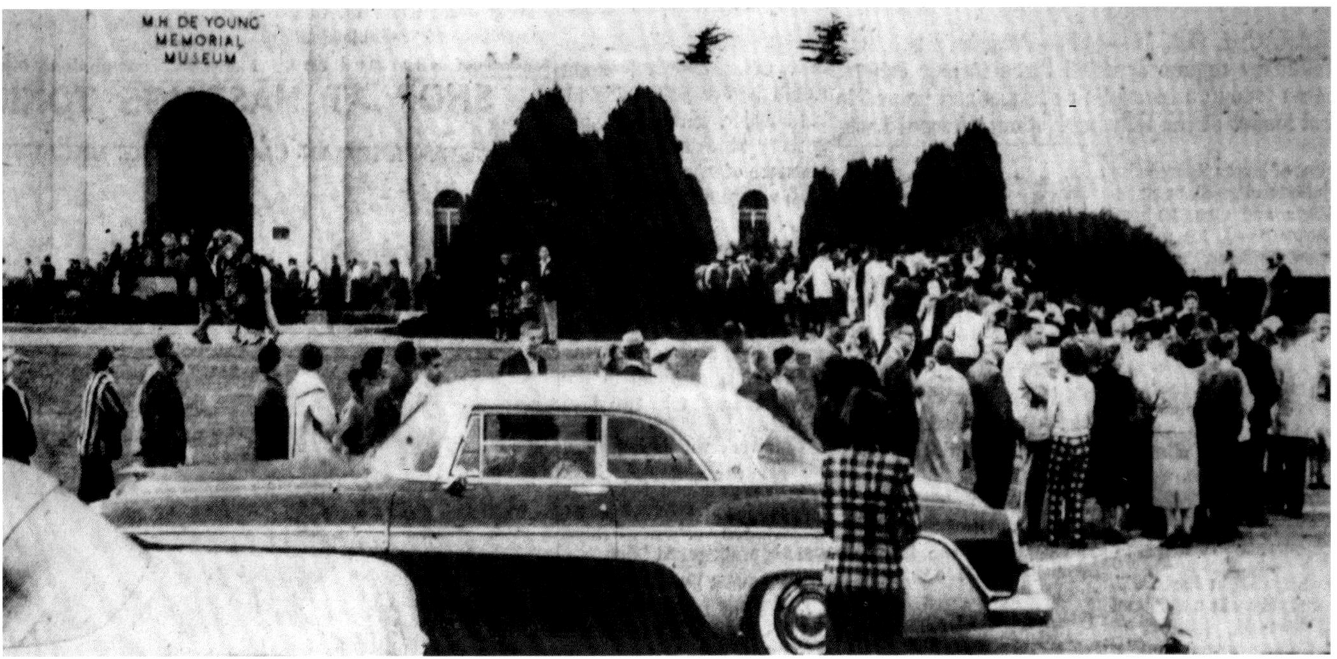

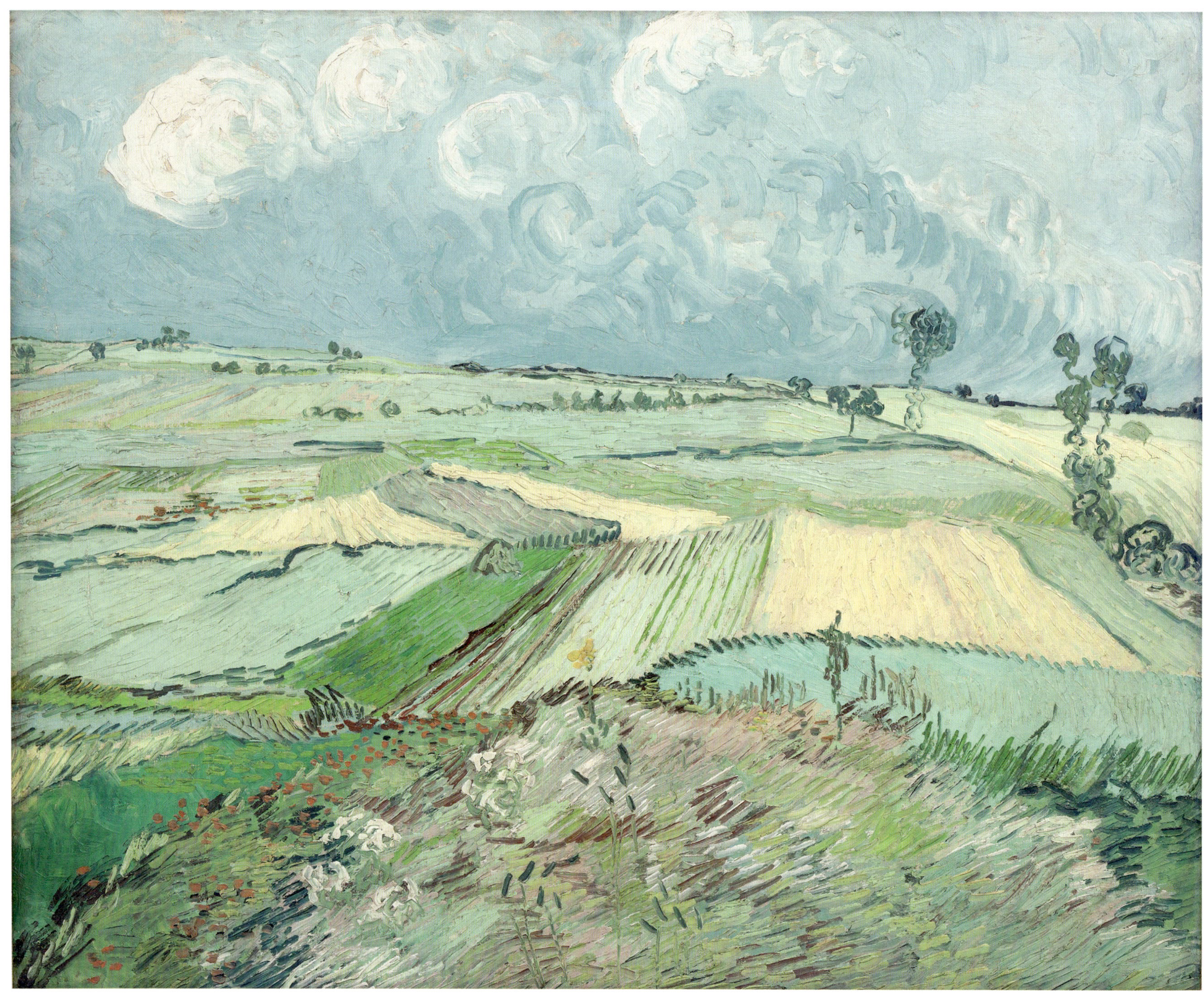

PLATE 68. *Wheat Fields after the Rain (The Plain of Auvers)*, 1890 (CAT. 69)

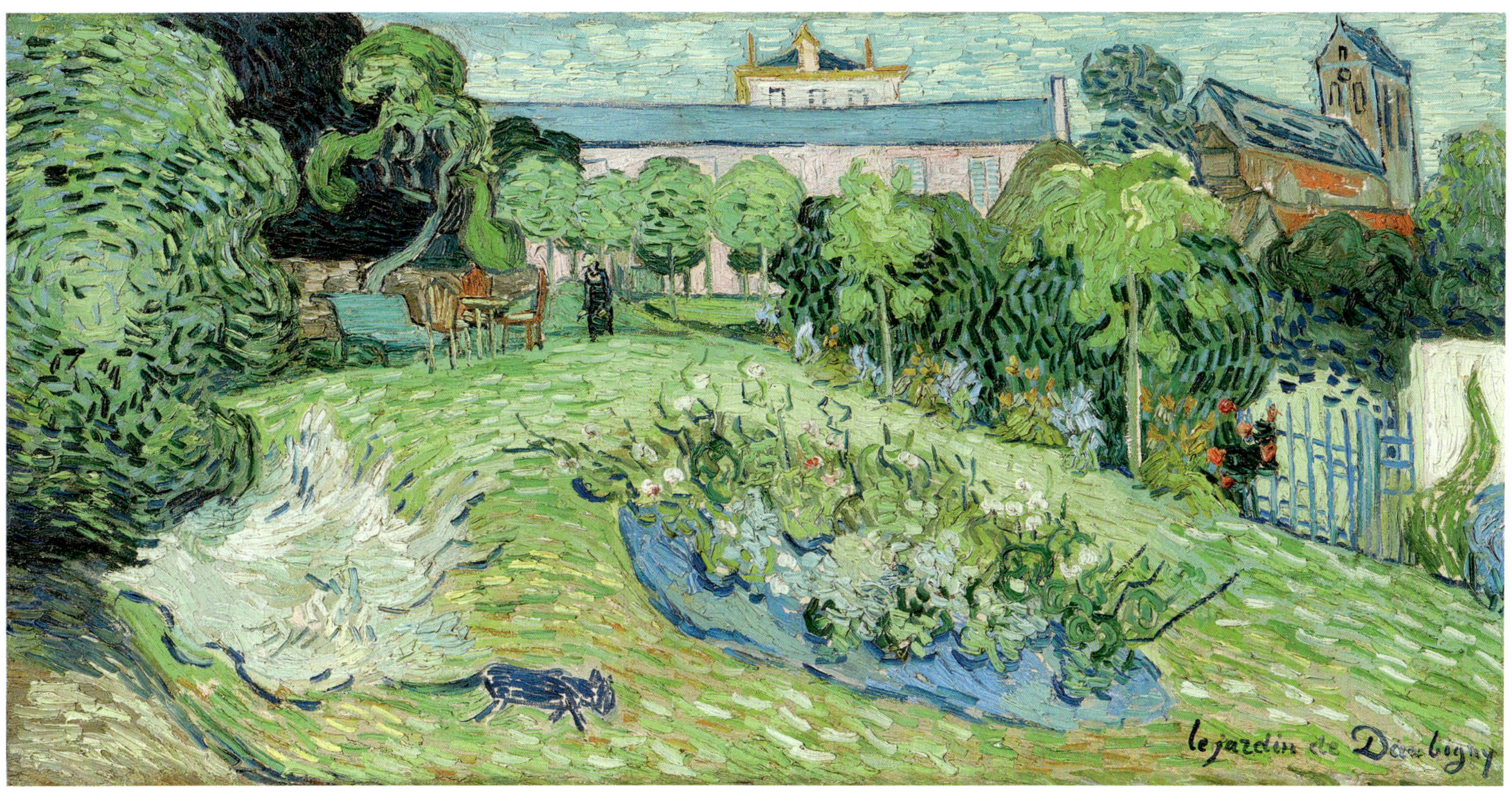

PLATE 69. *Daubigny's Garden*, 1890 (CAT. 70)

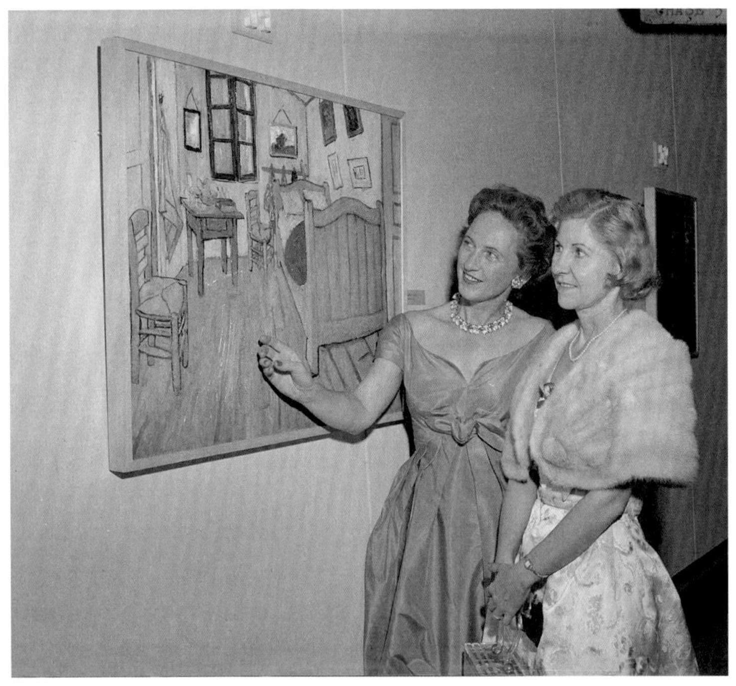

FIG. 4 Visitors in front of *The Bedroom* (F482) at the preview for *Vincent van Gogh: Paintings and Drawings* at the Los Angeles County Museum, *Los Angeles Times*, December 10, 1958.

the so-called 'blue-noses' and bohemians are the only people who are interested in great art haven't been to the De Young Museum in San Francisco recently." The article noted that the people attending the exhibition looked like a regular crowd at a baseball game: visitors were dressed in everything from fur coats to shorts, all fascinated by the art and many buying the catalogue.[24] Given the admission price of only fifty cents, this was probably precisely the outcome the museum had intended.

Having failed to bring the MoMA show to Los Angeles in 1935–36, the organizers this time around were determined that if nothing else, the exhibition would prove once and for all that the West Coast institutions were the equals of their East Coast counterparts when it came to cultural capital. Although much of the local press focused on the value of the works on display, the streams of visitors, and the fact that (probably for the first time) the pictures had been transported to California by airplane rather than ship or train, a significant number of articles showcased the involvement of the city's cultural elite, often accompanied by photographs of them admiring one of the artworks (fig. 4). The *Los Angeles Examiner*, for example, saw the show as the ultimate proof that Los Angeles could now legitimately call itself "a city of culture."[25]

It would then be ten years before San Francisco or Los Angeles would host another large-scale Van Gogh retrospective. Between 1969 and 1971, the two cities welcomed a traveling exhibition that more or less duplicated the 1958–59 show, with sixty-eight paintings and forty-six drawings from the collection of Vincent Willem van Gogh.[26] If anything, the hype surrounding the show was greater than ever before: as several newspapers noted, Amsterdam was now building its own Van Gogh museum, which would undoubtedly make major events like this one nearly impossible in the future. The reviews indicate a slight shift in the image of the artist, with critics seeking to align Van Gogh with the current *Zeitgeist* and make his art more relevant to the times. A new generation had grown up since the release of *Lust for Life* and the earlier retrospectives. The art world, too, had changed, with Abstract Expressionism having made way for the more cerebral works of Pop and Conceptual Art. Although many critics still defaulted to the myth of the tortured and suffering artist, wearing the "nimbus of one of the early saints of modern art,"[27] others sought to relate Van Gogh's life and work to the concerns of the generation of 1968. Van Gogh had "lived a life of prodigious spiritual intensity,"[28] while his works carried in them "a sense of rebirth."[29] Much emphasis is put on the artist's interest in the poor and downtrodden, and

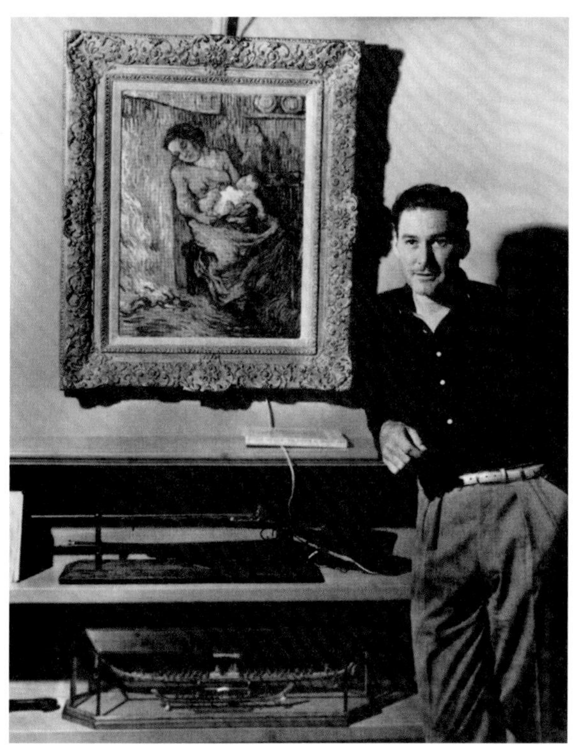

FIG. 5 Actor Errol Flynn at home with his Van Gogh painting, *The Man Is at Sea* (F644).

especially on his quest for transcendence. An article in the *Beverly Hills Courier*, for example, describes the crowds waiting to get into the exhibition as coming from all walks of life, both "hippie and haute couture," each wanting to get a glimpse of the art of a "high-school dropout" and "alcoholic." The critic writes: "His story provides an obvious lesson for the disillusioned youth of today. At the very depth of his deprivation, he still sought and clearly identified the beauty in the world."[30] *Los Angeles Times* critic Henry J. Seldis, too, made explicit reference to the current cultural climate: "We are living in a moment when Van Gogh's lonely and agonizing search for peace through an identification with the cosmological unity of nature has become the focal point of a new generation which speaks of love, of flowers and of peace with a faith that transcends today's atmosphere of hate and fear. Van Gogh belongs to them."[31]

The Collectors

Another intriguing chapter in Van Gogh's afterlife on the West Coast concerns his collectors. It should come as no surprise that many of them were celebrities in their own right, or deeply involved in the world of Hollywood film production. Los Angeles had no "old money" elite, and there can be little doubt that what these *nouveaux riches* hoped to gain from associating themselves with Van Gogh's life and legend was first and foremost cultural status. As a consequence, they sometimes made purchases that to our eyes may seem questionable. The Van Gogh pictures in Hollywood collections frequently have a whiff of scandal about them—even if only in regard to the reputation or life circumstances of the owner.

The best-known West Coast owners of Van Gogh pictures were the movie stars themselves: Errol Flynn, Edward G. Robinson, and Elizabeth Taylor.[32] Flynn's picture, *The Man Is at Sea* (F644), came into his possession via a circuitous route, passing from Paul Cassirer in Amsterdam through the art dealer Paul Graupe, who, with his business partner Arthur Goldschmidt, brought the work from Nazi-occupied Europe to the United States.[33] The actor purchased the picture from another dealer, Caesar R. Diorio, between July 1943 and 1944.[34] Flynn, the consummate on-screen swashbuckler, seems to have conjured his own story of the work's "rescue," describing it as having been "smuggled out of Holland just before the Nazis moved in."[35] The actor was apparently very fond of the picture and was always happy to show it off to his famous friends (fig. 5). In 1944 he opened a gallery with the equally flamboyant John Decker, an artist and set designer who

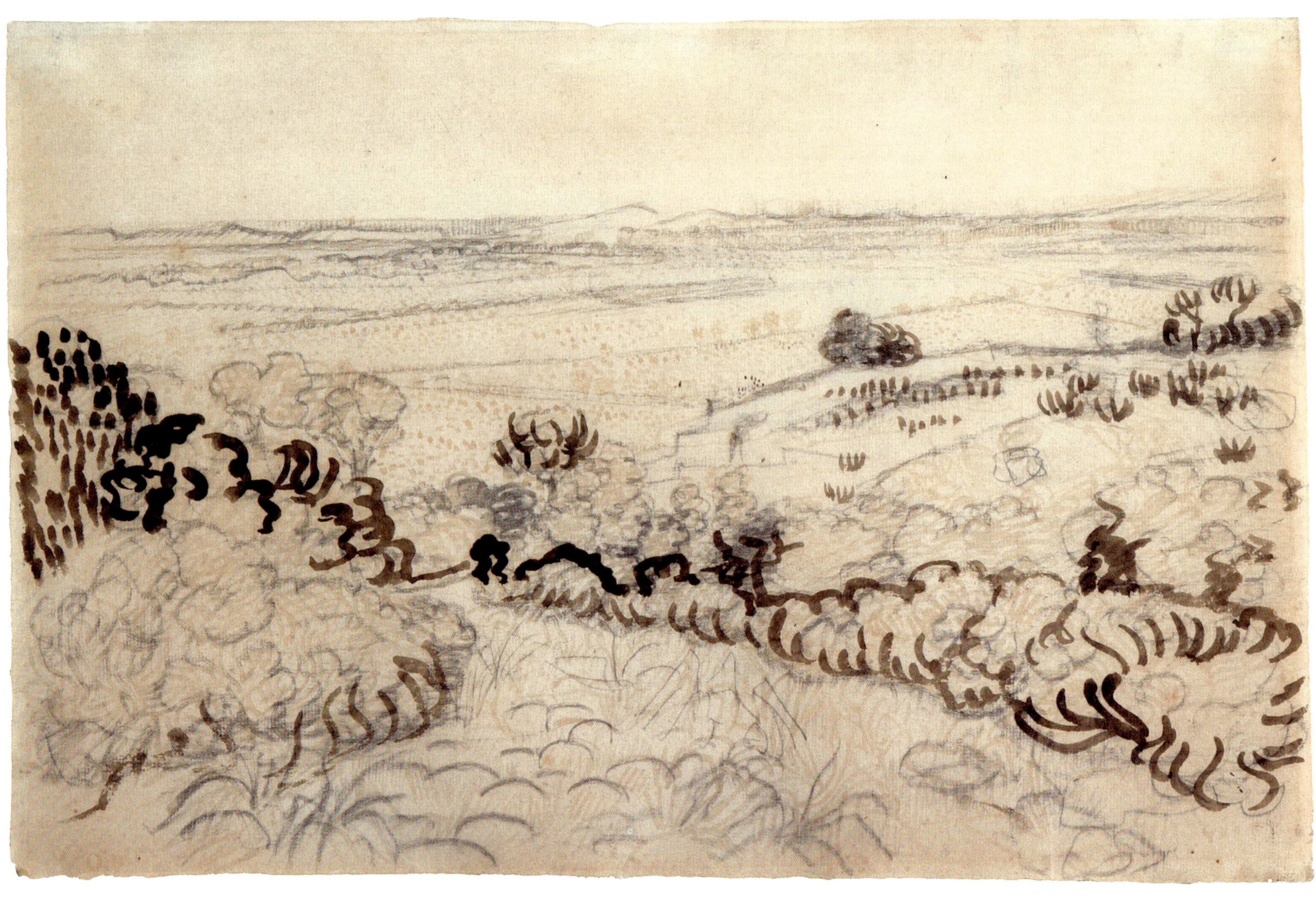

PLATE 70. *The Plain of La Crau*, 1888 (CAT. 30)

was apparently overly fond of "gold trinkets, salted butter, brass artifacts [and] Van Gogh canvases."[36] Their first show included not only *The Man Is at Sea* and Flynn's Gauguin, but also works by Courbet, Renoir, and Manet (*The Escape of Rochefort*), as well as some eighteenth-century Venetian paintings. The *Los Angeles Times* wrote: "Two of the most important paintings in the show, Gauguin's large and famous *At the Beach*, and Van Gogh's painting of a fisherman's wife, *The Man Is at Sea*, belong to Flynn personally, who explained that he is in partnership with Decker because he loves paintings and wants to make fine ones available to Hollywood folk."[37] In this, he certainly succeeded: the opening was attended by, among others, Michael Curtiz, director of the Flynn vehicles *Captain Blood* (1935) and *The Adventures of Robin Hood* (1938); the actress Faye Emerson; and actor and director Erich von Stroheim.[38] A few years later, the picture featured in an article on movie-star collectors in *Life*, with a color reproduction and the caption: "Superb Van Gogh is owned by Errol Flynn who bought it just after it was smuggled out of Nazi-dominated Holland. Flynn has been offered as much as $68,000 for his 'Woman by Fire with Child.'"[39] The picture would only be sold, however, in 1964.[40]

The story of Edward G. Robinson's two canvases by Van Gogh, *Portrait of Père Tanguy* (F364; fig. 1) and *The Old Willows* (F520) is somewhat less spectacular but no less typically Hollywood. *Portrait of Père Tanguy* was acquired in or around 1941,[41] while *The Old Willows* was purchased following a 1938 exhibition at Alex Reid & Lefevre in London titled, perhaps not surprisingly, *The Tragic Painters*.[42] Robinson's autobiography suggests a link between his interest in collecting and a desire to (posthumously) support (avant-garde) artists like Van Gogh, on the one hand, and, on the other, to boost his cultural capital and that of his city and country. An encounter with an exhibition of a private collection in Dresden had proven inspirational: "I immediately felt…that the role of collector had been given a definition I'd been striving to find all my life. A man who is not an artist yet is impelled to support, encourage, and, in effect, subsidize the artist—to make his work available to the public eye—what is he? An egotist? An investor? An exhibitionist getting his kicks by displaying not himself but his ownership? No, said the [exhibition] catalog, a man who 'can influence the artistic climate of a milieu, of a city, of a country.'"[43] In a 1941 article for *The Art News* (with the punning title "The Most Moving Pictures"), Robinson described his relationship to his collection as primarily affective: "intellectual" and abstract works were of no interest to him; rather, he felt attracted to works in which color and light were

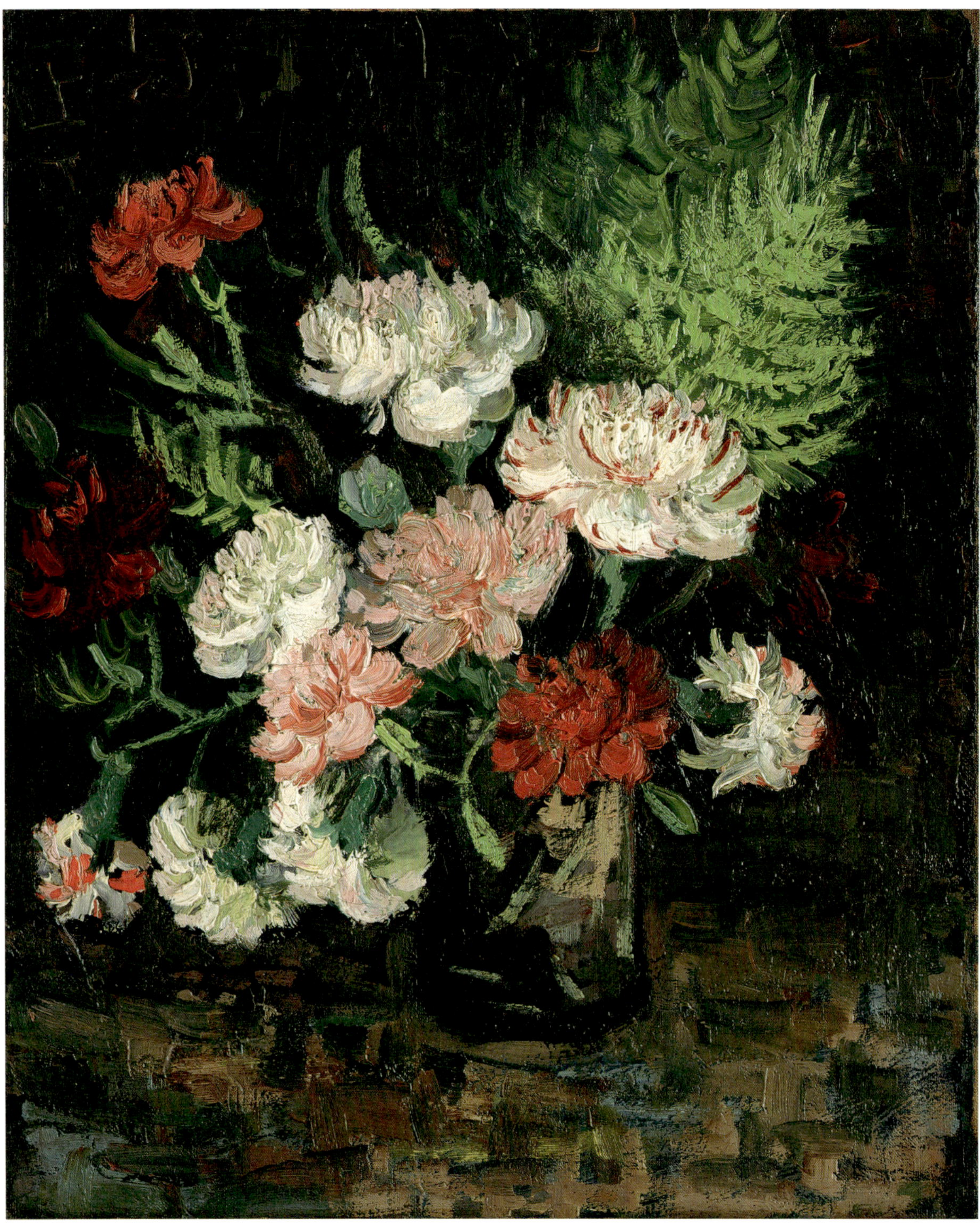

PLATE 71. *Vase with Carnations*, 1886 (CAT. 18)

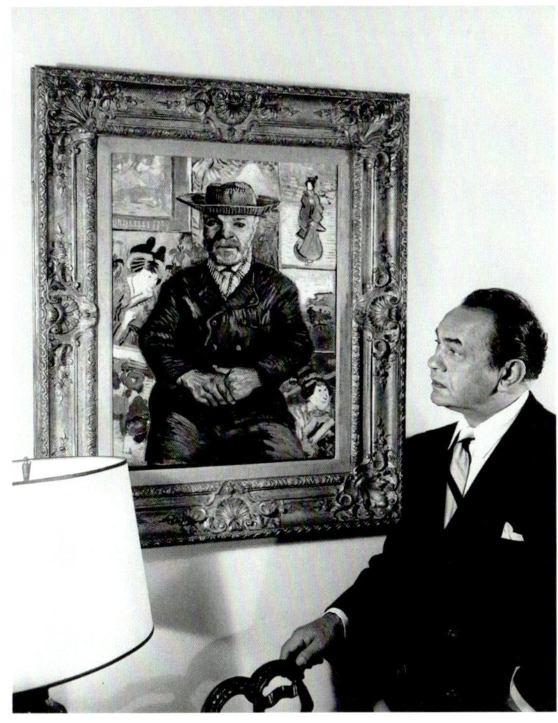

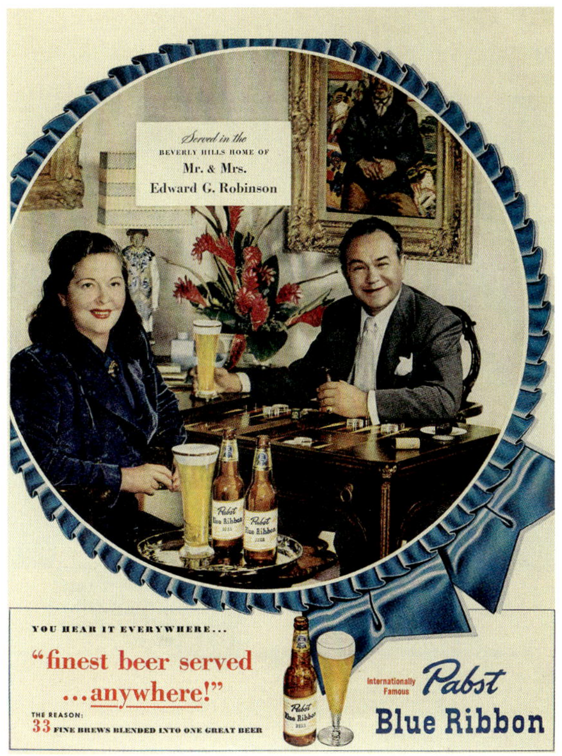

FIG. 6 Actor Edward G. Robinson at home with his Van Gogh painting *Portrait of Père Tanguy* (F364), c. 1950.

FIG. 7 Gladys and Edward G. Robinson posing with *Portrait of Père Tanguy* (F364), in an advertisement for Pabst Blue Ribbon Beer, c. 1949.

predominant and that embodied a certain stillness: "As I have gone ahead getting more and more paintings I have discovered that all really fine pictures, while they may be full of action, are very still. But it isn't a dead stillness. It's more like the world going round—so fast and so perfectly even that you don't notice it. Maybe the motion of a spinning top gives the idea. It's rhythm and timing, which are also things actors use in their work. Anyway, the result is strength and serenity." Robinson's favorite activity was sitting at home in front of the works, imagining himself as the artist (fig. 6). He elaborated: "You asked me...to write down what I think about the paintings I hang in my home. Well, I don't do much intellectual thinking about them at all. I just sit there in front of them and have the supreme pleasure of imagining I am painting. It's the actor cropping out, I suppose, but then I love to act—even in front of a great painting."[44]

Portrait of Père Tanguy appeared in a number of Los Angeles exhibitions during the 1930s and 1940s, and in 1949 was featured—together with its owner and his wife, Gladys—in an advertisement for Pabst Blue Ribbon beer (fig. 7). The harmony the couple conveys here would not last much longer, however, and the collection became a bone of contention in the acrimonious divorce that occupied Hollywood in the late 1950s. In order to "protect" it from Gladys's (supposed) avarice, Robinson arranged—without her knowledge—to have it displayed at the Los Angeles County Museum in 1956, just before it was to be sold. Her attempt to repossess the pictures was unsuccessful, but she did manage to force the museum to change the title of the show to include her name. The pictures were briefly returned to the couple's home before the sale, and Gladys organized a kind of farewell party to which she invited numerous celebrity friends. As Leonard Spiegelglass notes in his epilogue to Robinson's autobiography: "'Invitations to the good-bye party went out by the hundreds'.... 'Apparently everybody wanted to come to see the end of an era, the dissolution of a royal house.' As...many others have pointed out, movie stars were American royalty.... The party was 'the gayest funeral any family ever had.'"[45] Robinson subsequently tried to obtain a loan to buy his wife out and keep the pictures for himself. This proved impossible, however, and in one of the most spectacular coups the art world had witnessed up to that point, the Greek shipping tycoon Stavros Niarchos acquired the entire collection in February 1957.

In addition to the collectors who appeared in front of the camera, several important (and sometimes controversial) Van Gogh pictures also belonged to those who worked behind the scenes. Aside from apparently having been a member of the American Communist Party in the late 1930s—and therefore having

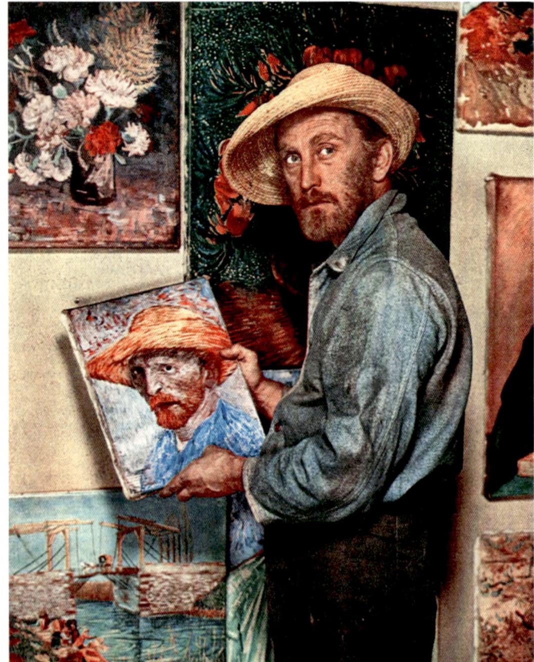

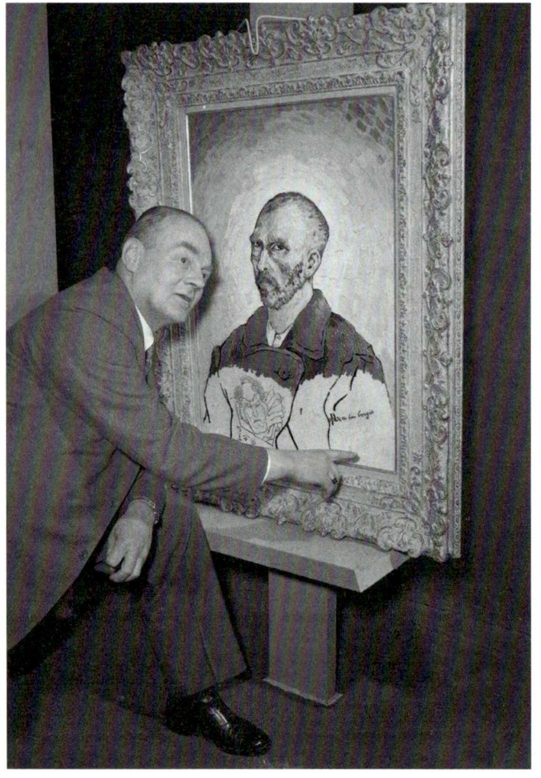

FIG. 8 Promotional photograph for Vincente Minnelli, *Lust for Life* (1956), showing the Detroit Institute of Arts' *Vase with Carnations* (F243; plate 71), and *Self-Portrait* (F526; plate 44).

FIG. 9 Van Gogh expert Jacob-Baart de la Faille with *Study by Candlelight* (F476a), a picture later deemed inauthentic.

to testify before the House Un-American Activities Committee in 1953[46]—both film producer Harold Hecht (among others, *Marty*, 1955) and his paintings had unblemished reputations. Hecht owned the drawing *The Plain of La Crau* (F1448; plate 70), and his lovely painting *L'Arlésienne* (F540), incorrectly listed as F712, even served as the frontispiece to the catalogue of the 1957 Van Gogh exhibition at the Los Angeles Municipal Art Gallery.[47]

The same cannot be said, however, for the works owned by Hecht's colleague William Goetz, one of the founders of Twentieth Century Pictures (after 1935, 20th Century Fox) and later head of Universal Pictures. Both works formerly in Goetz's collection have been subject to contention. Although *Vase with Carnations* (F243; plate 71) was accepted as authentic in the 1920s and, after Goetz's possession, even featured in several scenes in Minnelli's *Lust for Life* (fig. 8), it was contested in the 1990s following its donation to the Detroit Institute of Arts. It is now definitively recognized as authentic.[48]

Goetz's other work, *Study by Candlelight* (F476a), however, is another story.[49] Similar to the Arles sketchbook in *At Eternity's Gate*, the painting was "discovered accidentally" in 1948 in a Parisian café by one Charles Reeves Lewenthal, director of the Associated American Artists gallery. That same year, he sold it for $50,000 to the film producer, who put it on display in Beverly Hills in February 1949. Having been authenticated by the author of the Van Gogh catalogue raisonné, Jacob-Baart de la Faille—who praised it as "poignantly honest" in an article celebrating the discovery[50]—and by Paul Gachet, its presence caused a stir, prompting visits to the exhibition by both the author Thomas Mann and the actress Shirley Temple.[51]

Doubts were soon raised, however, and not from the least of sources: William Sandberg, director of the Stedelijk Museum in Amsterdam, which had recently been entrusted with the collection of Vincent Willem van Gogh, and from the artist's nephew himself. The pushback from Goetz was immediate, with threats of lawsuits and accusations of defamation. Much was at stake on the Dutch side, with the conflict threatening to jeopardize a planned exhibition of the collection in New York and Chicago later in the year, as well as diplomatic relations. Things heated up considerably, but in November 1949 a panel comprising several American museum directors refuted the work's authenticity. This was not the end of the story, however, as De la Faille stood by his original assessment and in 1950 even put together his own commission, which came to the opposite conclusion (fig. 9).

Several other factors helped Goetz to persist in his claim, including the intervention of the US Department of the Treasury and a previously unpublished letter by Van Gogh to his sister Willemien, which De la Faille interpreted to suit his argument.[52] Goetz himself continued to exhibit the work as authentic (fig. 10), and in 1959 it was included in a show of his collection at San Francisco's Palace of the Legion of Honor.[53] In the introduction to the catalogue, director Thomas Carr Howe praised the collection as a whole, calling it "the most distinguished of its kind in the West." He complimented the Goetzes on their faultless taste and "unerring connoisseurship." On the presumed self-portrait, he noted: "Occupying a commanding position among the Goetz pictures is the striking Van Gogh *Self-Portrait*, known as Étude à la Bougie, in which the artist has portrayed himself with the features of a Japanese, according to a recently-published letter written at Arles to his sister, Willemien. Despite its essential starkness, the canvas glows with striking luminosity."[54]

The 1970 edition of De la Faille's catalogue, completed by committee after his death, passes no judgment on the work, but the authors cite an article by Irving Stone as an argument for its authenticity[55]—proving once again that *Lust for Life* was a powerful tool of interpretation. The issue was definitively laid to rest only recently: following extensive technical research that delivered a negative verdict in 2013, the Goetz heirs are now satisfied that the picture is indeed a forgery.[56]

FIG. 10 Edith (Mayer) and William Goetz in their living room in Beverly Hills in front of *Study by Candlelight* (F476a), January 1, 1952.

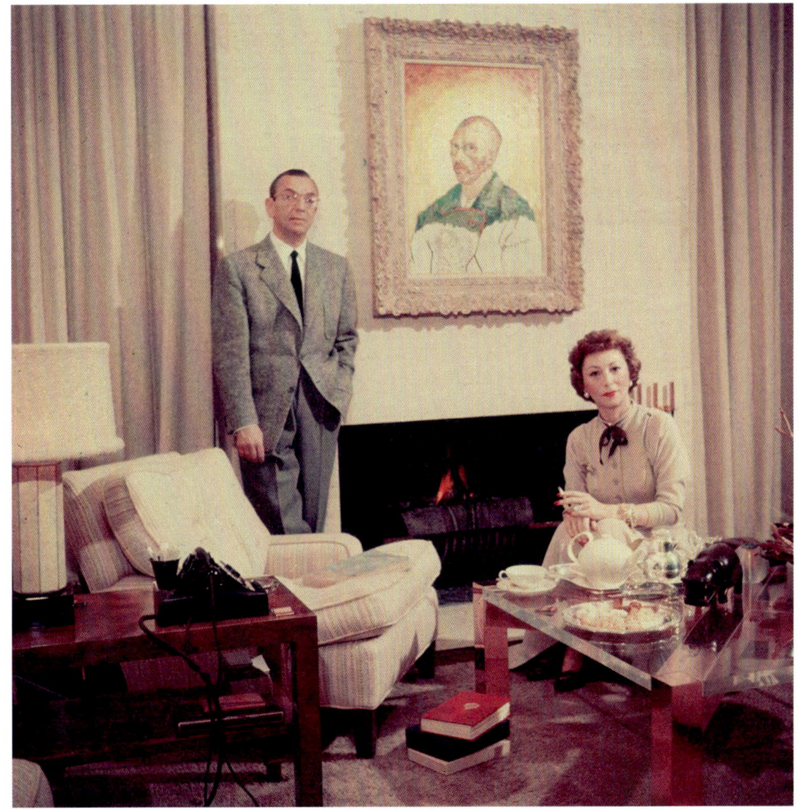

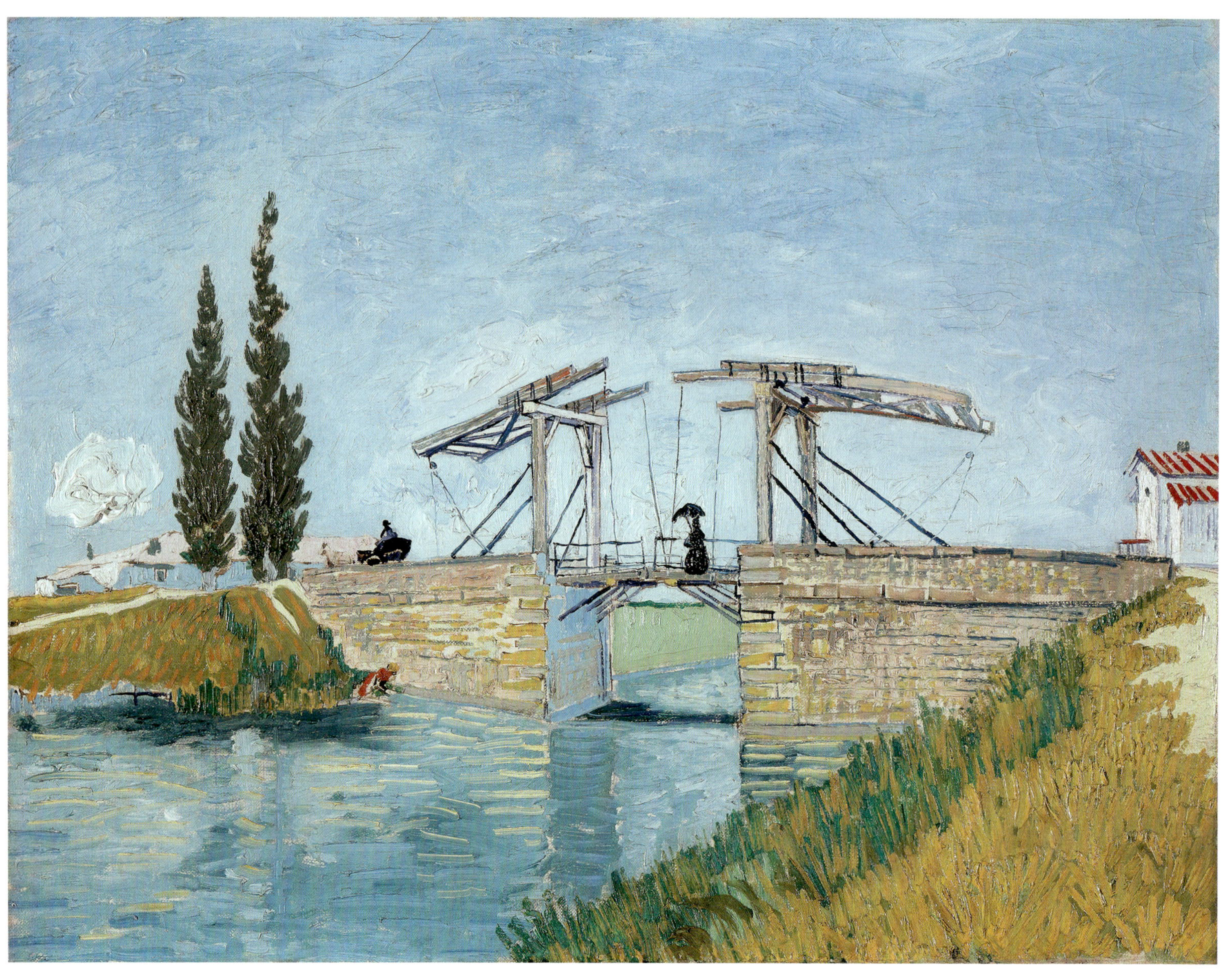

PLATE 72. *The Drawbridge*, 1888 (CAT. 29)

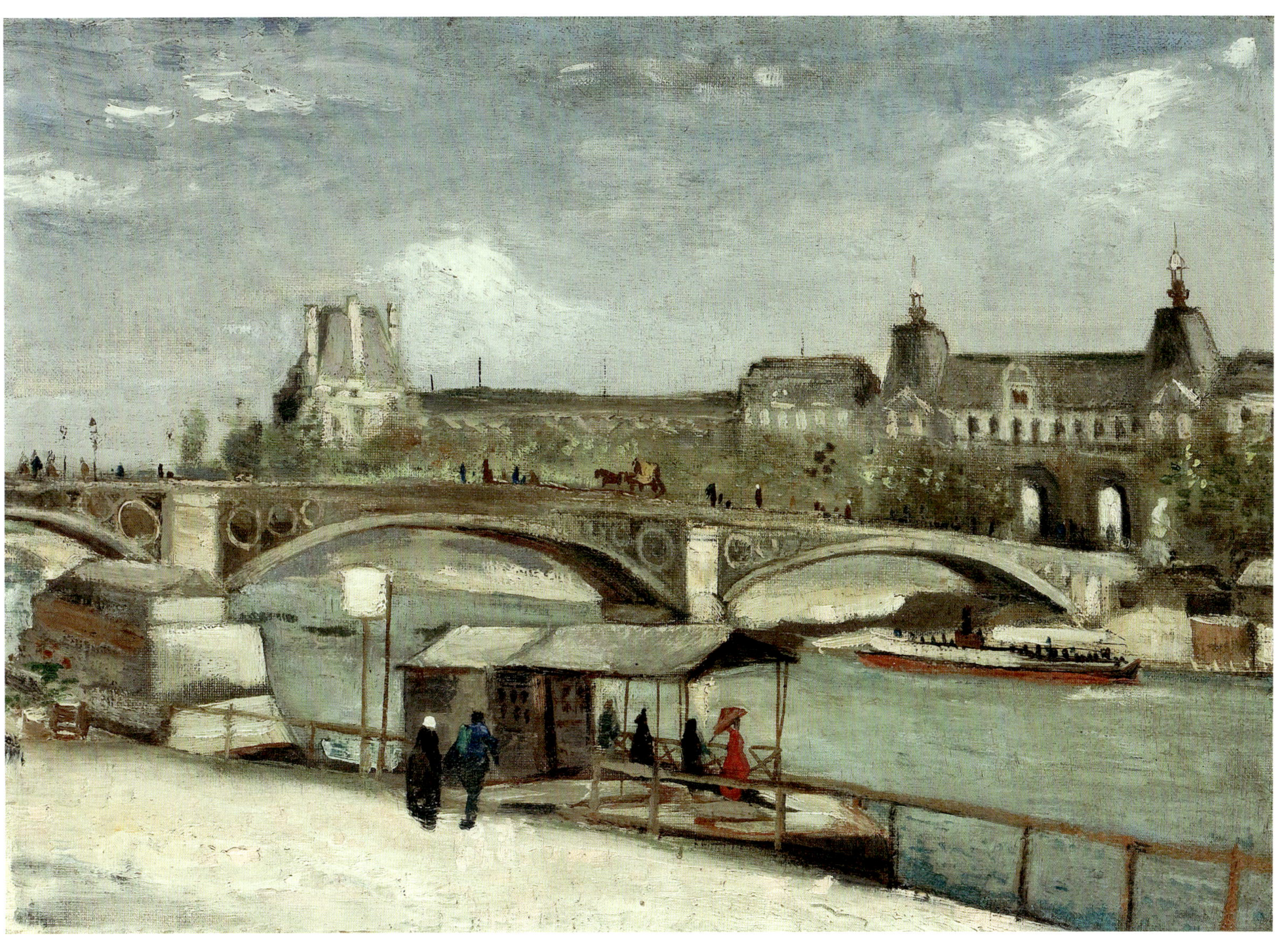

PLATE 73. *Pont du Carrousel and the Louvre*, 1886 (CAT. 17)

"Buddy" (George Gard) De Sylva, a songwriter whose hits include the classic "California, Here I Come," film producer, and record executive, was also the proud owner of three works by Van Gogh. Two of these—the drawings *The Postman Roulin* (F1459) and *The Bridge at Langlois* (F1471; for a related painting, see plate 72), which were also among his first purchases[57]—he donated early on to the Los Angeles County Museum. The third, the painting *Chestnut Trees in Flower: Pink and White Blossoms* (F751), was acquired after 1936.[58] It was exhibited at the Los Angeles County Museum in the spring of 1948 and featured on the cover of the museum's quarterly,[59] and again in 1950, in an exhibition showcasing the De Sylva collection.[60] According to a *New York Post* article published in March that year, "Before Buddy da [*sic*] Sylva sent his Van Gogh off to the museum exhibition, he painted his own copy of the masterpiece, 'The Chestnut Tree,' to hang in its place"—an anecdote that received considerable press coverage.[61] This story undoubtedly belongs to the category of eccentric behavior around Van Gogh and his work, but seems otherwise completely innocent. At the same time, however, as noted by Aline B. Loucheim in *The Art News* in 1946, De Sylva's interest in collecting was closely connected to his work in the theater: "This is a collection of a man who has lived in the world of the theater. No sham or glitter betrays this fact. But the link lies in Buddy De Sylva's choice of paintings, which call forth response by their color and by the immediacy of their vision. Surely preoccupation with people determines his apparently unconscious predilection for figure pieces and portraits."[62]

Not all Van Gogh collectors were situated inside the Hollywood cinema circuit, however: Armand Hammer (F575a, plate 26; and F643) and Norton Simon (F443 and F637) were somewhat controversial figures in themselves, but no scandals have arisen around their Van Gogh pictures. And although the Van Gogh owned by Los Angeles developer and collector Ernst G. Herman (F221; plate 73) did make news in 1984 when it was stolen from the collector's Bel-Air home, the painting itself has never been questioned. In this sense, they were all somewhat atypical Los Angeles collectors.

As amusing or disturbing as the stories of these collectors and their works may be, more interesting is what they indicate about Van Gogh's reception in the hothouse that was Hollywood in the middle of the twentieth century. As with the exhibitions and the reactions they elicited among the critics and the public, the Van Gogh myth surely played a role here as well. From Robinson's desire to support the struggling artist—albeit retroactively—to Flynn's heroic tales of rescue, or Goetz's unflagging faith in his picture, we can easily see how the artist's fictionalized life story, as told in print and film, informed his collectors' desires.

Vincent van Gogh was a highly sought-after commodity in Hollywood, and not only for the monetary value his work represented. Owning a piece of him bestowed a form of status that was closely bound up with the personalities of the collectors themselves, as well as their self-conception as actors of various kinds: in front of the camera, behind the scenes, or simply as cultural philanthropists. This was undoubtedly true of collectors in other areas of the United States and probably around the world as well, but it takes on a particular flavor in Hollywood, where the lines between fact and fantasy are perhaps more blurred than elsewhere. Hollywood invested heavily and in multiple forms in Van Gogh and the various myths and legends surrounding him: financially, certainly, but also as a means of garnering cultural capital for both individuals and institutions. In this arena, the artist was required to perform various roles: the tragic hero, the self-made man, the guru—and his work needed to be understood as perfectly aligned with these personas. That these "characters" were actually created out of highly fictionalized biographical material and supported by the performances of real actors who understood themselves (and were understood by others) to be literal embodiments of the painter, only thickened the fog of deception Hollywood created around Van Gogh's life and work. Hollywood's hybrid figure—an interplay between a real and an imagined Van Gogh—is still alive and kicking. And, as Schnabel's *At Eternity's Gate* demonstrates, it is still being deployed to questionable ends. Hollywood has yet to be cured of its Van Gogh illusion.

NOTES

I would like to thank Monique Hageman and the staff of the library and archive of the Van Gogh Museum, Amsterdam, Jill Shaw and Dorota Chudzicka of the Detroit Institute of Arts, as well as Larry Harnisch, Joost van der Hoeven, Julia Krikke, Susan Alyson Stein, and Henk Tromp for their assistance in the research for this essay.

1 Michel 2019, https://www.monacomatin.mc/vie-locale/comment-la-decouverte-de-dessins-de-van-gogh-par-un-commissaire-priseur-de-monaco-devient-un-grand-film-de-cinema-303816, accessed March 29, 2019. With thanks to Teio Meedendorp of the Van Gogh Museum for drawing my attention to this article.

2 See Welsh-Ovcharov and Pickvance 2016.

3 "Found Sketchbook with Drawings Not by Van Gogh, According to Van Gogh Museum," November 15, 2016, https://www.vangoghmuseum.nl/en/news-and-press/press-releases/found-sketchbook-with-drawings-is-not-by-van-gogh-according-to-van-gogh-museum; "Response to *Vincent van Gogh: The Lost Arles Sketchbook*: Drawings Not by Van Gogh and Notebook Unreliable," November 29, 2016, https://www.vangoghmuseum.nl/en/news-and-press/press-releases/response-to-vincent-van-gogh-the-lost-arles-sketchbook-drawings-not-by-van-gogh-and-notebook-unreliable; both accessed March 29, 2019.

4 See, among others, Berger 2014; Taylor 2002; Walker 1993; Custen 1992; and Hayward 1988. In relation to Vincent van Gogh, the classic case in point is Vincente Minnelli's *Lust for Life* (1956), starring Kirk Douglas. As the actor recalls in his autobiography, his physical resemblance to the artist caused older villagers at the locations in France where some of the scenes were filmed to cross themselves when they saw him in the streets, muttering "he has returned." More importantly, the experience of playing Van Gogh was somewhat disconcerting, as Douglas found it impossible to distance himself from the artist: "I felt myself going over the line, into the skin of Van Gogh. Not only did I look like him, I was the same age he had been when he committed suicide." Douglas, quoted in Walker 1993, 41. The film's influence on both the public's and the historian's understanding of the artist is the subject of a seminal essay by art historian Griselda Pollock; see Pollock 1980.

5 This theory was first proposed in Naifeh and Smith 2011.

6 San Francisco 1915, no. 4031.

7 Laurvik 1916, 2.

8 San Francisco 1924–25.

9 Tross 1933, n.p. The show was a loan exhibition from Wildenstein in New York; the Van Gogh works are nos. 50 and 51. On the interpretation of Van Gogh as a "northern" artist, see Manheim 1989. A few months before, Van Gogh's work had also been included in another Los Angeles show, Los Angeles 1933a, but nothing further is currently known about this exhibition.

10 San Francisco 1934, nos. 156–63. Nos. 159 (ill.) and 162, lent by Mr. and Mrs. W. W. Crocker of Hillsborough, would appear again at the first large Van Gogh retrospective in 1936 (see below). Also present was *Portrait of Père Tanguy* (F364), again lent by Wildenstein (no. 163, ill.). Van Gogh is described by Walter Heil in the foreword to the catalogue (p. 29) as "a Dutchman—but active in France and so decisively influenced by the Impressionists that he is rightly counted among the French painters—is a genius of strange and tragic greatness. Of violently passionate nature, he does not shrink from the deliberate forcing of the natural forms in his desire to intensify formal or coloristic impression to the highest degree. He symbolizes the movements and luminosity of the real by means of agitated outlines and powerful brush strokes; he 'draws' with paint in striking and pure colors. There is something stirring, even moving about the pictures of this man who died of madness at an early age." See also Los Angeles 1934 and San Diego 1936; nothing further is currently known about these exhibitions.

11 New York and other cities 1935–36.

12 See New York 1936 exhibition file, Van Gogh Museum Documentation, Amsterdam (hereafter VGMD).

13 The Crockers had purchased *Ploughing* in 1929 from Knoedler. Both paintings were also shown in San Francisco 1935 (nos. 43 and 44); and in San Francisco 1936 (nos. 36 and 37). See San Francisco 1935 exhibition file and San Francisco 1936 exhibition file, both VGMD.

14 *San Francisco Chronicle* 1936.

15 Stone 1936.

16 Frankenstein 1936a.

17 Frankenstein 1936b.

18 These included San Francisco 1939, nos. 169–82, all loaned by Vincent Willem van Gogh and apparently shipped to San Francisco from Batavia (see *San Francisco Chronicle* 1939); and San Francisco 1939–40, nos. 122–27. For Robert Neuhaus, writing in the foreword to the catalogue (p. 13), Van Gogh "symbolizes in our time the 'subjective' current of expressionism and symbolism. He calls to mind a statement by a great living French writer: 'It is from our substance that we imagine and that we make a stone, a plant, a movement, an object; no image whatever is more perhaps than a beginning of ourselves.' In looking at Van Gogh's 'Wheatfield' we re-experience the words of Valéry, this melting into a new cast of the vision of the world without and the life rhythm of the artist within. Colors become vitalized, forms strengthened, and the underlying rhythm in forms and in perspective itself are accentuated. The compositional pattern which had been gone for a while in the snapshot fragments of Impressionistic painting reappears." See also San Francisco 1940a; San Francisco 1940–41, nos. 51–53; Los Angeles 1941a, no. 57 ("Le Père Tanguy," F364); Los Angeles 1941b, nos. 25 and 26. Most interesting in the context of this essay is undoubtedly San Francisco 1940b. This show included F743 ("Cypress and Flowering Tree, St. Rémy," no. 8); F419 ("Les Saintes-Maries: White Houses," no. 10); and F625 ("Ploughing", no. 12), lent by the Crockers; no. 9 ("The First Steps, After Millet," F668), no. 11 ("Ploughed Field at Sunset," F737), and no. 13 ("Portrait of Mlle Ravoux," F768), were lent anonymously, but at the time were in the possession of Frank Oppenheimer (brother of the physicist J. Robert Oppenheimer), then resident in San Francisco. Somewhere between 1945 and 1949,

Oppenheimer sold F668 to the legendary Los Angeles gallerist and collector Dalzell Hatfield, who owned it until 1955. See F668 object file, VGMD.

19 A small and short-running "retrospective" was, however, held in the early 1950s: Los Angeles 1952.

20 Although in the foreword to San Francisco and other cities 1958–59, Walter Heil writes: "Only a few of these works have previously been shown in San Francisco and many of them have never been seen in America," the works are indeed largely the same as those on view in the late 1930s. The exhibition included eighty-four paintings and seventy-one drawings; it traveled to the Los Angeles County Museum, the Portland Art Museum (Oregon), and the Seattle Art Museum.

21 Rewald 1957, 7–8. Los Angeles 1957, which took place in cooperation with the Wildenstein gallery, was made up of thirty-eight works. It included "Bridge over the Seine—Pont du Carrousel" (F221; plate 73) (no. 7, lent by Lilli Schocken, New York). The Crockers' "Cypress and Flowering Tree" (no. 13 [ill.]) appeared again as well. Two drawings in the show (nos. 36 [ill.] and 37) were loaned by the Los Angeles County Museum of Art: "The Postman Roulin" (F1459), and "The Bridge at Langlois" (F1471), gifts in 1946 from film producer George Gard De Sylva, who also owned F751, "Chestnut Tree in Flower" (see Loucheim 1946); "The Postman Roulin" is illustrated on p. 32. Despite the apparently poor conditions in the Frank Lloyd Wright–designed Barnsdall Park pavilion, the show was a huge success, welcoming some 59,061 visitors by the end of the run; see *Los Angeles Times* 2007, accessed April 23, 2019.

22 The clippings can be found in the Los Angeles 1958–59 exhibition file, VGMD.

23 *De Young Muse* 1958b.

24 *De Young Muse* 1958a.

25 *Los Angeles Examiner* 1959.

26 Los Angeles and other cities 1969–71.

27 *San Bernardino Sun* 1969. A large selection of clippings is kept in the library of the Los Angeles County Museum and is the source for what follows. See Los Angeles County Museum of Art Publicity (press clippings), 1969.

28 *Fountain Valley Daily Pilot* 1969.

29 Seldis 1969.

30 Byrens 1969.

31 Seldis 1969.

32 Taylor's Van Gogh, *View of the Asylum and the Chapel at Saint-Rémy* (F803), was purchased for her by her father, Francis Taylor, a London art dealer, in 1963, but led a quiet existence until 2004, when it became the subject of a restitution dispute between the actress and the descendants of a previous owner, the German-Jewish collector and author Margarete Mauthner. The case, well documented in the press, was decided in favor of Taylor in 2007, who put the work up for auction in 2012. Its Hollywood "biography" thus falls outside the purview of this essay.

33 Nicholas 1995, 165, states that Graupe would be investigated by the Treasury Department, and the FBI apparently made a notation of Flynn's purchase, including its price. See McNulty 2015, 186.

34 See Sotheby's, London, February 5, 2014, lot 39, http://www.sothebys.com/en/auctions/ecatalogue/2014/impressionist-modern-art-evening-sale14002/lot.39.html, accessed July 11, 2019; see also Paris, New York, and Amsterdam 1999, 214.

35 Errol Flynn in Wood 1944; cited in McNulty 2015, 186n134.

36 Fowler 1954, 5, cited in McNulty 2015, 135. On the opening of the gallery, see *Art Digest* 1944: 14.

37 *Art Digest* 1944.

38 McNulty 2015, 186.

39 *Life* 1948: 64.

40 Paris, New York, and Amsterdam 1999, 214.

41 According to Susan Alyson Stein of the Metropolitan Museum of Art, it was probably acquired shortly before it appeared in an *Art News* article written by Robinson himself: Robinson 1941: 19 (ill.), 28.

42 See F520 object file, VGMD.

43 Robinson 1973, 175.

44 Robinson 1941. Interesting here is also the article's lead, which states that Robinson's collection proves that "you can collect as seriously in Beverly Hills as in Paris or Florence."

45 Leonard Spiegelglass, epilogue, in Robinson 1973, 287.

46 See https://archive.org/stream/investigationofco1unit/investigationofco1unit_djvu.txt, accessed April 13, 2019.

47 See note 21.

48 Hendriks and Van Tilborgh 2011, 572.

49 For a detailed history of the controversy, see Tromp 2010, 213–29. See also Koldehoff 2003, 166–68.

50 De la Faille 1948: 215.

51 *Time* 1949; cited in Tromp 2010, 214.

52 The letter was first included in Van Gogh Letters 1952–54. It does indeed mention "a new portrait of myself, as a study, in which I look like a Japanese," but this is a reference to F476, now in the Fogg Art Museum in Cambridge, Massachusetts. See Van Gogh Letters 2009, no. 678, http://vangoghletters.org/vg/letters/let678/letter.html, accessed April 14, 2019.

53 San Francisco 1959, no. 57.

54 Howe 1959.

55 De la Faille 1970, 216. The article in question is an interview held with Stone in July 1949 in Amsterdam that appeared in *De Waarheid* (July 18, 1949). Although Stone insists he is "not an expert" and in no position to "scientifically" pass judgment on the picture, his "gut feeling" tells him it is the real thing.

56 Reno 2013 was an exhibition devoted to the question of the painting's authenticity. For the research that led to establishing the work as a forgery, see Tromp 2010, coda to chapter 8 in the Chinese translation; see also Henk Tromp, email to the author, April 14, 2019.

57 See Loucheim 1946: 32, with an illustration of *The Postman Roulin*.

58 See W. Feilchenfeldt 2009, 253.

59 *Los Angeles County Museum Quarterly* 1948.

60 Los Angeles 1950, no. 20 (ill.).

61 *New York Post* 1950. For this and related clippings, see F751 object file, VGMD.

62 Loucheim 1946: 33.

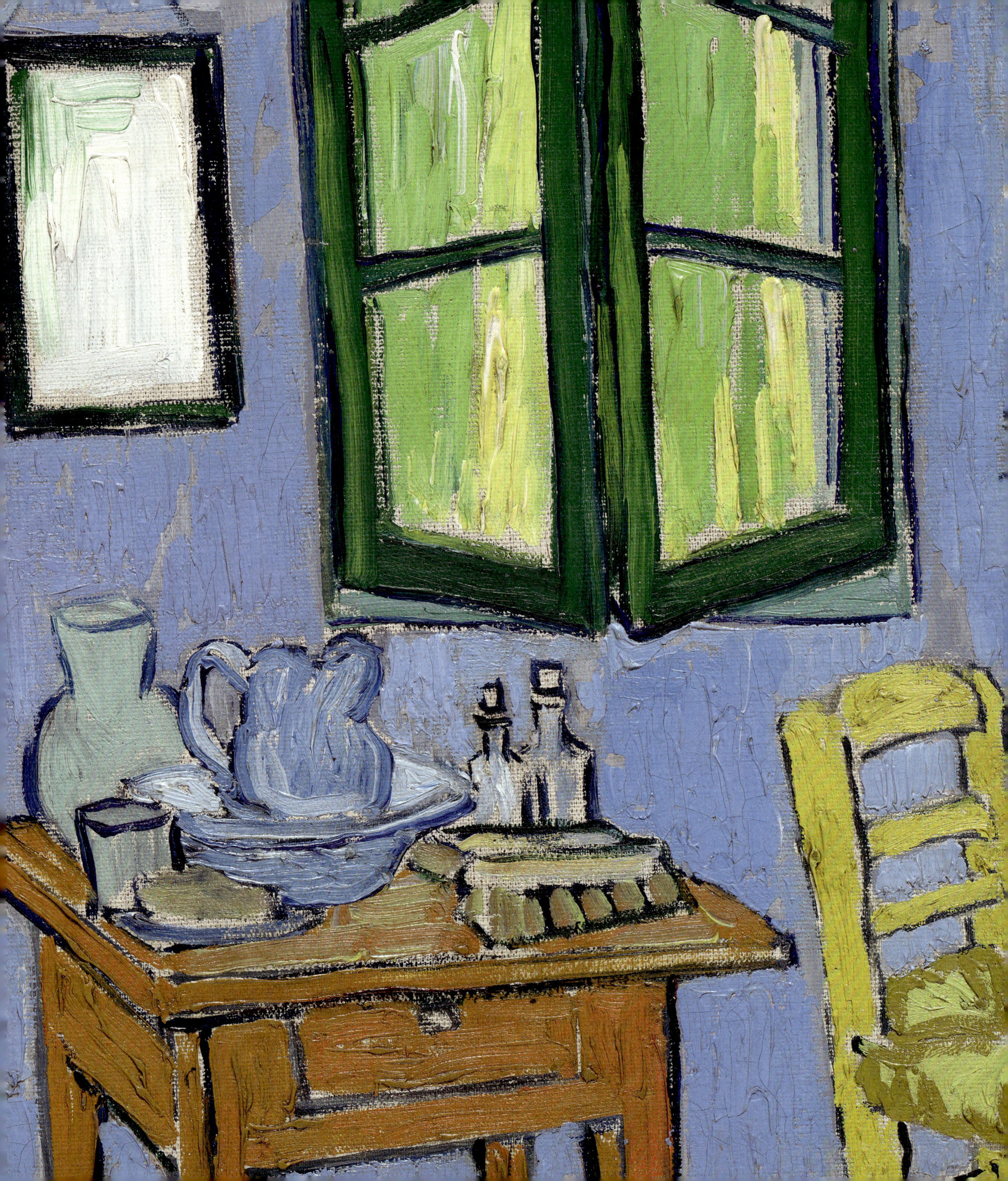

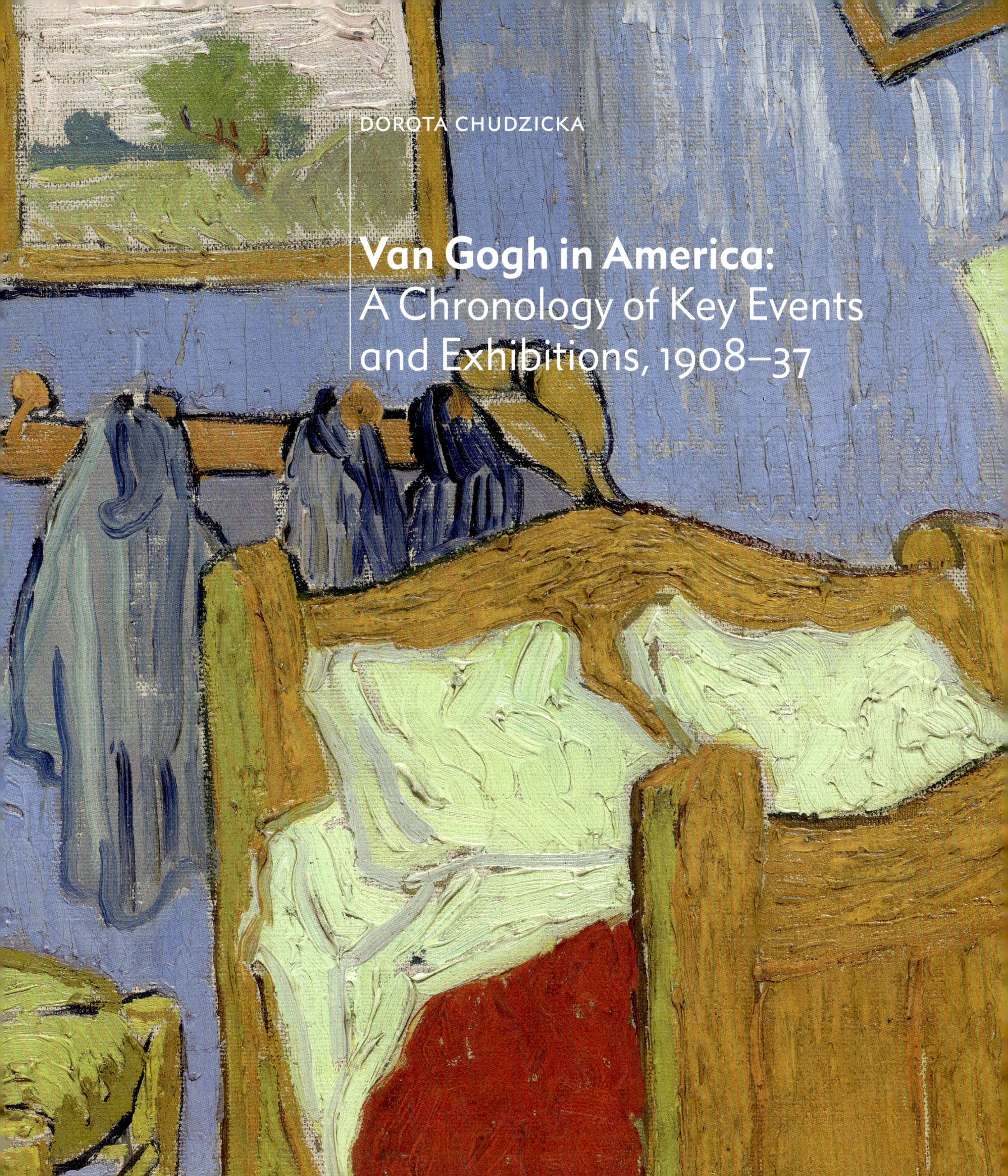

DOROTA CHUDZICKA

Van Gogh in America: A Chronology of Key Events and Exhibitions, 1908–37

1908

Julius Meier-Graefe's *Modern Art: Being a Contribution to a New System of Æsthetics* is published in two volumes in an English translation of the 1904 German edition. Meier-Graefe discusses Van Gogh in detail in a chapter devoted to the artist in the section "From Delacroix to Courbet" (fig. 1).[1]

1910

NOVEMBER 8. The first Post-Impressionist exhibition, *Manet and the Post-Impressionists*, opens at the Grafton Galleries in London. The exhibition, which will close on January 15, 1911, features works by Van Gogh in a room together with those by Cézanne and Gauguin. It provokes a robust and varied response from American journalists and critics.[2]

NOVEMBER AND DECEMBER. Rudolf Meyer-Riefstahl's two-part article on Van Gogh, illustrated with photographs of the artist's works by Eugène Druet, appears in *The Burlington Magazine for Connoisseurs*.[3]

202 THE DEVELOPMENT OF MODERN ART

VINCENT VAN GOGH

Lux mea crux—
Crux mea lux!
NIETZSCHE.

Van Gogh got nearer to the root of the matter. There has perhaps, indeed, never been any one who, quite unconsciously, penetrated so deeply into what we are now agreed to recognise as artistic. He himself turned to it merely as the most natural means of expression.

Van Gogh came from Holland, and was of the generation of Israels. He was born at Groot Zundert on March 30, 1853, and up to his thirtieth year had not found his vocation. Everything and nothing revealed the artist in him; everything, because he had within him a consciousness of the divine fire, a veritably elemental craving to express himself; and nothing, because painting by no means presented itself to him as the natural manifestation of this craving. He was of the stuff of which, in earlier days, the great benefactors of the human race were made; he was essentially an idealist, consumed with a yearning affection for humanity, a man who, under all circumstances, would always have been eager to do good. A natural inclination, the sole commercial element in which was a desire to occupy himself usefully with beautiful things, led him as a young man to seek employment with art-dealers. For several years he was with the well-known firm of Goupil in London, Paris, and the Hague. In 1876 he renounced business; and, obeying his dearest instincts, became a teacher in a school in England, working till the end of the year at Ramsgate and at Isleworth. Difficulties of all kinds only served to strengthen his convictions, and finally to make him resolve to extend his sphere of usefulness by becoming a clergyman. He was a Protestant; his father, the pastor of a small congregation, encouraged him in his determination, and in 1877 Vincent went to Amsterdam to begin his theological studies. But the struggle with all the forms and superficialities that overlie the essentials of faith, became too irksome to him. These were dark days; he felt impelled to change his calling once more; his family looked upon him as a castaway. The following year he left his native land again, this time for Brussels, and accepted a mission from the Protestant congregation to the workmen in the Borinage, reading the Scriptures to them, and expounding the primitive Gospel as he himself understood it.

This period, about the year 1880, was a decisive one in his life. His experiences among his miners were those of every warm-hearted person who is brought into contact with miners for the first time. Intelligent enough not to blind himself to the fact that his unpractised speech could offer little indeed to these mute victims of a sombre lot, everything that he saw increased his longing for a medium of expression; for him there was but one idea in these surroundings, where everything tended naturally to become a symbol to him; this was, to

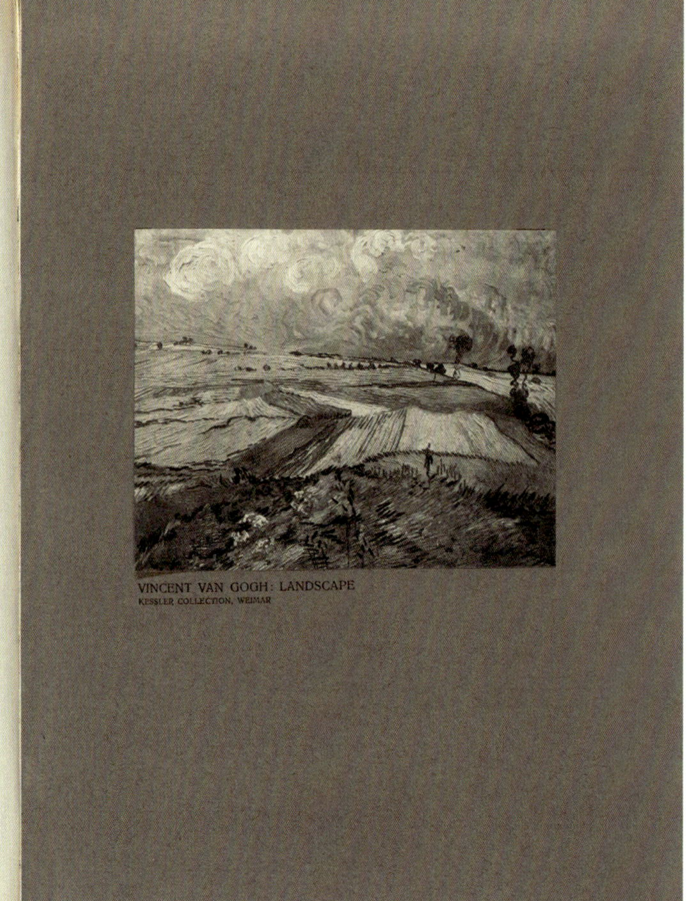

FIG. 1 Illustration of *Wheat Fields After the Rain (The Plain of Auvers)* (F781; plate 68) in Julius Meier-Graefe's *Modern Art: Being a Contribution to a New System of Æsthetics*, 1908, vol. 1.

1911

DECEMBER. The *New York Times* reports that William Van Horne (1843–1915), the American-born president of the Canadian Pacific Railway and prominent collector in Montreal, acquires "a garden picture by Van Gogh."[4] Over the next four years, Van Horne will expand his collection, advised by Stephan Bourgeois, a German-born art dealer newly established in New York.[5]

DECEMBER 14. The photographer and advocate for modern art Alfred Stieglitz publishes a letter to the editor of the *New York Evening Sun*, in which he points to the responsibility of the Metropolitan Museum of Art to organize a major exhibition of the works by Cézanne, Van Gogh, Matisse, and Picasso.[6]

1912

FEBRUARY. The physician and entrepreneur Albert C. Barnes (1872–1951) instructs the painter and friend William Glackens from Philadelphia to buy works by Renoir, Sisley, and "others of the modern painters."[7] Soon after, Glackens, aided by Alfred Maurer, an American painter in Paris, acquires *The Postman (Joseph-Étienne Roulin)* (F435; see Stein, New York, fig. 2). Shipped at the beginning of March, it will be the first Van Gogh to enter a collection in the United States and one of seven that Barnes will eventually own and donate to the Barnes Foundation.

MAY 25. The Sonderbund exhibition, with no fewer than 117 paintings and 17 works on paper attributed to Van Gogh, opens in Cologne and runs until September 30 (fig. 2).[8] The artist is presented as the central figure for early twentieth-century avant-garde art. The painter and future founder of the Société Anonyme Katherine S. Dreier (1877–1952) visits the exhibition; she will acquire *Adeline Ravoux* (F786; plate 18) through Artz & De Bois from Van Gogh's family in November.[9]

SEPTEMBER. John Quinn (1870–1924), a New York collector and staunch supporter of modern art, begins negotiations with the Parisian dealer Ambroise Vollard to buy *Self-Portrait* (F268; plate 17); the sale will be concluded with the shipment of the painting to New York in January 1913.[10]

SEPTEMBER 15. The Berlin Photographic Company makes public its plans to display a collection of Van Gogh's paintings in its gallery in New York. The *New York Times* quips, "The public very probably will quail before their stark logic and their uncompromising color."[11] The exhibition, however, does not take place.

OCTOBER. Excerpts from Van Gogh's letters translated into English by American journalist and collector Agnes Ernst Meyer appear in the October issue of Alfred Stieglitz's periodical *Camera Work*.[12]

FIG. 2 Installation of works by Van Gogh in Room 3, Sonderbund exhibition, Cologne, 1912, featuring *Entrance to the Public Gardens in Arles* (F566; plate 57) just left of the entrance to the next gallery.

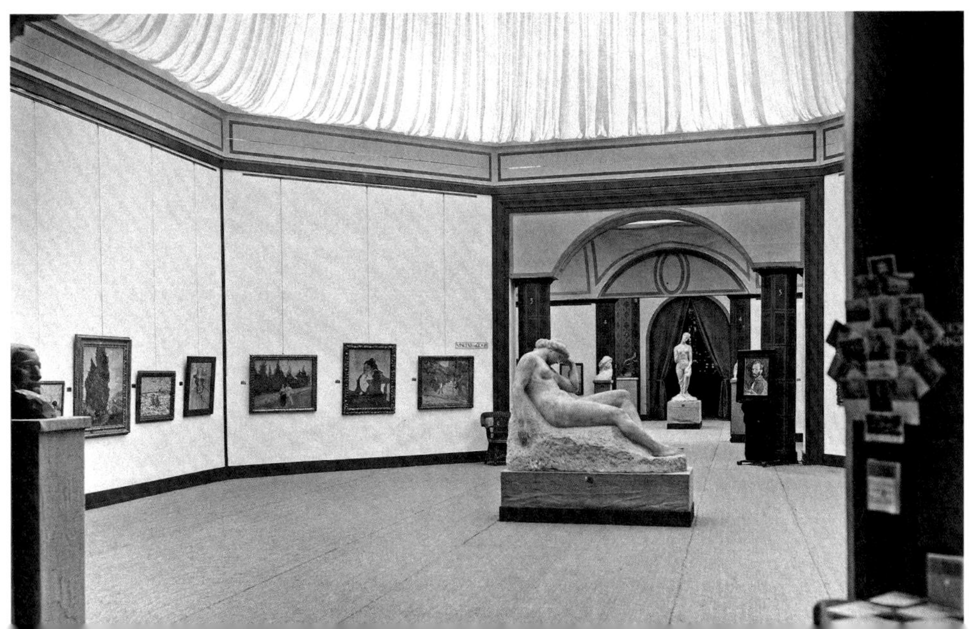

1913

A selection of Van Gogh's letters is published in English by Houghton, Mifflin and Company, translated by Anthony M. Ludovici from Margarete Mauthner's German edition, first issued by Bruno Cassirer in 1906. Fifteen drawings (see, for example, fig. 3) and one painting are reproduced in the English edition. Low sales of the book disappoint the American publisher.[13]

FEBRUARY 17–MARCH 15. The *International Exhibition of Modern Art* (Armory Show), organized by the Association of American Painters and Sculptors, takes place in New York, and travels in reduced form to the Art Institute of Chicago, March 24–April 16; and Copley Hall, Boston, April 28–May 19. Eighteen works by Van Gogh are listed in the catalogue and exhibited in all three venues. Three additional works are likely on view;[14] and, in New York, a Van Gogh portfolio of nine collotype reproductions of paintings is offered for sale. None of Van Gogh's works or the reproduction portfolio finds a buyer.

JUNE. Alfred Stieglitz's periodical *Camera Work* runs an article critical of the selection of Van Gogh's works in the Armory Show and publishes an illustration of his *Cypresses* (F613; fig. 4), exhibited in the Sonderbund exhibition in Cologne the previous year but absent from the Armory Show.[15]

NOVEMBER. Katherine S. Dreier's initiative to publish her English translation of *Personal Recollections of Vincent van Gogh* by the artist's sister Elisabeth du Quesne-Van Gogh comes to fruition. Furnished with a foreword by artist Arthur B. Davies and an introduction by Dreier, the book is illustrated with twenty-four plates of Van Gogh's paintings, drawings, and a letter (Letter 587); *Sunflowers* (F457) is on the cover.[16]

Royal Cortissoz, an art critic for the *New York Tribune*, publishes *Art and Common Sense*, in which he denounces the modernist art presented at the Armory Show and in negative terms describes Van Gogh's work as only "moderately competent" and "unimportant."[17]

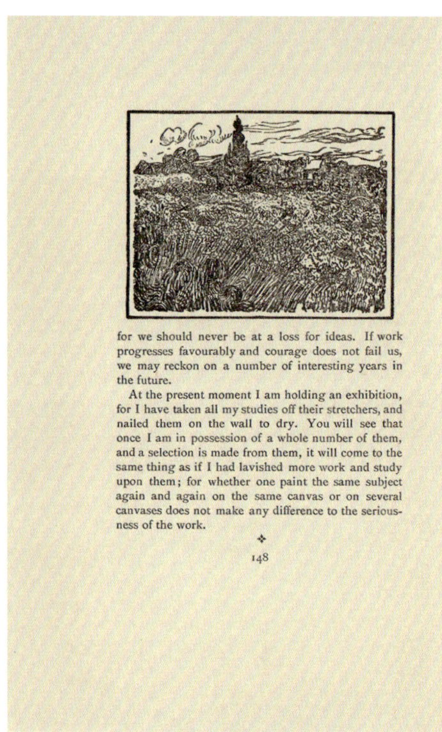

for we should never be at a loss for ideas. If work progresses favourably and courage does not fail us, we may reckon on a number of interesting years in the future.

At the present moment I am holding an exhibition, for I have taken all my studies off their stretchers, and nailed them on the wall to dry. You will see that once I am in possession of a whole number of them, and a selection is made from them, it will come to the same thing as if I had lavished more work and study upon them; for whether one paint the same subject again and again on the same canvas or on several canvases does not make any difference to the seriousness of the work.

148

FIG. 3 Illustration of *Wheatfield, Saint-Rémy de Provence* (F1548; plate 40) in *The Letters of a Post-Impressionist. Being the Familiar Correspondence of Vincent van Gogh*, 1913.

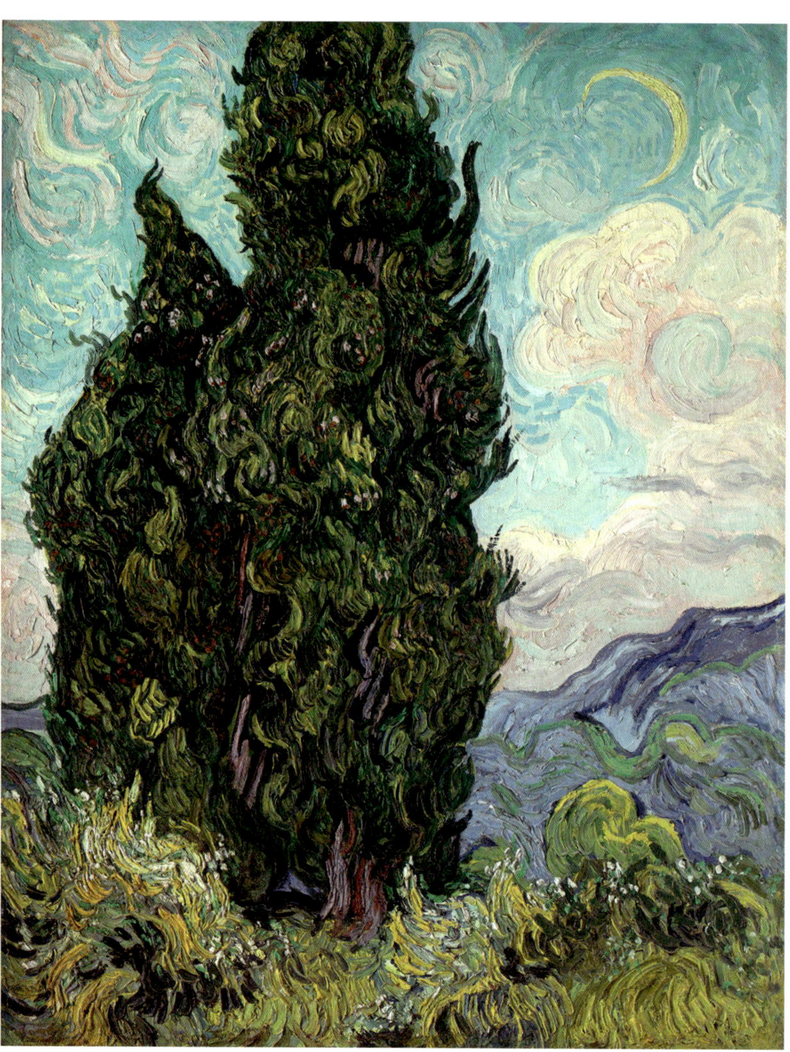

FIG. 4 *Cypresses* (F613), 1889. Oil on canvas, 36¾ × 29⅛ in. (93.4 × 74 cm). The Metropolitan Museum of Art, New York.

1914

FEBRUARY. Stephan Bourgeois mounts in his gallery an exhibition featuring four paintings under Van Gogh's name (F228, plate 63; F279, plate 24; F513; and a work called "Field Flowers in a Vase") among pieces by other artists, including Cézanne, Manet, Monet, Monticelli, and Toulouse-Lautrec as well as Old Masters (fig. 5).[18]

Arthur Jerome Eddy (1859–1920), a Chicago collector, writer, and promoter of modern art, publishes *Cubists and Post-Impressionism*. In this first history of modern art written by an American, Eddy identifies Van Gogh together with Gauguin as the artistic descendants of Cézanne and precursors of Fauvism.[19] Four of Van Gogh's works are illustrated (F529; F463, fig. 19; F176; F498, plate 47).

FIG. 5 Cover of *Exposition de tableaux anciens et modernes*, Galleries Bourgeois, New York, 1914.

1915

Willard Huntington Wright, a critic and brother of the American avant-garde painter Stanton MacDonald-Wright, champions modern artists in his book *Modern Painting: Its Tendency and Meaning*. Van Gogh is discussed in the chapter called "Neoimpressionism."[20]

FEBRUARY 20–DECEMBER 4. *Le Moulin de la Galette* (F228; plate 63) is the only work by Van Gogh exhibited in the *Panama-Pacific International Exposition* at the Palace of Fine Arts in San Francisco (fig. 6).[21]

MARCH 8–APRIL 3. The *Third Exhibition of Contemporary French Art* at the Carroll Galleries in New York features a still life said to be by Van Gogh lent by the Parisian dealer and critic Théodore Duret.[22]

NOVEMBER 22–DECEMBER. The first solo Van Gogh exhibition in the United States marks the opening season of the Modern Gallery in New York run by Marius de Zayas. New York newspapers take notice of eight paintings selected by De Zayas from Parisian dealers, accompanied by several works from the family of the artist, added to the display after the opening date. The exhibition's run is extended past its official closing date on December 12.[23]

DECEMBER. Mary Mowbray-Clarke's series of lectures "Ultra Modern Movements in Painting and Sculpture" is accompanied by a display of photographs of paintings by Cézanne, Gauguin, Van Gogh, Picasso, Redon, and Renoir in the reading room of the 58th Street branch of the New York Public Library.[24]

1916

FEBRUARY 12—MARCH 1. Marius de Zayas exhibits a flower still life attributed to Van Gogh (see Stein, New York, fig. 5) in the Modern Gallery's *Exhibition of Paintings by Cézanne, Van Gogh, Picasso, Picabia, Braque, Desseignes* [sic], *Rivera*. De Zayas will include Van Gogh in two other group exhibitions of nineteenth- and early twentieth-century international modern art in April–June and, on a more ambitious scale, in October.[25]

APRIL 3—29. The *Exhibition of Modern Art Arranged by a Group of European and American Artists in New York* opens at the Bourgeois Galleries in New York. The exhibition, organized by the artist and critic Walter Pach, features paintings, works on paper, and sculptures, including two oils and five drawings by Van Gogh.[26]

1917

The bequest of the collection assembled by John G. Johnson (1841–1917), a distinguished Philadelphia lawyer, comes to the city of Philadelphia with the provision that it will be exhibited in one of his residences acquired for that purpose. Among works by European masters from the fourteenth to the nineteenth centuries assembled by Johnson is *Still Life with a Vase of Flowers* (Philadelphia Museum of Art, inv. no. 2322), erroneously believed to be an example of Van Gogh's work from his early period but later revealed to be inauthentic.[27]

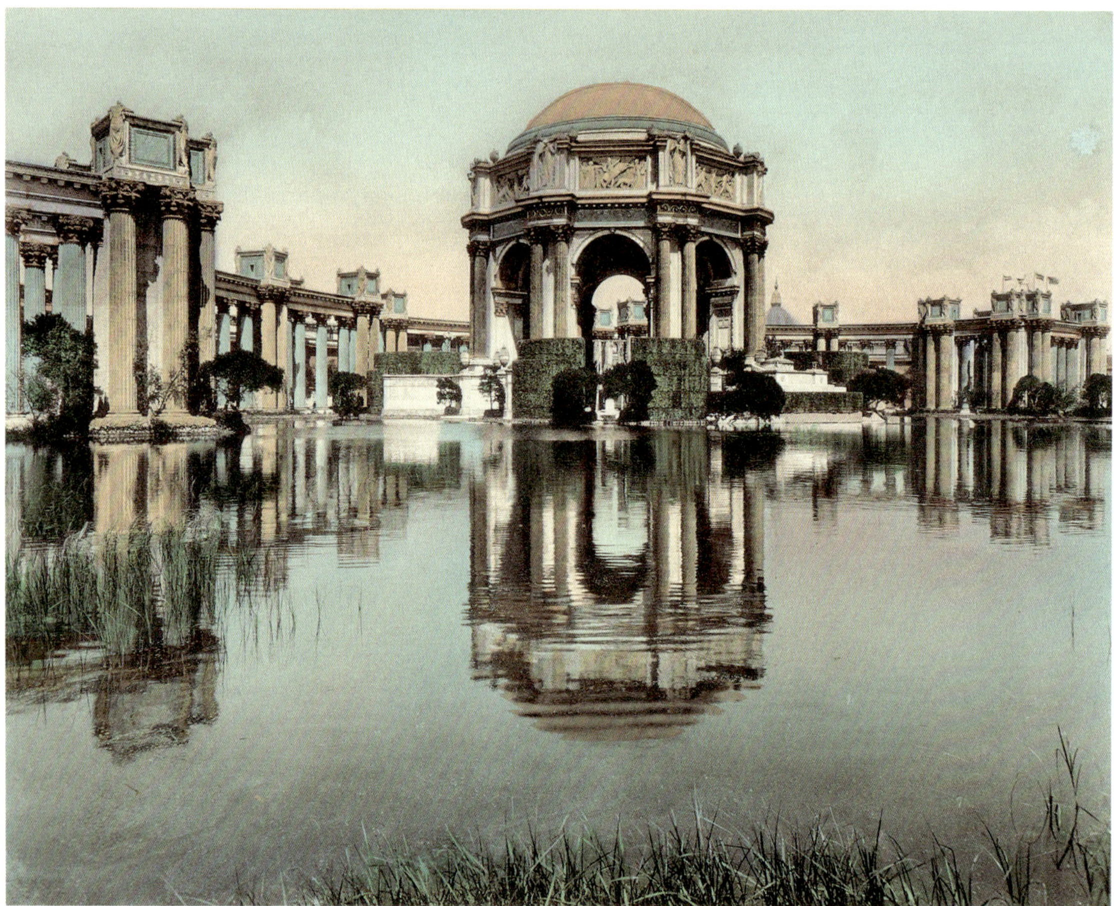

FIG. 6 The Palace of Fine Arts, hand-colored photograph from *The Splendors of the Panama-Pacific International Exposition* (San Francisco: Robert A. Reid, 1915).

1918

Extracts from Van Gogh's letters selected by the artist's sister-in-law, Jo van Gogh-Bonger (1862–1925), and prepared for publication by Walter Pach are published in the July 1918 and August 1919 issues of the anarchist magazine *The Modern School* (fig. 7).[28]

The Ryerson Library at the Art Institute of Chicago acquires the reproduction portfolio of one hundred drawings by Van Gogh in the collection of Dutch collector Hidde Nijland, on view at the Dordrechts Museum, *Vincent van Gogh 100 teekeningen uit de verzameling Hidde Nyland in het Museum te Dordrecht* (Amsterdam: W. Versluys, 1905).[29]

THE MODERN SCHOOL

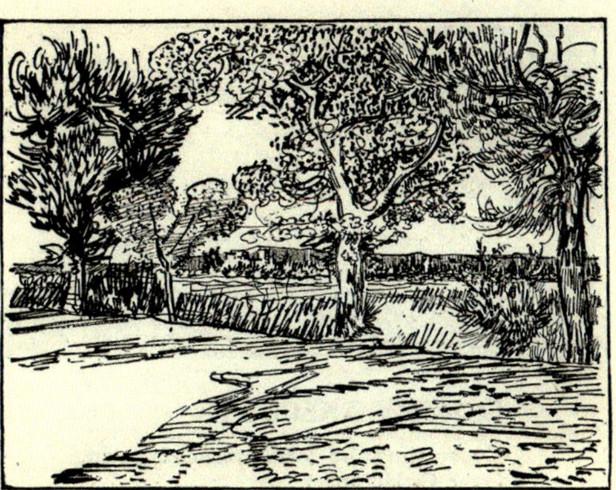

EXTRACTS FROM THE LETTERS OF VINCENT VAN GOGH
HITHERTO UNPUBLISHED IN ENGLISH

BORINAGE, 26 DECEMBER, 1878

Here in the Borinage (the famous mining districts of Belgium) there are no pictures, speaking in general, one does not even know what a picture is, so of course I have not seen anything in the art line since I left Brussels. But in spite of this, the country is very picturesque and very peculiar here, everything speaks as it were, and is full of character. These days, the dark days before Christmas, there was snow on the ground; everything then reminded me of the mediaeval pictures of the Peasant Breughel, for instance, and so many others who have known how to express so remarkably well that peculiar effect of red and green, black and white. At every moment I am reminded of the work for instance of Thys,

PAGE 194

FIG. 7 "Extracts from the Letters of Vincent van Gogh," published in *The Modern School*, July 1918.

1919

JANUARY 15–FEBRUARY 12. The Brooks Reed Gallery in Boston presents *Post-Impressionists*, an exhibition of twenty-eight paintings and drawings by "well-known luminaries of post-impressionism," the term loosely applied by the organizers to Cézanne, Van Gogh, Seurat, Matisse, Picasso, and other artists. One Van Gogh still life is on view.[30]

By the end of the year, the Arts Club of Chicago, a private club devoted to the advancement of modern art, exhibits Van Gogh's still life of "herrings and melon,"[31] seen as "typifying the aims of the 'modernist' school," in *Modern Paintings by Branchard, Friedman, Van Gogh, Rodin, Stella, and Sterne, Sculpture by P. Auguste Renoir, Statuettes by Derujinsky*, on view December 15–31.[32] The painting was probably a work (now reattributed to an imitator of Van Gogh; see Stein, New York, fig. 9) that would be given by Helen Birch Bartlett (1883–1925) to her husband, the painter and modern art collector Frederic Clay Bartlett (1873–1953), in January 1921,[33] and later donated to the Art Institute of Chicago.

1920

APRIL 30. Katherine S. Dreier opens the first exhibition of the Société Anonyme—an organization dedicated to exhibiting, publishing, and lecturing about avant-garde art—in two rooms at 19 East 47th Street in New York, decorated by Marcel Duchamp and Man Ray. The selection of artworks borrowed from collectors, dealers, and artists is augmented by Dreier's own collection, including *Adeline Ravoux* (F786; plate 18), classified as a Post-Impressionist work. Reportedly a popular exhibition, it remains on view until June 15.[34]

MAY 7—NOVEMBER 1. John Quinn lends *Self-Portrait* (F268; plate 17) to the *Fiftieth Anniversary Exhibition*, commemorating the founding of the Metropolitan Museum of Art in New York. The painting, placed in the gallery presenting "modern French painting," is the sole work by Van Gogh on display (see Stein, New York, fig. 7).[35]

OCTOBER 23—DECEMBER 31. *Vincent van Gogh Exhibition*, the first retrospective of the artist's work in the United States, opens at the Montross Gallery in New York. Drawn from the Van Gogh family's collection, the exhibition is reviewed extensively in newspapers and magazines, from the influential *Dial* to the niche *Freeman*.[36] Three works from the exhibition (F575a, plate 26; F769; F929a, plate 13) are acquired by the clergyman, philanthropist, and collector Theodore Pitcairn (1893–1973) of Bryn Athyn, Pennsylvania; they are paid for in October 1921.[37]

1921

FEBRUARY—MARCH. After showing a selection of Van Gogh's works in January, Montross Gallery restages its Van Gogh exhibition from the previous year, this time without charge for admission to attract more visitors.[38] The gallery's owner, Newman E. Montross, will continue to promote the artist throughout the early 1920s, including Van Gogh's works in *Special Exhibition of Contemporary Art* in April 1922[39] and mounting a smaller version of the 1920 retrospective in March 27–April 14, 1923.[40] Other New York galleries follow suit: Marius de Zayas will feature Van Gogh's works at the De Zayas Gallery in February 26–April 9, 1921,[41] and the Weyhe Gallery will include him in its *First of April Show* of drawings and reproductions by Old and Modern Masters in April 1922.[42]

FEBRUARY 8—14. The art dealer Dikran Kelekian's collection of fifty-nine modern paintings is briefly on view at the Brooklyn Museum in New York.[43] In a few weeks, the collection would be shown again at the same venue in the larger *Exhibition of Modern French Masters Representing the Post Impressionists and Their Predecessors*, including Van Gogh's *Self-Portrait* (F526; plate 44) and *Women Picking Olives* (F655; see Shaw, Heartland, fig. 3), from March 26 to April 1. "Brooklyn is stealing a march on its big neighbor in Manhattan," Alfred Stieglitz remarks in reaction to the exhibition.[44]

APRIL 7—21. The critic and curator Forbes Watson organizes *Second Annual Exhibition of American and European Art* for the Dallas Art Association at the Adolphus Hotel in Dallas. An extensive presentation of over three hundred works, it includes Van Gogh's "Portrait of a Boy" (F537; plate 15) lent by Marius de Zayas, formerly in the collection of conductor and dealer Josef Stransky. In November, De Zayas will exhibit the painting again together with "The Farmhouse at Auvers" (F623) in the *Modern French Paintings* exhibition at the Minneapolis Institute of Arts.[45] The portrait will be on view once more among "quite a roster of radicals" at the New Gallery exhibition in New York in January 1923[46] before it is sold along with "The Farmhouse at Auvers" at the auction of De Zayas's collection on March 23, 1923.[47]

APRIL 23—MAY 7. The Holland-America Society for Arts, Science and Friendly Relations presents *Modern Art of Holland: An Exhibition of Paintings, Etchings, Wood Engravings, Sculpture, and Batik Work* at the Anderson Galleries in New York. Van Gogh "occupies the place of honor," with six paintings and three drawings on view.[48]

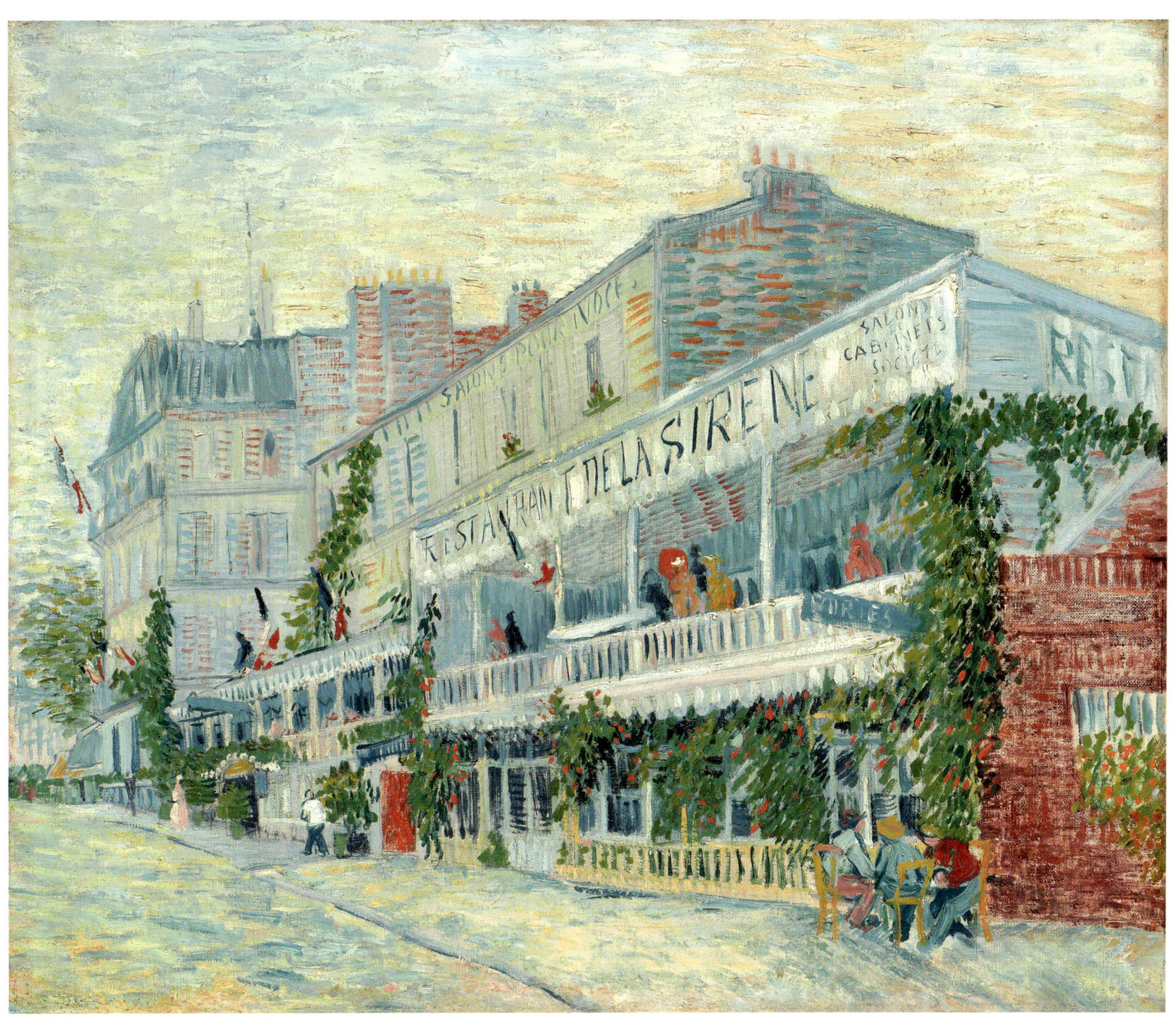

PLATE 74. *Restaurant de la Sirène at Asnières*, 1887 (CAT. 23)

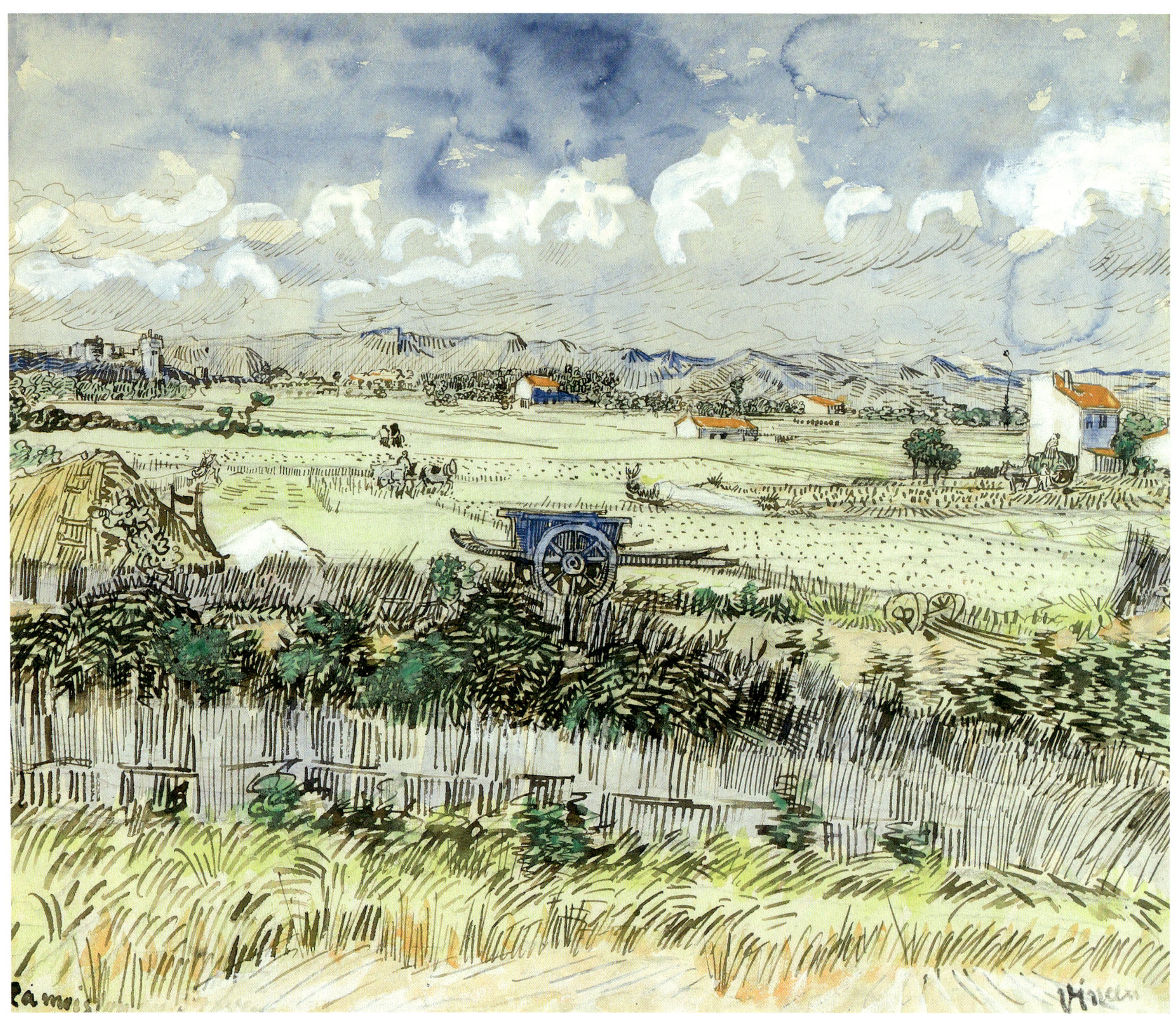

PLATE 75. *Harvest in Provence*, 1888 (CAT. 32)

MAY 3—SEPTEMBER 15. Seven of Van Gogh's works lent by John Quinn, Marius de Zayas, and Jo van Gogh-Bonger are on display in the Metropolitan Museum of Art's *Loan Exhibition of Impressionist and Post-Impressionist Paintings* in New York. *Still Life: Melon, Fish, Jar* (later deemed inauthentic; see Stein, New York, fig. 9), lent by Frederic Clay Bartlett from Chicago in August, expands the presentation.[49] An additional three drawings are lent by Van Gogh-Bonger to a complementary exhibition of works on paper.[50] The paintings exhibition ignites controversy and protests against modern art.[51]

MAY 26. The Musée du Louvre in Paris accepts a bequest of *Restaurant de la Sirène at Asnières* (F313; plate 74). American newspapers report on the first Van Gogh that enters the collection of this institution.[52]

NOVEMBER 3—DECEMBER 5. Katherine S. Dreier organizes *Exhibition of Paintings by Members of the Société Anonyme* at the Worcester Art Museum in Massachusetts with Van Gogh's *Adeline Ravoux* (F786; plate 18) among the avant-garde works of American and European artists on display. Dreier will offer the exhibition to several American institutions, but only Smith College, the Detroit Institute of Arts, and the MacDowell Club in New York will accept it.[53]

NOVEMBER 21—DECEMBER 12. Forbes Watson assembles *A Selected Group of American and French Painters*, with six of Van Gogh's works, at the Arts Club of Chicago.[54] The Chicago critic Hi Simons calls it "the most significant exhibition of modern art that has been in this city since the International Exhibition of 1913–14 [the Armory Show]."[55]

1922

Julius Meier-Graefe's *Vincent van Gogh: A Biographical Study*, originally published in Munich in 1921, appears in an English edition, with 102 reproductions of the artist's works (see, for example, F1483; plate 75).[56] The publication will be reissued in 1926, 1928, 1933, and in numerous editions after 1936.

JANUARY. The Art Institute of Chicago publicizes its acquisition and exhibition of a landscape drawing by Van Gogh.[57] The drawing will later be recognized as inauthentic.

JANUARY 31. At the sale of the Dikran Kelekian collection, held by the American Art Galleries in New York, the president of the City of Detroit Arts Commission Ralph H. Booth (1873–1931) successfully bids on behalf of the Detroit Institute of Arts for *Self-Portrait* (F526; plate 44). Pronounced "courageous" by *The Arts*, it is the first purchase of a Van Gogh painting by an American public museum (figs. 8 and 9).[58] The second Van Gogh painting in the sale, *Women Picking Olives* (F655; see Shaw, Heartland, fig. 3), goes to the dealer and collector Joseph Brummer, who bought it back for Kelekian.[59]

MARCH 1—31. The Detroit Institute of Arts mounts *Exhibition of Modern Art*, derived from Katherine S. Dreier's Société Anonyme show in Worcester, Massachusetts, on view the previous year. *Adeline Ravoux* (F786; plate 18) is joined by the DIA's recently acquired *Self-Portrait* (F526; plate 44) and *Still Life: Melon, Fish, Jar* from Frederic Clay Bartlett's collection.[60] Other works by modern artists from the DIA's collection as well as a selection of African sculptures are on view. On March 8, Forbes Watson delivers the lecture "The Significance of Modern Painting"; in the press coverage, Van Gogh is alternatively accepted as a modern master or "the saner and more skilled...of the [younger generation] extremists."[61]

NOVEMBER 15—DECEMBER 12. A touring exhibition of the Goudstikker collection of Dutch and Flemish paintings organized by Jacques Goudstikker and the Netherlands-America Affiliation, is shown at the City Art Museum of St. Louis. Initiated by a trustee of the St. Louis museum, the exhibition—the contents of which would differ significantly at each venue—travels to the Cleveland Museum of Art, December 16, 1922–January 7, 1923, and then to the Detroit Institute of Arts, January 13–February 15, 1923.[62] In Detroit, it is shown in two separate installations; the modern section, expanded by five of Van Gogh's works from Jo van Gogh-Bonger's collection, is on view February 1–15, 1923. The tour ends at the Anderson Galleries in New York, March 10–April 7, 1923, where the five Van Goghs are displayed again.

1923

JANUARY. In his role as a new editor of *The Arts*, Forbes Watson contributes an article on the Barnes Foundation, illustrated with Charles Sheeler's photographs of *The Postman (Joseph-Étienne Roulin)* (F435; see Stein, New York, fig. 2) and *The Smoker* (F534) as well as works by other artists in the collection.[63] *The Arts*, a magazine published between December 1920 and October 1931, with the mission to bring art and culture to the American people, will champion Van Gogh's art, frequently featuring reviews and reproductions of the artist's works on its pages and covers.

JUNE. The Detroit Institute of Arts mounts an exhibition of recent acquisitions and works from private collections, dubbed by the press "Exhibition of 'Ultra-Modern Art.'"[64] It is Henri Matisse's *The Window* (plate 49) that stirs controversy and forces the museum officials to defend their recent acquisitions, including *Self-Portrait* (F526; plate 44).[65]

SEPTEMBER 8–OCTOBER 22. *Group of Modern Paintings from the Birch-Bartlett Collection*, including *Madame Roulin Rocking the Cradle (La Berceuse)* (F506), acquired by Frederic Clay Bartlett in August, is shown at the Art Institute of Chicago.[66] Bartlett's collection will be displayed there again the following year from September 3 to October 22. As Bartlett adds new works to the collection,[67] its reputation grows, prompting the Minneapolis Institute of Arts to request it for a loan. The Birch Bartlett collection will be exhibited in Minneapolis in April 1925 and at the Art Institute of Chicago, September 8–October 8, before it travels to the Boston Art Club, December 9–26 that year.

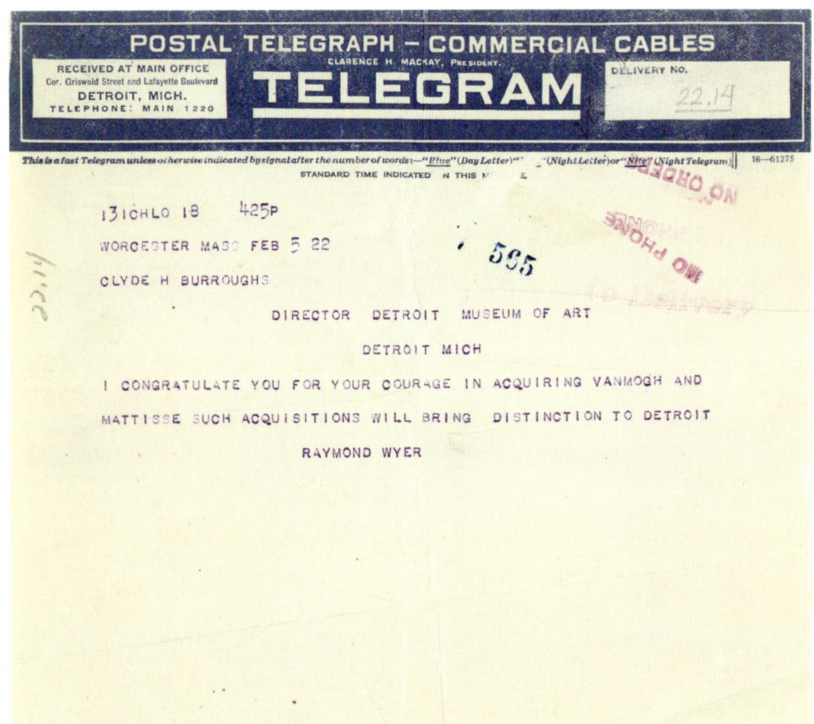

POSTAL TELEGRAPH – COMMERCIAL CABLES
CLARENCE H. MACKAY, PRESIDENT.

RECEIVED AT MAIN OFFICE
Cor. Griswold Street and Lafayette Boulevard
DETROIT, MICH.
TELEPHONE: MAIN 1220

TELEGRAM

DELIVERY NO. 22.14

131CHLO 18 425P

WORCESTER MASS FEB 5 22

CLYDE H BURROUGHS

DIRECTOR DETROIT MUSEUM OF ART

DETROIT MICH

I CONGRATULATE YOU FOR YOUR COURAGE IN ACQUIRING VANMOGH AND MATTISSE SUCH ACQUISITIONS WILL BRING DISTINCTION TO DETROIT

RAYMOND WYER

FIG. 8 Congratulatory telegram on the purchase of *Self-Portrait* (F526; plate 44) from Raymond Wyer, Director, Worcester Art Museum, to Clyde H. Burroughs, Director, Detroit Institute of Arts and Secretary to the Arts Commission of the City of Detroit.

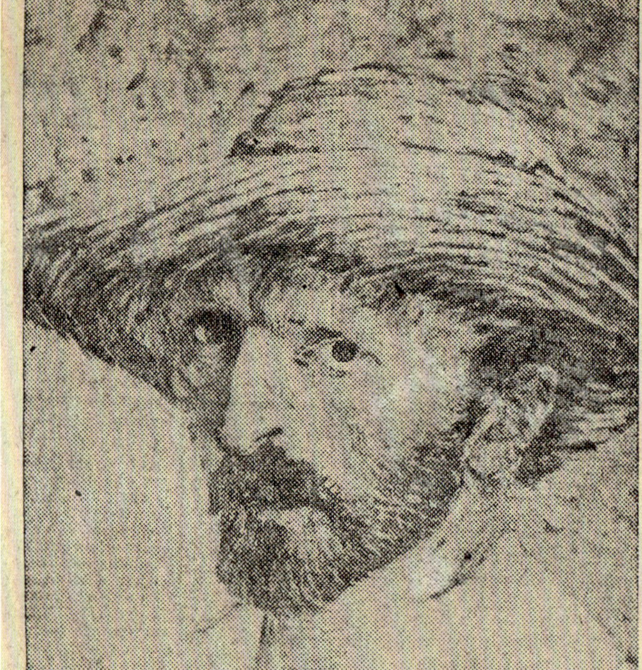

A MODERN AT THE ART INSTITUTE

THE portrait of Vincent Van Gogh by himself was acquired by the Detroit Institute of Arts at the Kelekian sale at New York, and is a good example of the artist's work. The black and white reproduction fails, naturally, to show the colorful nature of the painting, but gives a good idea of the painter's brushwork.

FIG. 9 Newspaper clipping reporting on Detroit's purchase of *Self-Portrait* (F526; plate 44).

1924

MARCH–APRIL. In his newly opened Printroom at 19 East Fifty-Seventh Street in New York, the German dealer J. B. Neumann shows Van Gogh's etching *Portrait of Dr. Gachet (Man with a Pipe)* (F1664; for example plate 42) among "early woodcuts, etchings, and lithographs by famous European masters," including Goya, Delacroix, Daumier, Gauguin, Cézanne, and others.[68] Neumann will continue to feature Van Gogh in group exhibitions of prints in his gallery, later named New Art Circle Gallery, which becomes a popular meeting spot for artists.[69]

MARCH 17–31. In New York, the Reinhardt Galleries host a small presentation of works from Tilla Durieux's collection, which includes at least one painting by Van Gogh, "The Railway Bridge" (F480).[70] Tilla Durieux (Ottillie Godefroy, 1880–1971), a well-known Austrian actress, and her husband, Paul Cassirer (1871–1926), the German art dealer who was critical to introducing Van Gogh's art to Germany, visited the United States the previous spring to tour "the museums and famous private galleries in America."[71] Durieux returns to the United States for her theater performance at the beginning of 1924, which coincides with the exhibition.

NOVEMBER. *Inaugural Exposition of French Art* marks the opening of the California Palace of the Legion of Honor in San Francisco, a new museum planned since 1915. This large survey of French art from French public and private collections included two Van Goghs: "Room of the Painter in Arles" (probably F484; plate 45) and "Rose Bushes in the Garden of Daubigny at Auvers" (F580).[72]

1925

JANUARY 9–FEBRUARY 1. Katherine S. Dreier lends *Adeline Ravoux* (F786; plate 18) to *An Exhibition of Modern French Art* at the Baltimore Museum of Art.

MARCH. Van Gogh is featured in *The Great Influences of the XIX Century* exhibition at the Rosenberg Galleries in New York.[73]

Albert C. Barnes publishes *The Art in Painting*, advertised as "the epoch-making study of modern and contemporary painters."[74] Accompanying Barnes's text on the educational value of works of art are 106 illustrations, among them a reproduction of Van Gogh's *Houses and Figure* (F674) from his collection.[75] The remaining four Van Goghs in Barnes's collection at the time (F435, F534, F318, and F330) are discussed in the section "Analysis of Paintings."[76] On March 19, the Barnes Foundation will open its doors to the selected public in Merion, Pennsylvania, near Philadelphia (fig. 10).

An English translation of *The Tragic Life of Vincent van Gogh* by Louis Piérard is published. Piérard's lively account of Van Gogh's life and work "succeeds in rekindling [the readers'] interest and deepening [their] sympathy" for the artist.[77]

FIG. 10 Gallery installation at the Barnes Foundation, Merion, Pennsylvania, featuring Van Gogh's *Houses and Figure* (F674) at the lower far right, 1928.

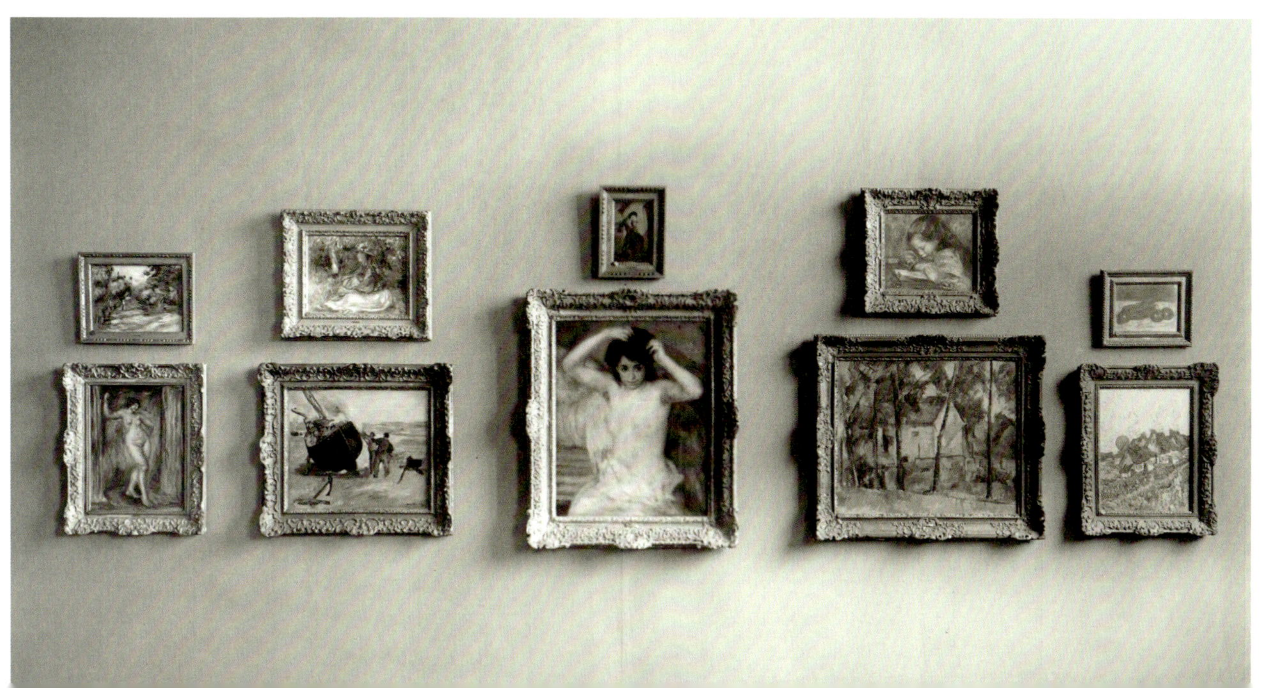

1926

JANUARY 7–30. A small portion of the collection assembled by the recently deceased John Quinn goes on display at the New York Art Center in the *Memorial Exhibition of Representative Works Selected from the John Quinn Collection*. Van Gogh's *Self-Portrait* (F268; plate 17) is on view. The painting will be sold by the Quinn Estate during the exhibition and will enter the collection of Josephine S. Goodwin (1850–1939) of New York and Hartford.[78] The new owner will exhibit it in the *Loan Exhibition of Modern French Painting* at the Wadsworth Atheneum in Hartford, April 20–May 5, 1928;[79] it will be given to the museum by her son Phillip L. Goodwin in 1954.

MAY. Frederic Clay Bartlett gifts the Helen Birch Bartlett Memorial Collection to the Art Institute of Chicago. The collection of twenty-four modern paintings includes four works by Van Gogh (one of them, *Still Life: Melon, Fish, Jar*, would later be deemed inauthentic); *The Bedroom* (F484; plate 45), acquired from Paul Rosenberg in May, was Bartlett's most recent addition of the artist's work.[80]

OCTOBER 29—NOVEMBER 29. The Cleveland Museum of Art presents *Fifty Years of French Art*; two works attributed to Van Gogh were lent by the galleries Scott and Fowles and Wildenstein & Co.[81]

NOVEMBER 20—DECEMBER 11. Adolph Lewisohn lends his newly acquired *L'Arlésienne: Madame Joseph-Michel Ginoux (Marie Julien, 1848–1911)* (F488; plate 29; fig. 11) to Reinhardt Galleries' *French Paintings: Three Hundred Years of Art* exhibition. The painting will return to the same gallery for the presentation of *El Greco and Rembrandt to Cézanne and Matisse* in January 15–February 5, 1927.

Paul-Émile Colin's *Van Gogh* is published in an English translation as part of a popular series of monographs on artists who influenced the modern art movement. The volume contains forty reproductions and a biographical and critical introduction to the artist's oeuvre.[82]

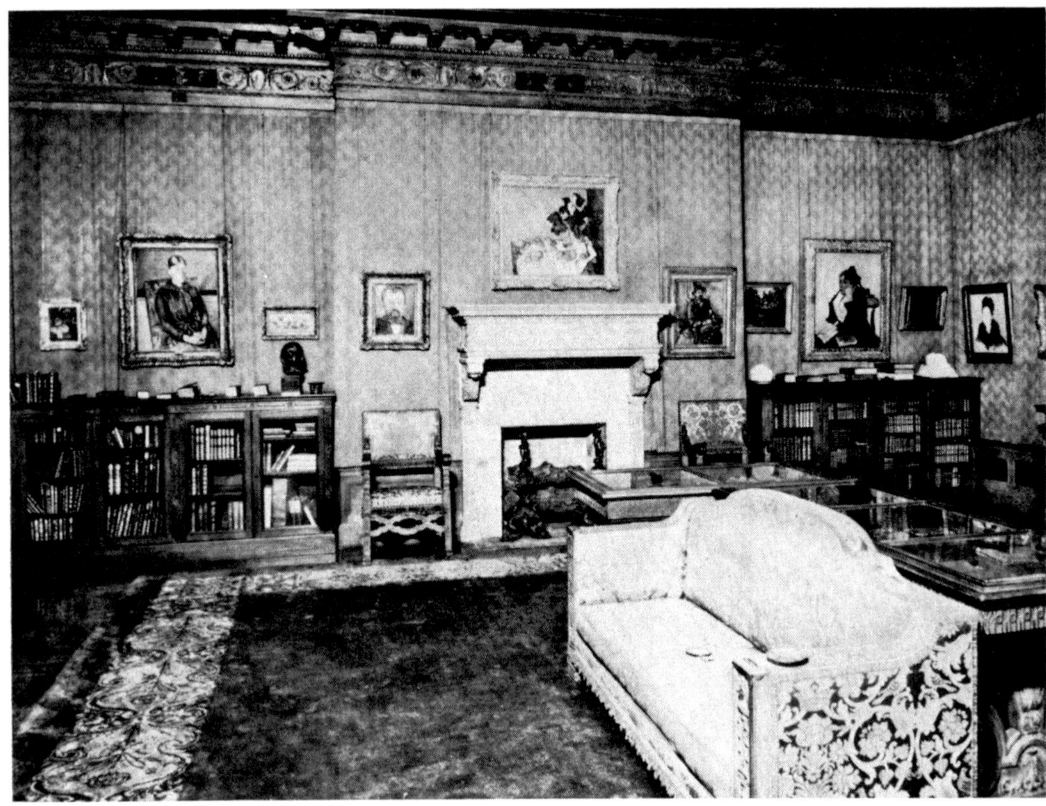

FIG. 11 Interior of Adolph Lewisohn's house at 881 Fifth Avenue, New York. *L'Arlésienne: Madame Joseph-Michel Ginoux (Marie Julien, 1848–1911)* (F488; plate 29) is third from the right.

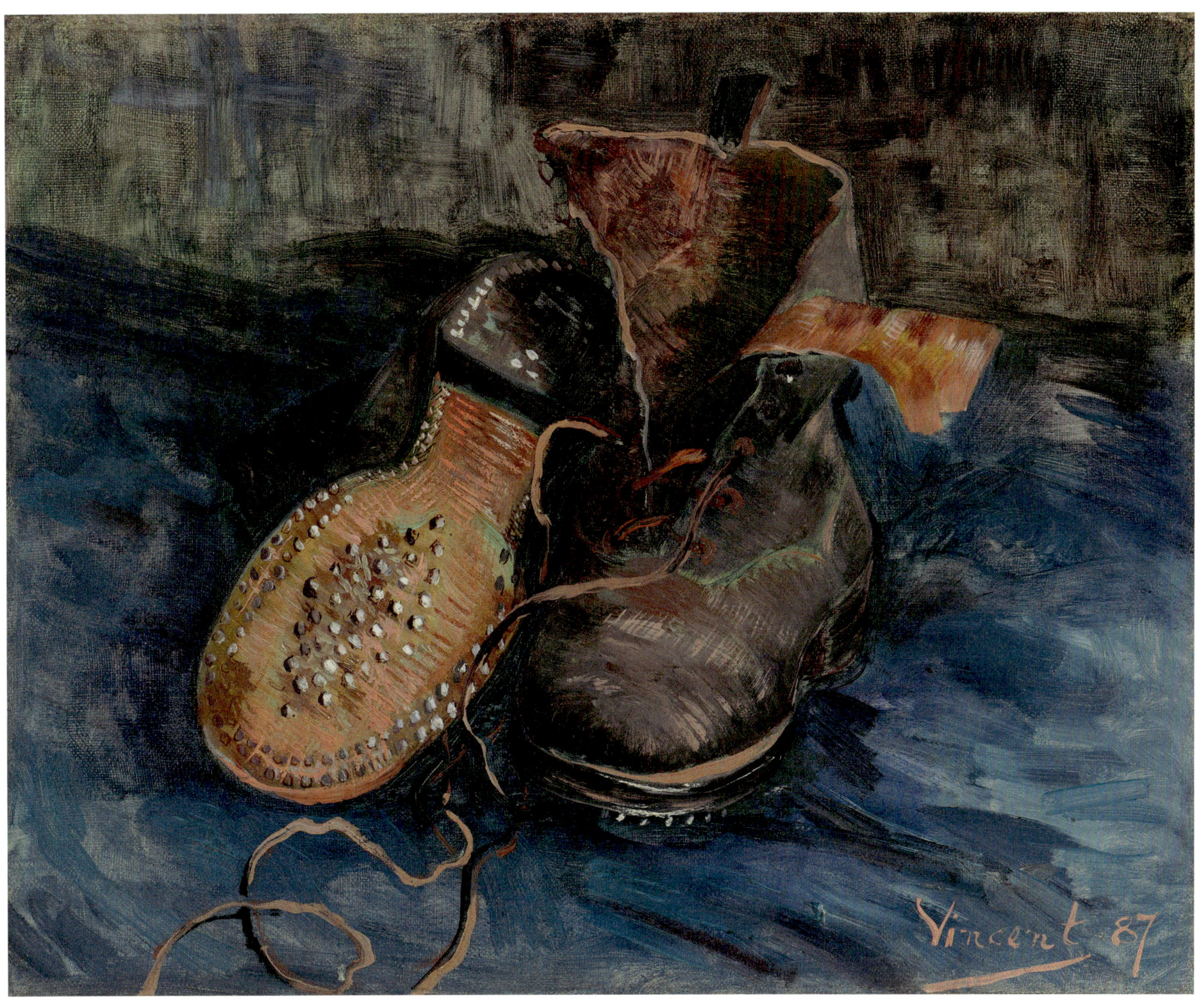

PLATE 76. *A Pair of Boots*, 1887 (CAT. 20)

1927

The first two volumes of *The Letters of Vincent Van Gogh to His Brother 1872–1886, with a Memoir by His Sister-in-law, J. van Gogh-Bonger* appear in an English translation prepared by Jo van Gogh-Bonger. The publication will be followed by the third and final volume, *Further Letters of Vincent van Gogh to His Brother, 1886–1889*, in 1929.[83]

MARCH. Van Gogh is featured as one of "the French masters of the nineteenth century" by Wildenstein Galleries in New York.[84]

By March, William G. Russell Allen (1882–1955) in Boston adds to his collection the etching *Portrait of Dr. Gachet* (F1664; see plate 42 for an exemplary work), which will come to the Museum of Fine Arts in Boston as part of the William G. Russell Allen Bequest in 1960.[85]

APRIL 12–23. César De Hauke stages *The Classics of Modern Painting* at the modern art branch of the Seligmann Galleries in New York. The exhibition features "The Tall House" (F550; plate 27), sent from Paris by De Hauke's French partner, Galerie Bernheim-Jeune. Shown for the first time in the United States, the work is erroneously touted by the press as "Van Gogh's last painting."[86] In December, Bernheim-Jeune will sell the painting to Anson Conger Goodyear (1877–1964), a Buffalo patron and later president of the Museum of Modern Art in New York;[87] it will come to the Albright-Knox Art Gallery in Buffalo as part of Goodyear's bequest in 1966.

MAY 25–JULY 1. *Flower Pictures (1568–1927)*, an exhibition at the Knoedler Galleries in New York, includes two still lifes of flowers attributed to Van Gogh. Popular with visitors, floral still life by Van Gogh and other French artists will be periodically revisited by the gallery in its exhibitions.[88]

AUGUST. Notable Baltimore collector Claribel Cone (1864–1929) informs her sister Etta (1870–1949) about her purchase of *A Pair of Boots* (F333; plate 76) from Paul Vallotton in Lausanne.[89] After a misstep with a purported Van Gogh bought from the Reinhardt Galleries the same year, Etta Cone will acquire *Landscape with Figures* (F818; plate 1) by August 1934.[90] The two paintings and the watercolor *Beach at Scheveningen* (F1038), in addition to works by other artists assembled by the Cone sisters in Baltimore, will come to the Baltimore Museum of Art upon Etta Cone's death in 1949.

OCTOBER 8–22. *Exhibition of Modern French Paintings, Water Colors and Drawings* inaugurates C. W. Kraushaar Art Galleries' season in New York. The catalogue lists "Coucher de soleil, Auvers" (unidentified) under Van Gogh's name; the drawing *Corridor in the Asylum* (F1529) is also on view.[91] In October 1–18 the following year, the gallery will assemble a "large all star cast" for their second exhibition of modern French art.[92] It includes *Landscape under a Stormy Sky* (F575) and two drawings, *Cottages with a Woman Working in the Middle Ground* (F1642) and "Orchard" (unidentified). The Chicago collector Annie Swan Coburn (1856–1932) will briefly own the first drawing.

Robert Allerton (1873–1964), a trustee of the Art Institute of Chicago and later its honorary president, gifts the drawing *Cypresses* (F1524) to the museum's permanent collection.

1928

Julius Meier-Graefe's *Vincent van Gogh* (1922) is issued in a one-volume inexpensive edition published by Payson and Clarke.

JANUARY. Jacob-Baart de la Faille (1886–1959), a trained jurist, art critic, and researcher, produces the first standard catalogue of the work of Van Gogh, *L'Œuvre de Vincent van Gogh. Catalogue Raisonné*, published in four volumes by Les Éditions G. van Oest in Brussels in a limited edition of 650.[93]

JANUARY 15. An exhibition of Van Gogh's works occasioned by the publication of De la Faille's catalogue raisonné opens at Paul Cassirer's gallery in Berlin. Several paintings lent by the art dealer Otto Wacker are revealed to be forgeries and are pulled from the exhibition. Wacker, to whom eventually thirty-three suspect works will be traced, is investigated and convicted of fraud after a public trial in April 1932 (fig. 12). The event draws attention to questions of authenticity of other Van Goghs in circulation.[94]

The same month in New York, Wildenstein Galleries holds an exhibition of works by Picasso as well as a show called *Modern French Paintings*. Van Gogh is included in the latter exhibition and is considered a "venerable" artist in contrast with the avant-garde Spaniard.[95]

FEBRUARY 27–MARCH 17. Howard Young Gallery lends *Orchard in Blossom with Yellow Enclosure* (F551) to an inclusive presentation of *Loan Exhibition of Paintings from Memling, Holbein and Titian to Renoir and Picasso*, held at Reinhardt Galleries in New York. The work is singled out by a reviewer for its "nervous intensity."[96]

MARCH 26. The partial opening of the new building of the Pennsylvania Museum of Art (later renamed Philadelphia Museum of Art) in Fairmount is celebrated with an inaugural installation that includes loans from Philadelphia collectors, among them *Portrait of Adeline Ravoux* (F769) and *Portrait of the Artist's Mother* (F477) from Theodore Pitcairn.[97]

JUNE 17–AUGUST 5. The Albright Art Gallery in Buffalo presents *Selection of Paintings of the French Modern School from the Collection of A. C. Goodyear and Other Single Loans*, among them *Landscape near Saint-Rémy* (F726). Goodyear acquired the painting two years earlier with the intention of donating it to the Albright Art Gallery.[98] Two other Van Goghs from Goodyear's collection on view this summer are *House on the Crau (The Old Mill)* (F550; plate 27) and "Self-Portrait" (unidentified). *Landscape near Saint-Rémy*, whose authenticity will come under suspicion in the wake of the Wacker affair, will be donated to the Museum of Modern Art in New York in December 1948.

SEPTEMBER 17. New York pediatricians Harry and Ruth Morris Bakwin acquire *L'Arlésienne, Madame Ginoux* (F543; plate 41) after viewing the picture at the Thannhauser Gallery in the summer.[99] In November of the following year, the painting will be on display at the Museum of Modern Art's inaugural exhibition in New York. Before its acquisition by the Bakwins, *L'Arlésienne* had been considered by a number of collectors as well as museum directors in Europe and the United States.[100] Ralph H. Booth, instrumental for the Detroit Institute of Arts' acquisitions and himself a collector, expressed interest in the painting during his visit to the gallery branch in Lucerne in the summer of 1928.[101]

FIG. 12 Berlin trial of Otto Wacker (far right), 1932.

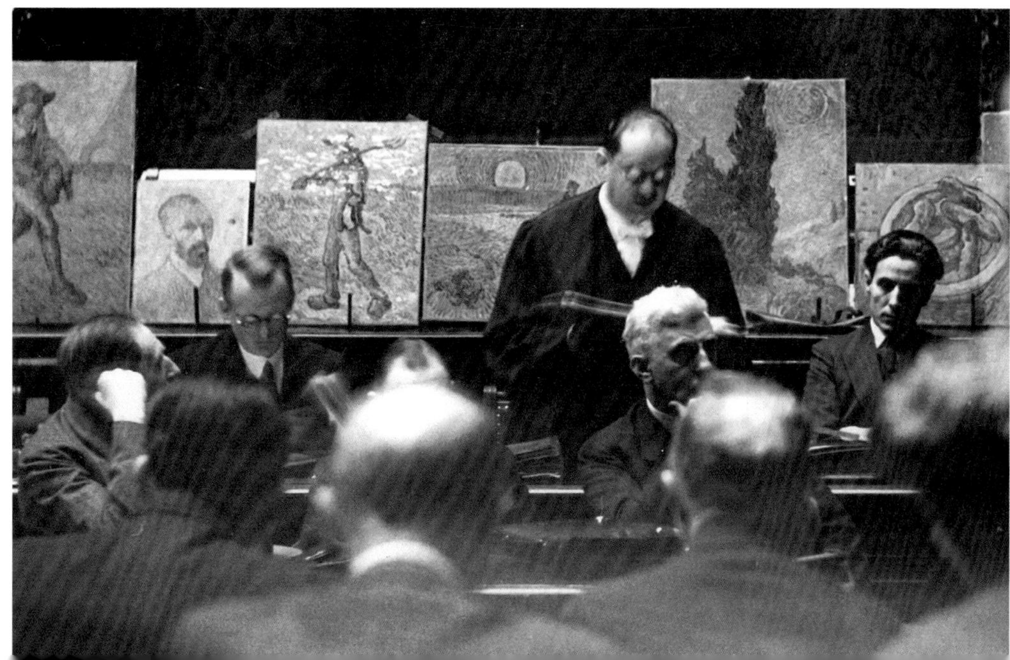

OCTOBER. *Modern French Art from the Chester Dale Collection* is shown at the Wildenstein Galleries. The New York collectors Chester Dale (1883–1962) and his wife Maud Murray Dale (1875–1953) had been acquiring works by modern French artists since 1926. The Dales bought *Roulin's Baby* (F440) from Kraushaar in June 1927[102] and "Self-Portrait" (F523, later reattributed to an imitator of Van Gogh) from Josef Stransky in the spring of 1928.[103] The self-portrait was illustrated and exalted in the press as "the best thing [Van Gogh] ever did" and an "outstanding canvas" in the collection;[104] later scholarship will trace its provenance to Otto Wacker. In a portrait commissioned from Diego Rivera, Dale is depicted in front of a book opened to an image of the painting (fig. 13).[105] Upon Chester Dale's death, the painting was bequeathed to the National Gallery of Art, Washington, DC.

OCTOBER 19–NOVEMBER. With the support of the Chicago patron and philanthropist Kate L. Brewster (1879–1947), *Exhibition of Modern French Paintings* opens at the Chester H. Johnson Galleries in Chicago, featuring *Grapes, Lemons, Pears, and Apples* (F382; plate 55).[106] Brewster, together with her husband, Walter (1872–1954), acquired the painting just before the exhibition and would lend the work three times the following year: to the Arts Club of Chicago's *Loan Exhibition of Modern Paintings Privately Owned by Chicagoans* in January 4–18, Harvard's Fogg Art Museum in Cambridge in the spring, and finally to the Museum of Modern Art's inaugural exhibition in New York.

OCTOBER 27. Providence collector Dorothy Sturges (1889–1933) buys *View of Auvers-sur-Oise* (F800; plate 77) together with a Berthe Morisot watercolor called "Springtime" from De Hauke & Co. in New York.[107]

NOVEMBER 12–DECEMBER 8. The New York collector Anna Eugenia La Chapelle Clark (1878–1963) buys *Oleanders* (F593) from Knoedler, shortly after the close of the gallery's exhibition *A Century of French Painting*, in which Van Gogh is situated within the French art canon.[108] Two other works on view are *Postman Joseph Roulin* (F432; see Stolwijk and Krikke, fig. 7) and *The Bridge at Trinquetaille* (F426). Clark will acquire the latter as well before May 1929, when she lends her two new acquisitions to the Corcoran Gallery in Washington, DC.[109]

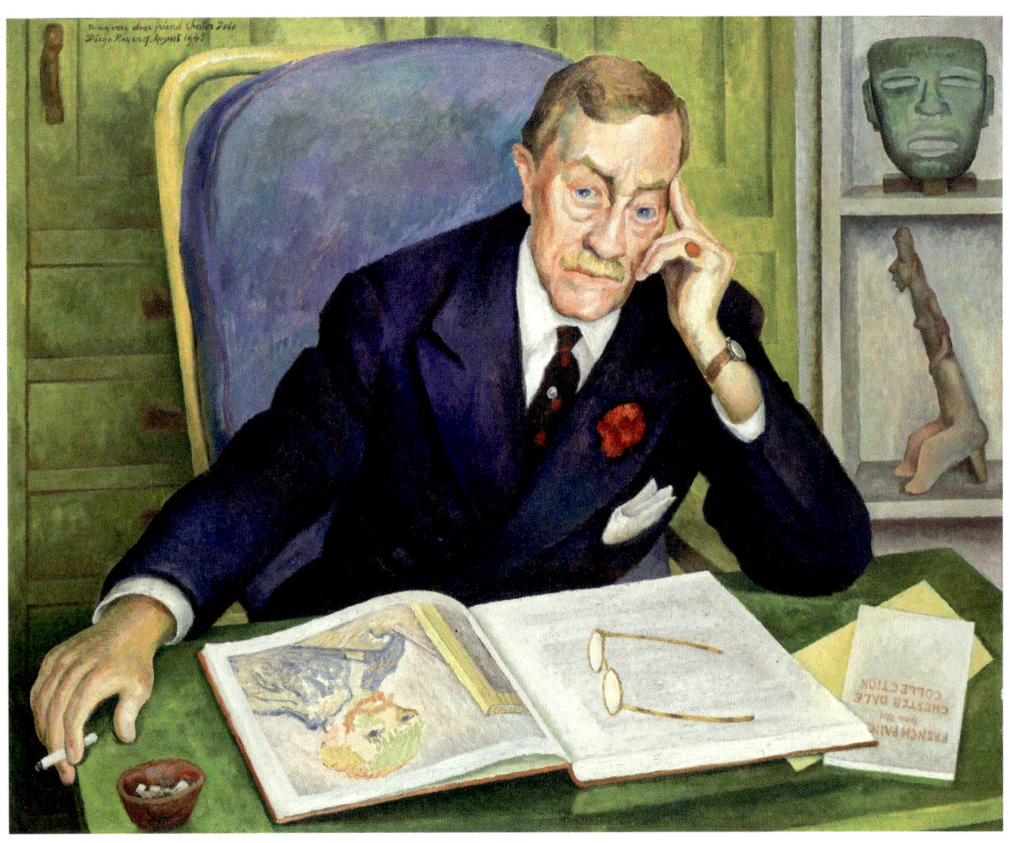

FIG. 13 Diego Rivera (Mexican, 1886–1957), *Chester Dale*, 1945. Oil on canvas, 39½ × 49$\frac{15}{16}$ in. (100.3 × 126.8 cm). National Gallery of Art, Washington, DC.

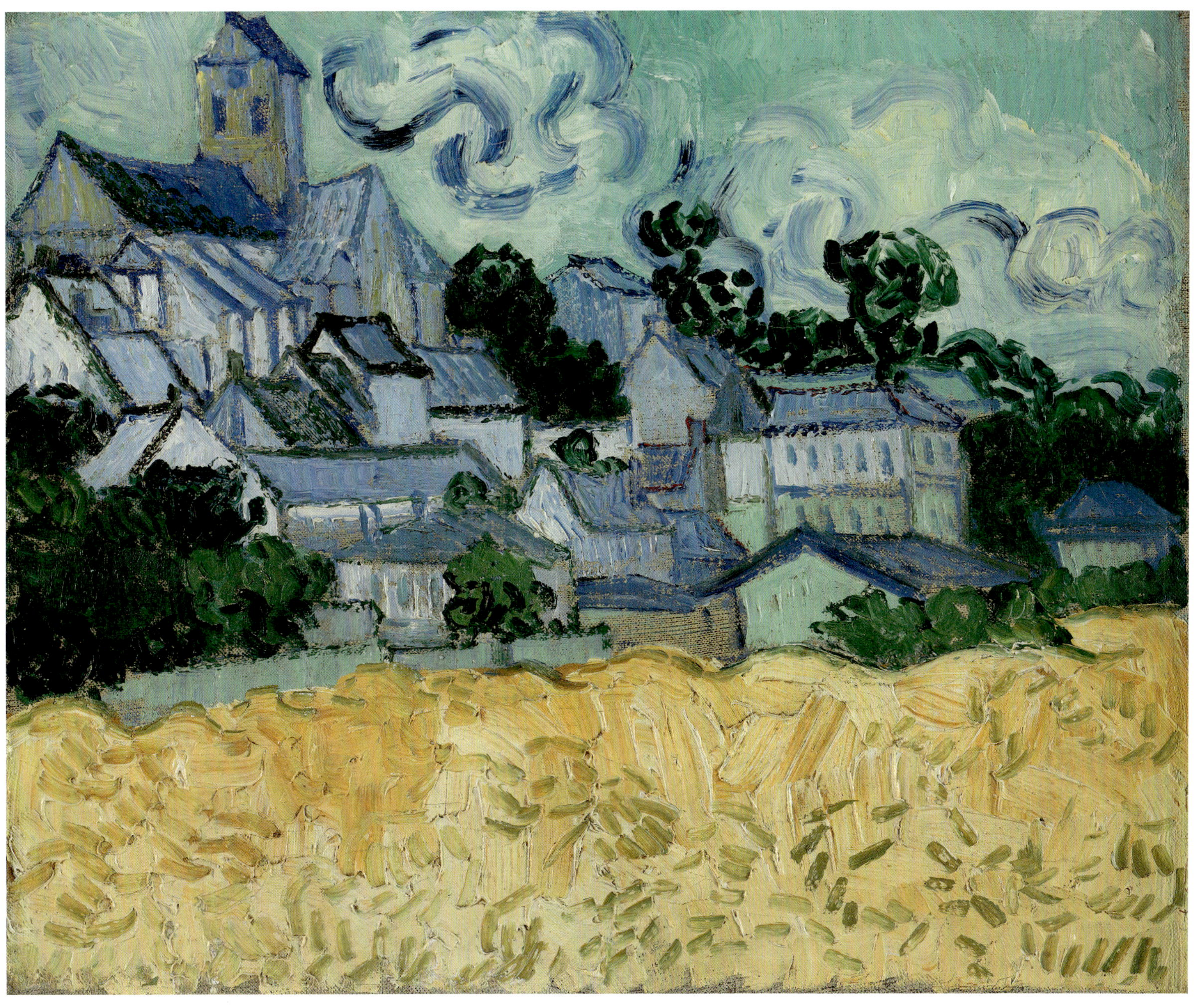

PLATE 77. *View of Auvers-sur-Oise*, 1890 (CAT. 73)

1929

Anthony Bertram's *Vincent van Gogh* appears in the World's Masters series published by Studio Publications in New York and London. A second edition will be issued in 1934, with Bertram's brief essay denigrating the "psychological school of [Van Gogh's] critics."[110]

FEBRUARY 3–24. The Toledo Museum of Art in Ohio presents *Exhibition of French Paintings*. Van Gogh is represented by "Walking Through the Fields" (probably F819; plate 58), lent by Wildenstein Galleries, as well as a still life lent by the Marie Sterner Gallery.[111]

MARCH 6–APRIL 6. The loan exhibition of *French Painting of the Nineteenth and Twentieth Centuries* opens at the Fogg Art Museum in Cambridge, Massachusetts (fig. 14). Occupying five galleries, the installation includes a significant section on Post-Impressionism, with ten works by Van Gogh. *La Berceuse* (F508; plate 22), acquired by the Boston collector John Spaulding the previous year and thought by the Fogg Museum's director Arthur Pope to be "perhaps the climax of [Spaulding's] collection," is on view along with other "glorious Van Goghs some of them familiar."[112] A smaller version of the exhibition, with seven Van Gogh works, will be staged at the Museum of Fine Arts, Boston, in August.[113]

MARCH 23. Collector and philanthropist Edith Wetmore (1870–1966) buys the drawing *Sand Barges Moored at the Quay, Arles* (F1462) from De Hauke & Co.'s *Exhibition of Works by Nineteenth Century and Contemporary French Artists: Watercolors and Drawings*, March 1–23.[114] In May De Hauke will sell the watercolor *The Zouave* (F1482; plate 20), featured on the November cover of *The Arts*, to Walter E. Sachs.[115] In December the gallery shows two drawings: "Seated Zouave" (F1443) and "The Bridge at Langlois" (F1471).[116]

MAY 1. Duncan Phillips (1886–1966) acquires *Women Crossing the Fields* (F819; plate 58) for the Phillips Memorial Gallery (later renamed Phillips Collection). Phillips opened his collection of modern European and American art to the public in his Washington, DC, mansion in 1921. In 1926 he admitted that "[a] number of brilliant European modernists are as yet absent," and he wished "to find examples of the inventive genius of Van Gogh."[117] Phillips had previously bought *The Fields* (F812) in 1927 and exhibited the painting in *Survey of Painting from Chardin to Derain*, February–May, 1928;[118] after its attribution was questioned following the Wacker scandal, it was returned to Wildenstein Galleries in January 1929, and subsequently exchanged for *Women Crossing the Fields*.[119]

FIG. 14 Installation of *French Painting of the Nineteenth and Twentieth Centuries*, Gallery XIV, Fogg Art Museum, Cambridge, Massachusetts, 1929, featuring *La Berceuse* (F508; plate 22) on the back wall.

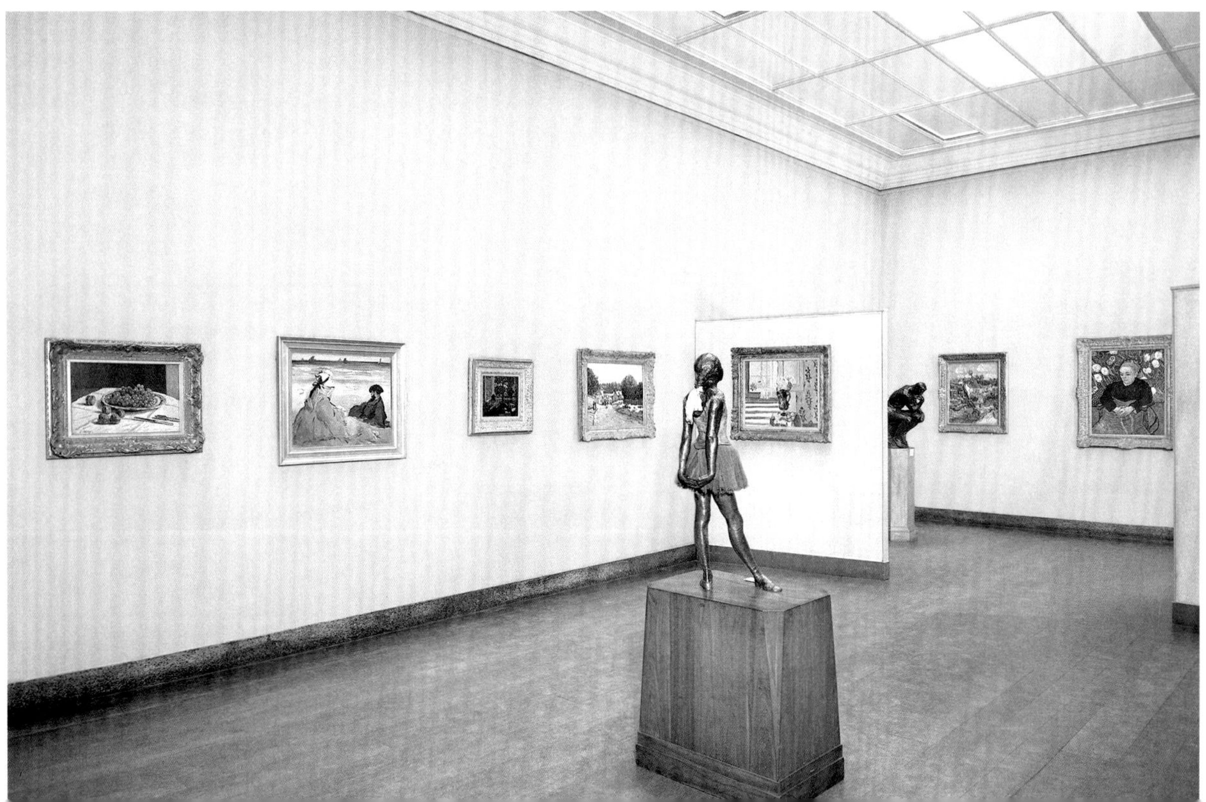

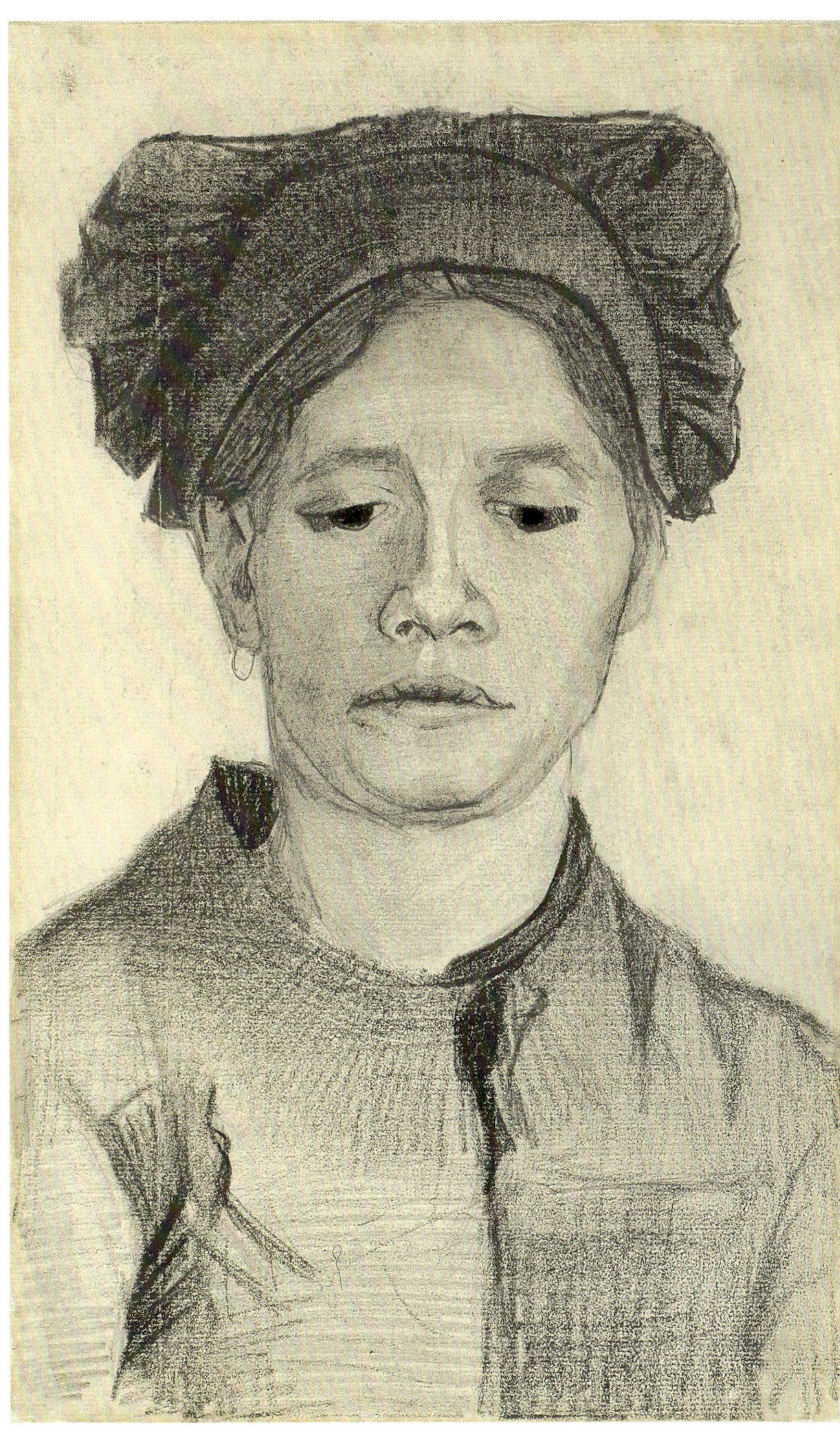

PLATE 78. *Head of a Peasant Woman*, 1884–85 (CAT. 8)

AUGUST 10. Industrialist Charles J. Liebman and his wife, painter Aline Liebman, buy the drawing *Head of a Peasant Woman* (F1175; plate 78) from Thannhauser Galleries. The drawing had been previously exhibited by Thannhauser in one of Otto Wacker's traveling exhibitions, but its provenance is traceable to Van Gogh's family and thus impeccable. A few months after its acquisition, the drawing will be shown at Salons of America at the Anderson Galleries, New York, in the spring of 1930. For nearly three decades it will remain in the Liebmans' collection of modern art in New York.[120]

NOVEMBER 7–DECEMBER 7. *First Loan Exhibition: Cézanne, Gauguin, Seurat, van Gogh* celebrates the inauguration of the Museum of Modern Art in midtown Manhattan. The exhibition is the first extensive display of Van Gogh's works at an American museum. The catalogue prepared by the museum's director Alfred H. Barr Jr. includes twenty-seven Van Gogh paintings and drawings, mainly from American private and institutional collections (among them, F382, plate 55; F432, Stolwijk and Krikke, fig. 7; F464, Van der Hoeven and Zwikker, fig. 3; F484, plate 45; F488, plate 29; F526, plate 44; F543, plate 41; F550, plate 27; F566, plate 57; F786, plate 18; F1003, plate 28; F1482, plate 20) and one work erroneously attributed to Van Gogh (see Stein, New York, fig. 9).

NOVEMBER 8–DECEMBER 8. The Cleveland Museum of Art organizes *French Art since 1800*, an exhibition that offers, in the words of the museum's director, William M. Milliken, "the opportunity to...become acquainted with the men who have made tradition."[121] The museum's trustee and committed modern art collector Ralph M. Coe (1882–1959) lends *The Park of Saint Paul's Hospital* (F640; see Shaw, Heartland, fig. 7); another Van Gogh loan comes from Edith Wetmore, who sends her recently purchased drawing *Sand Barges Moored at the Quay, Arles* (F1462).

The Arts offers for sale color reproductions of Van Gogh's works, advertised by the magazine as "exact copies of the original" suitable for "a Christmas Gift which...will afford the recipient lasting pleasure" (fig. 15). In *The Arts Portfolio Series*, only Cézanne and Van Gogh are represented by more than one reproduction.[122]

1930

JANUARY 3–17. The Arts Club of Chicago presents *Loan Exhibition of Modern Drawings and Sculpture Privately Owned by Chicagoans*. The drawing *Cottages with a Woman Working in the Middle Ground* (F1642), exhibited as "Landscape," comes from Walter S. and Kate L. Brewster, who acquired it in 1929 from Annie Swan Coburn. The Brewsters will lend the drawing again this year to *Modern European and Antique Oriental Art* at the Renaissance Society at the University of Chicago in April 7–21.

MARCH 11–31. Dorothy Sturges lends her *House at Auvers* (F804) and *View of Auvers-sur-Oise* (F800; plate 77) to the *Modern French Art* exhibition at the Rhode Island School of Design Museum in Providence. The catalogue accompanying the exhibition calls Van Gogh "the tragic great artist" who "at the present...is the most widely popularized painter of his group—and the most thoroughly documented."[123] Shortly thereafter, Sturges will acquire her third Van Gogh work, *The Road Menders* (F658; fig. 16), from the Wildenstein Galleries.[124] Sturges bequeaths the three works to her friend Elizabeth Hudson (1885–1973) of Syracuse.[125] Hudson, herself an enthusiastic admirer of Van Gogh, will donate *View of Auvers-sur-Oise* to the Rhode Island School of Design Museum in 1935, and sell the other two paintings to her cousin Duncan Phillips in 1949. In 1953 she will part with her drawing *Le Moulin de la Galette* (F1396a), which will become part of the Phillips Gallery's collection.

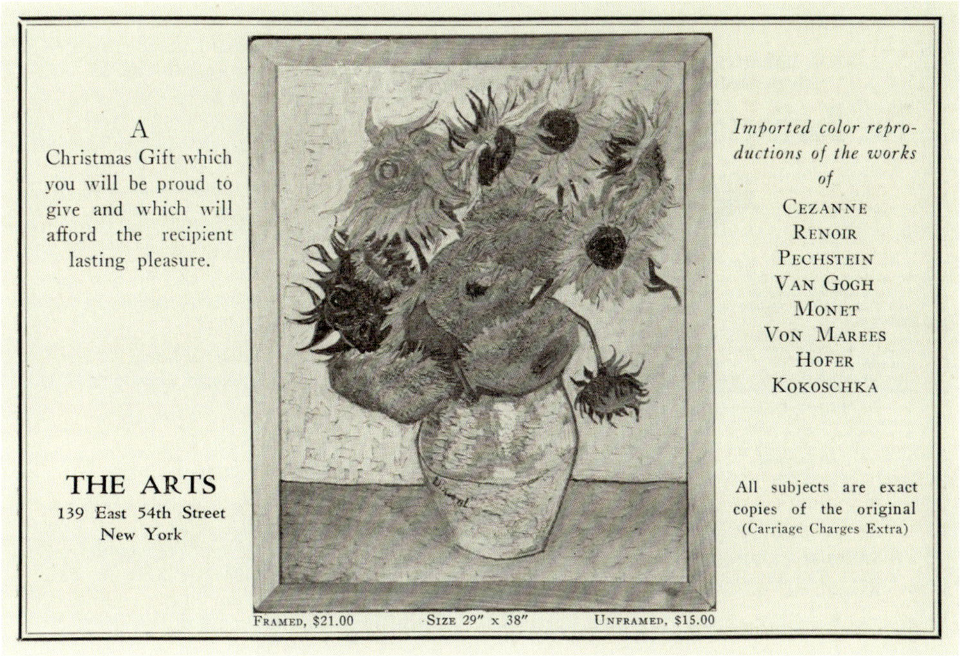

APRIL 12–MAY 8. The Minneapolis Institute of Arts organizes *Masters of Modernism: Loan Exhibition of French Paintings of the Past Fifty Years*. The exhibition brochure lists forty works by Braque, Cézanne, Degas, Van Gogh, Matisse, Picasso, and others, with an indication that many of the exhibited works are for sale.[126] Included is one Van Gogh work, "Rain" (F650?), lent by Wildenstein Galleries.

SEPTEMBER. Duncan Phillips exchanges *Women Crossing the Fields* (F819; plate 58), a painting by Derain, and two paintings by Daumier in a partial trade with Wildenstein Galleries for *Entrance to the Public Gardens in Arles* (F566, formerly in Arthur and Alice Sachs's collection; plate 57). The transaction documents "the tremendous rise in values" of Van Gogh's works.[127] In October the painting will be displayed together with other examples of "modern European and American masterpieces" in Phillips's collection in Washington, DC.[128]

OCTOBER. Marie Harriman opens her eponymous gallery on East 57th Street (close to the other international dealers Durand-Ruel, Knoedler, Wildenstein, and Reinhardt) with an exhibition of twenty-nine paintings by Cézanne, Derain, Gauguin, Van Gogh, Matisse, Picasso, Renoir, and Rousseau. One canvas by Van Gogh—*Roses* (F681; plate 59) from Harriman's own collection—is on view.[129] Harriman will lend the still life to a number of exhibitions in the 1930s.

FIG. 15 Advertisement of the color reproductions of Van Gogh's works in *The Arts*, December 1929.

DECEMBER. The Pennsylvania Museum of Art organizes *Nineteenth Century French Painting*, an exhibition of fifty-nine paintings, the majority of which are drawn from Philadelphia private collections. Theodore Pitcairn lends his pair of portraits: *Adeline Ravoux* (F769) and *The Artist's Mother* (F477).[130]

In an attempt to correct attribution mistakes made in his earlier publications, Jacob-Baart de la Faille publishes *Les faux Van Gogh*, a catalogue of paintings and drawings now considered by him to be forgeries. The publication draws attention to the continuing presence of fakes, forgeries, and misattributions of Van Gogh's works on the market and in existing collections.

FIG. 16 *The Road Menders* (F658), 1889. Oil on canvas, 29 × 36½ in. (73.66 × 92.71 cm). The Phillips Collection, Washington, DC.

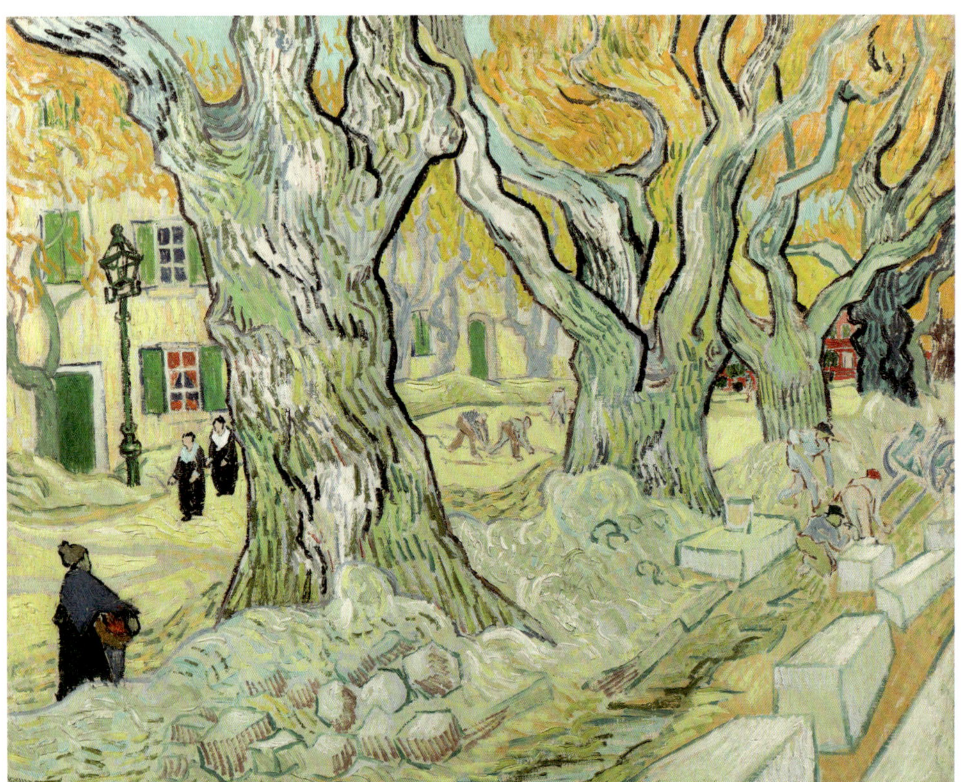

1931

JANUARY. The Museum of French Art, led by Maud Murray Dale under the auspices of the French Institute in the United States, organizes *Portraits of Women Loan Exhibition: Romanticism to Surrealism* in its gallery at 599 Fifth Avenue in New York. "Portrait of Mademoiselle Gachet" (F431) from Maud and Chester Dale's collection is included.

JANUARY 5–JANUARY 17. The Renaissance Society at the University of Chicago presents *Masters of Ukiyo-e and Nineteenth- and Twentieth-Century Western Prints*, showing the influence of Japanese art and calligraphy on Western art from before Impressionism to the present day. Van Gogh's fascination with Japanese art is evoked in the exhibition's brochure and illustrated by the inclusion of *Portrait of Dr. Gachet* (F1664; see plate 42 for an exemplary work).[131]

APRIL 4–26. The City Art Museum of St. Louis organizes *The Exhibition of Paintings and Prints by the Masters of Postimpressionism*, presenting "the leaders of the movement which dominates the art today."[132] The checklist features three paintings under Van Gogh's name: "The Olive Grove" (F708) lent by Wildenstein Galleries, "Flowers" lent by the Marie Sterner Gallery, and "Man with Pipe" from Gilbert E. Fuller; the prints section includes Van Gogh's etching *Portrait of Dr. Gachet* (F1664).[133]

MAY 22–JUNE 30. With the support of the collector Robert H. Tannahill (1893–1969) and catalogue contributions by Maud Murray Dale and Alfred H. Barr Jr., the Detroit Institute of Arts mounts *Modern French Painting*, "a survey of the most important painters in Paris who have been active in the last thirty years."[134] Van Gogh is presented as the artist who, together with Cézanne (including plate 79) and Gauguin, stimulated a later generation of artists, the Fauves in particular. *Self-Portrait* (F526; plate 44) from the Detroit Institute of Arts' collection is joined by *Olive Trees* (F708), lent by Wildenstein Galleries.[135]

1932

JANUARY. Responding to petitions to the trustees signed by about two hundred people, the William Rockhill Nelson Trust in Kansas City acquires the painting *Olive Trees* (F715; plate 56) from the dealer Durand-Ruel in anticipation of the opening of the William Rockhill Nelson Gallery of Art and the Mary Atkins Museum of Fine Arts in December 1933. It is the second purchase of a Van Gogh painting for an American encyclopedic museum.[136] The museum organizes *One Hundred Years: French Painting, 1820–1920*, on view March 31–April 28, 1935, in which *Olive Trees* is joined by two loaned still lifes: *Still Life, Basket of Apples* (F379) and *Bouquet of Flowers in a Vase* (F588).

APRIL 6–OCTOBER 9. *Exhibition of the Mrs. L. L. Coburn Collection, Modern Paintings & Water Colors* is organized under the auspices of the Antiquarian Society at the Art Institute of Chicago. Annie Swan Coburn assembled a collection dominated by Impressionist art, with examples of work by Cézanne, Gauguin, Van Gogh, Toulouse-Lautrec, Picasso, and others. *The Poet's Garden* (F468; fig. 17) and *Self-Portrait with a Pipe* (F527a; now attributed to an imitator of Van Gogh) are on view.[137] Upon her death, nearly two months after the opening of the exhibition, Coburn would bequeath her collection to the Art Institute of Chicago, the Fogg Museum, and Smith College Museum of Art.

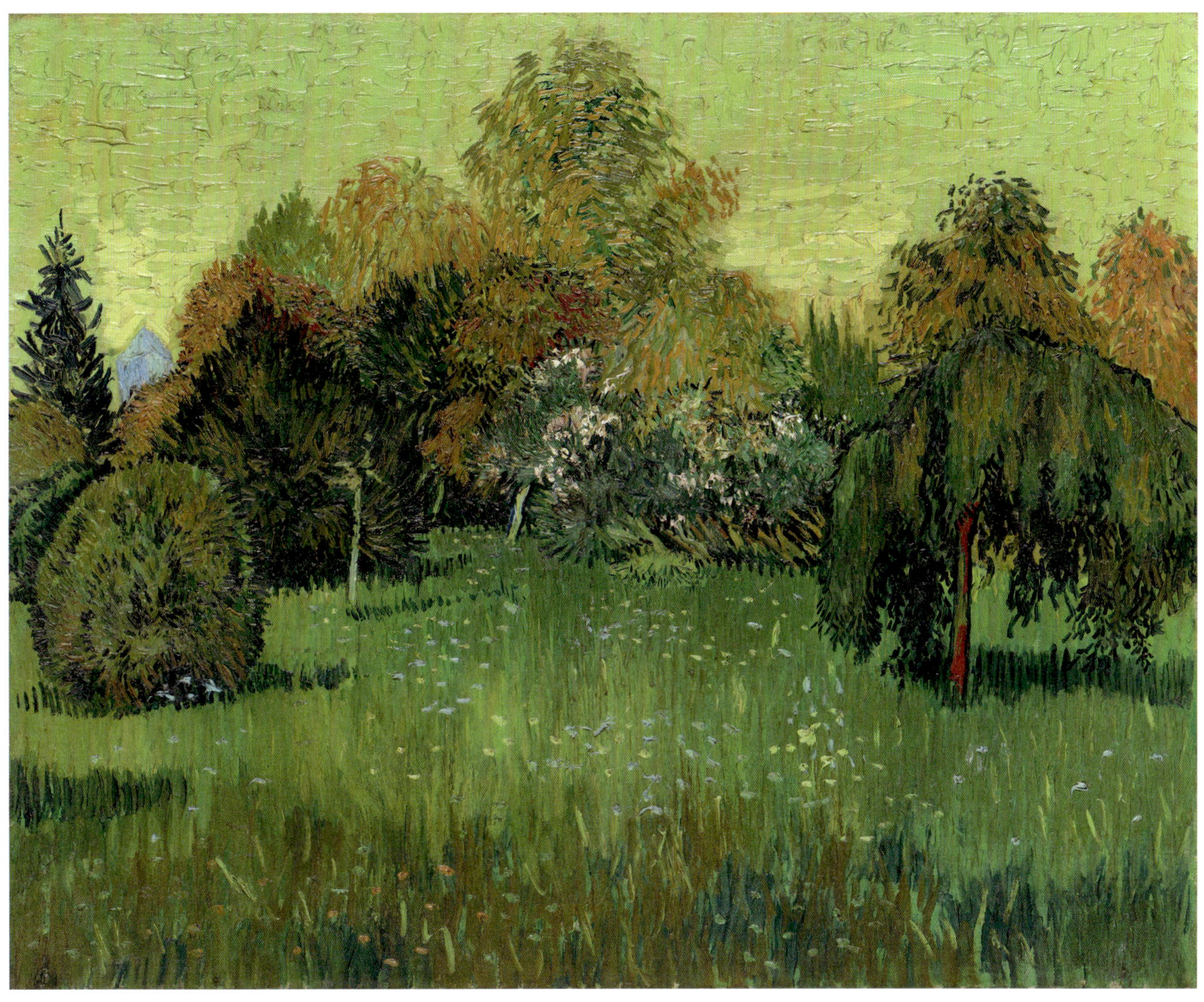

FIG. 17 *The Poet's Garden* (F468), 1888.
Oil on canvas, 28¾ × 36¼ in. (73 × 92.1 cm).
The Art Institute of Chicago.

1933

JUNE 1—NOVEMBER 1. *Exhibition of Paintings and Sculpture* opens at the Art Institute of Chicago as part of the *Century of Progress Exposition*, a world's fair commemorating the founding of the city of Chicago and designed to lift the nation's spirits during the Great Depression. The exhibition is assembled almost entirely from American sources to be a testament to the breadth and quality of American collections.[138] Fifteen of Van Gogh's paintings and drawings come from the Art Institute of Chicago; Phillips Memorial Gallery in Washington, DC; the New York collectors Julius Oppenheimer, Anson Conger Goodyear, and Chester Dale; Dorothy Sturges in Providence; and Robert Treat Paine II, in Boston. Dealers Marie Harriman, Knoedler, and Chester H. Johnson also contribute loans.[139] The *Century of Progress Exposition* is a resounding success (fig. 18) and reopens for a 1934 season, at the end of which over thirty million fairgoers had visited the exposition.[140] The second exhibition at the Art Institute of Chicago held from June 1 to November 1, 1934, presents seven of Van Gogh's works; this time examples from the Art Institute of Chicago's collection are joined by loans from Stephen C. Clark, the Detroit Institute of Arts, and Wildenstein Galleries.[141]

NOVEMBER 25—DECEMBER 31. The Los Angeles Museum presents *Five Centuries of European Painting*, "a collection of European paintings from the early Renaissance to the modernists," loaned by Wildenstein Galleries. *Wheat Fields with Reaper, Auvers* (F559; plate 60) and *Portrait of Père Tanguy* (F364; see Esner, fig. 1) are on view.[142]

1934

JUNE 8—JULY 8. *French Painting from the Fifteenth Century to the Present Day* at the California Palace of the Legion of Honor in San Francisco includes eight of Van Gogh's works; the loans come from Anna Eugenia La Chapelle Clark in New York (F426, F593), Marie Harriman Gallery (F588), Marie Sterner Gallery ("Malmaison Carnations"), and Wildenstein Galleries (F364; see Esner, fig. 1). Lenders also include the Crocker family from Hillsborough, California: Ethel and William Henry Crocker (F419) and Ruth and William Willard Crocker (F743, F625).[143]

NOVEMBER. *French Impressionists and Post-Impressionists* opens at the Toledo Museum of Art in Ohio. The exhibition includes *The Bedroom* (F484; plate 45) lent by the Art Institute of Chicago, *Wheat Fields with Reaper, Auvers* (F559; plate 60) from Wildenstein Galleries, and *Houses at Auvers* (F759; plate 61) from Durand-Ruel, shown at their New York gallery earlier in the spring.[144] The latter two paintings, along with Pissarro's *Peasants Resting*, also on view, will be acquired by the Toledo Museum of Art and accessioned in 1935.[145]

FIG. 18 Visitors to the *Century of Progress Exposition*, The Art Institute of Chicago, 1933.

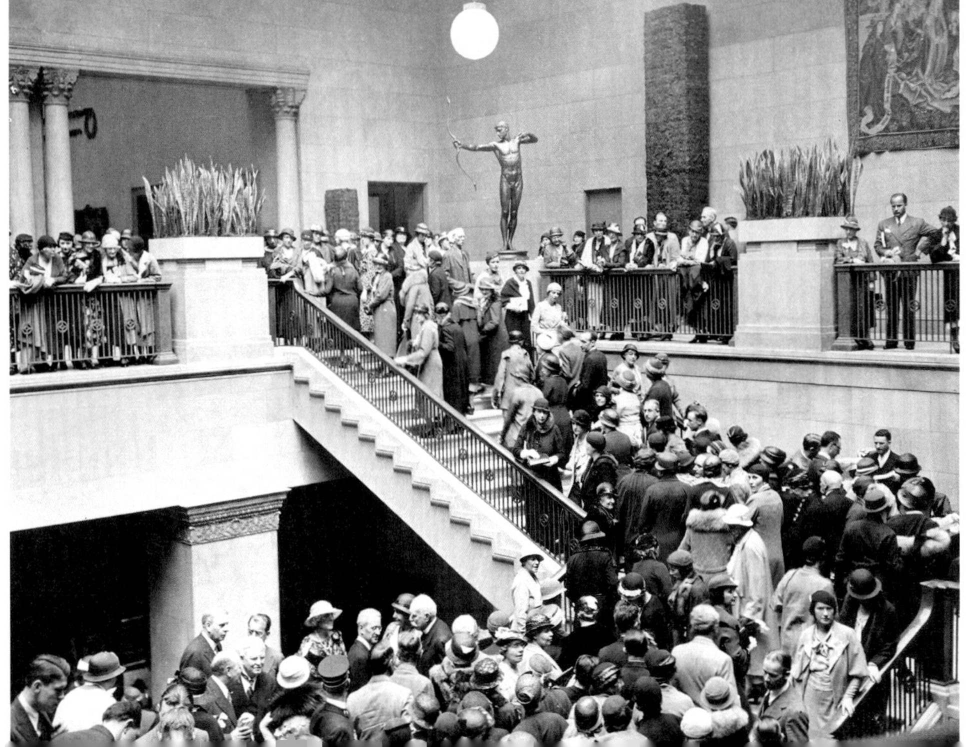

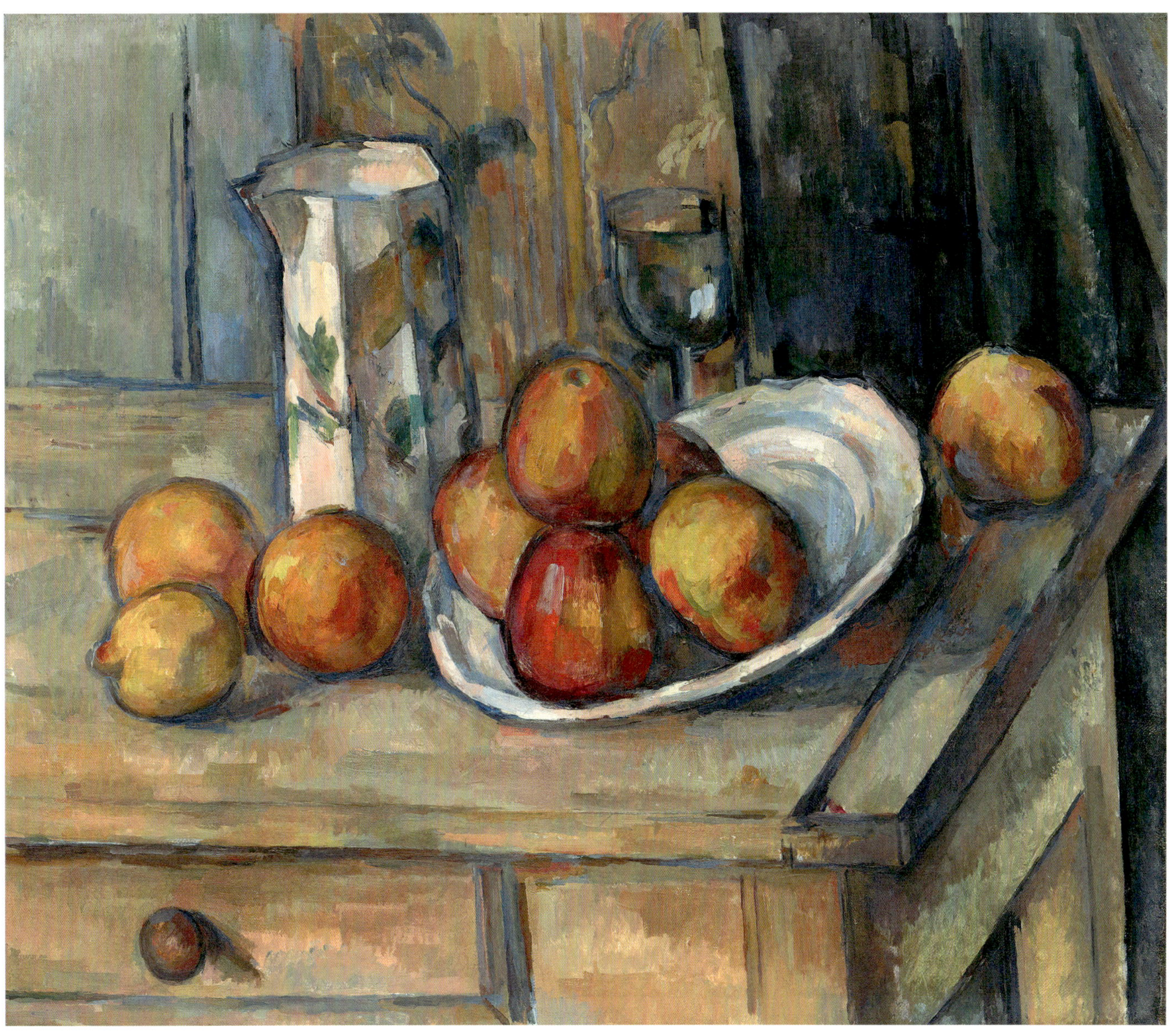

PLATE 79. Paul Cézanne (French, 1839–1906), *Still Life with Milk Jug and Fruit*, c. 1900 (CAT. 76)

NOVEMBER 2. The City Art Museum of St. Louis purchases *Stairway at Auvers* (F795; plate 62) from Paul Rosenberg.[146]

NOVEMBER 20–JANUARY 20. *Modern Works of Art* exhibition marks the fifth anniversary of the opening of the Museum of Modern Art in New York. Van Gogh is featured in the section "Pioneers of Modern Painting" with five works, including *The Night Café* (F463; fig. 19), which comes from Stephen C. Clark (1882–1960) of New York and Cooperstown. Clark's purchase of *The Night Café* the previous year from Knoedler, along with three other important works by Renoir, Degas, and Cézanne—all four paintings previously owned by the Museum of Western Art in Moscow—established his reputation as an important collector of modern masterpieces.[147] Clark's older brother Sterling (1877–1956), a passionate collector of nineteenth-century art, mainly Impressionist and Academic painting, will acquire *Terrace in the Luxembourg Gardens* (F223; plate 80) through Knoedler in 1937.[148]

Irving Stone publishes *Lust for Life*, a fictional biography of Van Gogh, which links individual works to dramatic events in the artist's life. A deluxe edition, illustrated with 150 black-and-white and color reproductions selected by J. B Neumann, will appear in 1936. The book, translated into many languages, becomes an international bestseller and a basis for Vincente Minnelli's film *Lust for Life* (fig. 20). Released in 1956, the film will have a lasting impact on the public image of the artist. Riding the wave of his novel's immense popularity, Stone will follow it with a compilation of loosely translated—and amplified for dramatic effect—letters from Van Gogh to his brother, issued in 1937 under the title *Dear Theo: The Autobiography of Vincent Van Gogh*.[149]

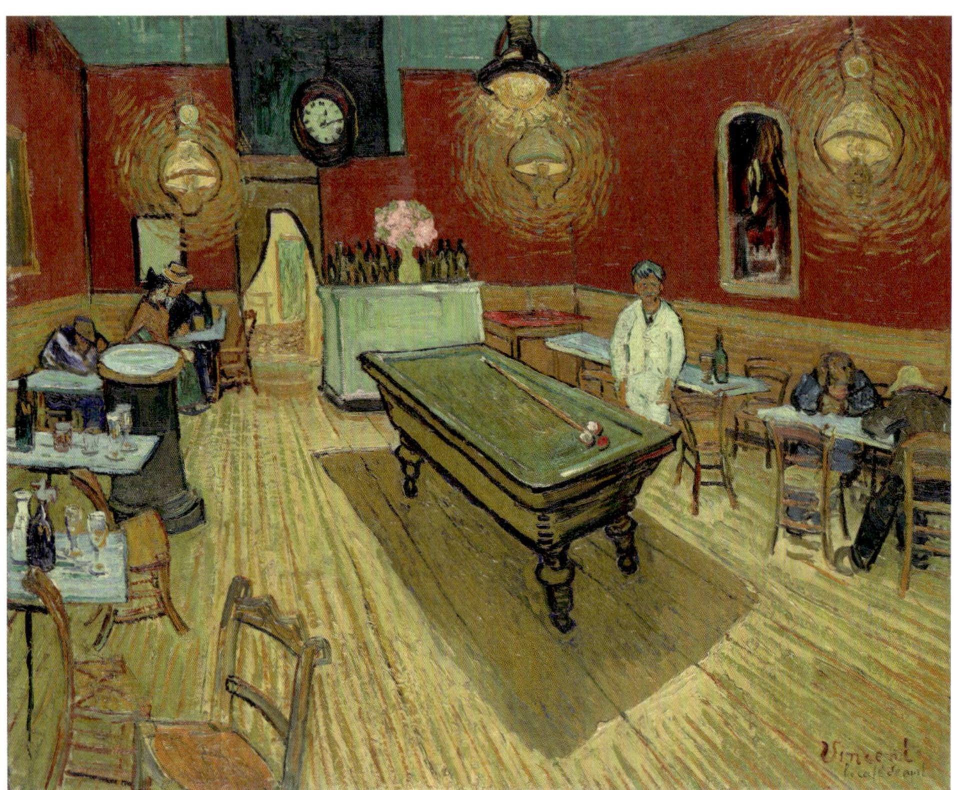

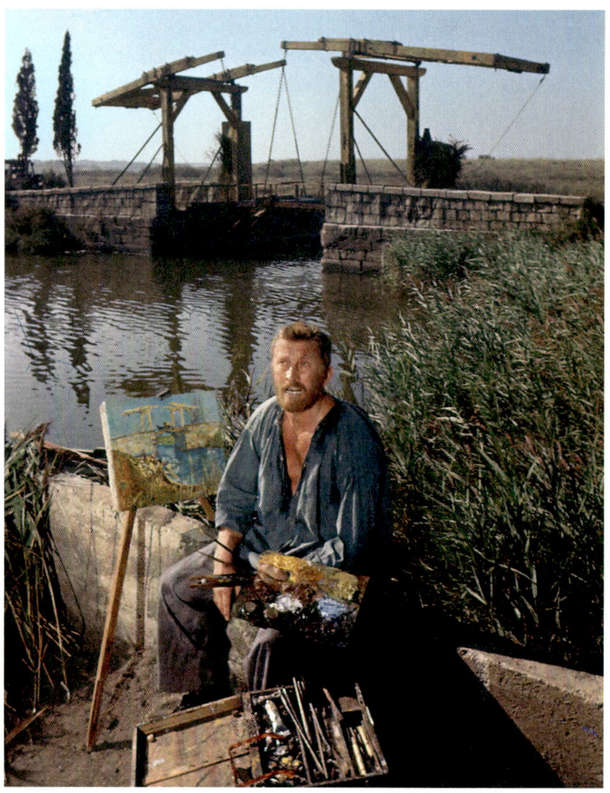

FIG. 19 *The Night Café* (F463), 1888. Oil on canvas, 28½ × 36¼ in. (72.4 × 92.1 cm). Yale University Art Gallery, New Haven.

FIG. 20 Kirk Douglas as Vincent van Gogh in a scene from Vincente Minnelli's *Lust for Life*, 1956.

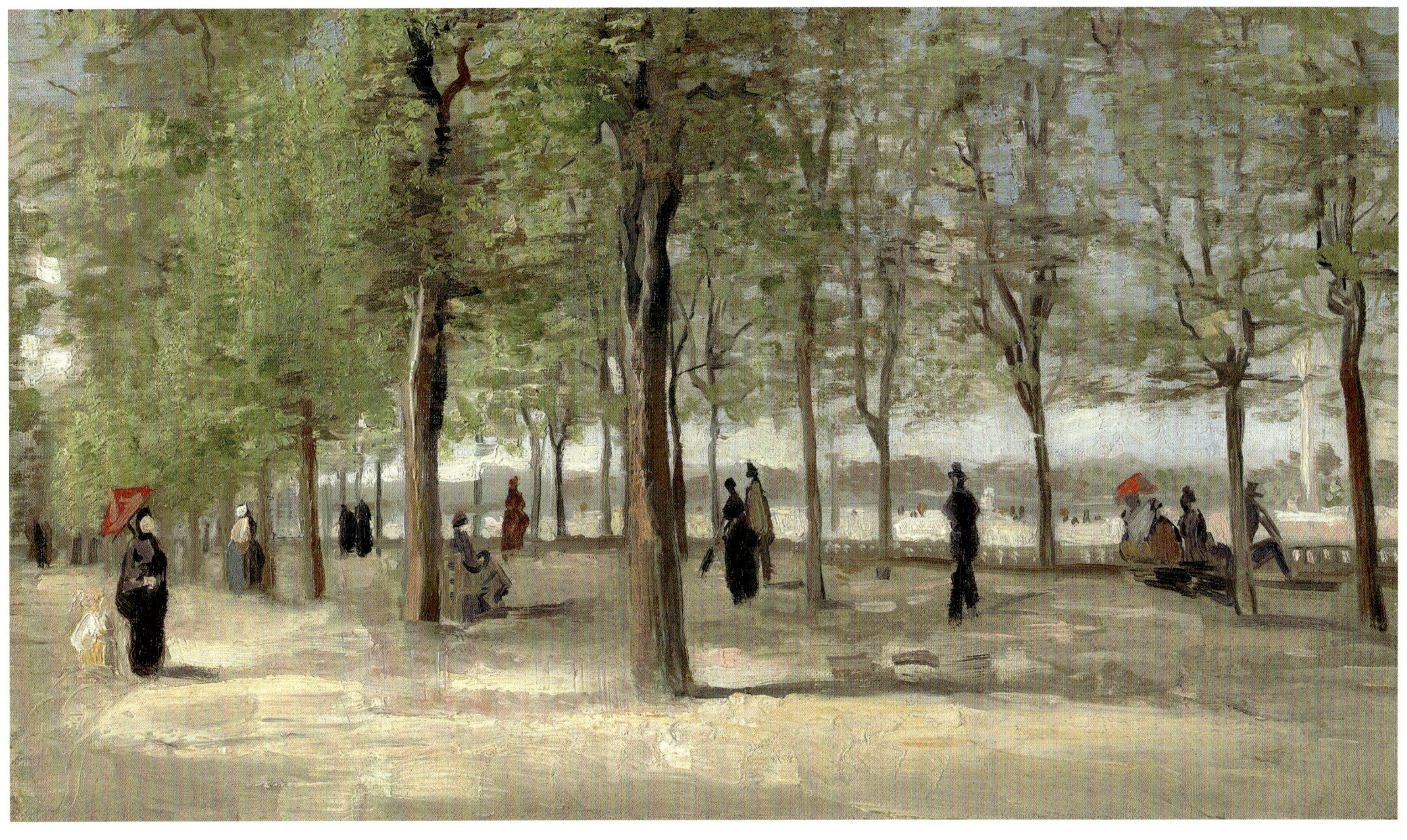

PLATE 80. *Terrace in the Luxembourg Gardens*, 1886 (CAT. 14)

1935–37

Van Gogh's first American museum retrospective featuring 127 works by the artist opens at the Museum of Modern Art in New York and is on view from November 4, 1935, to January 5, 1936 (fig. 21). The exhibition, a popular and critical success, travels to multiple venues across the country: Philadelphia Museum of Art, January 11–February 10; Museum of Fine Arts, Boston, February 18–March 15; Cleveland Museum of Art, March 25–April 19; California Palace of the Legion of Honor, San Francisco, April 28–May 24; and subsequently in a reduced format to the William Rockhill Nelson Gallery of Art and the Mary Atkins Museum of Fine Arts, Kansas City, June 12–July 10; Minneapolis Institute of Arts, July 20–August 17; The Art Institute of Chicago, August 26–September 23; Detroit Institute of Arts, October 6–28; and the Art Gallery of Toronto, November 10–December 9. The exhibition in its smaller version returns to the Museum of Modern Art early in 1937, from January 20 to February 2. Among several works added to this final presentation is *The Starry Night* (F612; see Shaw, America Wakes Up, fig. 1), lent from the collection of Georgette P. van Stolk in Rotterdam.[150] In 1941 the Museum of Modern Art will acquire this iconic work for its permanent collection.

In 1936 Walter Pach publishes *Vincent van Gogh, 1853–1890: A Study of the Artist and His Work in Relation to His Times*, a summary of the critic's ideas on Van Gogh's life and the universal value of his art. Hugely popular, the book is in its sixth printing by May of that year.[151]

The Van Gogh touring retrospective sparks a debate about the reception of the artist's work. The critic Payton Boswell inquires in the January 1936 issue of *Art Digest* whether the thousands of people who visited the Van Gogh exhibition at the Museum of Modern Art did so because of a sincere interest in Van Gogh's art or because they were drawn by "human interest."[152] The same month, *The American Magazine of Art* publishes Gertrude Benson's richly illustrated article poignantly titled "Exploding the Van Gogh Myth," in which the author notes that "apocrypha, part fact part fable associated with the name, Vincent Van Gogh, has grown to ominous proportions." Benson pleads for replacing sensationalism with careful interest in the painter's oeuvre and ideas.[153] In earlier correspondence with Katherine S. Dreier, concerned about the sensational publicity in the wake of the MoMA retrospective, Alfred H. Barr Jr. remarks: "We tried our best to keep the sensationalism of the 'insanity' and the ear story out of the newspapers but we were not successful....Our only compensation is that while some people may come to the Museum as sensation seekers they stay to look at pictures."[154]

FIG. 21 Installation of *Vincent van Gogh*, The Museum of Modern Art, New York, 1935–36, featuring *L'Arlésienne, Madame Ginoux* (F543; plate 41) on the left.

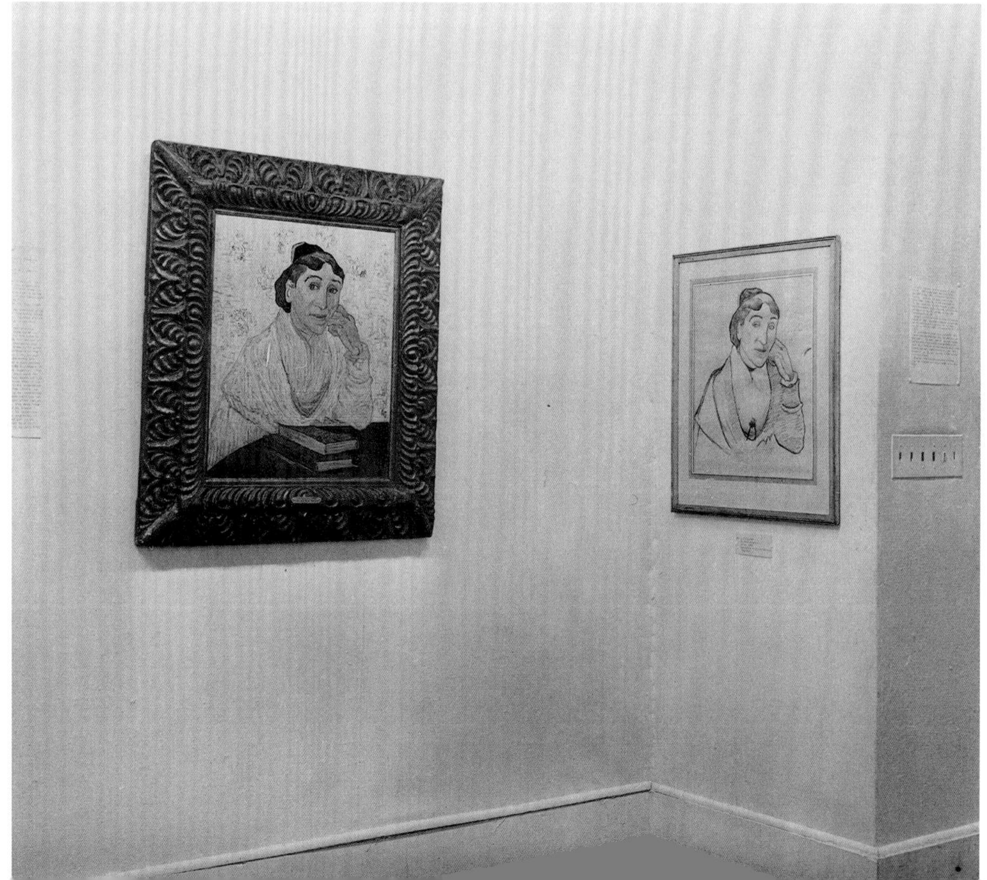

NOTES

After 1920, the frequency of exhibitions of Van Gogh's works in group shows significantly increased; only selected presentations after this date are included here.

The original research undertaken for this chronology was initiated by Jill Shaw and has been enhanced by the content of the essays published in this volume. I would like to extend my gratitude to the authors.

1 Meier-Graefe 1908, vol. 1, 202–12.
2 Nathanson 1985.
3 Meyer-Riefstahl 1910a; Meyer-Riefstahl 1910b.
4 *New York Times* 1911: SM15. See also Pach 1936a, vii. The attribution of Van Horne's only recorded purchase of Van Gogh is uncertain since the painting did not remain in his collection. The subject of the painting was identified as "Irises" by Van Horne's daughter, Adeline Van Horne, who stated that after the picture had been given to her brother Richard B. Van Horne, it perished in a fire in about 1930. "Excerpt from a letter of July 1, 1939 from Miss Adeline Horne (van) of Montreal, Canada" to Edward Buckman (b6951), Van Gogh Museum Documentation, Amsterdam. I am grateful to Monique Hageman for making the document available to us.
5 Bourgeois provided two alternative dates of 1910 and 1911 as the time of his arrival in New York. See Bourgeois, *Art Consultant & Advisor 'Art Research,'* brochure, 1961, 5, in Stephan Bourgeois papers, 1908–c. 1964, Archives of American Art, Smithsonian Institution, Washington, DC (hereafter AAA, SI), Box 4, Folder 27; and Bourgeois 1931: 405.
6 Cited in Nathanson 1985: 8, 10n65.
7 Wattenmaker 2010, 18–20.
8 The exhibition catalogue listed 125 works; see Cologne 1912, nos. 1–125. An additional nine (possibly eleven) works were exhibited but not listed in the catalogue; see Schaefer 2012, 533–53. The attribution to Van Gogh of seven works exhibited in Cologne has been rejected or questioned. Ibid.
9 Dreier 1913, xiii–xiv; Stolwijk and Veenenbos 2002, 190.
10 Zilczer 1978, 23, 100–101; Berman 2013, 415, 500n11; Rabinow and Warman 2006–2007, 286.
11 *New York Times* 1912: SM15.
12 *Camera Work* 1912.
13 Van Gogh Letters 1913. Publisher Constable & Co., Ltd., London, released the book in England in 1912. On the disappointing sales of the book in the United States, see Ferris Greenslet, Houghton, Mifflin and Company, letter to Katherine S. Dreier, April 23, 1913, in Katherine S. Dreier Papers / Société Anonyme Archive, Beinecke Library, Yale University, New Haven, YCAL MSS 101 (hereafter Dreier Papers / Société Anonyme Archive), Box 18, Folder 506.
14 Information is based on research in Stein, New York, p. 68. See also McCarthy 2013.
15 Bluemner 1913: 31, pl. IV; Rewald 1989, 181.
16 Du Quesne-Van Gogh 1913. Dreier had sought copyright to *Recollections* from the publisher of the German edition of the book, R. Piper & Co., who advised her to contact the author directly. She made her own selection of the image on the cover and substituted ten out of twenty-four reproductions in the German edition with new images.
17 Cortissoz 1913a, 153.
18 New York 1914; identification of "Field Flowers in a Vase" as inv. no. 2322 in the Philadelphia Museum of Art is according to Stein, New York, pp. 71, 87n33. This work is now considered to be inauthentic.
19 Eddy 1914, 37, 38–40.
20 Wright 1915, 182–86.
21 San Francisco 1915, no. 4031; Brinton 1916, 187 (ill.).
22 New York 1915a, no. 8; Théodore Duret, letters to Walter Pach, May 22, 1915, and December 29, 1915, both in Walter Pach papers, 1857–1980, AAA, SI, Box 1, Folder 47; see also McCarthy 2011, 72.
23 De Zayas 1996, 135; *New York Times Magazine* 1915b: 22. See also Stein, New York, p. 74.
24 *New York Times* 1915: E2.
25 De Zayas 1996, 138, 140, 122.
26 Perlman 2002: 243.
27 I am grateful to Jennifer Thompson for bringing this painting to our attention. The collection was not exhibited until 1920, first in a temporary arrangement, and then, from 1923, on a permanent basis at Johnson's house at 510 South Broad Street. In 1933 it was transferred to the Pennsylvania Museum of Art (later Philadelphia Museum of Art). Thompson 2018, accessed July 2, 2019. Johnson appeared not to have made any other Post-Impressionist acquisitions.
28 *Modern School* 1918 and *Modern School* 1919. See also Antliff 2001, 174.
29 *Bulletin of the Art Institute of Chicago* 1918: 133–34.
30 *American Art News* 1919: 6; Troyen 2013, 390.
31 Eleanor Jewett, Art column, no date, clipping, Arts Club of Chicago Records, Newberry Library, Chicago, Series 1, Box 1, Folder 2; and Jewett 1919: C11.
32 Stuart 1920: 5.
33 See the transcription of a handwritten note from the back of the painting in Curatorial Object File, 1926.201, The Art Institute of Chicago (hereafter AIC).
34 *American Art News* 1920a: 3; *American Art News* 1920c: 2.
35 New York 1920a, 10.
36 McBride 1920b: 631; Pach 1920b: 302–303; *Arts* 1921a: 42.
37 Stolwijk and Veenenbos 2002, 29–30.
38 *American Art News* 1921a: 6. The admission charge was lifted by February, see *Arts* 1921a: 42.
39 *American Art News* 1922c: 2; *New York Times* 1922b: 54.
40 *New York Times* 1923b: X7; *Art News* 1923b: 2.
41 De Zayas 1996, 155; *American Art News* 1921b: 3.
42 *American Art News* 1922b: 6.
43 "Preface," in New York 1921b, n.p.
44 Stieglitz 1921: 107.
45 Minneapolis 1921, nos. 17, 18.
46 *Christian Science Monitor* 1923: 6.
47 *The Collection of Marius de Zayas of New York City: Paintings, Etchings, Drawings, Sculpture*, sale cat., New York, Anderson Galleries, 1923, lots 84, 85.
48 Barnouw 1921: 7.
49 *New York Times* 1921a: 8; *Bulletin of the Art Institute of Chicago* 1921: 180.
50 *Metropolitan Museum of Art Bulletin* 1921: 126; Stein 2005, 37.
51 *New York Times* 1921b: 11; Jewett 1921a: F8; *Cincinnati Enquirer* 1921: B4; *Dial* 1921: 495–96. *Current Opinion* 1921: 789. See also Rabinow 2000, 6–8.
52 *American Art News* 1921d: 2.
53 On the genesis of the exhibition and ensuing negotiations with the Art Institute of Chicago; Cleveland Museum of Art; and the Department of Fine Arts, Carnegie Institute, Pittsburgh, as well as the Arts Club of Chicago, see Dreier Papers / Société Anonyme Archive, Box 20, Folder 585–587. The exhibition was shown at the Hillyer Art Gallery, Smith College, Northampton, Massachusetts, January 7–February 5, 1921; and the MacDowell Club, New York, April 25–May 8, 1921. See Herbert et al. 1984, 776.
54 Chicago 1921, nos. 51–56.
55 Simons 1921: 97.
56 Meier-Graefe 1922.
57 *Bulletin of the Art Institute of Chicago* 1922: 11 (ill.), 12; Jewett 1922: H5.
58 *Arts* 1922: 246.
59 *New York Times* 1922: 27.
60 Detroit 1922, nos. 77, 78, 78a.
61 Speyer 1922: 12.
62 *New York Times* 1923a: 14.
63 Watson 1923.
64 "Ultra Modern Art to Be Shown in June," *Detroit Times*, May 4, newspaper clipping, Detroit Institute of Arts Scrapbook 1923.
65 *Bulletin of the Detroit Institute of Arts* 1923: 72; [Poland] 1923b: 3–7.
66 Jewett 1923; on Bartlett's acquisition of *La Berceuse*, see Brettell 1986: 106.
67 By the end of 1924, in or after November, Bartlett buys his third Van Gogh painting, *Terrace and Observation Deck at the Moulin de Blute-Fin, Montmartre* (F272; plate 16) from Knoedler & Co. See Knoedler & Co.'s advertisement of the picture in *The Arts* 1924b: 294 and Stolwijk and Krikke, p. 53.
68 Brigham 1924: ES11; see also *New York Times* 1924b: SM12.
69 For example, January 20?–February 7, 1929, an exhibition of paintings and prints from the late Middle Ages to the present day, which included "a landscape and a figure subject" by Van Gogh, the latter possibly *Portrait of Dr. Gachet* (F1664; see plate 42 for an exemplary work), which would be reshown by J. B. Neumann in May that year, see *New York Times* 1929: X13; *Detroit Free Press* 1929: 8.
70 *New York Times* 1924a: X10; *Arts* 1924a: 235 (ill.).
71 *Art News* 1923a: 5; *New York Times* 1923c: E1. Tilla Durieux performed in New York in December 1923 and in 1924.
72 San Francisco 1924–25, nos. 64, 65. For identification of no. 65 as F580, see http://collection.nmwa.go.jp/en/P.1959-0193.html, accessed June 3, 2019.
73 Saber 1925: 180.
74 Harcourt, Brace and Company advertisement brochure in Dreier Papers / Société Anonyme Archive, Box 4, Folder 103.
75 Barnes 1925, 281 (ill.), 492.
76 Ibid., 492–94.
77 Piérard 1925; Parker 1924: 295.
78 *New York Times* 1926: E11. According to information kindly provided by Thomas P. Bruhn, Goodwin's acquisition of *Self-Portrait* (F268; plate 17) in 1926 was confirmed by her son, Phillip L. Goodwin, in correspondence with the Wadsworth Atheneum in 1954.
79 Zafran and Paret 2003, 63, fig. 47.

80 *The Bedroom* (F484; plate 45) was acquired by Bartlett from Paul Rosenberg, and paid in installments in May and December 1926. See the Art Institute of Chicago's memorandum, May 21, 1927, and Josef Stransky, Paul Rosenberg & Co., letter to Charles Burkholder, Secretary, AIC, May 25, 1927, in Curatorial Object File, 1926.417, AIC. See also Watson 1926: 306 (ill.).
81 Milliken 1926: 337.
82 Colin 1926.
83 Van Gogh Letters 1927–29.
84 *New York Times* 1927a: X10.
85 *Boston Daily Globe* 1927: A16. The *Boston Daily Globe* reported that the etching was presented to the Museum of Fine Arts in March 1927; however, it was still in Allen's possession when he died in 1955, and there is no record in the museum's documentation indicating a promised gift before that time. I am grateful to Victoria Reed, Museum of Fine Arts, Boston, for this information.
86 *New York Times* 1927b: 45.
87 Note to Germaine Seligmann about Jean and Claude Bernheim and Paul Ebstein's visit to De Hauke's offices, December 21, 1927, Jacques Seligmann & Co. records, 1904–1978, bulk 1913–1974 (hereafter Seligmann & Co. records), AAA, SI, Box 385, Folder 23.
88 New York 1927, nos. 38, 39; Salinger 1933: 26.
89 Hirschland and Hirschland Ramage 2008, 127.
90 Ibid., 128; W. Feilchenfeldt 2013, 257.
91 The work was mentioned and illustrated in several reviews of the exhibition; see newspaper clippings, Kraushaar Galleries records, 1885–2006 (hereafter Kraushaar Galleries records), AAA, SI, microfilm reel no. NK R1.
92 *New York Times* 1928d: 130.
93 The second revised edition of the painting portion of the catalogue would be issued in 1939 by Hypérion in Paris, London, and New York. In 1970 the third complete edition would be published posthumously, with revisions by the committee established by the Netherlands Institute of Art History in The Hague and led by A. M. Hammacher.
94 W. Feilchenfeldt 1988, 81–106; Koldehoff 2003, 80–159.
95 *New York Times* 1928a: X13; Watson 1928a: 35.
96 *New York Times* 1928b: 128.
97 Only F769 is listed in *Bulletin of the Pennsylvania Museum of Art* 1928: 15, but registration records at the Philadelphia Museum of Art confirm that F477 was exhibited as well. Information kindly provided by Catherine Herbert and Jane Joe, Philadelphia Museum of Art. See also [Barker] 1928: 263. Pitcairn will lend the two paintings again in November of the following year, and also in December 1930. *Bulletin of the Pennsylvania Museum of Art* 1929: 30. See also Weir 1930: 38.
98 On Goodyear's purchase, see Anson Conger Goodyear, letter to Beatrice Howe, Albright Art Gallery, August 13, 1926, Albright-Knox Art Gallery Archives, Buffalo. Information kindly provided by Gabrielle Carlo, Albright-Knox Art Gallery. See also Buffalo 1928, nos. 47–49; *New York Times* 1928c: 98.
99 The painting was sold by the Lucerne branch of Galerien Thannhauser and Else Tischer-von Durant, its previous owner who at the time of the sale owned a half-share of the painting. See Koldehoff and Stolwijk 2017, 204–205, no. 54.
100 Ibid.
101 Booth's client card records his visit under the date of July 23, 1928, with a note that he was again shown a photograph of the painting, Galerien Thannhauser records, ZADIK Archive, Cologne, A077_XIX_0033_0016.
102 Sales journal, Kraushaar Galleries records, AAA, SI, Box 76, Folder 2.
103 See https://www.nga.gov/collection/art-object-page.46628.html:#provenance, accessed June 3, 2019.
104 *New York Times* 1928e: F2 (ill.); *New York Times* 1928f: 132; Watson 1928b: 119–20; Watson 1928c: 267.
105 I am grateful to Susan Alyson Stein for bringing this painting to our attention.
106 Jewett 1928: 19.
107 De Hauke & Co., invoice, issued to Dorothy Sturges, October 27, 1928, in Seligmann & Co. records, AAA, SI, Box 390, Folder 11.
108 See https://www.metmuseum.org/art/collection/search/436530, accessed June 3, 2019.
109 *Washington Post* 1929: 9.
110 Bertram 1929; 1934 edition, 1.
111 Toledo 1929, nos. 57, 58.
112 Pope 1930: 98; Jewell 1929a: 142; Goodrich 1929a: 143.
113 Weir 1930: 25.
114 De Hauke & Co., letter to Edith Wetmore, March 23, 1929, Seligmann & Co. records, AAA, SI, Box 390, Folder 31.
115 On the sale of F1482, see De Hauke & Co., memorandum invoice to Walter E. Sachs, May 10, 1929, Seligmann & Co. records, AAA, SI, Box 389, Folder 17.
116 New York 1929b, nos. 20, 21; Goodrich 1929b: 262.
117 Phillips 1926, 9. Phillips's desire to own a Van Gogh was reported in dealers' exchanges, for example C. M. de Hauke, letter to Paul Ebstein, Bernheim-Jeune, February 26, 1927, Seligmann & Co. records, AAA, SI, Box 382, Folder 2.
118 Wildenstein & Co., invoice to Duncan Phillips, September 27, 1927, The Phillips Collection records, 1920–1960 (hereafter The Phillips Collection records), AAA, SI, microfilm reel 1938. *Bulletin of the Phillips Collection* 1928: 6.
119 W. Feilchenfeldt 2005, 82, 102. F812 was rejected in De la Faille 1930, no. 46, pl. XIII, but accepted as genuine by the editors of De la Faille 1970. On the exchange of pictures, see Josef Stransky, Wildenstein & Co., letter to Duncan Phillips, January 15, 1929; Phillips, letter to Stransky, April 25, 1929; and further correspondence between the collector and the dealer, April 25–May 1, 1929, The Phillips Collection records, AAA, SI, microfilm reel 1940.
120 Koldehoff and Stolwijk 2017, 192, no. 48 (ill.). Watson 1930: 628. The drawing was exhibited hors catalogue at Berlin, Vienna, and Hannover 1927–28.
121 [Milliken] 1929: 157.
122 *Arts* 1929a: 207; *Arts* 1929b: 281.
123 Providence 1930, n.p. Two additional Van Goghs were on view: *Postman Joseph Roulin* (F432; see Stolwijk and Krikke, fig. 7), lent by Robert Treat Paine II, Boston, and *Vineyard at Auvers* (F762), lent by Paul Rosenberg, New York. Ibid., nos. 42–45. No. 43 ("View of Auvers-sur-Oise") is identified as F762 in https://www.slam.org/collection/objects/820/, accessed July 10, 2019.
124 Koldehoff and Stolwijk 2017, 268.
125 Van Tilborgh and Van Maanen 2015: 24.
126 Weir 1930: 38.
127 Duncan Phillips, telegram to Josef Stransky, Wildenstein & Co., September 25, 1930; and further correspondence between the collector and the dealer, September 26–October 7, 1930, The Phillips Collection records, AAA, SI, microfilm reel 1940. The quotation comes from Stransky, letter to Phillips, April 27, 1929, ibid.
128 K. Sterne 1930: 46.
129 Ibid.; Barker 1930: 7–8.
130 Marceau 1930: 13.
131 "Renaissance Society Has Rare Prints on Display," January 9, 1931, press clipping, Renaissance Society at the University of Chicago records, 1917–1981, AAA, SI, microfilm reel 2401.
132 Rogers 1931: 2.
133 Ibid.: 10 (nos. 35–37), 11 (no. 77).
134 Valentiner 1931, 3.
135 Detroit 1931, nos. 46, 47. No. 47 ("Olive Trees") is identified as F708 in https://www.metmuseum.org/art/collection/search/437998, accessed July 18, 2019.
136 Meghan Gray, "Vincent van Gogh, *Olive Trees*, June/September 1889," documentation in Marcereau DeGalan 2021.
137 Chicago 1932, nos. 13, 14.
138 Harshe 1933, xiii–xv.
139 The following works were shown: F484 (plate 45), F506, F272 (plate 16), F1524, and "Pastoral (Harvesting)," which was later determined to be a forgery (The Art Institute of Chicago); F566 (Phillips Memorial Gallery; plate 57); F668 and F737 (Julius Oppenheimer); F550 (Anson Conger Goodyear; plate 27); F658 (Dorothy Sturges); F431 (Chester Dale); F432 (Robert Treat Paine II); F681 (Marie Harriman Gallery; plate 59); F798 (Knoedler & Co.; plate 7); and F819 (Chester H. Johnson Galleries; plate 58).
140 Rydell 1993, 106.
141 The following works were shown in 1934: F468, F484 (plate 45), F506, F272 (plate 16) (The Art Institute of Chicago); F463 (Stephen C. Clark); F526 (Detroit Institute of Arts; plate 44); and F559 (Wildenstein & Co.; plate 60).
142 Los Angeles 1933b, nos. 50, 51.
143 San Francisco 1934, nos. 156–63. No. 160, "Malmaison Carnations," not identified, was later illustrated in *Parnassus* 1936: 21 (ill.).
144 *Important Paintings by Great French Masters of the Nineteenth Century, Organized by Paul Rosenberg and Durand-Ruel* at Durand-Ruel Galleries, February 12–March 10, 1934, included three works by Van Gogh: *Still Life: Blue Enamel Coffeepot, Earthenware and Fruit* (F410), *Self-Portrait with Bandaged Ear and Pipe* (F529), and *Houses at Auvers* (F759; plate 61), see *Parnassus* 1934: 27.
145 Whiting 1935: 236; *New York Times* 1935a: 19; *New York Times* 1935b: N2.
146 See https://www.slam.org/collection/objects/33826/, accessed July 10, 2019.
147 Vincent and Lee 2006–2007, 156, 183.
148 Ganz 2006–2007, 80–81.
149 Stone 1937.
150 Museum of Modern Art press release, https://www.moma.org/documents/moma_press-release_325077.pdf, accessed July 18, 2019.
151 Pach 1936b; McCarthy 2011, 120.
152 Boswell 1936: 4.
153 Benson 1936: 6.
154 Alfred H. Barr Jr., letter to Katherine S. Dreier, November 29, 1935, Dreier Papers / Société Anonyme Archive, Box 26, Folder 733–738.

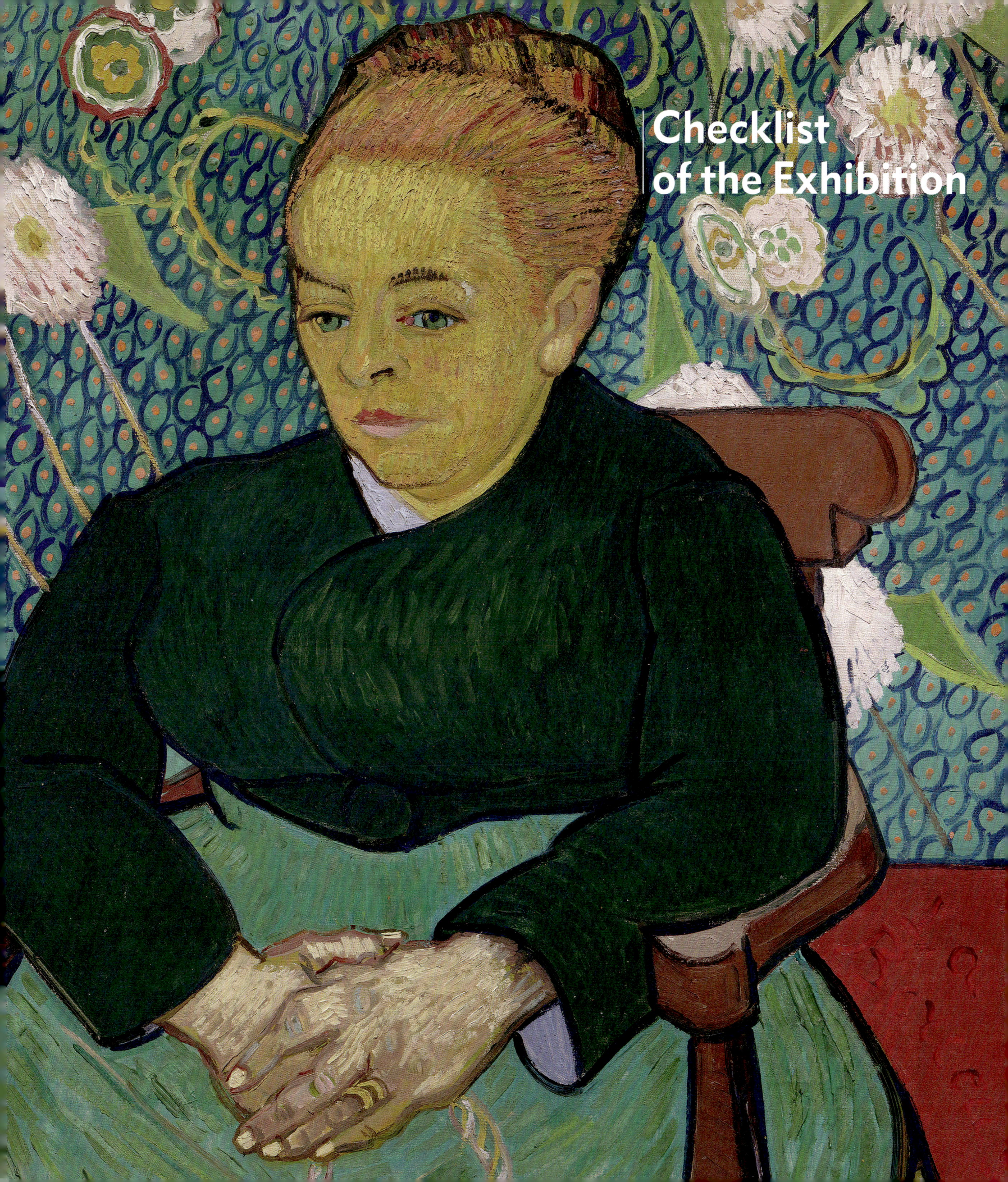

Checklist of the Exhibition

Works are by Vincent van Gogh (Dutch, 1853–1890) unless otherwise indicated. All are listed in chronological order.

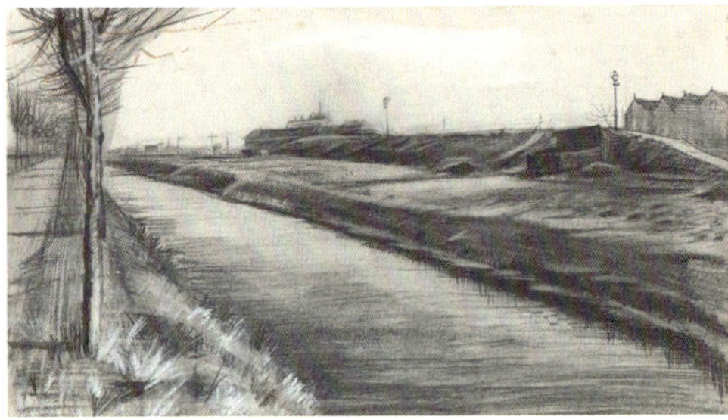

CAT. 1
Ditch along Schenkweg, 1882
Pencil, pen and brush in black ink, gray wash, white opaque watercolor, and traces of squaring on laid paper
7¼ × 13¼ in. (18.4 × 33.7 cm)
Kröller-Müller Museum, Otterlo, KM 113.904
F921 / JH116
Plate 33

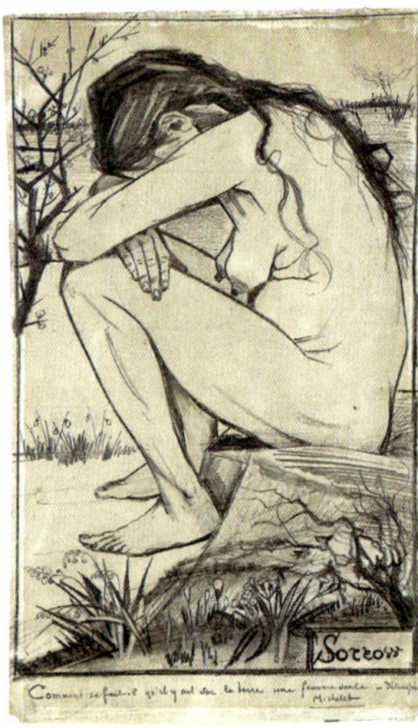

CAT. 2
Sorrow, 1882
Pencil and ink on paper
17½ × 10⅝ in. (44.5 × 27 cm)
The New Art Gallery Walsall, United Kingdom, The Garman Ryan Collection, 1973.128.GR
F929a / JH130
Plate 13

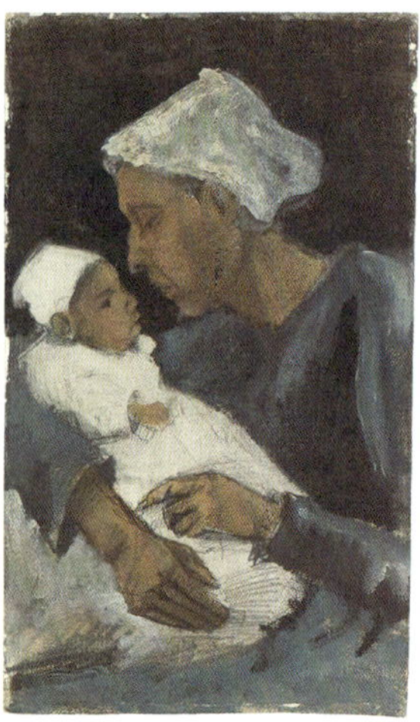

CAT. 3
Mother with Child, 1882
Pencil and oils on watercolor paper
16⅛ × 9¹¹⁄₁₆ in. (41 × 24.6 cm)
Kröller-Müller Museum, Otterlo, KM 112.180
F1061 / JH220
Plate 34

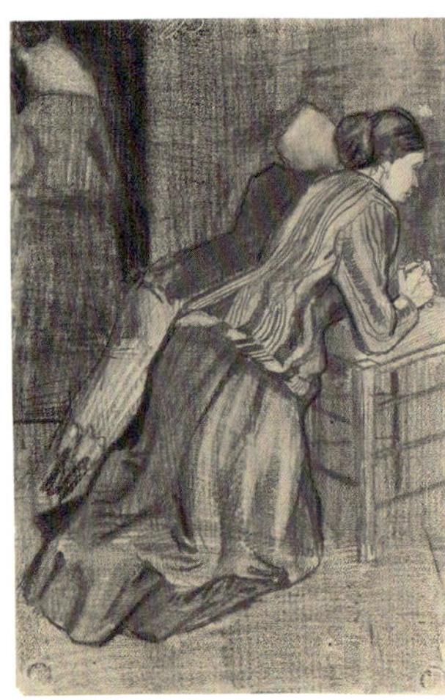

CAT. 4
Two Women Praying, 1882
Pencil and black lithographic crayon on laid paper
16¹³⁄₁₆ × 11⁵⁄₁₆ in. (42.7 × 28.7 cm)
Kröller-Müller Museum, Otterlo, KM 125.556
F1058 / JH348
Plate 35

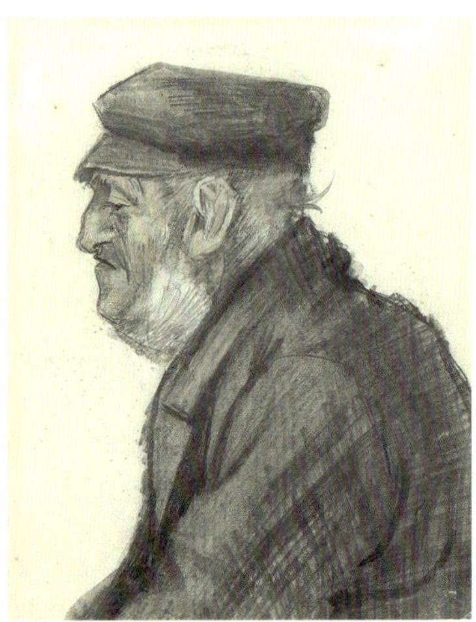

CAT. 5
Orphan Man, 1882–83
Pencil, ink, and watercolor wash on paper
13⅜ × 10¹³⁄₁₆ in. (34 × 27.4 cm)
Nancy and Sean Cotton Collection
F1018 / JH316
Plate 30

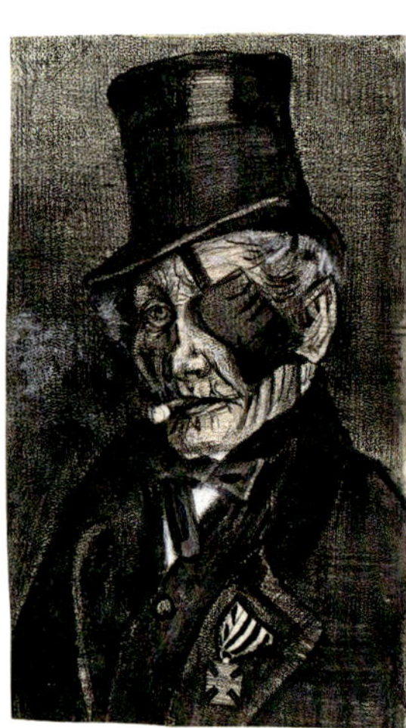

CAT. 6
The Wounded Veteran, c. 1882–83
Graphite, brown ink, black ink and wash, and white gouache on heavily textured white wove paper
18⅛ × 10¹³⁄₁₆ in. (46 × 27.5 cm)
Harvard Art Museums/Fogg Museum, Cambridge, bequest of Meta and Paul J. Sachs, 1965.289
F1003 / JH285
Plate 28

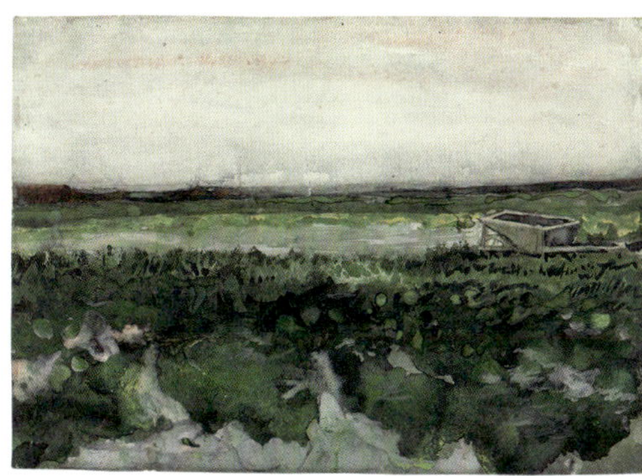

CAT. 7
***Landscape with Wheelbarrow*, 1883**
Watercolor and opaque watercolor with black chalk on cream wove paper
9 13/16 × 14 1/16 in. (24.9 × 35.7 cm)
The Cleveland Museum of Art, bequest of Leonard C. Hanna Jr., 1958.30
F1100 / JH400
Plate 50

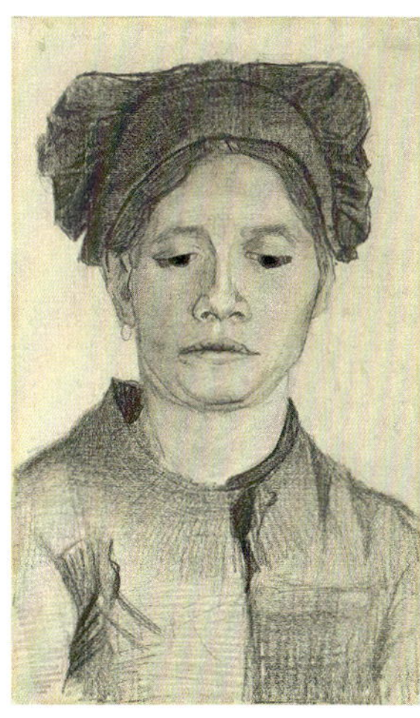

CAT. 8
***Head of a Peasant Woman*, 1884–85**
Pencil, conté crayon, and black chalk on paper
13 × 8 in. (33 × 20.3 cm)
Abelló Collection
F1175 / JH645
Plate 78

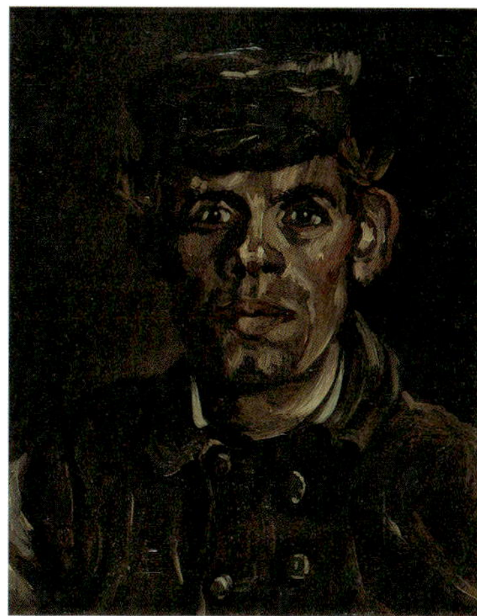

CAT. 9
***Head of a Peasant*, 1885**
Oil on canvas
15 3/8 × 12 in. (39 × 30.5 cm)
Royal Museums of Fine Arts of Belgium, Brussels, acquired through M. Jacob-Baart de la Faille (1886–1959), 1931, 4910
F163 / JH687
Plate 31

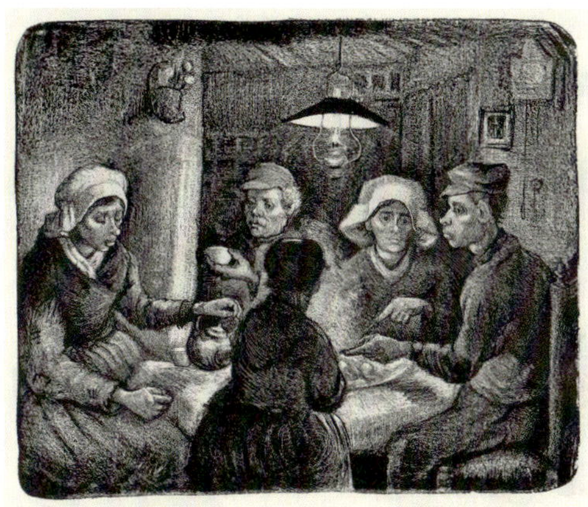

CAT. 10
***The Potato Eaters*, 1885**
Lithograph on Japan paper
Image: 10 7/16 × 12 13/16 in. (26.5 × 32.5 cm)
Museo Nacional Thyssen-Bornemisza, Madrid, 558, 1975.9
F1661 / JH737
Plate 32

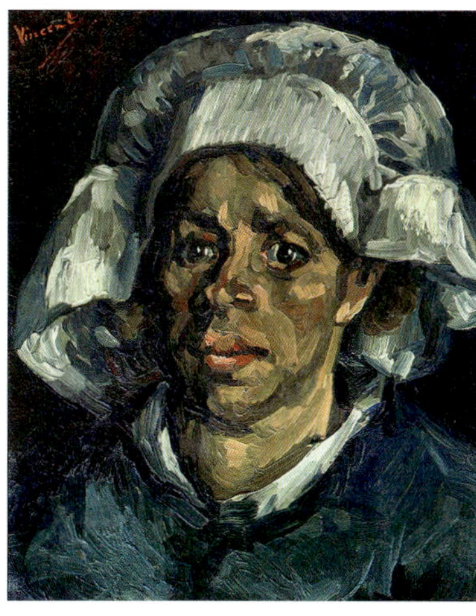

CAT. 11
***Head of Gordina de Groot*, 1885**
Oil on canvas
16 1/8 × 13 5/8 in. (41 × 34.5 cm)
Private Collection, courtesy of Eykyn Maclean
F141 / JH783
Plate 64

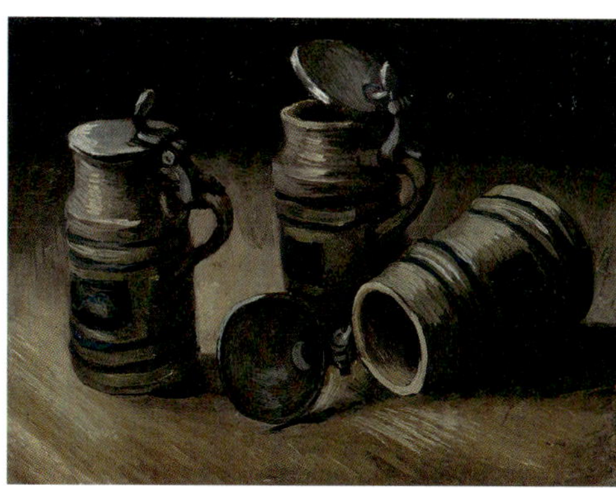

CAT. 12
***Beer Tankards*, 1885**
Oil on canvas
12 3/8 × 16 3/4 in. (31.5 × 42.5 cm)
Van Gogh Museum, Amsterdam (Vincent van Gogh Foundation), s0096V1962
F49 / JH534
Plate 23

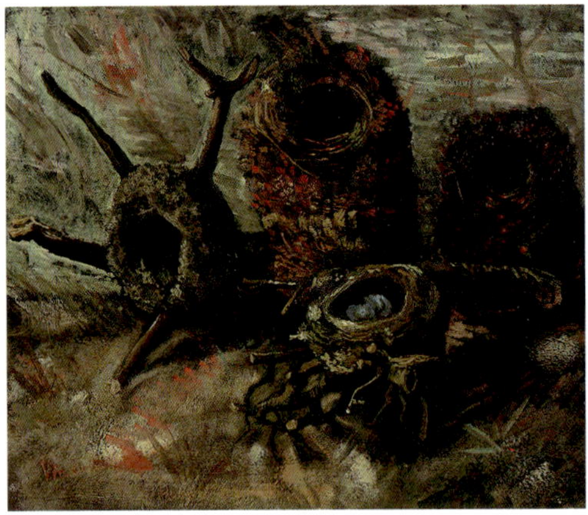

CAT. 13
Birds' Nests, 1885
Oil on canvas
15½ × 18$\frac{5}{16}$ in. (39.3 × 46.5 cm)
Van Gogh Museum, Amsterdam (Vincent van Gogh Foundation), s0001V1962
F111 / JH939
Plate 10

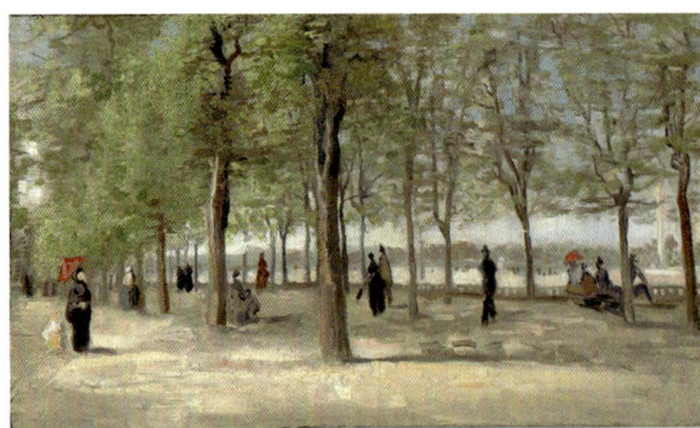

CAT. 14
Terrace in the Luxembourg Gardens, 1886
Oil on canvas
10⅝ × 18⅛ in. (27 × 46 cm)
The Sterling and Francine Clark Art Institute, Williamstown, acquired by Sterling and Francine Clark, 1939, 1955.889
F223 / JH1111
Plate 80

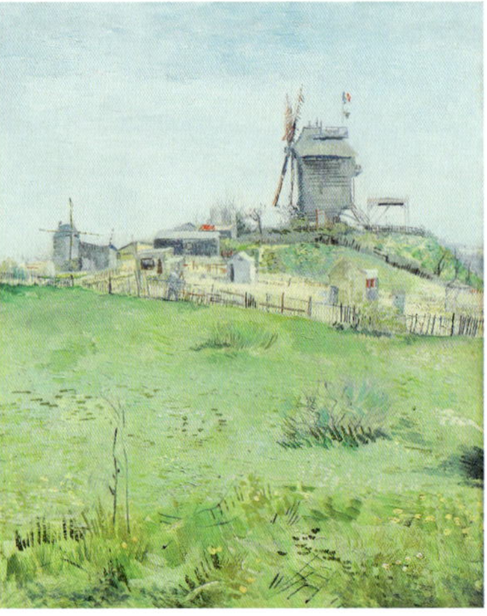

CAT. 15
Le Moulin de la Galette, 1886–87
Oil on canvas
18⅝ × 15½ in. (47.3 × 39.4 cm)
Carnegie Museum of Art, Pittsburgh, acquired through the generosity of the Sarah Mellon Scaife Family, 67.16
F348a / JH1221
Plate 65

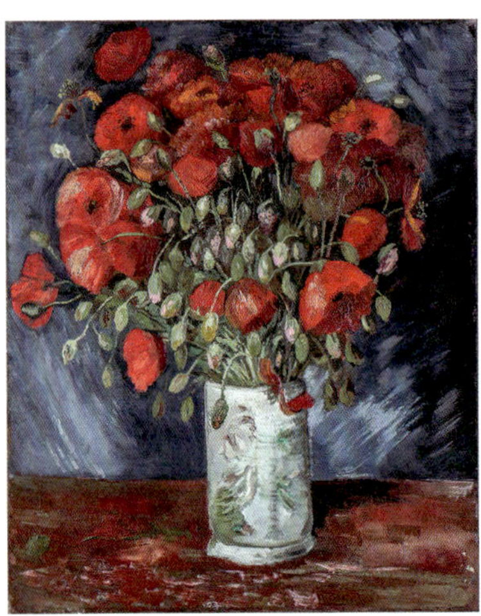

CAT. 16
Vase with Poppies, 1886
Oil on canvas
21½ × 17¾ in. (54.6 × 45.1 cm)
Wadsworth Atheneum Museum of Art, Hartford, bequest of Anne Parrish Titzell, 1957.617
F279 / JH1104
Plate 24

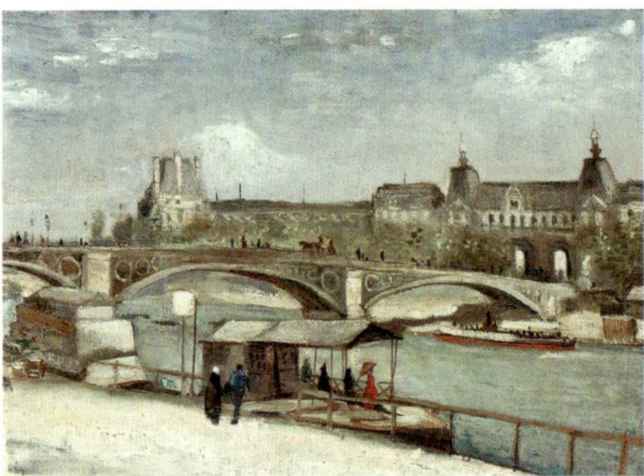

CAT. 17
Pont du Carrousel and the Louvre, 1886
Oil on canvas
12$\frac{3}{16}$ × 17$\frac{5}{16}$ in. (31 × 44 cm)
Ny Carlsberg Glyptotek, Copenhagen, MIN 3616
F221 / JH1109
Plate 73

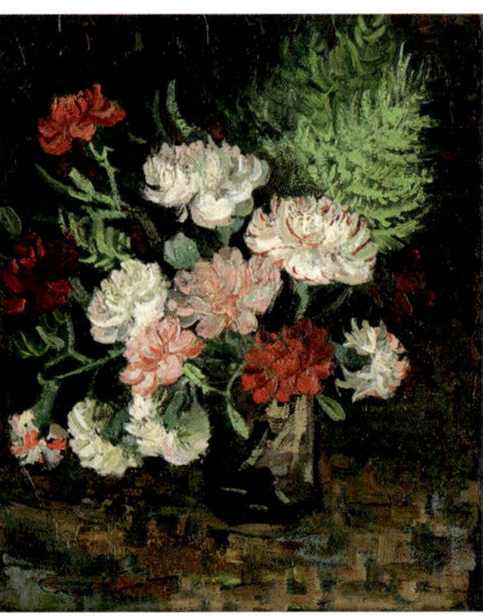

CAT. 18
Vase with Carnations, 1886
Oil on canvas
17 × 14 in. (43.2 × 35.6 cm)
Detroit Institute of Arts, gift of the Estate of Catherine Kresge Dewey, 2019.20
F243 / JH1129
Plate 71

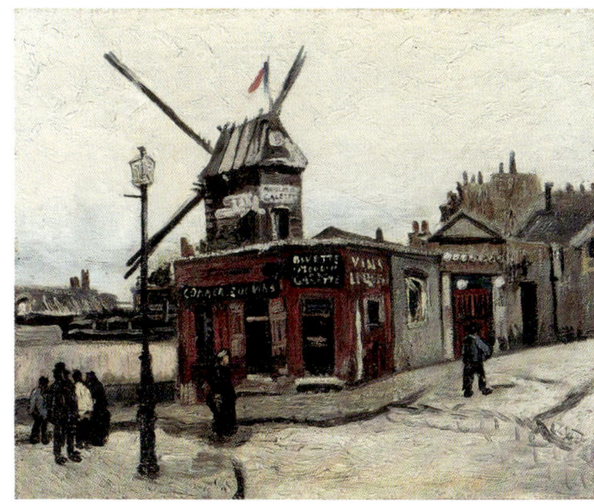

CAT. 19
Le Moulin de la Galette, 1886
Oil on canvas
$14\frac{15}{16} \times 18\frac{5}{16}$ in. (38 × 46.5 cm)
Staatliche Museen zu Berlin, Nationalgalerie, A II 687
F228 / JH1171
Plate 63

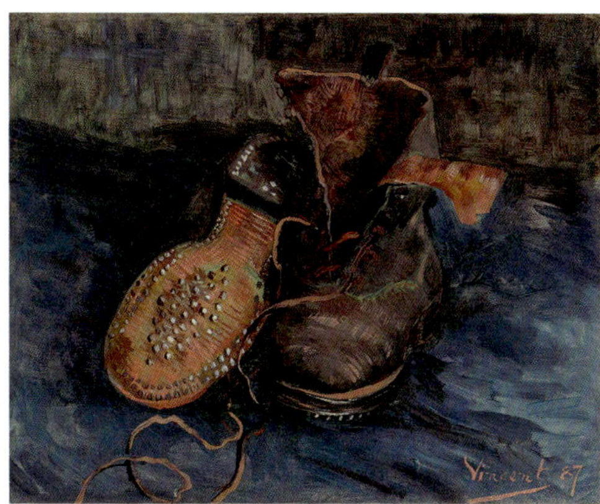

CAT. 20
A Pair of Boots, 1887
Oil on canvas
$12\frac{7}{8} \times 16\frac{1}{4}$ in. (32.7 × 41.3 cm)
The Baltimore Museum of Art, The Cone Collection, formed by Dr. Claribel Cone and Miss Etta Cone of Baltimore, Maryland, 1950.302
F333 / JH1236
Plate 76

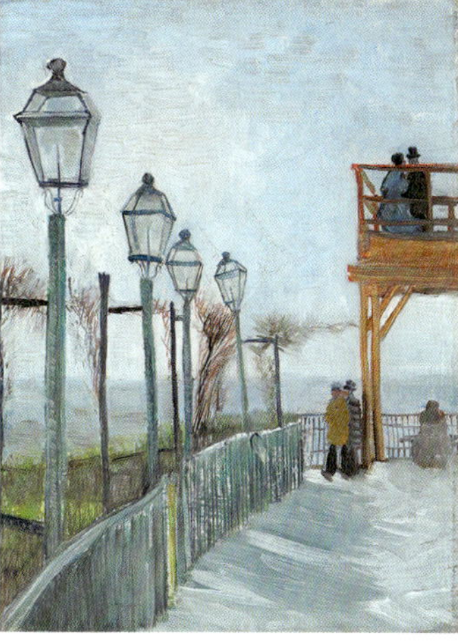

CAT. 21
Terrace and Observation Deck at the Moulin de Blute-Fin, Montmartre, 1887
Oil on canvas, mounted on pressboard
$17\frac{1}{8} \times 13$ in. (43.6 × 33 cm)
The Art Institute of Chicago, Helen Birch Bartlett Memorial Collection, 1926.202
F272 / JH1183
Plate 16

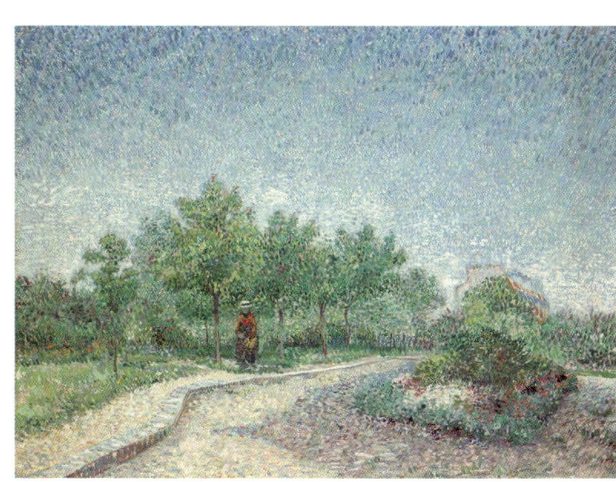

CAT. 22
Square Saint-Pierre, Paris, 1887
Oil on canvas
$23\frac{3}{8} \times 32$ in. (59.4 × 81.3 cm)
Yale University Art Gallery, New Haven, gift of Henry R. Luce, B.A., 1920, 1958.59
F276 / JH1259
Plate 3

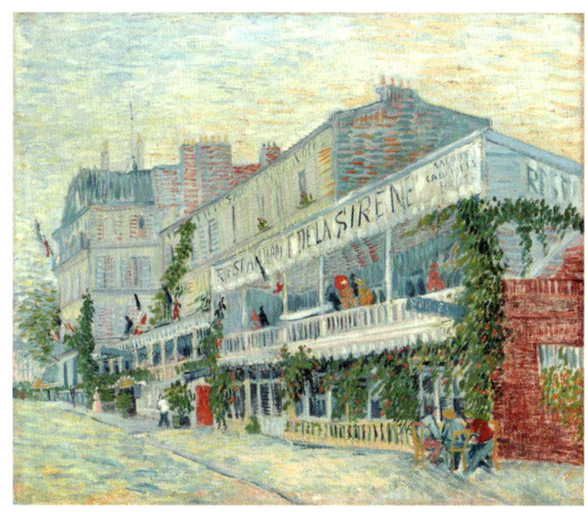

CAT. 23
Restaurant de la Sirène at Asnières, 1887
Oil on canvas
$21\frac{1}{4} \times 25\frac{13}{16}$ in. (54× 65.5 cm)
Musée d'Orsay, Paris, bequest of Joseph Reinach, 1921, RF 2325
F313 / JH1251
Plate 74

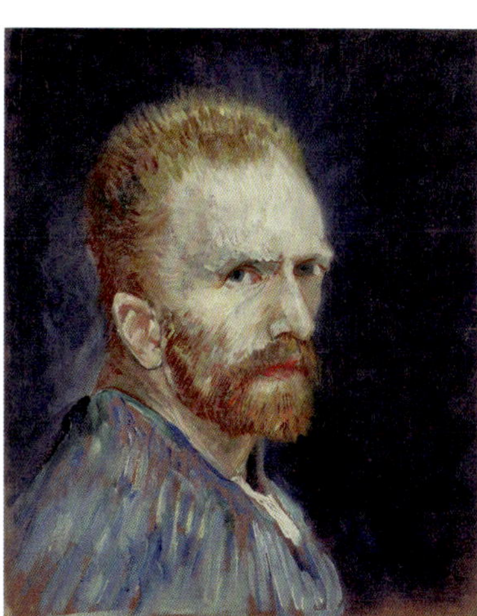

CAT. 24
Self-Portrait, 1887
Oil on canvas
$15\frac{15}{16} \times 13\frac{3}{8}$ in. (40.3 × 34 cm)
Wadsworth Atheneum Museum of Art, Hartford, gift of Philip L. Goodwin in memory of his mother, Josephine S. Goodwin, 1954.189
F268 / JH1299
Plate 17

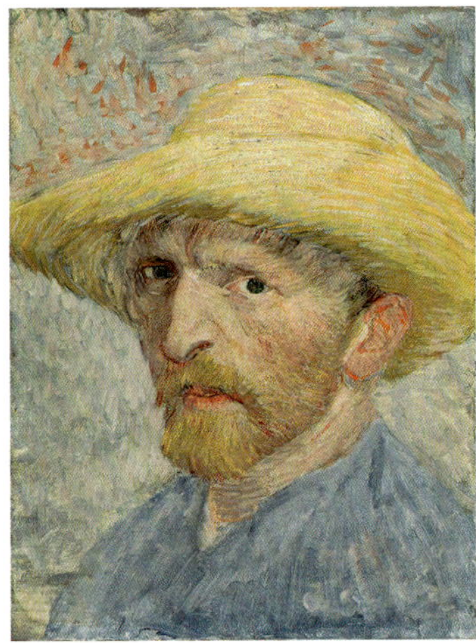

CAT. 25
Self-Portrait, 1887
Oil on artist board mounted to wood panel
13¾ × 10½ in. (34.9 × 26.7 cm)
Detroit Institute of Arts, City of Detroit Purchase, 22.13
F526 / JH1309
Plate 44

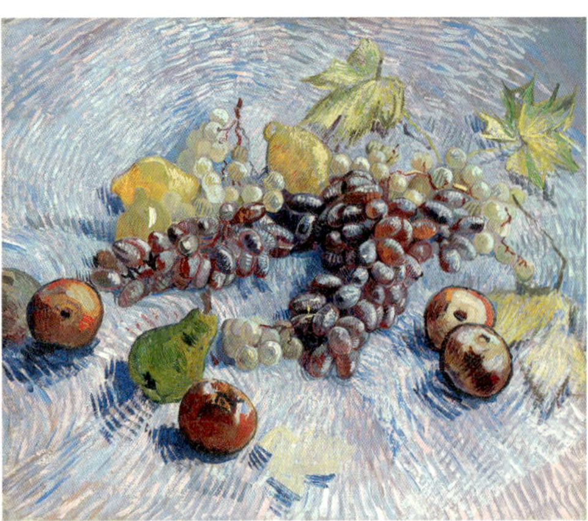

CAT. 26
Grapes, Lemons, Pears, and Apples, 1887
Oil on canvas
18¼ × 21¾ in. (46.5 × 55.2 cm)
The Art Institute of Chicago, gift of Kate L. Brewster, 1949.215
F382 / JH1337
Plate 55

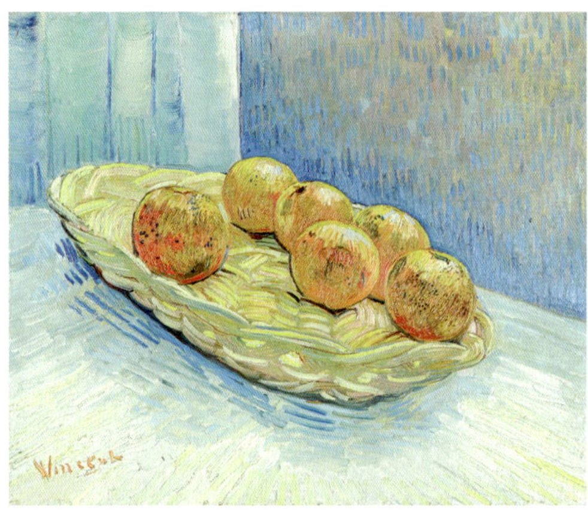

CAT. 27
Basket with Oranges, 1888
Oil on canvas
17¾ × 21¼ in. (45 × 54 cm)
Private Collection, courtesy of Heather James Fine Art, Palm Desert
F395 / JH1363
Plate 37

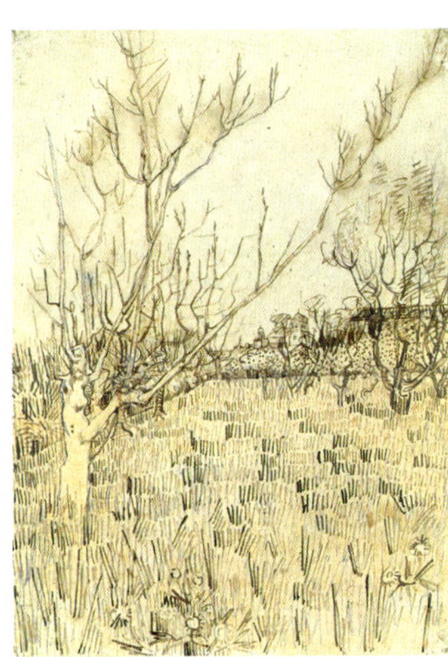

CAT. 28
Orchard with Arles in the Background, 1888
Reed pen, pen, ink, and graphite on laid paper
21 × 15⅜ in. (53.3 × 39.1 cm)
The Hyde Collection, Glens Falls, bequest of Charlotte Pruyn Hyde, 1971.81
F1516 / JH1376
Plate 43

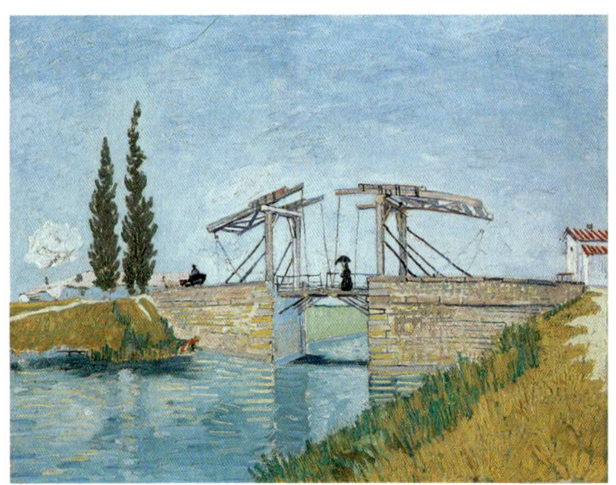

CAT. 29
The Drawbridge, 1888
Oil on canvas
19½ × 25⅜ in. (49.5 × 64.5 cm)
Wallraf-Richartz-Museum & Fondation Corboud, Cologne, WRM 1197
F570 / JH1421
Plate 72

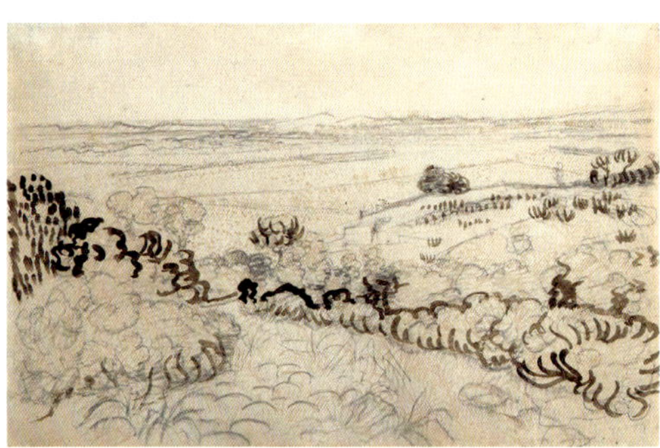

CAT. 30
The Plain of La Crau, 1888
Reed pen and ink with graphite on paper
1113⁄16 × 18 5⁄16 in. (30 × 46.5 cm)
Private Collection, Texas
F1448 / JH1432
Plate 70

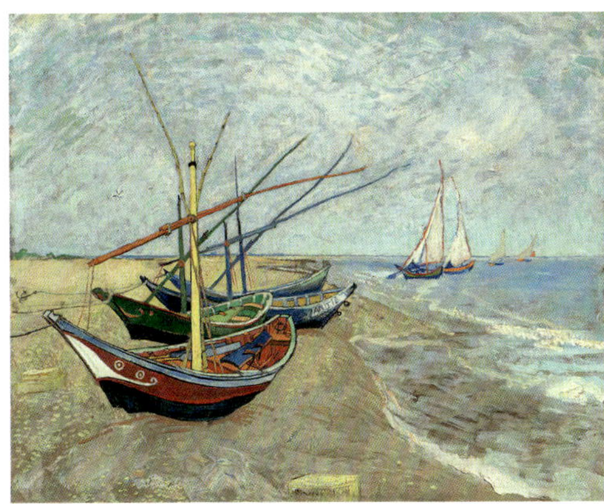

CAT. 31
Fishing Boats on the Beach at Les Saintes-Maries-de-la-Mer, 1888
Oil on canvas
$25\frac{9}{16} \times 32\frac{1}{16}$ in. (65 × 81.5 cm)
Van Gogh Museum, Amsterdam (Vincent van Gogh Foundation), s0028V1962
F413 / JH1460
Plate 39

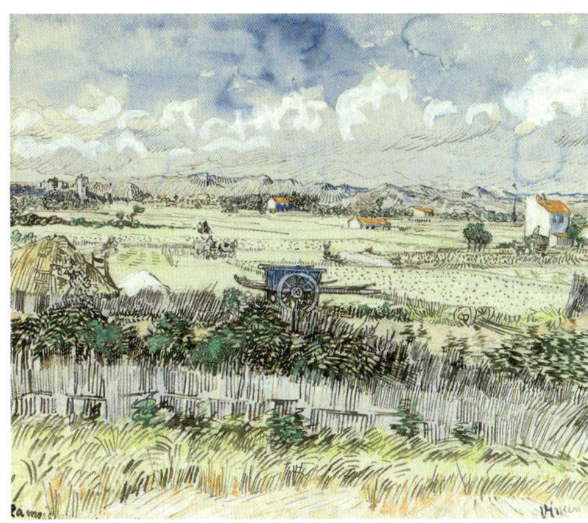

CAT. 32
Harvest in Provence, 1888
Watercolor, gouache, charcoal, reed and quill pen, and brown ink on off-white wove paper laid down on mill board
$19\frac{7}{8} \times 24$ in. (50.5 × 61 cm)
Private Collection, courtesy of Heather James Fine Art, Palm Desert
F1483 / JH1439
Plate 75

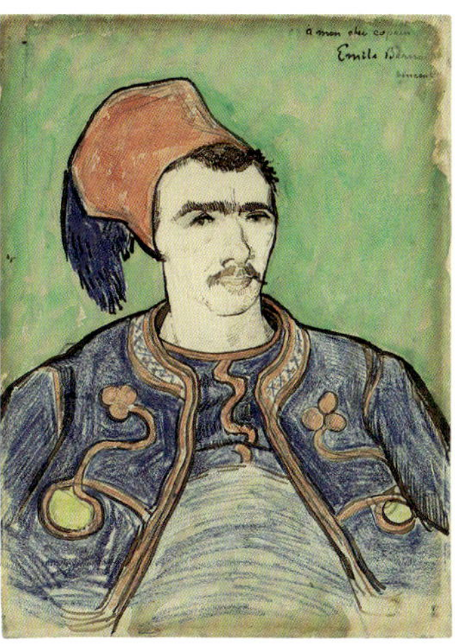

CAT. 33
The Zouave, 1888
Reed pen and brown ink, wax crayon, and watercolor over graphite on wove paper
$12\frac{3}{8} \times 9\frac{5}{16}$ in. (31.5 × 23.6 cm)
The Metropolitan Museum of Art, New York, gift of Emanie Philips, 1962, 62.151
F1482 / JH1487
Plate 20

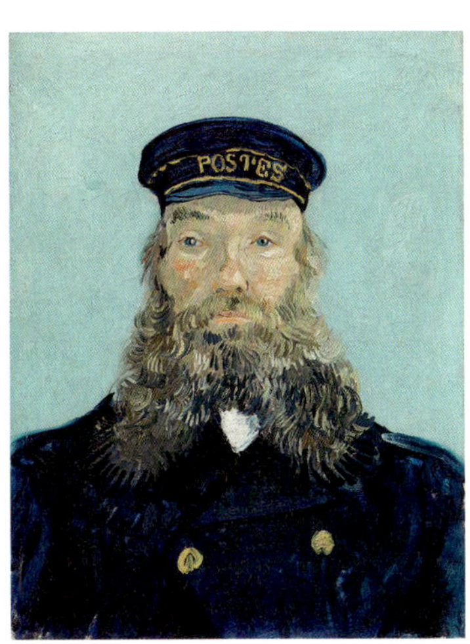

CAT. 34
Portrait of Postman Roulin, 1888
Oil on canvas
$25\frac{9}{16} \times 19\frac{7}{8}$ in. (65 × 50.5 cm)
Detroit Institute of Arts, gift of Mr. and Mrs. Walter Buhl Ford II, 1996.25
F433 / JH1524
Plate 51

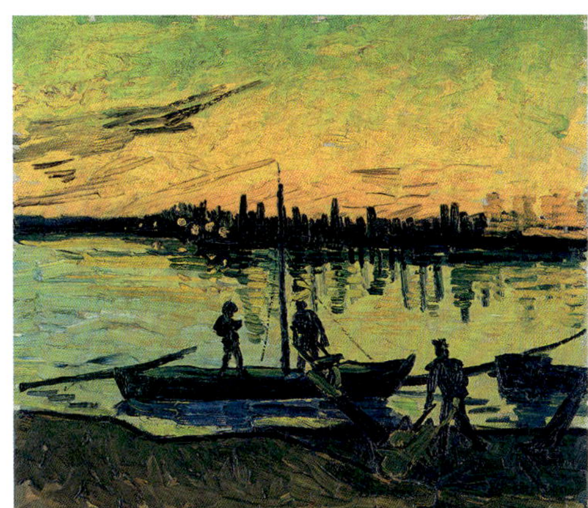

CAT. 35
The Stevedores in Arles, 1888
Oil on canvas
$21\frac{1}{4} \times 25\frac{9}{16}$ in. (54 × 65 cm)
Museo Nacional Thyssen-Bornemisza, Madrid, 557, 1965.7
F438 / JH1571
Plate 8

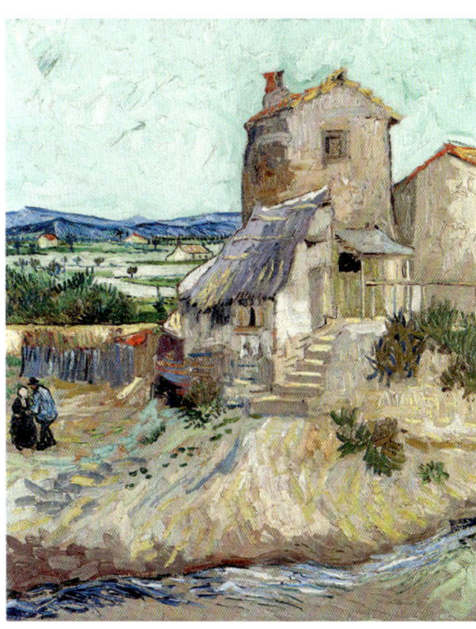

CAT. 36
House on the Crau (The Old Mill), 1888
Oil on canvas
$25\frac{1}{2} \times 21\frac{1}{4}$ in. (64.8 × 54 cm)
Albright-Knox Art Gallery, Buffalo, bequest of A. Conger Goodyear, 1966, 1966:9.22
F550 / JH1577
Plate 27

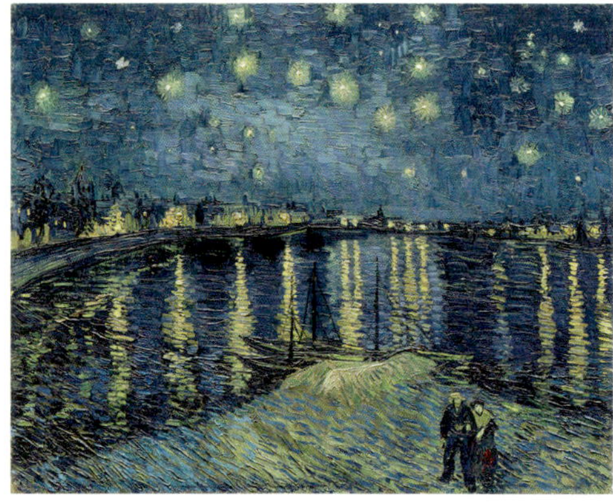

CAT. 37
Starry Night, 1888
Oil on canvas
28¾ × 36¼ in. (73 × 92 cm)
Musée d'Orsay, Paris, gift of M. and Mme Robert Khan-Sriber, in memory of M. and Mme Fernand Moch, 1975, RF 1975–19
F474 / JH1592
Plate 67

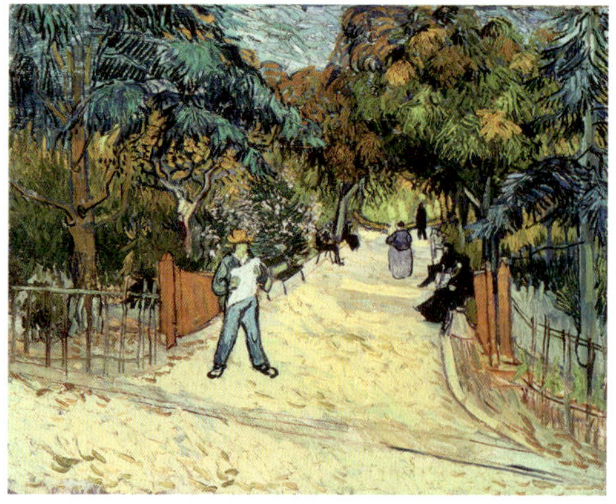

CAT. 38
Entrance to the Public Gardens in Arles, 1888
Oil on canvas
28½ × 35¾ in. (72.4 × 90.8 cm)
The Phillips Collection, Washington, DC, acquired 1930, 0796
F566 / JH1585
Plate 57

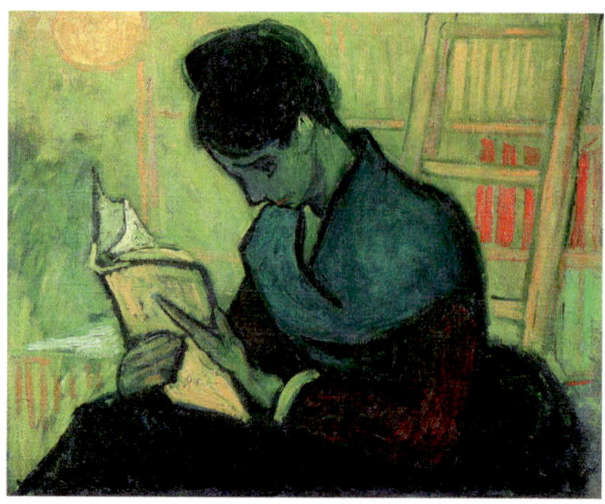

CAT. 39
The Novel Reader, 1888
Oil on canvas
28¾ × 36¼ in. (73 × 92.1 cm)
Private Collection, São Paulo
F497 / JH1632
Plate 46

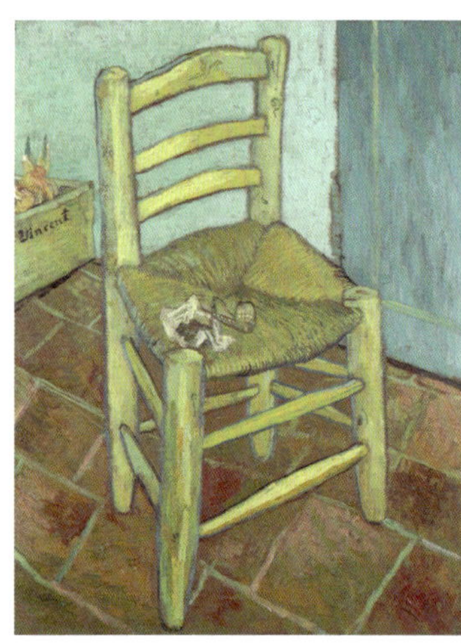

CAT. 40
Van Gogh's Chair, 1888
Oil on canvas
36⅛ × 28¾ in. (91.8 × 73 cm)
The National Gallery, London, bought, Courtauld Fund, 1924, NG3862
F498 / JH1635
Plate 47

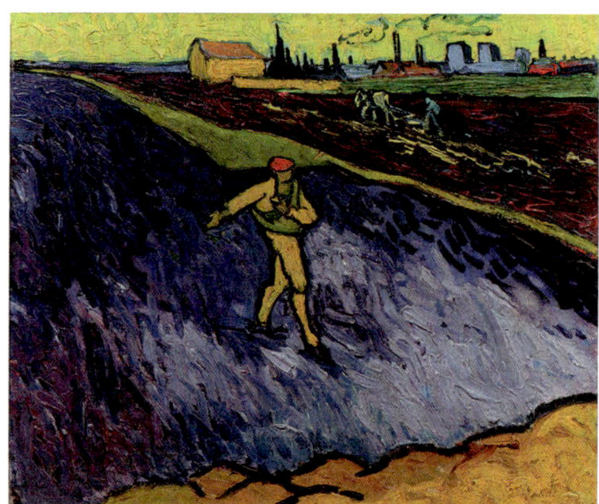

CAT. 41
The Sower, 1888
Oil on canvas
13¼ × 16 in. (33.7 × 40.6 cm)
Hammer Museum, Los Angeles, The Armand Hammer Collection, gift of Dr. Armand Hammer, AH.91.42
F575a / JH1596
Plate 26

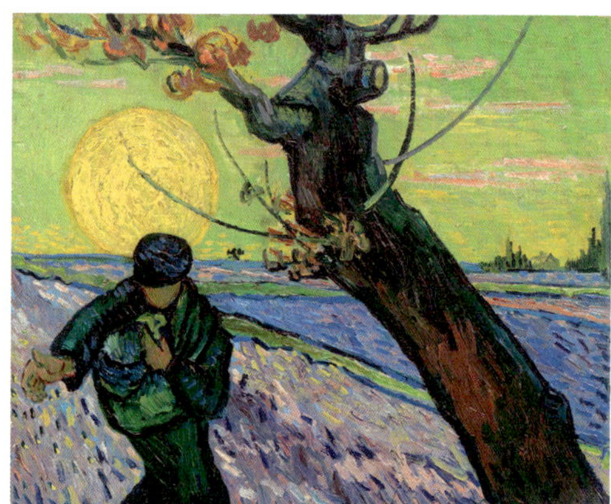

CAT. 42
The Sower, 1888
Oil on canvas
12¹³⁄₁₆ × 15⅞ in. (32.5 × 40.3 cm)
Van Gogh Museum, Amsterdam (Vincent van Gogh Foundation), s0029V1962
F451 / JH1629
Plate 11

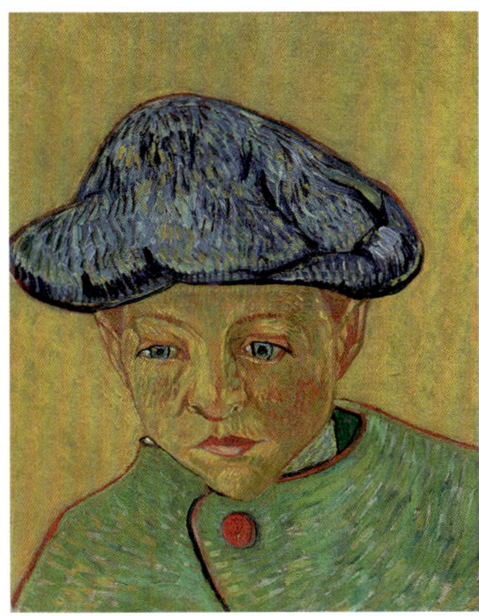

CAT. 43
Portrait of Camille Roulin, 1888
Oil on canvas
17 × 13¾ in. (43.2 × 34.9 cm)
Philadelphia Museum of Art, gift of Mr. and Mrs. Rodolphe Meyer de Schauensee, 1973, 1973-129-1
F537 / JH1644
Plate 15

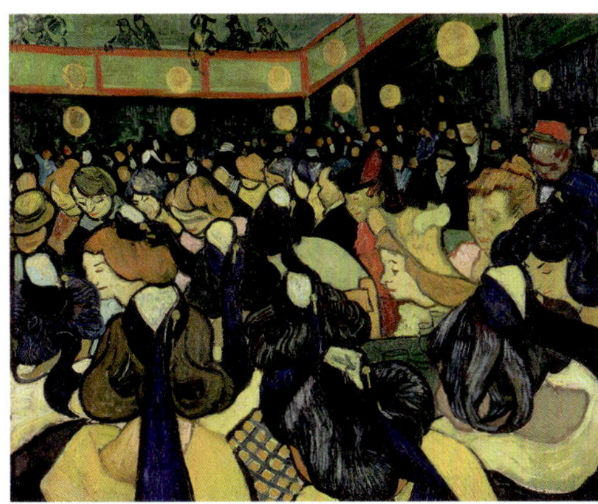

CAT. 44
The Dance Hall at Arles, 1888
Oil on canvas
25⅝ × 33⅝ in. (65 × 85.5 cm)
Musée d'Orsay, Paris, gift of M. and Mme André Meyer, 1951, RF 1950-9
F547 / JH1652
Plate 21

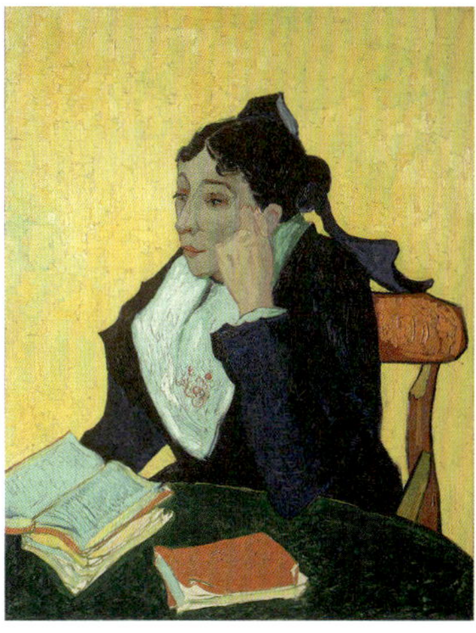

CAT. 45
L'Arlésienne: Madame Joseph-Michel Ginoux (Marie Julien, 1848–1911), 1888–89
Oil on canvas
36 × 29 in. (91.4 × 73.7 cm)
The Metropolitan Museum of Art, New York, bequest of Sam A. Lewisohn, 1951, 51.112.3
F488 / JH1624
Plate 29

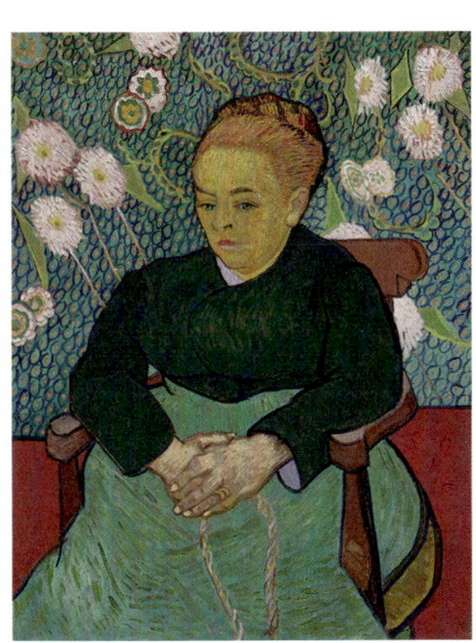

CAT. 46
Lullaby: Madame Augustine Roulin Rocking a Cradle (La Berceuse), 1889
Oil on canvas
36½ × 28⅝ in. (92.7 × 72.7 cm)
Museum of Fine Arts, Boston, bequest of John T. Spaulding, 48.548
F508 / JH1671
Plate 22

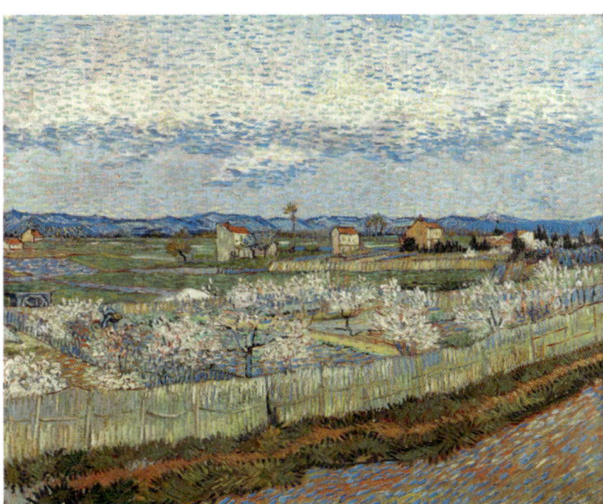

CAT. 47
Peach Trees in Blossom, 1889
Oil on canvas
25⁹⁄₁₆ × 31⅞ in. (65 × 81 cm)
The Samuel Courtauld Trust, The Courtauld Gallery, London, gift from Samuel Courtauld, 1932, P.1932.SC.176
F514 / JH1681
Plate 66

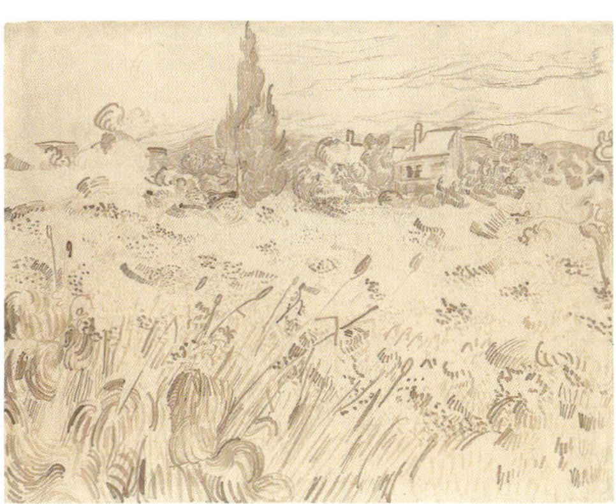

CAT. 48
Wheatfield, Saint-Rémy de Provence, 1889
Steel and reed pens and brown ink on paper
18⅜ × 24⅜ in. (46.7 × 61.9 cm)
The Morgan Library & Museum, New York, gift of Mrs. Gerard B. Lambert in memory of Gerard B. Lambert, 1973.13
F1548 / JH1726
Plate 40

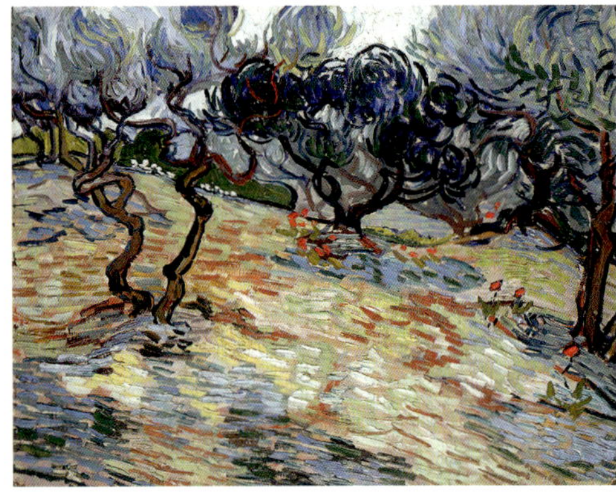

CAT. 49
Olive Trees, 1889
Oil on canvas
20⅟₁₆ × 25¹¹⁄₁₆ in. (51 × 65.2 cm)
National Galleries of Scotland, Edinburgh, purchased 1934, NG1803
F714 / JH1858
Plate 4

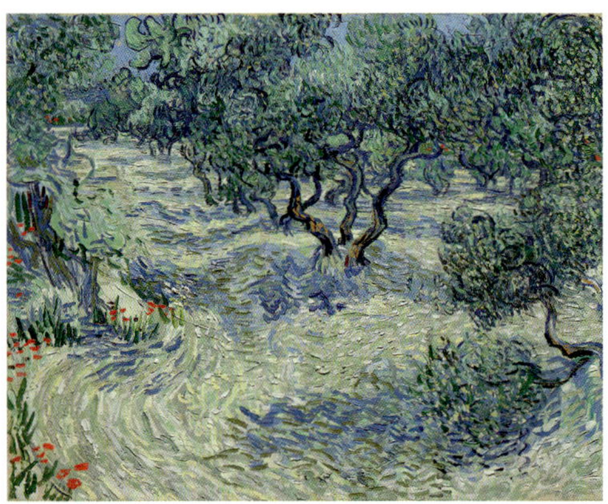

CAT. 50
Olive Trees, 1889
Oil on canvas
28¾ × 36¼ in. (73 × 92.1 cm)
The Nelson-Atkins Museum of Art, Kansas City, purchase, William Rockhill Nelson Trust, 32-2
F715 / JH1759
Plate 56

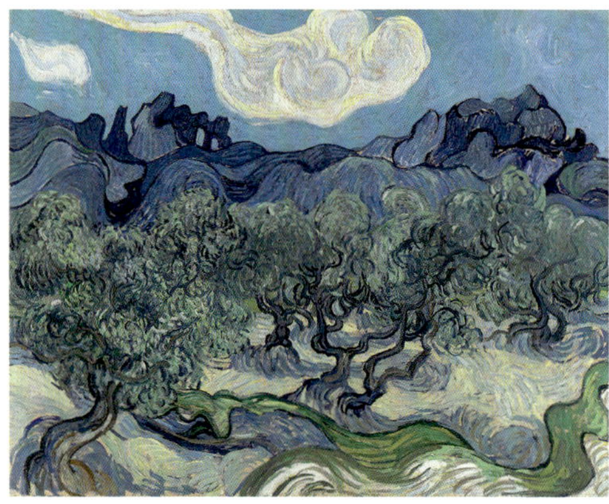

CAT. 51
The Olive Trees, 1889
Oil on canvas
28⅝ × 36 in. (72.6 × 91.4 cm)
The Museum of Modern Art, New York, Mrs. John Hay Whitney Bequest, 1998
F712 / JH1740
Plate 38

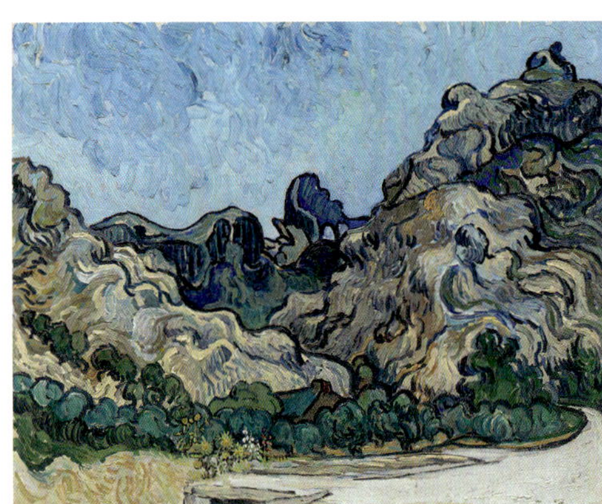

CAT. 52
Mountains at Saint-Rémy, 1889
Oil on canvas
28¹¹⁄₁₆ × 36¼ in. (72.8 × 92 cm)
Solomon R. Guggenheim Museum, New York, Thannhauser Collection, gift, Justin K. Thannhauser, 1978, 78.2514.24
F622 / JH1766
Plate 14

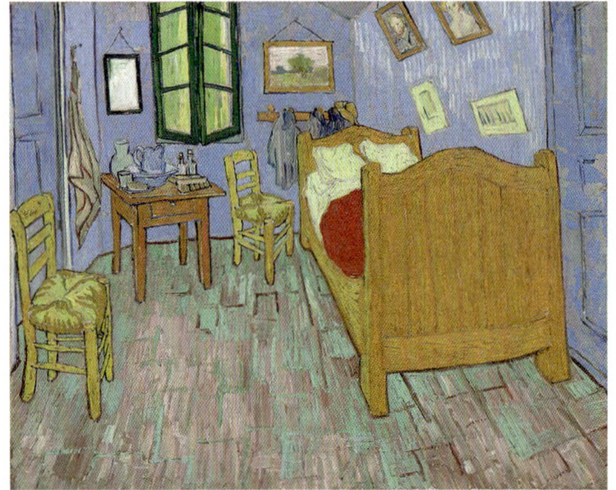

CAT. 53
The Bedroom, 1889
Oil on canvas
29 × 36⅝ in. (73.6 × 92.3 cm)
The Art Institute of Chicago, Helen Birch Bartlett Memorial Collection, 1926.417
F484 / JH1771
Plate 45

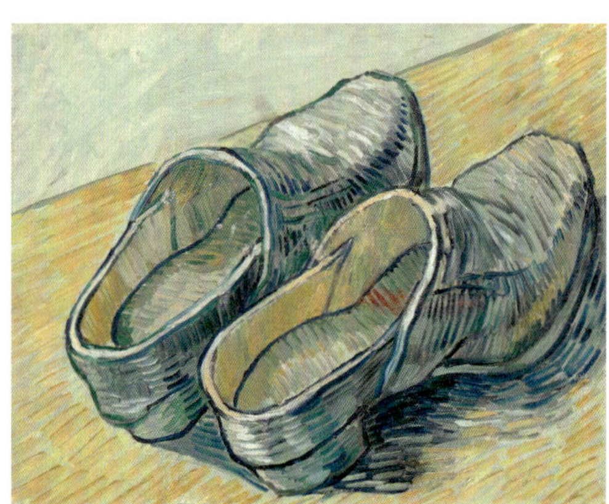

CAT. 54
A Pair of Leather Clogs, 1889
Oil on canvas
12¹¹⁄₁₆ × 15¹⁵⁄₁₆ in. (32.2 × 40.5 cm)
Van Gogh Museum, Amsterdam (Vincent van Gogh Foundation), s0120V1962
F607 / JH1364
Plate 19

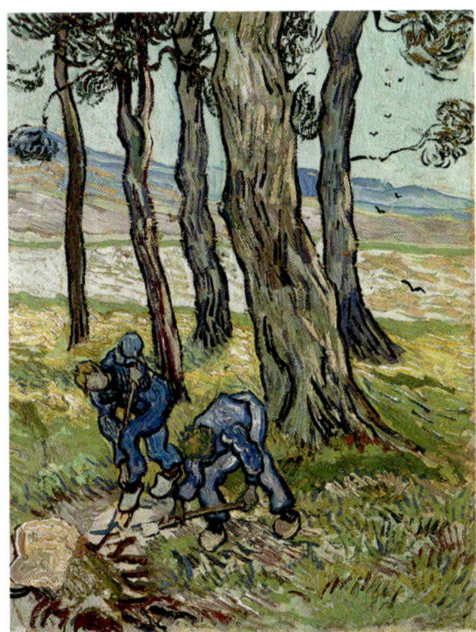

CAT. 55
The Diggers, 1889
Oil on paper lined onto canvas
25⅝ × 19¾ in. (65.1 × 50.2 cm)
Detroit Institute of Arts, bequest of Robert H. Tannahill, 70.158
F701 / JH1847
Plate 9

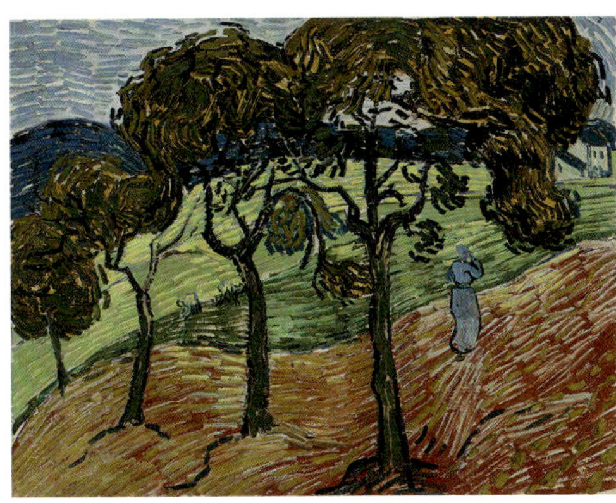

CAT. 56
Landscape with Figures, 1889
Oil on canvas
$19\frac{15}{16}$ × 26 in. (50.6 × 66 cm)
The Baltimore Museum of Art, The Cone Collection, formed by Dr. Claribel Cone and Miss Etta Cone of Baltimore, Maryland, 1950.303
F818 / JH1848
Plate 1

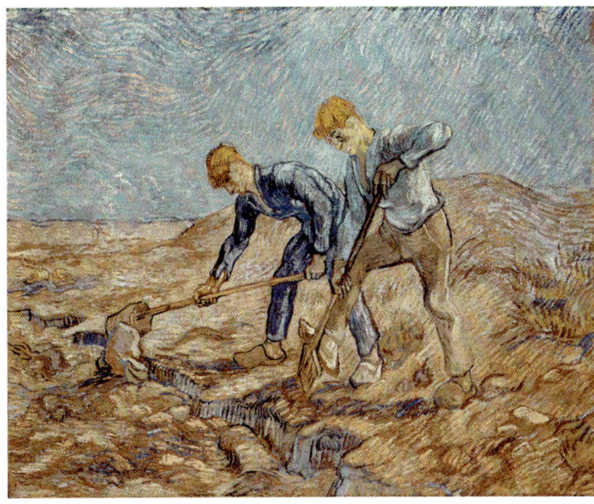

CAT. 57
Two Peasants Digging, 1889
Oil on canvas
29⅛ × 36⅝ in. (74 × 93 cm)
Stedelijk Museum, Amsterdam, A411
F648 / JH1833
Plate 25

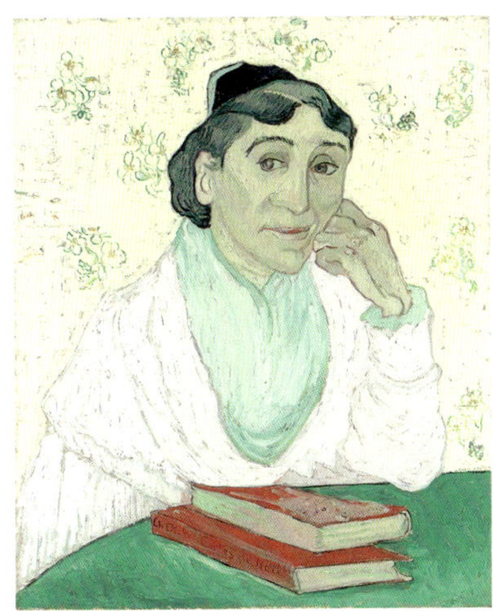

CAT. 58
L'Arlésienne, Madame Ginoux, 1890
Oil on canvas
$25\frac{5}{16}$ × 21¼ in. (65 × 54 cm)
Private Collection
F543 / JH1895
Plate 41

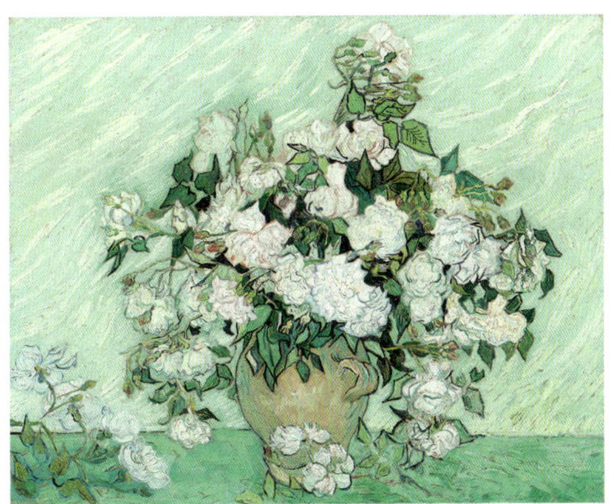

CAT. 59
Roses, 1890
Oil on canvas
$27\frac{15}{16}$ × $35\frac{7}{16}$ in. (71 × 90 cm)
National Gallery of Art, Washington, DC, gift of Pamela Harriman in memory of W. Averell Harriman, 1991.67.1
F681 / JH1976
Plate 59

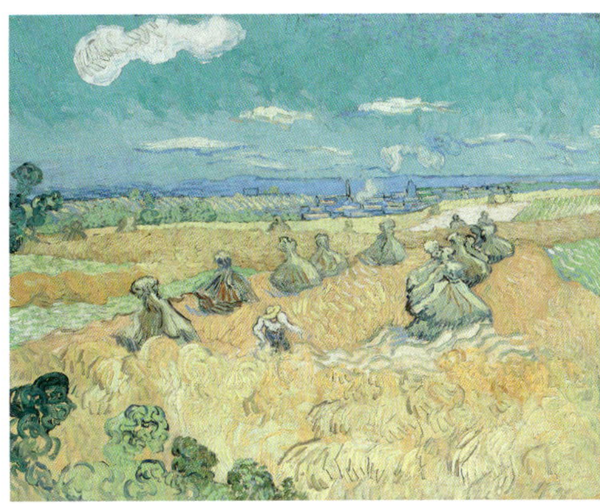

CAT. 60
Wheat Fields with Reaper, Auvers, 1890
Oil on canvas
29 × 36⅝ in. (73.6 × 93 cm)
Toledo Museum of Art, purchased with funds from the Libbey Endowment, gift of Edward Drummond Libbey, 1935.4
F559 / JH1479
Plate 60

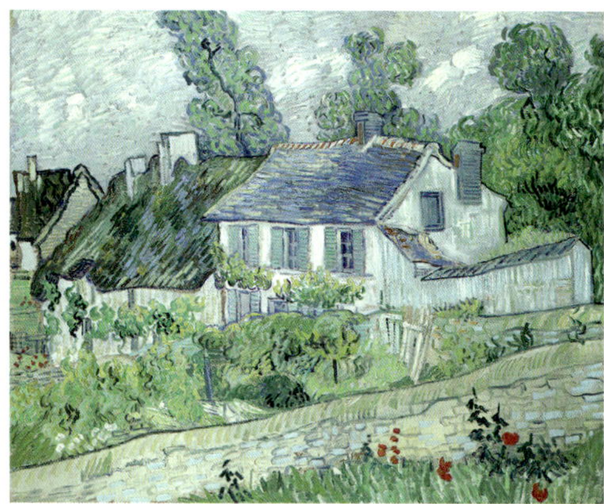

CAT. 61
Houses at Auvers, 1890
Oil on canvas
23⅝ × 28¾ in. (60 × 73 cm)
Toledo Museum of Art, purchased with funds from the Libbey Endowment, gift of Edward Drummond Libbey, 1935.5
F759 / JH1988
Plate 61

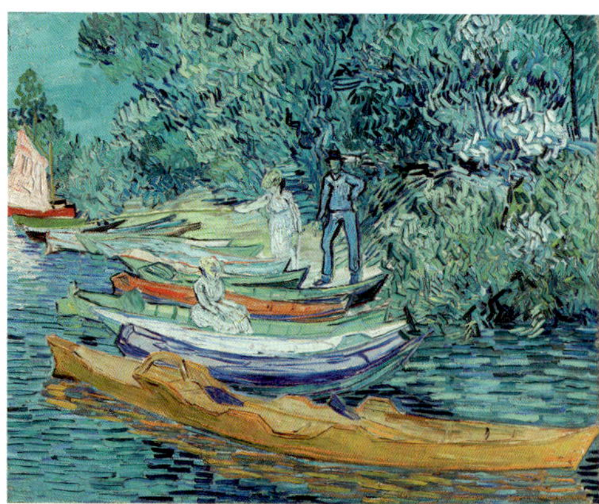

CAT. 62
Bank of the Oise at Auvers, 1890
Oil on canvas
28 × 36⅞ in. (71.1 × 93.7 cm)
Detroit Institute of Arts, bequest of Robert H. Tannahill, 70.159
F798 / JH2021
Plate 7

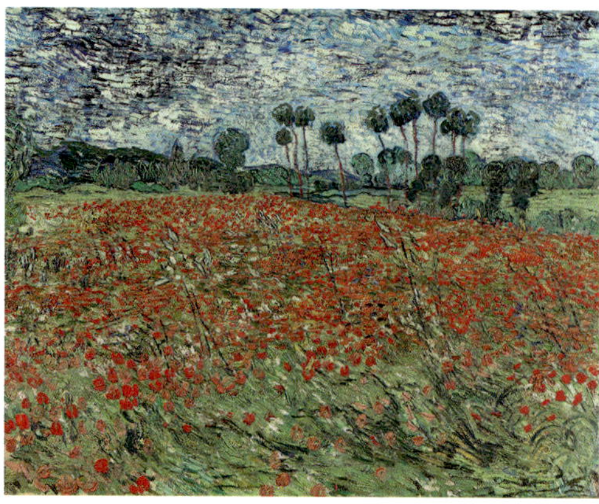

CAT. 63
Poppy Field, 1890
Oil on canvas
28¾ × 36⅛ in. (73 × 91.5 cm)
Kunstmuseum Den Haag, The Hague, long-term loan Cultural Heritage Agency of the Netherlands, SCH-1948x0003
F636 / JH2027
Plate 36

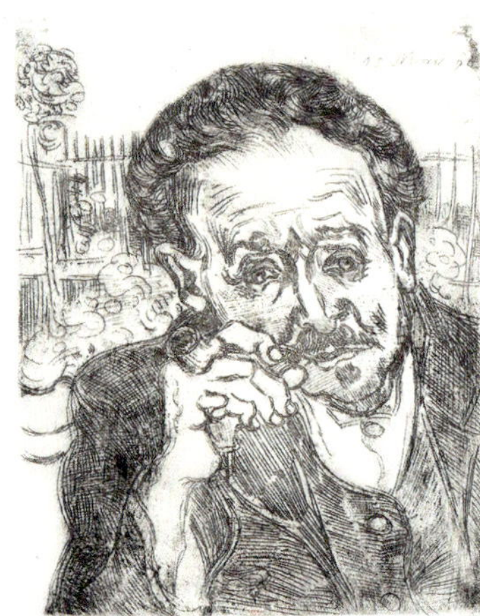

CAT. 64
Portrait of Dr. Gachet (Man with a Pipe), 1890
Etching on paper
Image: 7⅛ × 5 15/16 in. (18.1 × 15.1 cm); sheet: 13⅞ × 10⅜ in. (35.2 × 26.4 cm)
Des Moines Art Center Permanent Collections; purchased with funds from the Mildred M. Bohen Deaccession Fund and funds given by Harriet S. Macomber in memory of J. Locke Macomber, 2011.4
F1664 / JH2028
Plate 42

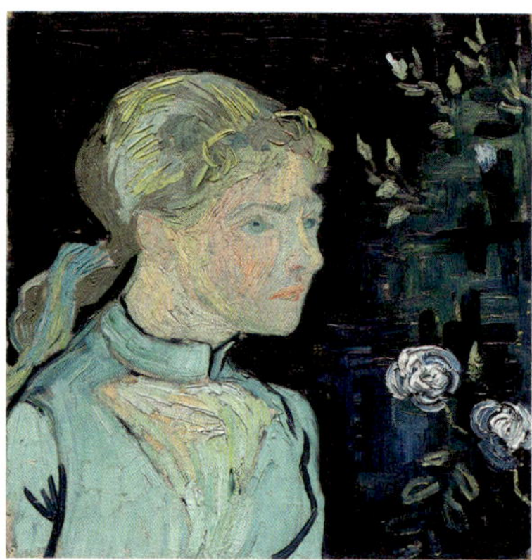

CAT. 65
Adeline Ravoux, 1890
Oil on fabric
19¾ × 19⅞ in. (50.2 × 50.5 cm)
The Cleveland Museum of Art, bequest of Leonard C. Hanna Jr., 1958.31
F786 / JH2036
Plate 18

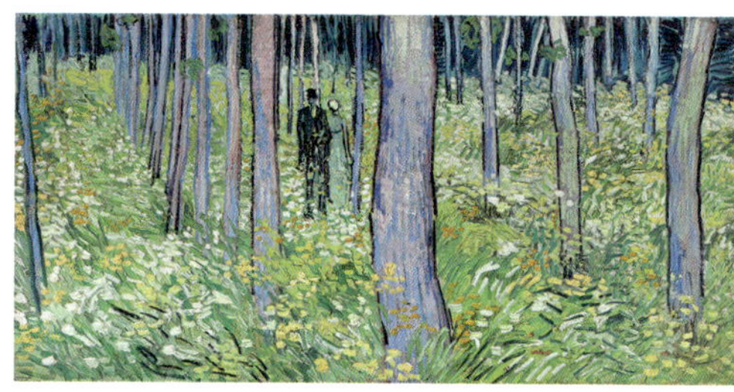

CAT. 66
Undergrowth with Two Figures, 1890
Oil on canvas
19½ × 39¼ in. (49.5 × 99.7 cm)
Cincinnati Art Museum, bequest of Mary E. Johnston, 1967.1430
F773 / JH2041
Plate 2

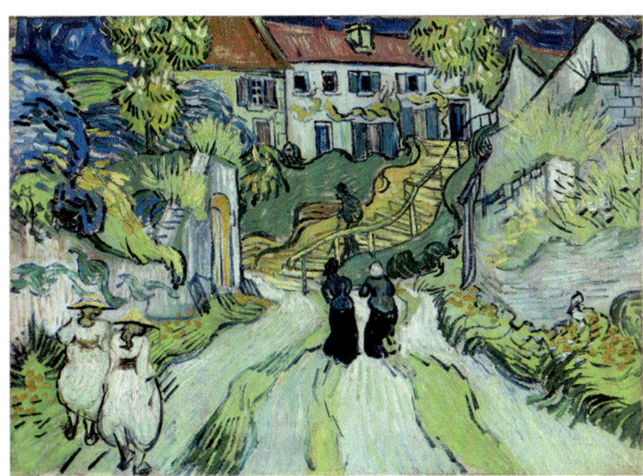

CAT. 67
Stairway at Auvers, 1890
Oil on canvas
$19\frac{11}{16} \times 27\frac{3}{4}$ in. (50 × 70.5 cm)
Saint Louis Art Museum, museum purchase, 1:1935
F795 / JH2111
Plate 62

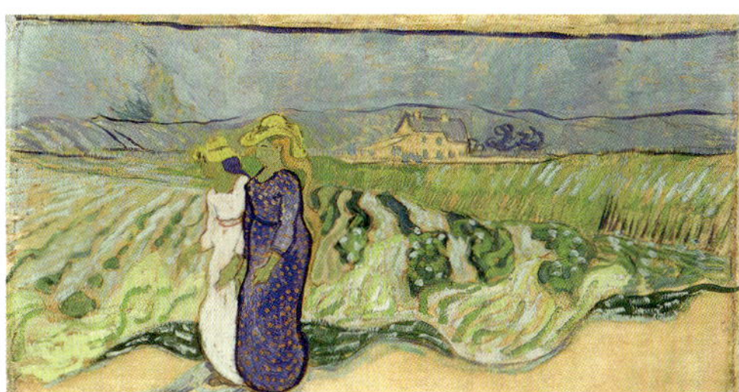

CAT. 68
Women Crossing the Fields, 1890
Oil on paper
$11\frac{15}{16} \times 23\frac{1}{2}$ in. (30.3 × 59.7 cm)
McNay Art Museum, San Antonio, bequest of Marion Koogler McNay, 1950.49
F819 / JH2112
Plate 58

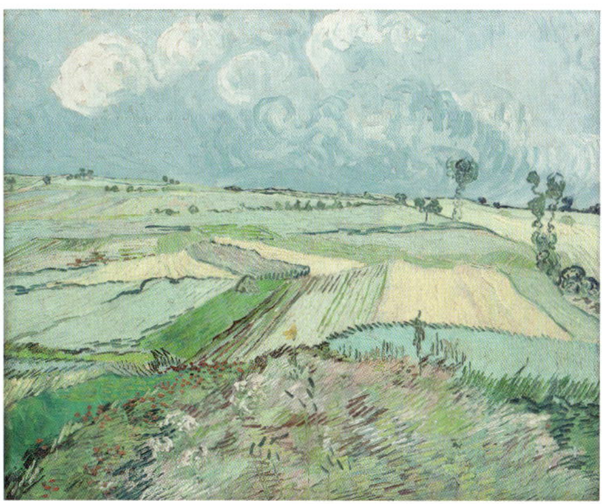

CAT. 69
Wheat Fields after the Rain (The Plain of Auvers), 1890
Oil on canvas
$28\frac{7}{8} \times 36\frac{3}{8}$ in. (73.3 × 92.4 cm)
Carnegie Museum of Art, Pittsburgh, acquired through the generosity of the Sarah Mellon Scaife Family, 68.18
F781 / JH2102
Plate 68

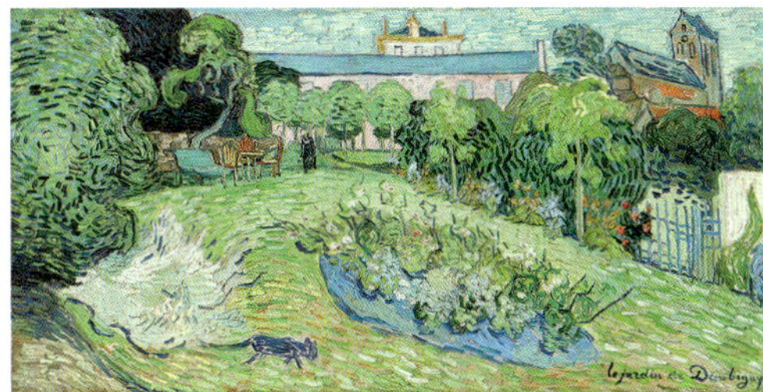

CAT. 70
Daubigny's Garden, 1890
Oil on canvas
$22\frac{1}{16} \times 39\frac{15}{16}$ in. (56 × 101.5 cm)
Rudolf Staechelin Collection
F777 / JH2105
Plate 69

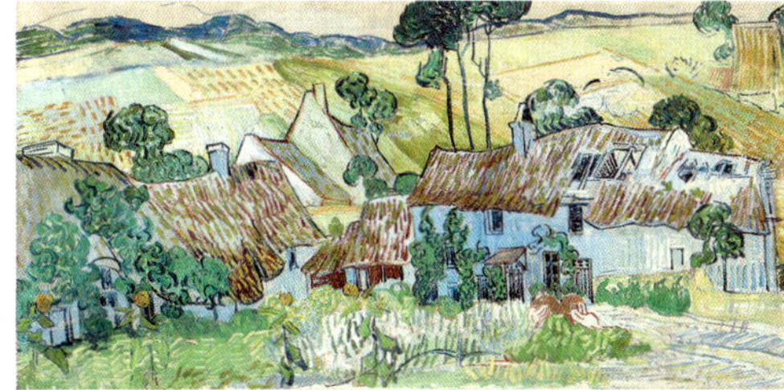

CAT. 71
Farms near Auvers, 1890
Oil on canvas
$19\frac{3}{4} \times 39\frac{1}{2}$ in. (50.2 × 100.3 cm)
Tate, London, bequeathed by C. Frank Stoop, 1933, N04713
F793 / JH2114
Plate 5

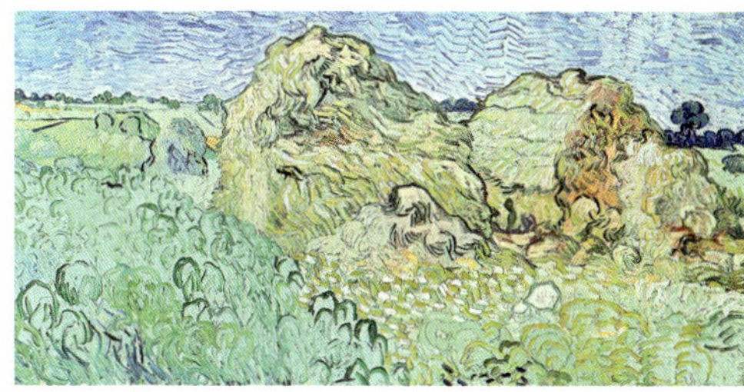

CAT. 72
Wheat Stacks, 1890
Oil on canvas
$19\frac{5}{8} \times 39\frac{3}{8}$ in. (50 × 100 cm)
Fondation Beyeler, Riehen/Basel, Beyeler Collection, 98.1
F809 / JH2098
Plate 6

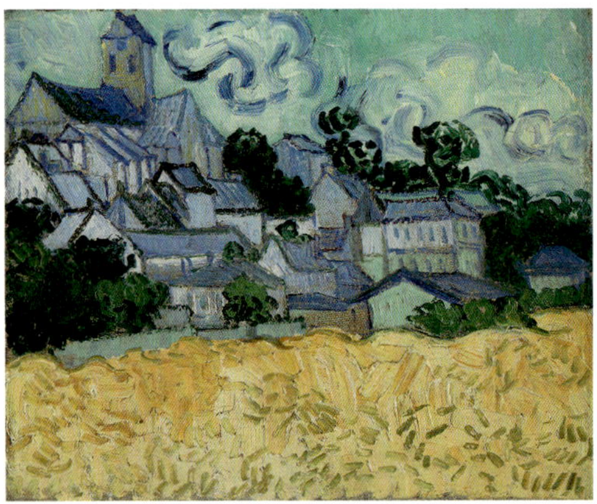

CAT. 73
View of Auvers-sur-Oise, 1890
Oil on canvas
13⅜ × 16⁹⁄₁₆ in. (34 × 42.1 cm)
Museum of Art, Rhode Island School of Design, Providence, given in memory of Miss Dorothy Sturges by a Friend, 35.770
F800 / JH2122
Plate 77

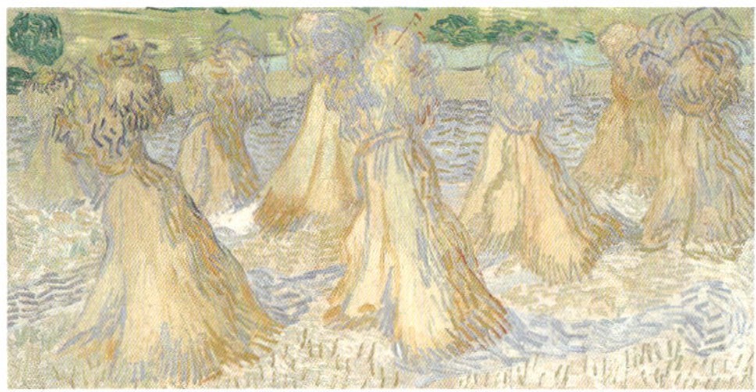

CAT. 74
Sheaves of Wheat, 1890
Oil on canvas
19⅞ × 39¾ in. (50.5 × 101 cm)
Dallas Museum of Art, The Wendy and Emery Reves Collection, 1985.R.80
F771 / JH2125
Plate 12

Other Artists in the Exhibition

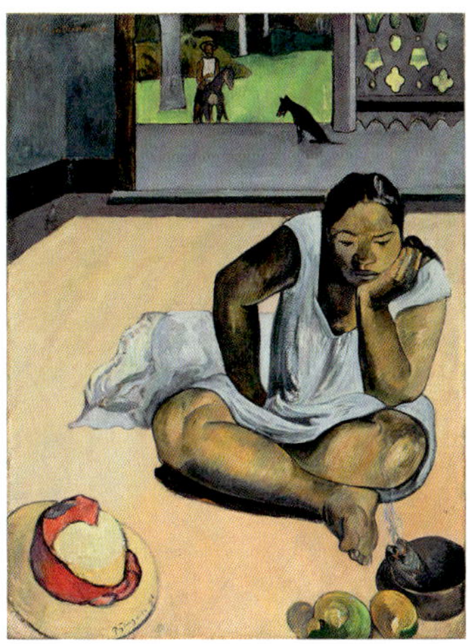

CAT. 75
Paul Gauguin (French, 1848–1903)
The Brooding Woman (Te Faaturuma), 1891
Oil on canvas
35⅞ × 27 1/16 in. (91.1 × 68.7 cm)
Worcester Art Museum, museum purchase, 1921.186
Plate 52

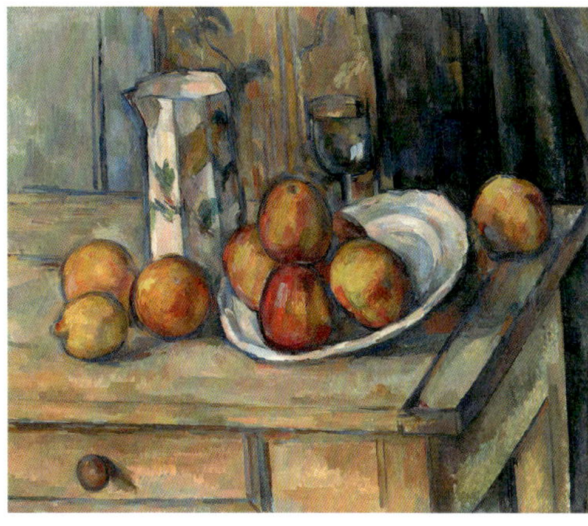

CAT. 76
Paul Cézanne (French, 1839–1906)
Still Life with Milk Jug and Fruit, c. 1900
Oil on canvas
18 1/16 × 21⅝ in. (45.8 × 54.9 cm)
National Gallery of Art, Washington, DC, gift of the W. Averell Harriman Foundation in memory of Marie N. Harriman, 1972.9.5
Plate 79

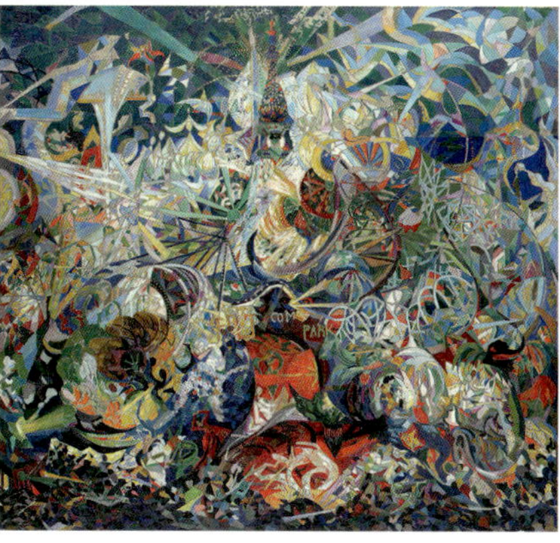

CAT. 77
Joseph Stella (American, 1877–1946)
Battle of Lights, Coney Island, Mardi Gras, 1913–14
Oil on canvas
77 × 84¾ in. (195.6 × 215.3 cm)
Yale University Art Gallery, New Haven, gift of Collection Société Anonyme, 1941.689
Plate 53

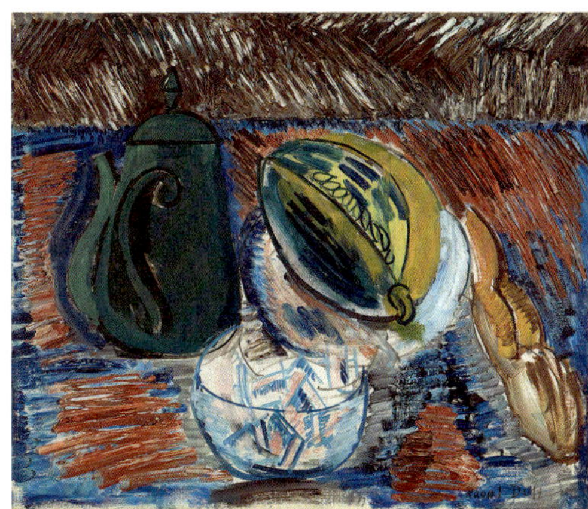

CAT. 78
Raoul Dufy (French, 1877–1953)
Still Life, c. 1914
Oil on canvas
18 × 21½ in. (45.7 × 54.6 cm)
Detroit Institute of Arts, City of Detroit Purchase, 22.15
Plate 48

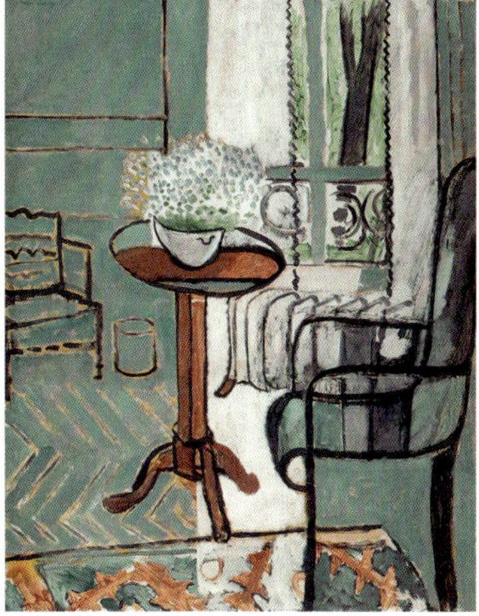

CAT. 79
Henri Matisse (French, 1869–1954)
The Window, 1916
Oil on canvas
57½ × 46 in. (146.1 × 116.8 cm)
Detroit Institute of Arts, City of Detroit Purchase, 22.14
Plate 49

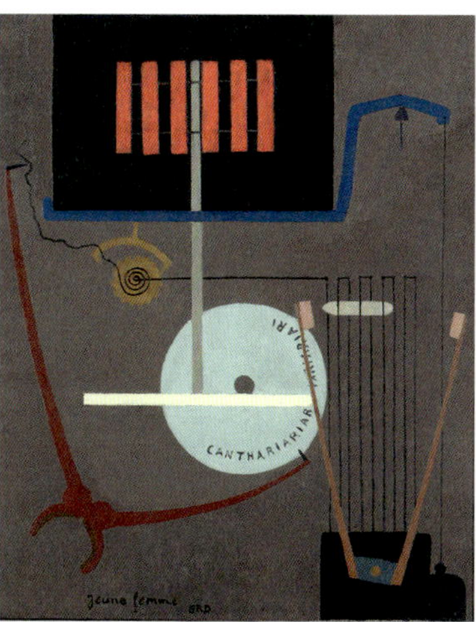

CAT. 80
Georges Ribemont-Dessaignes (French, 1884–1974)
Young Woman, 1919
Oil on linen
28 15/16 × 23¾ in. (73.5 × 60.4 cm)
Yale University Art Gallery, New Haven, gift of Collection Société Anonyme, 1941.665
Plate 54

Selected Bibliography

A

Adler et al. 2006
Adler, Kathleen et al. *Americans in Paris, 1860–1900*. London: National Gallery, 2006.

Van Adrichem 2001
Adrichem, Jan van. *De ontvangst van de moderne kunst in Nederland, 1910–2000: Picasso als pars pro toto*. Amsterdam: Prometheus, 2001.

Algemeen Handelsblad 1920
Algemeen Handelsblad, November 8, 1920: 10.

Algemeen Handelsblad 1921
"Moderne Hollandsche schilderkunst in New York." *Algemeen Handelsblad*, May 11, 1921: 9.

Algemeen Handelsblad 1923
"De collectie Goudstikker in de Anderson Galleries." *Algemeen Handelsblad*, March 28, 1923: 9.

Algemeen Handelsblad 1940
"Tentoonstellingen en concerten als ambassadeurs van 'Goodwill.'" *Algemeen Handelsblad*, March 2, 1940: 2.

American Art News 1914
"New Bourgeois Galleries." *American Art News* 12, 20 (February 21, 1914): 1, 4.

American Art News 1915
"Van Gogh at the Modern Gallery." *American Art News* 14, 8 (November 27, 1915): 6.

American Art News 1919
American Art News 17, 16 (January 26, 1919): 6.

American Art News 1920a
"Modern Art in New Gallery." *American Art News* 18, 29 (May 8, 1920): 3.

American Art News 1920b
M. C. "Paris Letter." *American Art News* 18, 30 (May 15, 1920): 4.

American Art News 1920c
"French Painters at De Zayas." *American Art News* 18, 36 (June 26, 1920): 2.

American Art News 1921a
"Special New York Exhibitions." *American Art News* 19, 12 (January 1, 1921): 6.

American Art News 1921b
"French Painters at De Zayas." *American Art News* 19, 24 (March 26, 1921): 3.

American Art News 1921c
"Museum Opens Its Modernist Show. Feature of Exhibition Is Introduction to Catalogue by Mr. Burroughs, Who Explains Significance of Movement." *American Art News* 19, 30 (May 7, 1921): 5.

American Art News 1921d
"Louvre Gets Its First Van Gogh." *American Art News* 19, 34 (June 4, 1921): 2.

American Art News 1921e
"Chicago." *American Art News* 20, 8 (December 3, 1921): 9.

American Art News 1922a
"America to Have Its First Great Auction of Modernist Art in Dispersal of Superb Collection Formed by D. K. Kelekian." *American Art News* 20, 15 (January 21, 1922): 7.

American Art News 1922b
"Anonymous Drawings Test Critics." *American Art News* 20, 25 (April 1, 1922): 6.

American Art News 1922c
"A Comprehensive Modern Show." *American Art News* 20, 26 (April 8, 1922): 2.

American Magazine of Art 1929
F. W. C. "Boston Happenings." *The American Magazine of Art* 20, 10 (October 1929): 591–92.

Antliff 2001
Antliff, Alan. *Anarchist Modernism: Art, Politics, and the First American Avant-Garde*. Chicago and London: University of Chicago Press, 2001.

Art and Archaeology 1920
"The Van Gogh Exhibition at the Montross Gallery." *Art and Archaeology* 10, 5 (November 1920): 198–99.

Art Digest 1936
"123,339 Visitors." *The Art Digest* 10 (January 15, 1936): 9.

Art Digest 1944
"Artist Decker, Actor Flynn, Open Gallery." *The Art Digest* 18 (July 1, 1944): 14.

Art News 1923a
"Cassirer to View Art in America." *The Art News* 21, 25 (March 31, 1923): 5.

Art News 1923b
"Reshowing Vincent Van Gogh." *The Art News* 21, 25 (March 31, 1923): 2.

Art News 1935a
"The Toledo Museum Buys Fine Van Gogh from Wildenstein." *The Art News* 33, 20 (February 16, 1935): 8.

Art News 1935b
"Toledo Acquires French Paintings." *The Art News* 33, 21 (February 23, 1935): 8.

Arts 1921a
"Comments on the Arts." *The Arts* 1, 3 (February–March 1921): 33–53.

Arts 1921b
"The Kelekian Collection." *The Arts* 2, 3 (December 1921): 132–48.

Arts 1922
"The Auction Room." *The Arts* 2, 4 (February 1922): 246–53.

Arts 1924a
The Arts 5, 4 (April 1924): 235.

Arts 1924b
The Arts 6, 5 (November 1924): 294.

Arts 1929a
The Arts 16, 3 (November 1929): 207.

Arts 1929b
The Arts 16, 4 (December 1929): 281.

Les Arts 1928
Les Arts 16 (November 1928): 147.

Arts and Decoration 1914
G.P.B. "Exhibitions at the Galleries: A New Gallery on Fifth Avenue." *Arts and Decoration* 4, 6 (April 1914): 238–46.

Arts and Decoration 1916
"Exhibitions in the Galleries." *Arts and Decoration* 6, 3 (January 1916): 136–38.

B

Bailey 2007
Bailey, Martin. "A Friend of Van Gogh: Dodge Macknight and the Post-Impressionists." *Apollo* 166, 545 (July–August 2007): 28–34.

Bailey 2019
Bailey, Martin. "On the Road: Van Gogh in England." In London 2019, 15–18.

Balk 2006
Balk, Hildelies. *De kunstpaus H. P. Bremmer*. Bussum, The Netherlands: Thoth Publishers, 2006.

[Barker] 1928
V. B. [Virgil Barker]. "A New Museum in Philadelphia." *The Arts* 13, 4 (April 1928): 254–70.

Barker 1930
Barker, Virgil. "October Exhibitions." *The Arts* 17, 1 (October 1930): 7–23, 50–52.

Barnes 1925
Barnes, Albert C. *The Art in Painting*. New York: Harcourt, Brace & Co., 1925.

Barnouw 1921
Barnouw, Adriaan J. "Modern Dutch Art at the Anderson Galleries." *Articles in Holland and Her Colonies: A Monthly Magazine Devoted to the Promotion of Closer Relations between the United States of America and Holland and Her Colonies*, May 1921: 7–9.

A. Barr 1929a
Barr, Alfred H., Jr. "Foreword." In New York 1929a, 11–27.

A. Barr 1929b
Barr, Alfred H., Jr. "A New Museum Which Will Devote Itself to the Masters of Modern Art." *Vogue*, October 26, 1929: 85, 108.

M. Barr 1987
Barr, Margaret Scolari. "'Our Campaigns': Alfred H. Barr, Jr., and the Museum of Modern Art: A Biographical Chronicle of the Years 1930–1944." *The New Criterion*, Summer 1987: 23–74.

Barter 2013
Barter, Judith A. "'The Great Confusion': The Armory Show in Chicago." In New York 2013–14, 363–73.

Bartlett 1965
Bartlett, Frederic Clay. *Sortofa Kindofa Journal of My Own*. Chicago and Crawfordsville, Indiana: The Lakeside Press, R. R. Donnelley & Sons Company, 1965.

Benson 1936
Benson, Gertrude. "Exploding the Van Gogh Myth." *The American Magazine of Art* 29, 1 (January 1936): 6–16.

Ten Berge et al. 2003
Berge, Jos ten et al. *The Paintings of Vincent van Gogh in the Collection of the Kröller-Müller Museum*. Otterlo: Kröller-Müller Museum, 2003.

Berger 2014
Berger, Doris. *Projected Art History: Biopics, Celebrity Culture, and the Popularizing of American Art*. New York and London: Bloomsbury, 2014.

Berman 2013
Berman, Avis. "'Creating a New Epoch': American Collectors and Dealers and the Armory Show." In New York 2013–14, 413–25.

Bertram 1929
Bertram, Anthony. *Vincent van Gogh*. London: The Studio Ltd.; New York: The Studio Publications, 1929.

Bluemner 1913
Bluemner, Oscar. "Audiator et Altera Pars: Some Plain Sense on the Modern Art Movement." *Camera Work*, special number, June 1913: 25–38.

Bohan 1982
Bohan, Ruth L. *The Société Anonyme's Brooklyn Exhibition: Katherine Dreier and Modernism in America*. Ann Arbor: UMI Research Press, 1982.

Bonte 1936
Bonte, C. H. "Famous Van Gogh Show Comes to Art Museum." *Philadelphia Inquirer*, January 12, 1936: 12.

Borgmeyer 1913
Borgmeyer, Charles Louis. "The Master Impressionists: Chapter IX." *The Fine Arts Journal* 29, 2 (August 1913): 447–76.

***Boston Daily Globe* 1927**
"Fine Prints and Etchings Presented to Art Museum." *Boston Daily Globe*, March 13, 1927: A16.

Boswell 1936
Boswell, Peyton. "Curiosity or Art?" *Art Digest* 10, 8 (January 15, 1936): 3–4, 17.

Bourgeois 1931
Bourgeois, Stephan. "Art Dealers." *Creative Art* 9 (November 1931): 403–407.

Brettell 1983
Brettell, Richard R. "The Diversity of French Nineteenth-Century Painting." *Apollo* 117, 253 (March 1983): 234–43.

Brettell 1986
Brettell, Richard R. "The Bartletts and the Grande Jatte: Collecting Modern Painting in the 1920s." *The Art Institute of Chicago Museum Studies* 12, 2, The Helen Birch Bartlett Memorial Collection (1986): 102–13.

Brettell and Prince 1990
Brettell, Richard R. and Sue Ann Prince. "From the Armory Show to the Century of Progress: The Art Institute Assimilates Modernism." In Prince 1990a, 209–25.

Brigham 1924
Brigham, Gertrude Richardson. "Art and Artists of the Capital." *Washington Post*, March 2, 1924: ES11.

Brinton 1915a
Brinton, Christian. "Foreign Painting at the Panama-Pacific Exposition [1]." *The International Studio* 56, 223 (September 1915): xlvii–liv.

Brinton 1915b
Brinton, Christian. "Foreign Painting at the Panama-Pacific Exposition [2]." *The International Studio* 56, 224 (October 1915): lxxxix–xcvi.

Brinton 1916
Brinton, Christian. *Impressions of the Art at the Panama-Pacific Exposition*. New York: John Lane Company, 1916.

Brooker and Thacker 2012
Brooker, Peter and Andrew Thacker, eds. *The Oxford Critical and Cultural History of Modernist Magazines: Volume II: North America 1894–1960*. Oxford: Oxford University Press, 2012.

***Brooklyn Daily Eagle* 1915a**
"The World of Art." *The Brooklyn Daily Eagle*, November 26, 1915: 18.

***Brooklyn Daily Eagle* 1915b**
"Eight New Van Gogh Pictures Shown." *The Brooklyn Daily Eagle*, December 11, 1915: 9.

***Brooklyn Daily Eagle* 1921**
"At the De Zayas Gallery." *The Brooklyn Daily Eagle*, February 27, 1921: 34.

***Brooklyn Daily Eagle* 1922**
"Modern Art at Its Best at Montrose [*sic*] Gallery." *The Brooklyn Daily Eagle*, April 9, 1922: 40.

***Brooklyn Daily Eagle* 1923**
"Art Announcements." *The Brooklyn Daily Eagle*, March 25, 1923: 24.

***Brooklyn Daily Eagle* 1936**
"Van Gogh Exhibit Viewed by 5,961 On Closing Day." *The Brooklyn Daily Eagle*, January 6, 1936: 7.

Brown 1963
Brown, Milton W. *The Story of the Armory Show*. [Greenwich, Connecticut]: Joseph H. Hirshhorn Foundation, 1963.

Brown 1988
Brown, Milton W. *The Story of the Armory Show*. New York: Abbeville Press, 1988.

***Bulletin of the Art Institute of Chicago* 1918**
"Library Notes." *Bulletin of the Art Institute of Chicago* 12, 8 (November 1918): 133–34.

***Bulletin of the Art Institute of Chicago* 1921**
"Gifts, Loans and Prizes." *Bulletin of the Art Institute of Chicago* 15, 6 (November–December 1921): 180–81.

***Bulletin of the Art Institute of Chicago* 1922**
"Notes." *Bulletin of the Art Institute of Chicago* 16, 1 (January–February 1922): 11–15.

***Bulletin of the Art Institute of Chicago* 1925**
"The Birch-Bartlett Loan Collection." *Bulletin of the Art Institute of Chicago* 19, 7 (October 1925): 80–82.

***Bulletin of the Cleveland Museum of Art* 1929**
"Lists of Objects in the Exhibition." *The Bulletin of the Cleveland Museum of Art* 16, 9 (November 1929): 159–72, 175.

***Bulletin of the Detroit Institute of Arts* 1923**
"Museum Notes." *Bulletin of the Detroit Institute of Arts of the City of Detroit* 4, 8 (May 1923): 72.

***Bulletin of the Museum of Modern Art* 1941**
B. "Van Gogh's 'Starry Night.'" *The Bulletin of the Museum of Modern Art* 9, 2 (November 1941): 2–3.

***Bulletin of the Pennsylvania Museum of Art* 1928**
"The New Museum of Art Inaugural Exhibition." *Bulletin of the Pennsylvania Museum of Art* 23, 119 (March 1928): 2–31.

***Bulletin of the Pennsylvania Museum of Art* 1929**
Bulletin of the Pennsylvania Museum of Art Bulletin 25, 129 (November 1929): 27–31.

***Bulletin of the Phillips Collection* 1928**
A Bulletin of the Phillips Collection Containing Catalogue and Notes of Interpretation Relating to a Tri-unit Exhibition of Paintings & Sculpture. Washington, DC: Phillips Memorial Gallery, February–May 1928.

Bulliet 1929
Bulliet, C. J. "Current Exhibits in Chicago." *Chicago Evening Post*, October 22, 1929: 2.

[Burroughs] 1922
C.H.B. [Clyde H. Burroughs]. "Exhibit of Ultra Modern Painting." *Bulletin of the Detroit Institute of Arts of the City of Detroit* 3, 5/6 (February and March 1922): 61.

Byrens 1969
Byrens, Ellen. "200,000 Demonstrators March on Wilshire." *Beverly Hills Courier*, November 28, 1969.

C

Caffin 1904
Caffin, Charles H. "The Art Display of Holland at the St. Louis Exposition." *The International Studio* 23, 90 (August 1904): cccxxv–cccxxxi.

***Camera Work* 1912**
"From Van Gogh's Letters." *Camera Work: A Photographic Quarterly* 40 (October 1912): 37–41.

***Chicago Daily Tribune* 1913a**
"Cubists Invade City Today." *Chicago Daily Tribune*, March 21, 1913: 12.

***Chicago Daily Tribune* 1913b**
"Varieties of Modern Art Shown at Chicago Exhibition." *Chicago Daily Tribune*, March 25, 1913: 7.

***Chicago Daily Tribune* 1913c**
"Chicago Artist Starts Revolt." *Chicago Daily Tribune*, March 26, 1913: 15.

***Christian Science Monitor* 1913**
"Art Productions of Many Sorts Shown in International Exhibition." *The Christian Science Monitor*, February 24, 1913, https://www.aaa.si.edu/collections/items/detail/walt-kuhn-scrapbook-press-clippings-documenting-armory-show-vol-2-14643.

***Christian Science Monitor* 1920**
"The Van Gogh Show in New York." *The Christian Science Monitor*, October 25, 1920: 12.

***Christian Science Monitor* 1923**
"New York Art News." *The Christian Science Monitor*, January 23, 1923: 6.

***Cincinnati Enquirer* 1913**
"The Week in Art Circles." *The Cincinnati Enquirer*, June 29, 1913: B8.

***Cincinnati Enquirer* 1921**
"The Week in Art Circles." *The Cincinnati Enquirer*, September 18, 1921: B4.

Colin 1926
Colin, Paul-Émile. *Van Gogh*. New York: Dodd, Mead and Company, 1926.

***Collector and Art Critic* 1906**
The Collector and Art Critic 4, 3 (January 1906): 78–82.

[Cortissoz] 1893
[Cortissoz, Royal]. "Art at the World's Fair VII: Dutch Pictures and Their Good Qualities." *New York Tribune*, June 29, 1893: 2.

Cortissoz 1913a
Cortissoz, Royal. *Art and Common Sense.* New York: Charles Scribner's Sons, 1913.

[Cortissoz] 1913b
[Cortissoz, Royal]. "Matters of Art. Post-Impressionist and Cubist Vagaries. Vincent Van Gogh and His Crudities." *New York Tribune*, February 23, 1913: 6.

Cortissoz 1920
Cortissoz, Royal. "Vincent van Gogh Seen at His Best and His Worst." *New York Tribune,* November 7, 1920: 7.

Cortissoz 1929
Cortissoz, Royal. "The New Museum of Modern Art, French Painting in the Opening Show." *New York Herald Tribune,* November 10, 1929: 10.

***Current Opinion* 1913**
"The Greatest Exhibition of Insurgent Art Ever Held." *Current Opinion* 54, 3 (March 1913): 230.

***Current Opinion* 1921**
"Analyzing the Explosive Quality in Post-Impressionism." *Current Opinion* 71, 6 (December 1921): 789.

Custen 1992
Custen, George F. *Bio/Pics: How Hollywood Constructed Public History*. New Brunswick, New Jersey: Rutgers University Press, 1992.

D

D'Alessandro 2013
D'Alessandro, Stephanie. *Picasso and Chicago: 100 Years, 100 Works*. Chicago: The Art Institute of Chicago, 2013.

F. Davis 1921
Davis, Forest. "Art and Artists." *Detroit Free Press*, September 18, 1921: 8.

G. Davis et al. 1893
Davis, George R. et al. *The World's Columbian Exposition: A Full Description of the Buildings and Exhibits in All Departments*. Philadelphia and Chicago: International Pub. Co., 1893.

Dekkers 1996
Dekkers, Dieuwertje. "'Where are the Dutchmen?' Promoting the Hague School in America, 1875–1900." *Simiolus* 24, 1 (1996): 54–73.

De la Faille, Jacob-Baart, see F

Dell 1913
Dell, Floyd. "Post-Impressionism." *The Chicago Evening Post*, March 28, 1913.

Delliquadri 1994
Delliquadri, Lyn. "A Living Tradition: The Winterbothams and Their Legacy." *The Art Institute of Chicago Museum Studies* 20, 2, The Joseph Winterbotham Collection at The Art Institute of Chicago (1994): 102–10.

***Detroit Free Press* 1922**
"Three Frenchmen and Mary Cassatt." *Detroit Free Press*, February 26, 1922: D4.

***Detroit Free Press* 1929**
"J. B. Neumann Gallery." *Detroit Free Press*, May 5, 1929: 8.

***Detroit News* 1923**
R. P. [probably Reginald Poland]. "An American on Dutch Art." *The Detroit News*, February 4, 1923: 12.

De Vries, G. E., see V

***De Young Muse* 1958a**
De Young Muse 1, 4 (November 1958).

***De Young Muse* 1958b**
De Young Muse 1, 5 (December 1958).

De Zayas, Marius, see Z

***Dial* 1921**
"Comment." *The Dial* 71 (October 1921): 494–96.

Donnell 1986
Donnell, Courtney Graham. "Frederic Clay and Helen Birch Bartlett: The Collectors." *The Art Institute of Chicago Museum Studies* 12, 2, The Helen Birch Bartlett Memorial Collection (1986): 84–101.

Dooley 1935
Dooley, William Germain. "Van Gogh with Full Strength in New York." *Boston Transcript*, November 16, 1935.

Dorn 1990
Dorn, Roland. "The Artistic Reception of Vincent van Gogh's Work—Prologue." In Essen and Amsterdam 1990–91, 189–91.

Dreier 1913
Dreier, Katherine S. "Introduction." In Du Quesne-Van Gogh 1913, xiii–xxiv.

Dumas 2006–2007
Dumas, Ann. "Ambroise Vollard, Patron of the Avant-Garde." In New York, Chicago, and Paris 2006–2007, 2–27.

Du Quesne-Van Gogh 1910
Du Quesne-Van Gogh, Elisabeth. *Vincent van Gogh: Persoonlijke herinneringen aangaande een kunstenaar*. Baarn: J. F. Van de Ven, 1910.

Du Quesne-Van Gogh 1913
Du Quesne-Van Gogh, Elisabeth. *Personal Recollections of Vincent van Gogh*, translated by Katherine S. Dreier, with a foreword by Arthur B. Davies. Boston and New York: Houghton Mifflin, 1913.

E

Eddy 1914
Eddy, Arthur Jerome. *Cubists and Post-Impressionism*. Chicago: A. C. McClurg, 1914.

Edelman 2012
Edelman, Hendrik. *The Netherland-America Foundation, 1921–2011: A History*. New York: The Netherland-America Foundation, 2012.

Erens 1979
Erens, Patricia. *Masterpieces: Famous Chicagoans and Their Paintings*. Chicago: Distributed by Chicago Review Press, 1979.

***Evening Post* 1913**
"International Art. The Sixty-ninth Armory Exhibition Is Fulfilling Its Main Purpose in Stimulating Thought and Ardent Discussion—The Foreign Work. First Notice." *The [New York] Evening Post*, February 20, 1913: 9, http://nyshistoricnewspapers.org/lccn/sn83030384/1913-02-20/ed-1/seq-9.pdf.

***Evening Post* 1915**
"Art Notes." *The [New York] Evening Post*, November 27, 1915: 9, http://nyshistoricnewspapers.org/lccn/sn83030384/1915-11-27/ed-1/seq-9.pdf.

F

De la Faille 1930
Faille, Jacob-Baart de la. *Les Faux Van Gogh*. Paris: G. V. Oest, 1930.

De la Faille 1948
Faille, Jacob-Baart de la. "Een merkwardige zelfportret van Vincent van Gogh." *Phoenix, maandschrift vaor beeldende kunst*, September 1948: 215.

De la Faille 1970
Faille, Jacob-Baart de la. *The Works of Vincent van Gogh: His Paintings and Drawings*. Amsterdam: Meulenhoff, 1970.

De la Faille 1992
Faille, Jacob-Baart de la. *Vincent van Gogh: The Complete Works on Paper: Catalogue Raisonné*. 2 vols. San Francisco: Alan Wofsy Fine Arts, 1992.

R. Feilchenfeldt and Brandis 2002
Feilchenfeldt, Rahel E. and Markus Brandis. *Paul Cassirer Verlag, Berlin, 1898–1933: Eine kommentierte Bibliographie*. Munich: K. G. Saur Verlag, 2002.

W. Feilchenfeldt 1988
Feilchenfeldt, Walter. *Vincent van Gogh & Paul Cassirer, Berlin: The Reception of Van Gogh in Germany from 1901 to 1914*. Cahier Vincent 2. Zwolle: Uitgeverij Waanders, 1988.

W. Feilchenfeldt 1990
Feilchenfeldt, Walter. "Vincent van Gogh—His Collectors and Dealers." In Essen and Amsterdam 1990–91, 39–46.

W. Feilchenfeldt 2005
Feilchenfeldt, Walter. *By Appointment Only: Cézanne, Van Gogh and Some Secrets of Art Dealing: Essays and Lectures*. New York: Thames and Hudson, 2005.

W. Feilchenfeldt 2009
Feilchenfeldt, Walter. *Vincent van Gogh: Die Gemälde, 1886–1890: Händler, Sammler, Ausstellungen. Frühe Provenienzen*. Wädenswil, Switzerland: Nimbus, Kunst und Bücher, 2009.

W. Feilchenfeldt 2013
Feilchenfeldt, Walter. *Vincent van Gogh: The Years in France: Complete Paintings, 1886–1890*. London: Philip Wilson Publishers, 2013.

Field 1920a
Field, Hamilton Easter. "News and Reviews in the Worlds of Music and Art…Van Gogh Exhibition at the Montross Gallery." *The Brooklyn Daily Eagle*, October 31, 1920: 39.

[Field] 1920b
[Field, Hamilton Easter.] "Current Art Exhibitions." *The Arts* 1, 1 (December 4, 1920): 25–48.

Flack 1904
Horace Flack [pseud.]. "Wereldtentoonstelling te St. Louis." *Het nieuws van den dag: Kleine courant*, May 25, 1904: 1.

***Fountain Valley Daily Pilot* 1969**
"Van Gogh on View." *Fountain Valley Daily Pilot*, October 10, 1969.

Fowler 1954
Fowler, Gene. *Minutes of the Last Meeting*. New York: Viking Press, 1954.

Frankenstein 1936a
Frankenstein, Alfred. "A Gesture to Separate Van Gogh's Art from His Luxuriant Biography." *San Francisco Chronicle*, May 3, 1936.

Frankenstein 1936b
Frankenstein, Alfred. "Van Gogh Captures S. F. Interest." *San Francisco Chronicle*, May 25, 1936.

G

Ganz 2006–2007
Ganz, James A. "From Paris to Williamstown: Robert Sterling Clark's Life as a Collector." In Williamstown and New York 2006–2007, 35–121.

Germer 1990
Germer, Stefan. "Traditions and Trends: Taste Patterns in Chicago Collecting." In Prince 1990a, 171–91.

Glasier 1922
Glasier, Jessie C. "Old and New Dutch Paintings of Masters Displayed at Art Museum." *Cleveland Plain Dealer*, December 17, 1922: 71.

J. van Gogh 1987
Gogh, Johan van. "The History of the Collection." In *The Rijksmuseum Vincent van Gogh*, edited by E. van Uitert and M. Hoyle. Amsterdam: Meulenhoff/Landshoff, 1987, 1–8.

Van Gogh Letters 1913
The Letters of a Post-Impressionist: Being the Familiar Correspondence of Vincent van Gogh, translated by Anthony M. Ludovici. Boston and New York: Houghton Mifflin Co., 1913.

Van Gogh Letters 1914
Vincent van Gogh: Brieven aan zijn broeder, published and annotated by his sister-in-law, J. van Gogh-Bonger. 3 vols. Amsterdam: Mij. voor Goede en Goedkoope Lectuur, 1914.

Van Gogh Letters 1927–29
The Letters of Vincent Van Gogh to His Brother, 1872–1886, with a Memoir by His Sister-in-Law, J. van Gogh-Bonger. 2 vols. London: Constable & Co.; Boston and New York: Houghton Mifflin Co., 1927. *Further Letters of Vincent van Gogh to His Brother, 1886–1889*. London: Constable & Co.; Boston and New York: Houghton Mifflin Co., 1929.

Van Gogh Letters 1936
Letters to an Artist: From Vincent van Gogh to Anton Ridder van Rappard, 1881–1885, translated by Rela van Messel, introduction by Walter Pach. New York: Viking Press, 1936.

Van Gogh Letters 1952–54
Verzamelde brieven van Vincent van Gogh. Amsterdam: Wereldbibliotheek, 1952–54.

Van Gogh Letters 2009
Jansen, Leo, Hans Luijten, and Nienke Bakker, eds. (2009), *Vincent van Gogh—The Letters*. Version: December 2010. Amsterdam and The Hague: Van Gogh Museum and Huygens ING, www.vangoghletters.org.

Goodrich 1929a
Goodrich, Lloyd. "About Town: What Some of the Galleries Have to Offer." *The New York Times*, March 24, 1929: 143.

Goodrich 1929b
Goodrich, Lloyd. "Exhibitions." *The Arts* 16, 4 (December 1929): 254–70.

Goodyear 1943
Goodyear, Anson Conger. *The Museum of Modern Art: The First Ten Years*. New York: 1943.

Gregg 1913
Gregg, Frederick James. "Letting in the Light." In *For and Against: Views on the International Exhibition Held in New York and Chicago*, edited by Frederick James Gregg. New York: Association of American Painters and Sculptors, 1913, 17–25.

Groom 2006–2007
Groom, Gloria. "Vollard, the Nabis, and Odilon Redon." In New York, Chicago, and Paris 2006–2007, 82–99.

Groom and Druick 2008
Groom, Gloria and Douglas Druick. *The Age of Impressionism at the Art Institute of Chicago*. Chicago: The Art Institute of Chicago; New Haven: Yale University Press, 2008.

Groom and Shaw 2014
Groom, Gloria and Jill Shaw, eds. *Monet Paintings and Drawings at the Art Institute of Chicago*. Chicago: The Art Institute of Chicago, 2014, https://publications.artic.edu/monet/reader/paintingsanddrawings/section/135470/135470_anchor.

H

Hale 1913
Hale, Edward E. "Vincent van Gogh: Post-Impressionist." *The Dial* 54, 647 (June 1, 1913): 455–58.

Harshe 1933
Harshe, Robert B. "Foreword." In Chicago 1933, xiii–xv.

Hayward 1988
Hayward, Phillip, ed. *Picture This: The Media Representation of Art and Artists*. London: J. Libbey, 1988.

Heijbroek and Wouthuysen 1993
Heijbroek, J. F. and E. L. Wouthuysen. *Kunst, kennis en commercie: De kunsthandelaar J. H. de Bois, 1878–1946*. Amsterdam and Antwerp: Contact Publishers, 1993.

Heil 1958–59
Heil, Walter. "Foreword." In San Francisco and other cities 1958–59, n.p.

Heinich 1996
Heinich, Nathalie. *The Glory of Van Gogh: An Anthropology of Admiration*, translated by Paul Leduc Browne. Princeton: Princeton University Press, 1996.

Hendren 2019
Hendren, Claire. "French Impressionism in the United States' Greater Midwest: The 1907–8 Traveling Exhibition." *Nineteenth-Century Art Worldwide* 18, 1 (Spring 2019), https://doi.org/10.29411/ncaw.2019.18.1.3.

Hendrickson 2013
Hendrickson, Julia V., ed. *Freak Art Scrapbook: Chicago's Armory Show in Print, 1913*. Chicago: Corbett vs. Dempsey, 2013.

Hendriks and Van Tilborgh 2011
Hendriks, Ella and Louis van Tilborgh. *Vincent van Gogh: Paintings, Antwerp and Paris, 1885–1888*, vol. 2, translated by Michael Hoyle. Amsterdam: Van Gogh Museum; London: Lund Humphries, 2011.

Herbert et al. 1984
Herbert, Robert L. et al. *The Société Anonyme and the Dreier Bequest at Yale University: A Catalogue Raisonné*. London and New York: Yale University Press, 1984.

Hirschland and Hirschland Ramage 2008
Hirschland, Ellen B. and Nancy Hirschland Ramage. *The Cone Sisters of Baltimore: Collecting at Full Tilt*. Evanston: Northwestern University Press, 2008.

Howe 1959
Howe, Thomas Carr. "Introduction." In San Francisco 1959, n.p.

Hulsker 1985
Hulsker, Jan. *Lotgenoten: Het leven van Vincent en Theo van Gogh*. Weesp: Agathon, 1985.

Hulsker 1996
Hulsker, Jan. *The New Complete Van Gogh: Paintings, Drawings, Sketches*. Amsterdam: J. M. Meulenhoff; Philadelphia: John Benjamins, 1996.

I

***De Indische Courant* 1938**
"De Van Goghs." *De Indische Courant*, December 3, 1938: 13.

***International Studio* 1921a**
"January in the Galleries: New York City." *The International Studio* 72, 286 (January 1921): 4.

***International Studio* 1921b**
"Second Thoughts." *The International Studio* 74, 293 (August 1921): III–V.

Ives 1904
Ives, Halsey C. "Introduction." In *Illustrations of Selected Works in the Various National Sections of the Department of Art*. St. Louis: The Louisiana Purchase Exposition Company for the Official Catalogue Company, 1904, v–xxix.

J

Jensen 1994
Jensen, Robert. *Marketing Modernism in Fin-de-Siècle Europe*. Princeton: Princeton University Press, 1994.

Jewell 1929a
Jewell, Edward Alden. "Notable French Show." *The New York Times*, March 24, 1929: 142.

Jewell 1929b
Jewell, Edward Alden. "A Museum of Modern Art for New York." *The New York Times*, September 22, 1929: SM7.

Jewell 1929c
Jewell, Edward Alden. "The New Museum of Modern Art Opens. A Superb Showing of Work by Four Pioneers: Cézanne, Gauguin, Van Gogh and Seurat—Contemporary Frenchmen." *The New York Times*, November 10, 1929: X14.

Jewell 1937
Jewell, Edward Alden. "Van Gogh's Works Are Again on View." *The New York Times*, January 20, 1937: 17.

Jewett 1919
Jewett, Eleanor. "Art: Toyland Wonders of American Make Shown at Institute." *Chicago Daily Tribune*, December 14, 1919: C11.

Jewett 1921a
Jewett, Eleanor. "Art and Architecture: New York Exhibit of Paintings Is Warmly Assailed." *Chicago Daily Tribune*, September 11, 1921: F8.

Jewett 1921b
Jewett, Eleanor. "Art and Architecture: 'The Appian Way' Is Highlight of Lachman Exhibit." *Chicago Daily Tribune*, November 27, 1921: G12.

Jewett 1922
Jewett, Eleanor. "Art and Artists: Ansfeld Drawings of Opera Settings Given to Institute." *Chicago Daily Tribune*, January 15, 1922: H5.

Jewett 1923
Jewett, Eleanor. "Art and Artists: Institute Opens Another Gallery to Japanese Art." *Chicago Daily Tribune*, September 23, 1923: F4.

Jewett 1928
Jewett, Eleanor. "Exhibit Depicts Ways to Link Architecture with Horticulture." *Chicago Daily Tribune*, October 20, 1928: 19.

Jewett 1929
Jewett, Eleanor. "Much Beauty among Modern Paintings in Current Loan Exhibit." *Chicago Daily Tribune*, January 5, 1929: 15.

Johnston 1992
Johnston, William R. "Alfred Sisley and the Early Interest in Impressionism in America, 1865–1913." In Cahn, Isabelle et al. *Alfred Sisley*. New Haven: Yale University Press, 1992, 55–67.

K

***Kansas City Star* 1931**
"In Gallery and Studio." *The Kansas City Star* 51, 199 (April 4, 1931): E.

Kantor 2002
Kantor, Sybil Gordon. *Alfred H. Barr Jr. and the Intellectual Origins of the Museum of Modern Art*. Cambridge: MIT Press, 2002.

Kelly 2012–13
Kelly, Simon. "'A Big, Good Enterprise': Van Gogh and His Markets." In Denver 2012–13, 55–69.

[Kirkland] 1921
Mme. X [Caroline Kirkland]. "News of Chicago Society." *Chicago Daily Tribune*, November 20, 1921: G4.

[Kirkland] 1924
Mme. X [Caroline Kirkland]. "News of Chicago Society." *Chicago Daily Tribune*, September 21, 1924: G1–G3.

[Kirkland] 1929
Mme. X [Caroline Kirkland]. "Only Few More Hunting Days Left This Fall." *Chicago Daily Tribune*, November 17, 1929: H1–H2.

Kōdera and Rosenberg 1993
Kōdera, Tsukasa and Yvette Rosenberg, eds. *The Mythology of Vincent van Gogh*. Tokyo: Asahi National Broadcasting Co., Ltd. and John Benjamins B. V., 1993.

Koldehoff 2003
Koldehoff, Stefan. *Van Gogh: Mythos und Wirklichkeit*. Cologne: DuMont Literatur und Kunst Verlag, 2003.

Koldehoff 2006–2007
Koldehoff, Stefan. "Van Gogh in Germany until 1918." In Amsterdam and New York 2006–2007, 168–77.

Koldehoff 2017
Koldehoff, Stefan. "Marketing Modernism: The Thannhauser Gallery and Its Clients." In Koldehoff and Stolwijk 2017, 56–81.

Koldehoff and Stolwijk 2017
Koldehoff, Stefan and Chris Stolwijk, eds. *The Thannhauser Gallery: Marketing Van Gogh*. Brussels: Mercatorfonds; Amsterdam: Van Gogh Museum, 2017.

Krul 2006
Krul, W. E. "De Haagse School en het nationale landschap." *Bijdragen en Mededelingen betreffende de Geschiedenis der Nederlanden* 121, 4 (2006): 620–49, https://doi.org/10.18352/bmgn-lchr.652.

Kruty 1987
Kruty, Paul. "Arthur Jerome Eddy and His Collection: Prelude and Postscript to the Armory Show." *Arts Magazine* 61, 6 (February 1987): 40–47.

L

Landon 1913
Landon, Herman. "Hark! Hark! The Critics Bark! The CUBISTS Are Coming to Town with CUBIST Hags and CUBIST Nags and Even a Cubist Gown!" *Jones's Daily Magazine: The Sunday Chicago Record-Herald* 1, 63 (March 23, 1913): 2.

Laurvik 1915
Laurvik, J. Nilsen. "The Art of the Netherlands." In San Francisco 1915, 102–103.

Laurvik 1916
Laurvik, J. Nilsen. "Introduction." In De Vries 1916, 1–18.

Leeman 1990
Leeman, Fred. "Van Gogh's Posthumous Rise to Fame in the Low Countries—Holland and Belgium." In Essen and Amsterdam 1990–91, 207–24.

Lees 2006–2007
Lees, Sarah. "List of Works Owned by Stephen Carlton Clark." In Williamstown and New York 2006–2007, 317–48.

***Life* 1948**
"Art in Hollywood." *Life* 24, 9 (March 1, 1948): 64–69.

Lloyd 1920
Lloyd, David. "At the Art Galleries; Large Group of Van Gogh's Paintings on Exhibition. Scorn Will Be Wasted Upon This Remarkable Artist's Work and Much Incense Will Be Burned—His Output Large Before He Died by His Own Hand." *The [New York] Evening Post*, October 23, 1920: 33.

***Los Angeles County Museum Quarterly* 1948**
Los Angeles County Museum Quarterly 7, 1 (Spring 1948).

***Los Angeles Examiner* 1959**
Los Angeles Examiner, January 19, 1959.

***Los Angeles Times* 2007**
"Van Gogh Show." The Daily Mirror Los Angeles History (blog), *Los Angeles Times*, June 21, 2007, https://latimesblogs.latimes.com/thedailymirror/2007/06/van_gogh_visits.html.

Loucheim 1946
Loucheim, Aline B. "Buddy de Sylva: Gift to Hollywood." *The Art News* 45, 7 (1946): 28–33, 53.

Lowrey 2007
Lowrey, Carol. *A Legacy of Art: Paintings and Sculptures by Artist Life Members of the National Arts Club*. New York and Manchester: National Arts Club, 2007.

Luijten 2019
Luijten, Hans. *Alles voor Vincent: Jo Bonger—een leven met Van Gogh*. Amsterdam: Prometheus, 2019.

M

***De Maasbode* 1936**
"Van Gogh in Amerika." *De Maasbode*, January 26, 1936.

Macbeth Gallery 1913
The Macbeth Gallery. *Exhibition of Paintings by Katherine S. Dreier.* New York: The Macbeth Gallery, 1913.

MacColl 1913
MacColl, W. D. "The International Exhibition of Modern Art: An Impression." *Forum* 1 (July 1913): 24–36.

Manheim 1989
Manheim, Ron. "The 'Germanic' van Gogh: A Case Study of Cultural Annexation." *Simiolus* 19, 4 (1989): 277–88.

Marceau 1930
Marceau, Henri Gabriel. "Nineteenth Century French Painting." *Bulletin of the Pennsylvania Museum of Art* 26, 137 (December 1930): 4–13.

Marcereau DeGalan 2021
Marcereau DeGalan, Aimee, ed. *French Paintings and Pastels, 1600–1945: The Collections of the Nelson-Atkins Museum of Art.* Kansas City: The Nelson-Atkins Museum of Art, 2021, https//doi: 10.37764/78973.

Marius 1903
Marius, G. H. *De Hollandsche schilderkunst in de XIXe eeuw*. The Hague: Martinus Nijhoff, 1903.

Marius 1907
Marius, G. H. "Isographische Reproducties van het Atelier Van Meurs en Van Gogh." *Het Nieuws van den Dag*, October 28, 1907: 6.

Marshall 2018
Marshall, Jennifer Jane. "Routes to Modernism, 1913–1943." In Taft and Cozzolino 2018, 57–93.

Martinez 1993
Martinez, Andrew. "A Mixed Reception for Modernism: The 1913 Armory Show at the Art Institute of Chicago." *The Art Institute of Chicago Museum Studies* 19, 1, One Hundred Years at the Art Institute: A Centennial Celebration (1993): 30–57, 102–105.

McBride 1920a
McBride, Henry. "Exhibition of Works of Vincent Van Gogh Touches All Phases of Artist's Career." *The New York Herald*, October 24, 1920: section 3, p. 8.

McBride 1920b
McBride, Henry. "Modern Forms: Van Gogh in America." *The Dial* 69 (December 1920): 631–33.

McBride 1921
McBride, Henry. "News and Reviews of the World of Art…Cezanne, Van Goghs, Others." *The New York Herald*, February 27, 1921: section 2, p. 5.

McCarthy 2011
McCarthy, Laurette E. *Walter Pach (1883–1958): The Armory Show and the Untold Story of Modern Art in America*. University Park: Pennsylvania State University Press, 2011.

McCarthy 2013
McCarthy, Laurette E. "Rediscovering Van Gogh in the 1913 Armory Show." Archives of American Art Blog, September 4, 2013, https://www.aaa.si.edu/blog/2013/09/rediscovering-van-gogh-the-1913-armory-show.

McCauley 1913
McCauley, Lena M. "Art and Artists." *Chicago Evening Post*, March 27, 1913.

McMahon 1935
McMahon, A. Philip. "Fame After Death." December 21, 1935: 16, 19.

McNulty 2015
McNulty, Thomas. *Errol Flynn. The Life and Career*. Jefferson, North Carolina: McFarland and Company, 2015.

Mechlin 1929
Mechlin, Leila. "Notes of Art and Artists: The International Exhibition of Paintings in Pittsburgh. New York Galleries Are Making Unusual Showings—Local Notes." *The [Washington, DC] Sunday Star,* November 24, 1929: 4, https://chroniclingamerica.loc.gov/data/batches/dlc_morton_ver01/data/sn83045462/0028065999A/1929112401/0539.pdf.

Meedendorp 2007
Meedendorp, Teio. *Drawings and Prints of Vincent van Gogh in the Collection of the Kröller-Müller Museum*. Otterlo: Kröller-Müller Museum, 2007.

Meier-Graefe 1908
Meier-Graefe, Julius. *Modern Art: Being a Contribution to Modern Æsthetics*, translated by F. Simmonds and G. W. Chrystal. 2 vols. London: W. Heinemann; New York: G. P. Putnam's Sons, 1908.

Meier-Graefe 1910
Meier-Graefe, Julius. *Vincent van Gogh: Mit 40 Abbildungen und dem Faksimile eines Briefes*. Munich: R. Piper & Co. Verlag, 1910.

Meier-Graefe 1921
Meier-Graefe, Julius. *Vincent*. 2 vols. Munich: R. Piper & Co. Verlag, 1921.

Meier-Graefe 1922
Meier-Graefe, Julius. *Vincent van Gogh: A Biographical Study*, translated by John Holroyd Reece. 2 vols. London, Liverpool, and Boston: The Medici Society, 1922.

***Metropolitan Museum of Art Bulletin* 1921**
W.M.I. Jr. "French Prints and Drawings of the Last Hundred Years." *The Metropolitan Museum of Art Bulletin* 16, 6 (June 1921): 126–32.

Meyer-Riefstahl 1910a
Meyer-Riefstahl, Rudolf. "Vincent Van Gogh-I." *The Burlington Magazine* 18, 92 (November 1910): 91–93, 96–99.

Meyer-Riefstahl 1910b
Meyer-Riefstahl, Rudolf. "Vincent Van Gogh-II: Van Gogh's Style in Relation to Nature." *The Burlington Magazine* 18, 93 (December 1910): 154–57, 160–62.

Michel 2019
Michel, Thomas. "Comment la découverte de dessins de Van Gogh par un Commissaire priseur de Monaco devient un grand film de cinéma." *Monaco-Matin*, March 6, 2019, https://www.monacomatin.mc/vie-locale/comment-la-decouverte-de-dessins-de-van-gogh-par-un-commissaire-priseur-de-monaco-devient-un-grand-film-de-cinema-303816.

Milliken 1926
Milliken, William Mathewson. "Fifty Years of French Art." *The Arts* 10, 6 (December 1926): 336–38.

[Milliken] 1929
W.M.M. [William Mathewson Milliken]. "French Art Since Eighteen Hundred." *The Bulletin of the Cleveland Museum of Art* 16, 9 (November 1929): 155–57.

***Modern Art* 1893**
"Some Impressions of the Art Exhibit at the Fair. I: The First View." *Modern Art* 1, 3 (Summer 1893): n.p.

***Modern School* 1918**
"Extracts from the Letters of Vincent van Gogh." *The Modern School*, July 1918: 194–203.

***Modern School* 1919**
"Extracts from the Letters of Vincent van Gogh." *The Modern School*, August 1919: 215–23.

Molnos and Geskó 2006–2007
Molnos, Péter and Judit Geskó. "Vincent van Gogh's Works in Hungary." In Budapest 2006–2007, 143–67.

Monroe 1913a
Monroe, Harriet. "Clark's Art Gains in Style and Aim." *Chicago Daily Tribune*, January 19, 1913: B4.

Monroe 1913b
Monroe, Harriet. "Davidson Sculpture Proves That Artist Has Ideas." *Chicago Sunday Tribune*, March 23, 1913: B5.

Monroe 1913c
Monroe, Harriet. "Art Exhibition Opens in Chicago." *Chicago Daily Tribune*, March 25, 1913: 7.

Monroe 1913d
Monroe, Harriet. "A Live Exhibit at the Art Institute: Visitors' Opinions Strong." *Chicago Daily Tribune*, March 30, 1913: B5.

***Museum Work* 1921**
"News from Art Museums." *Museum Work* 4, 1 (July–August 1921): 9–15.

N

Naifeh and Smith 2011
Naifeh, Steven and Gregory White Smith. *Van Gogh: The Life*. New York: Random House, 2011.

Nathanson 1985
Nathanson, Carol A. "The American Reaction to London's First Grafton Show." *Archives of American Art Journal* 25, 3 (1985): 2–10.

***New York Evening Telegram* 1920**
"French Art of the Great Show." *New York Evening Telegram*, May 10, 1920.

***New York Herald* 1922a**
"The American Art Association Will Hold during January and February the Following Very Important Unrestricted Public Sales of Art and Literary Properties." *The New York Herald*, January 1, 1922: section 2, p. 3.

***New York Herald* 1922b**
"Entire Kelekian Art Collection Brings $254,870." *The New York Herald*, February 21, 1922: 8.

***New York Post* 1950**
New York Post, March 15, 1950.

***New York Sun* 1908**
"Eight Painters: First Article." *New York Sun*, February 9, 1908: 8.

***New York Times* 1911**
"News and Notes of the Art World." *The New York Times*, December 31, 1911: SM15.

***New York Times* 1912**
"Art at Home and Abroad: Some Typical Pictures by Van Gogh, the Post Impressionist, Whose Works Will Be Exhibited Here This Season." *The New York Times*, September 15, 1912: SM15.

***New York Times* 1913**
"Art at Home and Abroad: Next Month's Exhibition of the Association of American Painters and Sculptors Especially Interesting as an Indication of National Progress in Creative Art." *The New York Times*, January 5, 1913: SM15.

***New York Times* 1915**
"Art Notes." *The New York Times*, December 5, 1915: E2.

***New York Times* 1921a**
"Cretan Art on View." *The New York Times*, August 11, 1921: 8.

***New York Times* 1921b**
"Panel Enters into Art War Here." *The New York Times*, September 8, 1921: 11.

***New York Times* 1922a**
"Cézanne Leads the French Modernists." *The New York Times*, February 1, 1922: 27.

***New York Times* 1922b**
"World of Art: Exhibitions and Still Exhibitions." *The New York Times*, April 9, 1922: 54.

***New York Times* 1923a**
"Old Masters Exhibition: Dutch and Flemish Paintings to Be Shown at Anderson's." *The New York Times,* March 9, 1923: 14.

***New York Times* 1923b**
"Art: Exhibitions of the Week—Foreign Notes." *The New York Times*, April 1, 1923: X7.

***New York Times* 1923c**
"Liner's Passengers Drink 'Exempt' Quarts." *The New York Times*, April 8, 1923: E1.

***New York Times* 1924a**
"Art: Exhibitions of the Week—Independents Show." *The New York Times*, March 16, 1924: X10.

***New York Times* 1924b**
"The World of Art." *The New York Times*, April 20, 1924: SM12.

***New York Times* 1926**
"52 Picasso Paintings Sold." *The New York Times*, January 10, 1926: E11.

***New York Times* 1927a**
"Seen in the New York Times Galleries." *The New York Times*, March 20, 1927: X10.

***New York Times* 1927b**
"Recalls Art Tragedy." *The New York Times*, April 12, 1927: 45.

***New York Times* 1928a**
"Landscape Odyssey from Primitives to Moderns." *The New York Times*, January 1, 1928: X13.

***New York Times* 1928b**
"Palettes Old and New." *The New York Times*, March 4, 1928: 128.

***New York Times* 1928c**
"Art in Other Cities." *The New York Times*, July 22, 1928: 98.

***New York Times* 1928d**
"Work of Many Masters." *The New York Times*, September 30, 1928: 130.

***New York Times* 1928e**
"Masterpieces of Modern French Art from the Chester Dale Collection on Exhibition for the Benefit of the French Hospital at the Wildenstein Galleries, Beginning Tomorrow." *The New York Times*, October 14, 1928: F2.

***New York Times* 1928f**
"Goya and Modern Art." *The New York Times*, October 21, 1928: 132.

***New York Times* 1929**
J. K. "A Round of Galleries." *The New York Times*, January 20, 1929: X13.

***New York Times* 1935a**
"Toledo Museum Acquires Here the Landscape 'Le Champ de Ble.'" *The New York Times*, February 12, 1935: 19.

***New York Times* 1935b**
"French Paintings Go to Ohio Museum." *The New York Times*, February 17, 1935: N2.

***New York Times* 1936a**
"Art Show Sets Record." *The New York Times*, January 6, 1936: 15.

***New York Times* 1936b**
"Chicago Beholds Van Gogh." *The New York Times*, August 30, 1936: X7.

***New York Times Magazine* 1915a**
"Art at Home and Abroad: Figure Subjects, Landscapes, Still Life by Van Gogh at the Modern Gallery." *The New York Times Magazine*, November 28, 1915: 17.

***New York Times Magazine* 1915b**
"Art at Home and Abroad: An Army of Prints and Drawings in the Field." *The New York Times Magazine*, December 12, 1915: 21–22.

***New York Tribune* 1921**
"Greek Art of Fifth Century B.C. to be Shown At Museum of Art." *New York Tribune*, August 11, 1921: 11, https://chroniclingamerica.loc.gov/lccn/sn83030214/1921-08-11/ed-1/seq-11.pdf.

Nicholas 1995
Nicholas, Lynn H. *The Rape of Europa: The Fate of Europe's Treasures in the Third Reich and Second World War*. New York: Penguin Random House, 1995.

***Nieuwe Rotterdamsche Courant* 1920**
"Van Gogh in Amerika en Mengelberg op komst." *De Nieuwe Rotterdamsche Courant*, December 17, 1920, Avondblad (Evening edition): B9.

***Nieuwe Rotterdamsche Courant* 1921**
"De filisters." *De Nieuwe Rotterdamsche Courant*, October 19, 1921, Avondblad (Evening edition): B1.

***Nieuwe Tilburgsche Courant* 1921**
"Kunst en Letteren. Hollandsche kunst naar Amerika." *Nieuwe Tilburgsche Courant*, March 5, 1921: 2.

O

Olson 2017
Olson, Liesl. *Chicago Renaissance: Literature and Art in the Midwest Metropolis*. New Haven: Yale University Press, 2017.

Op de Coul 2002
Op de Coul, Martha. "In Search of Van Gogh's Nuenen Studio: The Oldenzeel Exhibitions of 1903." *Van Gogh Museum Journal,* edited by Chris Stolwijk, 2002: 104–19.

P

Pach 1920a
Pach, Walter. "Vincent van Gogh." *The International Studio* 72, 284 (November 1920): xiii–xx.

Pach 1920b
Pach, Walter. "A Modern Artist." *The Freeman,* December 8, 1920: 302–303.

Pach 1936a
Pach, Walter. "Introduction." In Van Gogh Letters 1936, vii–xxi.

Pach 1936b
Pach, Walter. *Vincent Van Gogh, 1853–1890: A Study of the Artist and His Work in Relation to His Times.* New York: Artbook Museum, 1936.

Parker 1924
Parker, Robert Allerton. "La Vie tragique de Vincent van Gogh, par Louis Piérard." *The Arts* 6, 5 (November 1924): 295–96.

***Parnassus* 1934**
"A Descriptive Calendar of the New York Galleries." *Parnassus* 6, 3 (March 1934): 26–33.

***Parnassus* 1936**
Advertisement. *Parnassus* 8, 1 (January 1936): 21.

***Het Parool* 1949**
"Van Gogh-collectie naar Amerika." *Het Parool*, September 26, 1949: 5.

Patry 2015
Patry, Sylvie, ed. *Inventing Impressionism: Paul Durand-Ruel and the Modern Art Market.* London: National Gallery Company; [New Haven, Connecticut]: Distributed by Yale University Press, 2015.

Pattison 1913
Pattison, James William. "Art in an Unknown Tongue." *The Fine Arts Journal* 28, 5 (May 1913): 292–307.

Peck 1991
Peck, William H. *The Detroit Institute of Arts: A Brief History*. Detroit: Detroit Institute of Arts, distributed by Wayne State University Press, 1991.

Perlman 2002
Perlman, Bennard B. *American Artists, Authors, and Collectors: The Walter Pach Letters, 1906–1958.* Albany: State University of New York Press, 2002.

Phillips 1926
Phillips, Duncan. *A Collection in the Making*. New York: E. Weyhe; Washington, DC: Phillips Memorial Gallery, 1926.

Pickvance 1970
Pickvance, Ronald. "Van Gogh and America." *Lithopinion* 5, 4 (1970): 64–74.

Piérard 1925
Piérard, Louis. *The Tragic Life of Vincent van Gogh*, translated by Herbert Garland. Boston and New York: Houghton Mifflin Company, 1925.

[Poland] 1923a
R. P. [Reginald Poland]. "An American on Dutch Art." *The Detroit News*, February 4, 1923: 12.

[Poland] 1923b
R. P. [Reginald Poland]. "Modern Paintings Acquired." *Bulletin of the Detroit Institute of Arts of the City of Detroit* 5, 1 (October 1923): 3–7.

Pollock 1980
Pollock, Griselda. "Artists, Mythologies and Media—Genius, Madness and Art History." *Screen* 21, 3 (Autumn 1980): 57–96.

Pollock 2001
Pollock, Griselda. "Crows, Blossoms and Lust for Death." In *Looking Back to the Future: Essays on Art, Life and Death*. Amsterdam: OPA, 2001, 277–309.

Pope 1930
Pope, Arthur. "French Paintings in the Collection of John T. Spaulding." *The Art News* 28, 30 (April 26, 1930): 97–112.

Prince 1990a
Prince, Sue Ann, ed. *The Old Guard and the Avant-Garde: Modernism in Chicago, 1910–1940*. Chicago: University of Chicago Press, 1990.

Prince 1990b
Prince, Sue Ann. "Chicago Critics Take On Modernism." In Prince 1990a, 95–117.

Prins 2016–17
Prins, Laura. "Undergrowth with Two Figures." In Cincinnati 2016–17, 15–21.

R

Rabinow 2000
Rabinow, Rebecca A. "Modern Art Comes to The Metropolitan: The 1921 Exhibition of 'Impressionist and Post-Impressionist Paintings.'" *Apollo* 152 (2000): 3–12.

Rabinow and Warman 2006–2007
Rabinow, Rebecca A. and Jayne S. Warman. "Selected Chronology." In New York, Chicago, and Paris 2006–2007, 275–304.

Rewald 1957
Rewald, John. "Introduction." In Los Angeles 1957, 7–9.

Rewald 1986
Rewald, John. *Studies in Post-Impressionism*, edited by Irene Gordon and Frances Weitzenhoffer. New York: Harry N. Abrams, 1986.

Rewald 1989
Rewald, John with Frances Weitzenhoffer. *Cézanne and America: Dealers, Collectors, Artists and Critics, 1891–1921*. London: Thames and Hudson, 1989.

Riopelle 2006
Riopelle, Christopher. "American Artists in France / French Art in America." In Adler 2006, 207–22.

Robins 2010
Robins, Anna Gruetzner. "Manet and the Post-Impressionists: A Checklist of the Exhibition." *The Burlington Magazine* 152, 1293 (December 2010): 782–93.

Robinson 1941
Robinson, Edward G. "The Most Moving Pictures." *The Art News*, July 1941: 19, 28.

Robinson 1973
Robinson, Edward G. *All My Yesterdays: An Autobiography*. New York: Hawthorn Books, 1973.

Rogers 1931
Rogers, M. R. "Exhibition of Paintings & Prints by the Masters of Post-Impressionism." *Bulletin of the City Art Museum of St. Louis*, Supplement: Exhibition of Paintings & Prints by the Masters of Post-Impressionism 16 (April 1931): 1–11.

Rovers 2010
Rovers, Eva. *De eeuwigheid verzameld: Helene Kröller-Müller (1869–1939)*. Amsterdam: Bert Bakker Publisher, 2010.

De Ruiter 2000
Ruiter, Peter de. *A. M. Hammacher. Kunst als levensessentie*. Baarn, The Netherlands: De Prom, 2000.

Rydell 1993
Rydell, Robert W. *World of Fairs: The Century of Progress Expositions*. Chicago: University of Chicago Press, 1993.

S

Saber 1925
Saber, Gai. "Postscripts." *The Arts* 7, 3 (March 1925): 180.

Salinger 1933
Salinger, Margaretta M. "This Year's Yield." *Parnassus* 5, 4 (May 1933): 23–26.

***San Bernardino Sun* 1969**
"Van Gogh Exhibit Opens Oct. 15 at L.A. Museum." *San Bernardino Sun*, October 5, 1969.

***San Francisco Chronicle* 1936**
"Van Gogh Show to Be Open at Night." *San Francisco Chronicle*, May 10, 1936.

***San Francisco Chronicle* 1939**
"14 Van Gogh Canvases Go On View." *San Francisco Chronicle*, April 12, 1939.

Schaefer 2012
Schaefer, Barbara. "Sonderbundausstellung 1912: Rekonstruktion." In Cologne 2012, 533–617.

Scott and Rutkoff 1999
Scott, William B. and Peter M. Rutkoff. *New York Modern: The Arts and the City*. Baltimore and London: The Johns Hopkins University Press, 1999.

Seldis 1969
Seldis, Henry J. "'Lust for Death' in Artistic Drive of Vincent van Gogh." *Los Angeles Times*, October 19, 1969.

Shaw and Chudzicka 2008
Shaw, Jill and Dorota Chudzicka. "Impressionism and Post-Impressionism in Chicago." In Groom and Druick 2008, 10–25.

Simons 1921
Simons, Hi. "At Chicago." *The Arts* 2, 2 (November 1921): 95–98.

Smith 1993
Smith, John W. "The Nervous Profession: Daniel Catton Rich and the Art Institute of Chicago, 1927–1958." *The Art Institute of Chicago Museum Studies* 19, 1, One Hundred Years at the Art Institute: A Centennial Celebration (1993): 58–79, 105–107.

***Soerabaijasch Handelsblad* 1936**
"Propaganda voor Holland in Amerika. Van Gogh-expositie trekt veel publiek. Ivens' filmproducten maken goeden indruk." *Soerabaijasch Handelsblad*, May 2, 1936: Sheet II [16], see www.delpher.nl.

Soth 1994
Soth, Lauren. "Vincent van Gogh Reads Harriet Beecher Stowe." *Word and Image* 10, 2 (April–June 1994): 156–62.

Speyer 1922
Speyer, Edward. "The Wild Men Have Arrived: Institute of Arts Show Has Beautiful Pictures, but Is Mostly Otherwise." *The Detroit News*, March 5, 1922: 12.

Stein 2005
Stein, Susan A. "The Paper Trail." In Amsterdam and New York 2005, 21–39.

Sterling et al. 1966
Sterling, Charles et al., eds. *French Paintings: Catalogue of the Collection of the Metropolitan Museum of Art*, vol. 2. New York: The Metropolitan Museum of Art, 1966.

K. Sterne 1930
Sterne, Katherine. "New Notes." *Parnassus* 2, 6 (October 1930): 46.

M. Sterne 1980
Sterne, Margaret Heiden. *The Passionate Eye: The Life of William R. Valentiner*. Detroit: Wayne State University Press, 1980.

Stieglitz 1921
Stieglitz, Alfred. "Regarding the Modern French Masters Exhibition: A Letter." *The Brooklyn Museum Quarterly* 8, 3 (July 1921): 106–13.

Stolwijk 2006–2007
Stolwijk, Chris. "Such Expression and Atmosphere and Sentiment: Van Gogh's Early Ideas about the Expressive Power of Painting." In Amsterdam and New York 2006–2007, 29–36.

Stolwijk 2018
Stolwijk, Chris. "In vertrouwen aangeboden: Nederlandse kunst in internationale context 1800–1940." Inaugural lecture, Utrecht University, September 11, 2018, 28, https://issuu.com/humanitiesuu/docs/oratie-chris-stolwijk_2018_totaal.

Stolwijk and Veenenbos 2002
Stolwijk, Chris and Han Veenenbos. *The Accountbook of Theo van Gogh and Jo van Gogh-Bonger*. Amsterdam: Van Gogh Museum; Leiden: Primavera Pers, 2002.

Stone 1934
Stone, Irving. *Lust for Life: The Novel of Vincent van Gogh*. London, New York, Toronto: Longmans, Green and Co., 1934.

Stone 1935
Stone, Irving. "Van Gogh: Flaming Painter of Flaming Art." *The New York Times Magazine*, October 27, 1935: 12.

Stone 1936
Stone, Irving. "Van Gogh Exhibition Is Symbol in Pigment of a Spiritual Epic." *San Francisco Chronicle*, April 26, 1936.

Stone 1937
Stone, Irving, ed. *Dear Theo: The Autobiography of Vincent Van Gogh*. Boston: Houghton Mifflin Co., 1937.

Stott 1998
Stott, Annette. *Holland Mania: The Unknown Dutch Period in American Art and Culture*. Woodstock, New York: The Overlook Press, 1998.

Stuart 1920
Stuart, Evelyn Marie. "Chicago." *American Art News* 18, 11 (January 3, 1920): 5.

***The Sun* 1914**
"What is Happening in the World of Art." *The [New York] Sun,* February 22, 1914: 2.

***The Sun* 1915**
"Current News of Art and Exhibitions." *The [New York] Sun*, November 28, 1915: 7.

Sweet 1966
Sweet, Frederick A. "Great Chicago Collectors." *Apollo* 84, 55 (September 1966): 190–207.

T

Taft and Cozzolino 2018
Taft, Maggie and Robert Cozzolino, eds. *Art in Chicago: A History from the Fire to Now*. Chicago: University of Chicago Press, 2018.

Taylor 2002
Taylor, Henry M. *Rolle des Lebens: Die Filmbiographie als narratives System*. Marburg: Schüren, 2002.

***De Telegraaf* 1921**
"De Nederlandsche Tentoonstelling in New York: Dr. Barnouw over Vincent van Gogh." *De Telegraaf*, May 26, 1921, Avondblad (Evening edition): 9.

***De Telegraaf* 1923**
G. S. "De collectie Goudstikker. De Amerikaansche ontvangst." *De Telegraaf*, May 3, 1923: 7.

***De Telegraaf* 1949**
"Politie-Escorte voor 120 Van Goghs. Schilderijen te New York aangekomen." *De Telegraaf*, October 4, 1949: 1.

Ten Berge, see B

Thompson 2015
Thompson, Jennifer A. "Durand-Ruel and America." In Patry 2015, 134–51.

Thompson 2018
Thompson, Jennifer A. "The John G. Johnson Collection from 1917 to the Present." In *The John G. Johnson Collection: A History and Selected Works*, edited by Christopher D. M. Atkins. Philadelphia: Philadelphia Museum of Art, 2018, https://doi.org/10.29075/9780876332764/1917-to-the-Present/1.

Thomson 2012
Thomson, Richard. *Art of the Actual: Naturalism and Style in Early Third Republic France 1880–1900*. New Haven and London: Yale University Press, 2012.

Tibbe 2016
Tibbe, Lieske. "Holland op z'n mooist in Amerika: De Wereldtentoonstelling van 1876 in Philadelphia." *De Negentiende Eeuw* 40, 4 (2016): 334–50.

***De Tijd* 1949**
"New York stroomt naar Van Gogh." *De Tijd*, October 24, 1949: 3.

Van Tilborgh 2011
Tilborgh, Louis van. "The History of the Collection: Exchanges, Gifts, Sales and the Sacrosanct Core." In Hendriks and Van Tilborgh 2011, 17–36.

Van Tilborgh and Van Maanen 2015
Tilborgh, Louis van and Oda van Maanen. "Dominant and Disappearing Violets: Van Gogh's *View of Auvers-sur-Oise* Revisited." *Manual* 4 (Spring 2015): 24–33.

***Time* 1949**
"Vincent by Candlelight." *Time*, February 14, 1949: 58.

Tromp 2010
Tromp, Henk. *A Real Van Gogh: How the Art World Struggles with Truth*. Amsterdam: Amsterdam University Press, 2010.

Tross 1933
Tross, Ernst L. "Preface." In Los Angeles 1933b, n.p.

***Trouw* 1949**
"New York opende Van Gogh tentoonstelling: Buitengewoon grote belangstelling." *Trouw*, November 7, 1949: 5.

Troyen 2013
Troyen, Carol. "'Unwept, Unhonored, and Unsung': The Armory Show in Boston." In New York 2013–14, 379–91.

V

***Het Vaderland* 1921**
"Vincent van Gogh." *Het Vaderland*, January 25, 1921, Avondblad (Evening edition): B6.

Van Gogh, see G

Van Tilborgh, see T

Valentiner 1931
Valentiner, Wilhelm R. "Foreword." In Detroit 1922, 3.

Vincent and Lee 2006–2007
Vincent, Gilbert T. and Sarah Lee. "A Life with Art: Stephen Carlton Clark as Collector and Philanthropist." In Williamstown and New York 2006–2007, 123–99.

***Het Volk* 1905**
J. F. A. "Kunst en Letteren. Vincent van Gogh." *Het Volk: dagblad voorde arbeiderspartij* 6, 1624 (July 20, 1905): n.p.

***De Volkskrant* 1949**
"Grootse ontvangst voor Van Goghs." *De Volkskrant*, October 5, 1949: 3.

***De Volkskrant* 1950**
"Van Gogh populairste schilder in Amerika." *De Volkskrant*, January 17, 1950: n.p., see www.delpher.nl.

***De Volksvriend* 1921**
"Nederlandsche kunst in Amerika." *De Volksvriend* 27 (April 7, 1921): 41.

***Vossische Zeitung* 1901**
Vossische Zeitung 605, 1 (December 28, 1901), Beilage (Supplement).

De Vries 1936
De Vries, G. E. *Panama-California International Exposition: The Netherlands (Holland) Art Exhibition*. San Diego, 1916.

W

Walker 1993
Walker, John A. *Art and Artists on Screen*. Manchester: Manchester University Press, 1993.

***Washington Post* 1929**
"New Order in Paintings Shown Here." *The Washington Post*, May 12, 1929: 9.

Watson 1921
Watson, Forbes. "Note." In Chicago 1921, n.p.

Watson 1923
Watson, Forbes. "The Barnes Foundation." *The Arts* 3, 1 (January 1923): 9–22.

Watson 1926
Watson, Forbes. "A Note on the Birch-Bartlett Collection." *The Arts* 9, 6 (June 1926): 303–13.

Watson 1928a
Watson, Forbes. "Recent Exhibitions." *The Arts* 13, 1 (January 1928): 33–44.

Watson 1928b
Watson, Forbes. "The Logic of Taste." *The Arts* 14, 3 (September 1928): 119–20.

[Watson] 1928c
F. W. [Forbes Watson]. "Exhibitions in New York." *The Arts* 14, 5 (November 1928): 267–68.

Watson 1929
Watson, Forbes. "The Museum of Modern Art." *The Arts* 16, 3 (November 1929): 147–48.

Watson 1930
Watson, Forbes. "In the Galleries." *The Arts* 16, 9 (May 1930): 625–38.

Wattenmaker 2010
Wattenmaker, Richard J. *American Paintings and Works on Paper in the Barnes Foundation*. Merion, Pennsylvania: The Barnes Foundation, 2010.

Weir 1930
Weir, Irene. "A Cursive Review of Recent Museum Activities and Exhibitions outside New York." *Parnassus* 2, 5 (May 1930): 24–25, 38–39.

Welsh-Ovcharov and Pickvance 2016
Welsh-Ovcharov, Bogomila and Ronald Pickvance. *Vincent van Gogh: The Lost Arles Sketchbook*. New York: Harry N. Abrams, 2016.

Whiting 1935
Whiting, Philippa. "Speaking about Art." *The American Magazine of Art* 28, 4 (April 1935): 230–36.

Wood 1944
Wood, Virginia. "Errol Flynn Finally Talks." *Screenland*, December 1944: 20–21.

Wright 1915
Wright, Willard Huntington. *Modern Paintings: Its Tendency and Meaning*. New York: John Lane, 1915.

Z

Zafran 2007
Zafran, Eric M. "Monet in America." In Baillio, Joseph. *Claude Monet (1840–1926): A Tribute to Daniel Wildenstein and Katia Granoff*. New York: Wildenstein Galleries, 2007, 80–151.

Zafran and Paret 2003
Zafran, Eric and Paul Paret. *Surrealism and Modernism from the Collection of the Wadsworth Atheneum*. Hartford: Wadsworth Atheneum Museum of Art, 2003.

De Zayas 1996
Zayas, Marius de. *How, When, and Why Modern Art Came to New York*, edited by Francis M. Naumann. Cambridge, Massachusetts: MIT Press, 1996.

Zilczer 1978
Zilczer, Judith. *"The Noble Buyer": John Quinn, Patron of the Avant-Garde*. Washington, DC: Smithsonian Institution Press, 1978.

Zilczer 1982
Zilczer, Judith. "John Quinn and Modern Art Collectors in America, 1913–1924." *The American Art Journal* 14, 1 (Winter 1982): 56–71.

Zwikker 2020
Zwikker, Roelie. "An Offer You *Can* Refuse." *Van Gogh Museum Articles*, November 2020: 1–17, https://www.vangoghmuseum.nl/en/about/knowledge-and-research/van-gogh-museum-articles/an-offer-you-can-refuse, accessed May 17, 2022.

Selected Van Gogh Exhibitions

Amsterdam 1930
Vincent van Gogh en zijn tijdgenooten. Stedelijk Museum, Amsterdam, September 6–November 2, 1930. Catalogue foreword by C. W. H. Baard.

Amsterdam and New York 2005
Vincent van Gogh: The Drawings. Van Gogh Museum, Amsterdam, July 1–September 18, 2005; The Metropolitan Museum of Art, New York, October 12–December 31, 2005. Catalogue by Colta Ives, Susan Alyson Stein, Sjraar van Heugten, and Marije Vellekoop.

Amsterdam and New York 2006–2007
Van Gogh and Expressionism. Van Gogh Museum, Amsterdam, November 24, 2006–March 4, 2007; Neue Galerie, New York, March 23–July 2, 2007. Catalogue edited by Jill Lloyd and Michael Peppiatt.

Amsterdam and Paris 1999–2000
Theo van Gogh: 1857–1891: Art Dealer, Collector and Brother of Vincent. Van Gogh Museum, Amsterdam, June 24–September 5, 1999; Musée d'Orsay, Paris, September 27–January 9, 2000. Catalogue by Chris Stolwijk and Richard Thomson with a contribution by Sjraar van Heugten.

Berlin, Vienna, and Hannover 1927–28
Vincent van Gogh. Galerie Otto Wacker, Berlin, December 26, 1927–February 1, 1928; Neue Galerie, Vienna, February–March 1928; Kestner Gesellschaft, Hannover, April 3–30, 1928. Catalogue introduction by J.-B. de la Faille.

Boston 1919
Post-Impressionists. Brooks Reed Gallery, Boston, January 15–February 12, 1919. Catalogue.

Budapest 2006–2007
Van Gogh in Budapest. Museum of Fine Arts, Budapest, December 1, 2006–March 20, 2007. Catalogue edited by Judit Geskó.

Buffalo 1928
Selection of Nine Paintings by Pierre-Auguste Renoir from the Studios of Durand-Ruel Inc. Supplemented by A Selection of Paintings of the French Modern School from the Collection of A. C. Goodyear and Other Single Loans Also Important Examples of French Art in the Permanent Collection. The Buffalo Fine Arts Academy, Albright Art Gallery, June 17–August 5 1928. Catalogue.

Cambridge 1929
Exhibition of French Painting of the Nineteenth and Twentieth Centuries. Fogg Art Museum, Harvard University, Cambridge, Massachusetts, March 6–April 6, 1929. Catalogue foreword by Arthur Pope.

Chicago 1919
Modern Paintings by Branchard, Friedman, van Gogh, Rodin, Stella, and Sterne, Sculpture by P. Auguste Renoir, Statuettes by Derujinsky. The Arts Club of Chicago, December 15–31, 1919. No catalogue.

Chicago 1921
A Selected Group of American and French Painters. The Arts Club of Chicago, November 21–December 12, 1921. Catalogue note by Forbes Watson.

Chicago 1929
Loan Exhibition of Modern Paintings Privately Owned by Chicagoans. The Arts Club of Chicago, January 4–18, 1929. Catalogue.

Chicago 1930
Loan Exhibition of Modern Drawings and Sculpture Privately Owned by Chicagoans. The Arts Club of Chicago, January 3–17, 1930. Catalogue.

Chicago 1932
Exhibition of The Mrs. L. L. Coburn Collection, Modern Paintings & Water Colors. The Art Institute of Chicago, April 6–October 9, 1932. Catalogue by Daniel Catton Rich.

Chicago 1933
A Century of Progress Exhibition of Paintings and Sculpture. The Art Institute of Chicago, June 1–November 1, 1933. Catalogue foreword by Robert B. Harshe.

Chicago 1934
A Century of Progress Exhibition of Paintings and Sculpture. The Art Institute of Chicago, June 1–November 1, 1934. Catalogue foreword by Robert B. Harshe.

Cincinnati 2016–17
Van Gogh: Into the Undergrowth. Cincinnati Art Museum, October 15, 1916–January 8, 2017. Catalogue by Laura Prins, Simon Kelly, Jenny Reynaerts, and Cornelia Homburg.

Cologne 1912
Internationale Kunstausstellung des Sonderbundes westdeutscher Kunstfreunde und Künstler zu Cöln. Sonderbund Westdeutscher Kunstfreunde und Künstler, Cologne, May 25–September 30, 1912. Catalogue.

Cologne 2012
1912 Mission Moderne: Die Jahrhundertschau des Sonderbundes. Wallraf-Richartz-Museum & Fondation Corboud, Cologne, August 31–December 30, 2012. Catalogue edited by Barbara Schaefer.

Denver 2012–13
Becoming van Gogh. Denver Art Museum, October 21, 2012–January 20, 2013. Catalogue edited by Timothy J. Standring and Louis van Tilborgh.

Detroit 1922
Exhibition of Modern Art. Detroit Institute of Arts, March 1922. Catalogue foreword by Clyde H. Burroughs.

Detroit 1931
An Exhibition of Modern French Painting. Detroit Institute of Arts, May 22–June 30, 1931. Catalogue foreword by W. R. Valentiner.

Essen and Amsterdam 1990–91
Vincent van Gogh and the Modern Movement, 1890–1914. Museum Folkwang, Essen, August 11–November 4, 1990; Van Gogh Museum, Amsterdam, November 16, 1990–February 18, 1991. Catalogue edited by Georg-W. Költzsch, Ronald de Leeuw, and Inge Bodesohn-Vogel.

Frankfurt 2019–20
Making Van Gogh: A German Love Story. Städel Museum, Frankfurt, October 23, 2019–February 16, 2020. Catalogue edited by Alexander Eiling and Felix Krämer.

London 1910–11
Manet and the Post-Impressionists. Grafton Galleries, London, November 8, 1910–January 15, 1911. Catalogue.

London 2019
The EY Exhibition: Van Gogh and Britain. Tate Britain, London, March 27–August 11, 2019. Catalogue edited by Carol Jacobi.

Los Angeles 1933a
Modern Painting for the Past 50 Years. Los Angeles Museum, Exposition Park, September 9–30, 1933. No catalogue known.

Los Angeles 1933b
Five Centuries of European Painting: A Collection of European Paintings from the Early Renaissance to the Modernists, Loaned by Wildenstein & Co. Los Angeles Museum, Exposition Park, November 25–December 31, 1933. Catalogue preface by Ernest L. Tross.

Los Angeles 1934
European Paintings by Old and Modern Masters. Los Angeles Museum, Exposition Park, June 13–August 5, 1934. Catalogue.

Los Angeles 1941a
Aspects of French Painting from Cézanne to Picasso. Los Angeles County Museum, January 15–March 2, 1941. Catalogue.

Los Angeles 1941b
The E. G. Robinson Collection. Los Angeles County Museum, June–July 1941. Catalogue.

Los Angeles 1950
The Mr. and Mrs. George de Sylva Collection of French Impressionist and Modern Paintings and Sculpture. Los Angeles Museum, 1950. Catalogue introduction by William R. Valentiner.

Los Angeles 1952
Vincent van Gogh. Los Angeles County Museum, March 4–22, 1952. No catalogue.

Los Angeles 1957
Vincent van Gogh: A Loan Exhibition of Paintings and Drawings. Los Angeles Municipal Art Gallery, July 3–August 4, 1957. Catalogue introduction by John Rewald.

Los Angeles and other cities 1969–71
Vincent van Gogh: Paintings and Drawings. Los Angeles County Museum of Art, October 14–December 1, 1969; City Art Museum of St. Louis, December 20, 1969–February 1, 1970; Philadelphia Museum of Art, February 28–April 5, 1970 (paintings only); Columbus Gallery of Fine Arts, Columbus, Ohio, March 5–April 5, 1970 (drawings only); Baltimore Museum of Art, October 11–November 29, 1970; M. H. de Young Memorial Museum, San Francisco, December 11, 1970–January 31, 1971; Brooklyn Museum, New York, February 14–April 4, 1971. Separate catalogues were published for the Los Angeles, St. Louis, Philadelphia, and Columbus, Ohio, venues and for the Baltimore, San Francisco, and New York venues.

Minneapolis 1921
An Exhibition of Modern French Paintings. Minneapolis Institute of Arts, November 1921. Catalogue foreword by R.A.P. [Russell A. Plimpton].

New York 1914
Exposition de tableaux anciens et modernes. Bourgeois Galleries, New York, February 1914. Catalogue.

New York 1915a
Third Exhibition of Contemporary French Art. The Carroll Galleries, New York, March 8–April 3, 1915. Catalogue.

New York 1915b
Exhibition of Paintings by Van Gogh. Modern Gallery, New York, November 22–December 12, 1915, extended. Checklist in De Zayas 1996.

New York 1916a
Exhibition of Paintings by Cézanne, Van Gogh, Picasso, Picabia, Braque, Desseignes, Rivera. Modern Gallery, New York, February 12–March 1, 1916. Checklist in De Zayas 1996.

New York 1916b
Exhibition of Modern Art Arranged by a Group of European and American Artists in New York. Bourgeois Galleries, New York, April 3–29, 1916. Catalogue.

New York 1920a
Fiftieth Anniversary Exhibition: Loans and Special Features. The Metropolitan Museum of Art, New York, May 7–November 1920. Catalogue.

New York 1920b
Vincent van Gogh Exhibition. Montross Gallery, New York, October 23–December 31, 1920. Catalogue.

New York 1921a
Van Gogh. Montross Gallery, New York, February–March 1921. No catalogue.

New York 1921b
Paintings by Modern French Masters: Representing the Post Impressionists and Their Predecessors. Brooklyn Museum, New York, March 26–April 1, 1921, extended. Catalogue.

New York 1921c
Modern Art of Holland: An Exhibition of Paintings, Etchings, Wood Engravings, Sculpture, and Batik Work. Exhibition organized by the Holland-America Society for Arts, Science and Friendly Relations. Anderson Galleries, New York, April 23–May 7, 1921. Catalogue foreword by Adriaan J. Barnouw.

New York 1921d
Loan Exhibition of Impressionist and Post-Impressionist Paintings. The Metropolitan Museum of Art, New York, May 3–September 15, 1921. Catalogue introduction by Bryson Burroughs.

New York 1921e
French Prints and Drawings of the Last Hundred Years. The Metropolitan Museum of Art, New York, May 17–September 15, 1921. No catalogue.

New York 1922
Special Exhibition: Contemporary Art. Montross Gallery, New York, April 1922. Catalogue.

New York 1923
Paintings by Vincent Van Gogh. Montross Gallery, New York, March 27–April 14, 1923. No catalogue.

New York 1927
Flower Pictures (1568–1927). Knoedler & Co., New York, May 25–July 1, 1927. Catalogue.

New York 1928
Exhibition of Modern French Paintings, Water Colors and Drawings. C. W. Kraushaar Art Galleries, New York, October 1–18, 1928. Catalogue.

New York 1929a
First Loan Exhibition. Cézanne, Gauguin, Seurat, van Gogh. The Museum of Modern Art, New York, November 7–December 7, 1929. Catalogue foreword by Alfred H. Barr Jr.

New York 1929b
Exhibition of Watercolors and Drawings by Nineteenth Century and Contemporary French Artists. De Hauke & Co., New York, December 1929. Catalogue.

New York 1930
Summer Exhibition: Painting and Sculpture. The Museum of Modern Art, New York, June 15–September 28, 1930. Catalogue.

New York 1940
Exhibition of Paintings by Vincent van Gogh. Holland House, New York, June 6–28, 1940. Catalogue.

New York 2013–14
The Armory Show at 100: Modernism and Revolution. New York Historical Society, October 11, 2013–February 23, 2014. Catalogue edited by Marilyn S. Kushner, Kimberly Orcutt, and Casey Nelson Blake.

New York and Chicago 1949–50
Van Gogh Paintings and Drawings: A Special Loan Exhibition. The Metropolitan Museum of Art, New York, October 21, 1949–January 15, 1950; The Art Institute of Chicago, February 1–April 16, 1950. Catalogue by Daniel Catton Rich and Theodore Rousseau.

New York and other cities 1935–36
Vincent van Gogh. The Museum of Modern Art, New York, November 4, 1935–January 5, 1936. Traveled to Philadelphia Museum of Art, January 11–February 10; Museum of Fine Arts, Boston, February 18–March 15; Cleveland Museum of Art, March 25–April 19; California Palace of the Legion of Honor, San Francisco, April 28–May 24; and subsequently in a reduced format to the William Rockhill Nelson Gallery of Art and the Mary Atkins Museum of Fine Arts, Kansas City, June 12–July 10; Minneapolis Institute of Arts, July 20–August 17; The Art Institute of Chicago, August 26–September 23; Detroit Institute of Arts, October 6–28; The Art Gallery of Toronto, November 10–December 9; The Museum of Modern Art, New York, January 20–February 2, 1937. Catalogue edited by Alfred H. Barr Jr.

New York, Chicago, and Boston 1913
International Exhibition of Modern Art. 69th Regiment Armory, New York, February 17–March 15, 1913; smaller versions of the exhibition traveled to The Art Institute of Chicago, March 24–April 16, 1913; Copley Hall, Boston, April 28–May 19, 1913. Separate catalogues were published for different venues.

New York, Chicago, and Paris 2006–2007
Cézanne to Picasso: Ambroise Vollard, Patron of the Avant-Garde. The Metropolitan Museum of Art, New York, September 13, 2006–January 7, 2007; The Art Institute of Chicago, February 17–May 13, 2007; Musée d'Orsay, Paris, June 18–September 16, 2007. Catalogue edited by Rebecca A. Rabinow.

Oslo and Amsterdam 2015–16
Munch: Van Gogh. Munch Museum, Oslo, May 9–September 6, 2015; Van Gogh Museum, Amsterdam, September 25, 2015–January 17, 2016. Catalogue edited by Maite van Dijk, Magne Bruteig, and Leo Jansen.

Paris, New York, and Amsterdam 1999
Cézanne to Van Gogh: The Collection of Dr. Gachet. Grand Palais, Paris, January 28–April 26, 1999; The Metropolitan Museum of Art, New York, May 25–August 15, 1999; Van Gogh Museum, Amsterdam, September 24–December 5, 1999. Catalogue by Anne Distel and Susan Alyson Stein.

Providence 1930
Modern French Art. Rhode Island School of Design, Providence, March 11–31, 1930. Catalogue.

Reno 2013
A Real Van Gogh? An Unsolved Art World Mystery. Nevada Museum of Art, Reno, April 13–August 25, 2013. No catalogue.

San Diego 1936
California Pacific International Exposition. The Palace of Fine Arts, San Diego, February 12–September 9, 1936. Catalogue.

San Francisco 1915
Panama-Pacific International Exposition. Department of Fine Arts, San Francisco, February 20–December 4, 1915. Catalogue edited by John E. D. Trask and J. Nilsen Laurvik.

San Francisco 1924–25
Inaugural Exposition of French Art. California Palace of the Legion of Honor, San Francisco, 1924–25. Catalogue.

San Francisco 1934
French Painting from the Fifteenth Century to the Present Day. California Palace of the Legion of Honor, San Francisco, June 8–July 8, 1934. Catalogue foreword by Walter Heil.

San Francisco 1935
Opening Exhibition—Loan Exhibition of Modern Painting, Great Prints of Five Centuries, Chinese Art, Tapestries, Drawings. San Francisco Museum of Modern Art, January 1935. Catalogue.

San Francisco 1936
Survey of Landscape Painting. San Francisco Museum of Modern Art, June 3–30, 1936. Catalogue foreword by Grace L. McCann Morley; introduction by Alfred Neumeyer.

San Francisco 1939
Masterworks of Five Centuries. Golden Gate International Exposition, Palace of Fine and Decorative Arts, Department of Fine Arts, Division of European Art, San Francisco, February 18–October 29, 1939. Catalogue foreword by Walter Heil.

San Francisco 1939–40
Seven Centuries of Painting: A Loan Exhibition of Old and Modern Masters. M. H. de Young Memorial Museum, San Francisco, December 29, 1939–January 28, 1940. Catalogue by Walter Heil, Alfred Neumeyer, Thomas Carr Howe Jr., and Robert Neuhaus.

San Francisco 1940a
Fifth Anniversary Exhibition: Contemporary Art: Paintings, Watercolors and Sculpture Owned in the San Francisco Bay Region. San Francisco Museum of Art, January 18–February 5, 1940. Catalogue foreword by Grace L. McCann Morley.

San Francisco 1940b
Master Drawings: An Exhibition of Drawings from American Museums and Private Collections. Golden Gate International Exposition, Palace of Fine Arts, San Francisco, 1940. Catalogue foreword by Timothy L. Pflueger; introduction by Annemarie Henle.

San Francisco 1940–41
The Painting of France since the French Revolution. M. H. de Young Memorial Museum, San Francisco, December 1940–January 1941 (first showing); November 1941–January 1942 (second showing). Catalogue foreword by Walter Heil.

San Francisco 1959
The Collection of Mr. and Mrs. William Goetz. California Palace of the Legion of Honor, San Francisco, April 18–May 31, 1959. Catalogue foreword by Joseph W. Bransten and Mrs. Grover A. Magnin; introduction by Thomas Carr Howe.

San Francisco and other cities 1958–59
Vincent van Gogh: Paintings and Drawings. M. H. de Young Memorial Museum, San Francisco, October 6–November 30, 1958; Los Angeles County Museum, December 10, 1958–January 18, 1959; Portland Art Museum, Oregon, January 28–March 1, 1959; Seattle Art Museum, March 7–April 19, 1959. Catalogue foreword by Walter Heil.

St. Louis and other cities 1922–23
Exhibition of Dutch and Flemish Pictures XV to XX Century from the Goudstikker Collection of Amsterdam. City Art Museum of St. Louis, November 15–December 12, 1922 (works by Van Gogh not on view); traveled in different versions to Cleveland Museum of Art, December 16, 1922–January 7, 1923 (works by Van Gogh not on view); Detroit Institute of Arts, January 13–February 15, 1923 (works by Van Gogh on view February 1–15); Anderson Galleries, New York, March 10–April 7, 1923 (works by Van Gogh on view). Separate catalogues were published for three different venues: St. Louis, Detroit, and New York.

St. Louis, Philadelphia, and Toledo 1953–54
Vincent Van Gogh, 1853–1890. City Art Museum of St. Louis, October 17–December 13, 1953; Philadelphia Museum of Art, January 2–February 28, 1954; Toledo Museum of Art, March 7–April 30, 1954. Catalogue.

Toledo 1929
Exhibition of French Paintings. Toledo Museum of Art, February 3–24, 1929. Catalogue.

Toledo 1934
French Impressionists and Post-Impressionists. Toledo Museum of Art, November 1934. Catalogue.

Warwickshire and Edinburgh 2006
Van Gogh and Britain: Pioneer Collectors. Compton Verney, Warwickshire, March 31–June 18, 2006; Dean Gallery, National Galleries of Scotland, Edinburgh, July 7–September 24, 2006. Catalogue by Martin Bailey with an essay by Frances Fowle.

Washington 1982
The Hague School and Its American Legacy. Board of Governors of the Federal Reserve System, Washington, DC, April 19–June 11, 1982. Catalogue.

Williamstown and New York 2006–2007
The Clark Brothers Collect: Impressionist and Early Modern Paintings. Sterling and Francine Clark Art Institute, Williamstown, Massachusetts, June 4–September 4, 2006; The Metropolitan Museum of Art, New York, May 22–August 19, 2007. Catalogue by Michael Conforti et al.

Index

Page numbers in *italics* refer to illustrations.

A

B

E

F

G

H

I

J

K

L

M

N

O

P

Q

R

Photography Credits

Unless otherwise noted, photographs of artworks and archival documents appear by permission of the lenders or copyright holders mentioned in their captions. Every effort has been made to contact copyright holders and to ensure that all the information presented is correct. If proper copyright acknowledgment has not been made, or for clarification and corrections, please contact the publishers and we will correct the information in future reprinting.

Slim Aarons / Getty Images, p. 189
Albright-Knox Art Gallery / Art Resource, NY, p. 79
© The Art Institute of Chicago / Art Resource, NY, pp. 52, 67, 82, 131, 152, 154, 196–97 (cat. 53, detail), 221, 222, back cover
© 2018 Barnes Foundation. All rights reserved, pp. 59, 209
Robert Bayer, pp. 36, 181
bpk Bildagentur / Nationalgalerie, Staatliche Museen / Jörg P. Anders / Art Resource, NY, p. 171
© 2019 Carnegie Museum of Art, Pittsburgh, pp. 2 (cat. 69, detail), 176, 180
© Christie's Images / Bridgeman Images, p. 118
Cincinnati Art Museum / Bridgeman Images, p. 22
The Cleveland Museum of Art, pp. 61, 142
Collection Simonis & Buunk Fine Paintings, Ede, The Netherlands, p. 122
© Joaquín Cortes, p. 217
The Courtauld Gallery, pp. 168 (cat. 47, detail), 177
© CSG CIC Glasgow Museums Collection, p. 44
Dallas Museum of Art, pp. 16–17 (cat. 74, detail), 45
Detroit Institute of Arts, front cover (cat. 25, detail), pp. 26 (cat. 62, detail), 38, 41, 47, 129, 138, 139, 143, 186
Detroit Institute of Arts Research Library & Archives, pp. 73, 198, 208 (figs. 8 and 9)
Fine Arts Museums of San Francisco, p. 202
The Frick Collection, p. 49
Richard Goodbody, Inc., pp. 161, 162
Hammer Museum, p. 78
Harvard Art Museum Archives, p. 216
Heather James Fine Art, pp. 110, 206
HIP / Art Resource, NY, p. 150
Mitro Hood, pp. 21, 211
© Indien van toepassing, kontakt opnemen met Pictoright, Amsterdam, pp. 101, 105, 106, 113, 115
Kunstmuseum Den Haag – long-term loan Cultural Heritage Agency of the Netherlands, pp. 92 (cat. 63, detail), 109
Leemage / Corbis via Getty Images, p. 172
© Lefevre Fine Art Ltd., London / Bridgeman Images, p. 132
Joseph Levy, p. 120
Los Angeles Public Library Photo Collection, p. 174
Los Angeles Times Photographic Archive, Library Special Collections, Charles E. Young Research Library, UCLA, pp. 182, 188 (fig. 9)
Margaret Herrick Library, Academy of Motion Picture Arts and Sciences, p. 224 (fig. 20)
Mary Evans Library, p. 58
Robert Matzen and Michael Mazzone, "Errol Flynn Slept Here: The Flynns, The Hamblens, Ricky Nelson, and the Most Notorious House in Hollywood," p. 183
© McNay Art Museum / Art Resource, NY, p. 159
© The Metropolitan Museum of Art / Art Resource, NY, pp. 4 (cat. 45, detail), 54, 64, 77, 80, 84, 140, 200 (fig. 4), 201
© M.G.M. / Album, p. 23
Michael Tramis, Lowy, New York, p. 94
The Morgan Library & Museum, p. 116
Museo Nacional Thyssen-Bornemisza / Scala / Art Resource, NY, pp. 40, 99
© 2019 Museum of Fine Arts, Boston, pp. 53, 66, 229 (cat. 46, detail)
© The Museum of Modern Art / Licensed by SCALA / Art Resource, NY, pp. 18, 19, 83, 86, 112, 117, 146, 226
© National Galleries of Scotland, Dist. RMN-Grand Palais, p. 34
© The National Gallery, London, p. 135
National Gallery of Art, Washington, DC, pp. 8 (cat. 59, detail), 160, 223
National Gallery of Art, Washington, DC. © 2020 Banco de México Diego Rivera Frida Kahlo Museums Trust, Mexico, D.F. / Artists Rights Society (ARS), New York, p. 214
Nelson-Atkins Media Services / Jamison Miller, pp. 14 (cat. 50, detail), 155
The New Art Gallery Walsall, UK, p. 46
Ny Carlsberg Glyptotek, Copenhagen, p. 191
Pabst Brewing Company, p. 187 (fig. 7)
© Bridgestone Museum of Art, Tokyo. © 2020 Estate of Pablo Picasso / Artists Rights Society (ARS), New York, p. 137
Philadelphia Museum of Art, p. 51
Allen Phillips / Wadsworth Atheneum, pp. 60, 72
The Phillips Collection, Washington, DC, pp. 157, 220
Photo 12 / Alamy Stock Photo, p. 188 (fig. 8)
© Pictorial Parade / Archive Photos / Getty Images, p. 187 (fig. 6)
© President and Fellows of Harvard College, p. 81
Private Collection / Bridgeman Images, p. 151
Private Collection, courtesy of Eykyn Maclean, p. 175
Rheinisches Bildarchiv Cologne, pp. 33, 190, 199
Rhode Island School of Design Museum, Providence, RI, p. 215
Rijksmuseum, Amsterdam, p. 48
© RMN-Grand Palais / Art Resource, NY, pp. 56 (cat. 44, detail), 65, 178, 205
Royal Museums of Fine Arts of Belgium, Brussels / J. Geleyns – Art Photography, p. 98
Special Collections and University Archives, Rutgers University Libraries, p. 203
Saint Louis Art Museum, p. 164
Rich Sanders, Des Moines, p. 119
San Francisco Examiner Archive, p. 179
© The Solomon R. Guggenheim Foundation / Art Resource, NY, pp. 7 (cat. 52, detail), 50
Stedelijk Museum Amsterdam, pp. 68, 76
© The Sterling and Francine Clark Art Institute, USA / Bridgeman Images, p. 225
Sueddeutsche Zeitung Photo / Alamy Stock Photo, p. 213
Tate Britain, p. 35
Toledo Museum of Art, pp. 126 (cat. 60, detail), 161, 162
David Tunick, Inc., New York, p. 184
Van Gogh Museum, Amsterdam (Vincent van Gogh Foundation), pp. 24, 28, 42, 43, 62, 69, 74, 81, 97, 103, 108, 114, 123, 136
Worcester Art Museum, Worcester, MA, pp. 144, 145
Yale University Art Gallery, pp. 31, 147, 149, 224 (fig. 19)

VAN GOGH in AMERICA

is published in conjunction with an exhibition of the same title organized by the Detroit Institute of Arts.

EXHIBITION DATES
October 2, 2022–January 22, 2023

Van Gogh in America is organized by the Detroit Institute of Arts and is part of the Bonnie Ann Larson Modern European Artists Series.

Lead support is generously provided by the Founders Junior Council, The J. Addison and Marion M. Bartush Family Foundation, Bank of America, Cadillac, and Nancy and Sean Cotton.

Major support is provided by the William H. and Patricia M. Smith Family, Kenwal Steel, Frances and Kenneth Eisenberg, Nicole and Stephen Eisenberg, Alex Erdeljan, James and Sally Scapa Foundation, Marjorie and Maxwell Jospey Foundation, Spencer & Myrna Partrich, Friends of Art & Flowers, Joanne Danto, Arnold Weingarden & Jennifer Danto Shore, Huntington, Ford Motor Company Fund, DTE Energy Foundation, Jennifer Adderley, and The Family of Christopher R.W.D. Stroh.

Additional support is provided by the Community Foundation for Southeast Michigan, Wells Fargo, Gilbert Family Foundation, Nancy S. Williams Trust and executor, Sharon Backstrom, and Aaron and Carolynn Frankel.

This exhibition is supported in part by the National Endowment for the Arts, as part of the Dutch Culture USA program by the Consulate General of the Netherlands in New York, and the European Paintings Council.

Funding is also provided by Mrs. William Clay Ford, Mr. and Mrs. John W. Ingle, Jr., Mr. and Mrs. John W. Ingle III, Mr. and Mrs. John M. Sullivan, Jr., Eleanor and Frederick Ford, and Kathleen and Robert Rosowski.

Major funding for the exhibition catalogue is generously provided by Jo Elyn and George M. Nyman.

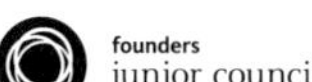

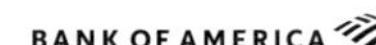

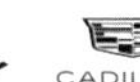

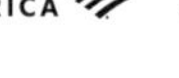
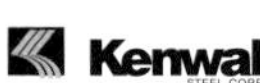

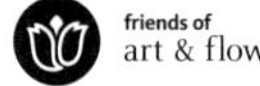

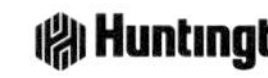

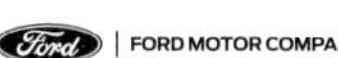

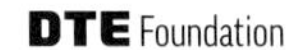

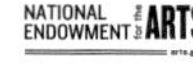

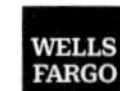

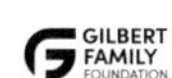

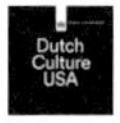

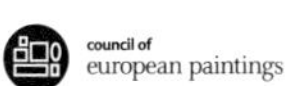

Edited by Terry Ann R. Neff, t. a. neff associates inc., Tucson, Arizona (2020), and Aaron Bogart (2022)
Designed by Lorraine Wild, Tommy Huang, with Xiaoqing Wang, Green Dragon Office, Los Angeles
Production and project management by Amanda Freymann, Glue + Paper Workshop (2020), and Aaron Bogart (2022)
Proofread by Sheila Majumdar, Chicago, Illinois
Index by Jane Friedman, Evanston, Illinois
Photography research by Elena Berry
Translations from Dutch by Lynne Richards and Diane Webb
Separations by Professional Graphics, Rockford, Illinois
Printing and binding by die Keure Printing and Publishing, Bruges, Belgium

FIRST EDITION
Printed in Belgium

Library of Congress Control Number: 2019949245
ISBN: 978-0-300-24709-1

PUBLISHED BY
Detroit Institute of Arts
5200 Woodward Avenue
Detroit, Michigan 48202-4094
www.dia.org

DISTRIBUTED BY
Yale University Press
302 Temple Street
P. O. Box 209040
New Haven, Connecticut 06520-9040
www.yalebooks.com/art